The WinEcon Workbook

Interactive Economics

Edited by
Jean Soper
Leicester University

and

Phil Hobbs
University of Bristol

First published 1996

2 4 6 8 10 9 7 5 3 1

Blackwell Publishers Ltd
108 Cowley Road
Oxford OX4 1JF,
UK

Blackwell Publishers Inc.
238 Main Street
Cambridge, Massachusetts 02142
USA

British Library Cataloguing in Publication Data

A CIP catalogue record for this book is available from the British Library

Library of Congress Cataloging-in-Publication Data

Soper, Jean.

The WinEcon workbook: interactive economics/Jean Soper and Phil Hobbs.
p. cm
Includes index.
1. Economics. I. Hobbs, Phil. II. Title.
HB171.5.S6448 1996
320–dc20 96-29123
CIP

ISBN 0-631-19795-8

Typeset in 10pt/13.5pt Helvetica by

Ian Foulis & Associates, Saltash, Cornwall

Printed in Great Britain by Hartnolls Ltd, Bodmin

This book is printed on acid-free paper

Contents

Preface

WinEcon is a computer software package offering a student-centred approach to learning economics. Many universities and colleges have WinEcon site licences, and an individual-user version of the package is available from Blackwell Publishers from Spring 1997. This workbook and the courseware together provide a complete, innovative and effective system for learning introductory degree level economics.

The WinEcon Workbook: Interactive Economics

This text is the WinEcon user's companion. If you are learning economics using WinEcon you will find it helpful. The book provides a structured guide to the software. It introduces the material contained in each WinEcon chapter, and adds depth to the economic analysis you discover in the screens. When you answer the questions in this book you are recording important analytical results from which you can later revise.

As you use the WinEcon software to study the topics of your choice, this book offers you additional relevant material and provides space for you to make notes about your work. You may like to read about the WinEcon topics before you begin to use the software. You will then know what you should discover and what input will be expected from you, the user, as you work through the screens. While you are working at the computer you should try the workbook questions that refer directly to WinEcon screens. In writing down your answers you will build up a record of the key results in economics that you have learnt.

The WinEcon Workbook helps you to make the most effective possible use of WinEcon. It prompts you to make a set of structured notes on the economic analysis as you learn. Additional commentary provided in this text on the analytical approach and diagrams forms a useful basis for writing essays.

WinEcon Workbook Chapters

The contents list for each chapter is applicable both to the software and to the workbook. Key words are provided to help you identify the subject matter of each chapter. Then follows an introduction setting out what you will study as you work through the chapter.

Each section of the workbook focuses on selected topics and the concepts they encompass. Descriptive information about the economic analysis is available and hints are given about what key information you should discover from the screens.

Multiple choice and true/false type questions are provided in the WinEcon software, so the questions included in the workbook are largely of other types. Some ask you about key results that you can record from the WinEcon screens. Others analyse alternative situations by posing a question with gaps for you to complete. You may be given alternative words from which to choose, or you

may find that the words you need are contained in some very similar text on the WinEcon screen. Many questions are designed to extend and develop your knowledge. There are tables for you to complete and opportunities for you to draw diagrams for yourself. Practising questions helps you to do well in examinations. Furthermore, developing your powers of reasoning and analysis provides you with transferable skills that are valuable in the job market. You will therefore find it useful to try lots of questions.

Each chapter concludes with a summary which provides a concise statement of the important analytical results you have learnt. Answers to questions are given at the back of the book.

Studying with WinEcon and the WinEcon Workbook

The WinEcon courseware comprises 21 chapters of tutorials on economics, giving comprehensive coverage of the material in a first year university degree course. There are also four further chapters containing mathematical and statistical techniques and examples. Associated with the economics chapters are corresponding test sections where you can try applying your knowledge of economics to new situations and to real world problems. The overall approach is user-friendly, offering you choice of what you study, the depth to which you take it, and the extent to which you revise and test your knowledge.

Learning economics involves understanding analytical diagrams. The WinEcon approach shows you how to draw them step by step. As you use the software to examine real world issues and case studies, you discover economics is a lively and relevant subject. WinEcon's interactive approach allows you to try applying your knowledge of concepts and techniques to these situations. Working with WinEcon lets you control the pace of your learning. You think out the implications of economic analysis as you respond to the many questions posed by the software.

If you are new to economics, you may find it helpful to work through the WinEcon screens sequentially, using the tutorials first and the tests later. If you have some previous knowledge of the subject you may prefer to select the topics you study from the tutorial menus. On some screens you can use a cross-reference button to move directly to another screen containing associated material. As you try the test questions you can get a hint and an explanation of the correct answer from the designated buttons, and if you would like more information you can click the tutorial button to move directly to the appropriate screen. To further extend your knowledge and give you material for assignments and projects, WinEcon includes data banks of information on key economic indicators, current tax rates, and company data.

About WinEcon

WinEcon is the first computer-based learning package to cover the whole of the syllabus for first years' degree courses in economics. In recognition of its

contribution, WinEcon was awarded a medal by the British Computer Society in the 1995 Software Awards – the computer industry's equivalent of the Oscars – and was a winner of a European Academic Software Award (EASA) in 1996.

The WinEcon software was developed over a period of three years by a consortium of eight UK economics departments funded under the UK higher education funding councils' Teaching and Learning Technology Programme. WinEcon's development entailed an estimated 40 person years of effort, involved 35 economic content authors and 17 programmers.

The WinEcon Workbook, together with the software, was authored by a team of university lecturers, known as the Economics Consortium, which is made up of eight member institutions, supported by over 150 Associate Members around the world.

Using WinEcon

WinEcon is started by clicking on the WinEcon icon in the Windows Program Manager. After you enter your password (if you haven't been given one, try user id 'student' and password 'student') you enter the Student Shell, a page with six tabs along the top of the screen from where you can navigate to any point in WinEcon. These six tabs are labelled as follows:

- Startup
- Using WinEcon
- Tutorials
- Tests
- Exams
- Tools

Clicking on these tabs takes you the relevant part of software. WinEcon is simple to use and you shouldn't need to spend very much time becoming familiar with the software and how it works. However, if you want to get the most from the software we suggest you click on the Using WinEcon tab the first time you use the software.

WinEcon and the World-Wide-Web

If you have access to the Internet, you may want to visit the WinEcon web site, where you will find updates and new materials, as well as the opportunity to feed back comments to the writers of WinEcon and the workbook. The URL is:

http://sosig.ac.uk/winecon/

We hope you enjoy Interactive Economics.

Jean Soper and Phil Hobbs
Editors

Workbook Authors

The *WinEcon Workbook* was written by the following team of authors:

Parvin Alizadeh, *London Guildhall University*

Pat Cooper, *University of Portsmouth*

David Demery, *University of Bristol*

Chris Elven, *London Guildhall University*

David Hawdon, *University of Surrey*

Ken Randall, *Staffordshire University*

Timothy Rodgers, *Coventry University*

Jean Soper, *University of Leicester*

Chapter 1:

What is Economics?

Economics is concerned with choice and with what provides the best value. As a subject, it stimulates a variety of intellectual, political and personal reactions. It can be seen as too simple or too complicated, left or right wing, and fascinating or boring. Some people see Economics as the key factor controlling people's lives, and others see it as much less important than, say family, culture, religion or ideology. WinEcon tries to make economic issues clearer by explaining graphically, and with as much input from the user as possible, how economists see the problems they are called upon to analyse. Whether we are looking at our own spending or at that of a firm or country, we explore the issues that arise when resources are limited. We discover a rational approach to making economic decisions.

If we want to know why some things are produced rather than others, why there is such high unemployment, and why some people are poor, then economics has at least some of the possible answers.

This book and the WinEcon software offer an interactive approach to learning economics. In WinEcon you can choose the topics you study, the analysis you master, and the test questions you attempt. This book will guide you and help you to make structured notes on what you learn.

KEYWORDS

- Choice
- Constraint
- Economic problem
- Methodology
- Models
- Objective
- Rational behaviour
- Resources
- Scarcity
- Theories

Section 1.1: Introduction to Economics

This chapter lets you discover what economics is about, and how you can learn economic analysis with WinEcon. You begin to understand what makes a problem 'economic', and what would be a 'rational' approach to solving such problems. The process involves identifying objectives (what we wish to achieve, such as satisfaction or security) and constraints (factors that restrict our freedom of manoeuvre, such as limited income) and producing a strategy which will ensure that the objectives are achieved as closely as possible given the constraints.

The introduction provided in this WinEcon chapter falls into four parts. We first define economics, and consider four crucial distinctions that are made in economics terminology. We next examine the idea of rationality, using three simple case studies. There are then three 'games' (simulations) in which you have to achieve objectives subject to different contraints, giving you an opportunity to try out the economist's approach. Lastly there is a brief outline of how economists set about creating their models (or theories).

As a subject, economics attracts interest because it analyses issues such as unemployment, inflation, poverty and international trade. It addresses questions about how decisions made by individual consumers and producers jointly determine prices and wages. Controversial issues include the appropriate role for governments in influencing economic decisions. WinEcon offers you the opportunity to discover economics for yourself. Using the computer mouse, you control the information presented to you and can study at your own pace.

The sections in WinEcon start with introductory blackboard screens which offer you Glossary, References, and Applications buttons, as well as a list of topics. As you move to other screens you find instructions and information on each of them. Economic concepts are demonstrated by animations which you activate by clicking a Show button or by entering values as requested. Sometimes you are asked to drag a point or marker to the position you believe to be correct. Questions within the WinEcon Tutorials and those accessed from the Tests tab (on the tabs page with the menu of tutorials) help you check your understanding as you proceed. The symbol on each button hints at what to expect when you click it. You move between WinEcon topics using the navigation bar at the bottom of each screen. An explanation of what each of these buttons does appears alongside when you pass the mouse pointer over the button.

This book provides a guide and companion to WinEcon. Its formative questions will help you to produce a set of structured notes. It introduces many of the WinEcon topics and indicates key points to look for on the screens. To help you with essay writing the book contains additional commentary on economic analysis.

Introduction to Economics

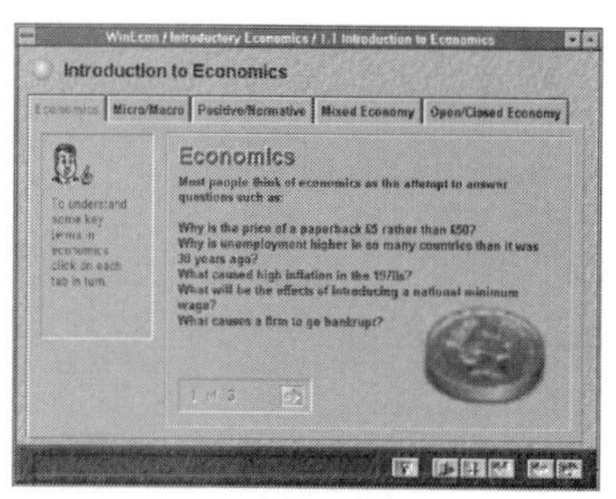

This topic lets you discover what economics is about and investigates four distinctions that are an important part of the language of economic analysis. Click on the tabs in any order you wish to view the information on each card, use the arrows to progress through the text, and try the questions by clicking the query buttons. When you are ready, use the appropriate button in the navigation bar to move either to the next page or back to the tabs page with the menu of tutorials. From the latter you can select any topic of your choice.

For concise definitions of economic terms you can use the WinEcon Glossary. You can access it by clicking the Glossary button available in the Introduction to each section, or from the Tools and Controls button menu at the foot of every screen.

Economics is concerned with questions about what goods should be produced in an economy and how the desired output should be achieved, given that there is a scarcity of productive resources. This does not necessarily mean that resources are in very short supply, but just that the quantity available is less than would be needed to make all the goods that people would like to have. Since people's wants are limitless, society needs a method of choosing for whom the goods that are made are produced. The main questions of economics are sometimes summarized as What?, How? and For Whom?. In other words, the major issues of economics are what should be produced, and how and for whom should the output be produced.

The Economics tab on this WinEcon screen lets you discover a range of economic problems that arise from the major issues described above. The Mixed Economy tab gives you access to information about alternative ways of finding solutions to economic problems.

On 'the economic problem'

01 **Summarize two aspects of the problem. (Compare your summary with the definitions of economics in introductory textbooks – you can get references to the main first year economics textbooks in WinEcon by clicking the References button or the Tools and Controls button.)**

About micro/macroeconomics

Microeconomic analysis is presented in chapters 2 to 8 of WinEcon, and macroeconomic analysis in chapters 9 to 16.

02 Define microeconomics.

03 Define macroeconomics.

Positive/normative economics

04 Define positive economics.

05 Define normative economics.

About a mixed economy

Suggested explanations of the roles of market and government are given in chapter 7, and a related topic, Nationalization and Privatization, is covered in chapter 20.

06 Define a command economy.

07 Define a market economy.

08 When answering the questions on this text card and deciding whether an activity was primarily a government or market affair, which was most important: (a) who produced the item; or (b) who bought the item? ______

Open/closed economy questions

The importance of the open/closed distinction in the macroeconomic area of economics is covered in chapters 10, 11, 13 and 15.

09 Define a 'closed economy' economic problem.

10 Define a 'open economy' economic problem.

11 What is the main way of deciding if a problem has to be analysed from the 'open economy' perspective?

The Economic Approach – Rationality

Economic analysis depends on the assumption that people are rational. Working through the cards on this screen will bring you first to a brief introduction to the concept of rationality, and then to three case studies.

These cases, on students and debt, advertising, and water shortages, illustrate different aspects of rationality, and allow you a first glimpse of problems as seen through the eyes of an economist. What makes the economist's approach different is the systematic analysis of the costs and benefits that decision-makers can expect if they take a particular decision. It is assumed that people typically consider fully all the information available and then act in the way that is most beneficial to them.

About rationality

12 **Define economic rationality.**

13 **Give two reasons why economists assume rationality.**

The issue of students and debt

14 **Does the case study suggest that getting into debt is rational or irrational?** ______

15 **How do interest rates affect this 'rational' decision?**

16 **What type of person is more likely to get into debt?**

17 **Is this type of person more rational?**

Advertising

18 **Does this case study suggest that advertising is rational or irrational?** ______

19 **For whom is advertising rational?** ______

20 **If voters sought a law to limit advertising to a small percentage of a product's price, would they be acting rationally?**

21 **What is the connection between rationality and the public interest.**

Causes of water shortages

22 **Does this case study suggest that water-metering (charging by the amount used) is rational or irrational?**

23 **Are water shortages produced by rational or irrational behaviour?**

24 **Who is being rational?**

25 **Who is being irrational?**

Objectives and Actions: The Squash Club

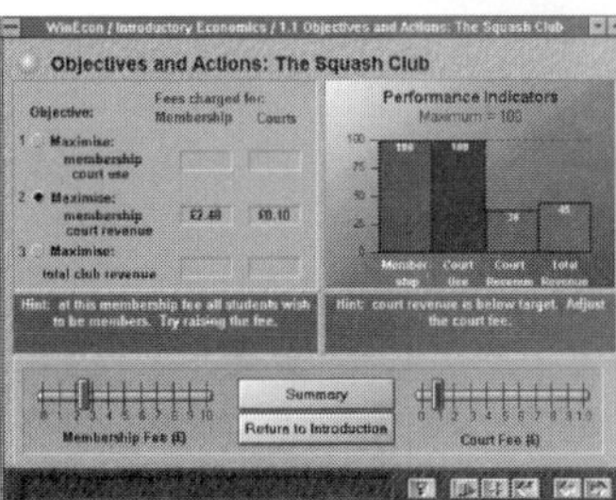

On this screen you can try out your skills in running a club, and discover how competent you are at achieving the three different objectives which you are given. The text cards help you to understand the effects of setting the club fees at different levels. Cards 4 to 6 then explain what each of the objectives entails. The Show button on card 8 brings up a screen that lets you choose membership and court fees and see the consequences of your choices. Notice the two hint windows. The one on the left gives information about your choice of membership fee. The right-hand one makes suggestions about the court fee. Use the hints to help you adjust the fees in a way that is consistent with the objective you select.

The game should make you think about the rationality of the squash club members, and your own rationality as a decision-maker. Learning how to set out a problem clearly is an important step in solving any problem, and your study of economics should provide good training in this skill, as this game illustrates.

Squash club prices

26 **What two assumptions did you make about the rationality of the club members?**

27 **In what two ways were your actions rational?**

28 Fill in each cell in the table with one of the following words: Higher/Lower/Irrelevant.

Objective:	Fees charged for:	
	Membership	Courts
Maximize: membership and court use		
Maximize: membership and court revenue		
Maximize: total club revenue		

Record what you learnt as you filled in the table. Does it shed light on your success (or failure) in achieving the different objectives?

Objectives and Actions: Allocating a Health Budget

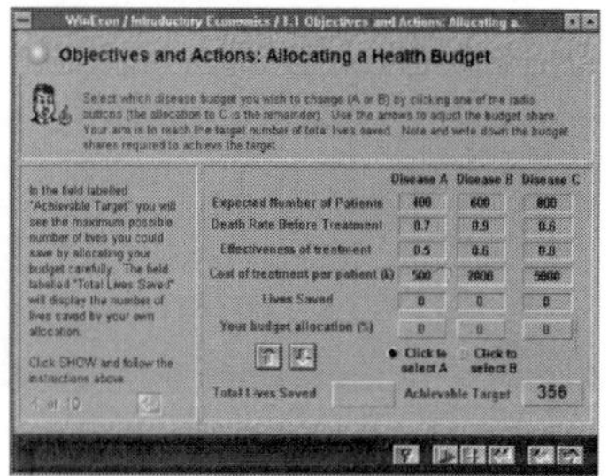

Most of us feel strongly about how both individuals and groups should spend money on healthcare. We are touched by the suffering of others, and afraid that when we are ill or old, perhaps we too will suffer. This leads us to try to make personal or social arrangements which will reduce our natural fears of the consequences of being ill. Historically, religious movements, charities and political parties have been involved in setting up ways of caring for the sick.

This game, or simulation, invites you to see whether you agree that even in this very emotional, or 'normative' area it is possible to apply the economist's idea of 'rational' decision taking. While clinicians would like to make decisions about the treatment each patient receives solely on the basis of clinical judgement, if a budget has been set by health service managers this limits the total spending on patients in a particular period of time. The economist's view then is that the budget should be used so as to gain maximum benefits for the patient group as a whole.

Your task in this simulation is to allocate a health budget of £1m between three competing groups of sufferers. Given the expected number of patients with each disease and the costs of appropriate treatment, you can calculate the total cost of treating all of the patients in a particular time period. Unfortunately you will find it is substantially greater than the budget, and so we cannot treat all of the patients. If we measure the benefits to patients in terms of the number of lives saved, the best we can do is to ensure that as many lives as possible are saved, given the budget constraint.

Card 4 of the screen lets you find the optimal budget allocation by clicking buttons to change how much is spent on each disease. As you alter the percentage of the budget spent on disease A or B, the figure for disease C changes to ensure the total remains at 100 per cent. It is also possible to work out the result numerically given the information on the screen.

Budgeting decisions

29 **For which of the three diseases was spending money most effective in saving a life (at first)?** ☐

30 Complete the table to show the optimal budget allocation:

	Disease A	Disease B	Disease C
Your budget allocation (%)			

31 **Can you explain why the above allocation is optimal?**

32 **At the treatment costs given on card 4, how much would it cost to treat all patients with diseases A, B and C?**
£ ☐

33 Fill in the table again for when the cost of treating disease C fell dramatically:

	Disease A	Disease B	Disease C
Your budget allocation (%)			

Objectives and Actions: Looking Ahead

People with an average education in the richer countries of the world have three main phases to their economically active lives: being educated and/or trained, working, and being 'retired' from work. This will mean that their incomes will vary significantly in these three periods. Their desire to spend money will also vary, but probably not as much as their income. So, we have an imbalance at different times of life between income and desired spending. Earlier we looked at the typical students' solution of going into debt, and suggested that this may be 'rational'.

Here we take the problem a little further by looking at how consumption spending might be planned over time. This is a very important issue in modern economics, and questions about how individuals smooth their income over time have been vigorously debated in the economic literature. The WinEcon screen lets you investigate the problem for a simple example using five time periods.

Planning your spending

34 What formula gives the optimum consumption in each time period?

For those of you who are not good at mathematics, there is a simple approximation to the right solution.

The simple approximation

35 Work out the average income for the five periods. This is approximately what can be spent in each period. The complication is that you cannot choose the actual consumption level, but have to express it as a proportion (1.0 = 100%) of the income of the period. (So you *do* need to be able to do simple arithmetic!) Now run the problem again and see if your solution works.

Economic Modelling

In common with the sciences and social sciences, economists use simple models of the problems they are studying. Simplifying a problem makes it easier to understand, definitions can be discussed and agreed, and the simplicity of the model makes it possible to make predictions which can then be tested.

Obviously the stages through which economists go when producing a new model will usually be complicated and detailed. This screen gives an overview of the modelling process. It sets out four important stages that are needed if a model is to provide a useful, though simplified, representation of how some aspect of the economy works. Once our model has been tested and has been shown to be useful we can use it to predict the effect of further changes that may occur.

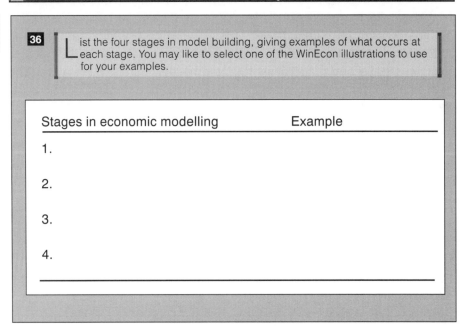

36 List the four stages in model building, giving examples of what occurs at each stage. You may like to select one of the WinEcon illustrations to use for your examples.

Stages in economic modelling	Example
1.	
2.	
3.	
4.	

Section 1.2: Summary

This chapter has encouraged you to discover what economics is about by using the WinEcon software. If you have noted down answers to the questions in this text you will have the beginnings of a set of structured notes that will be useful for future reference.

You have learnt that economics is concerned with situations where choices have to be made, and that people are assumed to act rationally in making decisions. You should understand the distinctions between micro- and macroeconomics, positive and normative questions, command and market economies, and open and closed economies. The three simulations available in WinEcon show you different aspect of economic problems and let you discover the approach that economists take to deciding what is the best action. Economic modelling has also been introduced, and you should understand why it is useful to study a simplified representation of the real world.

Chapter 2:

Supply and Demand

The big questions in economics — what is to be produced?, how is it to be produced?, and who is to have it? — are all affected by market forces, but what are these market forces?

When things go wrong with the economic system, and we suffer pollution, crime, inflation, unemployment and poverty, can we also trace their origins to the way markets operate? The short answer is 'yes'. However, we do not have to let markets which are generating problems operate unchecked. If we understand how they work, we can use markets rather than be used by them.

Supply and demand analysis is a brilliantly simple way of making sense of the way markets operate.

Contents

KEYWORDS

- Ceteris paribus
- Cross-price elasticity
- Price elasticity of supply
- Demand
- Income elasticity
- Price
- Quantity supplied
- Elasticity
- Price elasticity of demand
- Quantity demanded
- Supply

Section 2.1: Introduction

Is there a simple way of predicting what will happen to the price of a product when circumstances change? If price does change how will suppliers and customers react? At first sight the problem looks impossible – obviously suppliers and customers affect price, but how can we disentangle the effect they have on price from the effect it has on them? Supply and demand analysis, together with the concept of elasticity, provides an elegant solution to this problem.

One of the attractions of supply and demand analysis is that it can be used in many different markets, not just those for goods and services. We can apply supply and demand analysis to explaining wages, profits, interest rates, migration and exchange rates as well as the pollution, crime, inflation, unemployment and poverty that we mentioned earlier. However, the area where supply and demand analysis is easiest to understand is in markets for goods, and this is what we concentrate on in this chapter.

The most important simplifying assumption behind the analysis of supply and demand is that they can be considered as operating quite independently of each other. So we look first at the factors affecting demand, and then at those affecting supply. We next bring supply and demand together and show how they jointly determine the price of the product and how much is traded. Obviously the price sends signals to both suppliers and consumers. We then introduce the further concept of elasticity, which measures how responsive demand or supply is to changes in price, or to changes in other factors.

Section 2.2: Demand

The demand for a product is the amount of it that prospective purchasers wish to buy. Notice that this is different from the amount they would like to have. When we talk about demand we are concerned with what people are prepared to pay for. Demand may vary depending on a variety of factors, as you discover at the start of this section.

After this we show how the amount that someone would buy at different prices can be represented by a demand curve. We then look at what causes the demand curve to shift (move bodily to the right or left). Next we show how individual demand curves can be summed up to create a demand curve for a product as a whole. The last stage in developing a model of demand involves asking what might shift the product demand curve.

As you go through this section you will notice that the term 'quantity demanded' is used rather than just 'demand' in some circumstances. Try to discover why. Another key learning point is to be able to distinguish between a movement along a curve and a shift between demand curves.

Factors Affecting Demand

This WinEcon screen provides you with a definition of demand. Notice that we have to consider the amounts bought at all conceivable prices.

As you work through the text cards and choose your answers to the questions asked, you discover what affects the demand for peaches. Our model can conveniently be expressed as a demand function.

The concise notation $Q_d = f(P, Y, ...)$ is read as: quantity demanded (Q_d) is a function of price (P), income (Y), and other factors. This means that the left-hand side variable, Q_d, depends in our model on the variables specified in the brackets. The functional notation is generally useful in model building to set out the relationships that exist between variables.

The summary on card 4 lists several factors which economists have identified as affecting demand for most goods and services.

What affects demand?

01 **Demand is defined as:**

02 **It is affected by:**

03 **The term 'quantity demanded' is used to draw attention to the effect of ________.**

04 **So, economists sometimes say that 'demand' is not affected by ________.**

The Demand Curve of an Individual

The most important factor determining the quantity demanded of a good is likely to be its price. We therefore assume other factors affecting demand remain constant so that we can focus on the relationship between quantity demanded and price. This approach is typical of economic analysis, and the assumption that other subsidiary factors remain the same is called the 'ceteris paribus assumption'.

This WinEcon screen introduces the concept of the demand curve by looking at how an individual might react to changes in the price of a good. Notice that as the price of the good falls, the quantity demanded of it rises. This relationship between price and the quantity demanded is sometimes called the 'law of demand'.

There are two reasons why people wish to buy more of a good as its price falls. The first is that they feel better off. If they bought the same quantity as

You can learn more about substitute goods in the topic Cross Elasticity of Demand later in this chapter, and about income and substitution effects in section 3.7.

before they would have income left over, and they may choose to spend some of this on buying more of the good whose price has fallen. This is called the 'income effect' of a price change. The second reason is that the good whose price has fallen now seems cheaper by comparison with other goods. People may choose to buy less of other goods and to buy more of the one that is cheaper. They substitute the cheaper good for other goods. This is called the 'substitution effect' of a price change.

Clicking the Show button on card 6 of the WinEcon screen draws the demand curve through the plotted points. Notice that we talk in general terms about the demand curve, but that the curve shown is in fact a straight line. Modelling is simpler if we use linear relationships, and economists usually choose the simplest functional form that provides an adequate representation of the real world. Consequently many of the curves we talk about in economics will actually be represented as straight lines.

This diagram is drawn from plotted points to show you how it is built up. WinEcon presents many other economic relationships to you in the same way. Once, however, you are familiar with the typical shape of a particular curve it is usual to draw it as a sketch diagram. It is always important to label the axes, but usually we do not mark an exact scale on them. Curves are drawn on sketch diagrams without the need to plot individual points.

The demand curve of an individual

Fill in the table from the screen data

Helen's demand for peaches (per month)

	Price (£ per peach)	Quantity demanded (peaches)
A		
B		
C		
D		

Draw the demand curve

Price (£): 0, 0.1, 0.2, 0.3, 0.4, 0.5

Quantity (Peaches per month): 60, 120

05 **The quantity purchased tends to increase at ________ prices, and so the typical demand curve slopes ________ from left to right.**

06 **What assumption lies behind the WinEcon questions about demand when the price is 30p or 10p?**

Shifts in an Individual's Demand Curve

In drawing the demand curve we assumed that various factors which may affect demand remained constant. On this WinEcon screen you discover how changes in these factors cause a demand curve to shift so that we need a new demand curve.

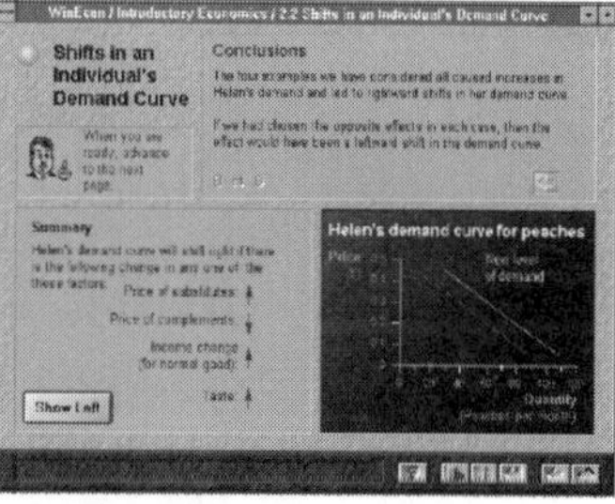

Notice that an increase in demand is said to occur when demand increases at all quantities and so the demand curve shifts to the right. This happens when there is a rise in the price of goods that might be used as substitutes for the one we are analysing, since these goods become relatively more expensive and so less attractive. Examples of possible substitutes are branded goods and supermarket own brands of the same items. Complementary goods are ones that are usually used together (e.g. CD players and CDs, bread and jam). A demand curve shifts to the right if the price of a complementary good falls, because a larger quantity of the complement is bought, and so more of the other good is needed to go with it. If your tastes change and you decide you like a particular product more, your demand for it increases. For example, if after a holiday in Spain you find you develop a passion for paella and olives, then your demand for these increases.

You learn more about the different possible effects of a change in income in the topic Shifts in the Product Demand Curve below.

An increase in income is also likely to increase demand because with more income you can afford to buy more. It is possible, however, that with more income you may choose to buy less of certain goods because you prefer to buy others instead. For example, your demand for chain store jeans may decrease as your income rises if you decide to buy branded jeans, such as Levi's, instead.

Factors shifting an individual's demand curve

07 **This topic covers situations when ________ does not change.**

08 **List the four factors named.**

09 **When the demand curve shifts to the left what does this represent?**

The Product Demand Curve

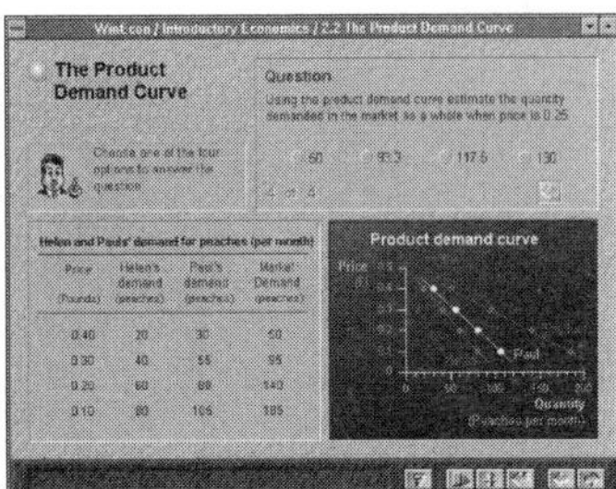

The product demand curve depicts the total amounts of the product demanded in the market as a whole at all possible purchase prices. Using an example of two purchasers, this WinEcon screen shows you how to find a total demand curve by adding together horizontally the individual demand curves. In a market that has more people demanding the product, all the individual demand curves must be summed in this way.

Constructing product demand curves

10 **At any possible purchase price, how is the total quantity demanded found?**

11 **How are product demand curves constructed?**

Shifts in the Product Demand Curve

This screen allows you to revise/review causes of shifts in demand. Use it to check whether the various factors listed have the effects that you would predict on the standard demand curve.

Notice the terms ‘normal’ and ‘inferior’ good. These are used in the description of how demand changes when income changes. When income rises, demand rises for a normal good. An inferior good is one which people prefer not to buy if they can afford something better, hence demand for it falls as income increases. It is just possible that at least part of the demand curve for an inferior good may slope upwards, and it is then called a ‘Giffen good’. Two conditions are necessary for this: the item must be exceptionally inferior, and people must spend a high proportion of their income on it. Rice could be a Giffen good in a poor country where it forms a high proportion of the staple diet. People might prefer other, more luxurious foodstuffs but give these up and buy more rice so as not to go hungry if the price of rice increases.

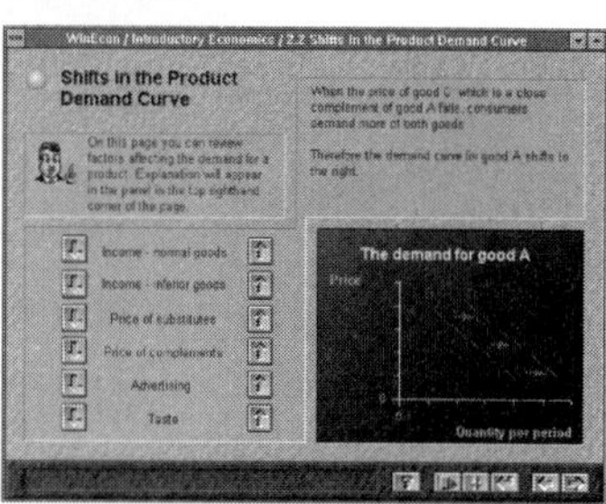

The implications of goods being normal or inferior are explored in greater detail in chapter 3, in the topics entitled The Income Effect and Inferior Goods.

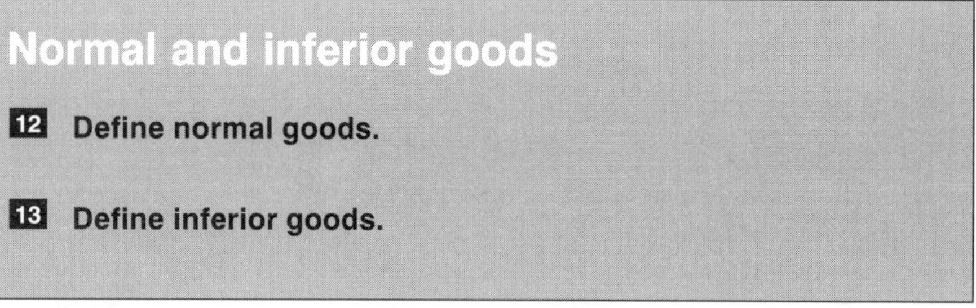

Normal and inferior goods

12 **Define normal goods.**

13 **Define inferior goods.**

Summary

Use this screen to check that you have understood the section, and note any points not covered elsewhere.

Section 2.3: Supply

Our analysis of how markets work requires us to model the behaviour of the sellers of the goods. A model of supply is developed in five stages in this section. First we look at the factors affecting the supply curve of an individual firm. We then draw its supply curve to represent what it would be willing to supply at different prices. The third stage looks what causes the firm’s supply curve to shift (move bodily to the left or right). Next we show how the supply curve for the whole industry can be constructed, and we finish by asking what might cause the industry supply curve to shift.

As with demand, a key learning point is the distinction between a movement along a curve and a shift to a new curve.

Factors Affecting Supply

The supply of a product is the quantities of it that either a single firm or the industry as a whole wishes to make available to the market at each of a possible set of prices.

Use this WinEcon screen to discover which factors commonly affect the supply of goods and services. Notice whether these are the same factors as affect the demand for these items.

What affects supply?

14 **Supply is defined as:**

15 **It is affected by:**

16 **The term 'quantity supplied' is used to draw attention to the effect of:**

17 **So, economists sometimes say that supply is not affected by ______.**

The Supply Curve of a Firm

This WinEcon screen introduces the concept of the supply curve by looking at how an individual firm might react to changes in the price of a good. The amounts it is willing to supply at various prices are plotted to form the supply curve. This curve has a typical upward slope, or we can say it is forward leaning. Other shapes of supply curves are possible, especially in the long run when a firm may experience increasing returns to scale.

See section 4.7 Economies of Scale.

Fill in the table from the screen data

Supply of loaves per hour

	Price (£ per loaf)	Quantity supplied (loaves)
A		
B		
C		

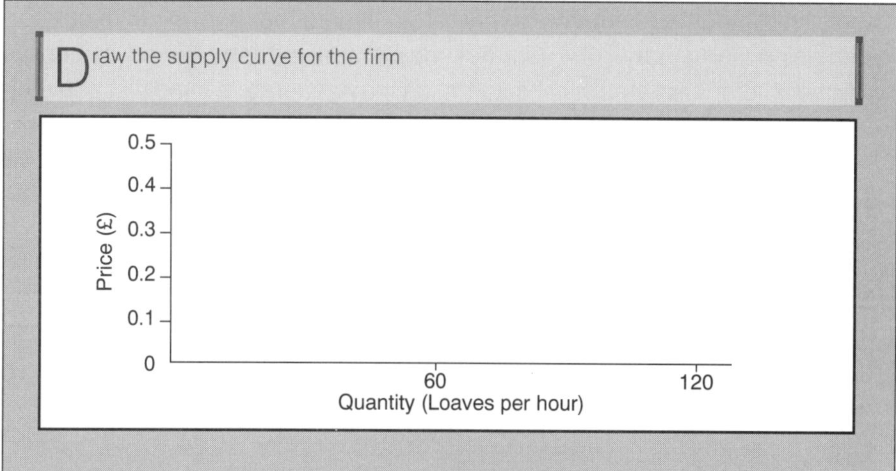

On consumer behaviour

18 **Revise the meaning of ceteris paribus.**

19 **Why is this assumption needed in this analysis?**

20 **What assumption lies behind the upward slope of the supply curve?**

21 **What assumption lies behind the calculation of point D on the final WinEcon diagram?**

Shifts in the Supply Curve of a Firm

Here you discover the circumstances that we must model by shifting the supply curve. Some of these stem from physical production relationships and actual market conditions. Included in these are changes in the costs of employing the factors of production required to make the product, and changes in technology. Some producers may be able to manufacture alternative products. If one of these products becomes more profitable to produce, supply of the others will fall. Some items are produced as a by-product of other goods. For example, the production of meat means that hides are also available for leather. A change in the quantity supplied of one good will alter the supply of other items produced jointly with it. Market conditions may be changed by government policy such as the imposition of a tax or subsidy. Such policy changes effectively shift the supply curve, and it is useful to analyse their effects in this way.

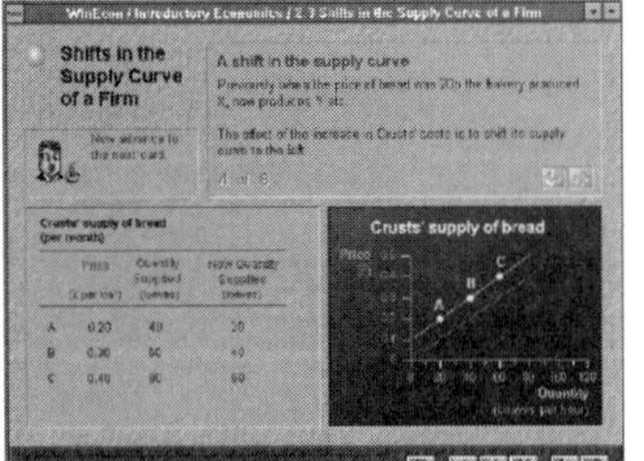

Other determinants of supply are particular events that happen to occur. For example, a particularly dry summer may mean reduced yields of certain crops, or a national celebration may generate a supply of souvenir items. The aims and expectations of producers are also relevant. For example, if they become more optimistic the supply curve will shift *outwards.*

Use the WinEcon screen to see first how a change in costs leads to a new supply curve, then check your understanding of the topic by answering the questions on text cards 5 to 7.

Factors affecting a firm's supply curve

22 This topic covers situations when ______ does not change.

23 List the four factors named.

24 When the supply curve shifts to the *right* what does this represent?

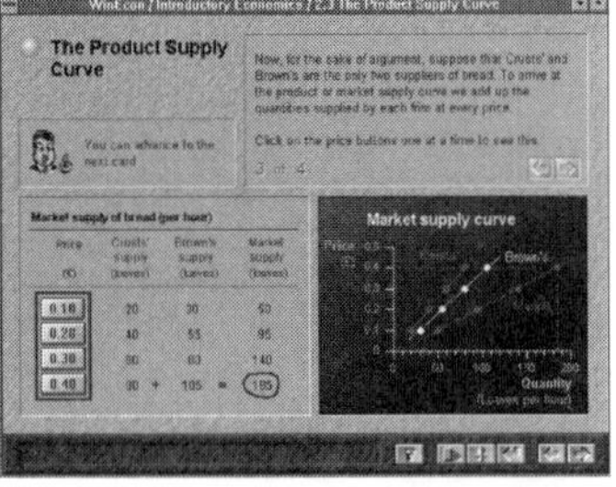

The Product Supply Curve

The procedure for obtaining a market supply curve parallels that for obtaining a market demand curve. We add the individual curves horizontally. The method is illustrated on this WinEcon screen using an example of two producers.

The hidden assumptions

25 What is the (implicit) definition of the product supply curve?

26 What assumption lies behind the WinEcon calculation of supply when the price is 0.25?

Shifts in the Product Supply Curve

You should now be able to predict how various causes shift the total supply of a product. Test your knowledge with this WinEcon screen.

Section 2.4: Supply and Demand Analysis

This section is where the two building blocks, supply and demand, are brought together to create a simple yet powerful model of how the price and the amount traded are determined in a competitive market.

In the previous sections you have seen two sets of factors which are assumed to operate independently of each other, one set affecting demand, and the other set affecting supply. They come together in the supply/demand interaction which can be represented mathematically as simultaneous equations or, as in the screens that follow, as curves. Because both supply and demand curves have been concerned with the effect of price on the quantity traded they can now be combined on one graph.

Supply and demand analysis is approached in this section in two ways. The main way is the conventional or 'comparative static' analysis built around the concept of 'equilibrium'. The other approach is to look at the 'cobweb' model which is a simple example of the alternative 'dynamic' approach.

Within comparative statics there are three stages. First we look at the concept of equilibrium and its implications for price and quantity. Next we consider how comparative statics is usually used. Then there are four examples or 'applications' which are found in most economics textbooks: agricultural support, rent controls, taxes, and subsidies.

The dynamic approach consists of a simple explanation of the cobweb model and the conditions under which it suggests prices will be stable.

Market Equilibrium

A diagram showing both the market demand and supply curves allows us to see how both purchasers and producers will behave at various possible prices. We compare the quantity demanded with that being supplied to see whether they are equal, and we consider whether there are any market forces that may cause the price to change.

As you work through the WinEcon cards, remember that a high price will be attractive to producers but not to purchasers. You will discover that there may then be excess supply. If producers are unable to sell all the goods they have produced, they may lower their prices to try to attract customers. There will therefore be a tendency for price to fall. A different disequilibrium situation is that of excess demand. When some customers are unable to obtain the goods they want to buy, they may offer to pay more to get some. In this case market forces tend to raise the price.

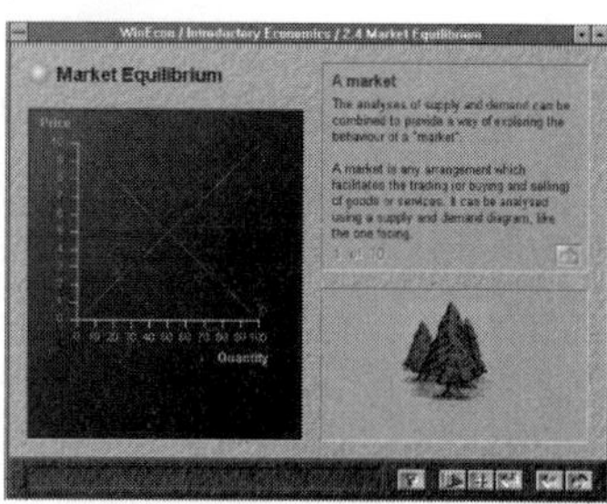

Equilibrium occurs when both purchasers and producers are satisfied with the quantity being traded at the market price. Notice where such a position occurs as you work through this screen. When a disequilibrium situation occurs, if market forces are generated that tend to return the market to equilibrium, the equilibrium is said to be stable. This occurs, for example, when a higher than equilibrium price initiates forces that lead to a fall in price.

What are markets and when are they in equilibrium?

27 **Define a market.**

28 **Define disequilibrium.**

29 **Give two disequilibrium states.**

30 **Why does an equilibrium occur?**

31 **What assumption is necessary for the idea of equilibrium to be a good explanation of why prices and quantities are what they are?**

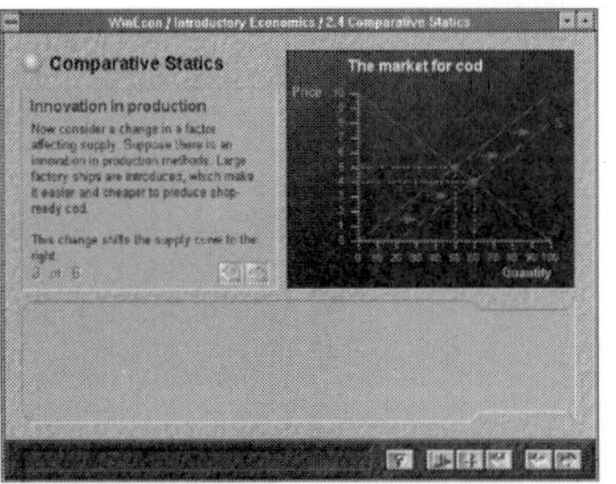

Comparative Statics

Comparative statics is concerned with comparing an initial equilibrium position with the new equilibrium postion that the market moves to after some change has taken place. This screen explores the simplest possible comparative static model in order to show you what it entails.

The underlying factors and assumptions

32 **What is the effect of an increase in income?**

33 **What is the effect of an increase in costs?**

34 **What is the crucial assumption behind the diagrammatic analysis in this topic of WinEcon?**

Agricultural Support

This topic gives you an opportunity to apply the comparative static demand and supply analysis of the previous topic to a policy problem which has faced governments in industrialized countries. You will discover the cost of interfering with the market mechanism in different circumstances.

Approaches to agricultural support

35 Give two reasons why agriculture has been supported.

Use the diagram to show how the 'deficiency scheme' approach works.

Price

S_{UK}

D_{UK}

0 Quantity

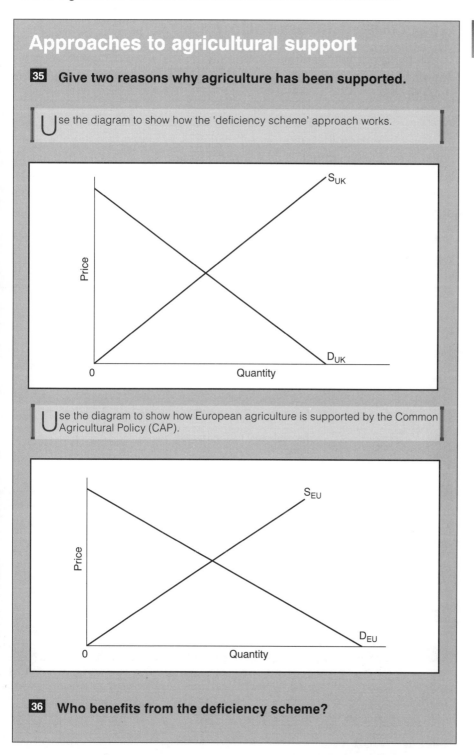

Use the diagram to show how European agriculture is supported by the Common Agricultural Policy (CAP).

Price

S_{EU}

D_{EU}

0 Quantity

36 Who benefits from the deficiency scheme?

37 **Who benefits from the CAP?**

38 **How could the 'mountains' produced by the CAP be reduced?**

Government Intervention

This topic gives you another opportunity to apply the comparative static demand and supply analysis to policy problems which have faced governments.

We consider first the market for housing space. Governments come under pressure to ensure that affordable housing is available to everyone. Rent controls may seem attractive as a way of keeping down the cost of housing, but they have further repercussions which are less desirable. Study the analysis shown in WinEcon to see the effect of rent controls on the availability of housing.

Subsidies and taxes provide another means for government to intervene in the market process. Cards 5 to 7 of this WinEcon screen demonstrate how you can use supply and demand analysis to explain who gains or who loses as a result of these policies.

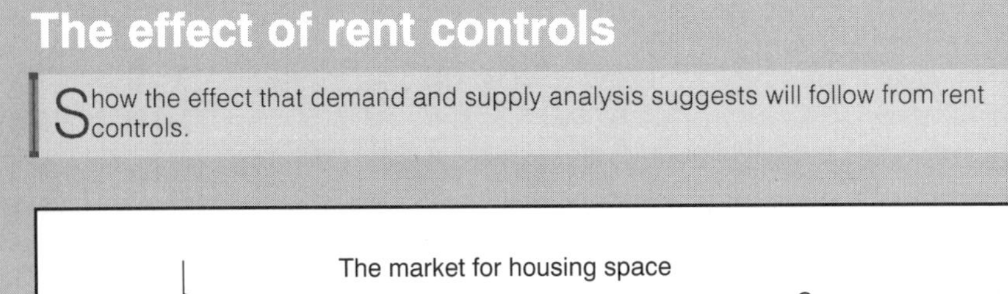

The effect of rent controls

Show the effect that demand and supply analysis suggests will follow from rent controls.

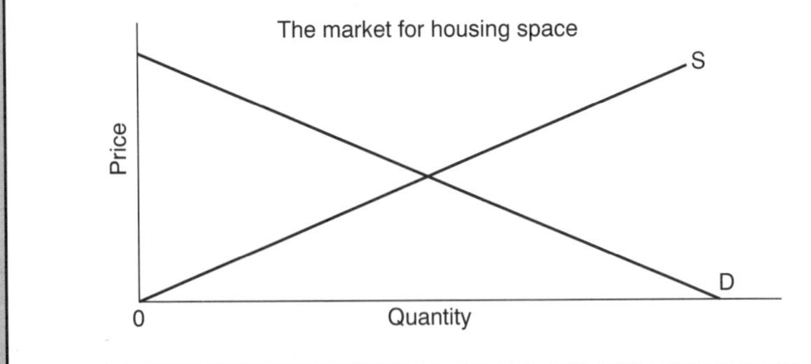

39 **What does this effect depend on?**

40 **If this effect occurs, why do many people support rent controls?**

The effect of subsidies

Show the effect of the imposition of a production subsidy.

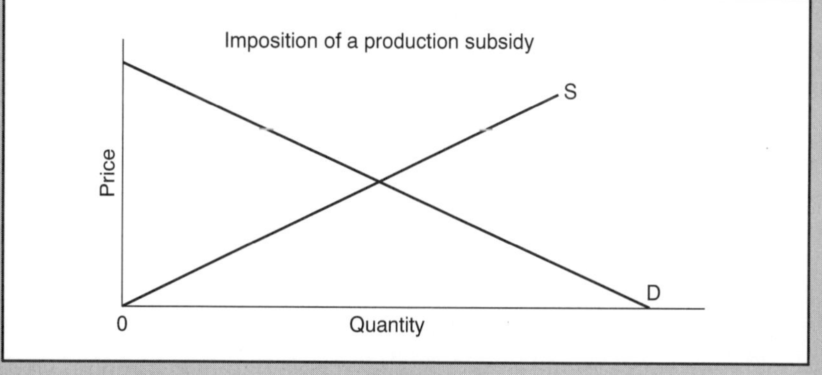

41 **What decides the size of the effect?**

42 **Would a demand subsidy have the same effect?**

Who suffers from VAT?

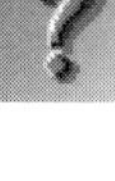

Show the effect of a VAT tax increase.

VAT increase

S

Price

D

Quantity

43 **Who suffers most and why?**

The Cobweb Model

The analysis of the cobweb model is concerned with how a market moves from one price/quantity combination to another in the next time period. The analysis starts from an initial disequilibrium situation and charts the path generated by the forces in the market. We look to see whether the market returns to equilibrium, or whether as is also possible the market diverges further from equilibrium. This is a simple dynamic model which is concerned with the process of change taking place. This contrasts with the topic Comparative Statics which compares an initial equilibrium situation with a new one without considering the process by which the latter is achieved.

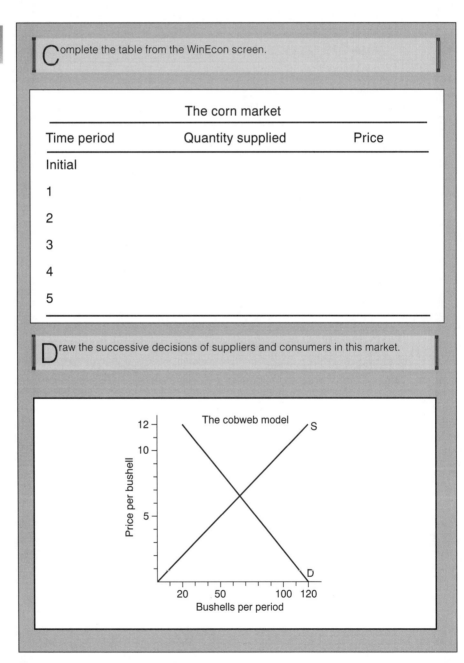

Complete the table from the WinEcon screen.

The corn market

Time period	Quantity supplied	Price
Initial		
1		
2		
3		
4		
5		

Draw the successive decisions of suppliers and consumers in this market.

The cobweb model

Price per bushell: 12, 10, 5

S

D

20, 50, 100, 120

Bushells per period

The assumptions of the cobweb model

44 What assumption is made about how producers decide how much they will supply?

45 How much flexibility do suppliers have to alter supply quickly?

46 What can you say about price and output in two adjacent time periods?

47 How does the market clear in each time period?

48 Which products are likely to be affected?

The Cobweb Model (2)

A cobweb need not diverge away from equilibrium. It may converge to equilibrium, or it may oscillate around it.

Move with the Next Page button to the second screen in the cobweb model topic. This screen shows a market diagram where the supply curve is fixed and has the equation given. Use the buttons provided to alter the slope and position of the demand curve, then click the Check Cobweb button to see the revised diagram and the cobweb it generates. As you investigate the stability of the cobweb model, try to discover a relationship between the demand equation for different types of cobweb and the supply equation given.

What makes cobwebs stable or unstable?

49 When will a cobweb be stable (converge to an equilibrium)?

50 When will a cobweb be unstable (diverge from equilibrium)?

51 When will a cobweb produce regular cycles of constant size?

Section 2.5: Elasticity

The concept of elasticity is defined and applied in this section. A price change of a particular amount may have very different impact depending on the conditions in the market for the good. You learn about various measures of elasticity which enable you to make predictions about the effects of possible

changes using comparative static analysis. For example, you may be interested in the impact of alterations in tax rates.

Whatever the units in which price and quantity are measured, elasticity is measured as just a number, so we can compare its value directly for different curves.

Elasticity is also useful in economic modelling. When two variables have a straight line relationship, this has a constant 'slope', and we can estimate this slope using linear regression. The simplest possible curved (non-linear) relationship has a constant 'elasticity', and we can again estimate this with a simple variant of linear regression.

You need to distinguish carefully between slope and elasticity. There is in fact a relationship between them, as you will discover.

The Concept of Elasticity

This WinEcon screen introduces the various concepts of elasticity you learn about in this section. Each is a measure of the responsiveness of one variable to changes in another variable – for instance, price elasticity of demand measures the responsiveness of quantity demanded to changes in price. (By implication, this means the price of the good itself.)

Other variables may also cause changes in the quantity demanded. Elasticities are commonly defined for two of them. Since the names of the elasticities indicate what the variables are, you are asked to select words to complete definitions of them on this screen. In the same way you obtain a definition of elasticity of supply.

Elasticity and Smoking

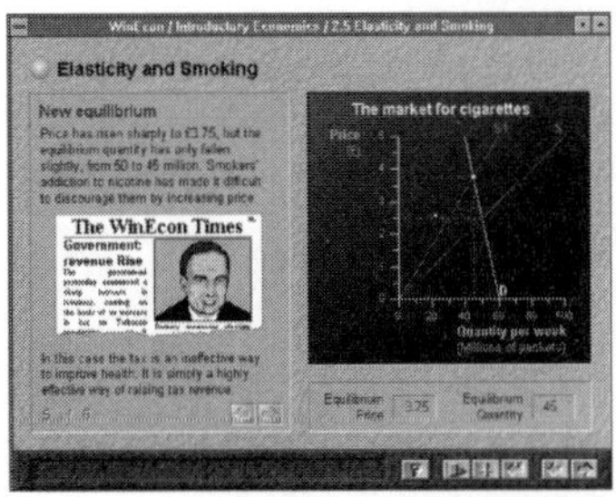

Here is an example of how the same change in price (in this instance caused by taxation) can have very different effects on the quantity demanded of a good. The analysis starts in each case from the same initial equilibrium position, but given the different shapes, and hence elasticities, of the demand curve we reach different conclusions.

Why knowledge of elasticity is important

Draw a diagram to show the different effects of a tax with two different price elasticities of demand.

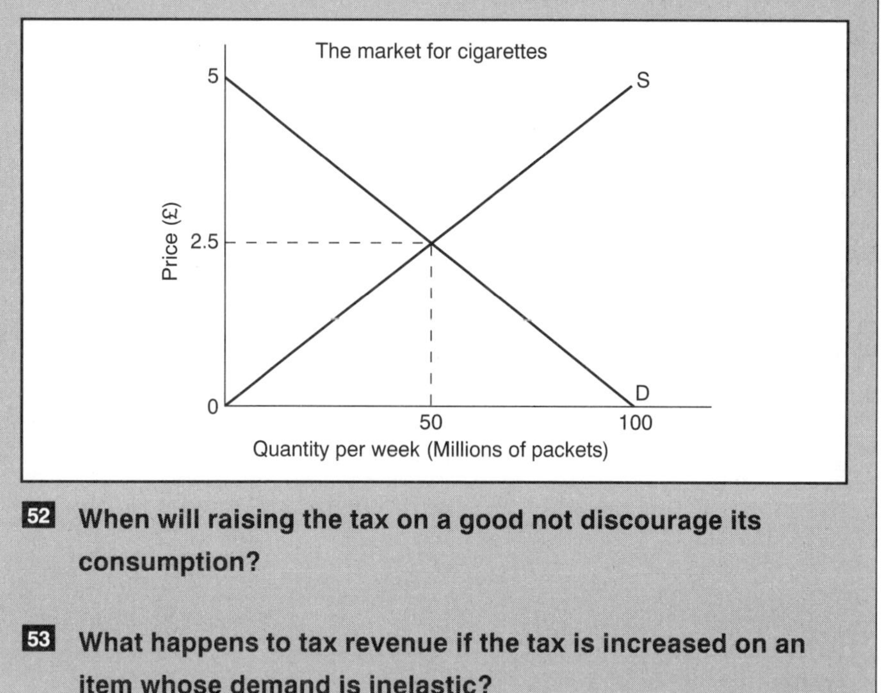

52 **When will raising the tax on a good not discourage its consumption?**

53 **What happens to tax revenue if the tax is increased on an item whose demand is inelastic?**

54 **Could increasing the tax on a good which has inelastic demand and whose consumption the government wishes to discourage be useful?**

Price Elasticity of Demand

You can discover on this screen how to calculate elasticity for a change between two points on the demand curve. This is called an arc elasticity. Notice that the change in quantity demanded is divided by the average of the new quantity and the old. Similarly we use the average of the new and old prices in the formula. These averages are used to ensure we obtain the same measure of elasticity over a particular range of the demand curve regardless of whether price increases from the lower price to the higher, or whether it falls between these same prices.

The price of a good and the quantity of it that is demanded have a negative relationship. As one increases, the other decreases. When you calculate price elasticities, therefore, their values are negative. In discussion it is convenient to ignore the negative sign. Remember that a price elasticity of (minus) 1 provides a benchmark. Elasticities that are numerically greater, ignoring the minus sign, are associated with elastic curves.

Work through the screen checking that you can do the calculations.

Check what you have learnt

55 Give a general formula in words for elasticity.

56 Distinguish between the terms arc and point elasticity.

57 What is the formula for arc elasticity?

Price elasticity and forecasting

If we have a reliable and stable estimate of the price elasticity of demand for a product over a reasonable price range we can use this to forecast how demand will change when prices change. Note that it is usual to use the current price and quantity as the basis for calculating percentage changes for forecasting purposes, rather than using the average of new and old values.

58 If the initial demand is 200 million litres, price elasticity is –1.2, and price is due to fall from 50 cents to 48 cents a litre, what will be the new level of demand?

59 If the initial demand is 500 tonnes, price elasticity is –0.5, and price is due to rise from \$2 to \$2.40 per tonne what will be the new level of demand?

Price Elasticity and Total Revenue

The firm's objectives are considered in section 5.3, Perfect Competition, in the topic Profit Maximization.

The total revenue obtained from a product is the price at which it is sold multiplied by the quantity traded. At different points on a demand curve price (indicated by a horizontal line to the demand curve) and quantity (indicated by a vertical from the same point) differ. Total revenue corresponding to a particular price/quantity combination is represented by the rectangle enclosed between these horizontal and vertical lines and the axes. This area differs for different points on the curve, and so total revenue varies with output.

Total revenue represents the return that the producer gets for selling its product, so a larger value would seem preferable to a smaller one. If, however, this requires a larger output to be produced, greater costs are incurred and these need to be balanced against the extra return.

This WinEcon screen asks you to identify which values of elasticity are appropriate to different demand curves. Work through the cards entering numbers when requested so that you will discover a relationship between price elasticity and total revenue. Check that you agree with the conclusion.

Maximizing total revenue

60 **At what point on a demand curve would total revenue be maximized?**

61 **Why is revenue maximized at that point?**

62 Draw a straight line demand curve which cuts the quantity axis at 500 visitors, and the price axis at £10 per visit. If you were advising the operators of this attraction which price to choose to maximize their revenue, what would you suggest?

Point Elasticity – Demand

Here we introduce another method of measuring elasticity. It is used when we want to know the price elasticity at or very close to a particular price. This WinEcon topic presents a method of calculating point elasticity. As part of the calculation it requires you to find the slope of the curve at the price at which you are estimating elasticity. For non-linear demand curves this is the same as the slope of the line (called a tangent) that just touches the curve at the point. A more general method uses the mathematical technique of differentiation.

There are three supplementary screens in this topic – Point Elasticity – Demand (2), Demand (3) and Demand (4).

Slope and elasticity

63 **What formula is used to find point price elasticity of demand?**

64 **What is the relationship between the slope of a demand curve and the point price elasticity of demand?**

Demand Curves with Constant Elasticity

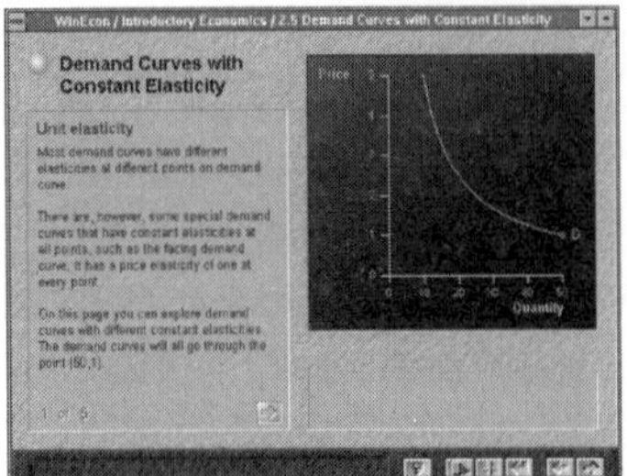

This screen shows demand curves with constant price elasticity. The first curve, with an elasticity of –1, is often used in economic modelling. Two linear curves follow, and then on the last card (card 6) you can see a whole family of curves. The two linear curves illustrated are in fact extreme examples of other similar curves. In mathematical terms they are limiting cases, pushing the elasticity to zero or minus infinity.

Constant elasticity of demand curves

You may wish to sketch here the three main kinds of demand curves with constant price elasticity.

Demand curves with constant elasticity

Price

Quantity

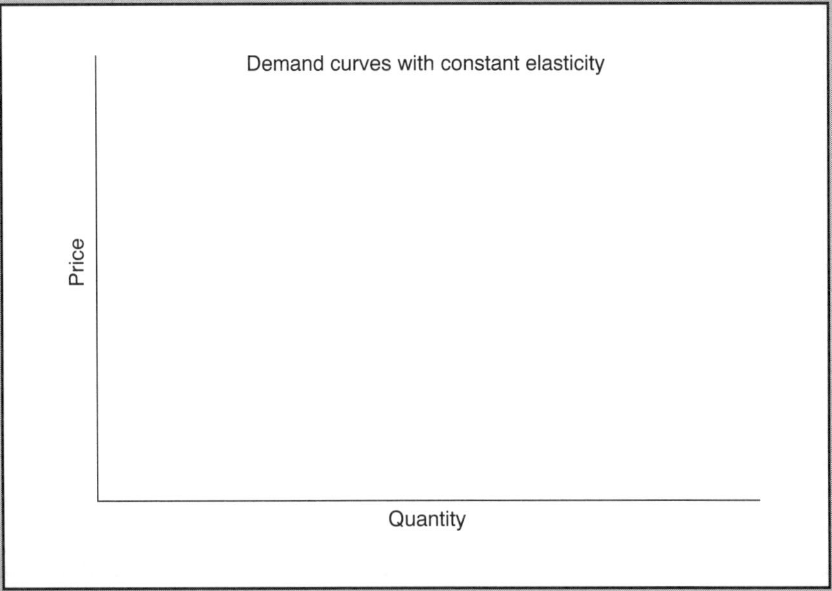

65 **What can you say about total revenue at various points on a demand curve with constant elasticity of –1?**

Factors Affecting PED

66 **Record the four main factors which increase the price elasticity of demand.**

Income Elasticity of Demand

We have seen that we can define elasticities with respect to various factors. We have also learnt to distinguish between normal and inferior goods.

This WinEcon screen lets you discover more about the income elasticity of demand. Notice that it can be either positive or negative, according to whether the good is a normal or an inferior one. A good which is income elastic has an elasticity of more than +1. One which is income inelastic has elasticity between 0 and +1, while an inferior good has negative income elasticity.

These terms are discussed in the topics The Concept of Elasticity (earlier in this section) and Shifts in the Product Demand Curve (section 2.2) respectively.

You find that the relationship between income and the quantity that is demanded of a good can be graphed as an 'Engel curve'. The shape of the Engel curve lets us distinguish between goods which are income elastic and those which are income inelastic. We can also see whether they are normal or inferior goods. It is sometimes useful to distinguish another category of goods called superior goods. The quantity bought of these items increases more than proportionately as income increases.

When we try to forecast the demand for a product or service we often find that income elasticity is even more useful than price elasticity. If we are trying to forecast for, say, three years ahead it is very difficult to forecast price changes. (See the earlier question on forecasting in the topic Price Elasticity of Demand.) However, we can assume that over a period of three years any annual fluctuations in income will have evened out, and income will have grown by a historically normal percentage. Thus we can forecast the change in demand if we know the 'income elasticity of demand' (IED).

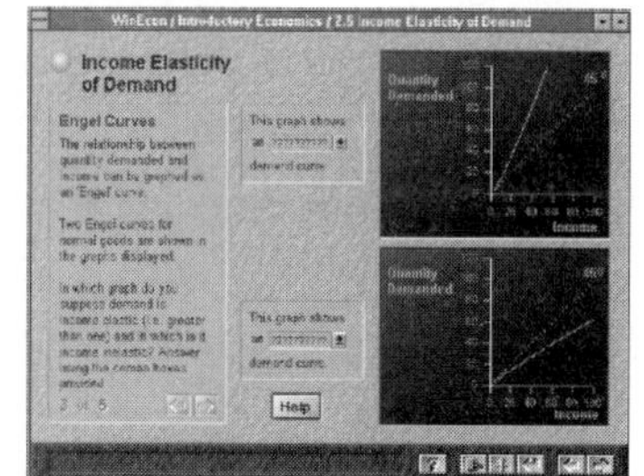

Research over many years enables us to be reasonably certain of the IEDs for a large number of products ranging from foods to cars. So IED is a useful forecasting tool in both the public and private sectors.

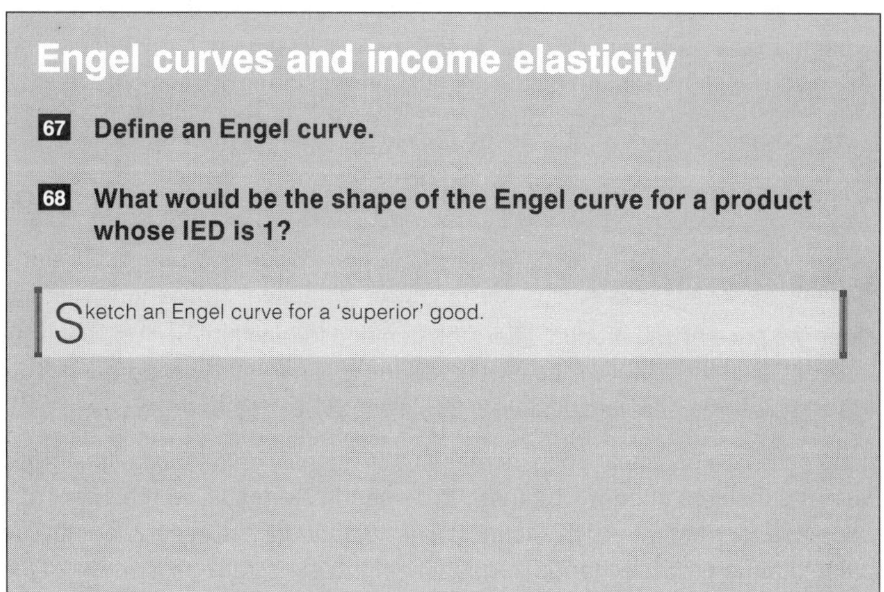

Engel curves and income elasticity

67 **Define an Engel curve.**

68 **What would be the shape of the Engel curve for a product whose IED is 1?**

Sketch an Engel curve for a 'superior' good.

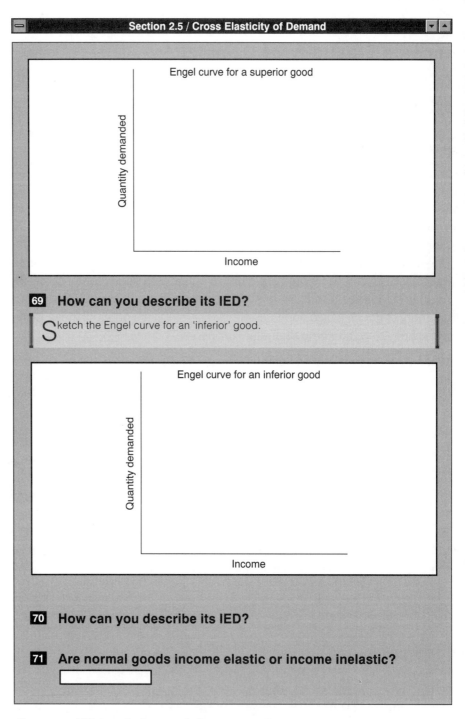

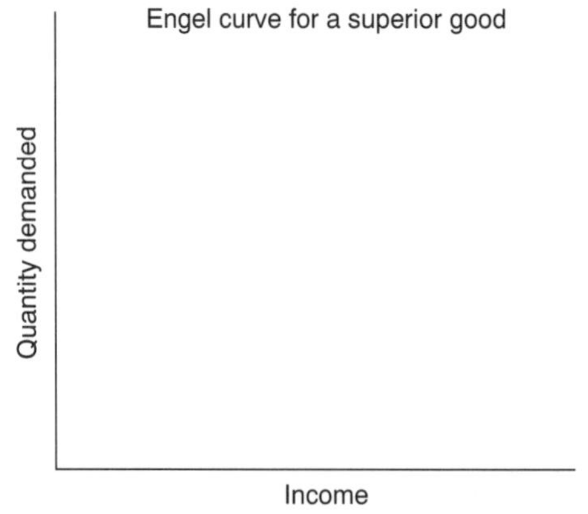

Engel curve for a superior good

Quantity demanded

Income

69 **How can you describe its IED?**

Sketch the Engel curve for an 'inferior' good.

Engel curve for an inferior good

Quantity demanded

Income

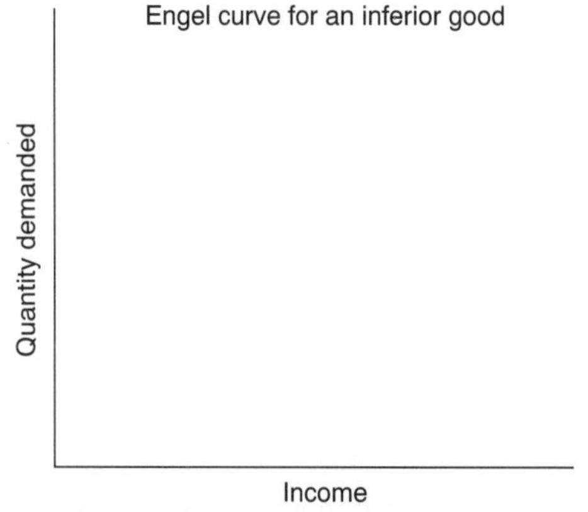

70 **How can you describe its IED?**

71 **Are normal goods income elastic or income inelastic?**

Cross Elasticity of Demand

Does the price of one product affect the demand for another? If it does we can forecast what the effect will be if we know the cross elasticity of demand. This topic shows you how to calculate cross elasticity of demand (XED).

If the price of a particular good increases, the quantity demanded of that good falls. A substitute good will be more in demand as a result, so the effect of a price rise for the first good is to increase demand for the second good. The price change and the change in quantity of the substitute good move in the same direction, so the cross elasticity of demand is positive for substitute goods.

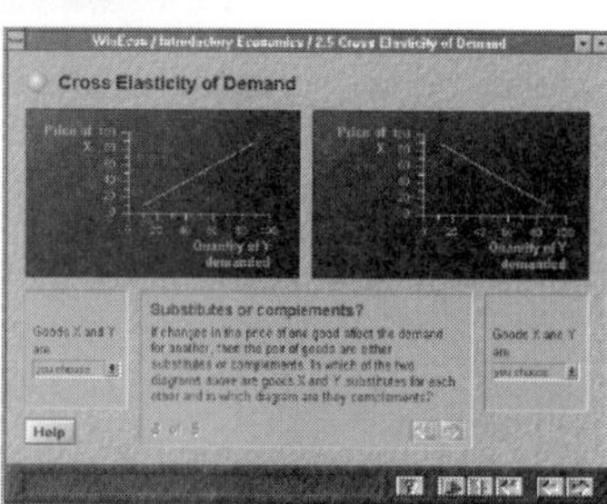

By a similar argument the price change and the change in quantity of a complementary good move in opposite directions, and so the cross elasticity of demand is negative for complements.

Use the screen and then answer the questions below.

Cross elasticity

72 **Define cross elasticity of demand.**

73 **Is XED for goods which are complements positive or negative?**

74 **Is XED for goods which are substitutes positive or negative?**

Elasticity of Supply

We use a simple example of how the effect of a change in demand depends on the supply curve to illustrate the importance of the next concept – price elasticity of supply (PES).

Ruby Earrings and PES

Work through the WinEcon text cards and then answer the questions below.

75 **For a given increase in demand, will price rise more if supply is elastic or if it is inelastic?**

76 **Do we need to know the PES to forecast how much price will rise if demand rises?**

Price Elasticity of Supply

As we look at PES we find it is analagous to PED. On this screen, for instance, we first define PES and then use the arc method of calculation. Note that we use the average price and average quantity as the base for our proportional change calculations.

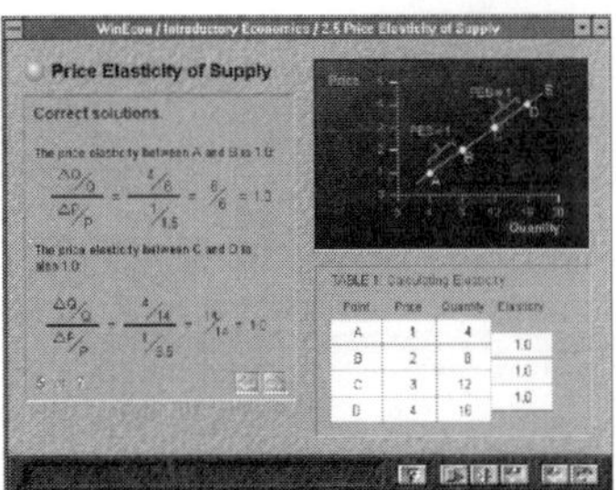

Since there is a positive relationship between price and the quantity supplied, the price elasticity of supply has a positive value. Curves with elasticities that are greater than 1 are said to be elastic, and those with elasticities of less than 1 are said to be inelastic. Notice that the supply curve on this WinEcon screen has unitary elasticity throughout its length, and try to discover why.

77 **Define price elasticity of supply.**

78 **When is PES constant?**

Price Elasticity and the Slope of the Supply Curve

When are supply curves elastic and inelastic?

79 **Is a steeper supply curve always less elastic?**

80 **Which straight line supply curves are price elastic?**

81 **Which straight line supply curves are price inelastic?**

Point Elasticity – Supply

This screen shows how point elasticity is calculated. If you have any queries look at the Show option on card 2. If you are still puzzled go through the calculations on card 3, writing down each step.

Test your understanding

82 **What is the formula for point price elasticity of supply?**

83 **Define price elastic supply.**

84 **Define price inelastic supply.**

85 **Which straight line supply curves have price elasticities which vary at different prices?**

Factors Affecting PES

This WinEcon screen looks at two factors which affect all supply curves.

Crucial factors

86 **Which are the two main factors which affect the price elasticity of supply of a product or service?**

87 **Is price elasticity of supply likely to vary positively or negatively with time?**

Section 2.6: Summary

Supply and demand analysis is a very simple but powerful tool for analysing economic issues. This chapter explains the approach and illustrates it using the market for goods.

You have discovered the factors underlying demand and supply curves, and learnt that in general a demand curve slopes downwards from left to right, while a supply curve slopes upwards. You have drawn curves both for individuals and for the market of a good as a whole and found that market equilibrium is achieved at the point where the supply and demand curves cross.

When one of the factors underlying either a demand or a supply curve changes, the appropriate curve shifts. We have studied the outcome in comparative static analysis. Applications have included government intervention with taxes, rent controls or agricultural support. A simple dynamic model where the equilibrium position may or may not be stable is the cobweb model.

Elasticity is a useful concept for measuring the reponsiveness of one variable (such as the quantity demanded or supplied) to changes in another such as price, income or the price of a different good. We have used the arc method to measure elasticity over a range, and also found point elasticity to measure responsiveness at a particular point. You should now understand the terms normal, inferior and superior good, and be able to interpret an Engel curve.

Chapter 3:

Intermediate Demand

When we see people shopping in Marks & Spencer or McDonald's, do we assume they are behaving rationally?

Why do people buy some products rather than others? Do they buy more at lower prices, or are much more subtle and strange processes going on? Will they behave totally differently next time they go shopping?

Intermediate demand analysis predicts how rational consumers would react to changing circumstances, and it concentrates on the two major influences on them, namely the price of the product and the size of their income.

Contents

KEYWORDS

- Budget line
- Income–consumption curve
- Price–consumption curve
- Engel curve
- Income effect
- Inferior good
- Rationality
- Utility
- Giffen good
- Indifference curve
- Marginal utility
- Substitution effect

Section 3.1: Introduction

In chapter 2 we discovered how suppliers and customers can interact, and represented this interaction through supply and demand curves. We now look at the reasoning that underlies the demand curve.

In trying to understand and predict consumer behaviour, economists are in intellectual competition with other social sciences, namely sociology and psychology. The marketing profession refers much more to the other social sciences than it does to economics. Is this justified, or is it because economists have not explained clearly enough what their theories about demand are actually saying?

Economists know that they are not qualified to say why consumers have particular needs and preferences (the role of sociology and psychology), but we can say what is a rational or logical way of going about satisfying those needs and preferences in the market-place. If we then assume that, in general, people behave rationally or logically we can predict how they will respond to changing circumstances. It is this predictive power of economics which can be used by marketing and other professions.

This chapter starts with another brief look at the crucial assumption of the rational (and consistent) consumer, followed by sections on 'utility' and 'indifference curve' analysis.

Assuming that consumers are rational and consistent in their buying decisions enables economists to predict demand reactions, using either the utility or indifference curve approaches. Utility theory produces strong predictions about how consumers will react to price changes, based on very simple assumptions about the satisfaction (utility) obtained from different levels of consumption. Indifference curve analysis extends the coverage to a second variable, income. The model is still very simple, but can now be used to explain many more situations, some of which are mentioned in WinEcon. The two approaches give an insight into how economics has developed.

You can revise your understanding of the assumption of rationality and consistency by looking again at chapter 1.

Section 3.2: Consumer Behaviour

The concepts of utility and consumer rationality are fundamental to intermediate demand analysis. You can learn about them in this section.

We often use words like 'logical' and 'rational' in an imprecise way, and this section allows us to explore rationality in particular. As you work through this section you might also think about 'consistency' – does it imply that consumers will make consistent choices? Consistency can have at least three meanings in this context:

To follow up these ideas consult first the relevant section in chapter 1, then look at introductory economics textbooks. To explore the topic further look at intermediate microeconomics textbooks, and references to consumer decision-making in managerial economics, marketing and social psychology textbooks.

(1) that consumers always choose the same items

(2) that they retain their original preferences but choose different items when, say, prices change

(3) that they may change their preferences, but retain the same strategy in making choices.

When economists say that consumers are consistent they usually use definition (3) – the choice made may change, but if preferences and prices etc. were the same, the choice would not change.

Consumption Decisions

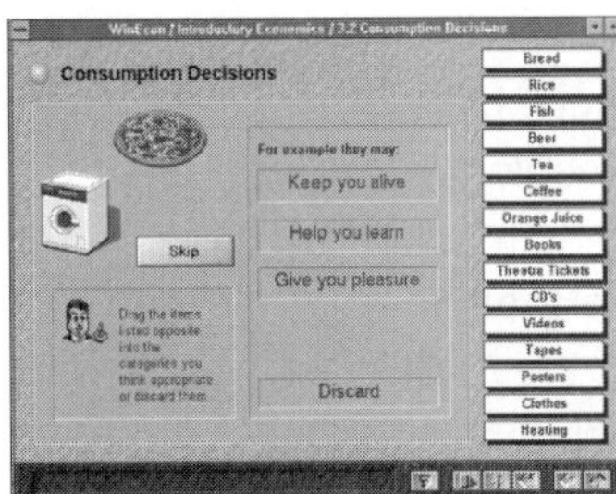

Do you consume the items listed on this screen? If you do, think about why. In WinEcon, use the mouse to drag each item to an appropriate category. When you have selected those that interest you, click Skip to see the reason economists give for your consumption decisions, and discover what it implies.

On consumer behaviour

01 **What units do economists use to measure utility?**

02 **What do economists mean by rational consumers?**

03 **Can we explain demand for one good on its own?**

04 **Are consumers rational?**

05 **If we make rational decisions why might we regret them later?**

06 **Are rational decisions good decisions?**

Section 3.3: Utility Analysis

Utility analysis is one approach to describing how consumers make choices. It dates from the mid-nineteenth century utilitarian philosophers, such as Jeremy Bentham and John Stuart Mill, who developed modes of thought spanning psychology, politics, penology, economics and social policy. Central to their ideas was the concept of 'man' as a rational creature seeking pleasure

and avoiding pain – and thus maximizing his 'utility'. So you could then explain human behaviour, but you could also influence it by applying the appropriate 'sticks' and 'carrots'.

This section sets out the concepts of 'total' and 'marginal' utility and shows which is more useful in explaining a consumer's demand curve. You can also discover an important result about which combinations of goods purchased maximize utility: this is called the 'equi-marginal' principle.

Total and Marginal Utility

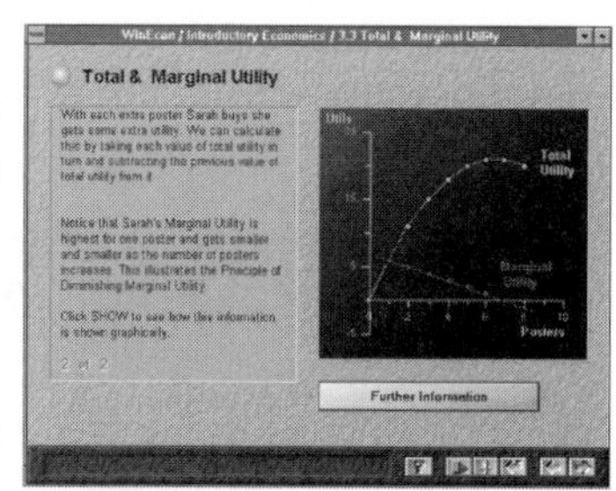

Given that different possible consumption situations yield different amounts of satisfaction, economists would like to compare the levels of utility achieved. These are assigned values in the example on this screen. We then focus on the changes in utility that occur as the consumption situation alters, finding the marginal utility in each case. You are asked to input some of these values, and can obtain an explanation of how to calculate them by clicking the appropriate button.

WinEcon shows you how to plot the graphs of total and marginal utility, and further information about them is then available to you.

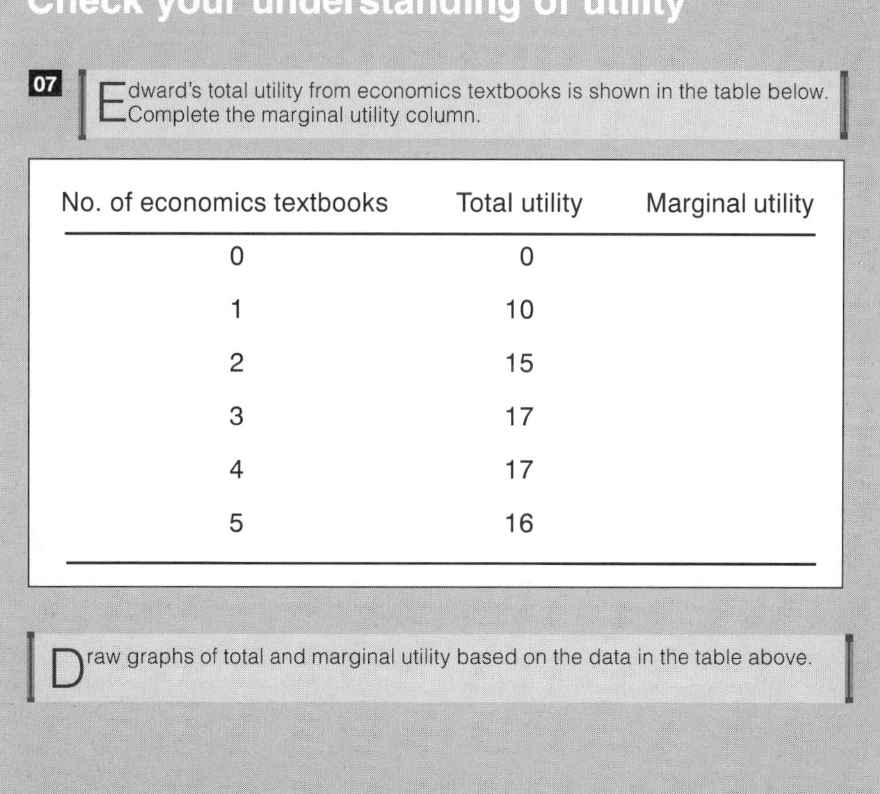

Check your understanding of utility

07 Edward's total utility from economics textbooks is shown in the table below. Complete the marginal utility column.

No. of economics textbooks	Total utility	Marginal utility
0	0	
1	10	
2	15	
3	17	
4	17	
5	16	

Draw graphs of total and marginal utility based on the data in the table above.

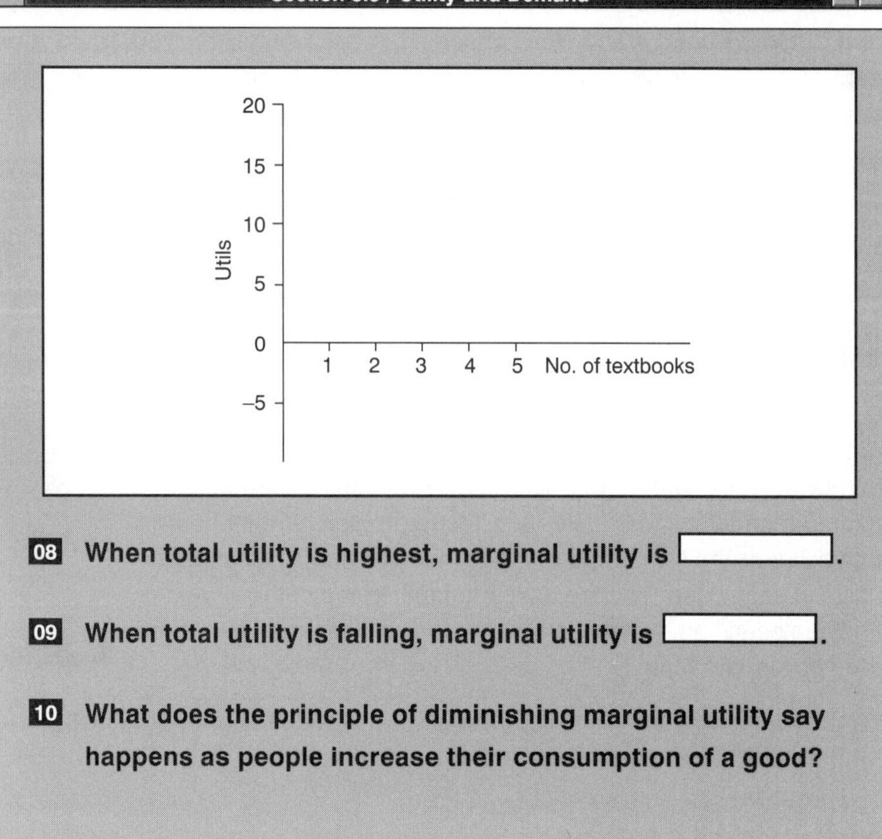

08 **When total utility is highest, marginal utility is ________.**

09 **When total utility is falling, marginal utility is ________.**

10 **What does the principle of diminishing marginal utility say happens as people increase their consumption of a good?**

Utility and Demand

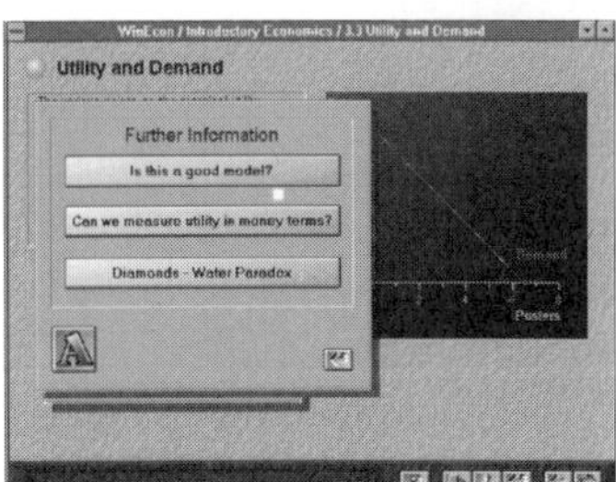

Applying utility analysis to a consumer's consumption pattern for a commodity lets us deduce a demand curve. You can discover the method by working through the cards in this topic. To find out how the model for one commodity might be extended and improved, look at the further information offered when the More button is clicked.

Looking at the utility of diamonds as compared with water, early economists found the relative values paradoxical. To understand why and find an explanation, click the appropriate buttons.

The relationship between marginal utility and demand

11 **Explain in two lines how utility and demand are related.**

12 **What assumption is made in order to keep this relationship simple?**

Choice of Goods

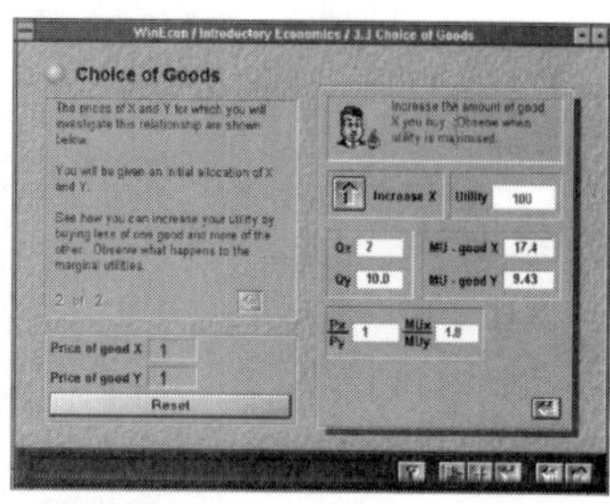

Rational consumers are assumed to choose a selection of goods that maximizes their utility. This topic shows you a relationship between prices and marginal utilities which holds when utility is maximized. As you start the analysis on this screen you are given particular amounts of two goods, X and Y. You can then increase your consumption of X, but have to trade it for Y at the market prices which are given. Alter your consumption of X, and notice when you obtain maximum utility. You can then discover the general result by clicking the button which appears.

Utility and choice

13 **Which concept in utility theory explains how consumers choose the relative amounts of different goods to buy?**

14 **What does it state?**

Section 3.4: About Indifference Curves

An alternative approach to explaining demand curves is by 'indifference curve analysis'. This was developed in the 1920s and 1930s from the work of John Hicks, and has three main advantages over utility analysis:

(1) it avoids the idea of measurable utility

(2) it explicitly introduces the idea of choosing between (two) goods

(3) it shows how choices are constrained and affected by changes in income.

Taken together these three factors produce a method of analysis which is often more complicated than utility theory, but which can provide explanations of a much wider set of circumstances.

This section explains what an indifference curve is, and lets you find out about the assumptions underlying them and their properties. These are used in the analysis which is developed in section 3.6.

Elements of the Consumer Choice Model

This topic lets you discover definitions of all the main terms used in indifference curve analysis. Details about, for example, the shape of the curves and the restrictiveness of the assumptions made are available from the More and Advanced buttons. You start exploring this screen by choosing a name from the list of those offered by the Names button.

Some points to remember about the indifference curve (IC) model

15 **Are ICs restricted to analysing choice between two goods? Explain your answer.**

16 **What is a general expression for the slope of the budget line?**

17 **Are consumers' tastes and preferences changed by changes in prices?**

18 **Why are ICs curved with the convex side to the origin of the diagram?**

19 **What is the mathematical term for getting on the highest IC that your budget line will allow?**

Discovering Indifference Curves

You begin using this screen in WinEcon by selecting a pair of goods to use in the analysis. Alternative consumption combinations are then considered. When someone likes different combinations of goods equally, so that he or she could be said to be indifferent between them, the points representing these different combinations of goods must lie on the same indifference curve. An indifference curve links all the possible combinations of two goods that give the consumer equal satisfaction.

It is implied that the consumption takes place within a particular time period, and this is a good example of a 'simplifying assumption'. The analysis of consumption in more than one time period would add extra details which might obscure the essential features of how indifference analysis works.

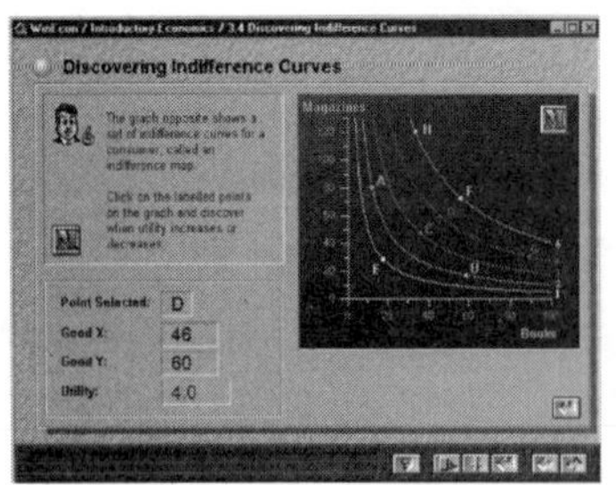

By obtaining points that give equal satisfaction you deduce one indifference curve. Then show the indifference map for your consumer from WinEcon card 3. The map is a set of non-intersecting curves, each representing a different level of satisfaction or utility. You can compare utility levels for the diagram on the screen by clicking on different points, and you find that the satisfaction level is greater for higher curves.

When two points on the same indifference curve are connected by a straight line, analytical conclusions can be drawn about other points on the line. This is possible because typically we assume indifference curves have the standard shape (i.e. convex to the origin). To find out about this click the More button.

The properties of indifference curves

20 What can you say about all points on an indifference curve?

After clicking the More button on the graph, what does each of the following buttons show?

21 Set of ICs

22 Position of ICs

23 Shape of ICs

24 Utility levels

Assumptions of Indifference Curves

The various assumptions made in drawing a standard indifference map are collected together on this WinEcon screen. The properties generated by each are stated and explanations of them are available.

Notice the basic assumptions of consumer rationality and ability to rank or compare different combinations of goods. These assumptions let us construct indifference curves and also imply that different curves cannot cross one another. The general downward (or negative) slope of indifference curves comes from the More assumption, which implies that alternative combinations giving equal satisfaction involve trade-offs of one good against the other. The specific curvature of being convex to the origin derives from the way in which such trade-offs take place, with the consumer becoming increasingly reluctant to take more and more of one good in exchange for the other. As we move from left to right along a curve its slope changes from steep to shallow, showing that the consumer becomes less and less willing to give up good Y in exchange for good X. The rate at which the consumer substitutes good Y by good X is called the marginal rate of substitution (MRS) and it diminishes as more of good X is obtained. The MRS is measured as the negative of the slope of the indifference curve. You can find the slope at any point as the slope of the line that forms a tangent to the curve, or you can use the mathematical technique of differentiation. When we model consumer utility, U, as a function of X and Y giving $U = f(X,Y)$, each indifference curve represents a constant level of utility and the MRS can be expressed as the ratio of the marginal utilities of the two goods. That is $MRS = MU_X/MU_Y$.

The assumption that the consumer prefers to have more of each good says that the goods we are comparing are things which the consumer wants to have. Sometimes we may be interested in using indifference curve analysis where

the choices involve one good which has negative utility for the consumer. An example is work, which we may wish to plot against income. To obtain standard-shaped indifference curves we look for another variable which is the opposite of the one giving negative utility. For example, instead of using hours of work, we plot hours of leisure instead.

The analytical results we obtain from indifference curve analysis rest on us being able to investigate the effects of a change in price or in the consumer's income while other factors are unchanged. In particular we require that tastes remain fixed so that the indifference curves do not alter. The objective of our analysis is assumed to be the achievement of the highest possible level of utility. The consumer therefore wishes to reach the highest possible indifference curve. We shall see that there is a restriction on how high a curve he or she can reach in terms of available income.

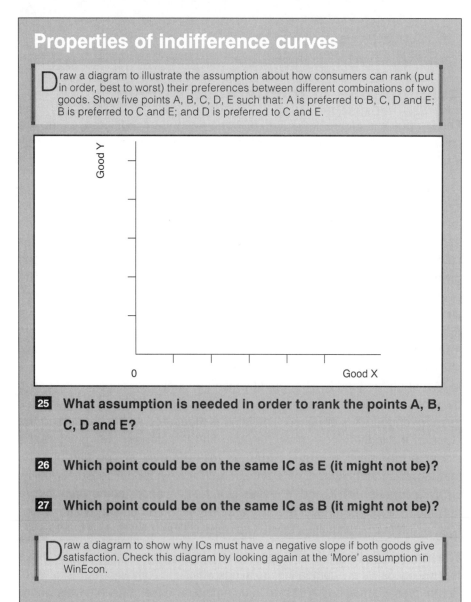

Properties of indifference curves

Draw a diagram to illustrate the assumption about how consumers can rank (put in order, best to worst) their preferences between different combinations of two goods. Show five points A, B, C, D, E such that: A is preferred to B, C, D and E; B is preferred to C and E; and D is preferred to C and E.

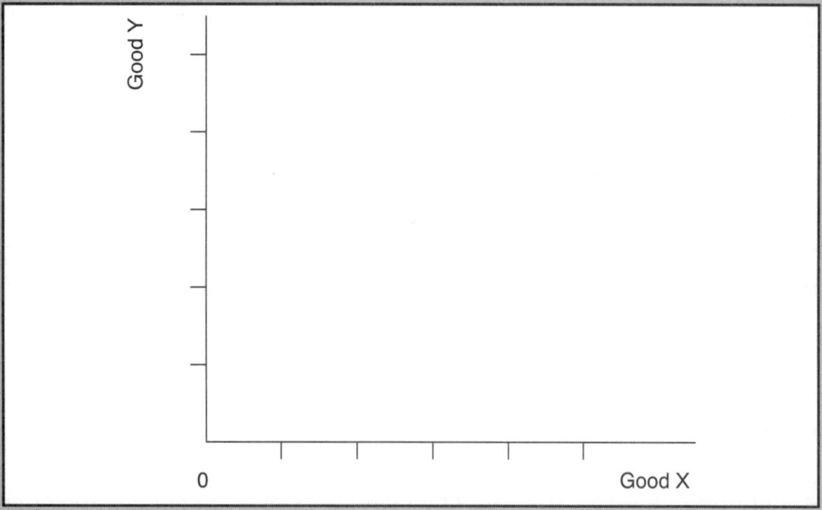

Good Y

0 Good X

25 **What assumption is needed in order to rank the points A, B, C, D and E?**

26 **Which point could be on the same IC as E (it might not be)?**

27 **Which point could be on the same IC as B (it might not be)?**

Draw a diagram to show why ICs must have a negative slope if both goods give satisfaction. Check this diagram by looking again at the 'More' assumption in WinEcon.

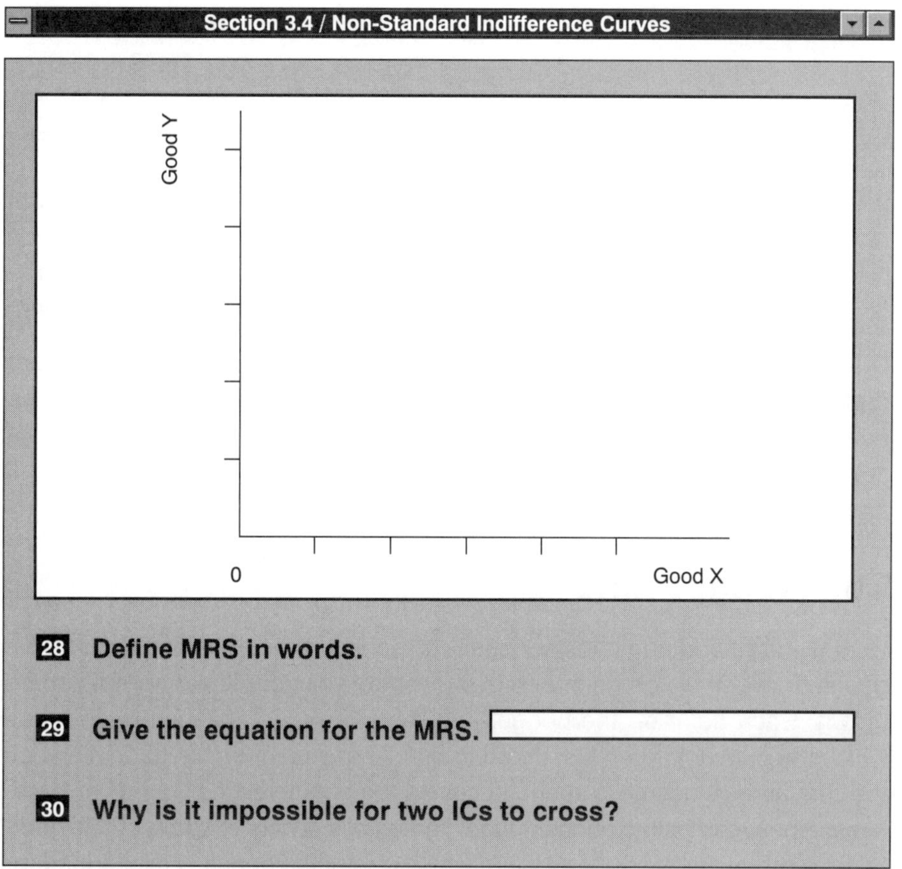

28 **Define MRS in words.**

29 **Give the equation for the MRS.**

30 **Why is it impossible for two ICs to cross?**

Non-Standard Indifference Curves

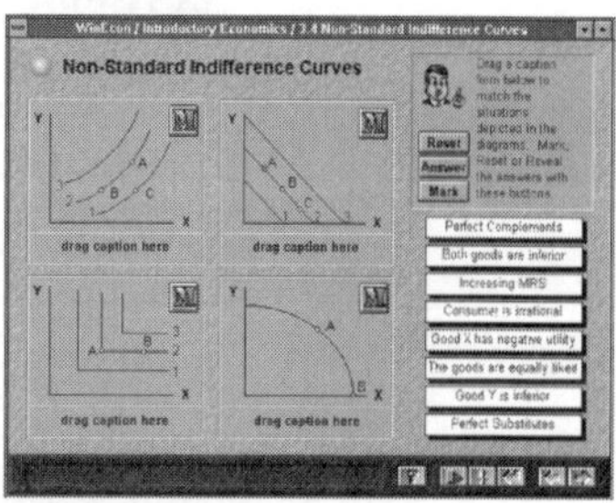

This WinEcon screen presents you with four non-standard indifference maps, and you are asked to identify situations in which they are applicable. The More buttons may be helpful to you, but if you do not name everything correctly you will have the opportunity to try again. Once you have placed the names correctly you can discover examples of when each type of map would occur.

31 In each of the cells below, give the caption and summarize the More button explanation to form a key to the corresponding diagrams.

Section 3.5: The Budget Line

We can show what consumers would like to have using indifference maps, but they are restricted by their budgets as to what they can actually obtain given the prices of the goods they would like to buy. This section shows how the constraint of what is affordable can be depicted graphically as a budget line.

Drawing the budget line emphasizes that the objective (what customers prefer – shown by the ICs) is completely separate from the constraints (which are summarized in the budget line). When the budget line is superimposed on a consumer's indifference map we have a powerful analytical tool, as explained in section 3.6.

The Budget Line

Given information about the consumer's income and about the prices of the goods between which he or she is choosing, a budget line diagram can be drawn. Each point on the budget line represents a combination of goods which the consumer can just afford to buy. At any point on the budget line all the consumer's income is spent on buying the combination of goods marked. Moving between points on the budget line entails giving up some of one good to get more of the other. The rate at which one of the goods is exchanged for the other depends on their relative prices, and so the slope of the budget line can be shown to be $-P_x/P_y$.

Drawing a continuous budget line assumes the consumer can buy fractional amounts of good X and good Y. If X and Y are, for example, kilos of apples and kilos of nuts, this assumption is satisfied. If instead they are numbers of apples and numbers of nuts, fractional quantities would not actually be bought but the continuous line provides a convenient approximation to the real world situation.

This WinEcon screen shows you how to draw the budget line by marking its end points and connecting them. Once the line has been drawn on the screen, move to the last card and drag the movable point. You can mark various combinations of the goods and compare the expenditures they entail. Notice whether or not they are affordable with the income available.

What a budget line shows

32 **What three items of information are needed to draw a budget line?**

33 **What determines whether or not a combination of goods is affordable?**

34 **What can you say about all points on a budget line?**

Drawing the Budget Line

Any two points on a budget line can be plotted. The line drawn through them and extended to the axes is the budget line. Use this WinEcon screen to check that you understand the concept of a budget line and how its position is determined. You can select an income and the prices of the goods. Next, for the first point, type in the amount of X to be bought. Click on successive boxes, make the required calculations and input your results so that the point can be plotted. Similarly, progress to the second point and type in values from which it can be plotted. Click to draw the budget line between the axes, passing through the points you have marked.

You can use this screen to investigate some of the properties of a budget line. The slope of the budget line depends on the relative prices of the goods, and its position depends on the consumer's real income, taking the prices of the goods into account. The initial screen has income, *M*, of 96, price of X, P_x, of 4, and price of Y, P_y, of 1. Plot this budget line, then plot another with the same income but with $P_x = 8$ and $P_y = 2$. The second line has the same slope as the first, but is nearer the origin. Next plot the line for $M = 48$, $P_x = 4$ and $P_y = 1$. It is identical to the second line because *M*, P_x and P_y have all been divided by the same amount, namely 2.

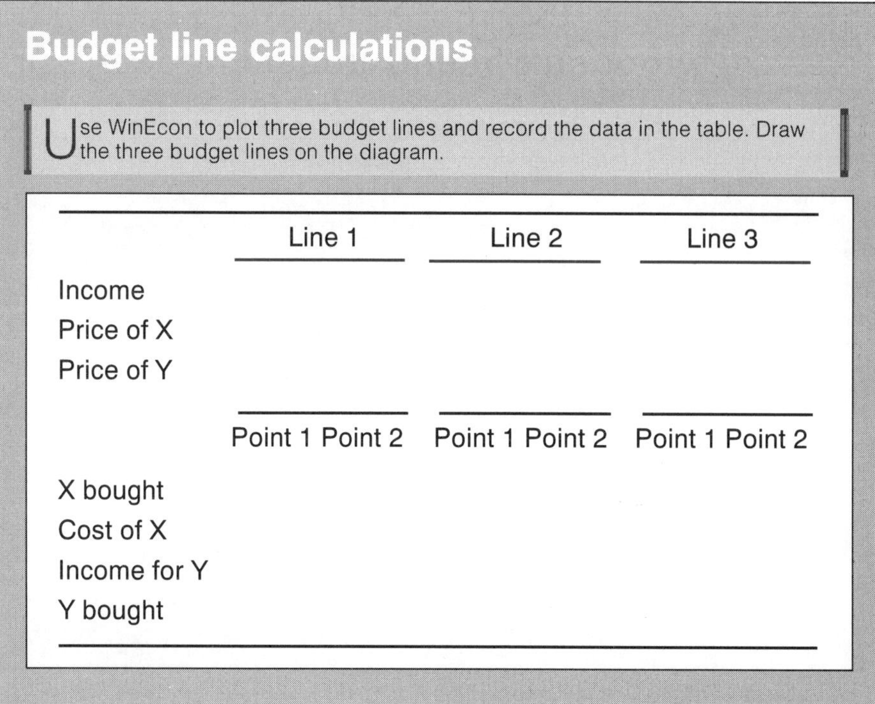

Budget line calculations

Use WinEcon to plot three budget lines and record the data in the table. Draw the three budget lines on the diagram.

	Line 1		Line 2		Line 3	
Income						
Price of X						
Price of Y						
	Point 1	Point 2	Point 1	Point 2	Point 1	Point 2
X bought						
Cost of X						
Income for Y						
Y bought						

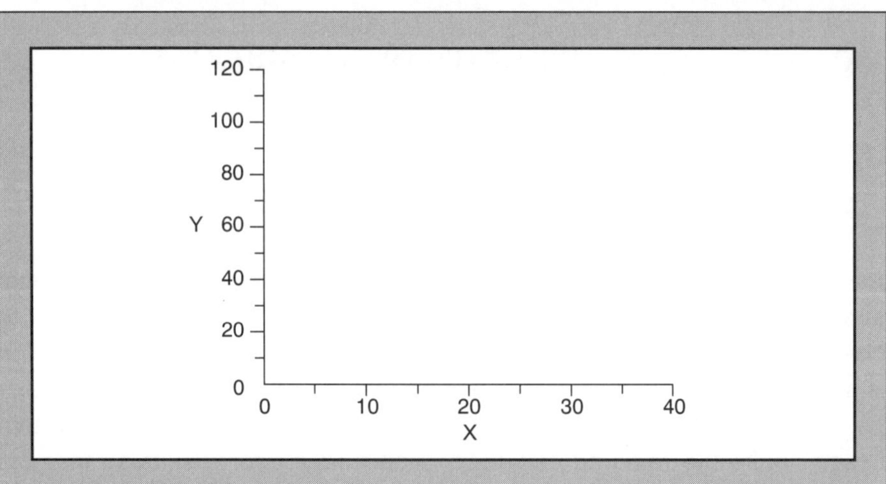

Changing the Budget Line

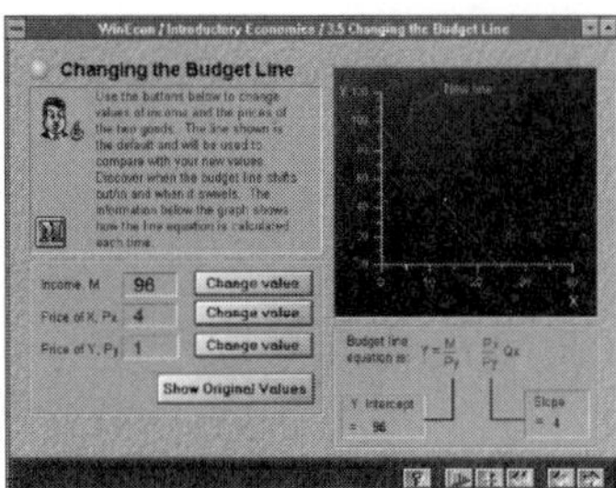

If there is a change in the consumer's income, or in the price of one of the goods which he or she buys, the budget line will change. You can discover when the budget line shifts and when it swivels using this WinEcon screen. Here you again have the opportunity to select values for income and prices, and then plot the budget line. On this screen, one particular budget line is always visible for comparison purposes. Notice that when a new line is drawn, information is given about its equation.

For more details on the equation of a line see the topic Linear Equations in chapter 22 (in WinEcon only).

The intercept of the budget line on the Y axis is the amount of Y the consumer can buy if all of his or her income is spent on buying Y. This amount is M/P_y, where M is the consumer's income and P_y is the price of good Y. The slope of the budget line is $-P_x/P_y$, because one unit of X can be exchanged for P_x/P_y units of Y at market prices.

Changes in income and prices

Record the data you use in WinEcon in the table, then draw and label each of the budget lines you plot.

	Original line	New line 1	New line 2	New line 3
Income				
Price of X				
Price of Y				

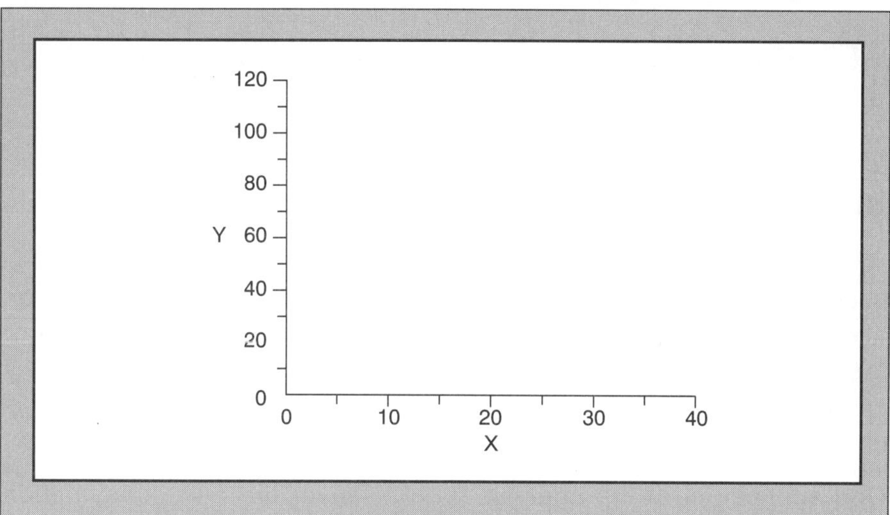

Section 3.6: Indifference Curve Analysis

In this section we bring together the indifference map and the budget line. From this we develop an analysis of how a consumer who is subject to a limited budget can maximize his or her utility. We then study the changes that would occur if the income of the consumer or the prices of the goods were to change. In this way we deduce the income–consumption curve, the Engel curve, the price–consumption curve and the demand curve for the consumer.

Optimal Consumption Choice

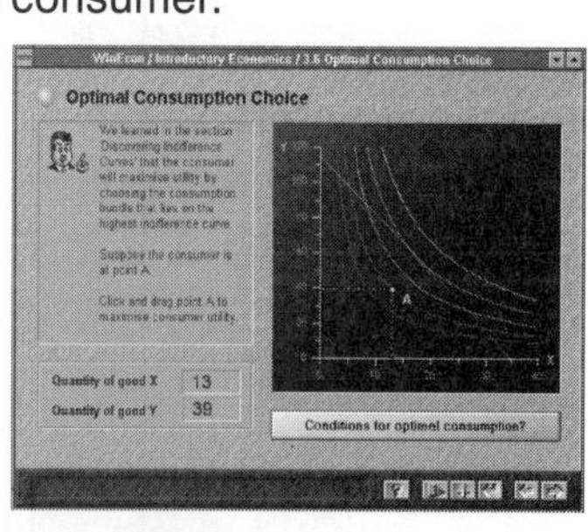

This WinEcon screen asks you to drag a point indicating a consumption combination to where the consumer achieves maximum utility. You need to consider what the consumer can afford, as indicated by the budget constraint, as well as what he or she would prefer. Use the button to discover a theoretical statement of the conditions under which optimal consumption is achieved.

The optimal choice

35 **Identify the two main mistakes that can be made when choosing an optimal position on the diagram.**

36 **Looked at from a diagrammatic point of view, what is an optimal choice?**

37 **Looked at from a mathematical point of view what is an optimal choice?**

38 **In terms of economic theory, what is an optimal choice?**

Income–Consumption Curve

You now know that a consumer chooses to consume at a point where the budget line just touches the highest possible indifference curve. This can alternatively be described as that consumption takes place at a point of tangency between the budget line and the indifference curve. This analysis can be used in many different situations to predict the effects of various changes that may occur.

One application of the analysis is to discover the new consumption combinations that arise as income changes, and these are depicted by the income–consumption curve (ICC). Work through this screen noting the changes that take place and so discover how the income–consumption curve is obtained.

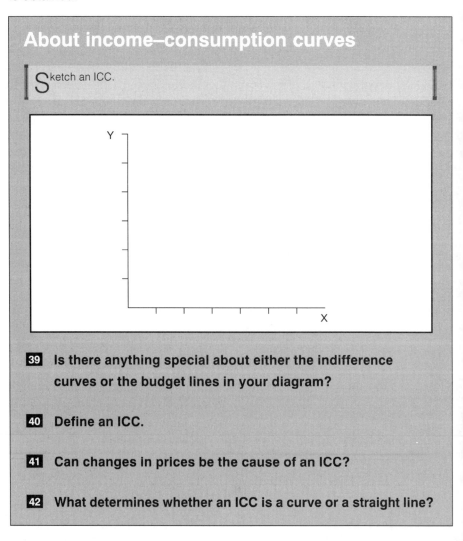

About income–consumption curves

Sketch an ICC.

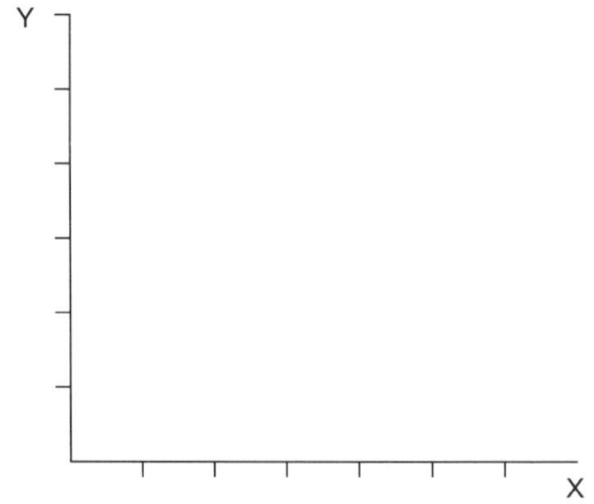

Y

X

39 **Is there anything special about either the indifference curves or the budget lines in your diagram?**

40 **Define an ICC.**

41 **Can changes in prices be the cause of an ICC?**

42 **What determines whether an ICC is a curve or a straight line?**

The Engel Curve

There are two main influences on demand; price and income. The Engel curve summarizes the effect of income changes, and so complements the demand curve which summarizes the effect of price changes. It shows the relationship between income and the amount of a good that is consumed. This WinEcon topic explains how it is derived using two linked diagrams. Notice what is plotted on the axes of each graph.

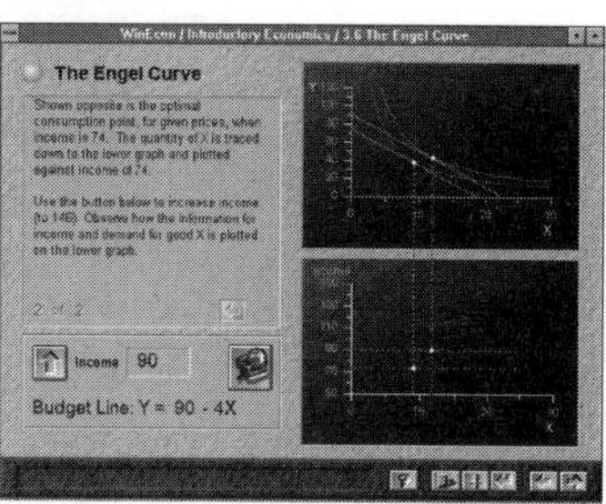

Engel curves are also discussed in the topic Income Elasticity of Demand in section 2.5. Notice that the axes are interchanged in this topic.

About Engel curves

Show how an Engel curve is derived from an ICC.

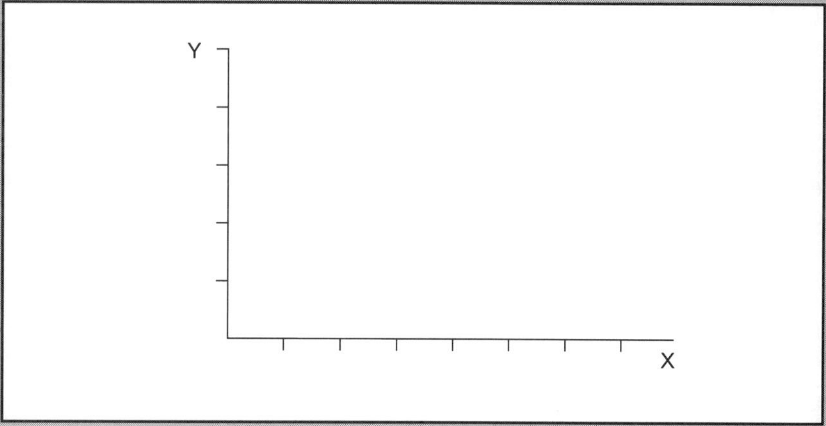

Y

X

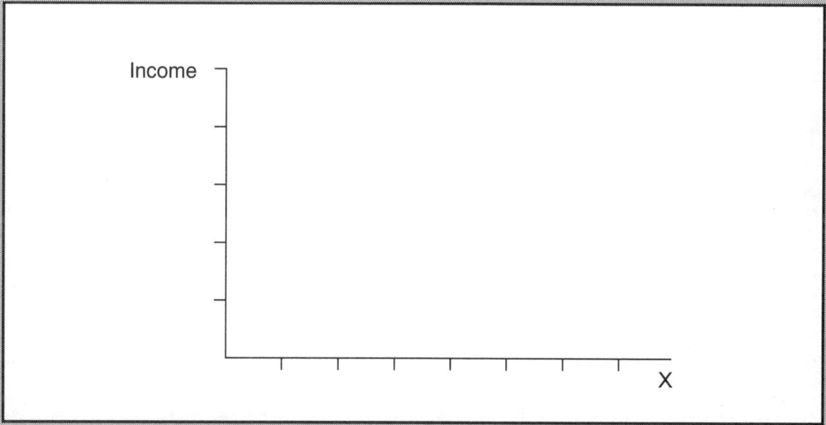

Income

X

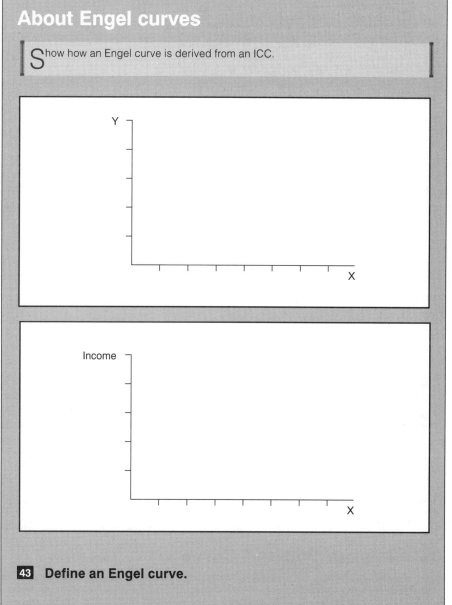

43 **Define an Engel curve.**

44 **Is there a connection between the slope of the ICC and the slope of the related Engel curve?**

Price–Consumption Curve

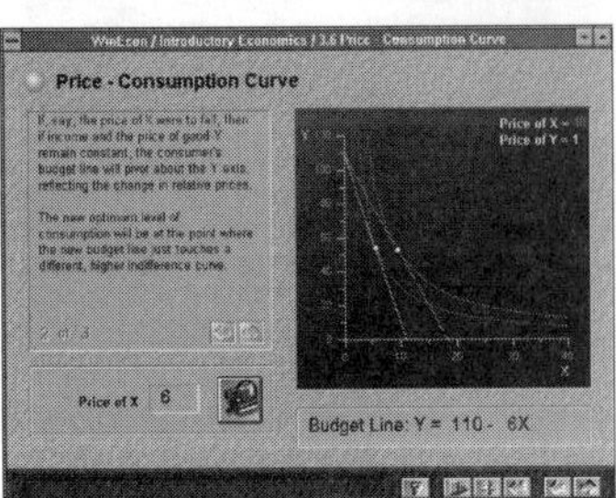

The price–consumption curve (PCC) represents on an indifference map diagram the pattern of consumption that occurs as the price of one of the goods is altered. Clicking the buttons on this WinEcon screen enables you to see how a price–consumption curve is obtained. Notice why the budget line changes, and how the quantities of goods bought alter.

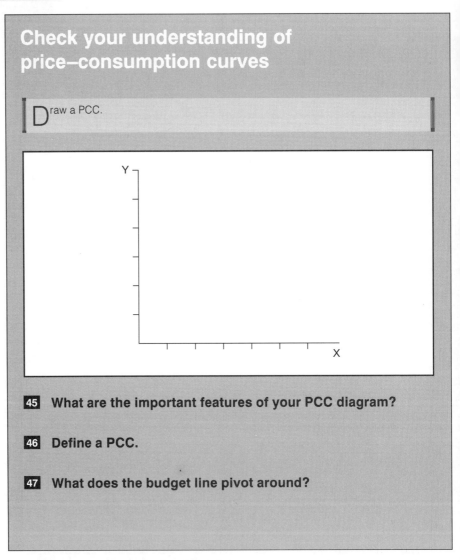

Check your understanding of price–consumption curves

Draw a PCC.

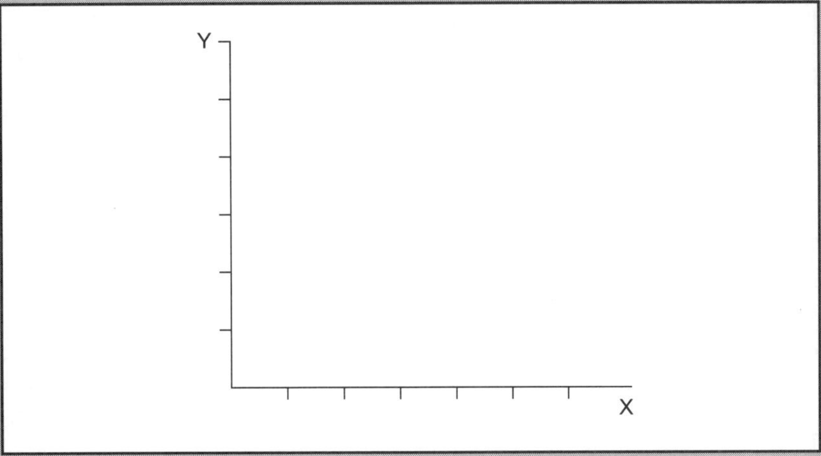

Y

X

45 **What are the important features of your PCC diagram?**

46 **Define a PCC.**

47 **What does the budget line pivot around?**

Deriving the Demand Curve

The demand curve shows the relationship between the price of a good and the quantities of it that are purchased, and this information is implicit in the price–consumption curve. We can therefore use the technique of two linked diagrams to derive the demand curve from the PCC. Notice how the values on each of the axes in the lower screen diagram are obtained.

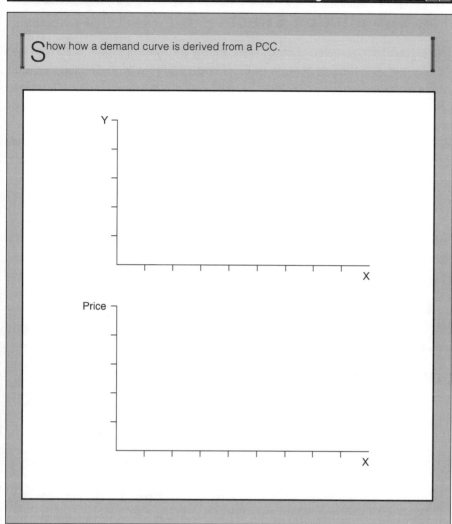

Show how a demand curve is derived from a PCC.

Section 3.7: The Income and Substitution Effects

This section provides an in-depth description of the effects of a price change. The overall effect is disaggregated into two parts, called the income and substitution effects. This analysis enables us to distinguish between normal and inferior goods. We can also identify which changes in the quantities of the goods purchased always accompany a price change in a particular direction, and which do not.

The Effect of a Price Change

Use this screen to test if you are ready to move on to the rest of this section. It asks you whether various statements are true when a price change occurs. If you are not sure of some of the answers, look back at earlier topics in sections 3.4, 3.5 and 3.6.

The Substitution Effect

Here you discover what economists mean by the substitution effect. It is concerned with the impact of a price change on the way the consumer feels about the good whose price has changed by comparison with the other good plotted on the indifference curve diagram. If the price of one good rises, this results in a different budget line. The substitution effect is concerned solely with the fact that the slope of the budget line is different. The change in relative prices makes the consumer tend to substitute away from the good whose price has risen and in favour of the other good.

Work through the WinEcon cards, noticing the construction that is used to enable us to define the substitution effect. As we consider the way in which the consumption combination alters, assuming the consumer stays on the same indifference curve, the important point to note is the direction of the change in the quantity chosen of the good whose price has changed. When the price of X rises, the budget line has a steeper slope. Since indifference curves are convex to the origin, the new line must touch the indifference curve at a point that is higher and to the left of the original position, implying that less X is purchased. When the price of X is higher, the consumer buys less X, and so we say the substitution effect is negative. The substitution effect is always negative, assuming indifference curves have the standard shape.

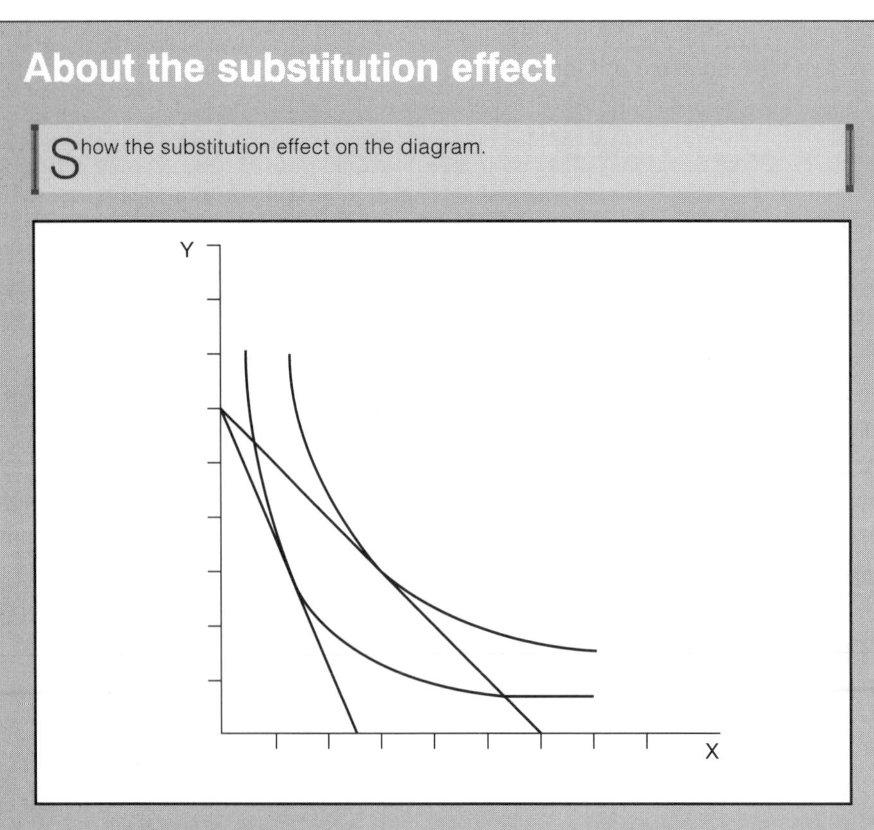

About the substitution effect
Show the substitution effect on the diagram.
Y
X

48 **Define the substitution effect.**

49 **How are ICs related to the substitution effect?**

50 **How are budget lines related to the substitution effect?**

The Income Effect

When the price of a good changes, the income effect is the part of the change in consumption of the good which is attributable to an alteration in how well-off the consumer is. After a price change, a new optimal consumption combination is chosen on a different indifference curve. To study the income effect of a price change we hold relative prices constant and look at the effect of moving from the original indifference curve to the one reached after the price change. The same change could be caused by a change in income, hence the term 'income effect'.

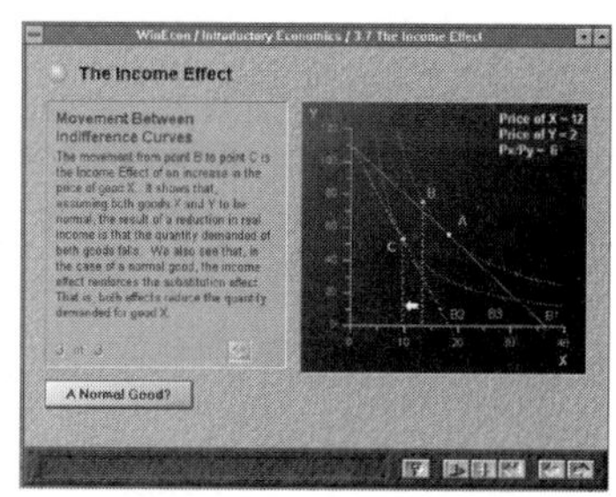

Use the WinEcon screen and notice that it recaps on the definition of the substitution effect so that you can then find the income effect. The income effect moves the consumer from a hypothetical position on the original indifference curve (chosen if the relative prices of X and Y were the post-price-change ones) to the position actually chosen after the price change. For a rise in the price of X, the new position is on a lower indifference curve, so the consumer experiences a decline in real income.

If X is a normal good, less of it is purchased as income declines. The decline in income is in this instance caused by a price rise. We say that the income effect of a price rise is that less of the good will be purchased, assuming it is a normal good. The income effect is therefore negative for a normal good, and it reinforces the substitution effect, which is also negative.

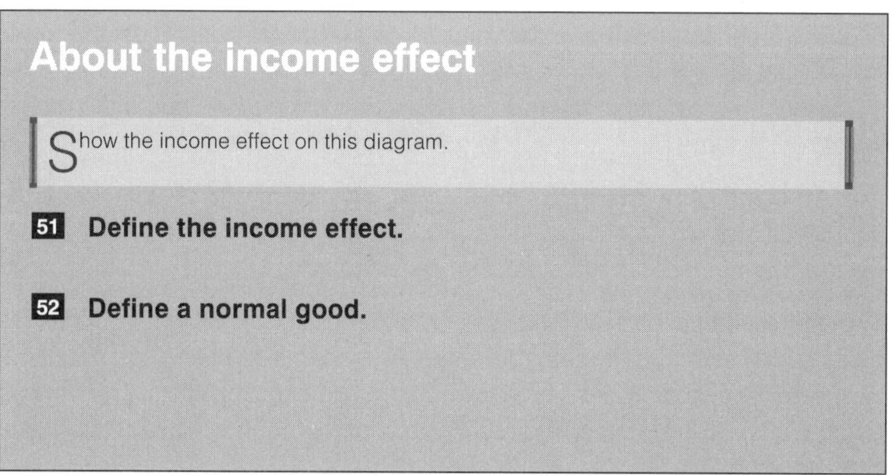

About the income effect

Show the income effect on this diagram.

51 **Define the income effect.**

52 **Define a normal good.**

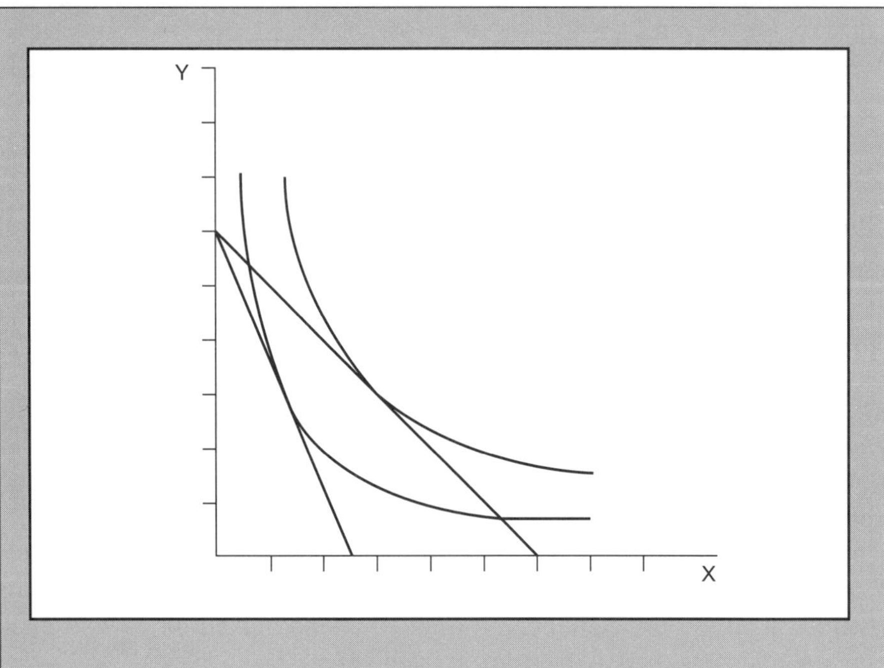

The Income and Substitution Effects

This WinEcon screen is a revision and summary of the previous two screens, letting you see both effects together.

Inferior Goods

See the topics Shifts in the Product Demand Curve and Income Elasticity of Demand in sections 2.2 and 2.5 respectively.

By comparison with a normal good, an inferior good has an unusual consumption pattern as income increases. Less of it is purchased rather than more, because the consumer prefers to buy other goods instead.

As you use the WinEcon screen, compare the pattern of indifference curves shown with those for a normal good. Notice that the lower indifference curve is more nearly vertical than the higher one. When a price change occurs, such pairs of curves generate a positive income effect. Comparing the points at which the parallel budget lines are tangential to the curves (so that relative prices are constant) we see that more X is chosen at point C on the lower curve than at point B where the consumer's real income is higher. This indicates that, for this consumer, X is an inferior good. A consumer with a lower real income tends to buy more X when X is an inferior good.

In this instance, the income effect of a rise in the price of X is to increase the quantity of X purchased. Since price and quantity move in the same direction, we say that the income effect is positive for an inferior good.

The overall effect of a rise in the price of X is that less of it is bought, so X has the usual downward-sloping demand curve. The reduction in the quantity of X demanded, however, is less than the substitution effect predicts. The income effect works in the opposite direction and partly counteracts the negative substitution effect.

A good which is extremely inferior generates a more exaggerated indifference map, and this can be constructed in such a way that point A corresponds to a lower value of X than point C. If this occurs, the positive income effect outweighs the negative substitution effect and the good has an upward-sloping demand curve, at least over part of its length. Such a good is very, very inferior – a 'Giffen good'. As we saw in chapter 2, for an item to be a Giffen good, not only must it be exceptionally inferior but it must also take up a large proportion of the consumer's income.

What is unusual about inferior goods?

53 **Define an inferior good.**

Show the substitution effect and the income effect for an inferior good.

Y

X

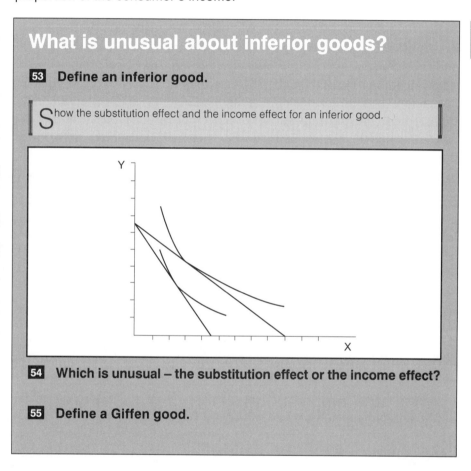

54 **Which is unusual – the substitution effect or the income effect?**

55 **Define a Giffen good.**

Section 3.8: Summary

The analysis of consumer behaviour which this chapter presents justifies the typical downward slope of the demand curve. It also gives us a powerful tool in indifference curve analysis which can be used to analyse choice in many different situations. The basis of the analysis is that consumers are rational and you see in this chapter some of the implications of this for consumer choice theory.

You discover the concept of utility and find that the principle of diminishing marginal utility yields a downward-sloping demand curve for a single good.

When choosing between two goods you find that utility is maximized if the amounts bought of each good are such that the ratio of their marginal utilities equals the ratio of their prices.

Another approach to analysing consumer choices is indifference curve analysis. Consumer preferences between two goods are represented by an indifference map. At all points on the same indifference curve the consumer has the same amount of utility, and higher curves denote higher levels of utility. Standard-shaped indifference curves are convex to the origin, but we have seen that other shapes of curves can also arise in special circumstances.

A budget line represents all possible combinations of two goods that the consumer can buy with a specific level of income. The slope of the line is the negative of the ratio of the prices of the goods, $-P_x/P_y$. When a budget line is superimposed on an indifference map the point of tangency between the budget line and the highest attainable indifference curve marks the combination of the two goods which maximizes the consumer's utility, given the budget constraint.

Using indifference curve analysis we can derive an Engel curve by considering changes in income, and a demand curve by considering changes in price. The effect of a price change is separated into its substitution and income effects. We find that the substitution effect of a price rise is that the consumer substitutes away from the good whose price increases, and tends to buy less of it. As price rises, quantity falls, and so the substitution effect is negative. The income effect for a normal good is such that less of it is bought as its price rises, so we say the income effect is negative for normal goods. With inferior goods, however, more is bought if income falls, and so the income effect tends to increase the quantity bought as price rises. The income effect for inferior goods is therefore positive. Giffen goods are exceptionally inferior goods for which the positive income effect is stronger than the negative substitution effect. Over the range of prices for which this occurs,the demand curve for a Giffen good is upward sloping.

Chapter 4:

Production and Costs

How should production be organized? What combination of factor inputs minimizes costs or maximizes profits? Since the birth of economics as a subject, economists have studied such questions. In 1817 David Ricardo began looking at different ways in which the profit-seeking entrepreneur could combine the use of land, labour and capital in the production process. The same questions are still of interest, because an understanding of production and costs allows us to analyse the firm's behaviour in the market-place.

Contents

KEYWORDS

- Average total cost
- Break-even analysis
- Cost minimization
- Diminishing returns
- Diseconomies of scale
- Economies of scale
- Expansion path
- Isocost
- Isoquant
- Marginal cost
- Minimum efficient scale
- Production function
- Target profit level

Section 4.1: Introduction

This chapter introduces the concept of a production function, and shows you how it determines the firm's costs. The ideas are presented from a historical perspective, so you learn about the contributions made by eminent economists in the past. We distinguish between the long run and the short run by how much flexibility there is in the use of resources.

You learn about the laws of diminishing returns and variable proportions, and discover what is meant by the marginal physical product of labour. In the next section you represent the production function by an isoquant map, and carry out an analysis of the optimal production decision for the firm. This is similar to the analysis of how a consumer achieves optimal utility. Average and marginal cost curves are then obtained and shown in diagrams. Cost–volume–profit analysis and its application follows. What happens when the firm chooses to increase its output either in the short or long run is then shown by the appropriate expansion path. In the long run we find that economies of scale may be available, and we consider how these may affect the organization of firms.

Section 4.2: Short-Run Production

To increase output the firm must use more of the factor inputs used in the production process. Some of these, however, are difficult to change quickly. For example, a new factory or new machinery may take time to obtain. When we analyse the production process we therefore distinguish between the 'long run' and the 'short run'. In the long run it is possible to change the quantity of any of the different types of factor inputs used in the production process, but in the short run it is not.

This section is concerned with the short run. We see what increase in production is brought about by a firm increasing the amounts used of just some of the factors it employs. The amounts of the other factors of production are assumed to be fixed. You learn about diminishing returns and variable proportions, along with important concepts such as total, average and marginal physical product.

Production and Factor Inputs

We begin by introducing you to the concept of the 'production function'. This is the tool economists use to analyse the relationship between the physical resources used in production and their associated output; it shows what output can be obtained from particular quantities of inputs.

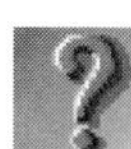

Develop your understanding of the production function

01 **David Ricardo said that production was a function of the amounts of ________, ________ and ________ used.**

Use WinEcon to find how we write a production function in algebraic form. Record this and try to explain in your own words what it shows.

The Short-Run Production Function

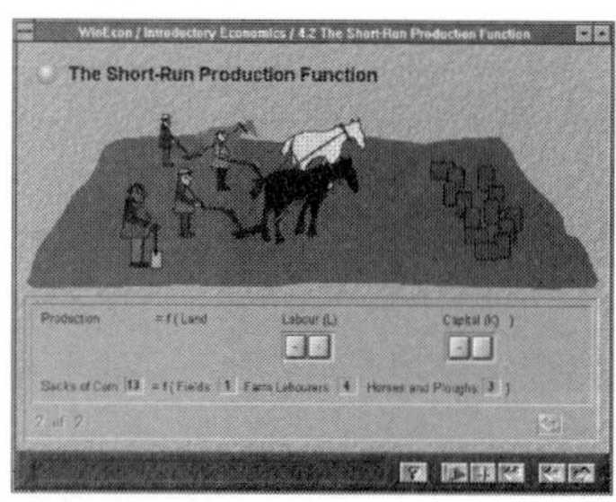

As you use this WinEcon screen you find that the output of corn depends on the amount of land, labour and capital used. (In this case capital is represented by horses and ploughs.) With the amount of land available being fixed (we only have one field) output can only be increased by using either more labour or more capital. Try changing the quantity of the two variable factor inputs in WinEcon and see what effect it has on production of corn.

Short-run production

02 **In the WinEcon example of the production of corn, ________ is in fixed supply which means that output can only be increased by changing the amount of ________ or ________ used.**

03 **What are the effects on the output of corn of adding the first unit of labour and the first unit of capital either separately or together? Can you explain the reasons for the changes in production that occur?**

Diminishing Returns in Production

When a firm's product is selling well it may decide to increase the rate of production. To do this it needs to employ more of the factors of production used. In the short run, although it may be able to buy more raw materials and perhaps more labour, it is unlikely to be able to obtain more machines or a larger factory. We say, then, that at least one of the factor inputs is fixed in the short run. This means that as output expands in the short run the proportions in which the factors are combined must change. It may be that more raw materials and labour are less effective unless they are used with more machinery.

Economists describe this situation as the problem of 'diminishing marginal returns' to the variable factor(s). You can see in this WinEcon topic that the problem may also arise in agriculture. When the amount of land is fixed if we add more and more units of labour to the production process the extra output produced by each additional labourer will eventually start to fall.

Apply the concept of diminishing returns

04 **Increasing the quantity of labour used when other ________ are ________ leads to the problem of ________ ________ ________.**

05 **What has to be fixed for the concept of diminishing returns to be applicable?**

06 **Economics gained the title of the 'dismal science' because Malthus said that the growth of population would outstrip the production of food and as a consequence people would die. What economic analysis lay behind Malthus' statement?**

The Law of Variable Proportions

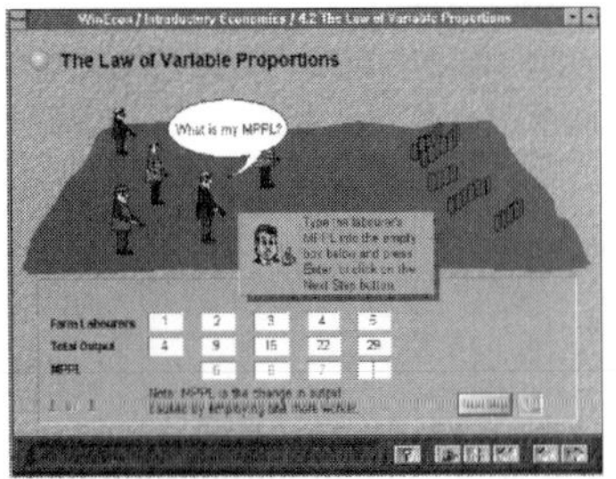

When a new firm is just launching into business, it may be that the smallest premises and machinery available have the capacity to produce more output than the firm's initial production level. In these circumstances, if the firm does choose to expand its output, it will initially be able to achieve a more favourable combination of inputs. If expansion continues with the same capital equipment diminishing returns will eventually set in.

In this case the 'law of variable proportions' is applicable. This states: when one factor of production is fixed (e.g. capital) we will observe firstly increasing returns to the variable factor (e.g. labour). This will then be followed by a period

of constant returns and then finally this in turn will be followed by decreasing returns.

To analyse what occurs in more detail we use the concept of the 'marginal physical product of labour' (MPPL). This shows us how 'total product' (output) changes as we add one more unit of labour. The WinEcon example asks you to enter values of the MPPL, which is calculated as the difference between the new total output and the previous value when one more labourer is employed.

Notice the different values that MPPL takes. At first there are increasing marginal returns with each MPPL being higher than the previous one. But as employment continues to increase, marginal returns become constant and then diminish.

Understanding the law of variable proportions

07 **Define the marginal physical product of labour.**

08 **If the additional output produced by adding one more labourer is higher than that produced when the previous labourer was added we can say that the MPPL is ______. If, however, the extra output is smaller the MPPL is ______.**

09 **Use WinEcon to find out how we define increasing, constant and decreasing marginal returns to labour and then record the definitions in your own words.**

Modern Production Methods

The factors of production that are most important in determining the output of most modern industrial firms are labour and capital. Production functions are therefore commonly written showing output to be simply a function of labour and capital.

Modern Production Methods: An Example

This WinEcon screen assumes that the production of micro-chips depends on the amounts of labour and capital employed. Use WinEcon to examine how the returns to labour vary at different output levels. You discover also how to plot 'total physical product' (TPP) and 'marginal physical product' (MPP) curves which are useful in further analysis.

Short-Run Production Functions: A Numerical Example

This WinEcon screen and the next are concerned with providing a numerical example of production functions. Work through these screens and undertake the numerical exercise which follows.

The production function is written as a function of labour and capital, and is similar to the function used in the WinEcon corn example. Since only one factor (labour) can be varied in the short run, we find capital always has the value 1. This value could be substituted for *K* in the production function, and the short-run function would then be written solely as a function of labour.

10a

The production function in this case is given as:

Short-run total physical product = $250L + 30L^2 - 1.55L^3$

Substitute in turn into the production function each value for labour given in the table. Use the WinEcon calculator to work out the corresponding value of TPP and record it in the total product column. You will use the other columns in the next topic.

Labour	Total product	Average product	Marginal product
1	278	278	
2	608	304	
3	978	326	
4			
5			
6			
7			
8			
9			
10			
11			
12			
13			
14			
15			
16			

Marginal and Average Physical Product of Labour: A Numerical Example

10b Complete the table in the previous topic by calculating values for average product and marginal product. Remember that when you write down the marginal product it should be placed between rows.

Sketch the APPL and MPPL curves from the values you have calculated above and indicate the points at which diminishing average returns and diminishing marginal returns set in.

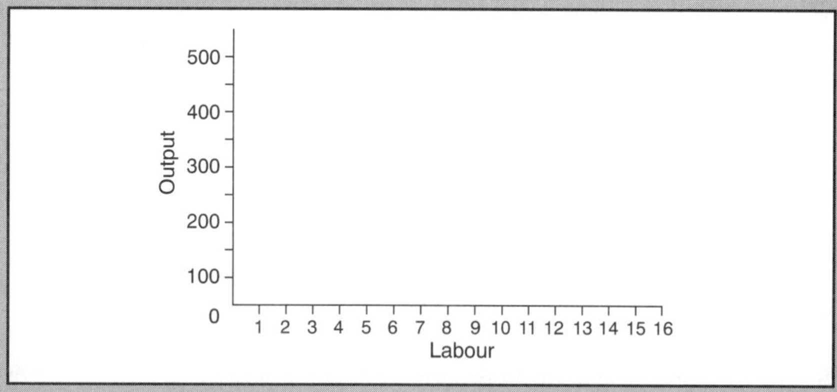

11 **Referring to WinEcon and using your own words, define the average physical product of labour.**

12 **In your own words, describe what happens to the average product of labour and the marginal product of labour as the number of labourers increases.**

13 **The production function shows what happens to _____ _____ _____ when the amount of land, _____ and _____ used in the production process is varied. If land and capital are fixed, as the amount of labour used increases output exhibits firstly _____ _____ then _____ _____ and then finally _____ _____ to labour.**

14 **Explain why diminishing returns occur in the above example.**

Section 4.3: Production at Minimum Cost in the Long Run

In this section we develop an analysis of production and costs in the long run using the tools of 'isocost' and 'isoquant' analysis. We use this to show how a profit maximizing firm will choose factor combinations which will minimize its costs in the long run. The firm is assumed to know the wage rate and the rate of interest, and also what different combinations of labour and capital could be used to produce a given level of output. This means that it will be able to determine what combinations of factors will produce the output it is intending to produce at the minimum cost.

The analysis of the firm's optimal production decision is similar to that of the consumer's optimal consumption decision. Isoquants are the equivalent of indifference curves, and isocost lines correspond to budget lines in indifference curve analysis.

Indifference curve analysis is presented in chapter 3.

The Long-Run Production Function

A profit maximizing firm aims to produce its chosen level of output in the most cost effective way. The longer its planning time period, the greater the flexibility it has in managing its combination of inputs.

Economists define the long run not as a specific time span, but as being the time period in which the amounts of all the factors of production used can be varied. This in practice means that the amount of capital can be varied as well as the amount of labour. This contrasts with the production function which we have just used in the previous section where the only way output could be varied was by altering the amount of labour used.

The Long-Run Production Function (2) is a supplementary screen in this topic that shows further how output can be altered by changing both labour and capital. The three output curves shown in the diagram each correspond to particular levels of capital, K, employed, namely 1, 2 or 3 units. They represent different short run production functions available to the firm, between which it can choose in the long run by altering its capital input.

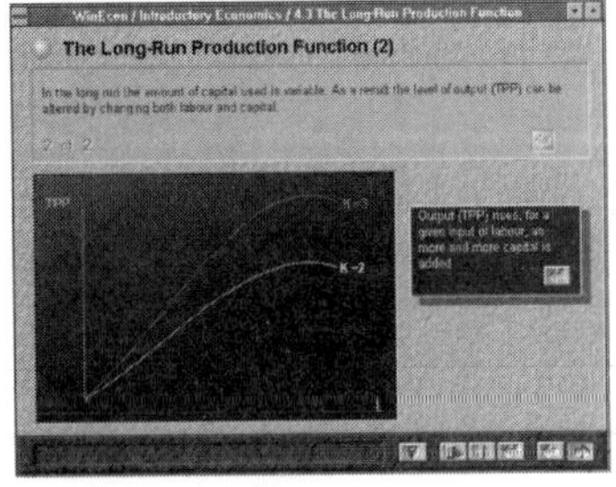

At a point on one of the curves we can read the quantity of labour, L, and capital, K, employed together with the TPP they yield. That output is the maximum that can be obtained from these inputs. It would, of course, be possible to produce less output from the same amounts of L and K. Both men and machines can be left idle. The production function assumes that such waste does not occur, and that firms use technologically efficient factor combinations.

The Isocost Line

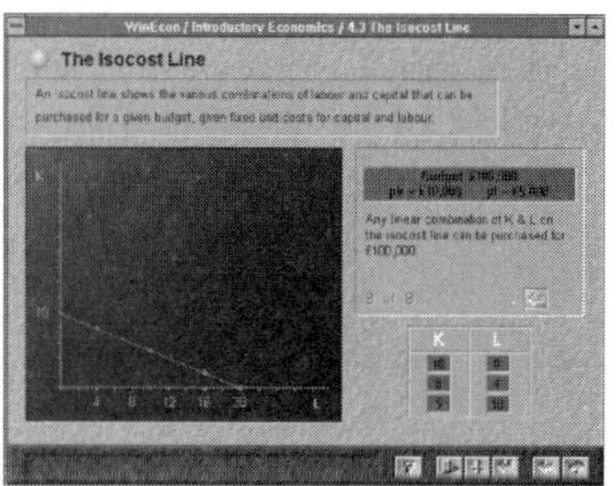

The firm may be able to produce a particular level of output with various different combinations of inputs. From these it would like to choose the one with the lowest cost. To obtain information about the costs of different factor combinations we draw up isocost lines. The prefix iso- means equal, so each isocost line shows us factor combinations that have the same cost.

The WinEcon screen helps you to understand that points along an isocost line represent different combinations of labour and capital which can be purchased from a given budget. From knowing the budget and also how much each unit of labour and capital costs, we decide on an amount of one factor and calculate how much of the other may be purchased. This gives us one point on the isocost line. Repeating the process yields further points which can be connected to the first giving the isocost line. The method is similar to that used to obtain budget lines in the analysis of consumer demand.

About isocost lines

15 **The isocost line shows the various combinations of ________ and ________ that can be purchased for a given ________. If a factor combination is chosen at the end of the isocost on the labour axis then zero ________ is being purchased. All the money will go into buying ________.**

Factors Affecting the Isocost Line and The Shape of the Isocost Line are two supplementary screens in this topic.

Isoquants and Production Rays

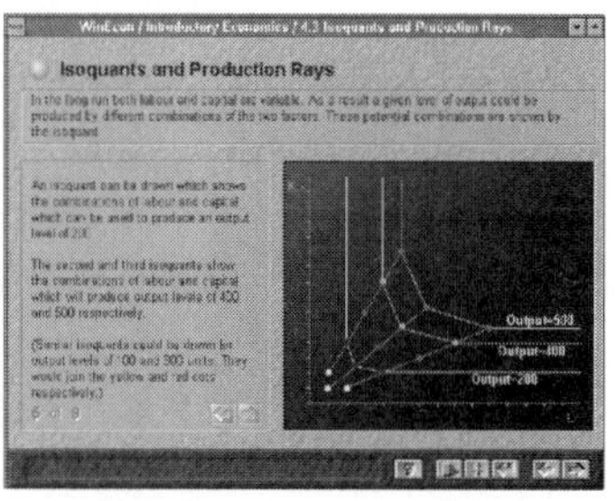

A firm may have available to it alternative production processes, each of which use labour and capital in specific proportions. If it continues to use the same production process as it expands output, a production ray is generated, as demonstrated on card 2 of this WinEcon screen. You can read the amounts of *L* and *K* used at any point on the line. Notice that on the ray shown, the number of units of capital is always double the number of units of labour.

Altering the ratio of labour to capital represents the use of a different technology; it gives a point on a different production ray. Other points on the new ray can be found by applying the new technology at different input levels.

This is illustrated on card 3 of the WinEcon screen. Comparing the proportions of inputs used on the two rays, you find that a ray lying closer to the *K* axis is more capital intensive than one that is farther from it.

Equal quantities of output are produced at all points on the same isoquant. We obtain an isoquant by choosing a particular output level and connecting up the points on different rays at which that output is produced. What an isoquant shows, therefore, is the different combinations of labour and capital which could be used to produce a fixed level of output. Normally we do not look at a single isoquant but at an isoquant map. This is analagous to the consumer's indifference curve map.

Use the following supplementary WinEcon screens (Technical Efficiency, The Shape of the Isoquant: factor substitutability, The Slope of the Isoquant: factor substitutability, and The Shape of the Isoquant: marginal rate of substitution) to discover more about isoquants and the different shapes they can take, then answer the following questions.

You find that isoquants are often drawn as smooth curves, implying that it is possible to make very small changes in the quantity used of either factor. While this may not always be realistic it is a convenient approximation. The marginal rate of substitution of capital by labour, MRS, is then defined and shown to equal the ratio of the marginal physical products of the factors. MRS = MPPL/MPPK.

Develop your understanding of isoquants

16 **At any two points on an isoquant, what is the same?**

17 **At any two points on an isoquant, what is different?**

18 **If an isoquant is higher than a previous one what has happened to output?**

19 The diagram below shows an isoquant curve and illustrates the different combinations of labour and capital which could be used to produce an output level of 100.

(a) **Choose five different combinations of labour and capital (including point X) which can be used to produce output level 100. Mark these points on the diagram and enter amounts in the table.**

(b) **Calculate what these different combinations will cost if labour costs £500 per unit and capital costs £500 per unit, and complete the table.**

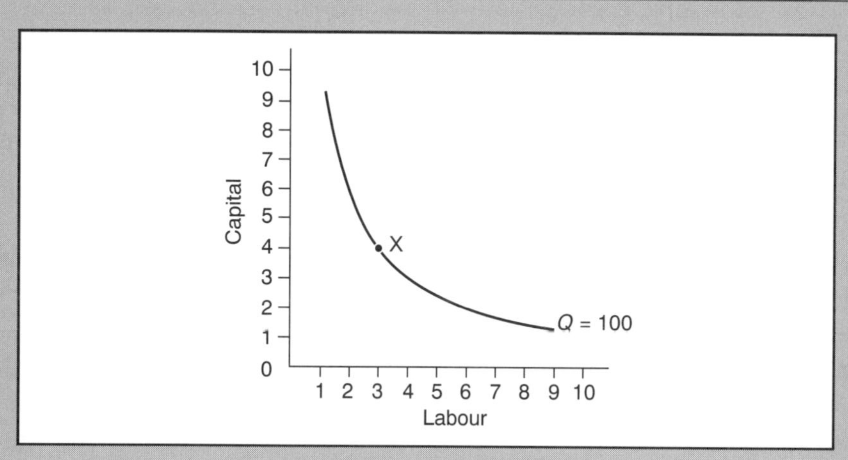

	Labour units	Capital units	Labour cost	Capital cost	Total Cost
1					
2					
3					
4					
5					

20 **The isoquant is normally shown as being convex to the origin. Can you explain why? (Remember that anywhere on an isoquant shows the combinations of labour and capital which may be used to produce the same output level.)**

21 **We normally draw isoquants as smooth curves. In practice do production relationships exhibit such smooth substitutability between factors?**

Producing at Minimum Cost

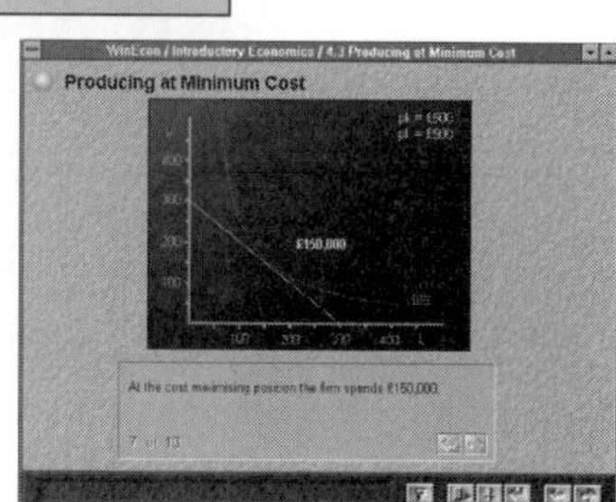

Isoquant and isocost analysis is now used to explain how a firm will go about the process of choosing the correct amounts of labour and capital to produce a particular output level at minimum cost. The firm will choose the factor combination where the isoquant for the chosen production level is tangential to an isocost. The cost associated with the isocost represents the minimum cost of producing the output level, because the factor combination at the point of tangency can just be bought for this money.

This WinEcon topic is concerned with producing an output level of 100. The isoquant is the same as that in the previous topic, where you completed a table listing the costs of different factor combinations. In the example on this screen you should have noted that the minimum cost combination of labour and capital involved a total expenditure of £150,000. You now discover that this corresponds to the point where the isoquant is tangential to the isocost. We have therefore proved in this case that the cost minimizing combination of labour and capital is given to us by the point where the isoquant is tangential to the isocost. We can, however, explain efficient factor combinations using more technical terms. At a point of tangency the marginal rate of substitution (MRS), which is the rate at which the two factor inputs can be substituted whilst keeping output constant, is equal to the ratio of the two factor prices (i.e. the rate at which the two factors can be substituted whilst keeping the total factor cost constant).

Work through the two supplementary screens, which cover Producing at Minimum Cost for a fixed output level and a fixed budget, and then try the following questions.

Minimizing costs

22 **The marginal rate of substitution is the negative of the ________ of the isoquant. It shows the rate at which the firm can substitute ________ for ________ whilst keeping output constant.**

23 **Cost minimizing combinations of labour and capital are given by the point where the ________ is tangential to the ________.**

24 **What can you say about the prices and marginal physical products of the factors when they are used in the optimal combination?**

25 **Explain why the firm is cost minimizing if it picks a factor combination where the isocost is tangential to the isoquant but is not cost minimizing if it chooses a factor combination where the isocost cuts the isoquant.**

Changes in Factor Prices

If the price of one of the factors changes relative to the other than factor substitution will occur. This will result in more of the relatively cheaper factor

being used and less of the relatively more expensive one. The new factor combination required to produce a given output will be found at the point where the existing isoquant is tangential to a new isocost line. This new isocost will have a slope which reflects the new relative prices of the two factors. This means that what will occur is a movement along the isoquant to the new equilibrium factor combination. Notice that the total expenditure associated with the new isocost line is likely to be different from that associated with the original isocost.

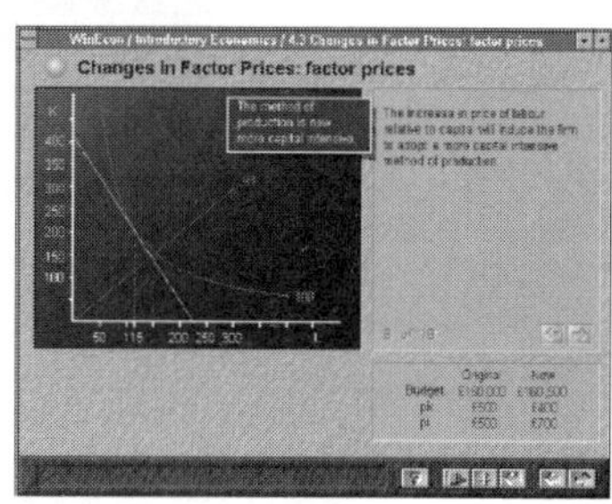

Develop your understanding of factor substitution

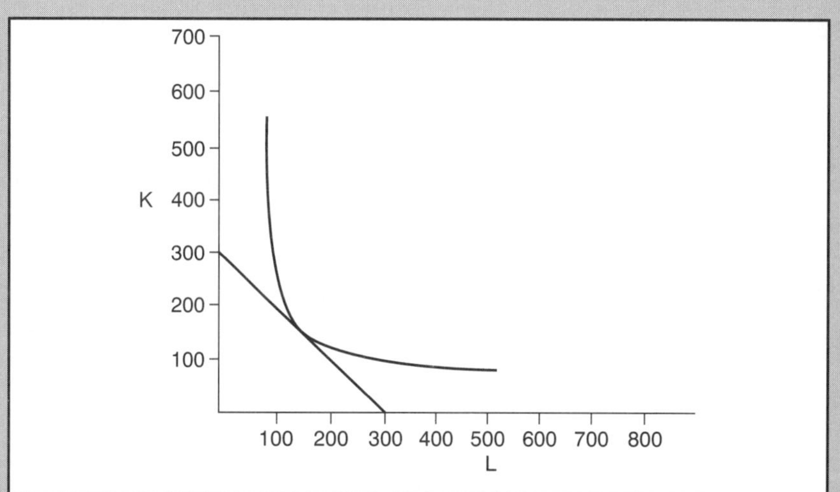

26 The diagram shown is from card 1 of this WinEcon screen. It shows an isoquant curve representing an output of 100 and the isocost line when labour costs £500 and capital costs £500. If the relative prices of the two factors change, then the slope of the isocost will change. For the following different factor prices, list the isocost slope in the table. Draw lines with these slopes on the diagram. If necessary, add other parallel isocost lines which just touch the isoquant. In each case estimate how much of each factor will be used to produce the output of 100.

Price of labour	Price of capital	Isocost slope	Capital used	Labour used
200	1000			
300	900			
800	200			

27 Explain in your own words why the amount of a factor used declines when its price increases relative to the price of the other factor.

(Hint: The firm is cost minimizing, given the output it wishes to produce.)

A supplementary screen in this topic shows another example of the effects of changes in factor prices.

Section 4.4: Short-Run Costs

The physical production relationship between the amounts of labour and capital used and the level of output is expressed by the production function. The costs of labour and capital let us translate the physical relationships that exist in the short run and in the long run into monetary cost relationships. We now derive various short-run cost functions and see that their shapes are determined by physical production relationships. For example, the 'U' shape of the 'short-run average total cost' curve is due primarily to the existence of diminishing marginal returns in production.

Short-Run Cost Definition

There are several important cost relationships in which we are interested. Use WinEcon to find out firstly how they are defined and secondly how we calculate them. Work through the two supplementary screens (Drawing Short-Run Cost Curves and Positioning Short-Run Cost Curves) and complete the table opposite.

For simplicity, economists often shorten ATC to AC (average cost). This convention is followed in most of the following sections.

Deriving Short-Run Total Cost Curves

The total cost of producing a particular level of output is the cost of employing the factors required to produce it. Given the unit costs of capital and labour and the production function we can find the cost of employing particular amounts of capital and labour and the associated total output. This gives one point on the total cost curve.

Discover short-run costs

28 **Record the names corresponding to the abbreviations given, the correct ways of calculating them and the correct cost definitions in the boxes below. Try to use your own words in explaining the definitions.**

TC Full name: Calculated as:
Definition:
Explanation:

FC Full name: Calculated as:
Definition:
Explanation:

VC Full name: Calculated as:
Definition:
Explanation:

ATC Full name: Calculated as:
Definition:
Explanation:

AFC Full name: Calculated as:
Definition:
Explanation:

AVC Full name: Calculated as:
Definition:
Explanation:

MC Full name: Calculated as:
Definition:
Explanation:

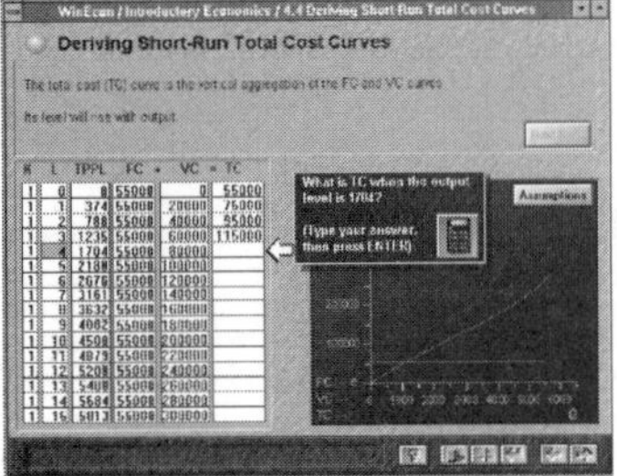

This WinEcon topic lists possible amounts of capital and labour that might be used in the short run. Notice that, because of the time period we are considering, the amount of capital does not alter. Employing capital therefore gives rise to fixed costs in the short run. Keeping the amount of capital fixed and substituting the various values for labour into the production function in turn gives the output obtained from each factor combination, as listed in the TPPL (total physical product of labour) column. The FC (fixed costs) column shows the cost of the capital employed. In addition to these fixed costs, there are VCs (variable costs) associated with employing labour. These increase as output increases. Total variable costs comprise the cost of a unit of labour multiplied by the number of units of labour employed, and are shown in the VC column. Finally we add together the fixed costs and total variable costs to give the total cost of producing each of the levels of output listed.

With the total cost curves calculated, we can now calculate their average cost counterparts by dividing by output. This is shown on the supplementary screen, Deriving Short-Run AFCs and AVCs.

The Shape of the Average Total Cost Curve

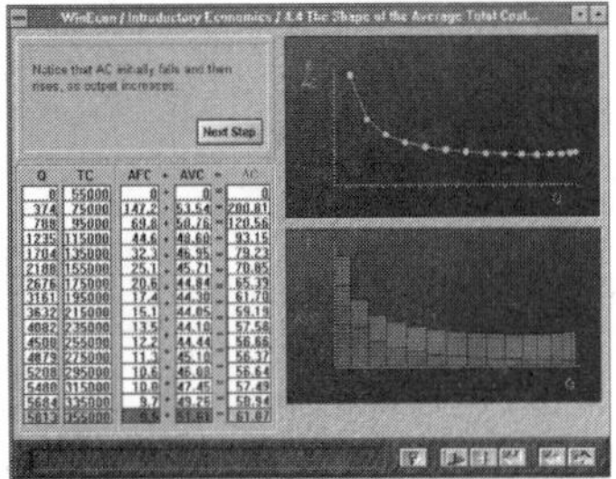

We have discovered in the topic Short-Run Cost Definition that average total cost (AC) consists of the sum of average fixed cost (AFC) and average variable cost (AVC). This composition has to be borne in mind as we examine what determines the shape of the AC curve. We find that its 'U' shape depends on the interaction between fixed and variable costs.

At low output levels, fixed costs represent a high proportion of total costs and will therefore dominate AC. AFC will be high at low output levels; this is because the fixed costs are being borne by relatively few units of output. As a consequence of this, AC will also be high. As output increases, AFC at first falls rapidly, causing AC to fall.

As output continues to increase the proportion of the firm's costs represented by fixed costs falls and that represented by variable costs increases. Therefore, at high output levels, variable costs are the dominant element in AC. As more and more of the variable factor, labour, is added to the same amount of the fixed factor, capital, the production process becomes less efficient, which leads to average variable costs beginning to rise. The WinEcon screen demonstrates this with a numerical example.

The shape of the average total cost curve is closely linked to that of the marginal cost curve, as you discover in the next topic.

The Shape of the Marginal Cost Curve

The marginal cost (MC) is the addition to total cost resulting from the production of one more unit of output. The MC curve's shape is closely related to that of the MPPL curve. Equally, MC can be described as the change in variable costs as one more unit of output is produced, since the fixed cost element of total costs remains unchanged.

See Marginal and Average Physical Product of Labour: a numerical example in section 4.2 to review MPPL curves.

As you use this WinEcon screen you discover that as MPPL increases then the MC falls. However, as soon as MPPL starts to fall then MC starts to rise. This means that there is an inverse relationship between the shape of the MPPL and AVC curves. MC initially falls and then rises.

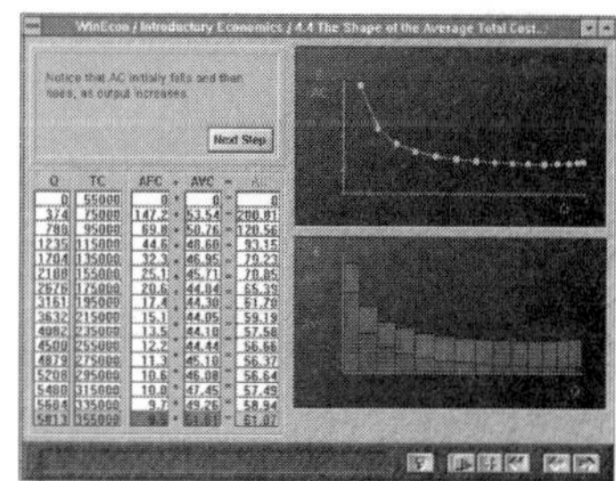

As output gradually builds up from zero, MC at first falls. AC also falls as output starts to rise, and we can now interpret this as being due to AFC and MC both falling. AC will continue to fall as long as MC is below it and this will occur even if MC itself is rising. AC represents the typical cost of one unit of output, while MC is the cost of the next unit. When the next unit is actually produced, the new value of AC incorporates the previous MC value. The value of AC is reduced by a MC value that is below it.

At some stage MC will begin to rise due to the existence of diminishing marginal returns. As soon as MC is above AC, the latter starts to increase. It is pulled up by the higher value of MC. This therefore explains the upward-sloping part of the U-shaped AC curve. It also implies that the MC curve always cuts the AC curve at the lowest point on the AC curve.

See what you have learnt about the MC and AC curves

29 **Explain in your own words why AC is high at low levels of output.**

30 **What is the relationship between MPPL and MC?**

31 **As output increases from a low level AC starts to fall because both ________ and ________ are falling. Even if MC is rising AC will continue to ________ as long as MC is ________ the AC curve. Once the MC curve cuts the AC the latter starts to ________. This is why AC is 'U-shaped.**

32 **Explain in your own words why AC can continue to fall even if MC is rising.**

Sketch on the same diagram the AVC, AC and MC curves. What is important about the points where the MC curve crosses the other curves?

Revenues and costs (£)

Quantity

Deriving the Short-Run MC and AC Curves: A Numerical Example

This WinEcon screen shows you how to calculate MC and AC for the function whose TC we found in the topic Deriving Short-Run Total Cost Curves.

Lab	TPP	APPL	MPPL	TFC	TVC	TC	AFC	AVC	AC	MC
1	278	278								
			329							
2	608	304								
			371							
3	978	326								
			403							
4	1381	345								
			425							
5	1806	361								
			439							
6	2245	374								
			443							
7	2688	384								
			438							
8	3126	391								
			424							
9	3550	394								
			400							
10	3950	395								
			367							
11	4317	392								
			325							
12	4642	387								
			273							
13	4915	378								
			212							
14	5127	366								
			142							
15	5269	351								
			62							
16	5331	333								

33 Here we develop further the exercise from the topic Short-Run Production Functions: a numerical example in section 4.2. You are now asked to calculate the various short-run values of total fixed cost, total variable cost, total cost, average fixed cost, average variable cost, average total cost and marginal cost. Record the values in the table opposite. The price of labour is £25,000 per unit and the cost of capital is £55,000 per unit with one unit being used. You may need to use the WinEcon calculator, and if you have forgotten the relevant formulas just refer back to the definitions you wrote down in the topic Short-Run Cost Definition.

From the values you have just calculated above plot the total cost curves on one diagram and the AFC, AVC, AC and MC curves on the second diagram.

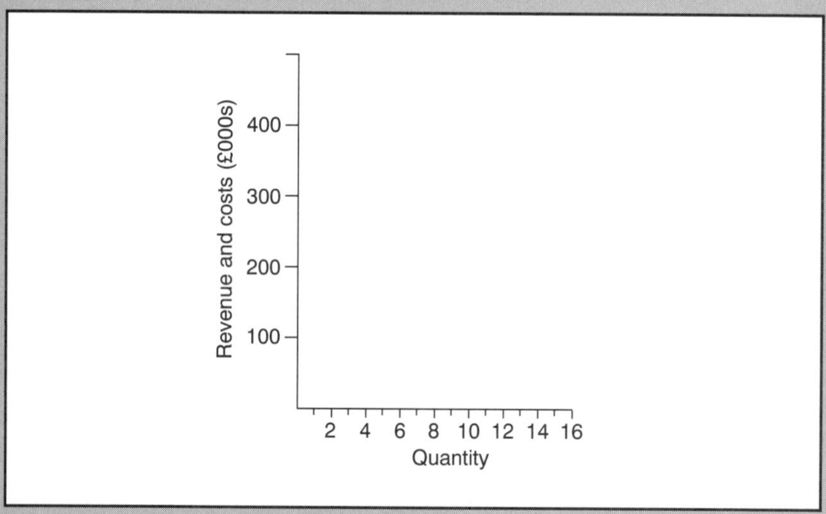

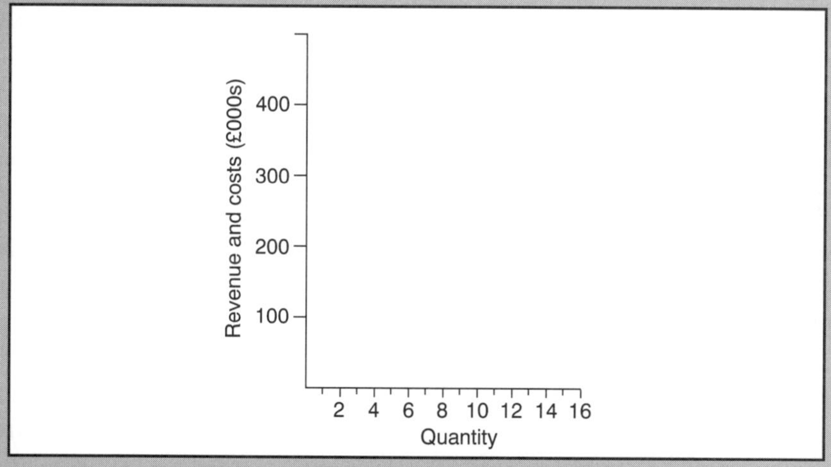

34 Explain what will happen to each of the curves plotted above if: (1) the cost of capital rises to £60,000; (2) the cost of labour rises to £30,000 per unit; and (3) the firm introduces more efficient technology.

Section 4.5: Cost–Volume–Profit Analysis

This section provides an introduction to a practical business application of cost theory, namely cost–volume–profit (CVP) analysis. This is concerned with the question of how an entrepreneur can calculate the quantity the firm needs to produce to break even or to achieve a target level of profit.

Cost–Volume–Profit Assumptions

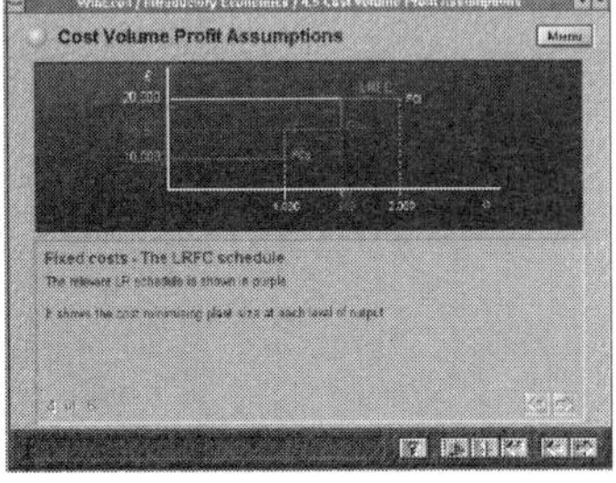

In undertaking this type of analysis we make the simplifying assumptions of the accountant regarding the nature of revenues and costs rather than using the more rigorous analysis of the economist. Demand (*D*) is assumed to be perfectly elastic which means that as the quantity the firm sells changes the revenue per unit is constant. In reality however, as we know from our economics, when the quantity sold increases then the price of the product will fall. It is also assumed by the accountant that variable costs per unit are constant. This also contradicts the economist's analysis of costs which shows that as output increases the variable cost per unit will initially fall and then subsequently increase.

CVP analysis may be undertaken either graphically or by using algebraic calculation. Both give the same results, as we will now show.

CVP: Graphical Analysis

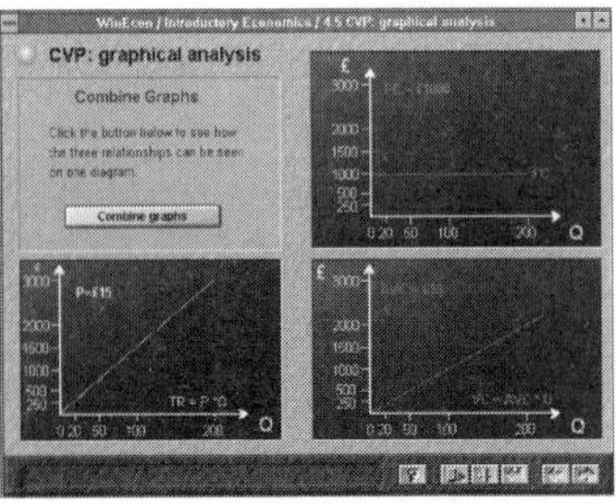

If you have problems with algebra try this graphical approach to find the break-even or target profit levels of output. The screenshot shows that the total revenues and total costs are calculated at each possible level of output, and we then just subtract the costs from the revenues at each output level to work out the profit or loss. You can see how to build up the graph by using the WinEcon screen.

Notice that at low levels of output the firm is making a large loss. This is because of the firm's fixed costs. The loss falls as output increases until break-even is reached. This happens because each unit sold will make what we call a contribution. The contribution is the difference between variable costs and price for the unit of output in question. At low output levels the sum of the contributions of all units of output is more than offset by fixed costs but as output rises the sum of the contributions will offset fixed costs.

Develop your understanding of break-even and target profit

35 **The contribution which each unit sold makes is defined as ☐ – ☐.**

36 **Why will the firm make large losses at low levels of output but become profitable at higher output levels?**

In the following example revenue and costs are no longer a linear function of output as the accountant's model would suggest. This is more in line with what the economist would believe. Plot these two curves on a graph for output levels between 1 and 12 and work out the break-even output level and the output level if the target profit level is £100. You should note here that both the revenue and costs are shown as a function of the output level and are therefore calculated rather differently than in the accountant's method as shown above.

$$TR = 41.5Q - 1.2Q^2$$

$$TC = 125 + 10Q - 0.5Q^2 + 0.02Q^3$$

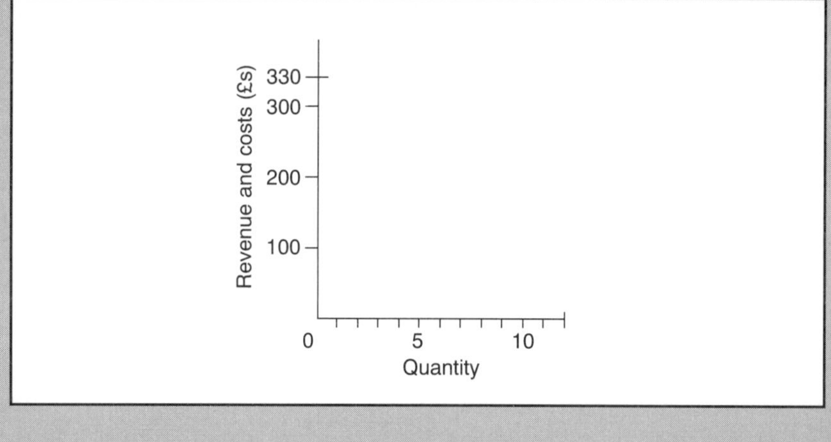

CVP: Algebraic Analysis

In this section we use a little mathematics to calculate break-even and target profit levels. Many students find mathematics difficult but in this section we hope to be able to show you that it can actually be quite easy. We start off with a few definitions of what costs and revenues we will be using. You should be already familiar with these from previous sections. TR = total revenue; TC = total cost; AVC = average variable cost; FC = fixed cost; Q = quantity; and P = price.

$$\text{Profit} = \text{TR} - \text{TC}$$

$$\text{TR} = P \times Q$$

$$\text{TC} = \text{FC} + \text{VC}$$

$$\text{VC} = Q \times \text{AVC}$$

The break-even quantity or the target profit quantity may be derived by algebraic manipulation. The only difference between the two is that to find break-even we are looking for the point where profit is zero while, clearly, if we are looking for a target profit the value will be above zero.

We can start our algebraic manipulation by taking the profit equation given above and then expanding it. This is done by breaking TR and TC down into their component parts. We then want to take Q to one side of the equation and everything else to the other side. (Remember the rule that whatever we do to one side of the equation, we must do to the other side also.) You discover that the break-even output is given by:

$$Q = (\text{Profit} + \text{FC})/(P - \text{AVC})$$

The profit level in the above equation will be set at zero if we want to calculate break-even output levels, or at the target profit level otherwise.

You can improve your understanding by working through the three supplementary screens – CVP: algebraic analysis (2), CVP: an illustration and CVP: a numerical example.

Show for yourself that the break-even output is given by:

$$Q = (\text{Profit} + \text{FC}) / (P - \text{AVC})$$

37 **If FC = 50,000, AVC = 20, P = 50 and the target profit is £30,000 calculate firstly the break-even quantity and secondly the target profit quantity.**

38 **If FC = 1,000,000, AVC = 25, P = 60 and the target profit is £50,000 calculate the break-even and target profit quantity levels.**

39 **If FC = 1000, AVC = 10, P = 20 and the target profit is £50,000 calculate break-even and target profit quantity levels.**

Section 4.6: Comparing Long- and Short-Run Costs

The isoquant and isocost analysis that we developed in section 4.2 can be extended using the concept of an expansion path. This shows the cost minimizing factor combinations used to produce at different output levels. We derive and contrast the expansion paths in both the long and short run. It should be remembered that in the short run the amount of capital which the firm can use is fixed, whilst in the long run both factors are variable.

Expansion Paths: Short- and Long-run Cost Curves

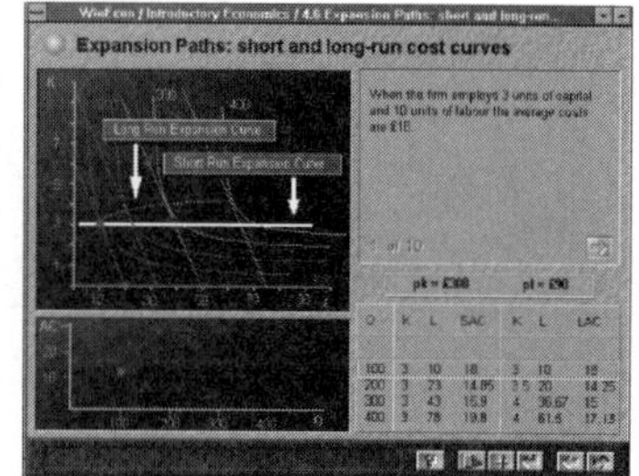

The screen shot shows both the long-run and short-run expansion paths. These expansion paths are used to trace the factor combinations a firm would use at different output levels in order to produce at minimum cost. The two preceding supplementary screens (Long-Run Expansion Path and Short-Run Expansion Path) show how expansion paths are plotted.

We consider firstly the long-run expansion path. This is derived by tracing the path to each higher isoquant through its point of tangency with the respective isocost line. This point of tangency gives the combinations of labour and capital which will produce each output level at minimum cost at the current prices of labour and capital. Because we are concerned with the long run, the quantities of both labour and capital change as output increases. As the prices of labour and capital are assumed to be fixed, however, the various isocost lines are parallel to one another.

The short-run expansion path, in contrast, shows what factor combinations could be used for different output levels in the short run. This, it should be remembered, is the period when the amount of capital which can be used is fixed. This means that the only way in which output may be increased is by increasing the amount of labour used. From the screen shot we see this means that the expansion path is a straight line with the level of capital being fixed, in this case at 3 units.

Notice the differences between the long-run and short-run paths. As output is increased the amount of capital used increases in the long run, but not in the short run. In the long run it is possible to continue to use capital and labour in the preferred proportions. There is only one output level in the short run where the isocost is tangential to the isoquant. At all other levels of output the isocost cuts the isoquant. This means that these levels of output are not being produced at minimum long-run cost.

The WinEcon screen shows you how to calculate both the long-run average cost (LAC) and short-run average cost (SAC) curves for each level of output. Isocost lines are used to find values of total cost TC whilst the isoquant curves give values of Q. You see that the LAC and SAC curves are tangential only at one point, namely where output is 100 units. We can explain why this is the case by looking at the isoquant and isocost diagram immediately above. Notice also that when capital is fixed at 3 units, 100 is the only output level where the point of tangency between the isocost and isoquant is actually on the short-run expansion path. If we wanted to increase output in the short run to 400 we would in contrast find that the isocost line cuts the 400 output isoquant rather than being tangential to it. This implies it costs more money to produce this output in the short run than in the long run. From this we are able to show that for the output level of 400, SAC is above LAC as it is on a higher isocost line. This is because in the short run the firm cannot adjust the quantity of capital it uses.

Develop your understanding of expansion paths

40 **In the ________ ________ the level of capital used is fixed. This means that the short-run expansion path will be a ________ ________.**

41 **If the wage rate falls, how would this affect the long-run expansion path? (Hint: factor substitution will occur as the price of labour relative to that of capital falls.)**

42 **Why is there only one output level on the short-run expansion path where the isocost is tangential to the isoquant rather than cutting it?**

43 **Explain in your own words why in the short run the expansion path is a straight line.**

(a) Draw the isocost line which goes through the point where the 400 isoquant cuts the short-run expansion path. Remember, the line must be parallel to the existing isocost lines, which are drawn for P_K = £300 and P_L = £90.

(b) Add to the diagram the new long-run expansion path if the price of labour falls to £70. How does this affect the cost minimizing capital and labour combinations?

Section 4.6 / Comparing Long- and Short-Run Costs: Conclusion

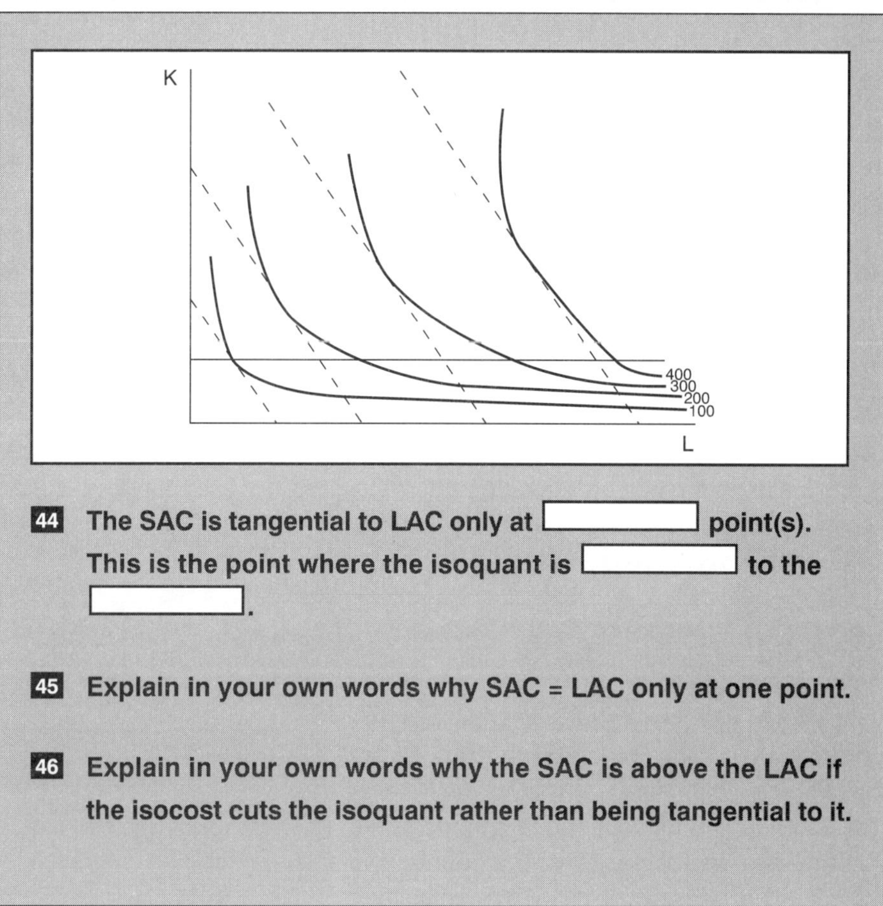

44 **The SAC is tangential to LAC only at ________ point(s). This is the point where the isoquant is ________ to the ________.**

45 **Explain in your own words why SAC = LAC only at one point.**

46 **Explain in your own words why the SAC is above the LAC if the isocost cuts the isoquant rather than being tangential to it.**

Comparing Long- and Short-Run Costs: Conclusion

The conclusion which we may draw is that for any fixed short-run quantity of capital there is only one output level where both the SAC = LAC and the isoquant is tangential to the isocost. At all other output levels associated with this fixed quantity of capital the isocost cuts the isoquant, and therefore the SAC is above the LAC as the firm is not on the lowest possible isocost line for this given output level.

Section 4.7: Economies of Scale

In this section we focus on the shape of the long-run average cost (LAC) curve. We also consider the effects of changes in technology on the LAC curve, and what effect the existence of economies of scale has on market structure.

Traditional economic theory suggests that the firm faces a U-shaped LAC curve. This means that as output increases from low levels, LAC initially falls (i.e. the firm is on the downward-sloping part of the U-shaped LAC curve). This fall in average cost happens because the firm is reaping the benefits of ‘economies of scale’.

Economies of Scale: Definitions

We can analyse economies of scale in terms of the relationship between factor inputs and outputs in the long run. These economies exist when the increase in factor inputs is less than proportionate to the increase in outputs generated; for example, if output doubles when all inputs increase by only 75 per cent. The traditional economic model suggests that after reaping all the economies of scale available, the firm will encounter 'constant returns to scale'. At this point LAC is constant and this is the point at the bottom of the U of LAC. Finally, as a firm grows beyond a certain size 'diseconomies of scale' will be incurred. This means that if, for example, the firm wants to double output it will need to more than double the inputs of labour and capital used. As we get into the region of diseconomies of scale, LAC starts to rise (i.e. we are on the upward-sloping part of the U on the LAC curve).

The Three Scale Effects

Constant Returns to Scale

When a firm operates under constant returns to scale it can achieve a particular percentage change in output by making that same percentage change in the use of each of its inputs. If the quantities of the factors used are increased repeatedly by equal amounts, the distances between successive isoquants along the production ray are all equal.

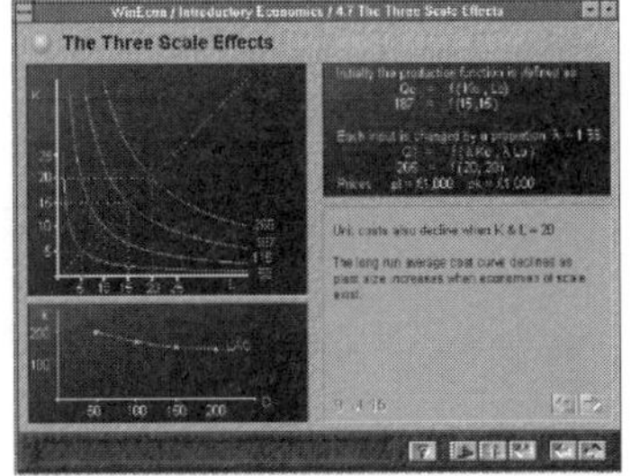

Increasing Returns to Scale

Economies of scale can take several forms, such as production economies and marketing economies. Normally, however, we concentrate on the former which are associated with the use of different types of technology for different output scales. For example, if we consider car production, a firm can use batch-production techniques to produce low-volume models such as Rolls Royce whilst more efficient and lower cost mass-production techniques are used by the high-volume manufacturers such as Ford.

Decreasing Returns to Scale

Diseconomies of scale are normally associated with managerial costs. As firms get larger and larger the management running the firm can become top heavy and inefficient and as a result the average costs can rise. It is argued by many economists, however, that such problems can be avoided (e.g. by splitting large companies into divisions to avoid the managerial diseconomies associated with size). This argument is backed up by empirical evidence taken from studies made by economists. These suggests that in practice the LAC curve is actually L-shaped rather than U-shaped because firms reap the economies of scale but avoid the diseconomies.

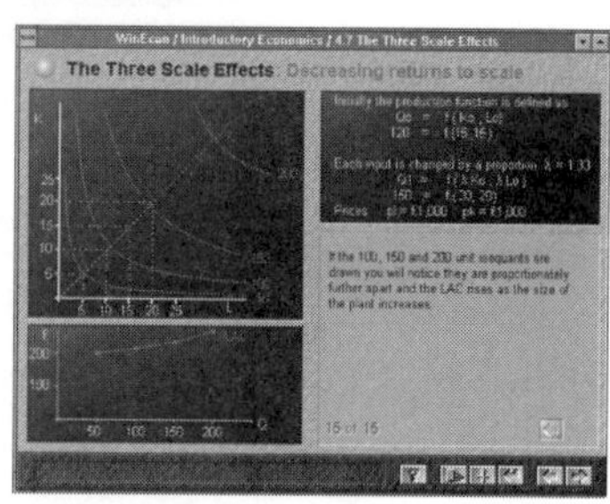

We can use isoquants to illustrate economies and diseconomies of scale. In the WinEcon screens the 200 isoquant represents a doubling of output as compared with the 100 one, and that represents a doubling of output as compared with the 50 isoquant. If the firm needs to less than double factor inputs to double output, then the firm is facing economies of scale. If, however, factor inputs need to be more than doubled to double output, the firm is facing diseconomies of scale.

Check your understanding of economies and diseconomies of scale

47 **Traditional theory suggests the LAC curve is ____-shaped. As output increases, LAC will initially ____. This occurs because the firm is reaping the benefits of ____ of scale. As output rises further the firm will be subject to firstly ____ ____ to scale and then finally ____ ____ ____ when average cost starts to ____.**

48 **Produce two lists, one of economies of scale and a second of diseconomies of scale.**

49 **The traditional view as to the shape of the LAC curve has been challenged by empirical evidence which suggests that the LAC is L-shaped. Explain why it is L-shaped.**

Long-Run Average Costs in Practice

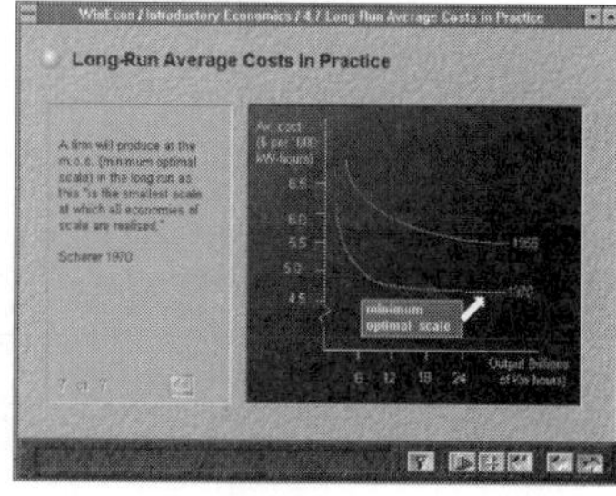

As well as considering how scale effects influence the LAC curve we must consider how technological change influences the curve. Over time, technologies become more efficient and this will result in a downward shift in the LAC curve. For example, with the introduction of computer and robot technology it now takes fewer inputs to manufacture a car. It is, however, often quite hard to distinguish changes in technology and scale effects, and as a consequence we sometimes show the two effects combined.

The LAC curve in practice tends to be L-shaped rather than U-shaped. This is because, in practice, managers can avoid diseconomies of scale. In order to survive in the competitive market the firm must reach the output scale at

the kink in the LAC curve. This point is known as 'minimum efficient scale'(MES). If the firm is smaller than this its costs will be higher than its competitors and it will be driven out of business.

Develop your understanding of technological change and MES

50 **Technological advances will shift the LAC ________.**

51 **The MES shows the output scale which a firm needs to reach in order to ________ ________ ________.**

Economies of Scale and Market Structure

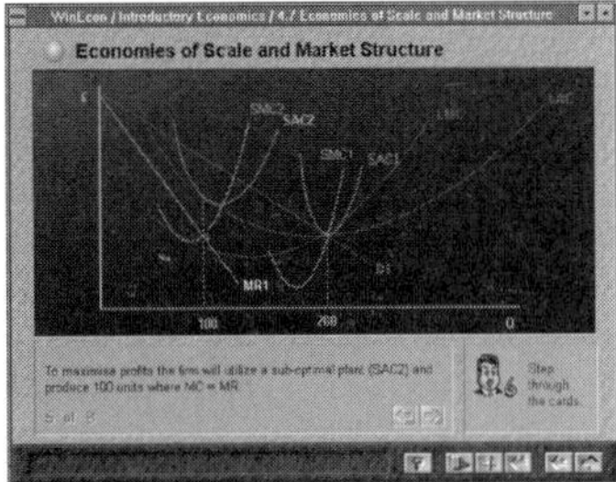

The size of the minimum efficient scale (MES) relative to the overall market is important in determining the type of competition in the market. If the economies of scale and, therefore, the MES are large relative to the size of the market, there will be few competitors and we will be faced with oligopolistic market structures. If, however, the scale economies are relatively small, then market structure will be akin to something more like perfect competition.

Notice the relationship between the various SAC and LAC curves. The LAC curve just touches each of the SAC curves, but only at the MES does it touch an SAC curve at its minimum point.

Minimum efficient scale and the market

52 **Explain why a market will support two firms with plants of optimal scale if the MES is 50 per cent of the market.**

53 **Work out how many firms will be in the market if the MES is the following percentages of the total market size: 100, 5, 12.5, 33 and 10 per cent.**

Section 4.8: Summary

This chapter looks at production and costs both in the short run and in the long run. We find that what a firm can produce is determined by its production function. This shows the relationship between factor inputs and the goods produced. In the short run at least one of the inputs, usually capital or land, is fixed, and so the firm experiences diminishing marginal returns or the law of variable proportions.

In the long run the amounts used of all factors can be varied and the firm can expand along a production ray. It may experience increasing, constant or decreasing returns to scale.

Cost functions show us the relationship between the cost of the inputs used and the quantity of output that is produced from them. Their shape depends largely on physical production relationships. In the short run we distinguish between fixed and variable costs. We also noted the relationship between total, average and marginal costs. The long-run average cost curve was shown to be the envelope of the short-run average cost curves.

Cost–volume–profit analysis provides a practical application of cost theory. It uses simple assumptions to analyse the break-even output level.

Chapter 5:

Perfect Competition and Monopoly

How should firms select the level of output at which to produce or the price at which to sell their goods or services? The choice affects profits and so is important if the best profit outcome is to be achieved. Costs of production and revenues from sales are clearly important, but in what way precisely? A lot depends on the type of market environment. A firm facing many competitors who produce identical products has less control of price than a sole producer of an item. But even a sole producer is influenced by what might happen in the longer term when other firms may enter the market.

Contents

KEYWORDS

- Barriers to entry
- Comparative statics
- Costs, total and marginal
- Marginal revenue
- Market structure
- Monopoly
- Normal profit
- Perfect competition
- Price discrimination
- Profit maximization
- Revenues: total, average and marginal
- Short and long run
- Supernormal profit

Section 5.1: Introduction

The type of market, or structure of the market as it is called in economics, has a vital bearing on a firm's price and output selection. This chapter brings together in a systematic way important relationships from cost and demand theory in two important market contexts – perfect competition and monopoly – to show how the firm makes decisions on which its profits depend.

Here we analyse two extreme types of environment in which a firm may operate: perfect competition and monopoly. Although these situations are rarely met in real life, many actual markets share vital characterisitics of these polar cases. By examining in depth the likely behaviour of firms in extreme cases, we can gain an insight into real-world behaviour. An advantage of this approach is that we learn what to look for in any market situation without being distracted by considerations which are specific to particular markets.

This chapter explains what is meant by total revenue and marginal revenue. Using these concepts with the corresponding cost functions, you discover the conditions under which a firm maximizes profit, and the distinction between normal and supernormal profit.

We then analyse the output that is produced in perfect competition considering individual firms and the industry as a whole. You discover the supply curve for a firm and find what conditions must be satisfied for a perfectly competitive industry to be in long-run equilibrium. Comparative static analysis uses these concepts to examine the effects of various changes in demand, or in costs, or with the imposition of a tariff. Our analysis is mainly graphical, using linear demand curves and U-shaped average cost curves.

Various assumptions that distinguish monopoly from perfect competition are set out and the profit maximizing output for a monopoly is obtained. This is compared with the output that would be produced by a perfectly competitive industry. The possibility that a monopolist may be able to charge different prices in different sections of the market is also analysed.

Section 5.2: Markets and Profits

We begin by considering the various types of markets which may be encountered in the real world. Obviously the markets for any two products differ in many respects – for example, the retail food market may be dominated by a few supermarkets and may be intensely local in character, whilst the world oil tanker market may contain thousands of firms and acknowledge no national boundaries. Although differences between markets can seem bewildering, there are relatively few characteristics which account for the really important economic differences. This section will introduce you to these factors and help you to assess their role.

Characteristics of Different Market Structures

The three most important characteristics of markets are the number and size of firms, the existence of barriers to entry, and the degree of product differentiation. Where there are many firms of an equal size, it is clear that the potential for competition is high. However, if there are large numbers of firms in a market and one or two are relatively large, the larger firms may exert a disproportionate influence on prices. Thus, size also matters in discovering firm behaviour.

Barriers to entry are anything which raises the cost to a potential newcomer of entering the industry. For example, high-tech biochemical firms raise competitors' costs by patenting genetic discoveries in an attempt to recover their research and development investments. This preserves a section of the market from competition because other firms will not be able to meet the extra cost of market entry.

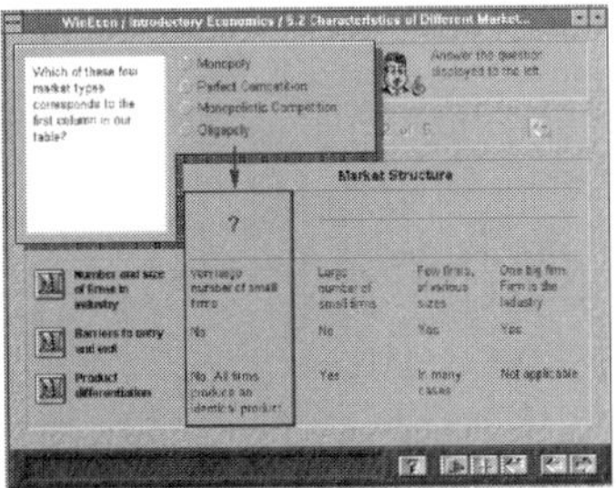

The final factor – product differentiation – refers to the extent to which products can be customized in order to create a less price elastic demand for the product. Sometimes the actual products are different (e.g. packets of biscuits) but in other instances the difference is largely in the packaging (e.g. porridge oats). Whatever the difference, it may be highlighted by marketing techniques.

Look at the Characteristics of Different Market Structures table on the WinEcon screen and attempt the questions it asks.

Market structures

01 **What market structure does an industry with many firms, no barriers to entry and differentiated products have?**

02 **What possible market structures describe an industry with barriers to entry?**

03 **A product is not differentiated. To which markets could it belong?**

04 **What distinguishes perfect competition from monopolistic competition?**

Profit Maximization

This topic lays the foundation for economic analysis of firms' decision making. We explain why profit maximization is assumed to be the major objective of

firms, and we discover how the concepts of either total revenue and total cost, or marginal revenue and marginal cost can help in analysing when this goal is achieved.

The ability of economics to produce clear predictions about the behaviour of firms depends on it making simplifying assumptions about firms' objectives. Each firm is viewed as a single decision-taker, whereas in reality the interests of many different groups within a firm may need to be satisfied before any decision is taken. In the economic model, the view of the ordinary shareholder is adopted and the interest is solely in the level of profit created by the firm.

But what are profits? The short answer is that they are simply the difference between total revenue and total cost facing the firm at any level of operation. The total revenue (TR) the firm receives from its output is the quantity of output it chooses to produce (Q) multiplied by the price at which that output is sold (P). Therefore, we have TR = $P \times Q$. Usually as Q changes, TR changes. We say total revenue is a function of output, and we can plot a curve showing the amount of total revenue associated with each level of output, as you discover on this WinEcon screen.

Total revenue is introduced in the topic Price Elasticity and Total Revenue in section 2.5. Total cost and marginal cost are described in detail in section 4.4 in the topics Deriving Short-Run Total Cost Curves and The Shape of the Marginal Cost Curve.

Related concepts which are also useful in this analysis are average revenue (AR) and marginal revenue (MR). The average revenue to the firm per unit of output is TR/Q = P. Since average revenue represents the price received for the particular quantity that is demanded, the average revenue function is another name for the demand function. Marginal revenue is the change in total revenue when output is increased by one unit. Marginal revenue is sometimes but not always equal to average revenue, as we shall see.

Use the WinEcon screen, answering the questions you are asked about costs and revenue. On card 3 we make the assumption that the firm faces a perfectly elastic or horizontal demand curve, which can alternatively be called the AR curve. This says that the firm can sell as much output as it likes, from zero units upwards, at a fixed price, P. Since TR = $P \times Q$ and P is a constant, TR is a straight line function of Q in this example. TR rises upwards from the origin with a slope of P.

Later in this chapter we revert to the downward-sloping demand curve that you learnt about in chapter 2 in the topic The Product Demand Curve. We shall see that different assumptions about the demand curve faced by a firm are amongst the features which distinguish the different market structures we analyse.

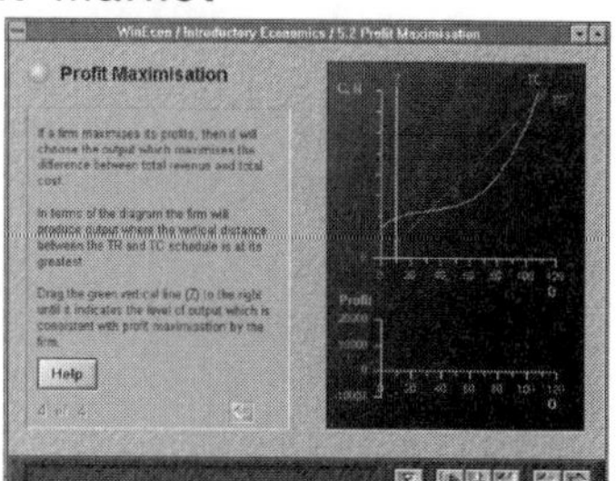

On card 4 you are asked to identify the profit maximizing output. This is found where the vertical gap between TR and TC is greatest. Click and drag the green line Z to mark the position. Note that costs rise more rapidly than revenues because it is assumed that this is a short-run curve showing diminishing marginal returns, so that as output increases costs increase more than proportionately.

Once you have correctly identified the output at which profit is maximized you will see the profit function itself displayed in the lower graph. At first profits are negative, then they rise, reach a maximum point and from then on they fall. Try the questions below and then use the Next Page button to move to the following supplementary screen which shows another aspect of profit maximization.

Revenue, cost and profit

05 **Complete the formulas:**

AR =

MR =

06 Ric's Privatized Railway Company sells tickets at 10p per ride. His analysis of total costs is as shown in the table. Complete the total revenue and profit columns. You will be asked to complete the remaining columns after using the next WinEcon screen.

Rides	Total revenues	Total costs	Profit	Marginal revenue	Marginal cost
10		114			
11		115			
12		116			
13		126			
14		140			
15		55			

07 **How many rides produce maximum profit?**

Sketch the TR and TC functions on the diagram, and mark the number of rides that gives maximum profit.

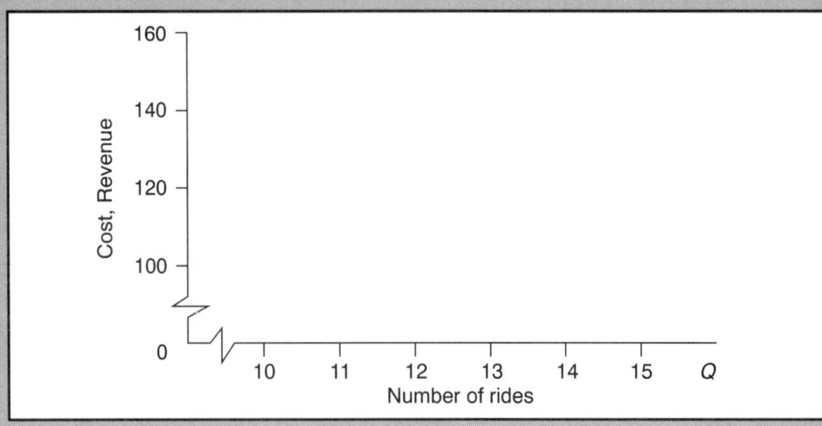

Profit Maximization (2)

This sub-topic introduces the concept of marginal revenue and uses it together with marginal cost to identify the profit maximizing output.

Any particular total cost (TC) curve changes in specific ways as output changes. Since marginal cost (MC) represents the rate at which total cost changes as output increases, any TC curve has a particular shape of MC curve associated with it. Usually MC is drawn as a U-shaped curve, although other shapes are possible. Card 1 of this screen asks you about a particular part of the TC curve shown on the screen and requires you to indicate what the corresponding section of the MC curve looks like.

As its name suggests, marginal revenue (MR) is defined as the change in total revenue (TR) that occurs when output is increased by one unit. The MR curve can be plotted, and is of a particular shape for a particular TR function. Often MR is drawn as a straight line, either horizontal or downward-sloping. Card 2 asks you to consider the shape of MR function that corresponds to the TR function on the screen, which has a perfectly elastic demand curve.

Work through the cards to find where profits are maximized, and notice also what the appropriate action is if output is firstly below or secondly above the optimum. At the optimum output the MC curve cuts the MR curve from below. At outputs below the optimum, MR is therefore greater than MC. Producing an extra unit of output adds more to revenue than it adds to cost when MR > MC, and so more output should be produced. It is worth while for the firm to continue to increase its output until the next unit of output just adds as much to revenue as it adds to cost, that is until MR = MC. If output is increased beyond this point, the addition to cost, MC, is greater than the addition to revenue, MR. Producing such extra units of output reduces profit, and so the firm would be better off producing less.

We see that the profit maximizing level of output can be found by equating marginal revenue and marginal cost. This is equivalent to the condition that the profit function should be at a maximum, and also to the requirement of there being the maximum difference between total revenue and total cost. So, rather than constructing profit curves, economists often find the marginal cost and marginal revenue curves. These curves may cross more than once. Notice that the profit maximizing position occurs when MC cuts MR from below.

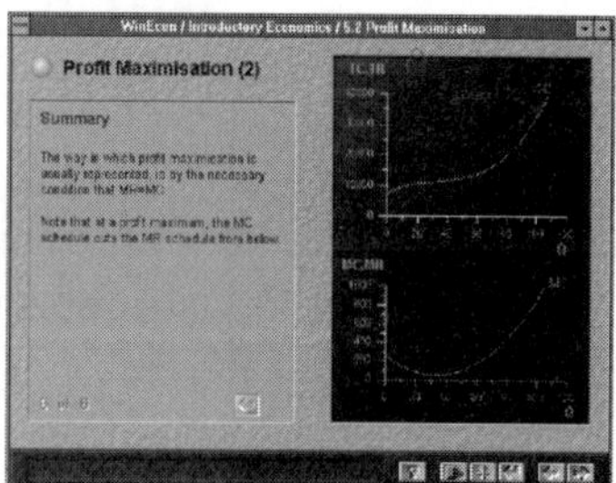

Using MC and MR to find the optimal output

Complete the table you began earlier for Ric's Railway, filling in the columns for marginal cost and marginal revenue.

08 What can you say about MC and MR: (a) below the profit maximizing output; (b) at the profit maximizing output; and (c) at outputs above the profit maximizing output?

Plot MC, MR and also AR, which is the demand curve, on this diagram. Mark the profit maximizing output.

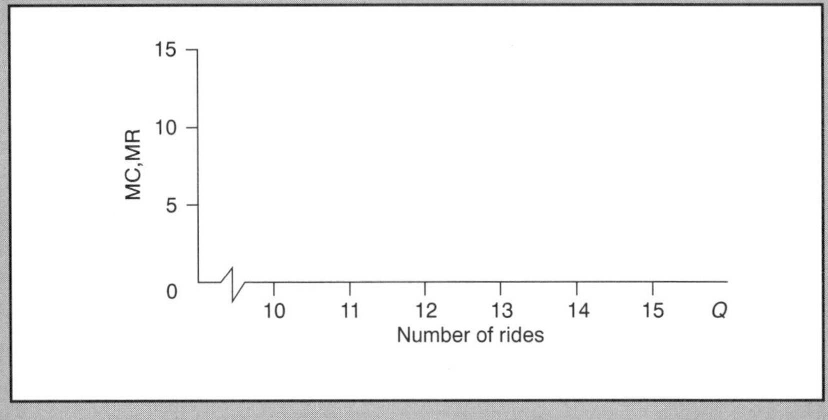

09 What can you say about MR and AR on your diagram?

Normal and Supernormal Profit

This WinEcon screen makes an important distinction between different types of profits. Work through the definitions until you understand the difference between normal profits, which are assumed to be earned in all economic activities, and supernormal profits, which are only earned in conditions of market power.

Test your understanding

10 Consider again Ric's Privatized Railway Company which you analysed in the last topic. Suppose Ric could earn 10 per cent by investing in government bonds, a safe investment. His railway company earns 14 per cent, but he estimates that the most he could earn for his managerial input elsewhere is equivalent to 2 per cent of the sum he is considering investing.

He believes that there is no risk facing his company. Is he making normal or supernormal profits? If he is making supernormal profits how much are they?

11 What is the connection between normal profits and production costs?

12 What is the relationship between supernormal profits and total cost?

13 The opportunity cost of capital services is called [ ] [ ].

14 For what are the terms 'abnormal profits' and 'pure profits' alternative names?

Section 5.3: Perfect Competition

Perfect competition is the first of the extreme cases of market behaviour studied in this chapter. It is important to realize that perfect competition is not the same as 'competitive'. For example, the UK newspaper industry is extremely competitive, but because there are relatively few separate companies involved it is not perfectly competitive. The essential characteristic of a perfectly competitive industry is that no one firm in it is large enough to have any influence on the price of the product. Clearly in the newspaper industry this is not the case. Perfect competition is studied because if it were to exist throughout an economy, the economy would be 'efficient'.

More on efficiency can be found in section 7.2 in the topics Allocative Efficiency and Perfect Competition and Allocative Efficiency.

Four Key Assumptions in Perfect Competition

In this topic you are asked you to try to work out the words required to complete four key assumptions about perfect competition. As you choose a word from each of the combo boxes you get feedback on whether your choice is correct, and more detailed information appears on the right of the screen.

Work through the screen to discover the assumptions that lie behind the model of perfect competition. The assumptions of large numbers of buyers and sellers are crucial. In such circumstances it is impossible for any individual to influence market price. Prices are then determined by the behaviour of all buyers and sellers in raising or lowering demand and jointly

supplying the market. The assumption about no barriers to entry helps to ensure that there are a large number of suppliers since firms can easily enter the industry if it is attractive to them to do so. As to products being homogenous, or alike, if every firm produced a differentiated product, clearly price would be under its control to a greater or lesser extent.

From the assumptions for perfect competition . . .

15 **What can you say about whether firms enter or leave the industry in the long run?**

16 **What is factor mobility? What can you say about it in a perfectly competitive industry?**

17 **What can you say about branded goods in a perfectly competitive industry?**

Firm and Industry Demand in Perfect Competition

The demand curve for the product of an industry is the total demand for a particular kind of good and, like demand curves in general, we assume it is downward sloping. For the separate firms, however, the situation is different. Individual firms in a perfectly competitive industry are each assumed to be so small that they could sell more output without having to reduce their price. Also, if one firm decides to supply less to the market, the market price will not rise. The demand curve facing an individual firm in perfect competition is therefore effectively horizontal. You can see an example of how this comes about by using the WinEcon screen.

How does the size of the firm relative to the size of the industry in which it operates affect whether the firm can influence the industry price? The WinEcon cards take you through an exercise in which a firm that is small in relation to the size of the industry changes its output by a given percentage (10 per cent in the example). It is important to realize that the exact percentage does not matter.

The example uses elasticities of market demand in a rather unusual way. Normally we use the elasticity of demand to calculate the effect of a given percentage change in price on demand. Here we run the calculation backwards to see how much price would have to fall so that a given increase in output could be sold in the market. The point of the exercise is to show that even with a moderate industry elasticity value, when the firm is small in relation to the industry (1/100th of the industry size in the example), changing its output has a negligible effect on price. Now work through the WinEcon cards to see this. You will probably need a pencil and paper to convince yourself of

the accuracy of the calculations. Remember that the elasticity of demand is defined as the percentage change in total quantity demanded divided by the percentage change in price, other things remaining constant.

Elasticity is explained in detail in section 2.5 in the topic Price Elasticity of Demand.

The very small change in industry price is translated backwards into a very large price elasticity of demand facing the firm. If this is so, only a minute change in price is required to absorb a large percentage change in the output of any one firm. In the limit, as each firm's share becomes smaller and smaller, the impact on price of quantity changes by any one firm becomes closer to zero. This implies that the demand curve facing an individual firm is horizontal. For this to hold we need the assumption that there are large numbers of firms in the perfectly competitive industry.

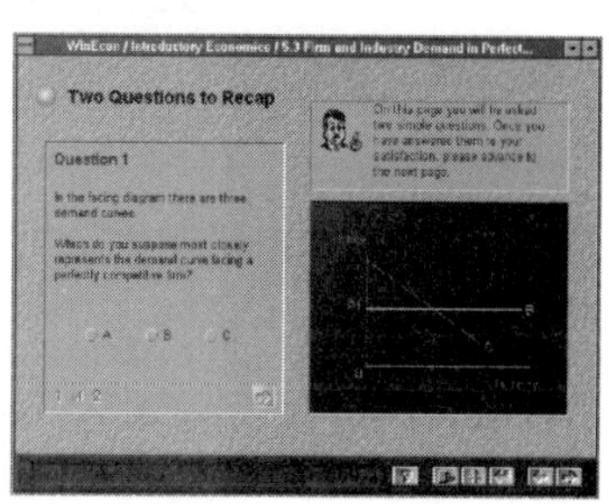

The following supplementary screen (Two Questions to Recap) shows two important conclusions about the firm's demand curve in perfect competition.

Demand in perfect competition

18 **What would be the effect on price if a firm which held 1/10,000 th of the market where elasticity of demand was –5 increased its output by 10 per cent?**

19 **What shape do we assume the market demand curve has for a perfectly competitive industry?** ______ ______

20 **What shape is the demand curve faced by any firm in a perfectly competitive industry?** ______

21 **What is the price elasticity of demand faced by one such firm?** ______

Profit Maximization in Perfect Competition

Finding the best level of output for the firm will enable us eventually to predict the response of the firm to changes in prices. In this topic you work through questions to remind yourself of the essential underlying relationships that we assume for costs and revenues.

Profit Maximization in Perfect Competition (2)

You have seen already that by varying output the firm can affect the level of profit it earns, and that the profit maximizing output is where marginal cost cuts marginal revenue from below. This screen investigates the implication of this condition for a firm in perfect competition which has a perfectly elastic

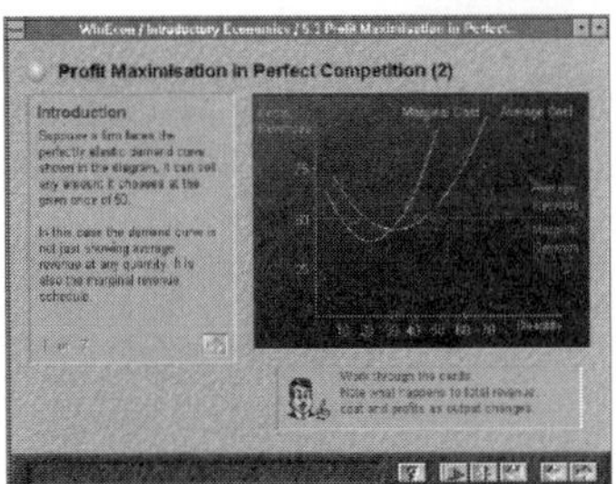

demand curve. Study closely the shapes of the marginal and average revenue and cost curves on the WinEcon screen and make sure that you understand them.

While the two marginal curves are useful for identifying when profit is maximized, it is the two average curves that immediately show us how much profit is made at any output level. Average revenue minus average cost (AR – AC) is the profit per unit of output. This is represented by the vertical distance between the average revenue and average cost curves, and is positive when AR is above AC. If we wish to find total profit we can multiply per unit profit by the quantity of output, Q.

WinEcon now allows you to discover the implications of the firm producing various possible output levels. This is one of the things you can only do on a computer. In real life such experimentation might have costly consequences for the firm. To answer the questions, compare the average revenue at each point with the average cost. Remember that when these are equal the firm just breaks even.

In the WinEcon experiment . . .

22 **At what level(s) of output does the firm break even?**

23 **Is MC higher or lower than MR at each break-even point?**

24 **Is the firm making normal or supernormal profits at the profit maximizing level of output?**

25 **In the diagram on the WinEcon screen, MC = MR at an output of 10. Is this the profit maximizing output? Explain.**

Fixed and Variable Costs

Steve's crab shipping company provides an exercise in identifying the types of cost which economists use to build up average and marginal cost curves. We need to distinguish between fixed and variable costs.

Fixed and variable costs are also discussed in section 4.4 .

Businesses usually have fixed costs over which they have no control in the short run. Fixed costs include items like factory and machine rental. The firm has to pay for these, even if it produces no output, and the amount paid for them is fixed regardless of the level of the firm's output. Variable costs are costs which increase as the firm increases its output. These include such items as the cost of raw materials and fuel.

Now work through the WinEcon exercise to identify costs correctly on card 3, and advise Steve whether to continue running his business on card 4. The important point to emerge is that a business should continue to operate in the short run providing it can cover its variable costs. Although it may be making a loss, it has to pay its fixed costs even if it ceases to trade. If by continuing in business it can at least cover its variable costs, its loss will be no greater and possibly smaller than would have been incurred if it had ceased trading. The optimal output for the firm, found in the usual way where marginal cost cuts marginal revenue from below, will in this instance be a loss minimizing output.

Using costs

26 **If total costs are expected to exceed total revenues, what determines whether the firm should stay in business?**

Short-Run Supply

The short-run supply curve for a perfectly competitive firm shows how much it is willing to supply at a range of possible prices. The optimal output for the firm will always be the quantity at which marginal cost equals marginal revenue (MC = MR), providing marginal cost cuts marginal revenue from below at that point. Since for the firm in perfect competition the demand curve is horizontal, price is equal to marginal revenue. The optimal output therefore occurs where price equals marginal cost. Whether it is actually worth while for the firm to produce that output in the short run depends on whether the price being offered is at least as great as the firm's average variable costs. If so, then the firm will produce the output.

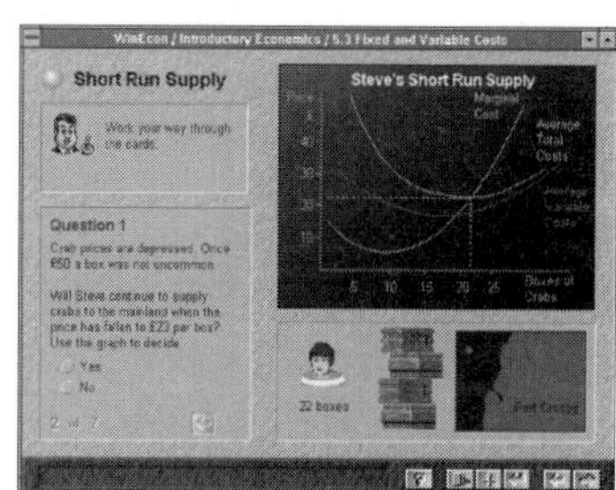

The interactive animation of this section is designed to make you think about the firm's situation and the likely decisions it will make in the short run. The 'short run' is a period where the firm is unable to adjust its stock of capital, for example by selling its boat if it is not covering total costs or by buying a new boat when it is making profits. The objective is to trace out in the diagram the relationship between price and the chosen output level of the firm in the short run. The animation assumes that the user has no problem in understanding that for prices above average total cost, the marginal cost line gives the output choice of the firm because here clearly all costs are covered. Now begin the animation.

You find that the firm's supply curve is that portion of the marginal cost curve lying above the firm's average variable cost. The firm's optimal output is therefore where its supply curve intersects the industry demand curve or price line. In the short run the firm produces so long as it is covering its average variable costs. If the market price is below average total costs its chosen output minimizes its losses.

27 **Will the firm continue to operate when the price lies below average total costs but above average variable costs?**

28 **When price is just covering average variable costs, is output the smallest or largest amount the firm will supply?** ______.

29 **Will the firm cease trading when price falls below AVC?**

Sketch the marginal cost curve on the diagram, and mark the short-run supply curve.

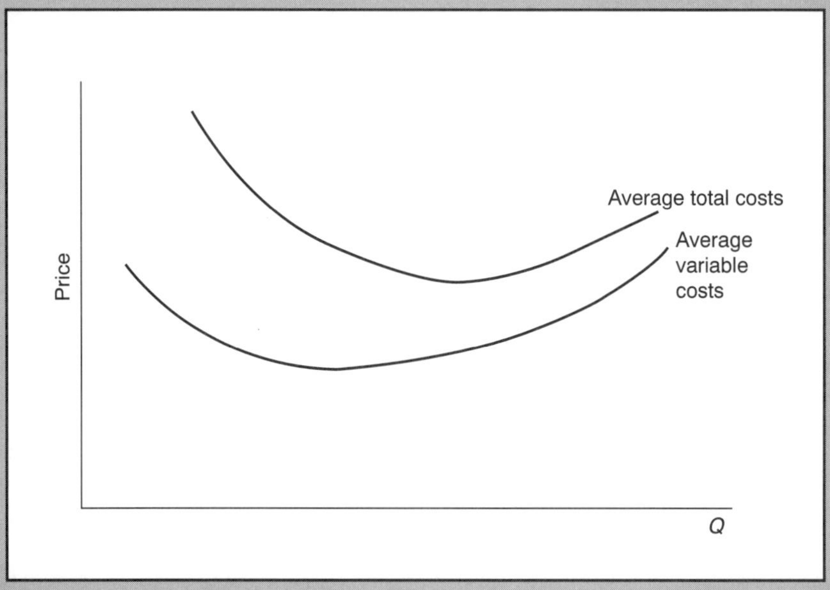

30 **The supply curve for a firm in a perfectly competitive industry is its ______ curve above ______.**

(Hint: The topic The Shape of the Marginal Cost Curve in section 4.4 explains where the MC curve cuts the AC curve.)

Section 5.4: Comparative Static Analysis of Perfect Competition

Comparative static analysis is a powerful technique for investigating the long-run or equilibrium impacts on markets of changes in demand, costs or taxation. The method works by taking one change at a time, rather than many changes together. It is sometimes known as partial equilibrium analysis because it ignores the subtler effects which come through the interaction of changes from different sources.

This method of analysis is also described in the topic Comparative Statics in section 2.4.

Since perfectly competitive firms sell their output at a price which is determined for the industry as a whole, to analyse the impact of changes we have to consider both the industry as a whole and typical firms within it. Price is determined by demand and supply in the industry diagram and that price is taken across to the diagram for an individual firm to use in that analysis.

You also discover what conditions must be met for an industry to be in long-run equilibrium. The long run is the time period in which firms can enter or leave the industry. For a perfectly competitive industry to be in long-run equilibrium, all existing firms in the industry must be willing to continue in production, and no new firms must wish to enter the industry. This implies that firms in the industry must be earning normal profits. They are then willing to continue in production, but the profits are insufficient to attract other firms to enter the industry.

The concept of normal profits is explained in the topic Normal and Supernormal Profit earlier in this chapter.

Profits and Losses in the Short Run

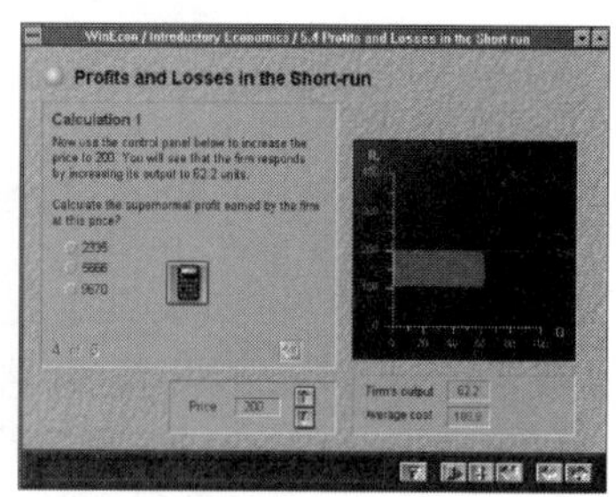

Diagrams showing the average and marginal cost and revenue curves can be used to depict the profit or loss made by the perfectly competitive firm. The firm determines its level of output, Q, which in this example is 62.2 when the price is 200, as the output at which the marginal cost and marginal revenue curves cross. Price minus average cost ($P - \text{AC}$) gives the profit per unit of output, or the loss per unit of output if average cost is greater than price. Here the value of $P - \text{AC}$ is $200 - 108.9 = 91.1$, which is the average profit made on each of the 62.2 units of output. When the unit profit or loss is multiplied by the quantity of output, Q, we obtain the total profit or loss. In this instance 91.1×62.2 gives the firm's total profit.

On the diagram the unit profit (or loss) is shown by the vertical distance between the price line and the average cost curve at the chosen output quantity. The rectangle formed between this line and the vertical axis, bounded at the top and bottom by price and average cost respectively when the firm is making a profit, represents the firm's total profit. It is coloured on the WinEcon screen. If average cost forms the top of the rectangle and price the bottom, then the firm is making a loss. The area of the rectangle is its height multiplied by its width, which is the unit profit or loss multiplied by the quantity of output, and so the area of the rectangle shows the total profit or loss of the firm. Use the WinEcon screen to discover the effect of price changes on the firm's output decision and the profit or loss it makes.

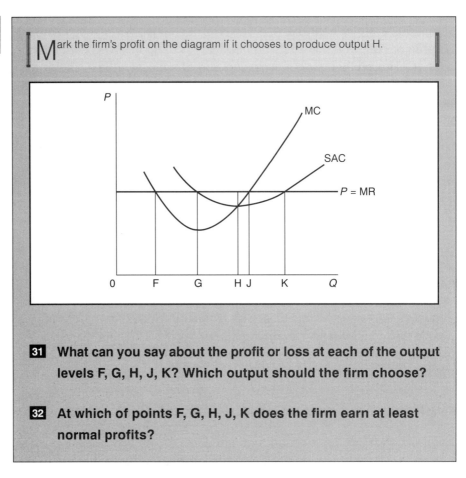

Mark the firm's profit on the diagram if it chooses to produce output H.

31 **What can you say about the profit or loss at each of the output levels F, G, H, J, K? Which output should the firm choose?**

32 **At which of points F, G, H, J, K does the firm earn at least normal profits?**

The Comparative Static Effects of Demand Changes

The first exercise in comparative statics examines the long-run impact of shifts in the industry demand curve. Although for any one firm in perfect competition the demand curve is perfectly elastic, the overall industry demand is of course downward sloping. Cards 1 and 2 of the WinEcon screen show the diagram for the industry as a whole. The supply curve drawn is the short-run supply curve. It is formed as the horizontal summation of the short-run supply curves for all the firms in the industry. It shows the total of what all the firms are willing to supply at the stated price.

We see that price rises in the short run from P_0 to P_1 as a result of an increase in demand. Before the increase in demand each firm in the industry sells its output at the price P_0. Card 3 shows you the diagram for a typical firm in the industry.

The analysis of what happens when demand increases can be broken down into the following steps:

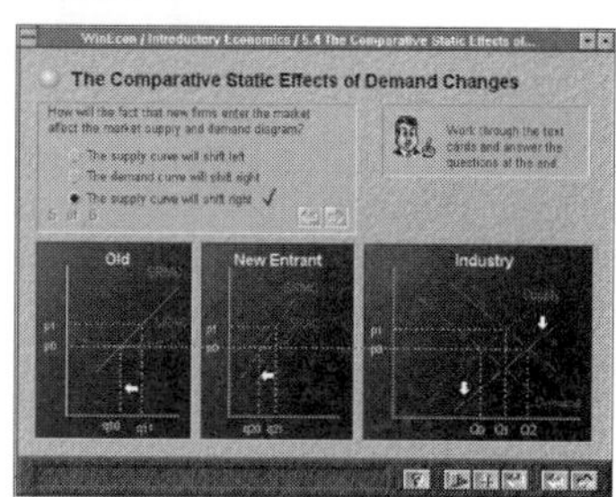

- Demand shifts to the right (i.e. demand is higher at every price).
- Prices rise in the short run as firms seek to recover costs along a rising supply curve.
- Old or existing firms will expand their output, and new firms will enter, causing the industry short-run supply curve to shift outwards.
- Finally prices fall as this new supply is sold.

It is important that you appreciate the strangeness or counter-intuitive nature of this result. It might be expected that increased demand would raise prices permanently. Comparative analysis predicts that in the long run there is no change in prices.

The long-run industry supply curve connects the original equilibrium at output Q_0 with the final one at Q_2. Clearly the long-run supply curve is horizontal in this example. This prediction depends, however, on assumptions about technology, namely that there are no economies of scale. You will see the impact of different technology assumptions in the next topic.

A change in demand

33 **When demand increases, why do firms in a perfectly competitive industry increase their output in the short run? And why do they then reduce output to its original level in the long run?**

34 **In 1973 and 1979, oil supply shifted to the left. Did the reverse process to that described above apply?**

The Effect of a Change in Demand (2)

Use the Next Page button to move to this supplementary screen which shows the influence of diseconomies of scale. Where there are diseconomies, the long-run price is higher after an increase in demand. Where there are economies of scale the reverse happens, and long-run prices fall. The long-run supply curve summarizes these responses:

- It is flat where there are no economies or diseconomies of scale.
- It rises but less steeply than short-run supply where there are diseconomies of scale.
- It falls where there are economies of scale to be enjoyed with expanded industry size.

Comparative Static Effects of Changing Costs

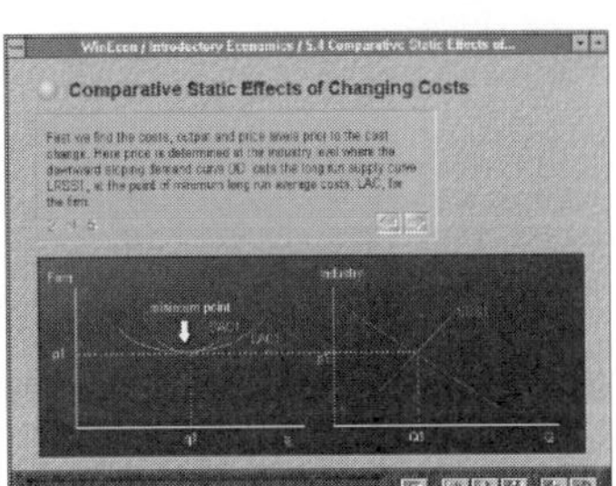

This topic analyses the impact of a change in costs which affects the industry as a whole. We begin by assuming that the industry is in long-run equilibrium. This means that there is no incentive for firms either to leave or to enter the industry. Firms in the industry must be earning normal profit, and they are operating at points on their long-run average cost curves.

We know from the topic Comparing Long- and Short-Run Costs in section 4.6 that the firm's long-run average cost curve is the envelope of all its short-run marginal cost curves.

For a firm in perfect competition average revenue equals marginal revenue (AR = MR). For long-run profit maximization, MR = LMC, where LMC is long-run marginal cost. And for the firm to be earning long-run normal profits, LAC = AR, where LAC is long-run average cost. This implies AR = MR = LMC = LAC. Since a marginal cost curve cuts the corresponding average cost curve at its lowest point, LMC = LAC at the minimum point of the LAC curve. In long-run equilibrium the firm operates at the minimum point of its long-run average cost curve, where the price line is tangential to it. It is also at the minimum point of one of its short-run average cost curves.

An increase in industry costs raises prices in two stages. Initially, firms continue production so long as average variable costs are covered. If, however, variable costs have risen so that SMC has shifted upwards, firms will reduce output in an attempt to cover their costs. In the long run, as losses are made, firms leave the industry reducing industry supply and raising price further until a new long-run equilibrium is reached. If costs have increased in the same way at all levels of output, the minimum point of the new LAC curve occurs at the same output as for the previous LAC curve. The firms that are left in the industry therefore expand their output back to its original level in the long run.

Comparative static effects

Try the test on card 5 to make sure that you understand the comparative static effects.

35 If a perfectly competitive industry is in long-run equilibrium, what can you say about: (a) the profits of the firms in the industry; (b) the point on its LAC curve at which a firm is producing; (c) the number of firms wishing to enter or leave the industry?

The Effect of a Tariff on Imports

International trade economics is particularly suited to comparative static analysis. Work through the cards to see that opening a previously protected domestic market to world trade will lower prices to consumers, reduce

domestic supply and increase imports. Note that no account is taken of changes in exchange rates which might accompany the adoption of a free trade policy. This is comparative statics.

36 **If the domestic price is 10 and the world price is 6, what is the level of tariff which would reduce imports to zero?**

Section 5.5: Monopoly

In contrast to perfect competition, monopoly refers to a market in which there is only one seller and in which there are significant barriers to entry. All the other assumptions we have made about markets remain the same. In spite of this, the consequences of the monopoly assumptions for the behaviour of the market are severe and have attracted the attention of policy-makers. Under monopoly conditions, profits, price and output levels differ from those which we might expect under perfect competition. Since perfect competition is sufficient to ensure the absence of supernormal profits in the long run, monopoly is traditionally portrayed as inefficient and distortionary. The effects of monopoly on economic welfare are fully explored in chapter 7 and chapter 18.

Two Key Assumptions in Monopoly

This WinEcon screen is designed to show you two important respects in which monopoly differs from perfect competition. Monopoly shares many of the features of perfect competition, but because the firm in monopoly is also the industry it faces the industry demand curve. The analysis determing the output at which profits are maximized is therefore somewhat different for a monopoly since marginal revenue is no longer equal to price.

About monopoly

37 **What shape is the monopolist's demand curve?**

38 **What impact do barriers to entry have?**

Barriers to Entry

The requirement that there is only one seller in a market is not sufficient to account for monopoly power over price. Suppose that there is a large number of potential entrants to an industry with identical costs to those of the incumbent monopoly. The reason they are 'potential' rather than actual entrants is that the monopolist is only making normal profits. Assume now that the monopolist attempts to raise its price. Immediately, some of the potential entrants would enter the industry to take advantage of the higher return now available in the monopolist's industry. Prices would fall so that this extra supply could be sold, and the monopolist's attempt to control market price would have failed. For the monopolist to remain the sole producer while making supernormal profits there must be barriers to entry which prevent other firms entering the industry.

WinEcon divides barriers to entry into two sorts – natural and legal. Natural includes not only natural physical characteristics of markets, such as oil fields, but also technologies, such as specific chemical processes. In natural monopolies, economies of scale are present which yield an advantage to an existing firm. By expanding to take up all economies of scale, the incumbent is able to produce at lower costs than would an entrant. This is a deterrent to entry at small levels of output. On the other hand, some barriers are artificial but are established by law and so have a similar effect in creating additional costs for entrants. Doctors for example possess sole legal rights to dispense certain medical treatments. Anyone wishing to enter this market has to undergo a lengthy and expensive training, the results of which are uncertain. Doctors therefore are protected against entry so long as their fees do not attract larger numbers into medicine than are lost each period through retirement from the profession.

Natural and legal barriers

39 Which items listed on the WinEcon screen have elements both of natural and legal monopoly?

A Monopolist's Revenue

The fundamental difference between perfect competition and monopoly lies in the shape of the demand curve facing both types of industry. Because there is only one firm, the monopolist faces industry demand, and has to consider the effect of changes in output with a downward-sloping demand curve. When demand is downward sloping, an increase in output has two effects:

(1) Price has to be lowered to sell the extra units;

(2) If the good is homogeneous, the price of existing units has to be lowered as well.

Thus, by increasing output the monopolist receives increased revenue from extra sales *minus* lower revenue from all existing sales. In consequence the net increase in revenue is less than the new price charged for the extra output.

For short-run operation, only average variable costs are relevant, whilst for longer term viability, average total costs must be covered by average revenues.

The aim of the Liz's Sandwich Shop case study on the WinEcon screen is to explore how concepts of monopoly firm behaviour can be applied in practice. WinEcon here makes a considerable simplification in assuming that all the shop's costs are met by a local supermarket selling inputs to Liz's sandwich production process. In this instance therefore the profit maximizing and revenue maximizing outputs coincide. You are told what prices and profits were on one day and have to discover the profit maximizing prices for the remainder of the week. The important point to note is that demand is not interrelated over the days of the week, so that each day is an independent experiment and can yield the correct price. Now try the experiment.

The questions below relate to the Liz's Sandwich Shop case study. You can see an example of the methods they use by moving with the Next Page button to the supplementary WinEcon screen, A Monopolist's Revenue (2).

Average revenue and marginal revenue

Use the Tuesday arrows to adjust price on the WinEcon screen A Monopolist's Revenue and so discover the demand curve faced by Liz's Sandwich Shop. Record in the table below each of the possible price/quantity combinations, starting with the highest price in the top row. Note that the starting values of 0 and 0 do not constitute a point on the demand curve. Use the values you record to calculate the values for total revenue (TR). Next calculate the change in TR as each price change occurs. Marginal revenue (MR) is defined as the change in TR when output is increased by one unit. Calculate the values of MR by dividing the change in TR figures by the change in quantity that accompanies them.

Price	Quantity	Total revenue	Change in TR	MR
160	0	0		
140	___	___	___	___
120	___	___	___	___
___	___	___	___	___
___	___	___	___	___
___	___	___	___	___
___	___	___	___	___
___	___	___	___	___

Plot the total revenue curve for this monopoly.

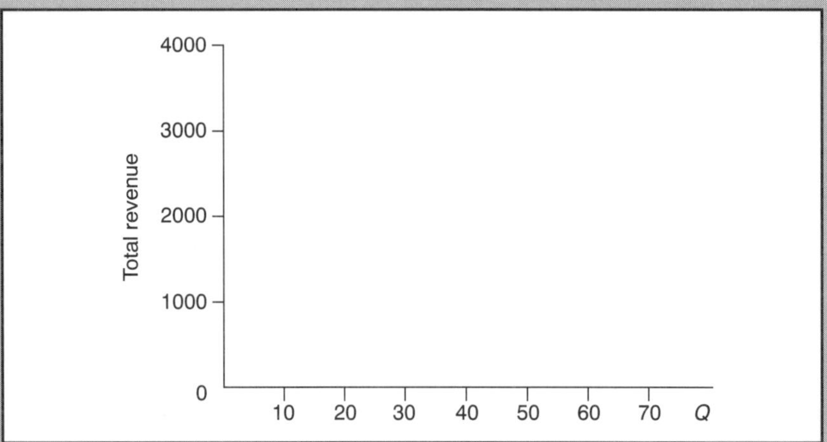

Plot the AR or demand curve for Liz's Sandwich Shop. On the same graph plot the corresponding MR curve. To do this, because the MR figures relate to the change between two quantity figures, plot them against a quantity half way between the two quantities in question.

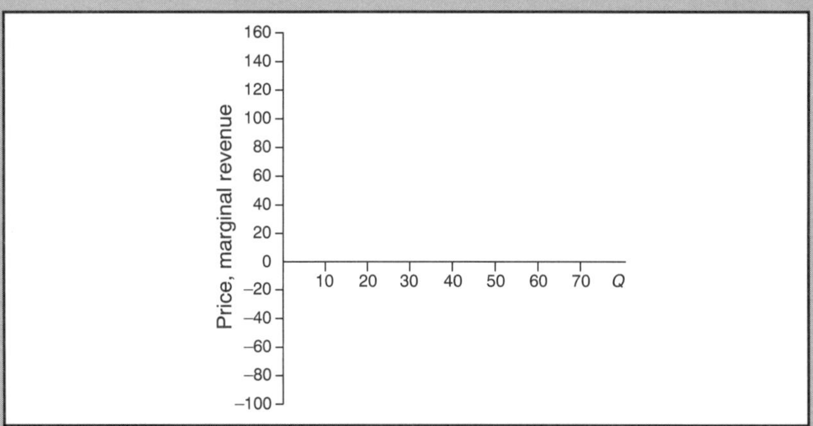

40 **Looking at your graphs, at what quantity is MR equal to zero? What can you say about the corresponding value of TR?**

41 **As quantity increases, how does the rate at which MR falls compare with the rate at which AR falls?**

42 **Which is lower, MR or AR? Can you explain why this is so?**

43 **Describe the shape of the TR curve when MR is negative.**

Profit Maximization by a Monopolist

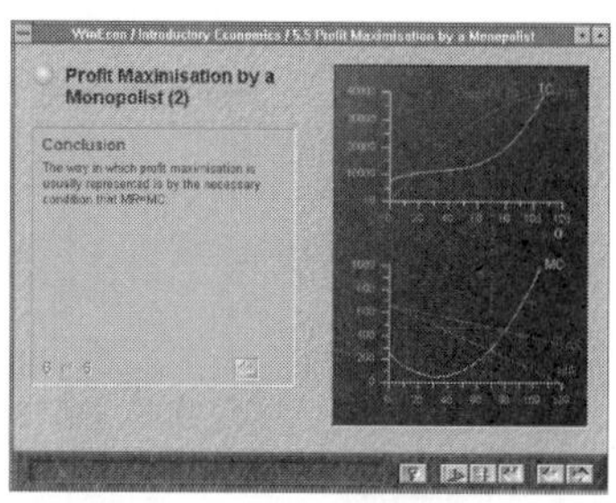

This WinEcon topic helps you to check your understanding of the shapes of various cost and revenue curves. Notice that profit maximization requires the fulfilment of the same condition as under perfect competition, namely the equalization of marginal total cost and marginal total revenue, with MC cutting MR from below. Once the profit maximizing output has been determined, the price at which it is sold is read from the AR curve. You should note that this is higher than MR for downward-sloping average and marginal revenue curves.

Since a monopolist has some control over price, we say that a monopoly has market power. But the monopolist can only decide either the output it wishes to sell or the price at which it will offer goods for sale. Once one of these is chosen, the other is determined by market forces as represented in the demand curve. The price/quantity combination that the monopolist sells must be a point on the market demand curve.

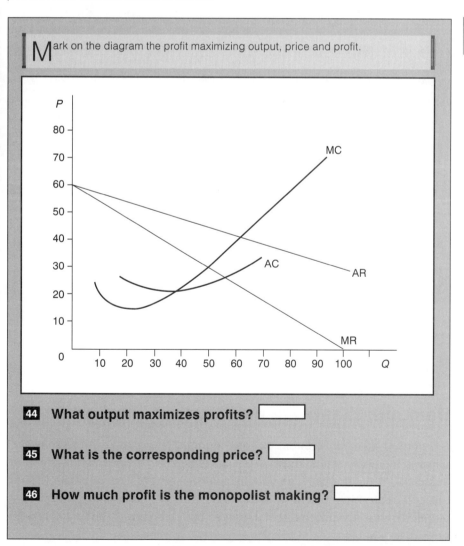

Mark on the diagram the profit maximizing output, price and profit.

44 **What output maximizes profits?** ______

45 **What is the corresponding price?** ______

46 **How much profit is the monopolist making?** ______

Monopoly and Supply

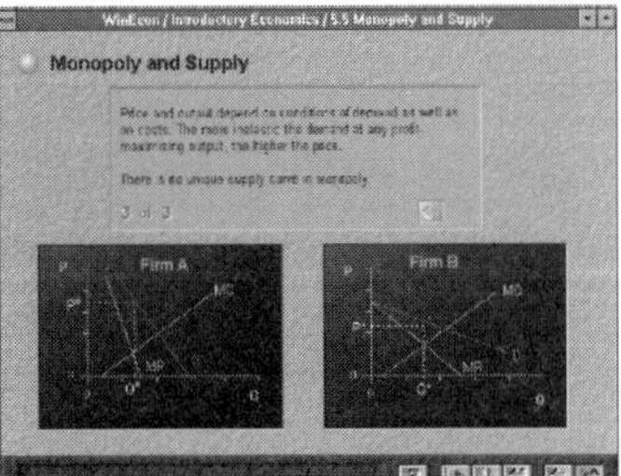

You have already seen that under perfect competition, there is a unique relationship between prices and outputs – the supply curve. Each firm will supply up to the point where its marginal cost is just equal to the market price so long as the price is greater than the firm's average variable costs of production. This result enables us to construct an industry supply curve by adding together the supply curves of individual firms. Unfortunately under monopoly there is no equivalent supply curve. This WinEcon topic shows that quantity produced depends on conditions of demand as much as upon the shape of the firm's marginal cost curve. To show this, we take a situation where two monopolists face identical costs but different demand curves, and find the profit maximizing level of output in each case.

Develop your understanding of monopolistic behaviour

47 **What can you say about the quantity supplied by a monopolist?**

48 **The steeper the demand curve, the more/less price elastic is demand.** ______

49 **Under perfect competition, lower prices would lead to lower supply. Consider monopolists A and B shown on the WinEcon screen diagram. If A's demand changed to look like that of B, prices would** ______ **and quantity produced would** ______**.**

50 **If you observed prices falling and outputs rising in a monopolistic industry, and you knew that costs had not changed, deduce whether demand was becoming more/less elastic.** ______

Demand, Elasticity and Monopoly

A common error is to suppose that monopolists exploit inelasticities of demand by keeping consumers on the inelastic part of their demand schedules. In fact this is not the case, as you discover on this WinEcon screen. To keep the explanation simple, it is assumed in the WinEcon exercise that the demand curve is linear and that it has a slope of unity (–1) so that it cuts the price and quantity axes at the same numerical values.

You find on card 5 that a monopolist who has zero marginal costs produces at the point where marginal revenue equals zero, which is the output at which the demand curve has unitary elasticity. The demand curve is inelastic only for outputs which are greater than this. At such outputs, however, marginal revenue is negative. Our condition for profit maximization is that marginal cost, which is positive or zero should equal marginal revenue. With a linear demand function it is therefore not possible that the profit maximizing position can occur at outputs where demand is inelastic.

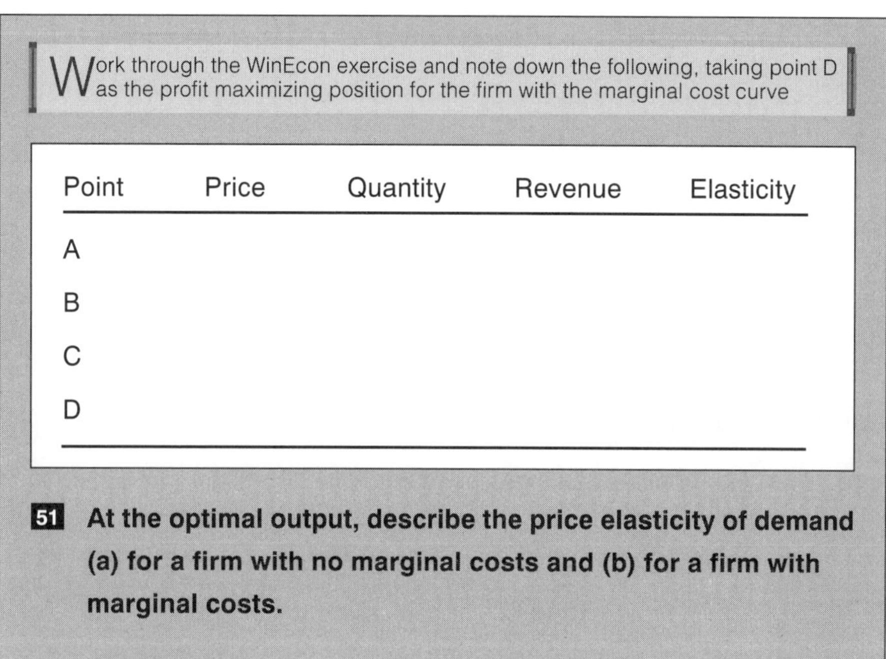

Work through the WinEcon exercise and note down the following, taking point D as the profit maximizing position for the firm with the marginal cost curve

Point	Price	Quantity	Revenue	Elasticity
A				
B				
C				
D				

51 **At the optimal output, describe the price elasticity of demand (a) for a firm with no marginal costs and (b) for a firm with marginal costs.**

Price Discrimination Under Monopoly

Why do firms sometimes charge different prices for the same good in different markets? For example, package holidays often cost more in the summer than in the winter for identical packages. The WinEcon exercise begins by finding the profit maximizing price and output where different prices are not allowed and then carries out the same exercise when prices are allowed to vary. It is interesting because the result is not intuitively obvious and yet it provides a good explanation for a real life situation.

One might expect that treating the two markets separately or together would produce the same answer. However, this is not the case where the demand in one market is zero at quite low prices. Here the second market dominates the aggregated calculation and the optimum quantities and prices are found on the second market's marginal revenue and cost curves alone. This has the effect of excluding the smaller market. Treating the two markets separately enables the firm to offer prices at which some of the smaller market demand is met, as well as that of the second market. Price discrimination then leads to a larger overall output, and to higher profits for the firm.

Customers in the larger market would of course prefer to pay the lower price at which the good is offered in the smaller market. If they are able to move between markets the differential pricing system breaks down. Price discrimination can only take place where the markets are separated, possibly in time, as with the winter and summer holidays, or where a personal service is offered to an individual, such as hairdressing or dental treatment. You will deal with welfare economics issues in chapter 18. Meanwhile, try the questions below.

Comparison of prices and quantities

52 **Does price discrimination represent an improvement over monopoly pricing for (a) consumers and (b) the producer?**

53 **From the consumer's point of view, is price discrimination better or worse than perfect competition?**

Perfect Competition and Monopoly Compared

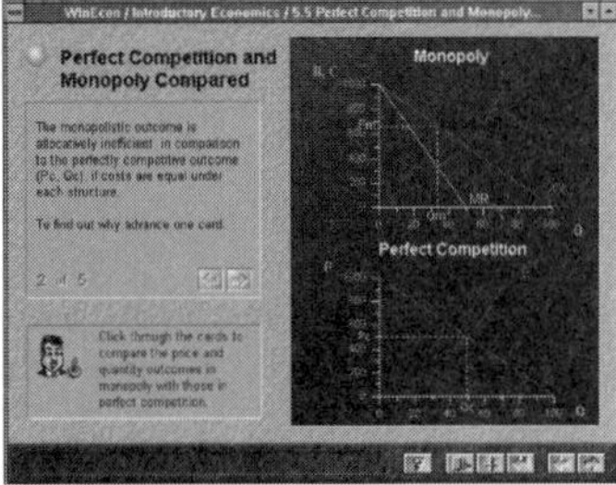

Monopolists can exercise market power and are often thought to act contrary to the public interest. The theoretical case against monopoly rests on a comparison of the same market being supplied either by perfectly competitive firms or by a monopolist. The basic analysis assumes that costs are the same under the two market structures, but we also see that the monopolist's costs would have to be lower, perhaps by a substantial margin, for the conclusion to change.

Use the WinEcon screen and notice that the monopolist, being both the firm and the industry, sets output at the level where marginal revenue equals marginal cost to maximize profits. Under perfect competition the industry supply curve would be the monopolist's marginal cost curve above average variable cost, assuming that costs are the same under the different market structures. The demand curve is identical with the AR curve for the monopoly. In perfect competition equilibrium occurs where supply equals demand in the market. The price thus determined, P_c, is the AR and also the MR for all firms in the industry. They each maximize their profits by setting this MR equal to MC, and the outputs they choose to produce total to the level Q_c shown on the WinEcon diagram.

With identical costs, price is higher and output is lower under monopoly as compared with perfect competition. It seems, therefore, that monopolists may exploit consumers and hence governments wish to control and regulate them.

An argument in favour of monopolies is that they may be able to reap economies of scale. WinEcon cards 4 and 5 suggest that these may have to be considerable to overturn the conclusion we have just reached. Lowering the marginal cost curve increases the monopolist's output and reduces price, but does not necessarily bring them to their competitive levels.

You will find more about this with a discussion of efficiency and examples of government action in chapters 7 and 18.

Main Differences between Perfect Competition and Monopoly

Use this supplementary WinEcon screen to check your understanding of the main differences between perfect competition and monopoly. Record the conclusions in the table below.

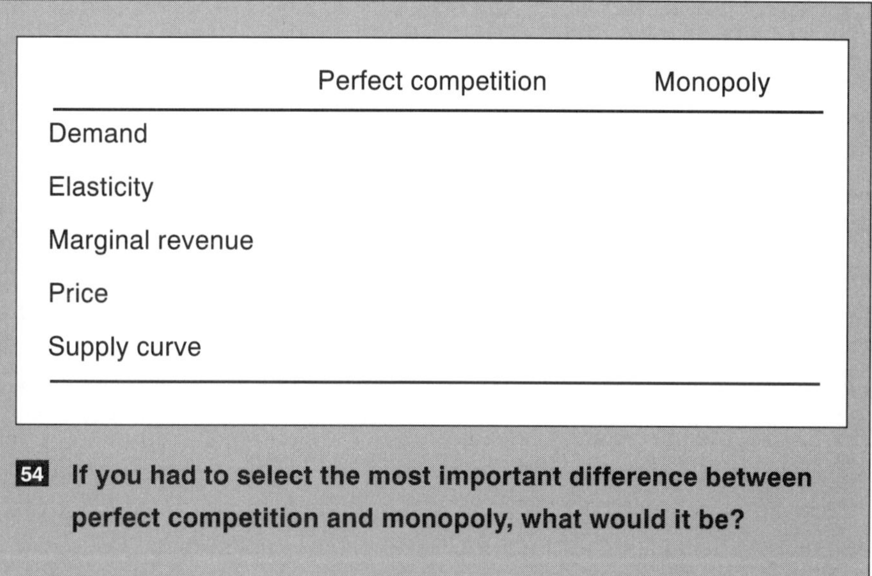

	Perfect competition	Monopoly
Demand		
Elasticity		
Marginal revenue		
Price		
Supply curve		

54 If you had to select the most important difference between perfect competition and monopoly, what would it be?

Section 5.6: Summary

Important general results for analysing market equilibrium are derived in this chapter.

When demand is perfectly elastic the average and marginal revenue curves coincide in the same horizontal line. The corresponding total revenue curve is an upward-sloping line through the origin. These curves are appropriate to individual firms in perfect competition.

If the demand curve slopes downwards so that price has to be lowered for a greater output to be sold, then the marginal revenue curve also slopes downwards and lies below the average revenue or demand curve. For simplicity we often use a linear demand function. In this case the corresponding marginal revenue curve is also linear and slopes down twice as fast as the line representing average revenue. With linear average and marginal functions, the corresponding total revenue function has an inverted U shape and reaches a maximum at the output at which marginal revenue equals zero.

Regardless of the market structure, we assume all firms aim to maximize profits. This implies they produce at the output at which marginal cost equals marginal revenue, with MC cutting MR from below. At this output firms maximize their profit or minimize their loss. The amount of profit (or loss) made by a firm is shown by an area on the diagram showing marginal and average cost and revenue curves. The area is a rectangle with a height equal to the difference between AR and AC and a width equal to the quantity of output. The profits which firms seek to maximize are known also as supernormal profits. The opportunity cost of capital services, or normal profit, is included in production costs.

Because of the large numbers of firms and consumers in perfect competition, firms see their demand curves as horizontal. All firms make the same homogenous product and there are no barriers to prevent firms entering or leaving the industry in the long run. In perfect competition the supply curve is the marginal cost curve above its intersection with average variable cost. This leads to the conclusion that a perfectly competitive industry will produce the output at the intersection of the aggregate MC curve and the demand curve.

Long-run equilibrium is achieved in a perfectly competitive industry when there is no incentive for firms either to enter or leave the industry. At such a point each firm operates where AR = MR = LMC = LAC, at the minimum point of its long-run average cost curve.

Comparative static analysis of a perfectly competitive industry uses linked diagrams for the industry and for individual firms. We find, for example, that an increase in demand raises prices in the short run but that in the long run new firms enter the industry and prices fall back to their original level. This is based on the assumption that the industry is operating at constant returns to scale.

The important features of monopoly are that there is only one seller in the market and that there are significant barriers to prevent other firms from entering the industry. The monopolist faces the market demand curve which is assumed to be downward sloping. Profits are maximized where MC = MR, but price is then higher than MR and so the monopolist makes supernormal profits. Because of the barriers to entry, these profits continue to be made in the long run.

A monopolist does not have a supply curve and produces at a point on the demand curve where demand is elastic. If the monopolist supplies separate markets with different demand curves, price discrimination is likely to be profitable.

By comparison with perfect competition, a monopolist produces less output and sells it at a higher price, assuming costs are the same under both types of market structure. If the monopolist can reap economies of scale this will induce a higher output from the monopolist, but it may still not be as high as under perfect competition.

Chapter 6:

Imperfect Competition

In practice, firms typically have some control over prices but have to take into account the behaviour of their competitors in deciding their actions. The jewellery business has many retail outlets offering different prices for similar looking products. By contrast, industries like oil and electricity sell very similar products but are dominated by a few large suppliers. Do these different market structures, known respectively as monopolistic competition and oligopoly, make a real difference to price and output decisions? Are the results optimal for consumers and producers? How effective are advertising and other forms of sales promotion in stimulating sales? This chapter explores such issues.

Contents

KEYWORDS

- Advertising
- Cartel
- Collusion
- Cournot
- Game theory
- Imperfect competition
- Kinked demand
- Monopolistic competition
- Nash equilibrium
- Non-price competition
- Oligopoly
- Price leadership
- Product differentiation
- Strategy

Section 6.1: Introduction

Monopolistic competition is where there are large numbers of firms whose products are not perfect substitutes for each other. Oligopoly is where there are few firms but the products may be similar.

This chapter extends the treatment of markets and prices to situations of imperfect competition. Imperfect competition is a generic term covering a range of situations from where products in an industry are differentiated (monopolistic competition) to those where firms are few in number (oligopoly). Each agent has some control over price, but clearly faces competition which would limit the prices set. The main purpose of the chapter is to show that economics is relevant to the study of realistic industrial situations and is not confined to idealistic markets such as those of perfect competition and monopoly.

Throughout the chapter we continue to assume that firms seek to maximize profits. This is an important feature of the economist's general approach because it allows clear predictions to be made about firms' behaviour. The advantage of this is that any predictions about behaviour are fully consistent with the incentives which owners of companies perceive in their markets. In this way economics makes rational predictions of behaviour.

We shall see that firms in monopolistically competitive and oligopolistic industries must consider the impact of a mix of price and non-price sales promotion activities. In oligopoly the actions of one firm affect others. Studying the interdependence between firms requires the consideration of strategic behaviour in which one firm explicitly takes into account the likely response of others to any decision it may make. The price and output decisions of firms in imperfect competition differ significantly from those that would be made under perfect competition. Since, as will be shown in chapter 7, perfect competition has many desirable qualities, it can be argued that social welfare might be improved if governments were to intervene in imperfectly competitive markets.

Our understanding of monopolistic competition is due largely to Joan Robinson of the UK and Edward Chamberlin of the USA. Oligopoly issues have received increased attention in recent years, although early results established by the nineteenth-century French economist Augustin Cournot and the twentieth-century German economist H. von Stackelberg remain important. Recently, the mathematical theory of games has been applied fruitfully to oligopoly situations.

Section 6.2: Monopolistic Competition

Monopolistic competition describes a market in which there are many sellers each selling a (slightly) different version of a good or service. Examples of such markets are cars, newspapers, housing, private hospitals, economic forecasters, TV production companies, booksellers, textile firms.

Although there are many similarities to perfect competition – the numbers of firms are large, each firm is small in relation to the market, there is freedom of entry and exit from the industry – monopolistic competition differs from perfect competition in that firms produce differentiated products. Two important features of the analysis are:

- Each firm faces a downward-sloping demand curve and needs to decide about the appropriate price for the product.
- Each firm is assumed to behave as if its actions do not provoke any response from other firms. The reason for this is that the effects of one firm's actions on the profits of any other firm are imperceptible.

If we can ignore the prospect of retaliation we can simply find the firm's optimal behaviour and then combine it with that of other firms to discover the likely behaviour of price and output in the monopolistically competitive market.

This section explores in more detail the assumptions of monopolistic competition, the nature of the demand facing a single firm in a monopolistically competitive industry, and the expected level of output and price of the firm and its relation to that of a perfectly competitive firm. As in the previous chapter on perfect competition we make an important distinction between how firms behave in the short and in the longer term. The existence of profits creates an incentive for long-run changes. Numbers of firms will change through entry or exit from the industry. Price and output will change as a result of investment decisions. We also examine the dynamic adjustments which are to be expected in monopolistically competitive markets.

Key Assumptions in Monopolistic Competition

Use the WinEcon screen to discover the main conditions which have to be satisfied by monopolistically competitive markets. Notice the greater detail on each condition that appears on the right. Now look at the question which takes the form of a case study where you decide on the appropriate market classification.

See what you have learnt

01 **Each individual firm produces ___ ______ ____ ____ of the total industry output, but does ___ ___ ___ price.**

02 **There are ____ barriers to entry created by ____ ______.**

03 Each firm produces a product which has ______ ______ ______ ______.

04 Firms have sufficient power to ______ ______ ______ ______.

05 Which is more monopolistically competitive, brewing or building?

06 Which of the following are differentiated products/services: steel bars; hairdressing services; crude oil; jewellery?

07 Are elasticities of demand the same or different for monopolistically competitive goods? ______

Short-Run Equilibrium of a Monopolistic Firm

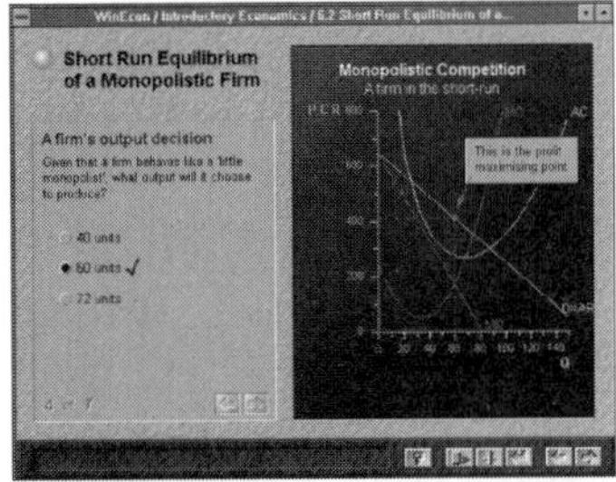

This WinEcon screen shows the demand curve for the differentiated product of one individual seller. (This is the demand for Doc Martens boots, not for footwear in general, or for Rolex watches rather than watches in general.) Notice that the diagram resembles that for a monopolist in that the marginal revenue lies below the average revenue curve. This implies the firm will choose to keep production below the level that would be produced under perfect competition.

Product differentiation is a key feature of monopolistic competition. A possible motive for it is the firm's wish to establish a degree of customer preference for the product. In an industry with few firms, it is relatively easy to establish such differentiation. For example, in the market for a new product like video cameras, the first few products quickly found specific market niches. As entry occurred, however, the differences between cameras became smaller, prices on average fell and the responsiveness of demand to price changed.

Notice the level of output and the price which are chosen by a monopolistically competitive firm. Discovering the appropriate levels is simply a matter of applying the rule that marginal cost equals marginal revenue for maximum profits. Look at the WinEcon screen diagram to see whether the firm shown produces at the point of minimum average costs. The diagram shows a monopolistically competitive firm in a position of short-run equilibrium. In general, such a firm will not be producing at the minimum point on its long-run average cost curve. Instead, it is likely to have excess capacity.

Profit maximization with a downward-sloping demand curve means we end up with a price higher than marginal revenue and marginal cost at the level of output where marginal revenue is equal to marginal cost. You will notice that this result is exactly what you would expect under monopoly conditions. You will discover in chapter 7 that an output where price does not equal marginal cost may be allocatively inefficient.

See section 7.4, in the topic Efficiency in Competition and Monopoly

Test your understanding by tackling these questions

08 **How does a monopolistically competitive firm choose its output?**

09 **Does a firm in monopolistic competition produce at minimum average cost (a) always, (b) under particular conditions, or (c) never?**

10 **What is the relationship between price and marginal cost in monopolistic competition?**

Adjustment to Long-Run Equilibrium

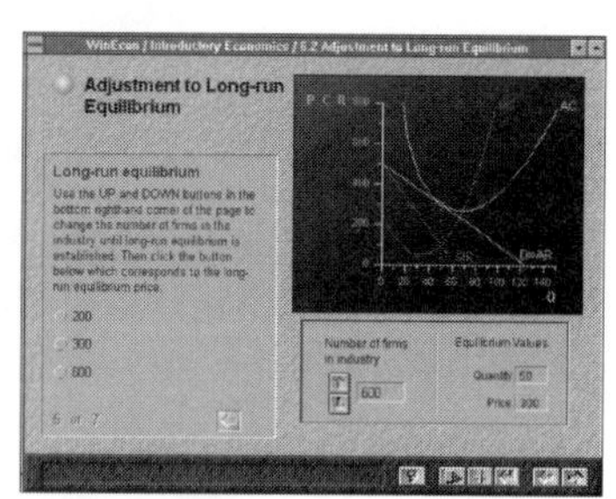

An important question is how inefficient the monopolistically competitive firm is likely to be. Not only is there usually inefficiency and excess capacity in the short run, but dynamic adjustment processes do not rectify the position. This topic develops a number of important points which you can see clearly by working through the adjustment process from short-run equilibrium to long-run equilibrium.

The major factor is that under monopolistic competition, although no supernormal profits are made in the long run, firms with standard-shaped cost curves will not produce at minimum costs. Thus excess capacity continues to exist under monopolistic competition. In the long run, the firm shown produces at less than the optimal level of output at prices which, although they merely cover costs, are higher than optimal. These are the main points made by economists in their criticism of monopolistic competition. It is possible, however, that these criticisms may be more than offset by the advantage that monopolistic competition has in offering consumers a variety of goods. A perfectly competitive industry might eliminate excess capacity and achieve allocative efficiency, but all firms would then offer identical products. Under monopolistic competition different brands and styles are available, and consumers may value these.

Do you understand the adjustment process?

Work through the WinEcon screen, completing the description below and marking output, price and profit on the diagram, both in the short run and in the long run.

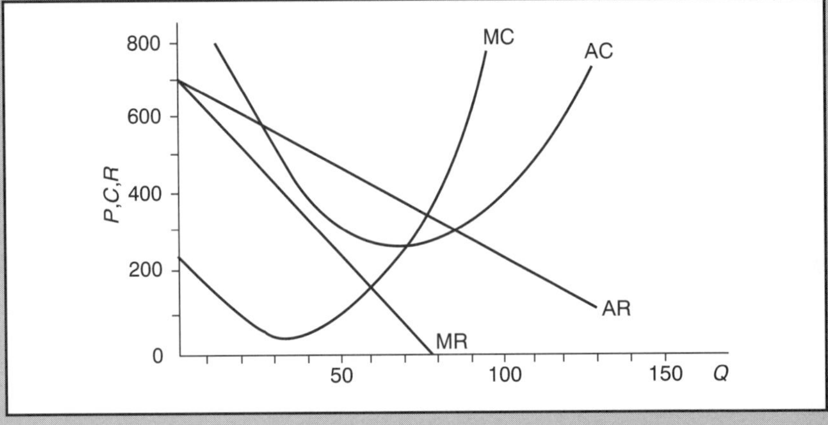

11 **The firm is in short-run equilibrium at output level ______ and price ______. At this output level profits are ______, amounting to ______. Other firms now ______ the industry and the demand curve shifts to the ______ as the share of each existing firm ______. The adjustment process comes to an end when the new demand curve is tangential to the old ______ curve because here the firm makes ______ supernormal profits. The new firm output level is ______ than before. Excess capacity persists because the new demand curve does not meet the average cost curve at its ______ point.**

12 **Does a firm in monopolistic competition produce at the minimum average cost if its average cost curve is (a) horizontal and (b) downward sloping?**

Quiz on Monopolistic Competition

Try the quiz on this WinEcon screen to check your knowledge about monopolistic competition.

Section 6.3: Oligopoly

Many real-life markets are dominated by a relatively small number of large producers. Examples are aircraft, washing powders, bicycles, electricity plant manufacturing, computer software and oil production. They are characterized by a scarcity of competitors and in consequence the fortunes of each firm can be significantly affected by the actions of the other firms. The existence of economies of scale is the principal reason for an industry characterized by few large firms. When economies of scale are coupled with similarity of products, then it is obvious that decisions made by one firm will affect the profits of its competitors. These are usually called 'rivals' to distinguish them from firms in perfectly competitive industries.

Since privatization, former public utilities like electricity and water are subject to some form of price regulation in areas where they possess a degree of market power. This takes the form of an RPI–*X* rule which caps the growth of prices by an efficiency factor *X* which is the percentage rate of efficiency achievement. Thus firms' freedom to set prices is restricted and they are not able to behave as unconstrained oligopolists.

For more details see the following WinEcon topics: Examples of Regulation in section 7.6 and Regulation of Privatized Utilities in section 20.3.

This section provides the theory which is needed to explain some important aspects of oligopoly behaviour in markets. Once the main features of oligopoly have been outlined, we distinguish two main ways in which oligopolies may operate. The firms may either collude or compete with one another. We study how cartels operate, and see that many restrictive practices are now prohibited by law.

A variant on the oligopoly theme is where a market contains a core of large firms surrounded by a fringe of competitive producers. The OPEC oil cartel is an example of this variant, where 46 per cent of world oil exports in 1994 came from OPEC members whilst non-OPEC countries like the UK, the US and Russia made up a competitive fringe of suppliers on the world market.

Non-collusive models of oligopoly include Cournot's duopoly model, the kinked demand curve, and game theory. We discover reasons for stable prices to exist in oligopoly, and so we investigate forms of non-price competition such as new models of goods and advertising.

The Key Assumptions of Oligopoly

The conditions for oligopoly shown on the screen should help you make comparisons between the various market types. The low number of suppliers is a particular feature of oligopoly and is linked with the existence of barriers to entry resulting from economies of scale and scope. These features make firms interdependent and give them the ability to exercise control over prices. Notice that the nature of the product is unimportant: it may or may not be differentiated.

Conditions for oligopoly

13 **What is the crucial difference between oligopoly and other market structures?**

14 **If firms in an oligopoly collude, they act as a ________.**

Interdependence in Oligopoly

The fact that individual oligopolists know that their actions affect the profits of other firms means that they must act strategically. They must try to foresee the consequences of various possible combinations of actions as each firm decides what steps to take to secure its best possible outcome.

Work through the WinEcon cards to find the two main possibilities. The first option is that the firms collude and make joint decisions. The alternative is to engage in rivalrous competition. This may seem unattractive in the short run as price competition reduces profits for all firms. In the longer term, however, low prices may drive competitors out of the market and increase the firm's market share. For example, the UK newspaper price war of 1994 and 1995 enabled Times Newspapers to establish a large market share at the expense of weaker papers.

Collusive Oligopoly

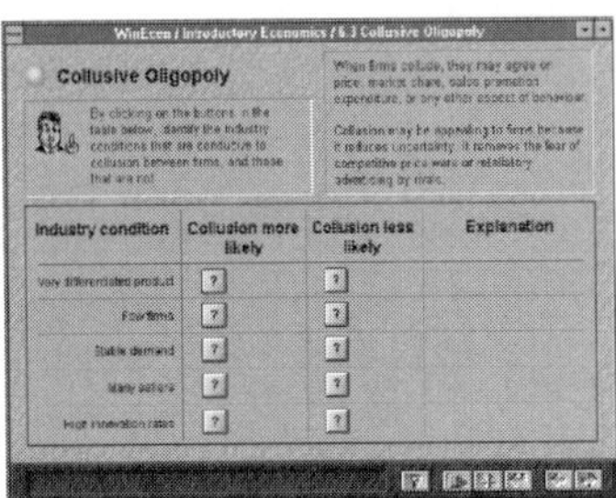

Collusion represents a co-operative solution to the firms' problem. It requires that the firms are able to bind themselves to an agreement to behave together, setting prices or outputs as a monopolist. The attraction of collusion is that it generates the greatest overall profit for the group of firms. Unfortunately such collusion is difficult to sustain both because governmental legislation is often hostile to cartels and because there are good economic reasons why co-operation should break down. We will explore these in a later section. This screen tests your knowledge of collusive oligopoly.

15 **Collusion is ________ likely when the industry's product is highly differentiated because the group ________ co-ordinate policy easily.**

16 **Large numbers of sellers find collusion ________ easy because cheating is ________ easily detectable.**

17 **Unpredictable demand makes collusion ______ likely because planning is ______.**

Cartels

A cartel is a production sharing agreement which results in quotas being assigned to each cartel member. One type of cartel is where firms agree on a monopoly price and market shares are determined by non-price competition. Domestic appliance and automobile markets often behave as if there had been an agreement on an industry price. Prices are publicized so that each producer can move rapidly to the industry standard price. Another sort of cartel is one which agrees the division of output among the members as well as its total size. Perhaps the best-known example of this type is that of OPEC. We saw this approach in action in June 1995 when the OPEC Council of Ministers allocated shares of the total output of 24.52 million barrels a day (mbd) amongst Saudi Arabia (8 mbd), Iran (3.6 mbd), Venezuela (2.36 mbd), UAE (2.16 mbd), Kuwait (2.0 mbd) and the rest to smaller members.

Cards 4 and 5 of the WinEcon screen are concerned with cheating in cartels. This is important because it explains why cartels are unstable. The basic reason is that members are tempted to cheat in order to increase their individual profits. As they do so the total profits of the cartel fall.

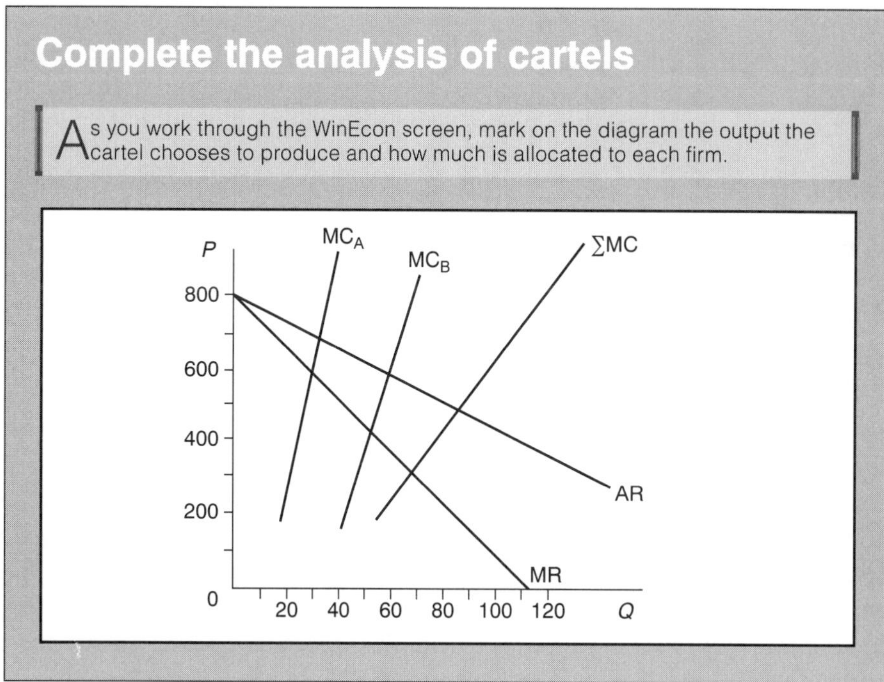

18 **How does the cartel choose its total output?**

19 **How does the cartel allocate output amongst its members?**

20 **If one firm chose to break the cartel, explain whether its output would change.**

21 **Why might a firm choose to cheat?**

To learn more about cartels, work through the following three sub-topics and the associated supplementary screens.

Cartel Disintegration

Suppose that a cartel breaks up due to cheating by its members. An important issue is what will happen to the price of the product or service covered by the cartel. We have seen that where an industry begins with a monopoly profit-sharing agreement, any firm has an incentive to shade its price below the joint profit maximizing price.

Try the questions on the WinEcon screen to check your understanding of how cartels work.

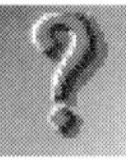

The effect of cheating

22 **Explain in your own words what happens when cartel members cheat.**

A Cartel Example – OPEC

We have already discussed OPEC as an example of a cartel. This sub-topic shows the problems facing OPEC in maintaining discipline amongst its members when market conditions changed.

One method by which the cartel handled cheating in the early 1980s was for the largest producer, Saudi Arabia, to make compensating reductions in its output as the output of the cheating members rose. This stabilized total supply for a while and maintained the market price. It failed ultimately because total revenue available to Saudi Arabia fell to an unacceptable level. The Saudis then retaliated by flooding the market with cheaper oil in 1986. This of course enabled them to retrieve some lost revenue as well as to punish cheating members. The cost was high for the Saudis and they vowed never again to act as the 'swing' producer for the market.

The example of OPEC

23 **High oil prices led to [ ] [ ] from producers outside OPEC.**

24 **The high price of oil also reduced demand for [ ] and [ ] [ ]. The world economy experienced [ ].**

25 **Wars between members (e.g. Iran versus Iraq) are an example of the [ ] [ ] which meant some members found it difficult to agree.**

Collusion in Practice

Since collusion may be deemed contrary to the public interest, governments often legislate against it. Firms which would choose to collude are therefore barred from doing so openly. They may, however, look for ways around the legislation which give them some of the benefits of collusion but which are not illegal. This sub-topic sets out some of the legislative background and then develops a model in which there is tacit collusion, namely the 'price leadership model'.

See also the related topic UK Regulation of Private Monopolies and Oligopolies in section 7.8.

Governments of most industrialized countries have taken steps to ban or control collusion. In the UK the appropriate legislation is the Restrictive Practices Act. Use the WinEcon screen to find an explanation of the main provisions of this and subsequent legislation.

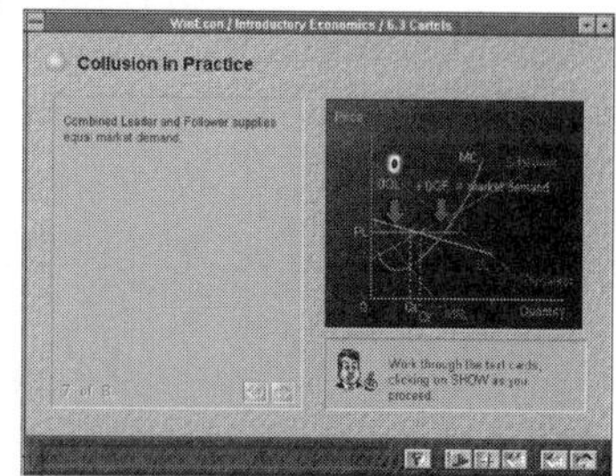

To avoid the penalties of the law, some firms behave according to a price leadership model. At any point in time, any firm can take the initiative and act as the leader. Usually, however, it will be a large firm with the expertise and resources to carry out the analysis that acts as the leader.

Develop your understanding of restrictive practices

26 **For a restrictive practice to be allowed in the UK, what is required?**

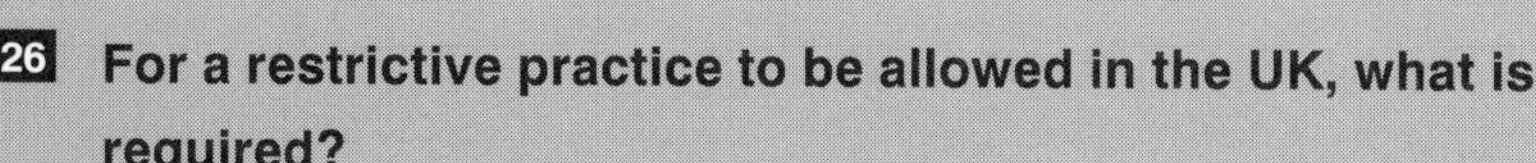
Work through the model developed in WinEcon, complete the diagram and answer the following questions:

27 **The leader begins by calculating the followers' ________ ________ curve ('S-followers').**

28 **The curve 'S-followers' is then subtracted from industry demand to get the ________ demand curve.**

29 **At the point where 'S-followers' cuts the demand curve the residual demand is ________.**

Price

0 Quantity

Non-Collusive Oligopoly

One example of non-collusive oligopoly is the price leadership model described in the previous sub-topic. There firms find it in their interests to select a price after anticipating how their rivals would react to such a price. This is an example of a more general approach involving estimating the reactions of a set of opponents before taking actions oneself. Taking account of opponents reactions is the essence of strategic decision making.

Use the WinEcon screen to learn more about strategic decision making, then move with the Next Page button to the supplementary screen (Equilibrium in Non-Collusive Oligopoly) to see how the concept of stable equilibrium is defined in oligopoly and discover why it may be unattainable.

One of the main incentives for collusion is the desire to reduce uncertainty. By agreeing on a common price, firms can then predict market demand and in the case of a quota agreement the demand for their own product. Where collusion is not possible, however, uncertainty will plague the firm's decision making. How competitor B will react will be the constant question asked by competitor A. Rather than panic in the face of such uncertainty, the economist will ask what actions will best serve the firms' interests, and will explore the implications of this rational behaviour.

Finding the rational behaviour of competing firms may well suggest a common set of strategies which is stable in the sense of being the best solution possible in the circumstances. For example, suppose two manufacturers of computer disks have to decide on the size of the disk before commencing production. They know that the total market will be bigger if both adopt the same standard size. Clearly if both firms adopt the standard then deviation by either one from this standard will reduce the overall market and affect profits of both badly. Suppose that if both adopt a common standard, profits are 100 each, but if the standards are different profits are only 20 each. Once one firm has announced a standard, not only does it pay the other also to adopt this standard but the first firm has no incentive to change the standard either. Where all the incentives point to a particular set of actions, and where the actions produce the expected levels of profits, the firms can be expected to adopt these actions. They have no incentive to make changes. Each is making a 'best response' to the other and this is the idea behind the 'Nash equilibrium'.

See what you have learnt

30 **When oligopolistic firms act independently, what always influences their actions?**

31 **In what sense is decision making in oligopoly like a game?**

32 **A Nash equilibrium exists if:**

33 **What can you say about the strategies planned by firms in a Nash equilibrium?**

34 **In what circumstances might the strategy of an oligopolistic firm not have its expected result?**

Models of Non-Collusive Oligopoly

Explanations of oligopolistic behaviour go back a long way in economics. This WinEcon screen introduces you to three such explanations which are frequently encountered in treatments of oligopoly. Augustin Cournot, the father of oligopoly theory, provided a solution to the simple case of duopoly – where two firms only are in competition. Although economists have reservations about the assumptions behind his work, Cournot laid the foundations for the more modern approach based on game theory. Game theory is the study of strategic behaviour and seeks to find equilibrium ideas like those of Cournot and Nash. The third approach, quite different from the first two, is that of Paul Sweezy who tries to explain the existence of sticky prices in oligopoly markets. Now use the WinEcon screen for more detail on the three approaches.

Assumptions of Cournot's Oligopoly Model

Your study of the Cournot model begins by using the WinEcon screen to discover the relevant assumptions. Then use the Next Page button to move to the supplementary screen.

Cournot's Model of Duopoly

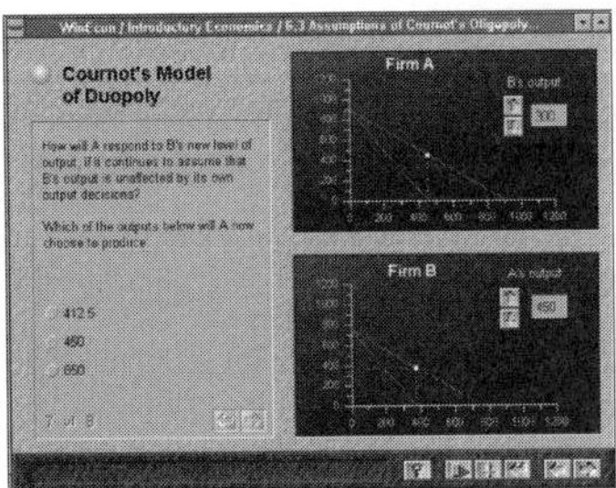

WinEcon provides a very full derivation of the response of one firm to the other's output selection as envisaged by Cournot. Work your way through the cards, noticing how each firm adjusts its own demand function to correspond to what it perceives its rival to be doing.

Cards 7 and 8 of the supplementary screen provide control buttons so you can make the appropriate adjustments. Use the buttons on the diagrams alternately. On the diagram relating to one firm you should set the other firm's output at the level you deduce from the other diagram, since this is how each firm is believed to view the other's activities. When you reach a Nash equilibrium it is no longer appropriate to use the buttons to alter the other firm's output, since each firm's expectation is being fulfilled. In equilibrium each firm is producing what its rival believes it will be producing. Theoretically each firm makes a long series of adjustments of ever diminishing magnitude. The WinEcon buttons only let you make changes of particular sizes, but it is possible to jump to the equilibrium position.

About the Cournot model

35 **In the Cournot model, what assumption is made about how each firm assumes its rival will react?**

36 **Why is the above assumption important?**

37 **What assumption is made about the firms' costs?**

38 **How does the first firm determine its initial output?**

39 **What proportion is this output of the maximum total output that would be taken up at a price of zero?** ☐

40 **How does the second firm initially determine its output?**

41 **What proportion of the maximum total output is then being produced by the two firms?** ☐

42 **How do the firm's prices compare?**

43 **Why does the first firm change its output? What happens to its price?**

44 **How does the second firm react in the output and price it offers?**

45 **In the equilibrium position, how much of the maximum total output is produced? How much of what is supplied is produced by each firm? What can you say about the firms' prices?**

Find the Cournot solution to this oligopoly problem

Helen and Jim sell identical surfboards on a small beach in north Cornwall. They have already paid for their stock of boards so that the marginal cost is zero. They face no competition other than from each other. Tom, their economic adviser, has estimated the market demand for surfboards as

Price = 100 – (quantity of surfboards)

where quantity of surfboards = quantity H + quantity J (i.e. the sum of the quantities sold by Helen and Jim).

(a) Using the Cournot model, and assuming Helen enters the market first show in the diagram her initial quantity and price.
(b) On the diagram for Jim, show his initial price/quantity combination when he enters the market.
(c) Adding information alternately to Helen's diagram and then to Jim's, show two iterations of the adjustment process.

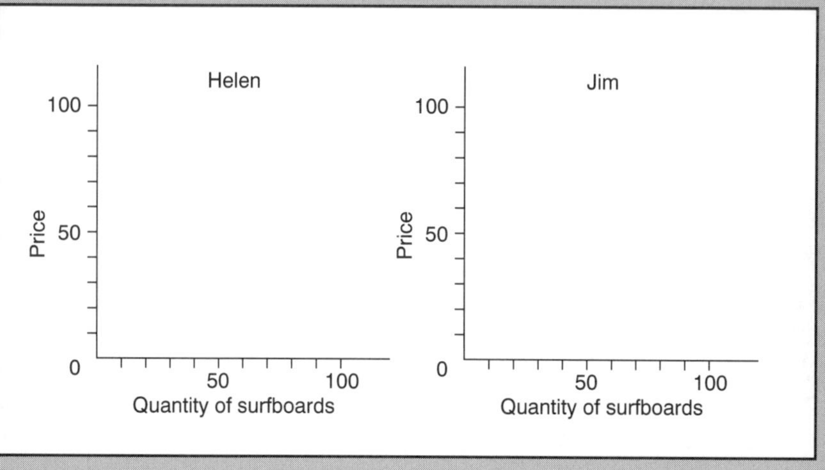

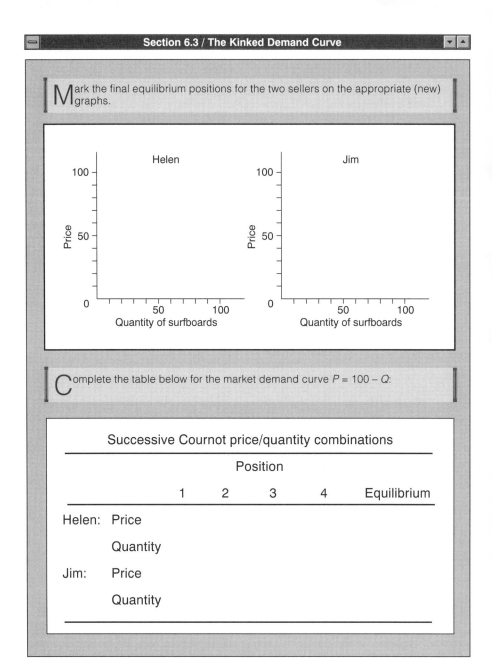

Mark the final equilibrium positions for the two sellers on the appropriate (new) graphs.

Helen

Price: 0, 50, 100

Quantity of surfboards: 50, 100

Jim

Price: 0, 50, 100

Quantity of surfboards: 50, 100

Complete the table below for the market demand curve $P = 100 - Q$:

Successive Cournot price/quantity combinations

		Position				
		1	2	3	4	Equilibrium
Helen:	Price					
	Quantity					
Jim:	Price					
	Quantity					

The Kinked Demand Curve

An implication of all theories of oligopoly is that output and price are likely to remain constant so long as the environment in which the market operates does not change. This price constancy or 'stickiness' is explained by the kinked demand theory as the result of the responsiveness of demand at the going price being different for a price rise and for a price fall.

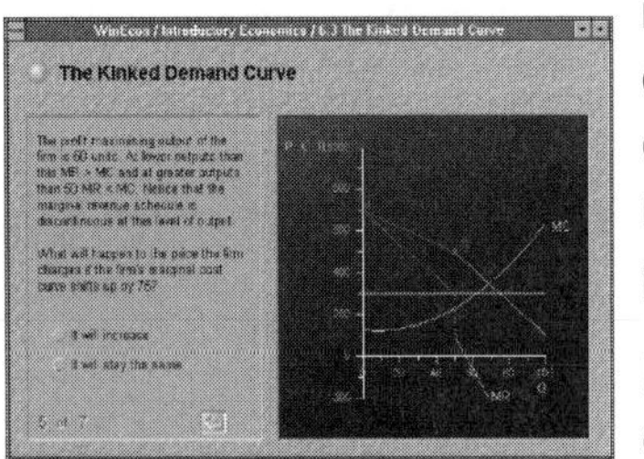

If a firm were to raise its price above the going rate, the quantity demanded would fall rapidly because of the availability of perfect substitutes at the going price. But if the firm were to reduce its price, competitors would be obliged to follow and the effect on the quantity demanded would be less. Thus the slope of the demand curve changes at the

going price. For price rises the curve is elastic, while for price decreases it is inelastic. The inelastic section of the curve corresponds to where competitors are assumed to match any price change.

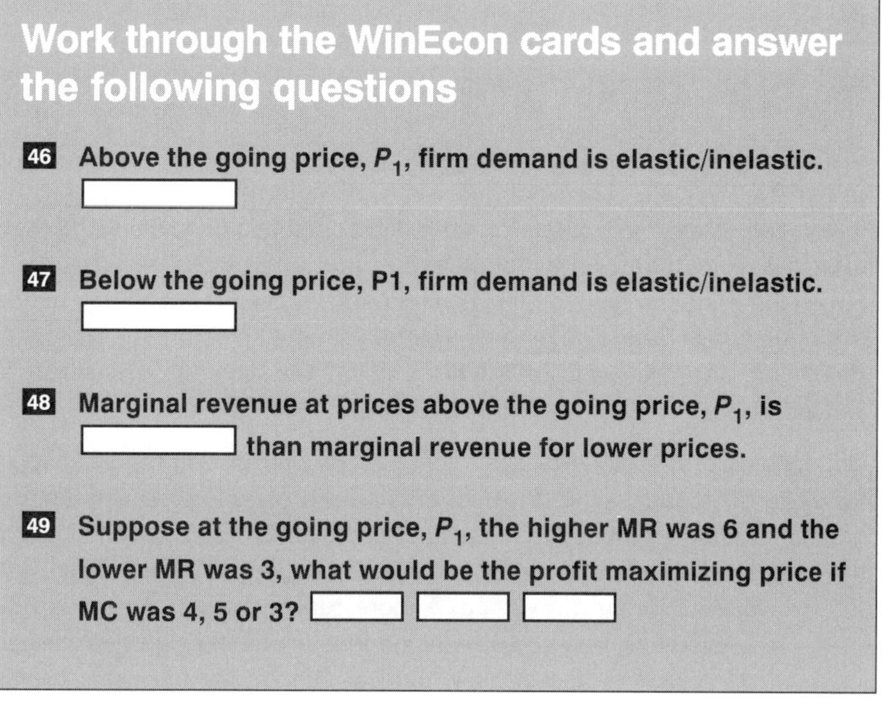

Work through the WinEcon cards and answer the following questions
46 Above the going price, P_1, firm demand is elastic/inelastic.
47 Below the going price, P1, firm demand is elastic/inelastic.
48 Marginal revenue at prices above the going price, P_1, is than marginal revenue for lower prices.
49 Suppose at the going price, P_1, the higher MR was 6 and the lower MR was 3, what would be the profit maximizing price if MC was 4, 5 or 3?

Other Explanations for Stable Prices

Although theories of oligopoly provide an explanation of sticky prices, it is important to realize that other explanations may be equally plausible. There are costs involved in changing prices, including direct costs of changing price lists as well as less obvious costs of damage to reputation and loss of trade. These factors might be expected to encourage price stability. In addition there are conventional price benchmarks which result in prices rising in a step-like manner rather than smoothly. Finally there is the practice of average cost pricing, which weakens the link between output and price, where a broad range of outputs can be produced at very similar average costs.

Work through the WinEcon screen and answer the following questions

50 **Which is likely to face higher costs of changing price, newspapers or petrol? Why?**

51 **Is benchmark pricing likely to be more important for personal computers or for apples? Why?**

52 **Which industry is more likely to have sticky prices because of constant average costs, clothing or glass? Why?**

Non-Price Competition

We have seen that in oligopolistic markets there are strong disincentives to the use of price as a competitive weapon. This topic provides a brief introduction to the main forms of non-price competition – advertising, new product development, new model styles, and after sales service. Work through the WinEcon screen to find out more, then use the Next Page button for further details about advertising on the three supplementary screens – Advertising, The Economics of Advertising and The Advertising Elasticity of Demand.

The economic role of advertising is a controversial one. Industry spokespeople can often be found saying that advertising merely supplies consumers' demand for information about products. From this viewpoint, advertising has an entirely passive role and should be regarded as a complementary good to the one which is being advertised. A more realistic point of view is that advertising is used as an instrument for stimulating sales through persuasive messages. Empirical support for this view comes from the fact that it is the producers of the advertised products who pay for advertising and not the consumers. If we accept this approach then we must realize that as well as providing sales opportunities for the firm, advertising complicates its decision processes. This is because advertising is a cost to the firm.

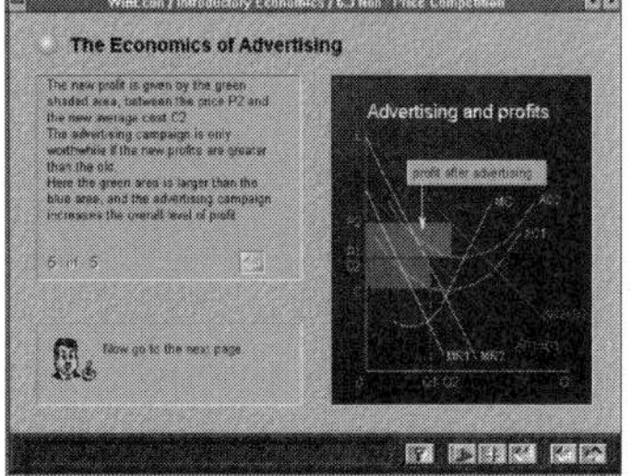

The firm must balance the extra cost of advertising against the benefits from advertising. Work through the WinEcon screen on The Economics of Advertising to find out how this balancing exercise is performed. The outcome of the exposition is that the firm will advertise up to the point where the marginal cost of advertising is equal to the marginal revenue from advertising. If the last unit of sales cost £2 to advertise but the value of this extra sale was £4, then it is clearly worth while to spend more on advertising.

When you have worked through all the screens in the topic, try these questions

53 **What two types of advertising can be distinguished?**

54 **What should determine whether the profit maximizing firm undertakes advertising?**

55 **Paul's Pizza Place is considering an advertising campaign to raise sales. Paul's estimates of sales and costs at various prices, either without advertising or spending £13.50 on advertising, are shown in the table below. Show whether the advertising campaign is worth while, assuming that total production costs can be calculated by summing successive values of marginal cost.**

Advertising = 0				Advertising = £13.50	
Sales	Marginal cost	Marginal revenue	Price	Marginal revenue	Price
0	1	6	6	10	10
1	1.5	4	5	8	9
2	2	2	4	6	8
3	4	0	3	4	7
4	6	0	2	2	6
5	10	0	1	0	5

56 **List nine circumstances in which advertising is likely to be more effective.**

Game Theory

Game theory, 'after thrilling a whole generation of post-1970 economists is spreading like a bushfire through the social sciences' (S.P. Hargreaves Heap and Y. Varoufakis (1994) *Game Theory: A Critical Introduction,* Routledge). It is not surprising therefore that it has something to say about oligopolistic behaviour. Despite its name, game theory is not trivial. It is a way of organizing one's thoughts about how rational people will behave in situations where interactions matter. In relation to the firm it provides guidelines for the choice of strategies when the number of firms is small.

Game theory uses the concept of 'pay-off' to describe the results of a choice of strategies for each of the players. Pay-off is simply another word for the utility derived from the outcome of the game. For example, if the outcome we are concerned with is profits, the pay-off is the utility of the various profit levels which result from the choice of particular strategies. If we feel that 100 units of profit provides 100 utility units whereas 200 units of profit only provides 150 utils, we use the numbers 100 and 150 as pay-offs rather than the crude profit values.

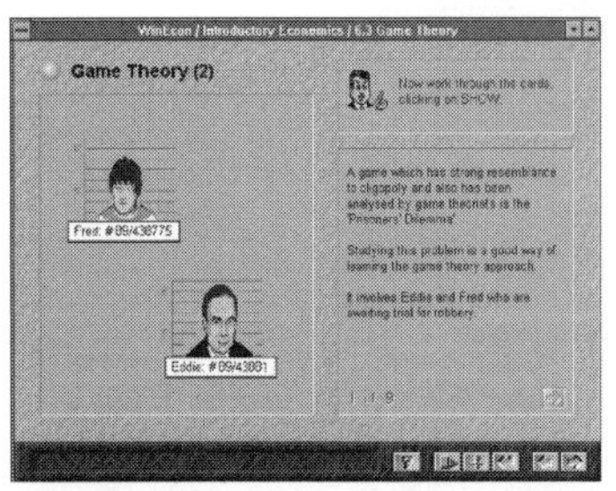

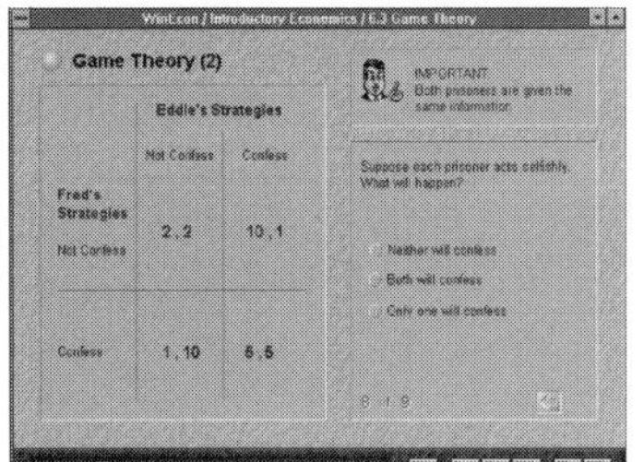

Now access the WinEcon supplementary screen Game Theory (2) using the Next Page button and begin studying the `prisoners' dilemma' game. In spite of its non-economic appearance, the prisoners' dilemma has much valuable insight to provide for firms in imperfect competition. The original prisoners' dilemma was conceived by Albert Tucker who made up the story for a talk on game theory at Stanford University in 1950. It shows that two prisoners acting rationally will fail to achieve the best of all possible outcomes for themselves – early release from jail. Instead they will end up with a very bad outcome – long imprisonment. Strange as it may seem at first, the analysis does have a bearing on the behaviour of firms.

As you work through the WinEcon screen check that you understand the pay-off figures that are placed in each cell of the table. The pay-offs in this game are years of imprisonment. In this case the two players, Fred and Eddie, would each like to minimize their pay-offs. The pay-offs appear in each cell of the table in pairs. The first of each pair is the pay-off to the person whose strategies are shown in the rows of the table (Fred in this case). The colour coding on the WinEcon screen will help you.

The dilemma arises because of the sentencing policy which is assumed. If either of the prisoners confesses but the other does not, the one who confesses is treated very leniently while the other is treated very severely. If both prisoners confess, their guilt is clearly established and both receive fairly severe punishment. If neither prisoner confesses the full extent of their guilt is not apparent, and fairly light sentences are meted out.

In looking for a solution to a game theory problem we assume the players are rational, and so in the case of Eddie and Fred we assume each wishes to minimize the length of his sentence. Each player must make some decision about which strategy to use. We consider the options for each, seeing what pay-off each strategy will yield when we take into consideration the other player's possible strategies. In the WinEcon example, each player has a dominant strategy. This is a strategy that always yields a better pay-off than any other strategy, regardless of what the other player does. The pop up on card 8 explains why to confess is the clearly preferred or dominant strategy for each player.

Each player, making a decision on rational grounds, chooses to confess. But the joint decision that is reached is not the best that could be achieved. Look for a combination of strategies that would give both prisoners a lighter sentence, and you can see that if both agree not to confess, both can benefit. But notice that then both have an incentive to cheat. Whenever one prisoner is certain that the other will not confess, he can lighten his own sentence by breaking the agreement and actually confessing.

A Duopoly Game Based on the Prisoners' Dilemma

To see how game theory applies to oligopoly, move with the Next Page button to the sub-topic A Duopoly Game Based on the Prisoners' Dilemma on the supplementary screen. As you work through the screen you find that the dominant strategy both for firm A and firm B is to lower price to £18.

The best possible market result, however, is achieved when both firms choose the contrary strategy and each keeps its price at £20. The highest overall profits are attained if the firms agree to the higher price and so behave together as a monopolist. However, any firm that cheats on the profit maximizing price and lowers its price unilaterally can improve its profits at the expense of the other firms. Work through the WinEcon screen and try the quiz to consolidate what you have learnt.

The implication of the game theory analysis is that firms do not co-operate because cheating always pays for the individual firm. This would always be true if firms met only once. However, firms are likely to make many transactions in any one market, often over long periods of time. This means that each firm should take into account the stream of profits which will arise from any strategy selection. When firms have a sufficiently high valuation of future profits it may be better to adopt behaviour which invites co-operation. One way of encouraging co-operation is to punish deviation from co-operative behaviour. A firm which deviates from the industry price then knows that it will face a substantial profit loss over time and will think twice about reneging on a deal.

Check your understanding of game theory

57 **What is a dominant strategy?**

Find the prisoners' dilemma solution for the oligopolist firms A and B. The pay-offs represent the utility derived from the profits generated by each pair of decision strategies. Mark the dominant strategies, and the rational outcome to the game if firms act individually.

Pay-offs to Firm A, Firm B

		Firm B	
		Low price	High price
Firm A	Low price	8, 8	200, 1
	High price	1, 200	150, 150

58 **Suppose firm A says that it will choose high price. Will firm B also choose high price?**

Section 6.4: Comparing Monopolistic Competition and Oligopoly

This section presents the case in favour of imperfectly competitive markets, showing that they have some advantages as compared with perfect competition. WinEcon also provides a screen which lets you check that you understand the important differences between different types of imperfect competition.

The Case for Imperfect Competition

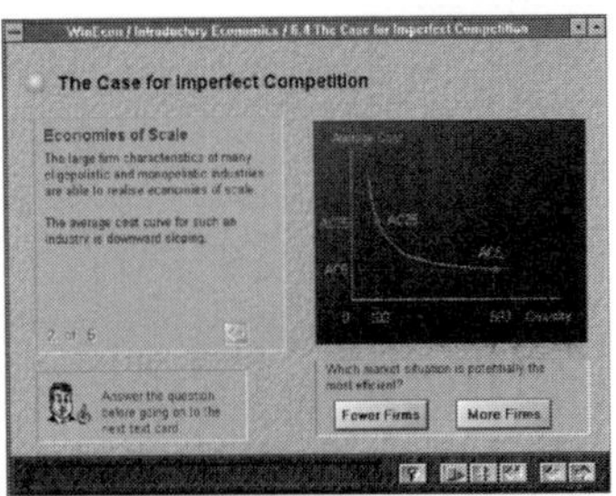

An oligopolistic industry, because of the small number of producers, may be able to achieve economies of scale. In an industry with a downward-sloping average cost curve, the point at which the industry operates may be associated with substantially reduced average costs if there are only a few firms. Card 2 of the WinEcon screen lets you discover this. Work through the screen to find various advantages of imperfectly competitive markets.

Test your understanding by trying these questions

59 As regards long-run costs, what possible disadvantage is there of having few firms in an industry?

60 Why are supernormal profits not necessarily undesirable?

61 Monopoly elements lead to inefficiencies measured by a deadweight loss. What may outweigh them?

62 What additional advantages accrue to investment and to research and development in markets which have some monopolistic characteristics?

63 What is advantageous about the products of monopolistically competitive firms?

Differences Within Imperfect Competition

This screen offers you various statements which are descriptive either of monopolistic competition or oligopoly. Click the appropriate button to indicate the market structure to which you think each should be assigned. When you complete the screen you have a set of comparisons of key analytical elements for the two types of market structure.

Summarize the differences listed on the WinEcon screen in the table below.

	Monopolistic competition	Oligopoly
Demand		
Elasticity		
Marginal revenue		
Price		
Supply curve		

Section 6.5: Summary

Monopolistic competition and oligopoly are two forms of imperfectly competitive market structures. The first of these is characterized by its firms producing products which are differentiated from one another, while the key feature of the second is the small number of firms in the industry. This chapter models these market structures, assuming firms wish to maximize profits.

A firm in monopolistic competition faces a downward-sloping demand curve and is usually assumed to have U-shaped average and marginal cost curves. The firm does not, however, have to consider the impact of its actions on other firms. We can therefore analyse an individual firm, and find that it selects its output and price as if it were a monopolist. In the short run the monopolistically competitive firm earns supernormal profits, but in the long run these are competed away. New firms enter the industry, reducing the first firm's demand curve until it is tangential to its average cost curve. Typically firms in monopolistic competition do not achieve either technical or allocative efficiency, either in the short or long run.

Theories of oligopoly explain how firms behave in a market when numbers of firms are small. The key concept is that of interdependence: the behaviour of each firm has a perceptible impact on the other competitors. No one firm can take decisions which ignore the likely effect on others since retaliation is always a possibility.

This interdependence is handled in two main ways: collusive arrangements between firms such as cartels, and non-collusive strategies such as Cournot competition, price leadership or the price stickiness suggested by the kinked demand model. Collusion may allow the industry as a whole to obtain maximum profits, and yet individual firms have an incentive to break the agreement. A firm which cheats can expect to increase its own profits at the expense of other firms in the industry. Cartels are therefore liable to break down and price wars may arise. The contribution of game theory to some of the more paradoxical features of oligopoly is discussed.

In oligopolistic markets, non-price competition is frequently advantageous because it avoids the need to change prices. The main types of non-price competition (namely, advertising, new product development, new model styles, and after sales service) are outlined and considered.

Imperfect competition can have advantages. It may enable lower costs to be achieved because economies of scale are reaped. Firms may undertake more investment and research and development because they gain greater benefits in imperfectly competitive markets. The differentiated products which are offered by firms in monopolistic competition, and sometimes by those in oligopoly, may be valued by consumers because they offer variety and choice.

Chapter 7:

Regulation of Markets and Market Failure

Why should the government regulate prices charged by the firms in certain industries (e.g. energy and telecommunications) when prices are usually determined by the market? Car exhaust systems must now meet strict emission requirements, but why are such regulations needed? Can they be justified by economic analysis? This chapter sets out to answer questions like these by explaining that market forces by themselves do not always achieve the social optimum. Government intervention may then be needed to improve the allocation of resources.

Contents

KEYWORDS

- Allocative efficiency
- Government policy
- Monopoly power
- Deadweight loss
- Marginal social benefit
- Regulation
- External costs and benefits
- Marginal social cost
- Social optimum

Section 7.1: Introduction

The main theme of this chapter is that government regulation may sometimes produce a better outcome for society than market forces alone. Regulatory bodies such as those set up in the gas and telephone industries (in the UK these are OFGAS and OFTEL) may be needed to ensure that firms which have some degree of monopoly power do not exploit consumers.

Since Adam Smith first suggested that a competitive market could produce the best possible outcome for society as a whole, the argument against government intervention has been developed and refined. Such analysis gives us a benchmark for comparisons. You will study it in this chapter in the section entitled Requirements for Allocative Efficiency. In some circumstances, however, the 'invisible hand' of the market does not allocate scarce economic resources so efficiently. We call this problem market failure. You can discover more about it in the section with that title. Subsequent sections are concerned with two of the important causes of market failure, monopoly power and externalities.

The analysis shown in this chapter has important implications for government policy. Later sections of this chapter discuss regulation, taxes and subsidies, and monopoly and merger policy. You will discover how these different forms of government intervention may be used to improve the allocation of resources, and the advantages of each in different circumstances.

Section 7.2: Requirements for Allocative Efficiency

The key concept in defining allocative efficiency is the idea that no resources are wasted. Given the factors of production available in the economy and the tastes and incomes of its consumers, the goods produced and their allocation are optimal from the point of view of society as a whole. In the topic entitled Allocative Efficiency you will discover that there must be efficiency both in the production process and in consumption.

In analysing whether a particular output is allocatively efficient, we first consider how consumers and the producer value different quantities of the good. You will discover this in the topic Marginal Private Cost and Benefit. From this analysis we derive a pricing policy which has been widely recommended for use in government owned or regulated industries.

In the topic Perfect Competition and Allocative Efficiency the analysis brings you to a key result. We show that in certain circumstances perfect competition delivers allocative efficiency. This makes perfect competition appear to be a desirable market structure, but as you may recall it only exists under certain rather restrictive assumptions. A topic which sets these out concludes this section.

Our main purpose in studying the various conditions for allocative efficiency is to be able to recognize when (from the point of view of society as a whole) they are not being met, because that is when market failure occurs.

Allocative Efficiency

To understand about market failure we first need to understand what is meant by allocative efficiency. The attainment of allocative efficiency is an economic goal, and when it is not achieved market failure occurs.

Economists are not primarily concerned with absolute efficiency, but with relative efficiency, and they judge one situation to be better than another if it makes use of less resources to achieve the same level of output, or it produces a higher level of output with the same resources. Similar comparisons are used to determine whether consumers as a whole are better off when goods are reallocated.

Most people have an intuitive understanding of technical efficiency – the selection out of the set of possible processes of those which produce the largest output from a given physical level of inputs. Economic efficiency includes technical efficiency and goes one stage further – it seeks to find processes which produce a given level of output at minimum cost. Clearly these must also be processes which maximize output for a given level of inputs, since if this were not the case it would be possible to substitute a more technically efficient process for a less efficient one and be better off. Allocative, or social efficiency, does not just require economic efficiency, as you will discover from the WinEcon screens.

More details about social costs and benefits will be found in section 7.5 on Externalities and Social Costs.

The concepts of social costs and benefits are introduced in this topic because they are used in a definition of allocative efficiency.

Begin by reading the first two paragraphs on the card to understand the concept of allocative efficiency. You can discover more details about the requirements for it by clicking the buttons on the screen. You may like to note down any unfamiliar definitions.

The top button introduces the Pareto criterion for making judgements about whether consumers are better off in one situation or in another. You discover how to recognize changes which do not bring about an improvement.

In specifying optimal conditions we recognize that there are fundamental distinctions between technical, economic, consumer and social efficiency. Clicking the remaining buttons will give you more information about these. Equalities that must be satisfied provide useful test rules. The last button discusses one that can be used to check whether allocative efficiency exists, namely marginal social cost (MSC) equals marginal social benefit (MSB).

The WinEcon cross-reference button takes you to chapter 18 where the topics The Pareto Principle and Pareto Optimality provide a more detailed analysis.

See what you have learnt

01 What is being allocated?

02 How do economists judge when an individual is better off?

03 What is technological efficiency?

04 What is technical efficiency?

05 How could you discover whether a particular allocation was Pareto optimal?

06 What can you say about social cost at the social optimum?

You can discover more about this in chapter 18.

07 Do you think the Pareto optimality condition means that incomes must not be changed?

08 List the three conditions for allocative efficiency

Marginal Private Cost and Benefit

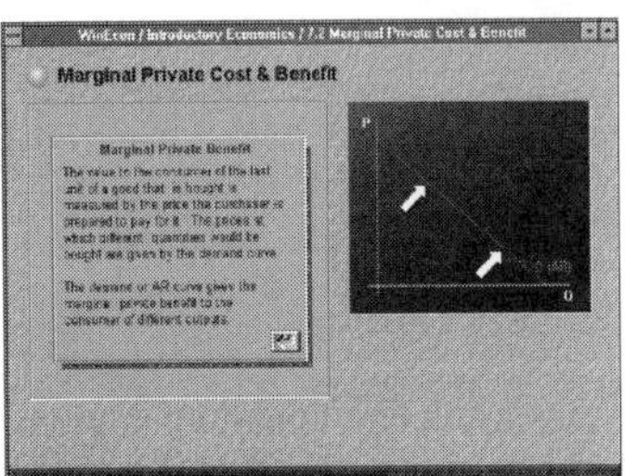

Marginal private cost and benefit play a key role in determining whether an efficient output is being produced. Before we can do this we need to understand how each of them is measured. In measuring private cost and benefit we are essentially concerned with discovering what the marginal unit of output is worth, both to the producer and to the consumer.

The screens in this topic, which evolve as buttons are clicked, focus on the value of the last unit of output bought and sold, both to the producer and to the consumer. We take the simplest case, namely where marginal cost is increasing over the relevant region of output and consumer demand is downward sloping with respect to price. This helps ensure an eventual stable point of equality between private costs and benefits. This is an example of the economist's method of abstraction in order to aid understanding.

About private efficiency

09 What is private about private efficiency?

10 Private efficiency occurs when ______ = ______ = ______.

Complete the diagram, adding the curves and labelling that appear as you click the buttons, before answering the following questions.

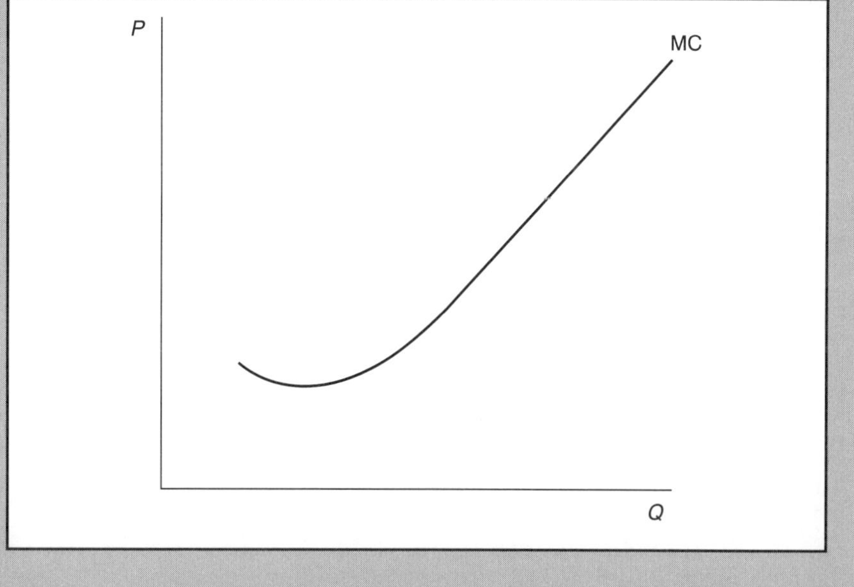

11 **Choose any point on the demand curve. What can you say about the value of the output which the point represents?**

12 **What pricing policy can be justified by this analysis of private efficiency?**

Perfect Competition and Allocative Efficiency

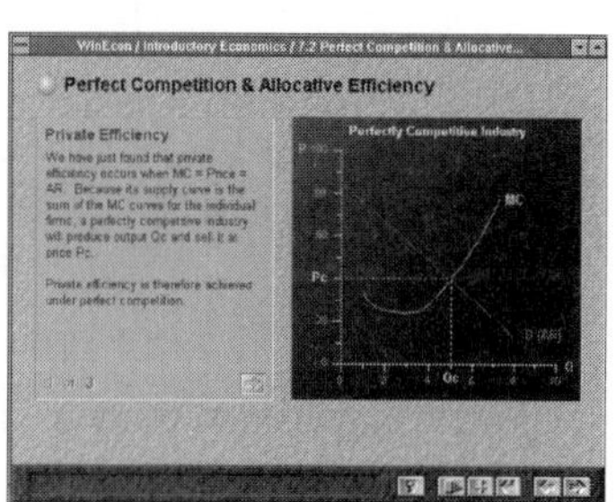

We can now derive an important result about the achievement of allocative efficiency in a perfectly competitive market. Our analysis here refers to the whole industry, so the cost curves for individual producers are summed horizontally to give the cost for the industry as a whole. Above the intersection with average variable cost the marginal cost curve so constructed represents the supply curve for the industry. Because the demand curve is for the whole industry, we can assume it is downward sloping. These curves are shown on the WinEcon screen diagram.

We look to see whether marginal social cost equals marginal social benefit at the market equilibrium. Social cost includes private cost but is not necessarily the same as it, and similarly with social benefit. The distinction between social and private costs and benefits involves externalities.

Details about externalities will be found in section 7.5 on Externalities and Social Costs.

The analysis shown is carried out in terms of product costs and prices and you should note that the conclusions require that perfect competition also holds in the markets for factors used to produce the product. If some factors

in the industry had monopoly power, marginal costs would include an element of monopoly profit. In this case overall welfare could be improved by removing this monopoly element and expanding the use of the factors.

Develop your understanding of perfect competition and allocative efficiency

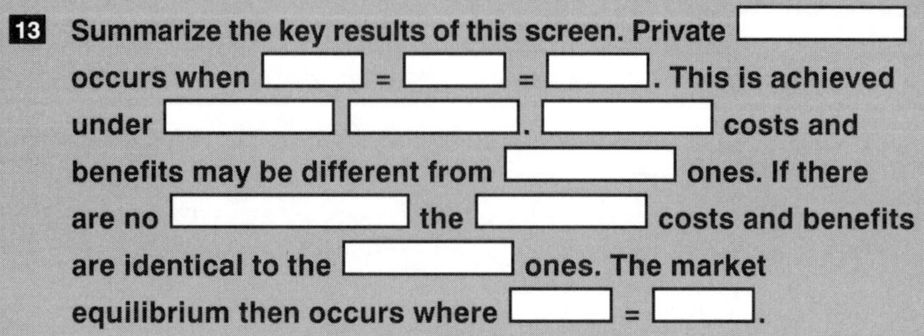

13 **Summarize the key results of this screen. Private ______ occurs when ______ = ______ = ______. This is achieved under ______ ______. ______ costs and benefits may be different from ______ ones. If there are no ______ the ______ costs and benefits are identical to the ______ ones. The market equilibrium then occurs where ______ = ______.**

The diagram shown appears when you move to card 2. Indicate on it the result which is revealed when the BUT button is clicked.

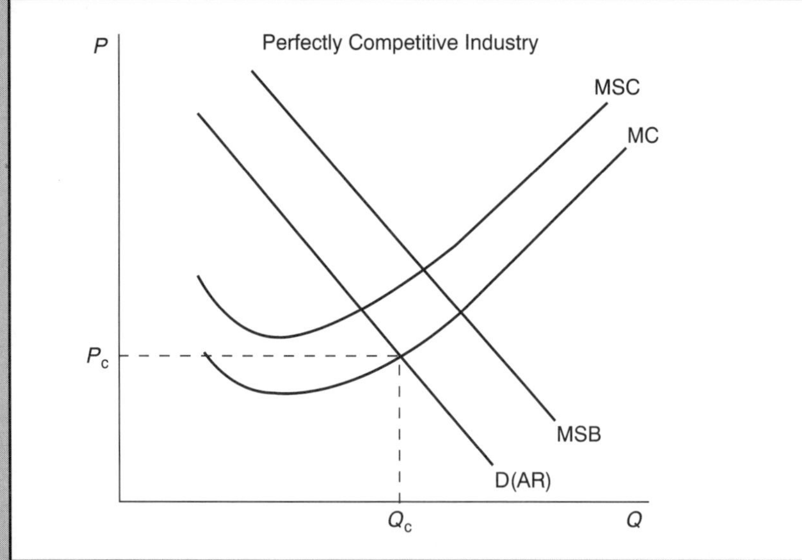

14 **Under what conditions does the result you have marked on the diagram occur? Why is it important?**

15 **Who incurs the private costs?**

16 **If there are no externalities, what can be said about the output produced in perfect competition?**

17 **When are social costs and benefits identical with private ones?**

18 **Perfect competition delivers allocative efficiency if there are [ ] [ ].**

The Six Competitive Market Assumptions

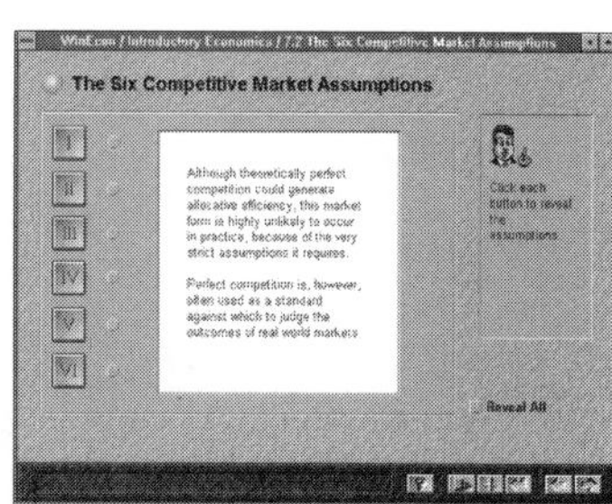

We now have an important result – perfect competition leads to allocative efficiency in certain circumstances – but its usefulness in practice depends on the occurrence of perfect competition. You may find it useful to check the assumptions necessary for perfect competition to see how likely it is that our result can be applied generally.

This screen lets you reveal and record the six assumptions required for a competitive market to exist. Economists also frequently assume a seventh requirement, namely that consumers and producers behave rationally. This means that when presented with a choice of possible actions they will pick the one which yields a surplus of marginal benefit over marginal cost. They will continue to choose in this way until there is no longer any surplus (i.e. until MB = MC).

In this context . . .

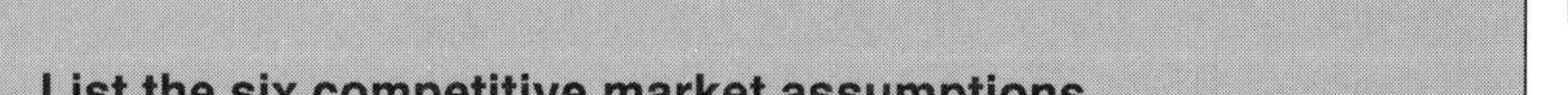

19 **List the six competitive market assumptions.**

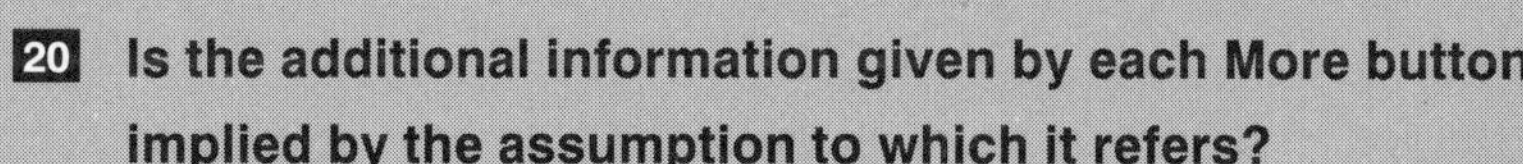

20 **Is the additional information given by each More button implied by the assumption to which it refers?**

Section 7.3: Market Failure

Market failure is the term used by economists to describe the situation which arises if the market does not achieve the social optimum. If we can identify the circumstances which give rise to scarce resources being wasted we can then see what action might be taken to improve allocative efficiency.

Market failure is discussed further in chapter 18.

This section sets out the reasons why allocative efficiency may not occur in practice. It defines market failure, then lets you discover which of its potential causes are actually the most important. Having identified two of them as monopoly power and externalities, we go on to investigate how they operate. If the market fails to reach a social optimum, government intervention may be required.

Reasons for Market Failure

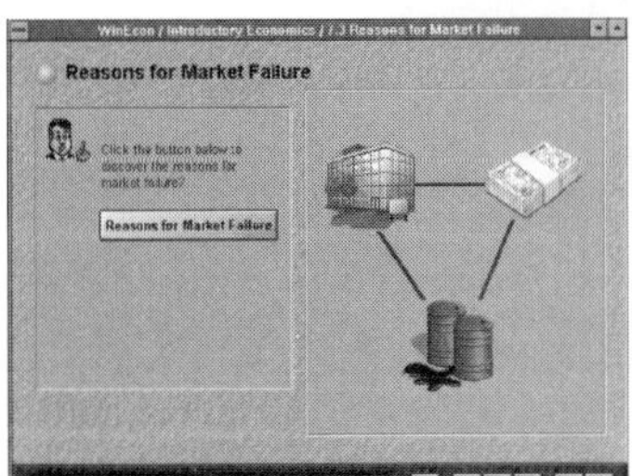

We can explain how market failure may arise by identifying requirements for a social optimum which are not being met. To say that this is wasteful is a statement of positive economics. A reallocation of resources could actually make someone better off without making anyone worse off.

This screen lets you discover the reasons for market failure. You will see that the various causes are classified as being of either more concern or less concern.

Test your understanding of market failure

21 **What have firms' objectives to do with whether market failure occurs?**

22 **What assumption about consumer behaviour affects whether market failure arises?**

23 **What is the problem of second best?**

24 **Which reasons for market failure are cause for more concern?**

Monopoly Power and Allocative Inefficiency

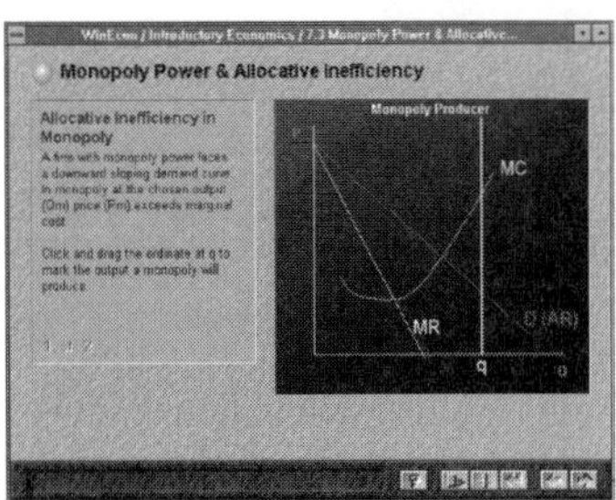

This topic and the next on externalities are making two separate points about allocative efficiency. In this section, monopoly by itself is shown to be allocatively inefficient. This is indicated in the first diagram where resources are not efficiently allocated between goods. The monopoly could, by sacrificing profit, bring about an expansion of consumer welfare greater than the reduction in profits. This is not likely to happen without structural change – either by way of breaking up the monopoly or by imposing price regulation.

This screen tests your understanding of a monopolist's production decision by asking you to mark the firm's chosen output by dragging a line to the appropriate position. The questions you are asked as you proceed through the screen will help your understanding of allocative efficiency.

Check these comparisons

25 **Do monopolies produce more, less or the same as the social optimum?** ☐

26 **Do perfectly competitive firms produce more, less or the same as the social optimum?** ☐

Mark on the diagram the socially efficient output.

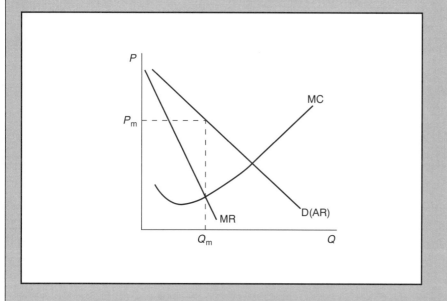

27 **Which outputs are allocatively inefficient and why are they so?**

Externalities and Allocative Inefficiency

This topic introduces the possibility of external costs. Whilst these are clear sources of inefficiency in competitive markets, they may well reduce the allocative impact of monopoly.

See what you have learnt

Complete the following diagram showing monopoly output, competitive output and socially optimal output.

Section 7.4 / Price, Output and Profit in Competition and Monopoly

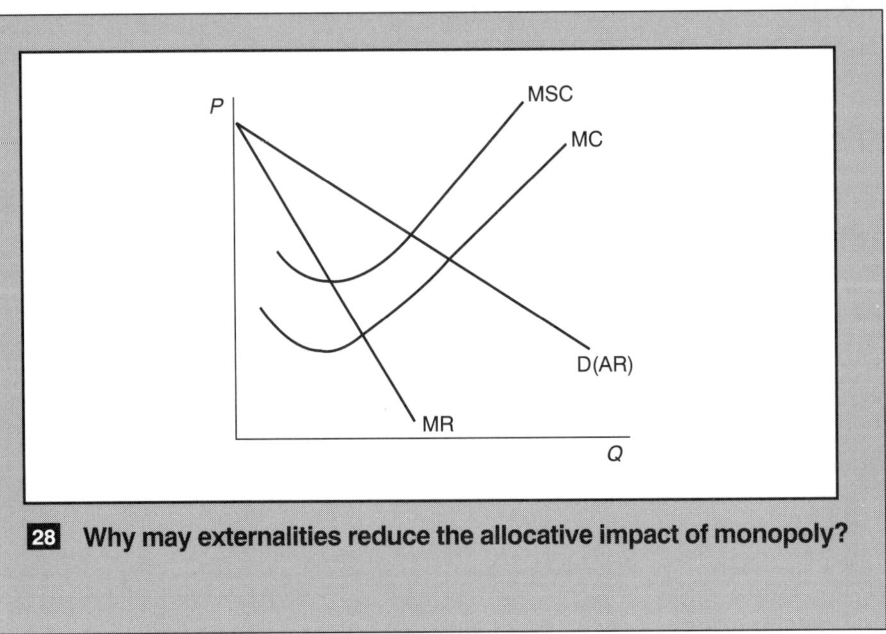

Section 7.4: Monopoly Power

You should already be familiar with key differences between perfect competition and monopoly. In this section your knowledge will be tested and extended, focusing on the implications of monopoly for market failure. If the output which a monopolist chooses to produce is not the socially optimal output for the industry, there may be scope for government intervention to reduce allocative inefficiency.

Price, Output and Profit in Competition and Monopoly

This is revision of material covered in more detail in chapter 5.

In this topic you will be asked to choose the curves to go on the diagram to determine equilibrium competitive output.

You should have no difficulty in understanding the level of output chosen in

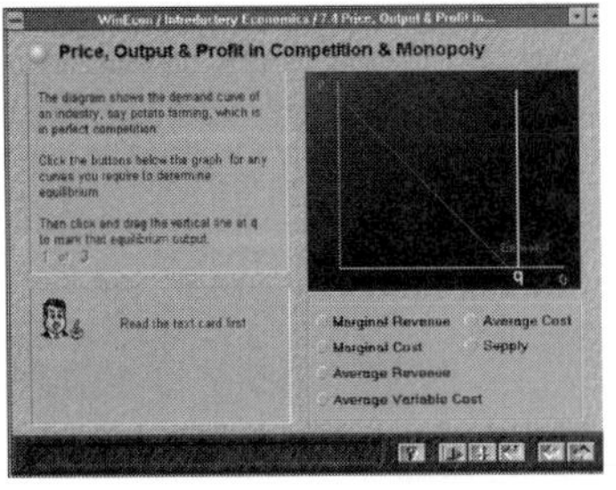

perfect competition. However, you will also need to be familiar with the average variable cost criterion. Clearly a firm needs to cover all its variable costs to remain in business in the short run. Hence price (average revenue, AR) must at least equal average variable cost (AVC). The firm's marginal cost (MC) curve cuts its average variable cost curve from below at the minimum point of the AVC curve. This should enable you to understand the appropriate position of the curve in the diagram.

First click buttons to choose any curves required. To mark the competitive equilibrium output you then click and drag a vertical line into the appropriate position. Proceed through the screen following the instructions. You will finally mark the monopoly output in a similar way.

Test your knowledge

29 **Equilibrium competitive output occurs at the intersection of the ______ curve and the ______ curve.**

30 **The competitive firm will produce, providing ______ is greater than or ______ ______ ______.**

31 **Equilibrium monopoly output occurs where ______ = ______.**

32 **What can we say about output and price under monopoly in comparison with perfect competition?**

33 **What are the assumptions used in reaching this conclusion?**

34 **What is the formula for the area of the profits rectangle?**

Efficiency in Competition and Monopoly

This topic introduces the concept of deadweight loss as a measure of the impact on efficiency of the monopolization of an industry. This is an indicator of how much society loses when an industry is run as a monopoly instead of by perfectly competitive firms. The analysis is often used to justify government intervention in markets. Notice that its validity rests on the assumption that a monopolist and a perfectly competitive market experience the same production costs.

From the initial WinEcon screen you see that under monopoly industry output is less than under competition (i.e. $Q_m < Q_c$) whilst prices are higher (i.e. $P_m > P_c$). Click the card 2 Show button to discover that units of output between Q_m and Q_c would all be worth more to society than they cost to produce, since MSB > MSC. Under monopoly, however, these units are not produced and so society loses the net benefit it would have received from them. This loss to society is called the deadweight loss of monopoly. It is measured, you discover, by the area between the MSB and MSC curves over the range of the lost output.

A more detailed explanation in terms of consumer and producer surplus is available in chapter 18.

Test your understanding of monopoly and efficiency

35 **How do we recognize the occurence of allocative efficiency on this screen?**

36 **For it to occur,which possible causes of market failure does the screen say do not occur?**

37 **Which other causes are implied to be absent?**

Label the curves on this diagram. Mark monopoly output, competitive output and the deadweight loss of monopoly.

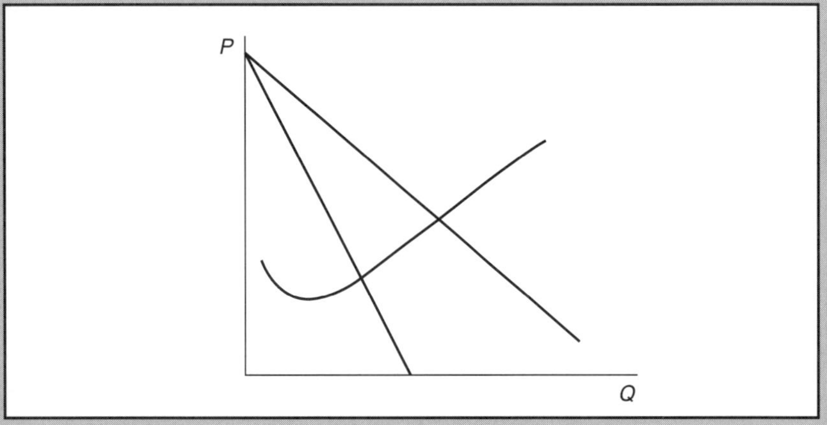

38 **What policy is supported by the concept of the deadweight loss of monopoly?**

Section 7.5: Externalities and Social Cost

The main issue discussed in this section is why the market fails to take account of certain costs and benefits that affect us all. Global warming and the capabilities of a skilled labour force are respectively detrimental and beneficial to everyone, and yet are largely ignored in the decision-making process about what should be produced. The topics in this section focus on where externalities arise, firstly on the production side and then on the consumption side. These are followed by a screen to test your understanding of the different concepts that have been presented, and then one that builds to give you a schematic summary comparing types of externalities and social costs and benefits.

The analysis you will work through adjusts the marginal cost curve when production side externalities arise, and the demand curve when there are externalities in consumption.

Another approach to choosing between alternative situations when externalities exist is cost–benefit analysis. This involves totalling all internal and external costs, and comparing them with the total of internal and external benefits. A measure of net social benefit is thus obtained which can be used for decision making. Cost–benefit analysis does not treat externalities arising as part of the production process separately from those associated with consumption.

Production Externalities

The analysis of production externalities is carried out by adjusting the marginal cost (MC) curve so that it represents marginal social cost (MSC). External production costs such as the build up of greenhouse gas raise the MC curve. Benefits to society as a whole occurring as a result of the production process are regarded as negative external costs. They are shown in the analysis by a lowering of the MC curve. In this case the relationship between MSC and MC is reversed (i.e. MSC < MC).

Another example of a situation where actions by one producer can reduce the cost of another good is that of the introduction of a bee hive into a fruit farm. The bee hive, which is used for the production of honey, reduces the costs of fruit pollination.

Notice that a production process can generate external costs or benefits affecting either consumers or other producers.

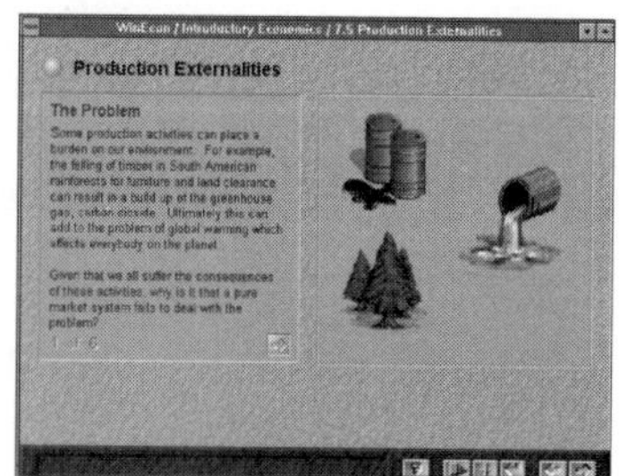

This screen presents the analysis of a market with production externalities, and tests your understanding of it. You are asked to choose a curve for the diagram, and to click and drag words to complete a statement about the social optimum.

More about the WinEcon examples

Complete the following diagram for the timber market.

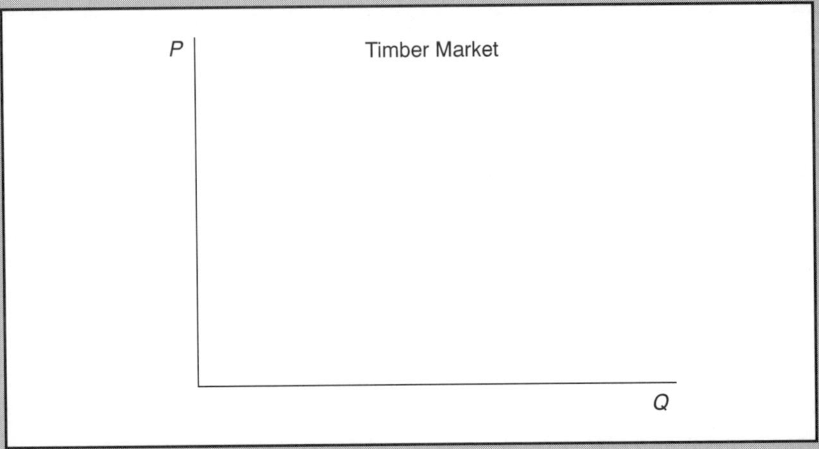

P

Timber Market

Q

39 **What does it show about the level of production?**

40 **Does the textile example suggest that training workers causes misallocation of resources? Explain your answer.**

Consumption Externalities

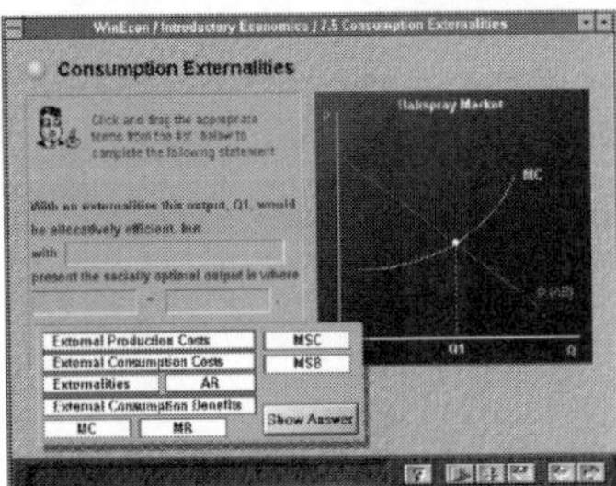

This screen discusses the effects of externalities arising during the consumption process. It is convenient to present the cases of positive and negative social benefits separately in order to illustrate the appropriate adjustment to the MSB line for each type of benefit. However, benefits can also change from positive to negative as quantities change. For example, fossil fuel consumption in relatively small amounts positively benefits gardeners by reducing the incidence of certain fungal plant diseases and by creating a supply of useful materials like sulphur and soot. In larger amounts the effects are outweighed by negative environmental impacts.

Follow the text cards to learn about consumption externalities, and test your understanding.

From what you have learnt ...

Complete the diagram showing why there may be over-consumption of hairsprays containing CFCs.

P

Hairspray Market

Q

41 **Does the train travel example on cards 5 and 6 suggest that to prevent misallocation of resources more travel should be by train?** ☐

Finding Marginal Social Cost and Benefit

Here is an exercise to help you revise your knowledge of marginal social cost and benefit. You select your choice of words to form a sentence and then click the button to have it marked. If you are correct your answer will be confirmed with a diagram.

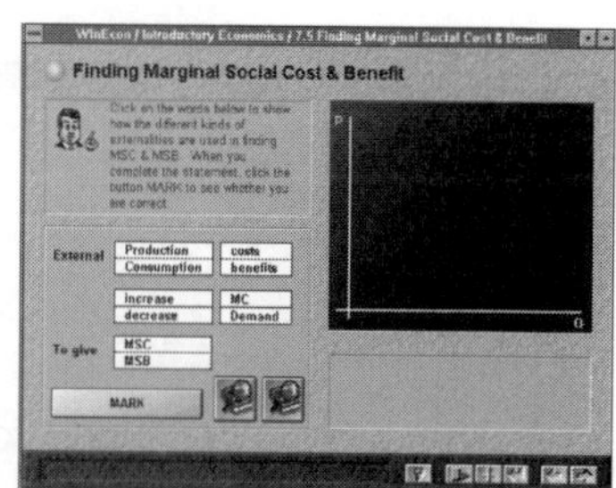

Check your understanding

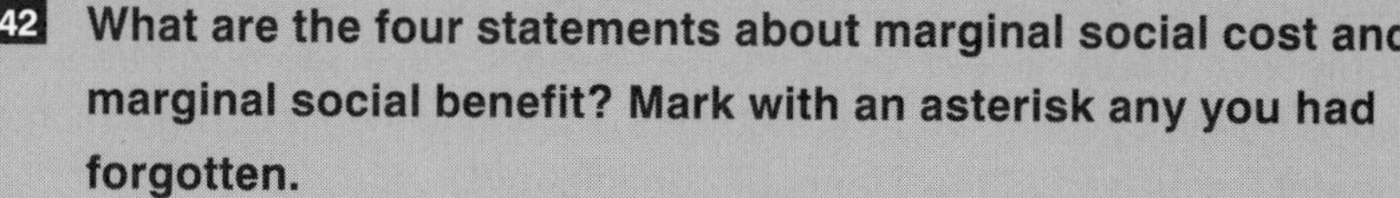

42 **What are the four statements about marginal social cost and marginal social benefit? Mark with an asterisk any you had forgotten.**

What are Social Costs and Externalities?

Use the buttons on the WinEcon screen to obtain the chart below, together with notes about the concepts you are investigating.

Consolidate your knowledge

Complete the chart showing the relationship between social costs and benefits and externalities.

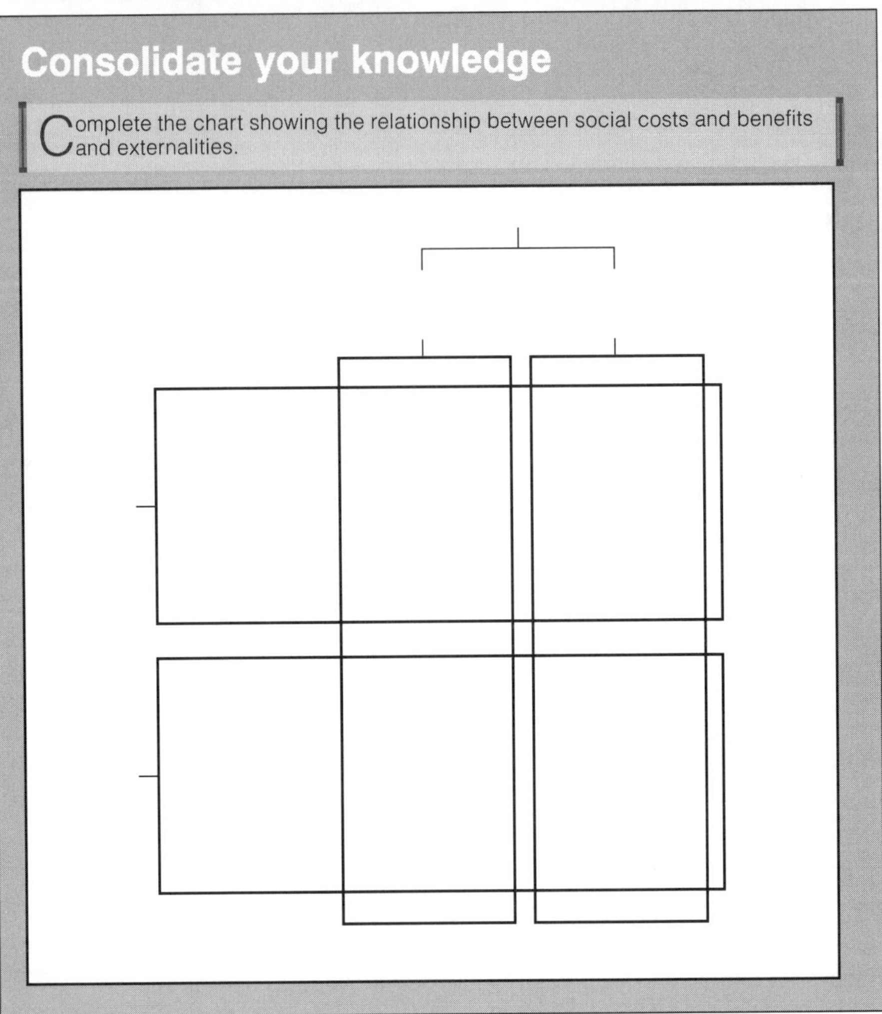

Section 7.6: Government Regulation

If market forces do not produce a social optimum, government intervention may be desirable. This section and those that follow will let you discover various ways in which the government can influence the output decisions of the economy through regulation, taxes and subsidies, and monopoly and merger policy.

Regulation can take many forms. It comprises rules set by a government authority, with the backing of legislation so that enterprises to which they apply are constrained by them. You will study the economic theory of regulation and see that it forms part of the theory of public choice.

You can use sliders to investigate which forces are more powerful in determining the demand for regulation. Similarly on the following screen you can discover which factors have most influence on the quantity of regulation the government will supply. Theories about the equilibrium quantity of regulation are then explained. After this you can look at the scope of regulation in the UK, seeing what regulations exist and why they are needed.

Demand for Regulation

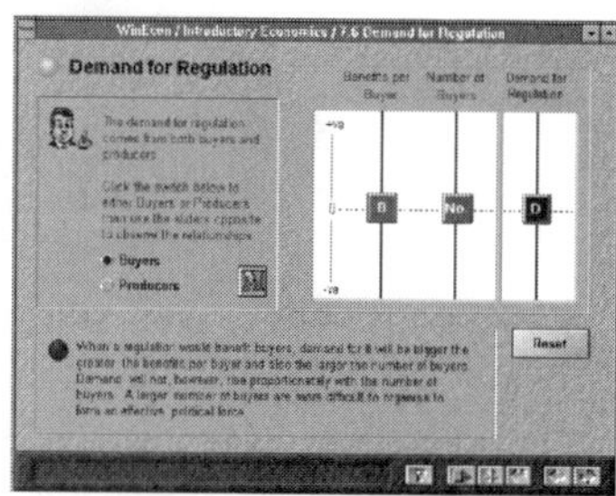

People who see regulation as beneficial will lobby the government to take action, so a demand for regulation arises. For example, environmentalists claim that bitumen-based fuel for power stations is dirty, causing asthma in children and crop damage. They are campaigning to have it banned. This would be a kind of regulation.

Use the switch and sliders to discover the particular nature of the demand for regulation.

Try this question

43 How is the demand for regulation expressed?

Supply of Regulation

As the former nationalized industries have been privatized, their potential monopoly power has been limited by the establishment of regulatory bodies such as OFGAS for British Gas and OFTEL for British Telecom in the UK. The motivation for privatization is to increase efficiency, but where many consumers are tied to a single supplier because of the nature of the product and the means by which it is supplied, governments have recognized the need for regulation to protect consumers against exploitation. As well as having power to limit prices, the regulators ensure that minimum levels of safety standards (for gas) and public service, such as public telephone boxes and emergency calls, are maintained.

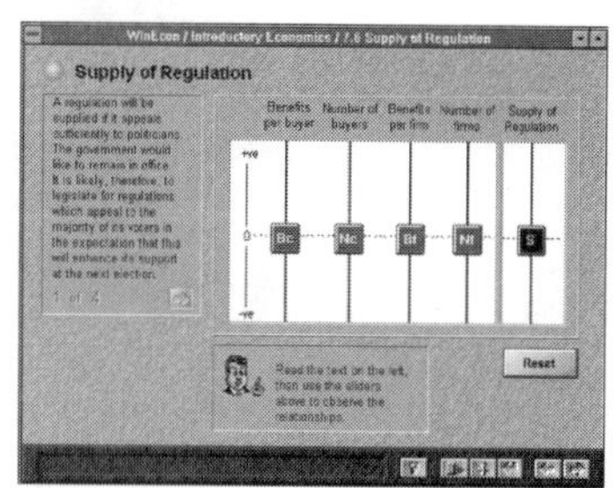

Proceed through the text cards and use the sliders to find what has most influence on the supply of regulation.

Check your understanding

44 Why are regulations that yield only inconspicuous net benefits not likely to be supplied?

Equilibrium Amount of Regulation

Political pressures determine the demand and supply of regulation, and when they are balanced equilibrium is achieved. Discover from the screen the conditions for equilibrium, and compare the descriptions you find of two alternative theories.

Test your knowledge of regulation

45 **When equilibrium exists, is everyone happy with the quantity of regulation?**

46 **Who or what is captured in the capture theory of regulation?**

47 **With regulation, will the socially optimal output be achieved?**

48 **What can be said about the quantity of regulation in equilibrium?**

Examples of Regulation

This WinEcon screen presents some examples of regulation grouped into different categories. Click on the picture denoting a group of interest to you to access information about regulations in that category.

Section 7.7: Taxes and Subsidies

Taxes and subsidies can alter the output decisions of firms, so they provide a possible approach to correcting for market failure. If an unregulated market is producing more than is socially desirable, taxing the product may be a way of reducing demand and moving output towards the optimal level. Conversely, if the government wants to encourage more output of a good to be produced, a subsidy may be an effective way of achieving this.

This section re-examines monopoly power and externalities and shows whether taxes or subsidies are needed to appropriately influence output. If both monopoly power and externalities exist, we say we are dealing with a second-best world, and we discover that different policies may be appropriate in different circumstances. As compared with alternative methods of government intervention, taxes and subsidies have both advantages and disadvantages. You can discover what they are at the end of this section.

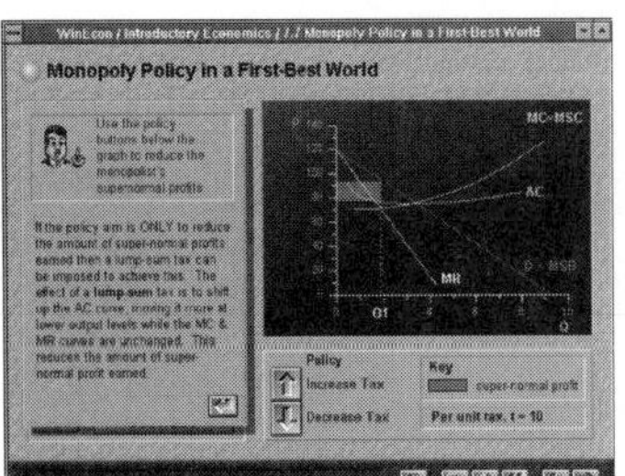

Monopoly Policy in a First-Best World

A monopolist chooses to produce less than the socially efficient level of output to maximize profits. But taxing these profits does not provide any motivation for increased output. This screen will let you discover the separate policies required to improve allocative efficiency and to reduce the monopolist's profits. Choose whether you want to investigate the use of taxes or subsidies, and read the accompanying dialogue.

See what policy is appropriate

49 **Do subsidies have a role in monopoly policy? If so, what is it?**

50 **What is the role of a lump sum tax in monopoly policy?**

Complete the diagram, showing how the monopolist could be influenced to produce the socially efficient output and how supernormal profits could be reduced. Record the policies that would be used to achieve this.

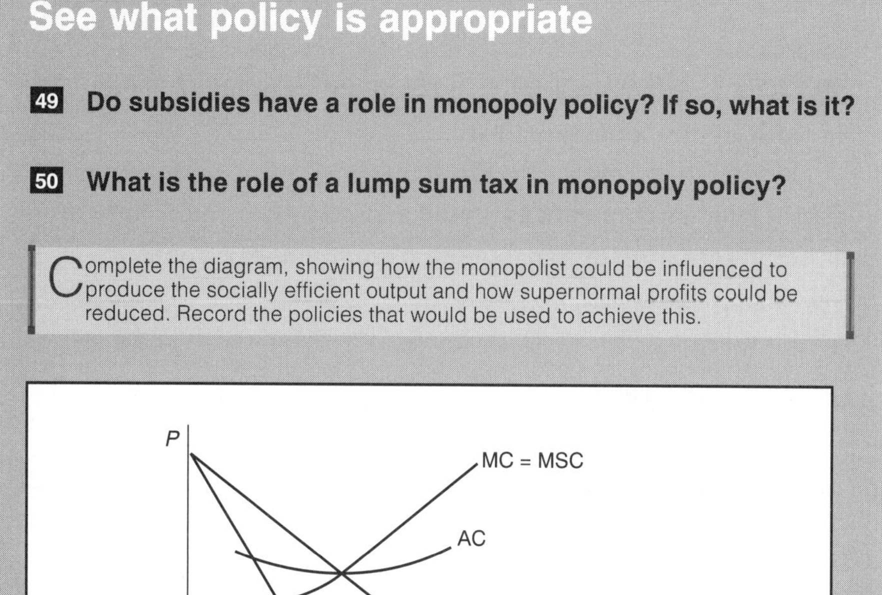

Externality Policy in a First-Best World

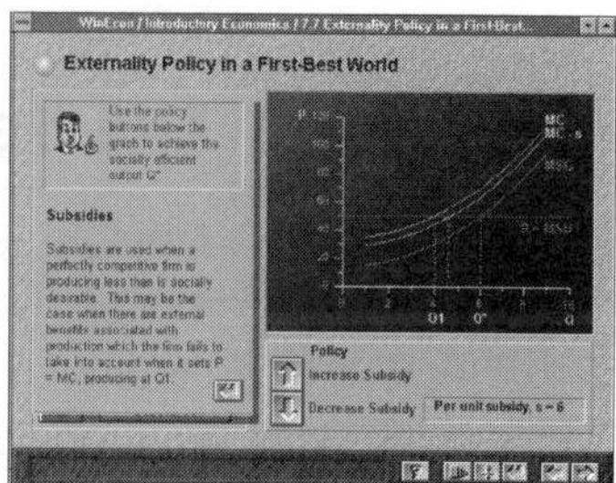

Here is another WinEcon screen that allows you to investigate the effects of different policies and discover the circumstances in which an improvement in resource allocation would be achieved. This screen relates to market failure caused by production externalities. Inefficiency arises because these are ignored by firms in making their production decisions. Depending on whether there are social costs or benefits, either a tax or a subsidy may be required. The firm's perception of its marginal cost is altered by the existence of a tax or subsidy so its output decision is changed.

Check how to correct for externalities

51 **Give an example of when a tax might be appropriate to correct for an externality.**

52 **In what circumstances would a subsidy be appropriate to correct for an externality? Can you think of a possible example of this?**

Complete the diagram for a firm that creates pollution. Show how the firm might be influenced to produce the socially optimal output , and note the policy used.

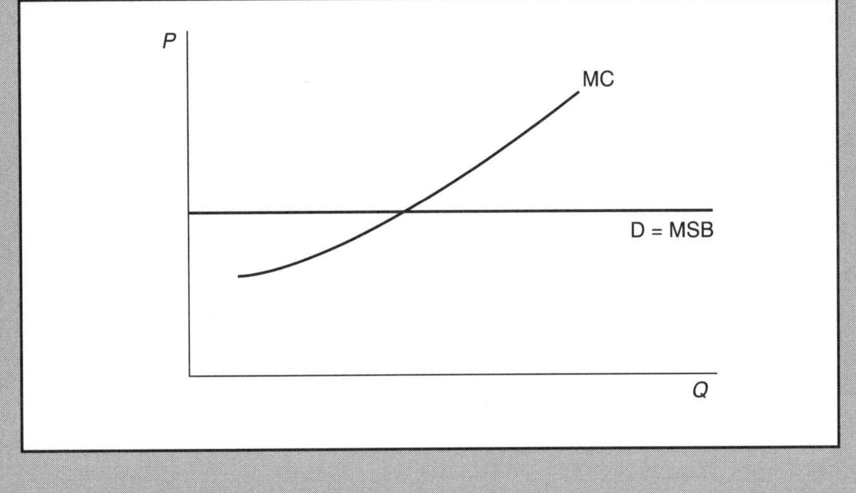

The Second-Best World

Although earlier topics in this section have shown policies that can correct monopoly power or externalities, the policies may in practice lead to results other than those described. This can occur if market failure is caused by more than one factor acting simultaneously. Suppose both monopoly power and externalities exist in a market. If the government attempts to correct just for one of them (perhaps because this is all that is possible in the complex conditions of the real world), a policy shown in a previous topic to improve the allocation of resources may in fact worsen the situation. This is known as the 'problem of second best'.

Use this WinEcon screen to discover the policies that would lead to an optimal allocation of resources in different types of second-best world situations.

The problem of second best

Complete this diagram to show a second-best situation in which a tax could lead to an optimal allocation of resources.

P

MR

D = MSB

Q

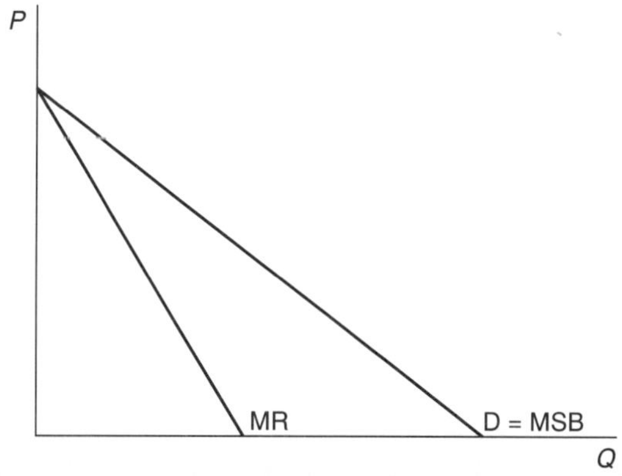

Consider a different second-best situation on this diagram. How could the government improve the allocation of resources in this market?

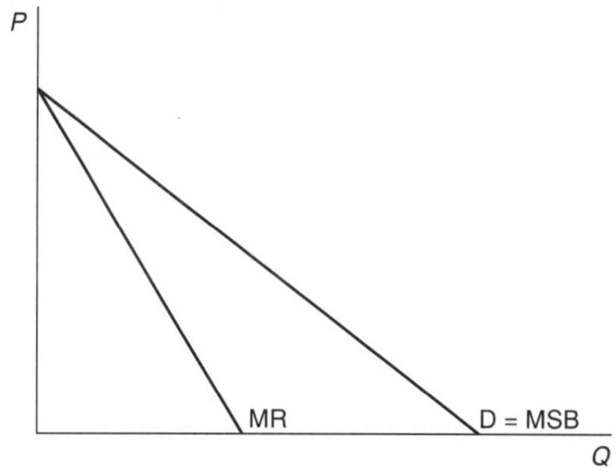

P

MR

D = MSB

Q

Advantages/Disadvantages of Taxes and Subsidies

Use this screen to discover the best ways of using fiscal policy, and also some possible difficulties.

Section 7.8: Monopoly and Merger Policy

This section describes the legal framework that exists in the UK for protecting the public interest in situations where monopoly power may exist.

UK Regulation of Private Monopolies and Oligopolies

Government policy towards monopolies and oligopolies is described on this screen. Notice the way in which it operates, and the two grounds on which a firm can be referred to the Monopolies and Mergers Commission (MMC).

Test your knowledge

53 **What process takes place when a firm is referred to the Monopolies and Mergers Commission?**

54 **What are the two possible grounds for referring a prospective merger to the Monopolies and Mergers Commission or the Restrictive Practices Court?**

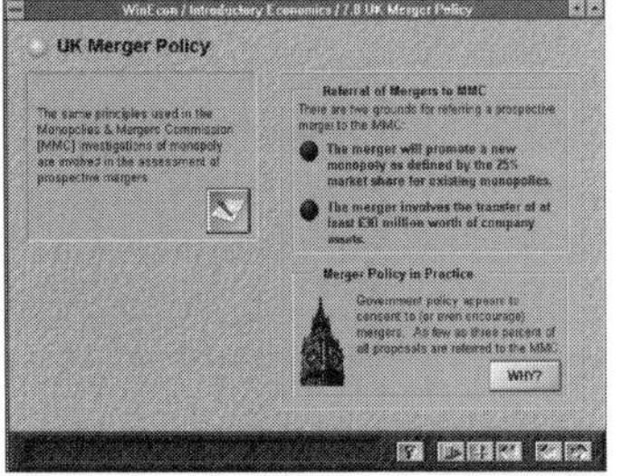

UK Merger Policy

This screen sets out the grounds on which a proposed merger may be referred to the Monopolies and Mergers Commission, and gives reasons why such a referral rarely takes place.

See if you know . . .

55 **What are the two limits beyond which a prospective merger can be referred to the Monopolies and Mergers Commission?**

56 **What are the three reasons why few mergers are actually referred to the MMC?**

Regulation due to Membership of the European Union

This screen outlines the European Union legislation relating to monopolies, mergers and restrictive agreements.

Test what you have learnt

57 **What are the grounds for prohibiting a merger on account of its world-wide and EU-wide turnover?**

Section 7.9: Summary

This chapter explains what is meant by market failure. The concept is contrasted with a socially optimal situation. For comparison purposes we study various aspects of economic and consumption efficiency that occur when a Pareto optimum is reached. We define social costs and benefits and show that MSC = MSB is a condition for a socially efficient level of output.

Since in a perfectly competitive market marginal private benefit, shown by the demand curve, is set equal to marginal private cost, perfect competition delivers allocative efficiency if there are no externalities.

Market failure occurs when resources are not all optimally allocated. It involves some waste of resources and can be due to various causes. One important reason for its occurrence is monopoly power. A monopolist produces less than the socially efficient level of output, and also earns supernormal profits. The deadweight loss of monopoly provides a measure of the cost to society of monopolization of the industry.

Externalities are another important cause of market failure. External production costs are shown to raise the marginal social cost curve above the private one. From the viewpoint of society as a whole it is the social cost and benefit curves that are relevant to determining efficient output.

Government policies to improve the allocation of resources in situations of market failure are demonstrated. The amount of regulation is seen as a political decision with the equilibrium amount of regulation being achieved when the pressure from groups wanting more regulation is balanced by those opposed to this.

The role of taxes and subsidies in improving allocative efficiency is demonstrated with examples. When an industry is operated by a monopolist you see that a subsidy may be appropriate to induce an increase of output, while taxation can be used to reduce profits.

Section 7.9 / Summary

We analyse production side externalities by their effects on the marginal cost curve. If they comprise external costs a tax is shown to improve allocative efficiency, while if they are external benefits a subsidy is required.

You see that if in fact there are various simultaneous causes of market failure, trying to correct one of them in isolation may have the opposite of the desired effect. This is the problem of second best.

Since monopolies may exercise monopoly power against the public interest, governments often regulate them. In the UK this operates through the Monopolies and Mergers Commission and the European Commission.

Chapter 8:

Factors of Production

What determines the wage rate? How do the markets for labour and capital operate? Questions like these are not new in economics and were studied by classical economists such as David Ricardo and Karl Marx. They thought wages would automatically be kept down to the minimum subsistence level necessary for people to survive. Modern economists, however, have shown that wages are determined by the market mechanism and the interaction between the forces of supply and demand.

Contents

KEYWORDS

- Arbitrage
- Internal rate of return
- Marginal revenue product
- Opportunity cost
- Economic rent
- Labour demand
- Minimum wage
- Transfer earnings
- Investment appraisal
- Labour supply
- Net present value
- Wage discrimination

Section 8.1: Introduction

The main issue in this chapter is what determines the price and output levels of factors of production. We concentrate on the labour market, showing how the market mechanism operates within a supply and demand framework.

We begin by examining what determines the amount of labour people are willing to supply and go on to consider what influences the amount of labour firms demand. The wage rate is found to depend on the interaction between the forces of supply and demand. The chapter then explores reasons for inequalities in the labour market in order to explain why people are paid different wage levels. The theme of inequality is continued as we examine the case for and against a minimum wage. The chapter concludes by briefly considering what influences the firm's demand for capital and looking at some of the investment appraisal techniques that the firm can use to decide how much capital it should employ.

Section 8.2: Factor Markets

There are parallels between the ways in which the factor markets and the goods markets operate, and there are therefore similarities in the ways in which economists analyse them. But there is also something distinctive about factor markets. The factors they deal in are not demanded for their own sake, but because of the end products that the factors can be used to produce.

Factor Markets: An Overview

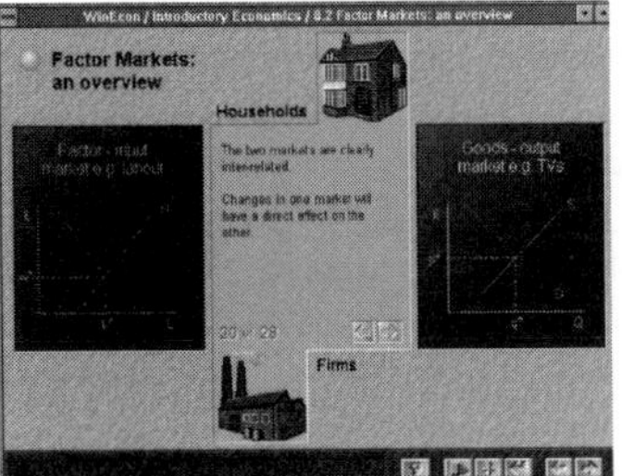

This WinEcon topic shows you that factor markets are closely linked with goods markets. Outcomes in one influence those in the other. The determinants of supply and demand in factor markets are indicative of the particular characteristics of such markets. Factors of production, such as labour or capital, are made available for use because this generates income for their owners. Firms demand factors of production because of the profits they can make by selling the goods or services in which the factors of production are used. We say that the demand for factors of production is a 'derived demand' (i.e. factors of production are only demanded if there is a demand for the products they make).

Section 8.3: Factor Supply: The Supply of Labour

This section looks at the individual person's decision about how many hours they wish to work. We use the framework of indifference curve analysis developed in chapter 3. Later we construct the market labour supply curve by adding the supply curves of individuals.

Supply of Labour: The Leisure/Work Trade-off

Economists look at the labour supply decision in terms of the choices individuals make in allocating their time between leisure and work. This is known to economists as the leisure/work trade-off. Whilst leisure produces utility, time spent working yields disutility, but also generates income. People get utility from the things they buy with their income. In looking at the labour supply decision we are therefore in effect studying the trade-off between utility from leisure time and utility from the things people buy with their income earned from work.

Supply of Labour: Derivation of the Budget Constraint

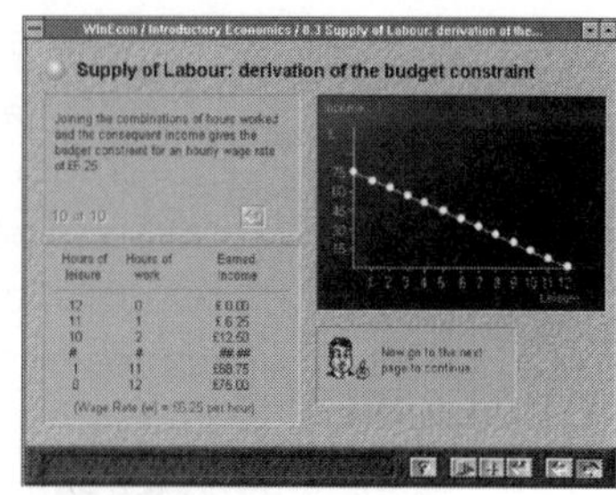

This WinEcon screen relates to an individual who has a 'budget' of 12 hours per day to spend on work and leisure combined. The diagram shows leisure time on the horizontal axis and the income generated by the hours worked on the vertical axis. If all the time available is used for leisure then 12 hours of leisure are consumed, no work is done and therefore no income is earned. This gives us the point at the end of the budget constraint on the horizontal axis. At the other extreme, at the other end of the budget constraint, where no leisure is taken (i.e. 12 hours are worked) £75 is earned.

The rate at which leisure time can be translated into income depends on the wage rate, and this is given by the slope of the budget constraint, ignoring the negative sign. At the wage rate of is £6.25 per hour, £75 is earned if all 12 hours are spent working (£6.25 × 12 = £75). The slope of the budget constraint becomes steeper as the wage rate increases because this raises the income level for any given number of leisure hours foregone.

The budget constraint for the labour supply of an individual

An individual can work for anything up to 10 hours per day at a wage rate of £8 per hour. Labelling the diagram appropriately, plot the budget constraint representing the choices available to him or her each day. Consider only the hours for which work is available.

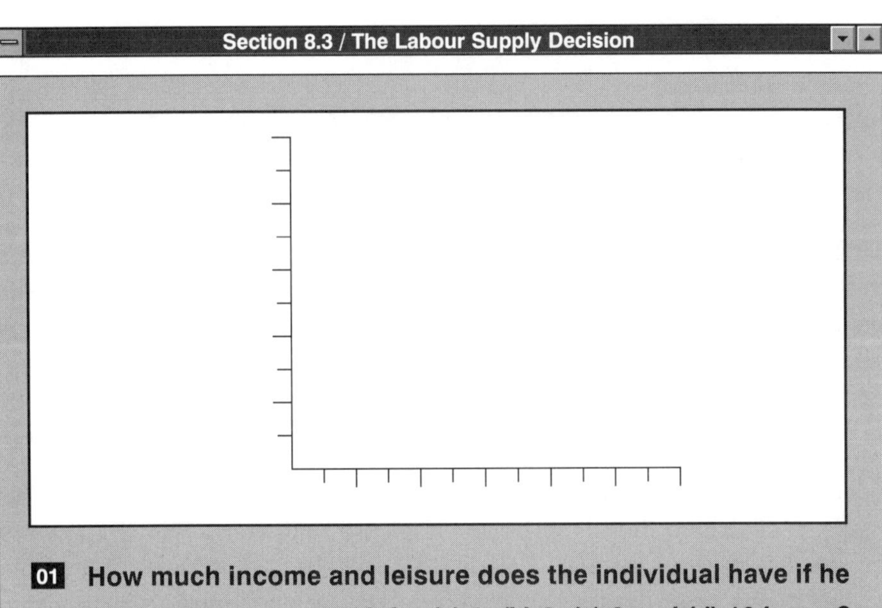

Section 8.3 / The Labour Supply Decision
01 How much income and leisure does the individual have if he or she chooses to work for (a) 0, (b) 2, (c) 8 and (d) 10 hours?

The Labour Supply Decision

We have seen that an individual is able to trade off leisure against income. Any trade-off which occurs depends on the person's income/leisure preferences as shown by his or her indifference curves. Each separate indifference curve marked on the WinEcon screen diagram shows different combinations of income and leisure which give a constant level of utility. Higher curves yield higher levels of utility, but the individual with a fixed number of hours available can only move onto a higher curve if the budget constraint becomes steeper. This requires an increase in the wage rate.

As explained in chapter 3, the individual maximizes utility by choosing the point where the budget constraint is tangential to an indifference curve. In the case of the labour supply model this determines how many hours are worked.

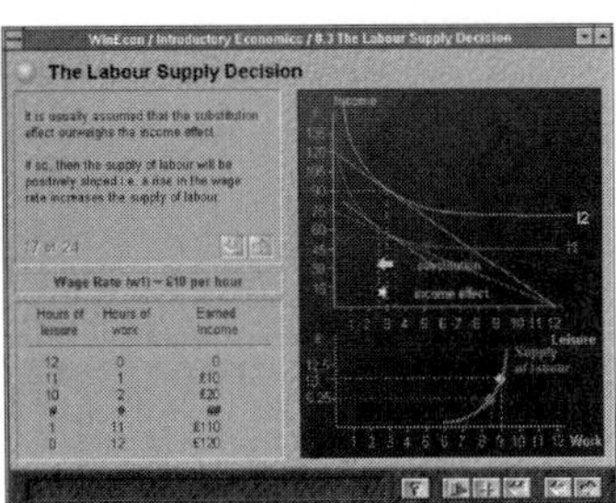

If the wage rate changes, income levels change along with the amount of work that people want to do. For example, increasing the wage rate rotates the budget constraint clockwise around the point where no work is done. The constraint pivots rather than shifting out parallel because the number of hours remains fixed at 12 whilst the potential income which can be earned if all 12 hours are used to work increases. A shift to a higher indifference curve occurs, meaning that a higher level of utility or 'real income' is reached.

The movement between the equilibrium position on the first curve and that on the second is made up of a substitution effect and an income effect. Whether the number of hours worked increases or decreases depends on the relative sizes of these effects, which go in opposite directions. When the wage rate increases, the substitution effect makes people want to work more because they earn more money for each hour of leisure which is given up. We can see this in terms of income being substituted for leisure. The income effect,

however, goes in the opposite direction – an increase in the wage rate makes people want to work less. This is because 'real income' (as defined in terms of the individual's utility) has risen and, given that leisure is a normal good, the individual wants to 'buy' more of this from his or her available real income.

It should be noted that we are using the term 'real income' in a rather specialist sense here. A rise in real income defined in terms of an increase in the person's utility is shown by his or her movement on to a higher indifference curve. We are not talking about the person's money income.

The net effect of a wage increase can be to increase or decrease the hours worked. If the substitution effect outweighs the income effect, the individual ends up taking less leisure time and working longer hours.

From our indifference curve analysis it is possible to calculate the individual's labour supply curve. This curve shows how many hours the individual is willing to work at each different wage rate. Since, as we have seen, an increase in wages may result in someone working either more or fewer hours, the curve may have either a positive or a negative slope. Normally, the labour supply curve slopes forwards at low wage rates, with the substitution effect dominating the income effect. At higher wage rates it may bend backwards with any increase in wages, resulting in a reduction in the hours worked. On this part of the supply curve the income effect outweighs the substitution effect. As you use the WinEcon screen, complete the table below.

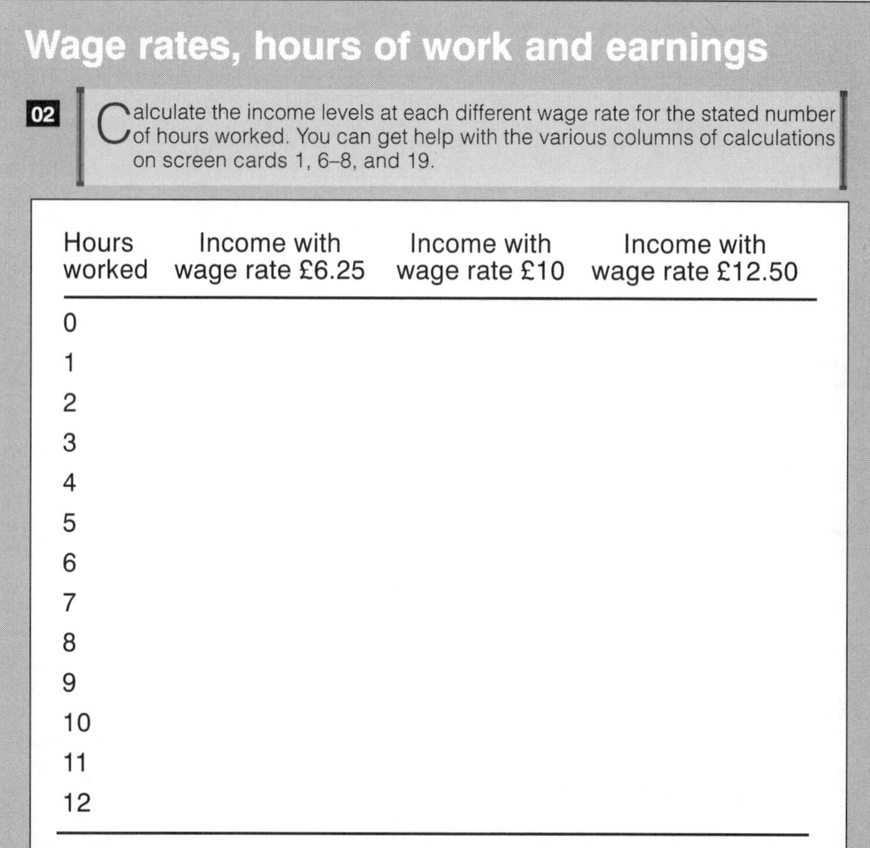

Wage rates, hours of work and earnings

02 Calculate the income levels at each different wage rate for the stated number of hours worked. You can get help with the various columns of calculations on screen cards 1, 6–8, and 19.

Hours worked	Income with wage rate £6.25	Income with wage rate £10	Income with wage rate £12.50
0			
1			
2			
3			
4			
5			
6			
7			
8			
9			
10			
11			
12			

Use the data in the above table to add three budget constraints to the diagram.

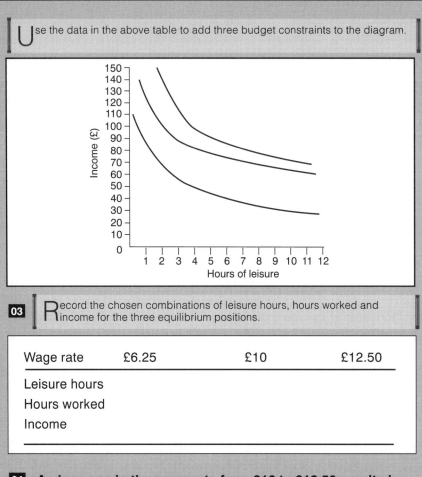

03 Record the chosen combinations of leisure hours, hours worked and income for the three equilibrium positions.

Wage rate	£6.25	£10	£12.50
Leisure hours			
Hours worked			
Income			

04 **An increase in the wage rate from £10 to £12.50 results in fewer hours being worked. Why do you think this occurs?**

About the income and substitution effects

05 **If the wage rate increases the substitution effect results in an ________ in hours worked whilst the income effect results in a ________ in hours worked.**

06 **Explain how the substitution effect influences the number of hours of leisure taken if the wage rate falls. (Hint: the income received per hour worked falls.)**

07 **Explain how the income effect influences the number of hours of leisure taken if the wage rate is reduced. (Hint: the level of real income is falling.)**

08 **How do we define 'real income' when we are using indifference curve analysis to look at the labour supply decision?**

09 **If the income effect is larger than the substitution effect, how does an increase in the wage rate affect the number of hours of leisure taken?**

What is the labour supply curve?

Use your figures from the above table of wage rates and hours worked to plot the labour supply curve. Annotate the curve to show the area where the substitution effect dominates and that where the income effect dominates.

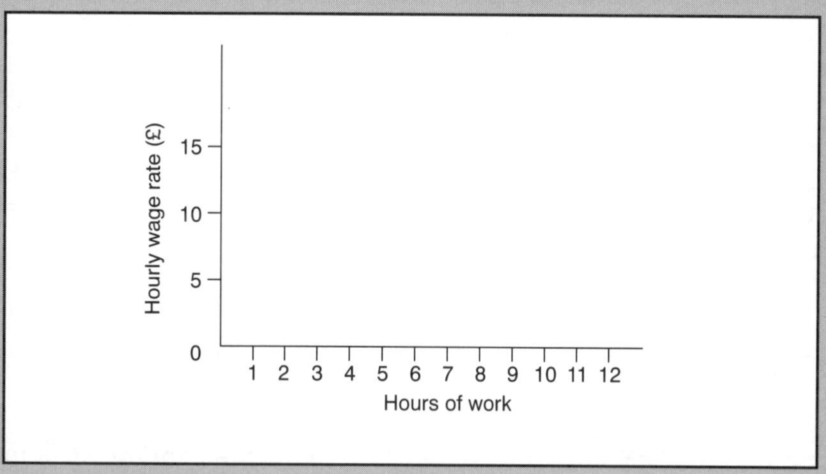

10 **On the forward-bending part of the labour supply curve does the income effect outweigh the substitution effect or vice versa?**

11 **Try to explain why the income effect outweighs the substitution effect at high income levels. (Hint: at high income levels, people's demand for goods tends towards saturation whilst demand for leisure time does not.)**

The Market Supply of Labour

So far this section has considered the labour supply decision of the individual, but it is the market labour supply curve in which economists are most interested. This is because we want to find out what happens in the economy as a whole if, for example, the government decides to increase or cut income taxes. To derive the market labour supply curve all we need to do is add together the labour supply curves of each individual. Referring to WinEcon, we see that we work out the amount of hours which each person is willing to work at a particular wage rate and then just add them together to find the market supply.

Section 8.4: Factor Demand: The Demand for Labour

We now turn our attention to factor demand and the question of how much labour a firm is willing to hire. A firm hires labour (and other factors of production, such as capital) in order to produce goods and services. Factor inputs will only be hired by a profit maximizing firm if the value of what they produce at least matches the cost to the firm of employing them (in the case of labour, this would be the wages paid). From this it follows that if we want to find out how much labour a firm will hire at a given wage rate we will have know two things: firstly how much each unit of labour will produce (i.e. the marginal physical product (MPP)) and secondly the marginal revenue (MR) from selling the additional goods that have been produced. We can see from this that analysing labour demand is quite complicated. We need to investigate the market for the firm's product (the goods market) as well as the labour market. We also need to consider the type of competition found in both of these markets, as this may affect both the wage rate and the price the firm gets for the goods it sells.

Factor Demand by a Firm Under Different Market Structures

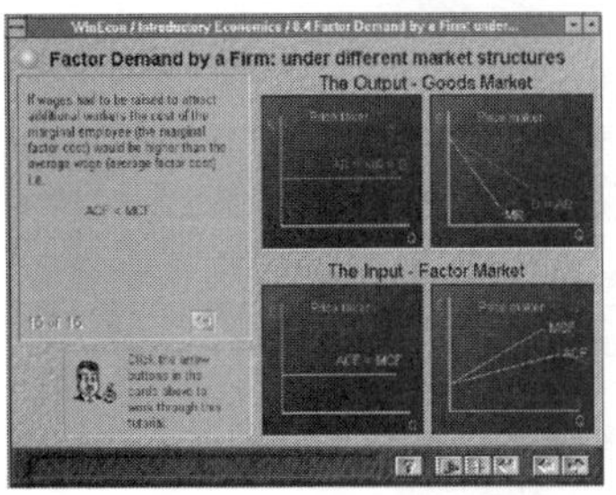

In WinEcon we look at four possible market structure combinations. Firstly, perfect competition could exist in both the goods (or output) and labour (or input) markets. Secondly, the goods market may be perfectly competitive whilst the labour market is imperfectly competitive. The third possibility is that the goods market could be imperfectly competitive whilst the labour market is perfectly competitive. The final possibility is imperfect competition in both markets. The WinEcon screen shows the potential market structures.

- Perfect competition in either market implies that the firm is a price-taker. In the goods market this means that the product demand curve is perfectly elastic. The consequence of this is that no matter how much the firm produces of its product, the price at which it can be sold does not change.
- If the goods market is monopolistic, the producer is then a price-maker. This means that the demand curve is downward sloping, so that as more and more of the good is produced for sale its price will fall.
- In the labour market, if the firm is a price-taker then no matter how much

labour the firm demands, the wage rate (or the price of labour) does not change. In this market we find the 'average cost of a factor' (ACF, which is also the wage rate) curve and the 'marginal cost of a factor' (MCF) curve are identical. Notice that under perfect competition both curves are perfectly elastic.

In the case of the imperfect labour market, however, it can be seen that ACF and MCF rise as the amount of labour used increases. This occurs because in order to attract more people to work for them the firm has to increase the wage rate offered to all.

Clicking the Next Page button takes you to a supplementary screen (The Firm's Demand for Factors) which summarizes these market conditions. As we will see, the effects of different market structures can be very considerable.

Short-Run Demand for Labour: Competitive Input and Output Markets

To determine how much labour a firm will demand we need to introduce the concepts of 'marginal revenue product' (MRP) and 'value of marginal product' (VMP). These are used as a measure of the worth to the firm of the output produced by the last unit of labour employed. They provide an indication of whether it is worth employing an additional person. The MRP is the change in revenue that the firm receives as a result of employing one more person, while VMP is the profit it makes by selling the output of that extra person. These amounts are the same in a competitive goods market, but would not be so in an imperfectly competitive market where the firm has to reduce its price to sell more output.

Before we can value the output of an extra person, we need to know how much the person will produce. The marginal physical product (MPP) measures the extra output of an additional worker. The size of the MPP is determined by the firm's production function. If the MPP is multiplied by the extra revenue the firm gets from selling this output we obtain the MRP, which is the measurement of the value to the firm of what the additional worker has produced. To obtain the VMP, we multiply the MPP by the price at which the good is sold. In perfect competition, price equals marginal revenue (MR) at all output levels, and so MRP = VMP.

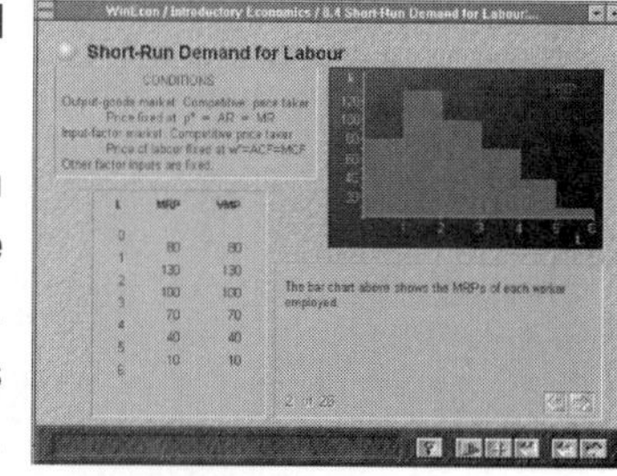

As you use the supplementary WinEcon screen (Short-Run Demand for Labour, accessed via the Next Page button), notice that beyond a certain point the MRP falls as output increases. This is a consequence of the law of diminishing returns which, as we saw in chapter 4, causes the MPP first to rise and then to fall.

We can now address the main question of this section, namely how much labour the profit maximizing firm will hire. This depends on the relationship between the MCF (which is also the wage rate where ACF = MCF) and the MRP. The firm will hire labour up to the point where MCF = wage rate = MRP.

Develop your understanding of labour demand in competitive markets

12 **The MRP is calculated as ☐ multiplied by ☐ .**

13 **The VMP is calculated as ☐ multiplied by ☐.**

14 **The firm will hire additional workers up to the point where ☐ = ☐.**

15 **Explain why MRP = VMP if the goods market is in perfect competition but not if it is in imperfect competition.**

16 From the data on the WinEcon screen, record in the appropriate column of the table the numbers that will be employed at each of the stated wage rates. (The column for competitive input and imperfect output markets will be used later.)

Input market: Output market:	Competitive Competitive	Competitive Imperfect
Wage rate	Workers employed	Workers employed
70		
40		
10		

Plot the labour demand curve for the firm when both the goods and labour market are in perfect competition and label it C-C.

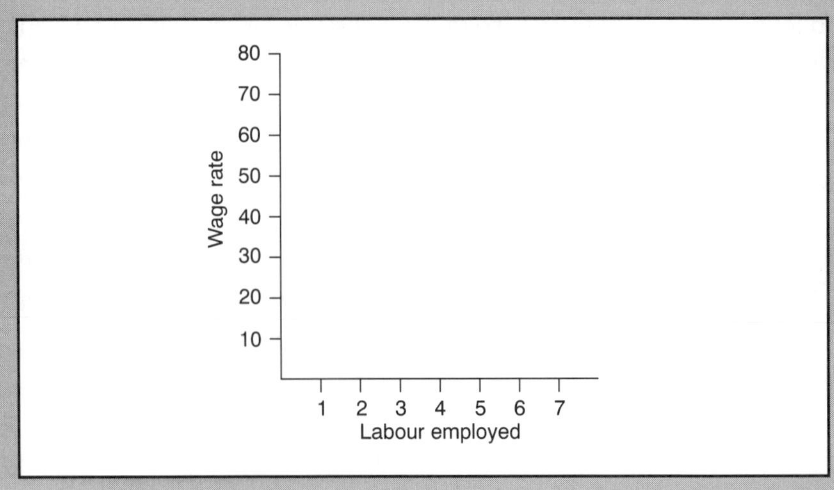

Competitive Input Market and Imperfect Output Market

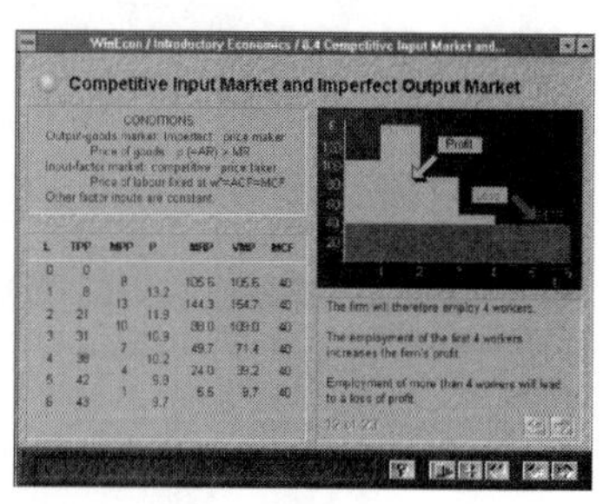

In the imperfectly competitive goods market the demand curve is downward sloping which means that if output is increased the price of the good falls. In this situation the MRP and VMP values differ, as you can see from the WinEcon screen. The result of this is that for a given wage rate the firm hires a different number of workers from those it would hire if both input and output markets were perfectly competitive. The labour demand curve is therefore also different. WinEcon shows you the calculations step by step.

Labour demand (imperfect goods market)

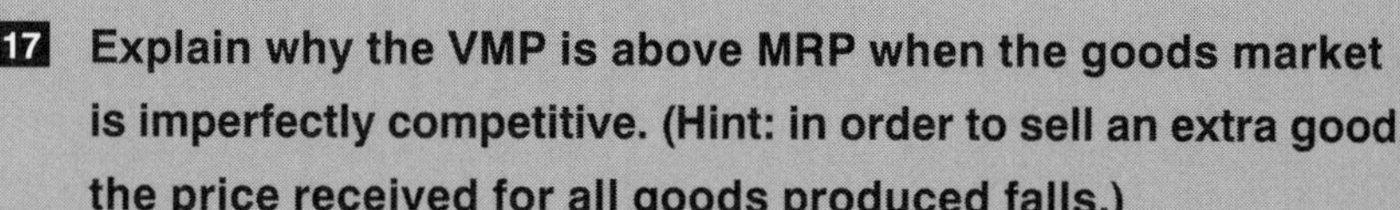

17 Explain why the VMP is above MRP when the goods market is imperfectly competitive. (Hint: in order to sell an extra good, the price received for all goods produced falls.)

18 Work out how many workers will be employed at wage rates of £70, £40 and £10 and complete the competitive/imperfect markets column of the table you started to fill in above. Plot the associated demand curve on the diagram above and label the curve C-I.

Imperfect Input Market and Competitive Output Market

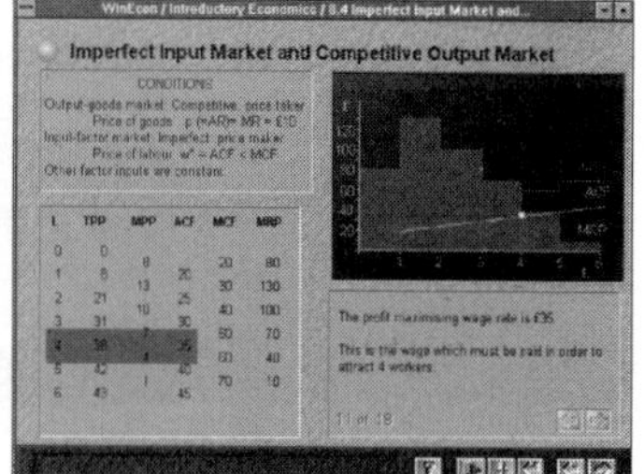

When the input market is imperfect, if the firm wants to employ more workers a higher wage will have to be offered to attract them. The MCF increases as the number of workers employed increases. A firm which is the sole buyer of a particular type of labour is described as a 'monopsonist'. It has power which is analagous to that of a monopolist, the sole seller in a market.

Since the goods market is perfectly competitive, the MRP and VMP values will be the same as in the topic Short-Run Demand for Labour: competitive input and output markets. The number of workers hired, however, must take account of the fact that the wage rate rises as the numbers employed increase. The firm still employs workers up to the point where MRP = MCF, but now MCF is not fixed. We can see this on the WinEcon screen.

Imperfect Input and Output Markets

This WinEcon topic deals with the case of imperfectly competitive goods and labour markets. In the goods market the demand curve is downward sloping. In the labour market the MCF will increase as the number of workers

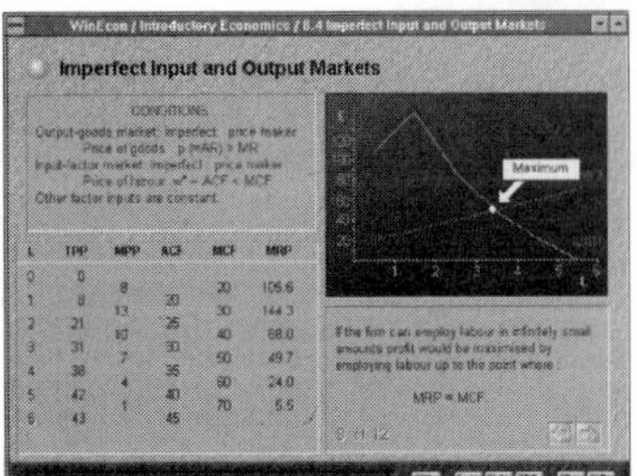

employed increases. The MRP and VMP values differ from each other, and the number of workers who are hired has to take account of the fact that the wage rate rises as employment rises.

Comparison of labour demand under different market structures

19 **Explain why the MRP curve is downward sloping under all the market structures we have analysed.**

20 **If you examine the two labour demand curves you drew on the diagram above, you should see that one is above the other. Can you explain why?**

21 **Why is the MRP curve the same as VMP when the goods market is competitive but not in imperfect competition?**

22 **What will happen to the MRP if there is a technological advance? (Hint: MPP rises.)**

23 **What is the ACF of labour? Explain why the curve slopes upwards when the labour market is imperfectly competitive but is horizontal when the labour market is perfectly competitive.**

Aggregate Demand for Labour

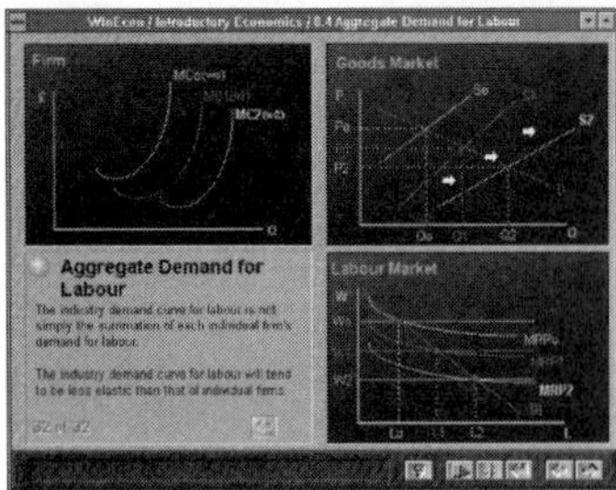

We now look at the aggregate labour demand curve which is the combined demand curve for all the firms in the market. This is quite complicated so we shall be limiting our analysis to the case where both the goods and labour markets are perfectly competitive. Even here, deriving the market demand curve is not as simple as you might think. We cannot just sum together the MRP curves of the individual firms in the market. This is because there is a different market MRP curve (i.e. sum of individual firms' MRP curves) for each different market wage rate. The aggregate labour demand curve is therefore made up of a series of points on individual market MRP curves, each of which corresponds to a different wage rate. We can look in detail at the process of deriving the labour demand curve on the WinEcon screen.

The top left-hand quadrant of the screen shows the marginal cost (MC) curve of an individual representative firm in the perfectly competitive goods market. This represents just one firm out of possibly several hundred, each of which will have similar MC curves. Notice that once the diagram is complete there are three MC curves, each of which relates to a different wage rate (i.e. wage rates W_0, W_1 and W_2 respectively on the diagram). The marginal cost is the cost of producing an additional unit of output, and in the short run this consists principally of the cost of employing more labour. Therefore, if the wage rate falls, as we see in the diagram, this will reduce the marginal cost.

The goods market supply curve in the top right-hand quadrant is derived by summing together, for each firm in the market, the part of the MC curve where average variable costs are covered. The goods market supply curve measures the quantity which the market will supply at each given price level. Notice that there is a new supply curve associated with each given wage level. This is because each reduction in the wage level shifts the MC curve for each individual firm which in turn will shift the supply curve. The significance of the movement of the supply curve is that the equilibrium price of goods in the market will fall and output will rise. The result of the fall in the wage rate is therefore a fall in the market price of the goods being produced.

Turning now to the bottom right-hand quadrant, what we notice here is that there is an MRP curve associated with each different wage level. Remember that the MRP is calculated as MPP × MR (MR = P in perfect competition) and, therefore, if the price of the product goes down, the MRP will also go down. The net result is that there is a different MRP curve associated with each different wage level.

Finally, we want to derive the short-run aggregate labour demand curve. This is obtained by finding a locus of points on different MRP curves. We have to find the quantity of labour at which a given wage rate intersects with its associated MRP curve. This point will show us the labour demand we are seeking. This process is repeated for all the other different wage rates and we finally join up the points to produce the demand curve, as seen on the last four text cards.

Develop your understanding of the market labour demand curve

24 **Why is there a different market MRP curve associated with each wage rate in perfect competition?**

25 **If the wage rate increases, what will this do to the market MRP curve?**

26 **Explain why a fall in the wage rate will result in a fall in MRP. (Hint: the fall in the wage rate shifts the goods market supply curve.)**

27 **If the wage rate increases the market supply curve shifts [____] . This will [____] the price of the good and [____] the quantity sold. This in turn will move the MRP curve [____] because MRP is calculated as [____] × [____].**

28 **If the wage rate falls the MC curve will shift [____]. This in turn will [____] the market supply curve which will cause the price of the product to [____]. This in turn will result in the MRP curve shifting [____].**

Section 8.5: Economic Rent and Transfer Earnings

The price which a firm has to pay for a factor of production, such as labour, depends on the interaction between the forces of supply and demand in the factor market. We define the concepts of 'transfer earnings' and 'economic rent' and can apply them to any factor of production, although we concentrate on the labour market.

People in different occupations can earn vastly different amounts of money. For example, if we look at the music industry we see that the supply of the music produced by top rock and pop stars is limited whilst the demand is high. As a result, these workers are very highly paid. At the other extreme, the supply of unskilled labourers such as bar staff is high relative to employer demand and therefore these types of workers are relatively poorly paid.

The payment made to a factor such as a worker can be shown to be made up of varying combinations of transfer earnings and economic rent. We show that the size of workers' transfer earnings depends on the 'opportunity costs' of their current jobs. The opportunity cost to workers of doing a particular job is the amount of money they could earn if they left their present job and got a new one. It is effectively, therefore, the money they would be paid in the next best job they could find. If workers' present earnings are less than the opportunity cost (i.e. if they could get a better paid job elsewhere), they will transfer their employment to this better paid job. We can define transfer earnings, therefore, as the minimum payment required to keep someone in their present job.

People such as rock stars are paid well above their transfer earnings. The additional amount they are paid is the economic rent and this can be seen as the amount they are paid over and above the amount which is necessary to keep them in their present job.

We can illustrate these concepts with a hypothetical example of a rock star who is paid £1 million a year, with his next best earning opportunity (i.e. his opportunity cost or transfer earnings) being bar work earning £7500 a year. We can see that the economic rent component of what he is paid is £992,500 per year which is the amount he is paid over and above his transfer earnings. The total payment to the rock star is comprised of transfer earnings of £7500 (the minimum he would accept to be paid as a rock star) and economic rent of £992,500.

At the other end of the earnings spectrum are people working in unskilled jobs, such as bar staff. They may, for example, be paid £7500, with their next best earning opportunity being a job as a gardener's labourer also earning £7500. In this particular example the transfer earnings are equal to the present pay and therefore the economic rent element of their pay is zero.

Surprising as it may seem, considering the labour market as a whole, there is likely to be an element of both transfer earnings and economic rent in most jobs. As long as the supply of labour is not perfectly elastic (i.e. as long as employers are not able to get as many workers as they want at a fixed wage rate) there is an element of economic rent in what some workers are paid.

The Market for Skilled Labour: TV Weather Presenters

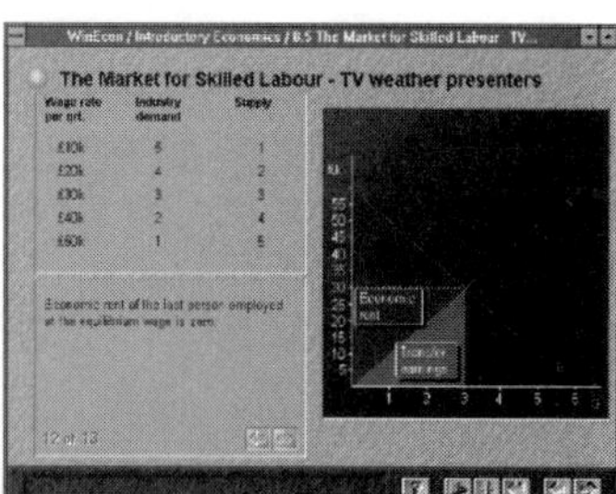

As you build the wage vs labour diagram by working through the WinEcon screen, notice how the economic rent element in the weather presenter labour market as a whole can be measured in terms of the gap between the labour supply curve and the actual payment made to the presenters. The WinEcon text cards explain why this is so, given that the wage rate at which someone is prepared to work represents their transfer earnings. Some of the people employed would be prepared to work for less than they are actually paid, and the difference between the amounts represents their economic rent.

The amount of economic rent in the market as a whole is given by the area above the supply curve and under the wage rate. The transfer earnings element is given by the area under the supply curve.

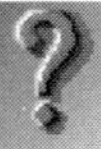

About economic rent and transfer earnings

29 **Find the definitions of opportunity cost, transfer earnings and economic rent. Using your own words, record these definitions.**

30 **Produce two lists of jobs, one where there is a high level of economic rent and another where the economic rent is low. Can you explain the difference between the two?**

31 **Explain why the area under the supply curve in the WinEcon diagram represents transfer earnings whilst the area above shows economic rent.**

32 **If a pop star earning £2 million a year could also get a job as a footballer earning £1 million a year, his transfer earnings are ______ and his economic rent is ______.**

33 If the equilibrium wage rate rose to £50,000 per quarter in the weather presenter labour market, work out and tabulate how much of the payment to each presenter would be transfer earnings and how much would be economic rent.

Presenter	Transfer earnings	Economic rent
1		
2		
3		
4		
5		

34 **If the next best job the first presenter could find paid £5000 per quarter, what would his or her transfer earnings and economic rent be if a presenter's pay was £15,000 per quarter?**

The Market for Unskilled Labour: Bar Staff

Early economists, such as David Ricardo and Karl Marx, assumed that there would be what Marx called a 'reserve army' of unemployed labour which would work for subsistence pay levels. This would effectively mean there was a limitless supply of labour for employers to hire at the subsistence-level wage rate. It has been argued by some present-day economists that unskilled labour, such as bar staff, represents the modern-day equivalent of Marx's reserve army. In effect there is a low, subsistence-based wage rate at which firms can hire an unlimited number of workers. Look at the WinEcon screen to see the shape of labour supply curve this implies.

If the labour supply curve is perfectly elastic there is no economic rent element to earnings whatsoever. No unskilled workers would be willing to work for less than the subsistence wage rate, and therefore none is being paid more than is necessary to keep them in their present job; all are paid just their transfer earnings.

About the unskilled labour market

Draw the labour market diagram for unskilled workers. Annotate it to indicate transfer earnings and economic rent.

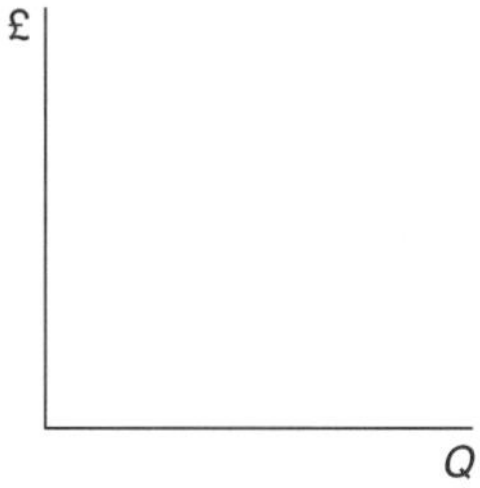

£

Q

The labour supply curve for unskilled workers is perfectly elastic. State in your own words what implications this has for the wage rate if the demand for labour increases.

35 **The economic rent element paid to workers on subsistence wage rates is ________. This is because the ________ ________ of working in this job are equivalent to the amount they is being paid currently.**

The Market for City Centre Office Space

We now turn to another factor of production – capital. An example is the supply of office space, which is fixed in the short run because the offices which already exist cannot be used for anything else and no new office blocks can be built. This means that the supply of space is perfectly inelastic.

As we can see from the WinEcon screen the consequence of this is that the supply curve is vertical. Therefore, irrespective of whether the rent is £1 or £125 per square metre, the supply is fixed.

For a factor in perfectly inelastic supply, any payments made for its use consist entirely of economic rent because transfer earnings are zero. This may seem strange at first until we remember that transfer earnings are based on the payment the factor could receive if it were used for another purpose. The office block has no other use in the short run so the transfer earnings it would receive are zero. From this we can conclude that any payments made for the use of the office block consist entirely of economic rent.

Perfectly inelastic factor supply

36 **If a factor of production has no other potential use, its transfer earnings are ______. This means that the payments made to the factor consist entirely of ______ ______. This will occur when the supply of the factor is perfectly ______.**

Draw a diagram to illustrate the market for a factor of production which is in perfectly inelastic supply. Annotate it to indicate economic rent and transfer earnings.

37 **Suggest some examples of factors of production in perfectly inelastic supply in the short run.**

Section 8.6: Discrimination in the Labour Market

In this section we use economics to explain why different people earn different amounts for doing similar jobs. Our analysis can be used to explain why women are paid less than men, why younger workers are paid less than older workers, why people working in different regions receive different wages, and why workers from the ethnic minorities can sometimes be paid less than white workers.

Employers can only pay different wage rates to different groups of workers doing the same job if they can separate the labour markets. This is necessary to prevent workers switching between the markets. If the workers can switch, a process called 'arbitrage' occurs which eventually equalizes the wage rates. For example, if car assembly workers in the north of England were paid less than those in southern England, workers from the north could move to the south for higher pay. This would increase the supply of car assembly workers in the south, reducing the wage rate in that area. At the same time the supply of labour in the north would be reduced, which would increase the wage rate there. Through this process of arbitrage the wage rates of the two groups would eventually become equal. Empirical evidence produced by economists suggests, however, that in the real world such a process of arbitrage does not work perfectly and employers are in fact able to discriminate to some degree between different groups of workers. In WinEcon we use our economic theory to examine the process of how the market determines the wage rate for these different groups.

Develop your understanding of wage discrimination

38 **The process by which market forces can equate the wage rate of different groups of people is called ________.**

39 **Give some examples of wage discrimination in practice.**

You learn in the following WinEcon screens that discrimination will occur because this enables the employer to increase profits. The example shows that a firm which acts as a discriminating monopsonist (the sole buyer of labour) in two different labour markets makes more profits than a non-discriminating monopsonist.

The Aggregate Supply Curve faced by a Monopsonist

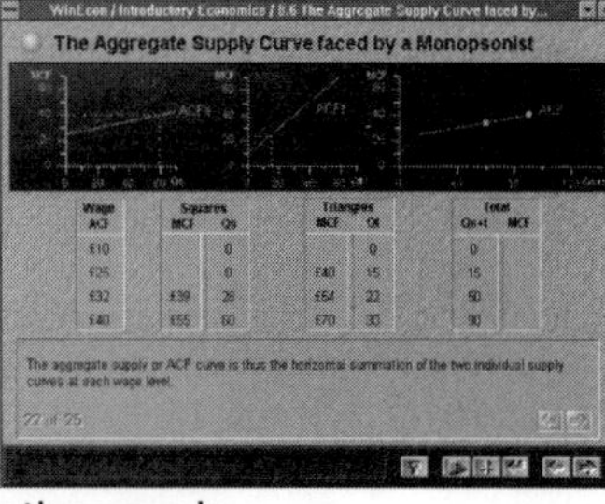

This WinEcon screen shows two different groups of workers in separate labour markets. These groups are called the 'squares' and the 'triangles'. If we wanted to, we could think of the squares as male workers and the triangles as female workers, or as some other such groups. Notice the positions of the average cost of a factor (ACF) and marginal cost of a factor (MCF) curves. The ACF curve shows us how many people are willing to work at a particular wage rate, and so is the labour supply curve. The MCF is above ACF because if a monopsonist wants to employ more workers an increased wage rate must be offered not only to the new workers but also to all the existing workers. Each labour market has its own ACF and MCF curves and the aggregate ACF and MCF curves which the monopsonist faces are found by adding together the respective curves from the two markets. The WinEcon text cards show you the method of finding both the aggregate labour supply curve and also the overall additional cost of employing another worker.

How labour market discrimination arises

40 **The WinEcon screen shows that at a market wage rate of £40 ____ 'squares' and ____ 'triangles' are willing to work. This leads to an aggregate labour supply of ____.**

41 **Explain why the MCF curve of the monopsonist is above the ACF curve. Would this be the case if the supply of labour was perfectly elastic in both markets?**

Discriminating and Non-Discriminating Monopsony Compared

Wage rates are determined by the forces of supply and demand. We have seen how the labour supply curve is derived and now we must consider the demand side of the equation. The number of workers the monopsonist will employ will depend on the workers' marginal revenue product (MRP). As each of the two types of workers are equally productive, we have a single MRP curve on the market diagram. The monopsonist will employ workers up to the point where the cost of employing an additional worker, the MCF, is equal to the MRP. This is the point on the market diagram where MRP = MCF.

The monopsonist could pay the same wage rate in the two labour markets or could discriminate with different wage rates. Work through the WinEcon cards, noticing the employee mix and the total wage bill in each case. You find that the total wage bill paid by a discriminating monopsonist is less than the bill paid by the non-discriminating monopsonist. We see, therefore, that discrimination increases the monopsonist's total profits by reducing the total wage bill. We conclude that the profit motive is one of the main reasons why wage discrimination between different ethnic or socio-economic groups exists in the real world.

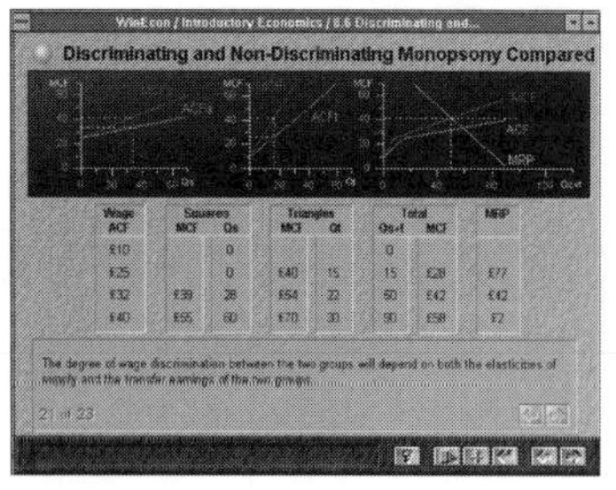

Develop your understanding of discrimination in the labour market

42 **In the WinEcon example, the discriminating monopsonist faces a wage bill of [ ]. Without discrimination the wage bill would be [ ]. Discrimination therefore increases profits by [ ].**

43 **Using your own words, explain why the profit maximizing monopsonist will decide to employ 16 'triangles' and 34 'squares' in the WinEcon example.**

Section 8.7: Labour Markets: Impact of the Minimum Wage

Minimum Wage

In countries such as France and Switzerland the government has set a minimum wage level which employers must pay, whilst in the UK the minimum wage issue continues to attract debate. This section uses supply and demand analysis to assess the impact of minimum wage legislation on wage levels and levels of employment. The effect of such legislation depends on whether the minimum is set above or below the market equilibrium wage level and whether the labour market is perfectly competitive or not. The latter point should be borne in mind in what follows, as our analysis only considers the effects in competitive labour markets.

As you work through the WinEcon text cards you should discover that a minimum wage rate which is set below the current market equilibrium rate has no effect whatsoever on the amount workers are paid or on the number of workers employed.

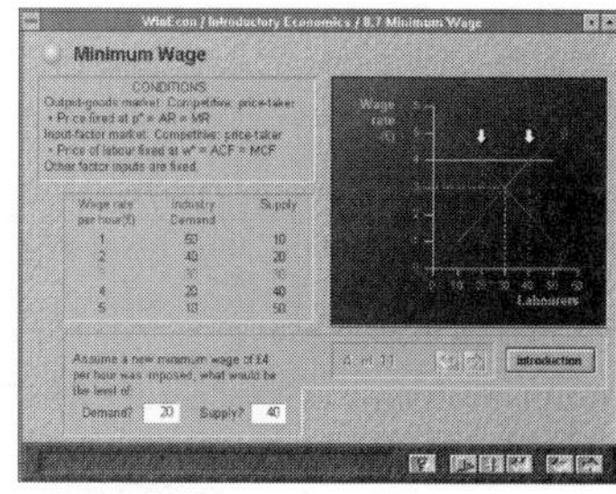

The diagram on card 5 is probably closer to what usually occurs in practice if a minimum wage is introduced. Those who support minimum wage legislation normally do so because they think market wages are below a socially acceptable level and workers should be paid more. The effect of imposing a minimum wage rate above the market equilibrium is to reduce the number of workers that employers demand so that employment levels fall. Another side to the effect is that the number of people who want to work increases at the higher wage rate. The overall result is an excess supply of labour and unemployment. Economists who oppose a minimum wage say that such a minimum wage would be bad for the economy as it would reduce the number

of jobs available and also increase the level of unemployment. We can see that the government faces a dilemma. Does it allow workers to live in poverty on low wages, or does it increase the standards of living of those who are working at the expense of increasing unemployment and reducing the level of economic activity?

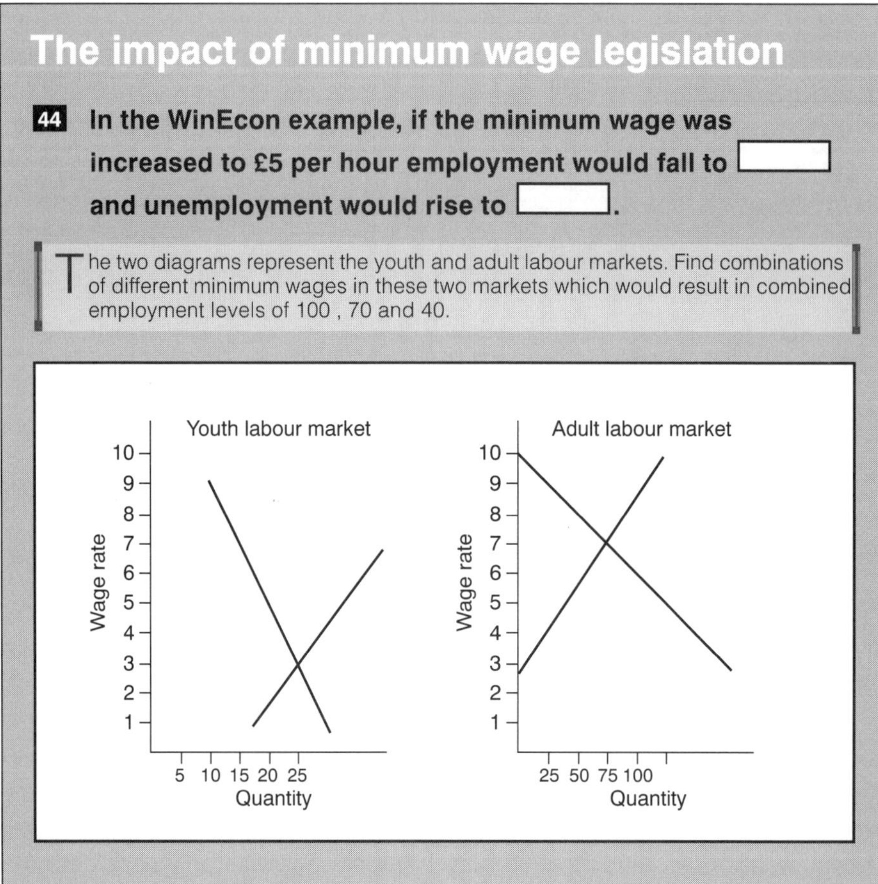

The impact of minimum wage legislation

44 **In the WinEcon example, if the minimum wage was increased to £5 per hour employment would fall to ______ and unemployment would rise to ______.**

The two diagrams represent the youth and adult labour markets. Find combinations of different minimum wages in these two markets which would result in combined employment levels of 100 , 70 and 40.

Section 8.8: Capital Investment Appraisal

In this section we turn our attention to the capital market, looking specifically at how firms determine the amount of capital they should use. There are a number of analytical techniques which can be used to appraise the viability of investment projects. We concentrate here on the discounting techniques of 'net present value' (NPV) and the 'internal rate of return' (IRR). These two approaches are closely related to each other as we shall see. The section concludes by briefly investigating the less sophisticated technique of pay-back which, although it is less theoretically sound than discounting techniques, is widely used in industry.

Net Present Value

NPV and IRR are investment appraisal techniques which take into account the fact that money has a time value. This means that the £100 you receive this year is worth more than £100 you receive in 10 years' time. The reason for this is straightforward: today's £100 can be put it in an interest bearing account so that in 10 years, with the interest added, it will be worth substantially more than £100. This is very important when looking at a firm's investment decisions because an investment in plant and machinery is likely to produce a stream of earnings or profits over a series of years. The value of each £100 profit which the investment produces in subsequent years of the investment's life will be less than the value of each £100 profit produced in year one. To take this into account, the value of the profits from subsequent years must be discounted to show their value in terms of today's money.

The amount by which the future earnings stream is discounted each year depends on the discount rate used. Each year's earnings will be shown in terms of today's money by using the following discounting calculation:

$$\text{PV} = P/(1 + r)^n$$

where PV = present value, P = cash flow, r = the discount rate and n = the number of years ahead. If, for example, the discount rate is 10 per cent (0.1) then the value of £100 received in one year's time in today's money will be £90.91 $(100/(1.1)^1)$. Likewise, at today's value, £100 received in two years' time will be worth £82.64 $(100/(1.1)^2)$ and in ten years' time it will be worth £38.55 $(100/(1.1)^{10})$.

We can see from this that the time at which the money is received makes a lot of difference to how much each £100 is worth to the firm. As a consequence if the time value of money is not taken into consideration when a firm is deciding whether or not to go ahead with an investment project, mistakes can be made.

In assessing the viability of a project the firm estimates the cost of the investment and also the projected annual income stream. It then discounts all future values to take into account the time value of money. The discounted earnings are added and the costs subtracted to determine the NPV. If this figure is positive then the investment will be profitable.

Develop your understanding of NPV by working through the two supplementary screens – Evaluate Your Own Project and The Meaning of Net Present Value – which can be accessed via the Next Page button.

Test your understanding of NPV

45 **Explain why money has a time value.**

46 **Write down a formula in words for the discount factor.**

47 **Why is it important for the firm to take account of the time value of money when making its investment decisions?**

48 Work out the NPV for an investment project with the cash flows shown, at each of the discount rates listed. Conclude in each case whether or not the firm should go ahead with the investment. When you work out the present value of each year's earnings use the discount rates of 10 per cent, 12.5 per cent and 15 per cent. Use the WinEcon calculator to do this, and check your answers using the Evaluate Your Own Project screen. Note that the initial cost is a negative value as it represents a cash outflow. Negative values are shown in brackets.

		Discount rate		
Year	Cost or earnings	10% Present value	12.5% Present value	15% Present value
0	(70,000)	(70,000)	(70,000)	(70,000)
1	20,000			
2	40,000			
3	30,000			
4	20,000			
5	10,000			
NPV		-----------	-----------	-----------
Decision		-----------	-----------	-----------

The Cost of Capital: An Introduction

One of the main problems associated with using the NPV method is to choose the discount rate to use. This should reflect the firm's opportunity cost of capital (i.e. the potential profits it could earn by using its capital elsewhere). A firm should only invest in a specific project if it cannot find a better use for its money elsewhere. The measure of opportunity cost used by most firms is the bank interest rate. If the NPV of a project is positive with this discount rate,

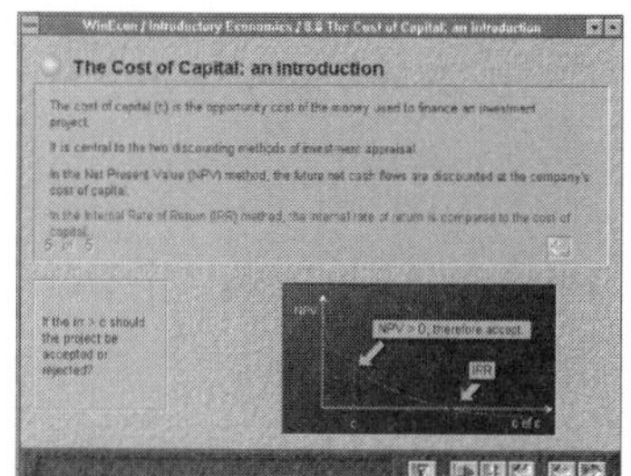

the investment is more profitable than putting the money in the bank and therefore should go ahead. In practice the situation may be more complex with the firm choosing from various projects, some of which are alternatives.

If the true opportunity cost is uncertain the internal rate of return (IRR) approach may be preferred. The IRR is found as the discount rate which produces a NPV of zero. It measures the discount rate at which the project is just viable and can be compared with the cost of capital which needs to be below IRR for the project to go ahead.

The IRR is relatively hard to calculate, but we can make an approximation by drawing a graph. We calculate the NPV of a project at two discount rates, one low rate where the NPV will be positive and one high rate where the NPV will be negative. We then plot the two points and draw a line between them. The discount rate at which this line cuts the NPV axis gives us an estimate of the IRR. An accurate result can easily be obtained using a computer spreadsheet. The WinEcon screen entitled Evaluate Your Own Project includes an IRR calculation, and also plots a graph of NPV at various discount rates.

Firms may prefer decision making using the IRR approach. It provides one possible way of choosing between alternative projects, but often in practice a slightly modified method is required, for example if there is capital rationing and the various possible projects have different costs. Use the Next Page button to move to the supplementary screen entitled Influences. This shows the circumstances influencing two companies considering an identical investment.

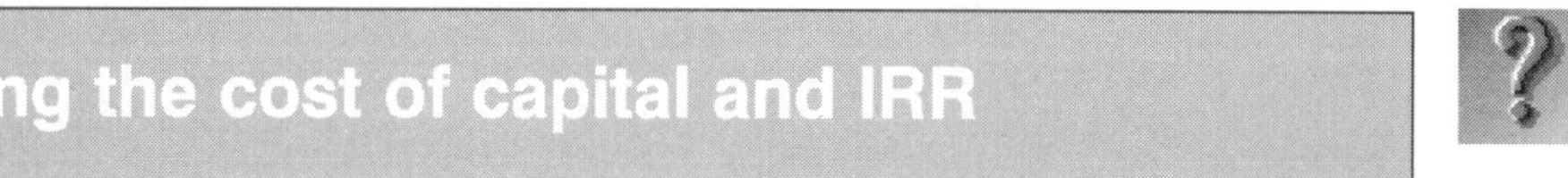

Using the cost of capital and IRR

49 **Explain the relationship between NPV and IRR.**

50 **If a potential investment has a positive NPV, does that mean that a firm should necessarily go ahead with it?**

51 Plot the following pairs of discount rates and NPVs and from these estimate the IRRs for projects 1–5. How might we choose which of the projects to undertake if we can only finance one of them?

Project	Discount rate	NPV	Discount rate	NPV
1	2	15,000	7	–25,000
2	3	20,000	9	–15,000
3	7	10,000	12	–10,000
4	1	10,000	12	–10,000
5	5	5000	11	–15,000

Section 8.8 / Pay-back

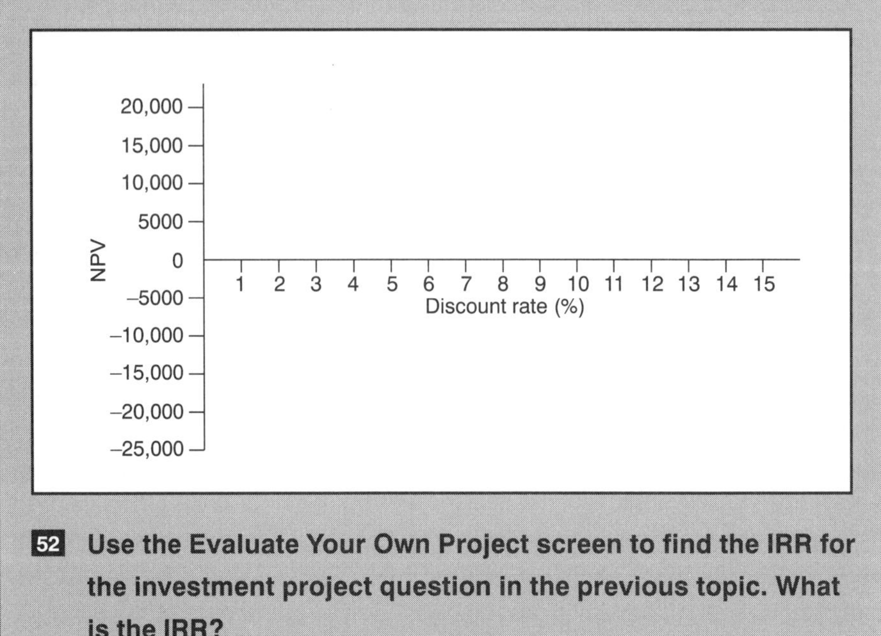

52 **Use the Evaluate Your Own Project screen to find the IRR for the investment project question in the previous topic. What is the IRR?**

Pay-back

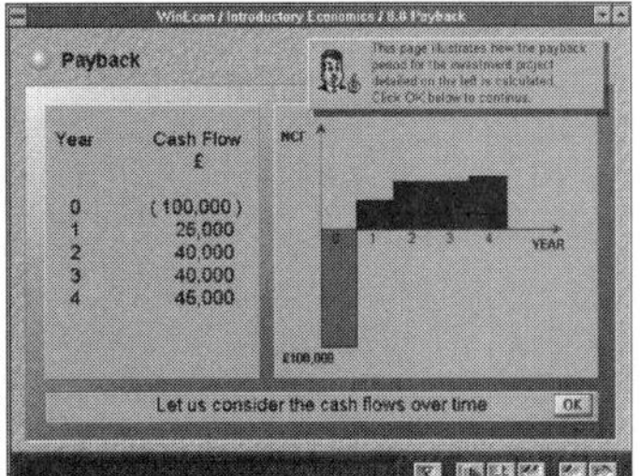

This is a simple method which firms sometimes use to make investment decisions. It looks at how long it will take for the cash flow from an investment to pay-back the cost of that investment. If, for example, a firm has to choose between several investment opportunities it would choose the option that pays back the investment most quickly. Theoretically this is an inferior method to discounting as it does not take into account the time value of money, and as a consequence it could result in wrong decisions being made. Its use is, however, sometimes justified by firms as being appropriate when their earnings streams are very uncertain or very risky. If, for example, the firm is investing in a politically unstable country, it may want to ensure that the investment is paid back as quickly as possible due to the potential risk of losing the whole investment.

Section 8.9: Summary

This chapter examines how factor markets operate, concentrating on the labour market. We see that factor markets interact with goods markets, and that the demand for factors of production is a derived demand.

The supply of labour is analysed using indifference curve analysis and plotting income against leisure. From this we deduce the labour supply curve. Usually it is upward-sloping at low wage rates. At higher wage rates it may bend backwards so that the individual works less hours as the wage rate increases

further. This occurs if the income effect of a change in the wage rate outweighs the substitution effect.

The short-run demand of a firm for labour is analysed under different market structures. We see that the firm chooses to employ labour up to the point where the marginal revenue product (MRP) of labour equals the marginal cost of the factor (MCF). The shapes of these curves are different under different market structures. The market demand curve for labour is quite complicated to obtain, even when both the goods and labour markets are perfectly competitive. This is because there is a different market MRP curve at different wage rates.

Economic rent is defined to be the amount a factor is paid over and above that which is necessary to keep it in its present job. As long as the supply of labour is not perfectly elastic there is an element of economic rent in what some employees are paid. If a factor supply curve is vertical, any payment made for its use consists entirely of economic rent.

When an employer has some monopsonistic power, we see it may be profitable for him to discriminate between different groups of workers in what they are paid.

We analyse the impact of minimum wage legislation. If the minimum wage is set above the market equilibrium, an excess supply of labour is created. The outcome is that unemployment is created and the level of economic activity is reduced.

The viability of an investment project can be judged using the appraisal techniques of net present value (NPV) or internal rate of return (IRR). A project should be undertaken if its NPV is positive, or if its IRR is greater than the cost of capital. A simple technique sometimes preferred for practical convenience is the pay-back method. This looks at how long it will take for the cash flow from an investment to pay back the cost of an investment. In choosing between projects the firm prefers the one that pays back most quickly.

Chapter 9:

Macroeconomic Data

Key macroeconomic variables often feature in news items. 'Unemployment rises to new post-war peak', 'Inflation up again', 'Trade Gap widens' and 'Pound under pressure' are all familiar newspaper headlines. Governments wait anxiously for the latest macroeconomic statistics, fearful of their political impact. Success in managing the economy is usually gauged by the behaviour of key data series, like the unemployment rate, the inflation rate and the exchange rate. The media ensure that just about everyone has a view of the government's economic performance. Our aim in this chapter is to make this an informed view.

Contents

KEYWORDS

- Comovements
- Cyclical
- GDP deflator
- Hyperinflation
- Lagging indicator
- Leading indicator
- Nominal
- Non-trended
- Price index
- Real
- Trended

Section 9.1: Introduction

Macroeconomic data provide information about the performance of the economy. The data comprise measurements of the values of variables at particular points in time. These are usually collected by an official statistical service, such as the Central Statistical Office in the UK.

The behaviour of one key variable led to the emergence of macroeconomics as a discipline within economics: Keynesian economics was devised to explain the rise and persistence of unemployment during the inter-war depression. Contemporary macroeconomics seeks to explain the behaviour of several key variables, the most important of which are summarized below.

Closed economy variables	Open economy variables
Unemployment	Balance of payments
Real GDP growth	Exchange rates
Inflation	
Interest rates	

The measurement of GDP, from which GDP growth can be calculated, is discussed in chapter 10.

We examine these variables in this chapter.

You begin by viewing the data to appreciate why some of the series may require de-trending while others do not. We then briefly examine two ways of de-trending data. You next learn how some key macroeconomic variables are measured, especially inflation and the balance of payments. Finally you see how macroeconomic variables interact with each other, both within a single economy and internationally.

Section 9.2: Macroeconomic Variables

The theme of this section is looking at data to see what information it gives, and noticing any patterns in it. As you examine the graphs it becomes clear that some macroeconomic variables have strong upward trends, and if we are to explain their short-run movements we need to de-trend the data (i.e. remove the influence of the variable's secular or long-run trend).

Trended and Non-Trended Variables

This WinEcon screen lets you view the data of your choice. Read the first two text cards and examine in turn each trended variable. Look for a pattern in the

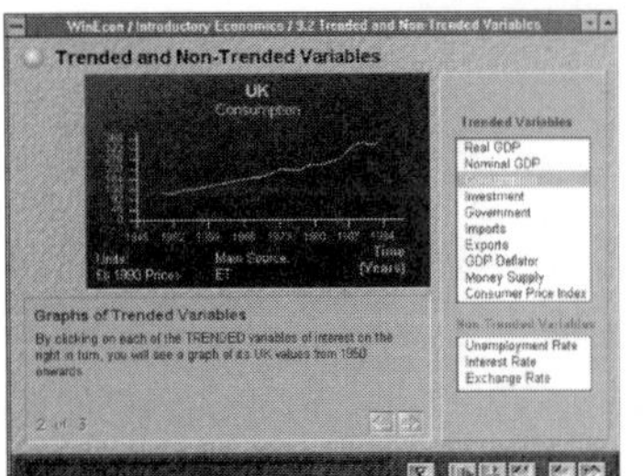

movement of each series over time. A variable which has a general tendency to move in a particular direction over a long period of time is said to have a trend.

The third text card invites you to view the behaviour of non-trended variables. In fact these series do appear to have mild trends – unemployment and interest upwards, and the exchange rate downwards. Of course, we would not expect these to be permanent trends: similar plots drawn in 20 years' time would not be expected to have the same trends. The unemployment rate has a natural upper limit of 100 per cent and we would not expect the exchange rate to reach zero. Notice how recent movements in the unemployment rate are far more volatile than other post-war changes.

What have you noticed about these trends?

01 Which trended variable appears to have the more volatile upward trend?

02 Briefly explain the main features of the exchange rate graph.

The Behaviour of Real and Nominal Variables

In this topic we distinguish between real and nominal variables. A nominal variable is expressed in current *money* terms. For example, if you were asked what your nominal spending was last week, you would simply add the money expenditures on each good and service you purchased – say, £20. You would not reply 'five pizzas'. If you were asked for your real spending on pizzas then you could reply five pizzas, and not £20. This is the basic distinction between nominal and real spending.

Note that changes in real spending indicate different quantities of goods being bought, and alter nominal spending in proportion. For example, a doubling of your real spending doubles your nominal expenditure if the price is unchanged. But changes in nominal spending may also arise from changes in the prices of goods – for example, a doubling of the price of pizzas doubles your nominal expenditure if your real purchases are unchanged.

Measurement of macroeconomic variables in real terms attempts to remove the 'price change' influence on the variable's nominal value. It is often convenient to measure expenditures rather than actual quantities of goods. A measure of real expenditure in different years is obtained by expressing each year's expenditure in constant prices (i.e. in the prices that were operative in the year that is chosen as a base year for comparison purposes). This is done by valuing expenditure at current prices to find nominal expenditure, and then adjusting this in line with the price changes that have

taken place between the base year and the current year. For example, if prices had doubled between 1970 (which we wish to use as the base year) and 1995, and your actual, nominal expenditure in 1995 was £500, your real expenditure in 1970 prices would be £500/2, or £250.

The distinction between nominal and real GDP is explained in section 10.4.

Work through the text cards and examine in turn the graphs of the real, nominal and 'ratio' variables.

Test your understanding of real and nominal variables

03 **Briefly explain the major differences in the trends of real and nominal variables.**

04 **'If prices are rising over time, the time trend of nominal consumption must be steeper than the time trend in real spending.' Is this statement true when real spending increases over time? Provide a brief explanation.**

Nominal and Real Interest Rates

The distinction between real and nominal has a special meaning when applied to interest rates, and this is the focus of this three-screen WinEcon topic. We are all familiar with the nominal interest rate – the rate of return we receive when we hold an interest-bearing deposit or some other financial asset. We may also pay a nominal interest rate on loans and overdrafts from the bank or building society. To illustrate the difference between nominal and real interest rates, we consider the nominal and real return an individual will receive from an interest-bearing deposit with a building society.

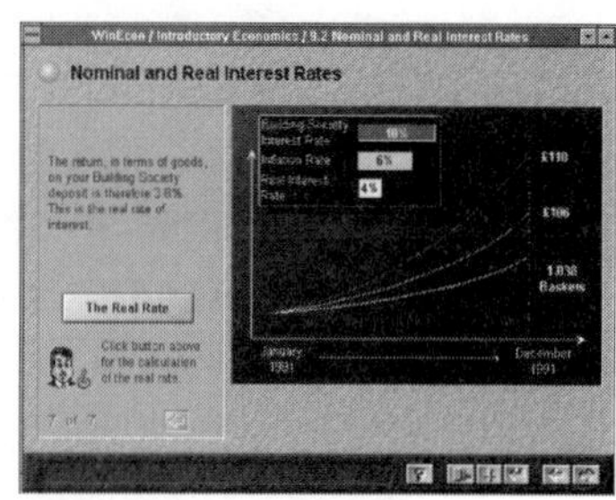

Work through the text cards on the first of these WinEcon screens to appreciate the difference in the two rates. On card seven you can discover the formula for the real interest rate by clicking The Real Rate button. Notice that as well as the correct formula there is a useful approximation which is very easy to calculate.

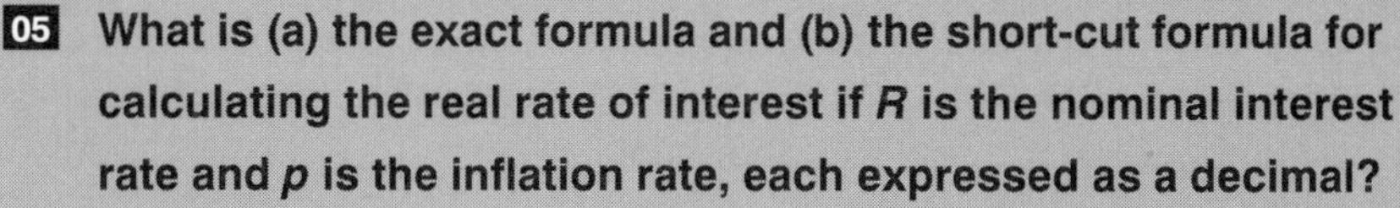

About interest rates

05 **What is (a) the exact formula and (b) the short-cut formula for calculating the real rate of interest if R is the nominal interest rate and p is the inflation rate, each expressed as a decimal?**

06 **'If prices are falling, the real interest rate and the nominal interest rates will be identical' – true or false? Provide a brief explanation.**

07 Calculate the real interest rate using the following data. (Use the correct and the short-cut methods.)

Interest rate (%)	Inflation rate (%)	Correct real rate (%)	Short-cut method (%)
5	2		
20	18		
10	15		
5	–1		

Nominal and Real Interest Rates (2) and (3)

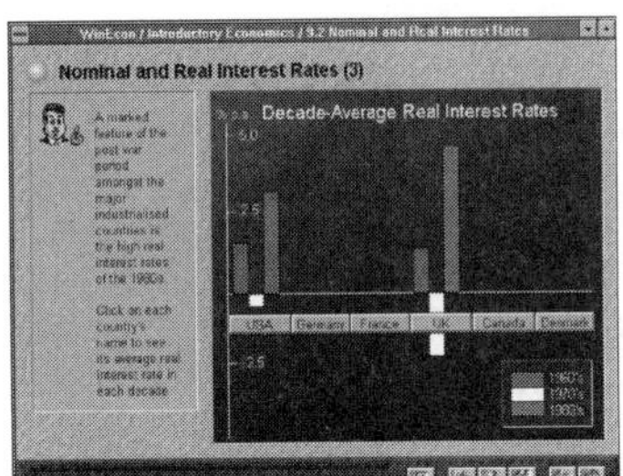

On the first of these screens you discover how real interest rates can be negative. On the next you find that real interest rates were negative in many countries during the 1970s, but that they generally have been quite high during the 1980s. A clue to understanding why this may have been the case lies in the fact that inflation was far higher in the 1970s than the 1980s. One question which naturally arises is 'Why should rational people hold an asset with a negative return when they could hold money?' To answer this question we have to determine the real return on holding money. The nominal return on money is zero – there is no interest paid on the cash that you hold. But the real return on money is the nominal return minus the inflation rate, or the negative of the inflation rate. The difference between the rate of return on an interest-bearing asset and money is (using the short-cut formula):

$$\begin{pmatrix}\text{Real return}\\ \text{on deposit}\end{pmatrix} \text{ minus } \begin{pmatrix}\text{Real return}\\ \text{on money}\end{pmatrix} \text{ equals } \begin{pmatrix}\text{Nominal interest}\\ \text{rate}\end{pmatrix}$$

$$(R - p) \quad - \quad (0 - p) \quad = \quad R$$

where R is the nominal interest rate and p is inflation rate.

So, even though the rate of return on the interest-bearing asset is negative it is still higher than the real return on money.

Test your understanding of real rates of return

08 Calculate using the full (not the short-cut) method the difference in the real return on an interest-bearing deposit and the real return on cash, which pays no interest.

Interest-bearing rate (%)	Inflation rate (%)	Deposit vs Cash real rate difference (%)
10	4	
20	14	
5	8	
10	–4	

Hyperinflations

Hyperinflations are periods of excessive increases in the price level. They have been experienced by western European countries (largely in the inter-war years), the eastern European countries (more recently) and Latin American countries (again more recently). On this WinEcon screen we provide you with some interesting examples of hyperinflation.

Step through the first five text cards and then click the country buttons to see how rapidly prices rose in these countries. Click the More button in the cases of Austria and Germany to see what life was like living in an economy experiencing hyperinflation. Card six describes the inflation rate in Hungary in 1945 and you are invited to guess the price of a loaf of bread under such a dramatic inflation rate.

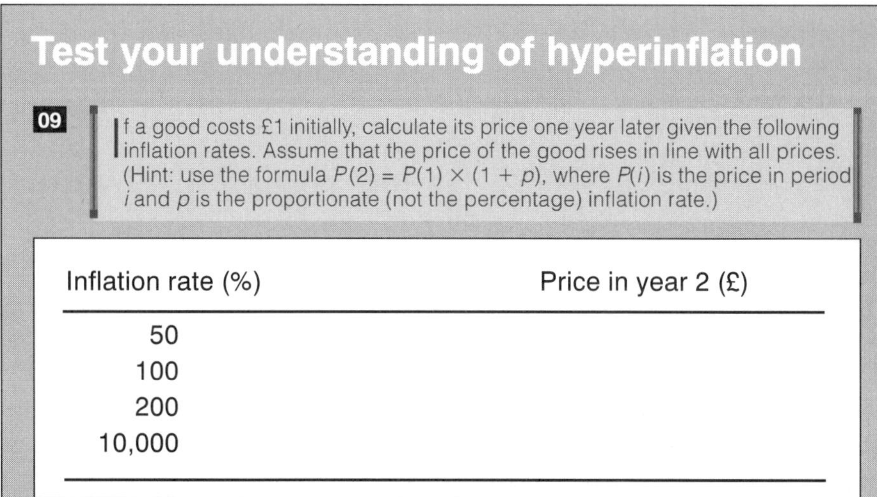

Test your understanding of hyperinflation

09 If a good costs £1 initially, calculate its price one year later given the following inflation rates. Assume that the price of the good rises in line with all prices. (Hint: use the formula $P(2) = P(1) \times (1 + p)$, where $P(i)$ is the price in period i and p is the proportionate (not the percentage) inflation rate.)

Inflation rate (%)	Price in year 2 (£)
50	
100	
200	
10,000	

Fitting Linear Trends

You can discover more about fitting a line to data in section 25.3 of WinEcon in the topics Fitting a Line to the Data and Linear Regression (or Fitting a Line to the Data). [N.B. These topics do not appear in this workbook.]

Many of the variables which macroeconomics seeks to explain are subject to secular or long-term trends. Real GDP, for example, has grown on average for many decades and most people expect this growth to continue into the indefinite future. Economists often find it necessary to remove the long-run trend from the data series so that they can focus on the variable's short-run or cyclical behaviour. In this topic you learn one way of achieving this separation of trend and cycle.

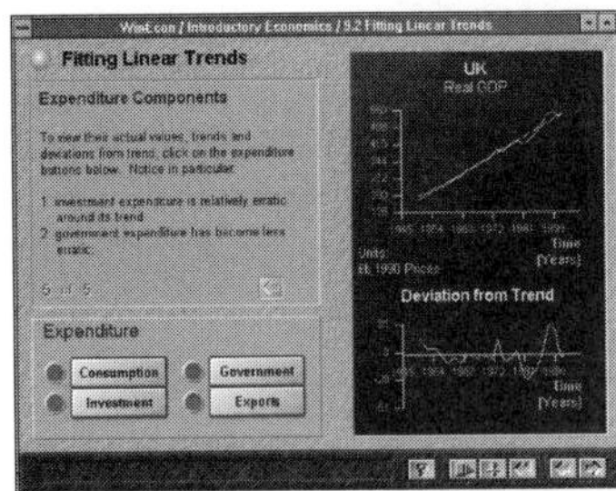

Step through the first four WinEcon text cards to see how the linear (or straight-line) trend can be fitted to real GDP, and deviations from this trend then calculated. When linear trends of this sort are fitted, it is assumed that the trend has not changed over the period. Some observers believe that the trend growth rate in the UK (and other countries) declined after 1972, following the first oil price shock, but the graph assumes a single, linear trend over the whole period. Notice that the deviations of output around this trend are more variable in the 1980s. On card five you are given the opportunity to observe the trend-cycle decomposition of the main components of GDP.

See what you know about a linear trend

10 Calculate the deviation from the linear trend of the following imaginary variable.

Year	Variable	Deviation from trend
1980	100	
1981	105	
1982	110	
1982	115	
1983	120	

The topic Logarithmic Functions in section 22.3 (in WinEcon only, not this workbook) defines and explains logarithms.

Trends in Levels and Logarithms

Macroeconomists often take logarithms of variables before they fit trends to them and on this WinEcon screen you will discover why. The spreadsheet contains imaginary data for a variable, Y. This variable increases at a constant growth rate of 0.25, or 25 per cent, per annum.

On the first text card click the Show button to graph the series for *Y* and then read the second text card for an explanation of its shape. Now step through the last two text cards, using the formula pop-up to calculate the logarithm of variable *Y*. You will find that the time series plot of the logarithm of *Y* is a straight line. To summarize: the logarithm of a variable with a constant growth rate has a constant trend. For many macroeconomic series, it is thought more appropriate to take trends of the logarithms of these variables.

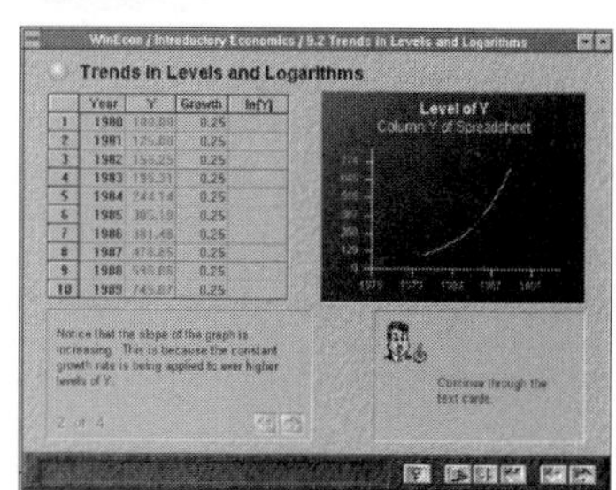

Applying a linear trend

11 Draw a linear trend through the series in the graph below (which is identical to that on the screen). Your trend need not be drawn too precisely.

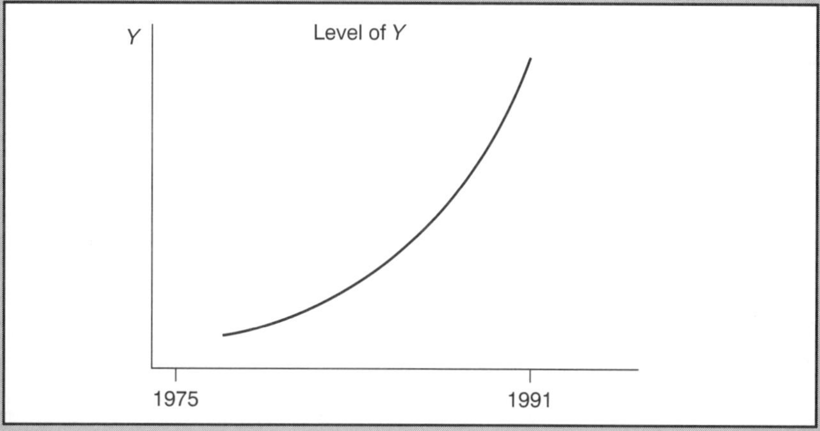

Y

Level of *Y*

1975

1991

12 **Would your trend be a useful way of predicting future values of *Y*? Briefly explain.**

13 **Which of the following best describes the deviations of *Y* from its linear trend on your graph?**

(a) Positive deviations at start and negative at the end ☐

(b) Negative deviations at start and positive deviations at the end ☐

(c) Positive deviations at start and end of the period and negative deviations in the middle ☐

14 **A variable grows at 10 per cent per period. If its initial value is 100, what is its value after one period and what is the difference between the new and initial value? Repeat the calculation, but assume the initial value is 500. What do you learn from your answer?**

15 **A variable grows at 10 per cent per period. Its initial value is 100. Calculate the natural logarithm of the initial value of the variable, the natural logarithm of its value after one period and the difference between the two. Repeat the calculation, but assume the initial value is 500. What do you learn from your answer?**

Deviations from Linear and Log-Linear Trends

The choice of de-trending variables either in levels or logarithms does make a difference to the de-trended series and on this screen you will see these differences for a number of variables. Before you read the cards, recall one important lesson from the previous topic. A variable which grows geometrically (i.e. at a constant rate) will have a log-linear trend. If we fitted a simple linear trend to such a variable, we would observe positive deviations from trend at the start and end of the period and negative deviations in the middle. Look out for this feature when we plot the data on this screen.

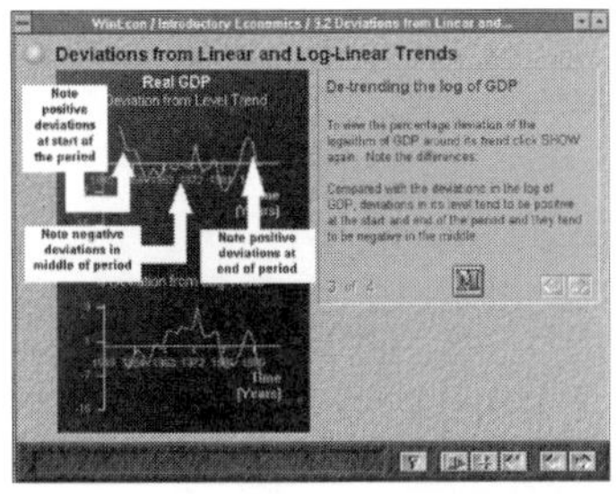

Work through the first three WinEcon text cards. The first noteworthy feature of the two graphs on the left of the screen is how different they look – the choice of taking trend in the level or the logarithm of the variable is clearly important. And, as the pop-up cards emphasize, deviations from the trend in the level of GDP do tend to be positive at the start and end, and negative in the middle of the period. This suggests that we should take logarithms of real GDP before fitting the trend. For information about how the deviations from trend are calculated click the More button. The last text card shows the differences between deviations from trend in levels and logarithms for a number of other variables.

16 **Which is the correct definition of a percentage deviation of the logarithm of real GDP ($\ln Y$) around its trend (Y^{**})?**

(a) $\ln Y/Y^{**}$ ☐

(b) $(\ln Y/Y^{**})100$ ☐

(c) $(\ln Y - Y^{**})100$ ☐

(d) $\ln Y - Y^{**}$ ☐

Linear Trends with Constant Growth

The exercise on this WinEcon screen is a reminder of the importance of taking deviations from the logarithm of variables which tend to grow geometrically. You are invited to create data for a series which grows at a constant growth rate (of your choosing). You will then be shown the deviation of your series around its trend in levels to reinforce a lesson from previous topics.

Annual Real GDP Growth Rates

We have seen that deviations around the trend in the logarithm of a macroeconomic variable may be an appropriate way of separating the short-run changes in a variable from its long-run trend. Economists have increasingly adopted an alternative method, which is the subject of this topic and the next. In this approach, the growth rate of the variable is calculated in each period. These growth rates may then be compared with the average or mean growth rate over the whole period.

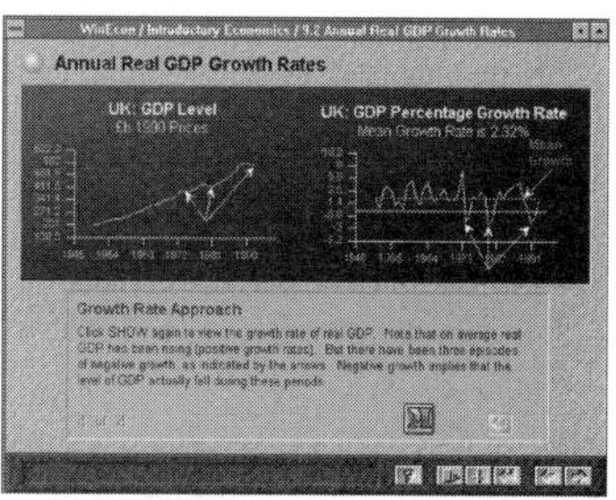

Work through the first three WinEcon text cards and the Show button on card three will reveal the level of GDP plotted against time. On card four, the Show button will reveal the growth rate of this series. Notice how variable growth rates are and how, on several occasions, growth can be negative (i.e. the level of real GDP actually falls).

Test your understanding of real GDP growth rates

17 Calculate the annual percentage growth rate of the following imaginary GDP.

Year	Real GDP ($m)	Growth rate (%)
1980	1500	–
1981	1800	
1982	1600	
1983	2500	
1984	3125	

The topic Logarithms and Growth Rates: A Review in section 14.5 also discusses growth rate calculations.

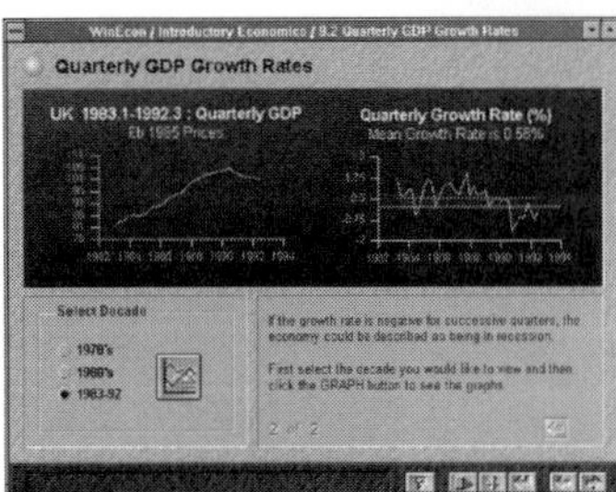

Quarterly GDP Growth Rates

Because annual data may hide growth rate variations within the year, this WinEcon screen allows you to view the quarterly growth rate of real GDP in the UK. The data are organized into sub-periods, which you view separately.

Identifying recessions

18 **If a recession is defined as a succession of negative quarterly GDP growth rates, identify (using the diagrams on the WinEcon screen) the periods of recession in the UK since 1979.**

Section 9.3: Measuring Macroeconomic Variables

The measurement of macroeconomic variables raises several practical and conceptual problems. The most important of these you will discover in chapter 10 in which we examine the problems associated with measuring a country's aggregate output, expenditure and income. In this section you examine the problems in measuring inflation and the balance of payments.

Measuring the Price Level and Inflation

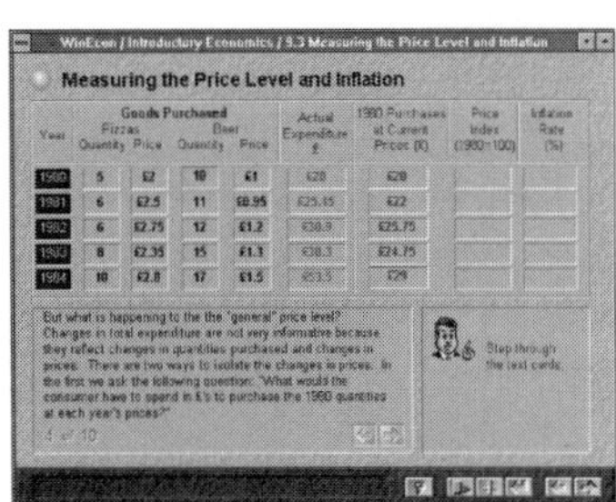

On this WinEcon screen you discover how to calculate a price index. If the economy produced and consumed only one commodity, say bread, there would be no problem in calculating the price index: it would simply be the price of a loaf in each period, possibly expressed as a ratio of some base-year price. The problem arises when we are confronted with a large number of goods and services whose quantities are measured rather differently (numbers of Boeing 747s, pints of beer, numbers of safety pins, litres of milk etc.).

The basic principles of price level calculation can be appreciated by considering the consumption of two goods, pizzas and beer. Our aim is to construct a price index for an economy consuming imaginary quantities of these two goods at imaginary prices.

As you step through the first three WinEcon text cards, the imaginary data are presented. Note how prices and quantities consumed combine to determine aggregate nominal expenditure. Changes in expenditure are due to two

factors: first the quantities purchased of the two goods may have changed and secondly their prices may also have changed. Our aim in devising a price index is to isolate and measure the influence of price changes alone. For overall information on the price level we have to combine price data for different goods, giving greater weight to items which are more important.

On this screen you discover two methods of computing a price index. In the first we ask the question ‘What expenditure would be required to purchase base year (i.e. 1980) quantities at current prices?’, and we compare this with the actual base year expenditure to form a price index. This method is explained in detail on the text cards four to six.

The price index we derive using this ‘base-weighted’ approach depends crucially on the quantities consumed in the base year because these quantities act as ‘weights’ in the calculation of the average price level. On card seven you can see what happens to the price index when these base year quantities change.

To calculate the price index by the second method we ask a slightly different question: ‘What would be total expenditure if prices remained at their 1980 level, given the actual quantities consumed?’ By comparing this hypothetical expenditure with actual expenditure, we can gain some idea of the increase in average prices. In effect, this method uses current quantities as ‘weights’ in the price level calculation. Work through cards eight to ten to find out about this second method of calculation. Make sure you understand why this method is referred to as a ‘current-weighted’ index.

The method of calculating index numbers described on this screen is called the ‘aggregative method’. You may be familiar with the UK ‘retail price index’, which is effectively a current-weighted index but calculated (for convenience) by a somewhat different method known as the ‘relatives method’.

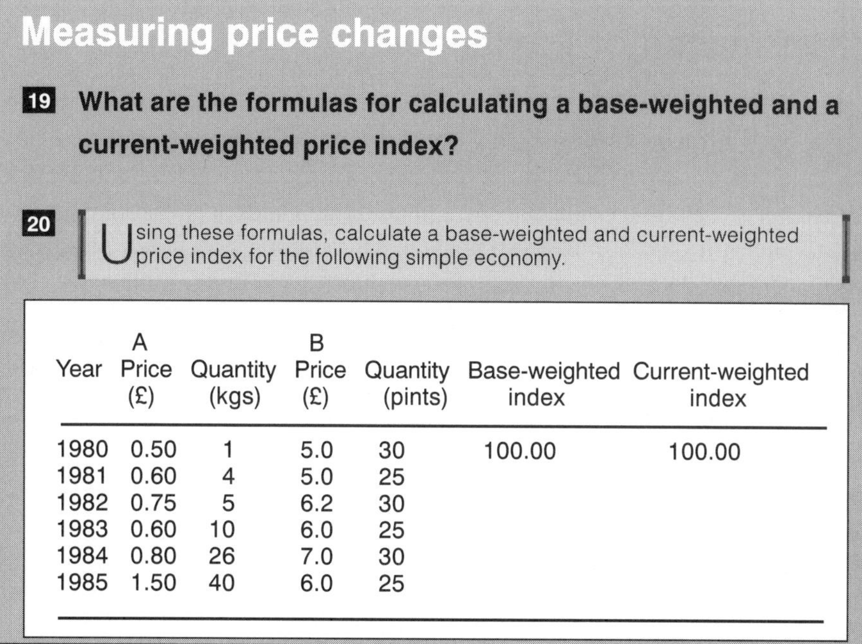

Measuring price changes

19 **What are the formulas for calculating a base-weighted and a current-weighted price index?**

20 Using these formulas, calculate a base-weighted and current-weighted price index for the following simple economy.

Year	A Price (£)	A Quantity (kgs)	B Price (£)	B Quantity (pints)	Base-weighted index	Current-weighted index
1980	0.50	1	5.0	30	100.00	100.00
1981	0.60	4	5.0	25		
1982	0.75	5	6.2	30		
1983	0.60	10	6.0	25		
1984	0.80	26	7.0	30		
1985	1.50	40	6.0	25		

21 **Measure the inflation rate in 1985 by both methods.**

22 **Explain the difference in the two indices for the year 1985.**

Calculating the GDP Deflator

Nominal and real GDP, between which the GDP deflator forms a link, are mentioned in section 10.4 in the topic The Expenditure Approach.

One widely used index of prices is the GDP deflator. This is simply the ratio of nominal GDP to GDP measured in constant base-year prices. This is similar to the second method of computing the price index (i.e. a current-weighted index). Since GDP is a measure of the total output of goods and services produced in the domestic economy, its coverage is very wide. For example, the GDP deflator will include the prices of Air Buses and high-speed trains as well as haircuts and orange juice. The consumer price index is more restricted in its coverage, including as it does goods purchased by the typical or average household. Complete the task set on this screen and answer the following questions.

Nominal and real GDP

23 **Real GDP is calculated using constant 1990 prices. What is the value of the GDP deflator in 1990?**

24 **In 1994, real GDP was £200 million and the GDP deflator was 150. What was the nominal GDP?**

The Balance of Payments

The balance of payments is a record of national transactions which take place over a given period involving residents of other countries. These transactions will cover purchases and sales of goods (visibles) and services (invisibles). They also cover transfers (including dividends, interest payments etc., which are also called invisibles) and purchases and sales of financial assets like bonds and shares (capital account).

On this WinEcon screen you can find further details of these items. Work through each one carefully, making sure you understand them all, and then answer the following questions.

Entering items in the balance of payments

25 **In the balance of payments of a hypothetical country, the balancing item is zero. You also know that the capital account surplus is $200 million and the surplus on the invisible account is $400 million. What is the current account deficit?**

26 **Where do the following transactions appear in the balance of payments accounts?**

(a) Life insurance policy purchased by UK individual from an Icelandic insurance company: ______

(b) Sale of personal computer by UK company to Danish resident: ______

(c) Purchase of personal computer by UK household from British company: ______

(d) Interest payment received by UK resident on account held in a German bank: ______

(e) Loan from a US bank to UK resident to purchase a German car: ______

Using the Next Page button takes you to The Balance of Payments (2), a supplementary screen which shows how currency devaluation is used to tackle a balance of payments deficit. The resulting J-curve is introduced and explained on the text cards.

Section 9.4: Interactions Between Macroeconomic Variables

Having examined the behaviour of a number of key macroeconomic variables and investigated problems of measurement in two of them, you will now have an opportunity to learn how these variables may interact with each other. Why is such interaction important? Economic theories often make distinct predictions about the behaviour of macroeconomic variables: for example, the Keynesian consumption function (in its simplest form) states that national income is the main determinant of aggregate consumption expenditure. If this theory were correct, we would expect to find an association in the data between GDP (which moves closely with national income) and consumption. Our main aim in this section is to discover and note key interrelationships amongst our macroeconomic variables.

We devote a topic each to two specific interrelationships which figure prominently in macroeconomic debate: the behaviour of inflation over the business cycle and the relationship between the money supply and the inflation rate. But we begin by investigating the comovements of several variables with real GDP growth.

Comovements with GDP Growth

'How do variables behave over the business cycle?' This is the question we ask on this WinEcon screen. You will discover three types of behaviour:

(1) Pro-cyclical: the variable moves in sympathy with the cycle.

(2) Counter-cyclical: the variable tends to fall when real output rises.

(3) A-cyclical: the variable displays no clear cyclical pattern.

Chapter 25, again in WinEcon only, explains more about the correlation coefficient.

On this WinEcon screen we use a statistical measure of association – the 'correlation coefficient'. If two variables are strongly associated, this coefficient is close to one (or minus one if the variables are negatively associated); where two variables are not associated with each other, the correlation coefficient is close to zero. Imagine that a keen cricketer noted his score and the number of hours training he had completed in the week before each match. We would expect to find a strong association between these two (i.e. the correlation coefficient would be close to one). The same cricketer might also keep a record of the number of drinks he had the evening before the game. Comparing the number of drinks with the number of runs scored, we might expect a negative correlation coefficient (close to minus one), excess drinking being associated with low scores. We would not expect to find any association between the number of runs scored and the length of his hair on the morning of the game – the correlation coefficient in this case would be zero.

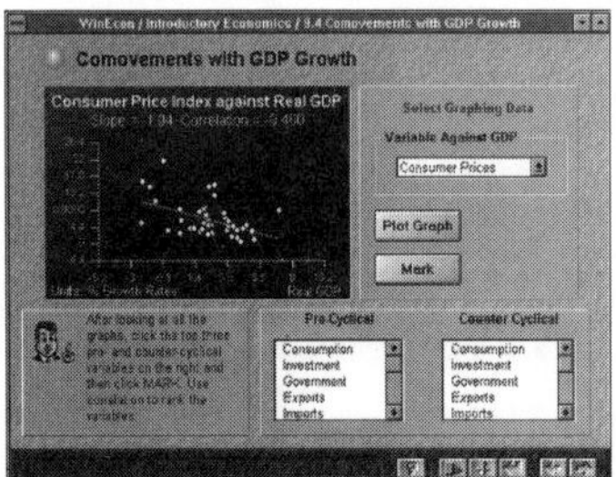

Work through the text cards to the end, and complete the exercise set on this screen.

About variable comovements

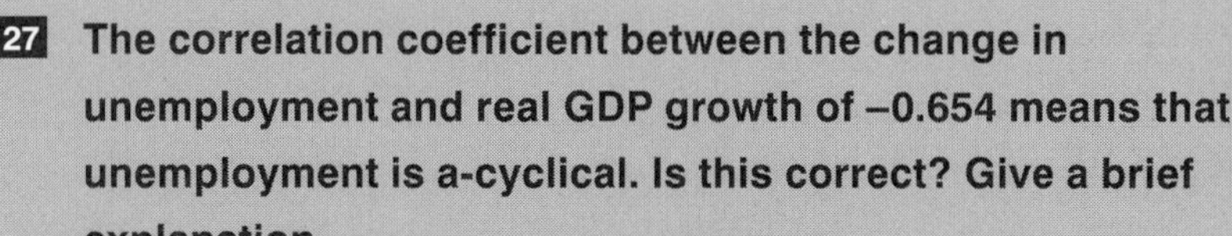

27 **The correlation coefficient between the change in unemployment and real GDP growth of –0.654 means that unemployment is a-cyclical. Is this correct? Give a brief explanation.**

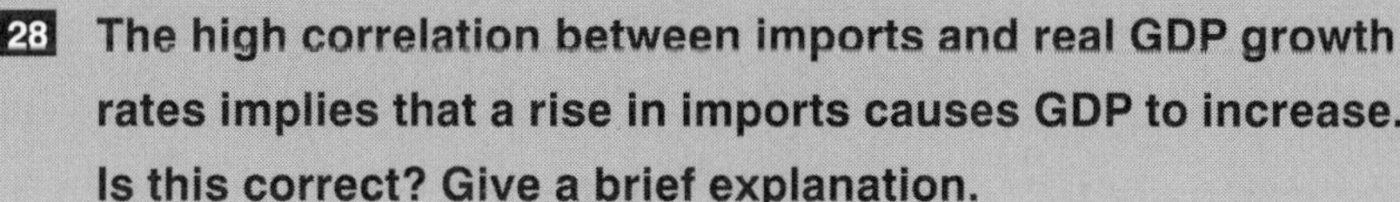

28 **The high correlation between imports and real GDP growth rates implies that a rise in imports causes GDP to increase. Is this correct? Give a brief explanation.**

Lead and Lag Comovements

Macroeconomic variables may show weak contemporaneous correlation, but they may be strongly correlated when one of the variables is lagged (say by one year). We refer to these comovements as leading or lagging. A variable has a lagging pro-cyclical comovement if its growth rate rises after GDP growth rises, and it has a lagging counter-cyclical comovement if its growth rate falls after GDP growth rises. A variable has a leading pro-cyclical comovement if its growth rate rises before GDP growth rises, and it has a leading counter-cyclical comovement if its growth rate generally falls before GDP growth rises.

Before you work through the tasks set on this screen, first ask whether you would expect each of the three variables considered – money supply, interest rates and unemployment – to have leading or lagging comovements with real GDP. Enter your selection below before examining the data. Next work through the screen and enter the correct answers in the space provided. (For obvious reasons, this workbook does not attempt to provide answers for your expectations!)

Enter what you expect the comovements with real GDP to be:

Interest rates (Lead/Lag/Both/Neither) ☐
Money supply (Lead/Lag/Both/Neither) ☐
Unemployment (Lead/Lag/Both/Neither) ☐

29 **Having worked through the screen, enter the actual comovements with real GDP:**

Interest rates (Lead/Lag/Both/Neither) ☐
Money supply (Lead/Lag/Both/Neither) ☐
Unemployment (Lead/Lag/Both/Neither) ☐

Test your understanding of lead and lag comovement

30 **The high negative correlation (of –0.722) between real GDP growth and changes in unemployment a year later means that unemployment changes are caused by changes in GDP. Is this correct? Give a brief explanation.**

31 **Is it possible for a variable to be both a leading and lagging indicator of the business cycle? Provide a brief explanation.**

Inflation over the Business Cycle

Theories of economic fluctuations, as we shall see in chapter 16, make distinctive predictions about the behaviour of inflation over the business cycle. Our task on this WinEcon screen is to determine the nature of this relationship from the data.

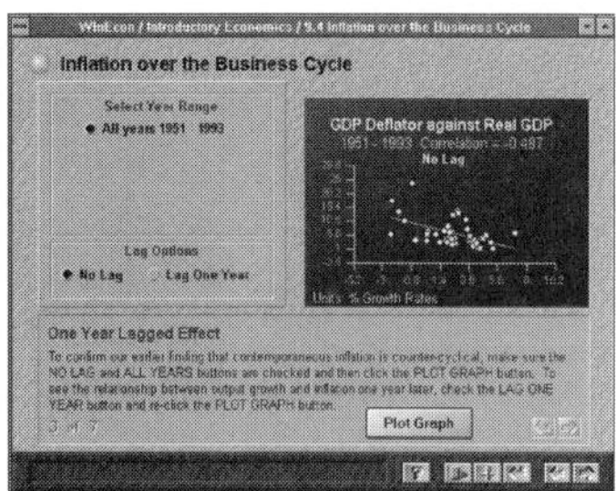

Read the first three text cards and then use the graph to establish the unlagged correlation between the inflation rate and real GDP growth (click the Plot Graph button). You will find that over the whole period, inflation is counter-cyclical (and more weakly so when inflation is treated as a lagging indicator). It is always possible that, taken overall, inflation is counter-cyclical, but within selected sub-periods it is pro-cyclical (i.e. GDP growth and inflation are positively associated). Work through the task set on card four and note the changing patterns of GDP growth and inflation within sub-periods, and when inflation is treated as a lagged indicator.

Money Supply and Inflation

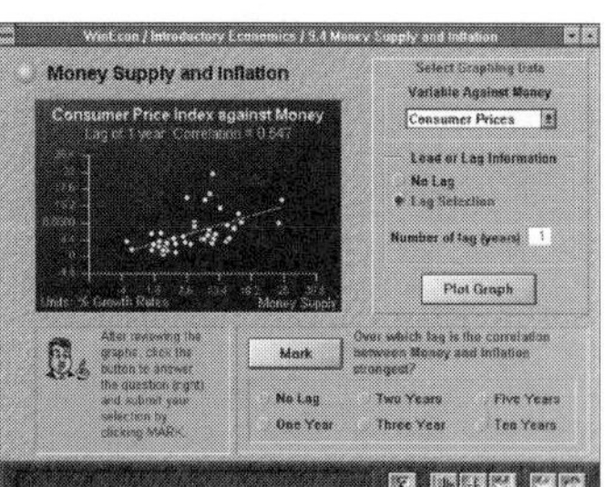

One of most controversial areas of macroeconomics concerns the relationship between the growth of the money supply and inflation. On this screen we examine the UK data on this relationship, taking as our measure of money the relatively wide M4 definition.

Read the first three text cards, and observe the contemporaneous correlation between inflation (the growth rate of the GDP deflator) and monetary growth (the growth rate of M4). The observed correlation coefficient of 0.331 suggests a positive (but not particularly strong) association between the two variables. Now follow the task set on card four.

Interpret this data

The high positive correlation (0.6) between money growth and inflation two years later means that monetary growth causes inflation. Is this correct? Give a brief explanation.

International Comovements

In this last topic you investigate the comovements in different countries' growth rates. It used to be said that 'when America sneezed, Europe caught a cold' and it is certainly true that politicians frequently blame 'world recession' for poor domestic economic performance. There is some truth to this defence, as this screen explains. Work through the tasks set in WinEcon and note carefully how international growth rates are closely correlated.

Section 9.5: Summary

The main aim of macroeconomic theory is to explain the performance of key macroeconomic variables and model relationships between them. In this chapter you have examined many of these data series and learnt to interpret the patterns which they show.

You have discovered what is meant by trend, and found that economists sometimes wish to remove it so that short-run fluctuations can be seen clearly. Methods for removing a linear or log-linear trend have been described, and you have seen examples of them using data on real GDP and exports. You have also learnt to distinguish between nominal and real variables, and seen a particular relationship between them in the case of interest rates. The impact of hyperinflations has also been explored.

You have seen how a price index is calculated and used to compare average price levels in different periods. An example of such an index is the GDP deflator. You have also learnt how to interpret the information in the balance of payments.

The correlation coefficient has been used to measure the extent to which various series move in line with GDP growth. Lead and lag relationships have been studied, and the pattern of inflation has been examined in the contexts of the business cycle and the money supply. You have also explored international comovements by plotting growth rates for different countries against one another.

Chapter 10:

National Income Accounting

The current level of economic activity and the rate of economic growth are central concerns in macroeconomics. They influence the level of unemployment, the state of the balance of payments and various other important macroeconomic variables. The actual level of economic activity (and its rate of change) are recorded in the National Income Accounts. These accounts contain a whole range of economic statistics relating to production and income and they provide a framework for analysing the level of economic activity.

Contents

KEYWORDS

- Circular flow of income
- Consumers' expenditure
- Expenditure approach
- Exports and imports
- Factor cost
- Government consumption
- Gross domestic fixed capital formation
- Gross domestic product
- Gross national product
- Income approach
- Inventory investment
- Market prices
- Measure of economic welfare
- Net national product
- Output approach

Section 10.1: Introduction

One of the central questions in macroeconomics is how the total level of production in any given period is determined. This question is examined in several of the chapters that follow this one. However, before you can examine theories relating to the determination of output, you must learn how output is defined and measured. In this chapter you will explore national income accounting – a subject largely concerned with the definition and measurement of the key macroeconomic variables which make up output, expenditure and income.

You will find that national income can theoretically be calculated in any of three ways. These are called the 'output approach', the 'income approach' and the 'expenditure approach'.

Since national income for a particular year represents the value of goods and services available during that time period for consumption and investment, comparisons of national income are used in discussing economic welfare. There are, however, other things that contribute to economic welfare which are not included in national income, while some of the items that are counted in national income may not actually increase welfare. Here, we will learn about the 'measure of economic welfare' (MEW), which has been proposed as a better measure of economic well-being.

Section 10.2: Defining Output

The national income of a country is the value of all final goods and services that become available to its citizens in a particular period of time, usually a year. Since the value of any output is measured either by how much is paid for it or how much it costs to produce, you might expect 'total product' simply to be equal to the sum of the values of all transactions in a period. Unfortunately, however, measuring total product is not quite so simple:

(1) Not all transactions reflect productive activity. A distinction must be drawn between those transactions which do and those, known as 'transfer payments', which do not.

(2) There is a further problem associated with adding up the value of all transactions. It would result in 'double counting'.

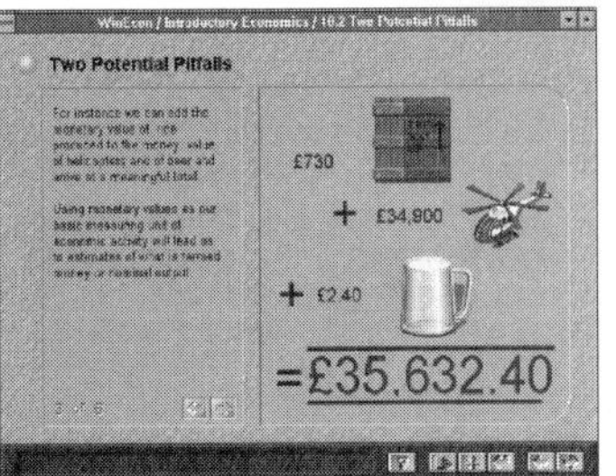

Two Potential Pitfalls

One of the main purposes of national income accounting is to measure the total product of an economy over a period. In order to do this we must find a common unit in which to measure many different kinds of output. Work through the screen and make a note of your findings by answering the questions below.

Record your findings

01 What is the common denominator used to measure total product?

02 Why can we not just sum the total monetary value of all transactions in order to estimate national output?

Transfer Payments

Certain economic transactions do not reflect productive activity, and must therefore not be included in any estimate of total output. Money is handed over in these transactions without any product or service being exchanged for it. Such payments, which include state pensions and social security benefits are called transfer payments.

It is not always obvious which category an economic transaction fits into. Indeed, certain transactions are defined as transfer payments even though a strong case can be made for their being designated as output. Explore the five questions on this WinEcon screen. They will help you to distinguish between transactions which reflect productive activity and transfer payments. Read carefully the comments provided by WinEcon on any answer you choose.

Test your understanding of transfer payments

03 'Double counting and transfer payments are basically the same kind of problem. They reflect activity which is not productive, so it is obvious that they should not be included as product.' Explain why this statement is untrue.

04 **Explain why purchases of new cars indicate current production but payments of pensions to senior citizens do not.**

05 **Transactions which contribute to (or reflect) productive activity generally involve two kinds of flow. What are they?**

06 **Transfer payments usually only involve one kind of flow: true or false?** ______

07 **Why is a spouse's housework not counted as production?**

08 **Write down one example of a transaction which reflects production, but which in fact counts as a transfer payment.**

09 **Write down one example of a transaction which might be thought to constitute a transfer payment, but which in fact counts as production.**

Double Counting: A Potential Error

The problem of double counting is different from transfer payments. It must be avoided to prevent certain outputs from being counted more than once. In this WinEcon topic there are two screens (A Potential Error and Avoiding the Problem). They show a simple example involving three firms. One firm produces coal and iron ore; the second produces steel; the third produces cutlery. Work your way through this example to learn about the danger that the iron, coal and steel will be double counted. Make sure you understand what is meant by the term 'value added'.

Check your understanding of the basic concepts

10 **In the cutlery example above, which commodity is raw material, which is the intermediate good and which is the final good? Give a definition of each category.**

11 **If the value of all transactions recorded in the WinEcon example were simply summed, how many times would the output of iron and coal have been counted? Explain.**

12 To avoid double counting when estimating national output we must ensure that any particular output is only counted once. There are two ways to do this. What are they? Write a sentence about each.

13 Agriphilia is a rural economy where production is concentrated solely on the production of foodstuffs. There are two collective enterprises, one a farming co-operative (Earth) which produces corn, grapes and milk, the other a manufacturing operation (Wind) which produces wine, bread and cheese. Wind buys grapes, corn and milk from Earth, from which it manufactures bread, cheese and wine.

This year, Wind produced and sold the following amounts of its three products: bread £10,000, wine £5000, and cheese £8000.

Earth produced and sold the following amounts of its three products: corn £8100, grapes £3600, and milk £4200.

Wind bought a third of Earth's output of each commodity.

Complete the table below and hence calculate the total product of Earth and Wind.

Firm/product	Value added	Final sales
Earth		
Corn		
Grapes		
Milk		
Wind		
Bread		
Wine		
Cheese		
Total product		

14 What are the incomes generated by each type of output in the table above and what is total income?

Section 10.3: Developing an Accounting Framework

In macroeconomics it is helpful to treat an economy as consisting of four large sectors: 'households', 'firms', 'government' and the 'foreign sector'. The key real and monetary flows between these sectors can be represented by the 'circular flow of income' diagram. Many useful concepts and definitions can be explored within this framework.

Developing an Accounting Framework

We begin by concentrating on the interaction of just two sectors: households and firms. (For simplicity we assume that there is no government or foreign sector.) Use the supplementary screens (The Households Sector and The Productive Sector) to identify the real and monetary flows that are centred on households on the one hand and firms on the other. These screens are accessed by using the Next Page button in WinEcon.

The Circular Flow of Income

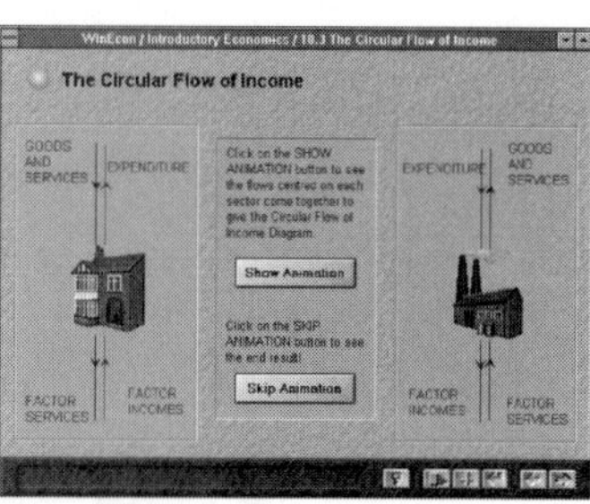

The 'circular flow of income' diagram brings the real and monetary flows between households and firms on to one diagram and shows how the spending of one sector provides income for the other. This topic also shows that there are three equivalent ways of measuring the total level of production over a period, namely the output method, the income method and the expenditure method.

About flows between households and firms

15 **Complete these statements to indicate how households and firms interact in the circular flow of income:**

Households provide firms with ________ ________. In return they receive ________ ________ in the form of ________, ________ and ________. Firms sell ________ ________ and ________ and in return they earn ________. They make ________ payments to households in return for ________ ________.

16 **Output and income are equal by definition. Explain why this is so.**

17 **Output and expenditure are equal by definition. Explain why this is so.**

Investment and Saving

To make the circular flow of income diagram more realistic, we need to recognize that there are injections into and leakages from the circular flow of income. Household saving is one example of a leakage from the circular flow. It is income received by households that is not passed on as expenditure on final goods and services. Investment is an example of an injection into the circular flow. It is spending received by firms which does not come from the spending of households. Text cards 3–6 of this screen show schematically how the introduction of saving and investment alters the circular flow of income diagram. We also see that, in a framework in which there is no government or foreign sector, saving must equal investment.

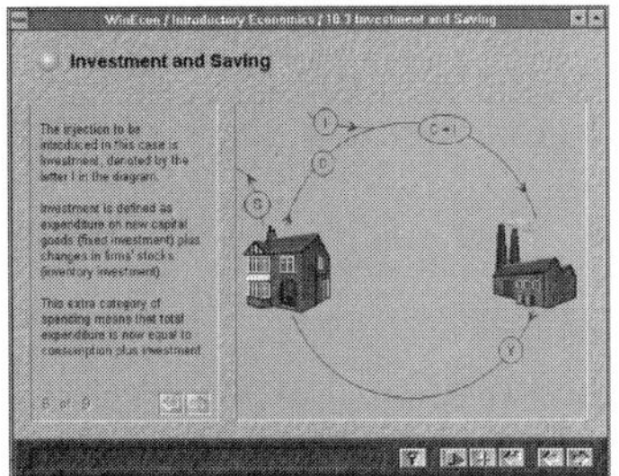

Check your understanding of these terms

18 **What is the definition of an 'injection' into the circular flow of income?**

19 **What is meant by 'household saving'?**

20 **What is 'consumers' expenditure'?**

21 **What is 'firms' saving'?**

22 **Define 'investment'.**

23 **Distinguish between 'fixed investment' and 'inventory investment'.**

24 **Output and expenditure are equal by definition. How can this be the case if firms fail to sell all the output they produce in a particular period?**

The Inclusion of Government

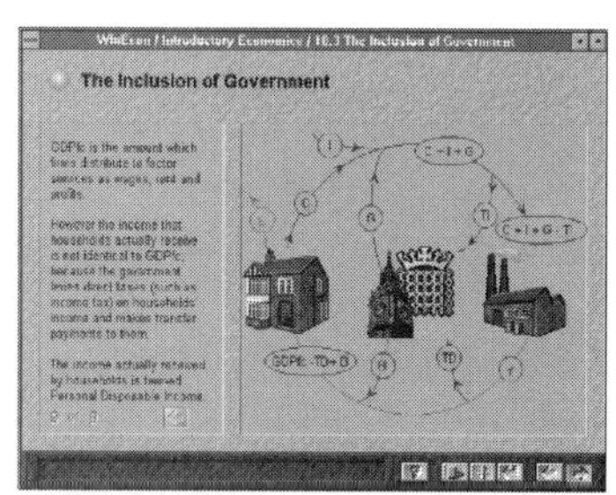

Introducing the government as a third sector makes the circular flow of income diagram more complex, but more realistic. The government participates via expenditure on final goods and services and this expenditure constitutes another injection into the circular flow. The government also causes a leakage from the circular flow of income, because it levies taxes. Refer to cards 3–5 to see how the inclusion of the government alters the circular flow of income diagram.

The government's effect on the circular flow

25 **Governments are said to drive a wedge between what is spent on final goods and services and what firms receive – how? Which definition of GDP is equal to actual spending on goods and services and which is equal to the amount received by firms?**

26 **Governments also drive a wedge between what firms make in the way of factor payments to households and what households have available to spend – explain.**

27 **Why does government consumption (government current expenditure on final goods and services) constitute an injection into the circular flow of income?**

28 **Why is taxation a leakage from the circular flow?**

29 **Which concept of output is equivalent to the factor income generated by the payments made by firms?**

30 **Is it true that output equals expenditure equals income? Explain.**

31 **Prove that total injections equal total leakages when the government sector is included.**

The Foreign Sector

The introduction of the foreign sector as the fourth component in the framework introduces an extra injection into, and further leakage from, the circular flow.

Payments made for imports amount to a leakage from the circular flow of domestic income while payments received for exports are injections.

Test your understanding of the foreign sector

32 **'Since exports are UK-produced goods and services being bought by overseas residents, they surely represent a leakage from the circular flow of income' – why is this the opposite of the truth?!**

33 **Following on from the previous question, are imports an injection or a leakage? Explain.**

34 **How many injections are there in the four sector economy? Name them.**

35 **How many leakages are there in the four sector economy? Name them.**

36 **Suppose you wanted to measure GDP at market prices in an open economy, what formula would you use to define GDP_{mp}? Make sure you can define all the terms and explain why there is now a negative term in the formula.**

37 **Prove algebraically that total injections equal total withdrawals when there are four sectors.**

Section 10.4: The Measurement of GDP in Practice

The topic GNP and NNP in section 10.5 explains how we adjust GDP to obtain GNP.

Gross domestic product (GDP) is the value of all final goods and services produced in a country during the accounting time period, which is usually a year. This measure takes no account of who owns the factors of production used to produce the output, and this distinguishes GDP from 'gross national product' (GNP), which we consider in the next section.

The circular flow framework represents the real and monetary flows in an economy and shows that there are three different, but equivalent, methods of measuring total product: by output, by income and by expenditure. In this section you will examine these three methods of measuring total product in

more depth to obtain estimates of the value of GDP. The output, income and expenditure measures of GDP are contained in the National Income Expenditure tables, popularly known as the Blue Book. In WinEcon you can learn about the categories that make up each aggregate and explore the difficulties associated with their measurement.

Real and Nominal GDP

It is important to distinguish between nominal measures (which reflect the *money value* of current production) and real measures (which indicate the *quantity* of current production) when measuring total product. This screen explores the distinction so we can move on to analyse the three approaches to measuring GDP.

The Output Approach

The output measure of GDP totals the output of seven broad industrial sectors. Use the three screens in this WinEcon topic to find out more about these seven sectors and to discover how data are procured and used to measure GDP (output). Notice the invitation on card 6 of the first screen to click on the various estimates in the table. You can discover more about how the estimates have been obtained.

In this method the problem of double counting could easily occur. In principle it is avoided by calculating value added for each sector, but you will find that in practice net changes in output cannot always be measured directly.

The real output of each of the industrial sectors is expressed as an index number, which is arbitrarily set at 100 in the base year. (This is 1985 in the WinEcon tables.)

See the topic Double Counting – a Potential Error in section 10.2 for further details.

Test your understanding of the output approach

The sectors in the output table are:

(1) ______

(2) ______

(3) ______

(4) ______

(5) ______

(6) ______

(7) ______

38 In 1990 the index number representing the real output in agriculture, forestry and fishing was 106.3, whereas it was 88.9 in energy and water. Does this imply that the former sector produced more than the latter? Explain.

39 In 1990 the index number representing the real output in agriculture, forestry and fishing was 106.3, whereas it was 100 in 1985. Does this imply that the output of the sector was higher in 1990 than in 1985? Explain.

40 In principle, the output of an industrial sector is equal to the value added by that sector. In practice, value added is difficult to estimate. Explain. (To answer this question you will need to click on the data displayed in the output table.)

41 The real outputs of certain services (e.g. healthcare) are difficult to measure and are often simply estimated by the level of spending on that service over a period. Other services, however, do present natural units of measurement. Find an example in the table, of a service whose real (gross) output is relatively straightforward to measure.

42 The output of the seven broad industrial sectors cannot simply be summed in order to arrive at a measure of GDP. How can they be combined to provide an estimate of GDP?

43 On The Output Approach (1) screen you learnt that it is not valid to compare the outputs of different sectors using real output data based on index numbers. Is it valid to compare the data based on nominal outputs, as shown on The Output Approach (2) screen? Explain.

The pie diagram on the The Output Approach (3) screen is linked to nominal output data over the period 1970–93. By clicking on each pie segment you can examine the trend in the share in GDP of that particular category of output over time.

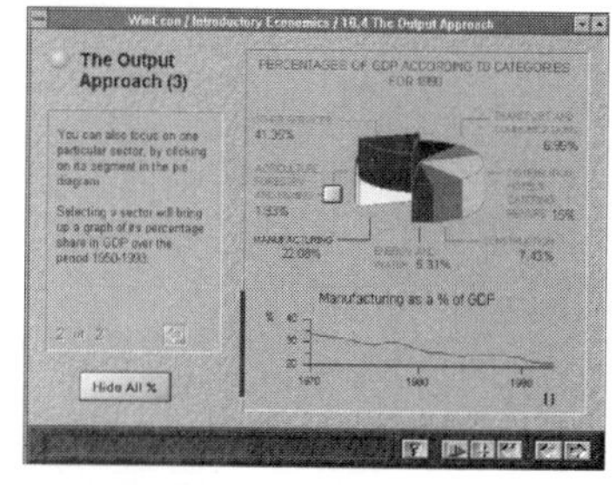

Nominal output data, 1970–93

44 **What do you observe about the trend in the 'manufacturing' share as compared with the trend in 'other services'?**

44 **Explain the pattern observed for 'energy and water supply'.**

45 **In 1970, GDP in the UK consisted of approximately 50 per cent goods and 50 per cent services. What were the shares of total goods and total services in 1990?**

The Expenditure Approach

GDP can be estimated by summing all the items in four categories of expenditure. We are counting the total of what is spent on final goods and services, and this will be measured at market prices. To obtain a measure of GDP at factor cost by this approach, after finding GDP at market prices we subtract indirect taxes (which raise prices to purchasers) and add subsidies (which lower the prices consumers pay). We are valuing what is produced in the domestic economy. This includes goods sold for export, and does not include the imports which people buy. Consequently, once total domestic expenditure has been calculated we add the value of exports and subtract what is spent on imports.

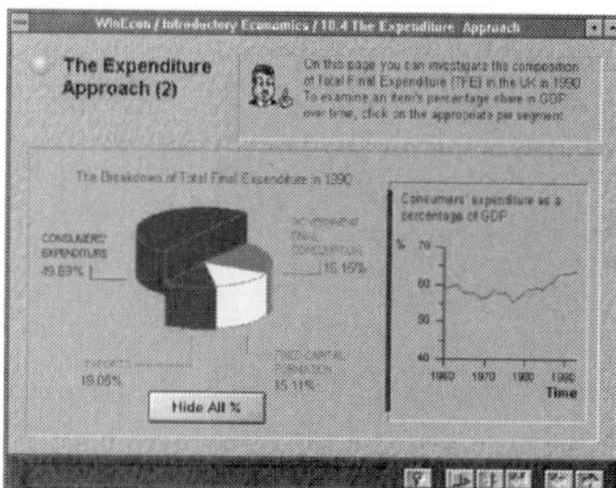

Work your way through The Expenditure Approach screen to discover more about the various categories of expenditure and how they are measured. The Next Page button takes you to The Expenditure Approach (2), a supplementary screen with a pie chart that shows the composition of 'total final expenditure' in the UK in 1990.

Test your understanding of the expenditure approach

47 What are the four categories of expenditure?

48 The national accounts include consumers' expenditure as one category of expenditure rather than consumption. Explain the distinction between these two concepts.

49 The accounts also include government consumption as a separate category of expenditure, but not government investment. Does this imply that the government carries out no investment? Explain.

50 Does the expenditure approach naturally lead to a measure of GDP at market prices or at factor cost? Explain.

51 In the UK what is the largest category of total final expenditure? What share of total final expenditure does it constitute?

52 Which is the most volatile component of expenditure?

53 In the UK which is the category of expenditure that is trending upwards the most strongly?

The Income Approach

For more details on transfer payments and why they are excluded from calculations of national income, see the topic Transfer Payments in section 10.2.

Another way of measuring GDP is to sum all the incomes generated by production over a period. These are the incomes that accrue to each of the factors of production. Notice that incomes that are not paid in exchange for a corresponding factor service are not included. Hence, for example, state pensions and National Lottery winnings are excluded. Such items are called transfer payments.

Work your way through The Income Approach screen to discover more about the various categories that comprise income and how they are measured and summed. You find that the income approach leads directly to a measure of GDP at factor cost.

The Income Approach (2) is a supplementary screen accessed via the Next Page button. It shows the composition of GDP by income type. By clicking on the various segments you can discover the share of each income category.

Test what you know about the income approach

54 What are the broad theoretical categories of income which first emerged in the circular flow of income diagram as payments for factor services?

55 Does the income measure lead most naturally to an estimate of GDP at market prices or at factor cost? Explain.

56 Which is the largest component of income?

57 Who is the most important provider of income data?

58 The share of profits on the one hand and income from employment and self-employment on the other has remained highly stable over the period 1960–90. There was, however, a conspicuous blip. When did this occur?

Section 10.5: GNP, NNP and Economic Welfare

In this section you learn about two other concepts of total product: 'gross national product' (GNP) and 'net national product' (NNP). You also learn that these concepts are imperfect measures of economic welfare.

GNP and NNP

The distinction between GDP, which we measured in the previous section, and GNP stems from the ownership of the factors of production. For example, lifts may be manufactured in Singapore but if the factory making them is owned by a UK company part of the profits will be transmitted to the UK and so form part of the UK's national income. Similarly, if immigrants send some of their earnings back to their home countries, that money is not available to the citizens of the UK and so does not form part of UK national income.

Adding all the inflows and subtracting all the outflows generated in this way gives net property income from abroad. When this is added to GDP at factor cost we obtain GNP at factor cost. Notice that net exports of goods and services (exports minus imports) are already included in GDP.

'National income' is the income generated by productive activity that is available to the people in a country during a particular time period. Some of the items of machinery and equipment that are counted in GNP are needed to replace other capital equipment which is worn out. Consequently the value of the capital stock used up in the time period, known as 'depreciation', is not available to anyone as income that can be spent. It should therefore be subtracted from GNP in calculating national income, otherwise known as 'net national product' (NNP).

Work through the GNP and NNP screen to learn how GNP and NNP are defined and see how they are related to GDP.

See what you have learnt about GNP and NNP

59 **What is the distinction between GDP and GNP? Explain.**

60 **What is the distinction between GNP and NNP? Why is NNP also termed national income?**

61 **Why is the concept of NNP not heavily used?**

GNP and Economic Welfare

Although it has many shortcomings, GNP is often used to measure economic welfare. Use the GNP and Economic Welfare screen of WinEcon to find out more.

Welfare comparisons using either GNP per capita or an alternative measure are also discussed in section 17.3 in the topic Development – Concepts and Measurements.

The Next Page button takes you to GNP and Economic Welfare (2). This supplementary screen shows how Nordhaus and Tobin developed a 'measure of economic welfare' (MEW) which adjusts GNP to give a better indicator of economic well-being. There are theoretical arguments for preferring MEW, but there are also considerable practical difficulties in obtaining the data required to make the adjustment. Consequently, GNP (or GNP per capita, to take account of population size) remains the main indicator used for welfare comparisons.

Explain the adjustments suggested

62 **Give four reasons why GNP is not a good measure of economic welfare.**

63 **What are regrettables? Are they included in the MEW or not?**

64 **What are intermediates? Are they included in the MEW or not?**

65 **What is non-market activity? Is it included in the MEW or not?**

Section 10.6: Summary

In national income accounting we may use any one of three methods (output, expenditure or income) to calculate GDP at factor cost. By adding net property income from abroad, we arrive at GNP. If we then subtract depreciation, this yields NNP, which is national income.

The reason why the three calculation methods all allow us to estimate GDP, and from it national income, is seen from the circular flow of income diagram. Production generates factor income and the sale of what is produced generates expenditure. The three methods are different ways of looking at the same flow.

Chapter 11:

The Income–Expenditure Model

How do we even begin to examine the working of an entire national economy? This is the concern of macroeconomics, a subject which has developed from the work of John Maynard Keynes in the 1930s. At its heart is an analysis of the income and expenditure flows between firms and households in the national economy. The basic income–expenditure model helps explain the level of economic activity (production, employment, income, spending) and also suggests what governments might do to reduce large-scale unemployment.

Contents

KEYWORDS

- Aggregate demand
- Aggregate output/income
- Circular flow
- Consumption function
- Equilibrium
- Factor market
- Firms sector
- Goods market
- Household sector
- Injections
- Marginal propensity
- Multiplier
- Withdrawals

Section 11.1: Introduction

An economic model is a simplified representation of the more complex real world. In this chapter we develop a macroeconomic model – a way of looking at the national economy which allows us to understand some of the cause and effect connections between different parts of the system. When specified in equation form, a model can provide more precise estimates of the scale of the effect when one change causes another, and we shall look at some examples of this.

Firstly, however, the chapter takes you through some basic ideas about firms, households and aggregate markets, and how they relate to each other. These concepts are needed for the model we shall build. Later in the chapter we look in more detail at patterns of economic behaviour of households and firms to enable us to model each of these sectors. These models can be combined to give a simple model of the aggregate demand for goods and services. In the model developed in this chapter, aggregate demand is the crucial determinant of the economy's aggregate output and employment.

The idea of a circular flow of income and expenditure has already been introduced in chapter 10. Here you will be reminded of the components of the circular flow and examine some of them in more depth.

Section 11.2: Circular Flow of Income and Expenditure

We begin by defining the sectors of the economy, and go on to examine the relationship between them. We obtain an overall view of the structure of a national economy, which is developed further in subsequent sections.

Basic Concepts: Firms and Households

The two fundamental sectors for this type of modelling are firms and households. Note that these do not have to be composed of different people: they are defined by the nature of their activity. The manager of a retail store (a firm) may go home to her family where she engages in domestic activity and leisure (a household). Firms are organizations which make goods and/or provide services. Another name for this sector is the production sector. Households are where we eat, sleep and conduct our private lives, which, in a modern industrial society, involves consuming goods and services produced in the firms sector. Hence, the households sector is also sometimes called the consumption sector.

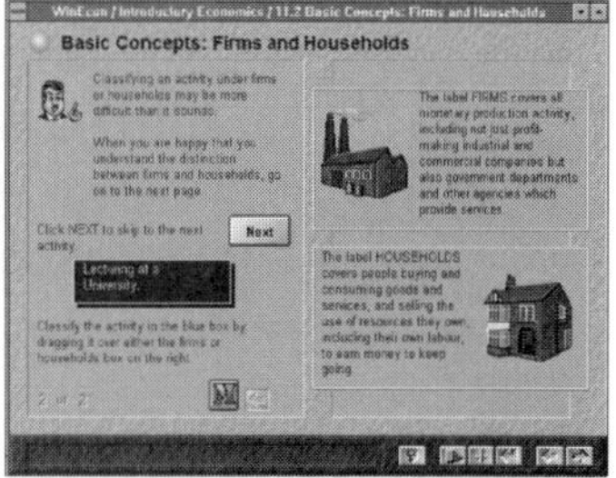

Move to the second WinEcon text card of this screen and confirm with the drag-and-drop examples that you can classify activities correctly.

Check your understanding of the distinction between firms and households

01 Firms [____] goods and services, households [____] them.

Here are a few more examples to try. Classify the following activities under households or firms:

02 A bricklayer putting his young children to bed. [____]

03 A bricklayer building a house. [____]

04 A bricklayer buying a drink at the pub. [____]

05 A nurse attending a patient in hospital. [____]

06 Students paying to go into a disco. [____]

07 An insurance salesman telephoning customers. [____]

Basic Concepts: Aggregate Markets

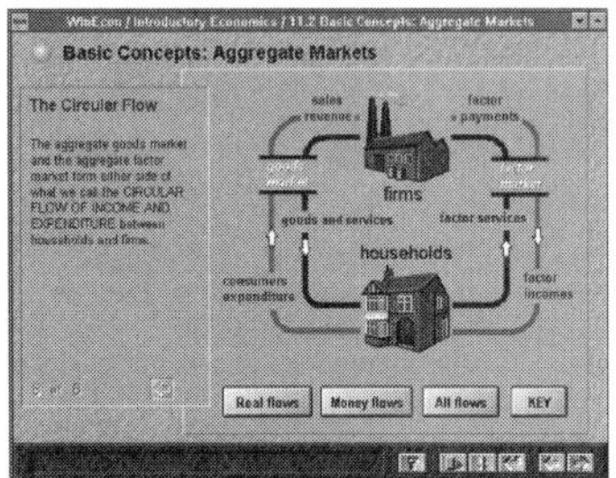

Production and consumption are related activities. What firms produce, households consume. Firms need to be paid in order to produce, because they in turn have to pay for materials, labour, and other costs of production (including profits for the owners). So money payments (expenditures) flow from households to firms in return for consumer goods and services flowing from firms to households. This is the goods market: consumers demand, firms supply. The aggregate goods market encompasses all varieties of goods and services traded.

In paying for materials, firms are purchasing from other firms. Such payments are contained wholly within the firms sector. But when paying for the factors of production – labour, land, capital – these payments (also known as factor payments) go to owners in the households sector. Thus we have an aggregate factor market: firms demand factor services, households supply factor services.

On this screen you build a model of how the two fundamental sectors of the economy (firms and households) interact. To help you understand the movements of money and goods you can animate the flows of your choice by clicking the buttons marked 'flows'. The circular flow diagram forms the core of our view of the structure of the economy.

Check your understanding of aggregate markets

08 **In the goods market, which are called real flows: (a) goods and services delivered from firms to customers, or (b) payments by customers to firms?** ☐

09 **What name do economists give to the money firms receive from customers who purchase what they produce?** ☐

10 **In the factor market, payments by firms to households for labour, land and capital used in the production process are ☐ flows, and the labour, land and capital provided by households to firms are ☐ flows.**

11 **What specific names are given to payments by firms (a) for labour, (b) for the use of land (and buildings), and (c) for the use of capital?**

12 **When firms pay households for factors of production, what is the general name for the money received by the households sector?**

Complete the diagram to show a simple closed circuit with two sectors and two markets between them, with real flows circulating round in one direction and money flows circulating in the other direction.

FIRMS

__________ market　　　__________ market

HOUSEHOLDS

The Simple Circular Flow of Income and Expenditure

This screen takes the simple circular flow of income and expenditure developed so far and specifically emphasizes the money flows in the economy. From here on we concentrate on money flows. Money is a common unit with which to measure a vast range of real goods and services, including factor services. Note that if prices are taken as given, changes in total money flows then correspond to changes in real quantities.

The Full Circular Flow of Income and Expenditure

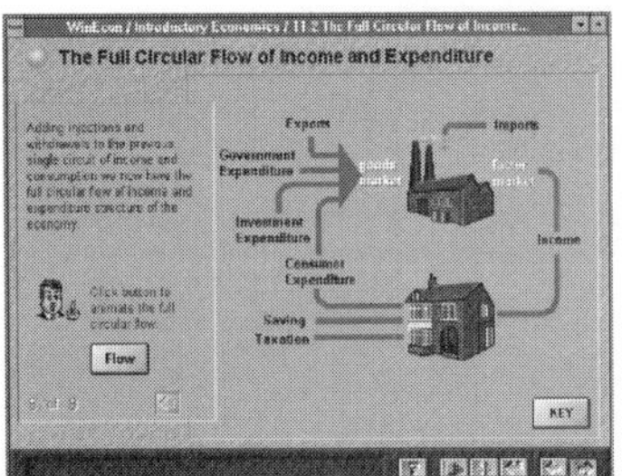

We now need to make the model more realistic by recognizing some other flows in the system, and this screen presents the full circular flow of income and expenditure in the economy. In the real world, households do not spend all of their current income, and firms do not sell only to households. WinEcon here identifies two further categories of flows, 'injections' and 'withdrawals', with three flows to be recognized in each category.

Section 10.3 of WinEcon builds up more gradually to the full picture by looking at these injections and withdrawals (or leakages) flows in pairs. Here, we include all of these flows at once, but you will see that we make certain simplifications in the case of government sector activities. Transfer payments (such as state pensions) are not included as a separate item but are treated as negative taxation. Net taxation is direct taxation minus transfer payments.

Test your knowledge of circular flows

13 Expenditures which do not come directly from our households, but which buy final goods and services produced by the firms sector, are called ______.

14 Money flows out of the inner circuit of income and consumption are called ______ or ______.

15 List the three injections flows.

16 List the three withdrawals flows.

Classify the following as withdrawals, *W*, or injections, *J*, and say which type:

17 Payments of VAT to the government. W/J ______

18 A British retail store buying shirts from India. W/J

19 A distillery selling whisky to Japan. W/J

20 A bank building a new office block. W/J

21 The government paying higher salaries to teachers. W/J

22 Putting money earned in a summer vacation job into a building society account to earn interest. W/J

23 Name two payments flows in the circular flow structure which are neither injections nor withdrawals.

Accounting Identities in the Circular Flow

Now that you appreciate the general structure of income and expenditure payments flows in our economy, we can derive some accounting relationships between them. You see that total sales revenue received by the firms sector ultimately (after taking account of inter-firm transactions) pays for imported goods and services or pays households for factor services. Total income to the households sector is either taxed, saved or spent on consumption. From these features of the circular flow structure we obtain some accounting relationships. These are 'identities', true by definition because for each sector actual money receipts (flows in) have to be fully accounted for in different uses (flows out).

The sequence of screens in section 10.3 also considers these relationships.

As you think about this screen, bear in mind that domestic output of goods and services requires factor services in production, and factor payments by firms are factor incomes to households. The money paid by firms to create value added in goods and services (including profits with other factor costs) gives the monetary value of that production. The money paid becomes household sector income of the same total amount. Incomes are received for contributions to the production process, and equate to the value of what is produced.

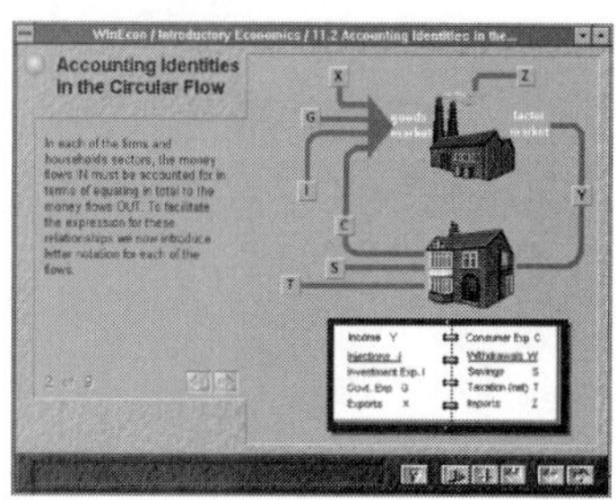

It is very important to note that aggregate output and aggregate income in an economy have the same monetary total. From now on we will frequently refer to aggregate output and income as *Y*. You should interpret *Y* according to the context as either firms sector output (i.e. goods market aggregate supply) or as household sector income.

For further details of national accounting see chapter 10.

Check your understanding of accounting identities

24 Make your own record of the notation being used. Write down what the letters stand for:

Y =

C =

J =

W =

I =

G =

X =

S =

T =

Z =

25 **In the firms sector, revenues are received from ______ expenditure, ______ expenditure, ______ expenditure, and ______.**

26 **In the households sector, income is used for ______ expenditure, or it is ______, or it goes to the government as ______.**

The diagram shown here illustrates the full circular flow structure of the economy. Mark on it the letter notation for each of the flows.

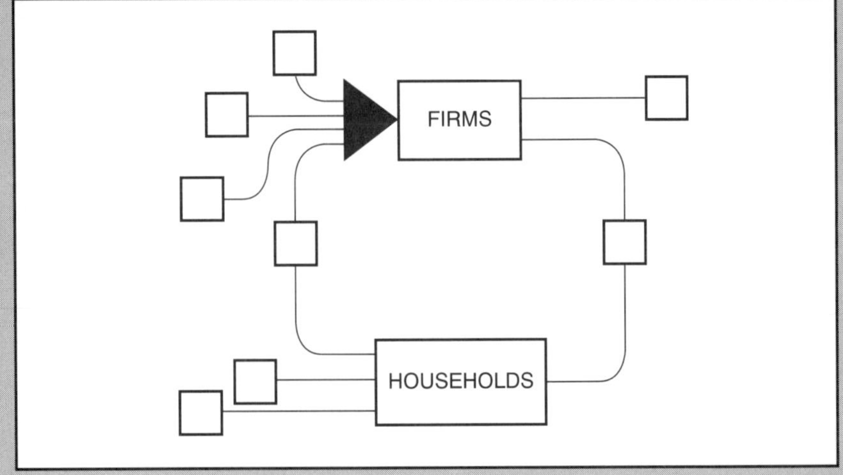

In the standard letter notation, complete the following accounting identities. (Remember, T is net taxation.)

27 $C + I + G + X =$ ______

28 $C + I + G + X - Z =$ ______

29 $C + S + T =$ ______

Planned Versus Actual Flows

An accounting system records actual values, after the event. Thus, for example, the UK official measure of GDP at factor cost records the value of aggregate production and income in the economy in a particular period – which corresponds to Y in our circular flow structure. Why was output at that recorded level rather than higher or lower? The accounts cannot tell us that. To understand many important economic questions like this one, we need more than a set of accounts. The circular flow diagram gives us some structural relationships, but it is not yet a model with explanatory content.

To develop the income–expenditure model we must now incorporate ideas about the behaviour of firms and households, described in terms of their plans or intentions rather than the actual outcome. The distinction between planned and actual values of variables is crucial. The plans of different economic agents (e.g. for quantities supplied and demanded) are not necessarily consistent, in which case it is the responses of those agents to the disequilibrium which explains why the economy ends up where it does.

From this point on, we shall concentrate on the planned values of variables in describing the economic behaviour of the firms and households sectors.

Record your findings

30 **Alternative terms with equivalent meaning to 'planned' include ______ and ______.**

31 **Alternative terms with equivalent meaning to 'actual' include ______ and ______.**

32 **For which variables are we concentrating on planned values?**

Section 11.3: The Household Sector

The core idea that we develop here is that the consumer expenditure of households is conditional on their income. We can model such expenditure plans with a 'consumption function' which can be represented in equation form or diagrammatically. Keynes considered that aggregate consumer behaviour would exhibit certain features, which are incorporated as properties of the Keynesian consumption function. We first examine these. After this we model taxation and saving flows in a similar manner.

The Consumption Function

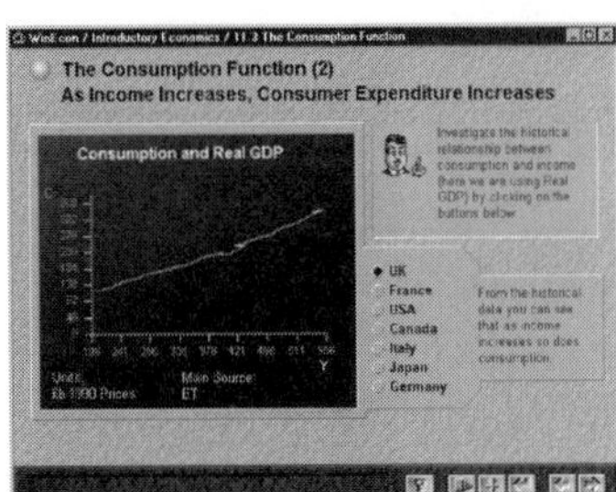

In the first of four screens on this topic you are asked to think about three different properties of the consumption function. More details and examples of these are provided in the following three screens, which are accessed using the Next Page button.

For modelling purposes we assume the 'marginal propensity to consume' (MPC) to be constant. (Later, the same assumption is made for the other marginal propensities.) Notice that the marginal tax rate, the marginal propensity to consume and the marginal propensity to save are all fractions, and they add up to 1. They show, respectively, the proportions of an increase in total income that would be taken in tax, consumed and saved.

Properties of consumer expenditure

We have identified three particular properties of aggregate consumer expenditure plans. Complete the following statements to record these.

33 **As income increases, consumer expenditure ________.**

34 **As income increases, ________ of the increase will be consumed.**

35 **As income increases, a ________ proportion will be consumed.**

Complete the following definitions, including a formula.

36 **The marginal propensity to consume is: ________**

37 **The average propensity to consume is:** ______

38 **If the marginal propensities to consume, save and be taxed are respectively 0.65, 0.11, and 0.24 then what are the changes in *C*, *S* and *T* if income increases by 200?**

The Consumption Function Diagram

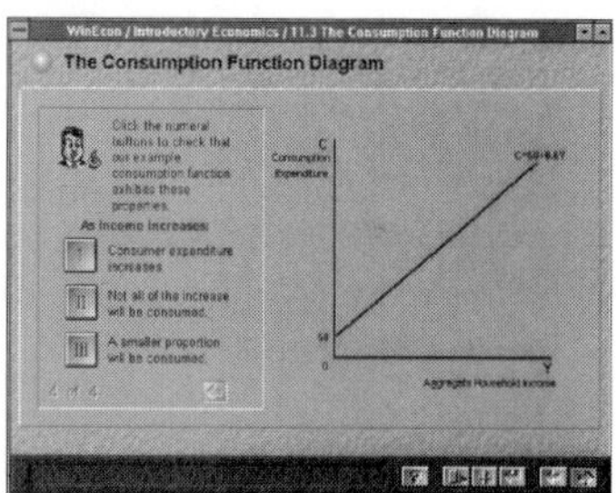

You can discover an example of a consumption function on this screen. It is useful to write the general form, which for the Keynesian consumption function is

$$C = a + bY$$

where a and b are constants. a is positive and b is the marginal propensity to consume.

Apply consumption functions

39 **On the WinEcon screen, what is the value of the constant a?** ______ **What value does b take?** ______

If $C = 800 + 0.7Y$:

40 **Calculate consumption *C* when *Y* = 8000 and when *Y* = 12,000.**

41 **What is the average propensity to consume at each of these points?**

42 **What is the marginal propensity to consume?**

Plot the consumption function $C = 800 + 0.7Y$ on this diagram, and mark the two points referred to in the questions above.

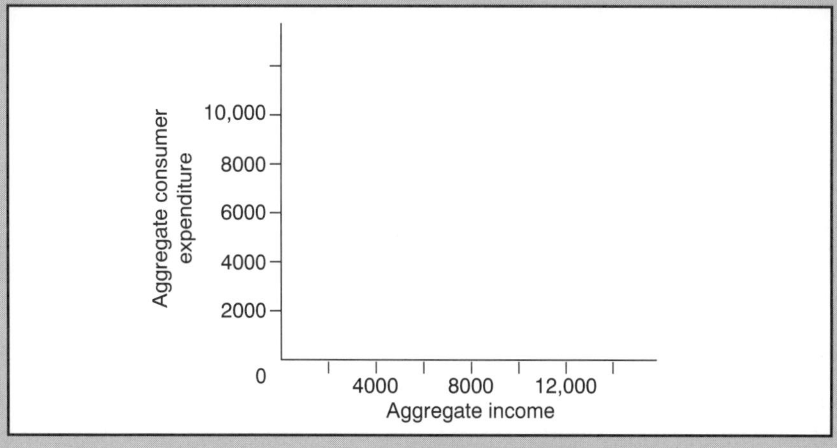

Consumption, Taxation and Saving

The total income of the household sector finances taxation payments and saving, as well as consumption. Increased consumer expenditure continues round the circular flow path to generate more production and income. However, the taxation and saving withdrawals from the flow are also functions of income. The next topics look in detail at these withdrawals flows.

Taxation

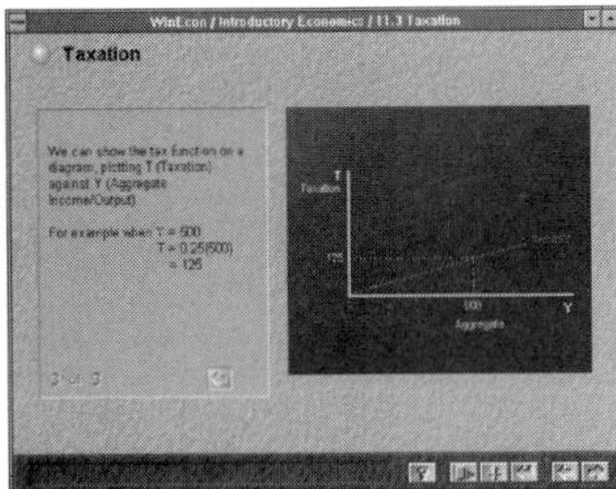

Household sector income is subject to taxation, often before it is received (e.g. workers' take-home pay is less than their gross pay). Many taxes are directly related to income or spending – hence, we can represent total taxation as a function of income. To simplify further, taxation revenue for the government is measured net of transfer payments such as social security benefits payments to households. Since the precise form of the tax function is not critical for our model, we will keep the mathematics as simple as possible by specifying that tax revenue is a constant proportion of income. For example, total taxation might take 20 per cent of total income, giving $T = 0.2Y$ as the tax function in the model.

A more disaggregated treatment is shown in section 10.3. It explicitly recognizes the different kinds of government payments and taxation flows, and shows you where they all fit in a circular flow diagram. Note, however, that we have now switched the emphasis from the accounting structure to explaining the size of the flows.

About taxation

43 The measure of the total taxation payments flow to the government being used in our model is net of government transfer payments. Give two examples of such transfer payments.

Saving

The after-tax net income of the household sector is known as disposable income. Disposable income is either consumed or saved (i.e. its use is split two ways). Total income is split three ways, namely into consumption and saving, and also into taxation. We usually relate the three flows (consumption, saving and direct taxation) back to the total income from which they are derived.

The saving flow is not necessarily just a residual of income left over after tax and consumption payments – it may well be undertaken as a positive and

deliberate choice. Indeed, saving and consumption require a joint decision about the allocation of disposable income. However, because of the accounting relationship between the three flows, any one can be derived from the other two. On the WinEcon screen, you see an example of how to derive the saving function.

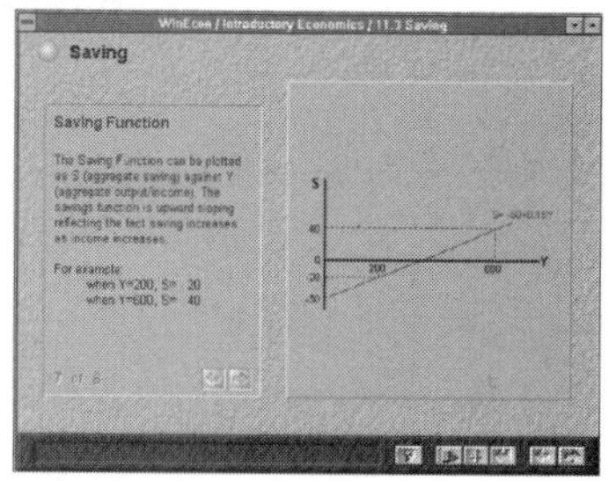

Check your understanding of saving

44 **Disposable income is [ ] [ ] minus [ ] [ ] .**

45 **The sum of the marginal propensities to consume and save relative to disposable income add to one, but for marginal propensities defined relative to total income it is the sum of the marginal propensities to consume, save and be taxed which add to one. True or false? [ ]**

Let $C = 800 + 0.7Y$ and $T = 0.2Y$

46 **Calculate saving S when $Y = 8000$ and when $Y = 12{,}000$.**

47 **What is the equation of the saving function in this case?**

48 **What is the marginal propensity to save from total income?**

When $T = 0.2Y$

49 **What is disposable income as a function of total income?**

50 **If the MPC from disposable income is 0.9, what is the MPC from total income?**

51 **If the MPS from disposable income is 0.1, what is the MPS from total income?**

Section 11.4: The Firms Sector and the Goods Market

This section brings together households and firms, and analyses the demand and supply of goods. The approach focuses particularly on the operation of the goods market, and begins with an explanation of the term aggregate demand.

In this income–expenditure approach to macroeconomics, firms are portrayed as changing their planned quantity of production in response to changes in the aggregate demand for what they produce. In effect, firms supply what will be bought in the market. This gives the income–expenditure approach description of aggregate supply. In this section you discover how we can represent aggregate demand and supply in equations, or as lines on a diagram.

The demand by firms for factors of production is dependent on the level of production, and the factor market is therefore of secondary importance.

Aggregate Demand in the Goods Market

Aggregate demand (AD) is the total of planned expenditures on domestic output (i.e. goods and services produced in our economy). From the circular flow structure we have seen that, for actual values, this total is given by $(C + I + G + X - Z)$. We now use this relationship for total planned expenditure, aggregate demand. Planned C is given by the consumption function.

With this screen you learn about the other components of aggregate demand, and how the equation for aggregate demand may be obtained. To keep the model simple we assume that the injections are exogenous variables (i.e. given amounts). A more advanced approach would model planned investment, and perhaps exports too, as endogenous variables (i.e. quantities to be explained as a function of other variables). Government expenditure is a matter of policy decision which makes it more truly exogenous. Our simplification leaves the quantities of I, G and X unexplained but, importantly, still allows us to investigate the consequences of changes in these quantities.

In the topic Investment Demand and Aggregate Output/Income in section 13.4 you begin to model investment as endogenous.

Imports almost certainly vary with the level of production and income in a country, and we model Z accordingly. If production and income rise, firms need more imported supplies and consumers can afford more purchases including purchases of foreign-made goods and services.

From the analysis on this screen we conclude that aggregate demand for goods and services is an increasing function of the level of aggregate output/income (Y). If income rises it will induce increased spending on domestic output. Notice that the marginal propensity to spend on domestic production can be read off from the AD equation. It is the coefficient against Y. Moreover, in this type of example it is the MPC (coefficient against Y in the consumption function) minus the marginal propensity to import (MPZ)

(coefficient against Y in the import function): $0.6 - 0.1 = 0.5$ in the example on screen. If Y increased by 100, C would increase by 60 but 10 of this would be spent on foreign goods, so the other 50 is the extra demand for domestic production.

Constructing the Aggregate Demand Function

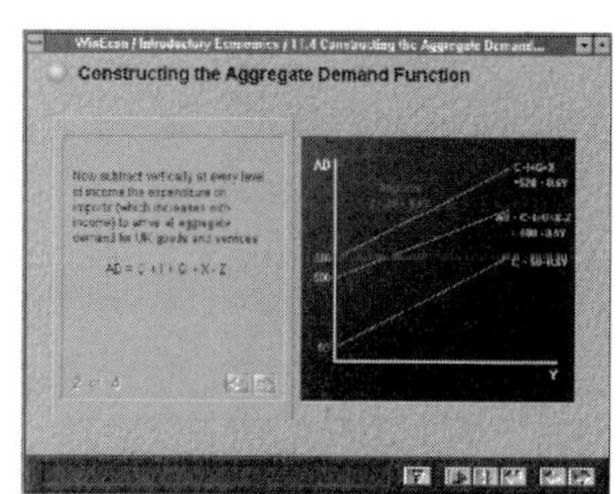

On this WinEcon screen you discover how to plot the aggregate demand function we have been analysing. Notice from the graph that the gradient of the AD function is less than the gradient of the consumption function. It is the deduction of imports, which increase as income increases, which explains why this is so.

Record what you have learnt about aggregate demand

52 **Why are imports modelled as a positive function of output/income Y?**

53 **Aggregate demand is the total of ______ ______ on our domestic production.**

54 **In terms of its components, AD = ______.**

Test your understanding by tackling the following numerical example. Given that $C = 800 + 0.7Y$, $I = 1200$, $G = 1500$, $X = 1800$ and $Z = 600 + 0.1Y$:

55 **What is the AD equation in this case?**

56 **What is the level of imports when $Y = 6000$, $Y = 8000$ and $Y = 10{,}000$?**

57 **What is the marginal propensity to import?**

58 **What is the marginal propensity to spend on domestic output?**

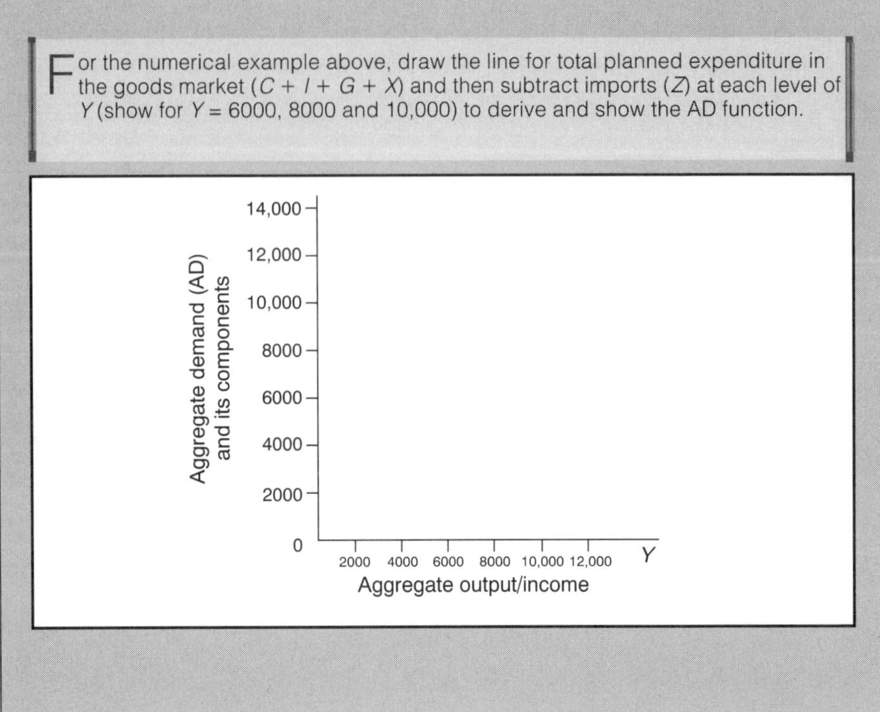
For the numerical example above, draw the line for total planned expenditure in the goods market ($C + I + G + X$) and then subtract imports (Z) at each level of Y (show for Y = 6000, 8000 and 10,000) to derive and show the AD function.
Aggregate demand (AD) and its components
14,000
12,000
10,000
8000
6000
4000
2000
0
2000 4000 6000 8000 10,000 12,000
Y
Aggregate output/income

The Firms Sector

We now move to the supply side of the goods market, and we begin by examining the behaviour of firms. We need to model producer behaviour. What determines the planned level of production by the firms sector? Most firms are in business to make a profit, indeed to maximize profits. So, what is the most profitable level of production? This depends on many things, but it is certainly not profitable to produce goods and services which do not find a buyer, and profits are not being maximized if customers have unsatisfied demands when more could be produced.

In the income–expenditure approach then, the firms sector will want to produce the aggregate quantity of output which they can sell at current prices – no more, no less. To do otherwise is to accept lower profits than are attainable. If demand rises, and firms can supply it with extra production, they will. If demand falls they do not want to have money tied up in unsold stocks, so they cut production.

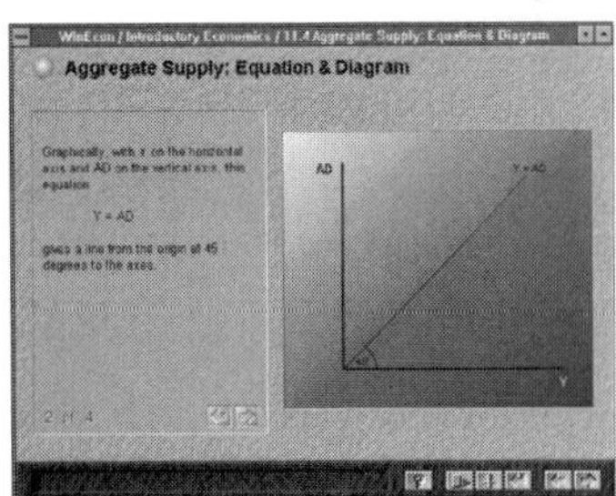
Aggregate Supply: Equation & Diagram

Aggregate Supply: Equation and Diagram

Assuming that suppliers respond to consumers' demand, we have a theory of supply in this model. Planned aggregate supply from the firms sector, which is domestic output, Y, will match aggregate demand, AD, giving Y = AD. In a diagram this gives a line from the origin at 45 degrees to the Y and AD axes.

Note the assumption, characteristic of this approach in macroeconomics, that the price level remains constant in the short run and that it is primarily quantities which are changed in response to changes in demand. For a modern industrial economy dominated by large firms this is a broadly realistic representation of what happens in the goods market. Firms publish price lists, and supply what quantity is demanded at those prices. Such prices are subject to revision over longer periods, but they do not fluctuate continuously like prices in, say, the stock market.

Chapter 14 provides a more advanced approach in which we allow the price level to vary and develop possible aggregate supply functions.

Test your understanding of aggregate supply

59 **If there is an unexpected increase in sales, stocks of finished goods will ________.**

60 **An unplanned increase or decrease in stocks of finished goods is a signal to producers to, respectively, ________ or ________ the quantity of output.**

61 **In the income–expenditure model, it is assumed that firms typically have some market power and publish ________ ________. This means that, in the short run, fluctuations in demand cause output ________ adjustment rather than ________ adjustment.**

62 **If AD = 8000, planned output will be ________.**

63 **The aggregate supply function is Y = ________.**

Plot the above equation on this diagram to show the aggregate supply function.

Section 11.5: Equilibrium in the Goods Market

We now have all the elements of the goods market aggregate demand and supply model in this income–expenditure approach. What remains is to put the parts together and understand how it all works. In this section, we discover how equations and diagrams can be used to calculate and illustrate the outcomes.

Goods Market Equilibrium

Producers and consumers behave in a way that brings the economy to an equilibrium level of activity where all plans are consistent. If current demand exceeds current output, and spare resources are available, firms will increase production to supply this demand. As they do so, more workers are employed and incomes to households increase, which induces an increase in consumer expenditure and hence in aggregate demand. But this process of increasing supply chasing increasing demand is convergent because only part of each increase in income is spent on domestic production (i.e. the marginal propensity fraction) so the changes become smaller and smaller until eventually the quantities supplied and demanded are equal. The economy can then operate without further change in the size of the flows. Notice that the level of output reached in equilibrium may not be the full employment level. The adjustment process brings the economy to equilibrium, but not necessarily to full employment.

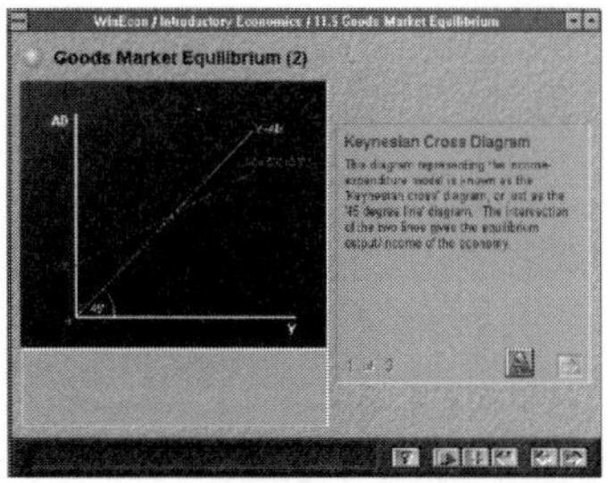

WinEcon has two screens for this topic. The first introduces the idea of goods market equilibrium, and explains why the system moves towards this equilibrium. The second card on the first screen asks you questions to check whether you understand how this process works. The second screen (Goods Market Equilibrium (2)) illustrates the analysis with a diagram and shows you how you can discover from the diagram whether the economy is in equilibrium and, if it is not, what adjustment will take place.

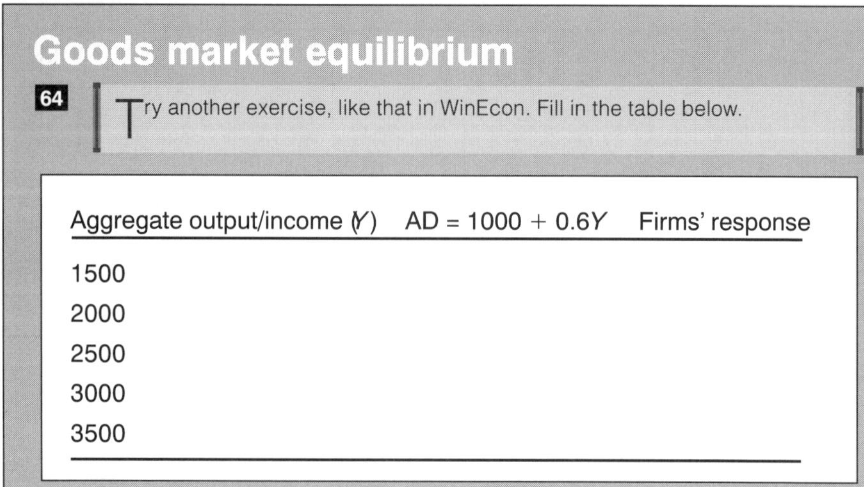

Goods market equilibrium

64 Try another exercise, like that in WinEcon. Fill in the table below.

Aggregate output/income (Y)	AD = 1000 + 0.6Y	Firms' response
1500		
2000		
2500		
3000		
3500		

The adjustment process operates in a downward direction if initially supply exceeds demand. Check you understand the sequence of adjustments in the case of excess supply:

65 **Firms [(increase/decrease/do not change)] production;**

66 **employment and household income [(increase/decrease/do not change)];**

67 **consumption then [(increases/decreases/stays unchanged)];**

68 **aggregate demand [(increases/decreases/stays unchanged)];**

69 **firms [(increase/decrease/do not change)] production;**

70 **and so on until the economy reaches [ ].**

71 **In the Keynesian cross 45 degree line diagram, positions to the left of equilibrium *Y* correspond to excess [ ] (insufficient [ ]) in the goods market, and positions to the right of equilibrium correspond to excess [ ] (insufficient [ ]).**

The Formal Model: Equations and Solutions

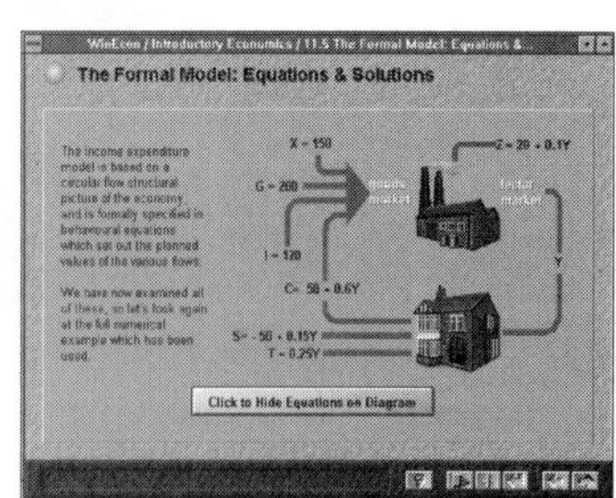

WinEcon now leads you through a series of five screens which let you discover two methods of calculating the equilibrium output/income. These are alternative but equivalent methods – two ways of looking at the same thing. Method 1 makes direct use of the aggregate goods market equilibrium condition that planned output must equal planned demand. Method 2 is indirect, using the fact that a constant income flow in the circular flow structure requires an equality between total planned injections (which increase the flow) and total planned withdrawals (which decrease it). The first screen has the circular flow graphic and shows the equations for our numerical example.

Solution Method 1: Aggregate Demand equals Aggregate Output/Income

This WinEcon screen works through the example to illustrate solution method 1. It is based on the goods market equilibrium condition that aggregate demand equals aggregate output/income.

Introduction to Solution Method 2

Here you see why total withdrawals must balance total injections when the system is in equilibrium. This provides an alternative basis for getting the equilibrium result.

Solution Method 2

Using the same equation model, this WinEcon screen demonstrates solution method 2 based on the equilibrium requirement that total planned withdrawals equal total planned injections.

Equilibrium Values for Other Variables

Finally you see how to find the values of other variables in equilibrium. The WinEcon screen takes you through the required calculations in steps.

Check your understanding of the solution methods

72 Equilibrium in the income–expenditure model requires that, in planned values, aggregate output supplied in the goods market equals ______ ______, and that in the circular flow structure, the total of ______ equals the total of ______.

Now try for yourself another example using method 1. Let $C = 600 + 0.72Y$, $I = 700$, $G = 1500$, $X = 1300$ and $Z = 500 + 0.12Y$.

73 Derive the AD equation.

74 Put Y = AD and solve.

Now use method 2. In addition to the equations already given, let $S = -600 + 0.08Y$ and $T = 0.2Y$.

75 Derive the W equation.

76 Put $W = J$ and solve for Y.

77 Now calculate the equilibrium values for C, S, T and Z.

78 The government budget balance is defined as ______ minus ______ ______.

79 **The foreign trade balance is defined as ______ minus ______.**

80 **In the numerical example above, calculate (a) the government budget balance and (b) the foreign trade balance.**

The Formal Model: Diagrams

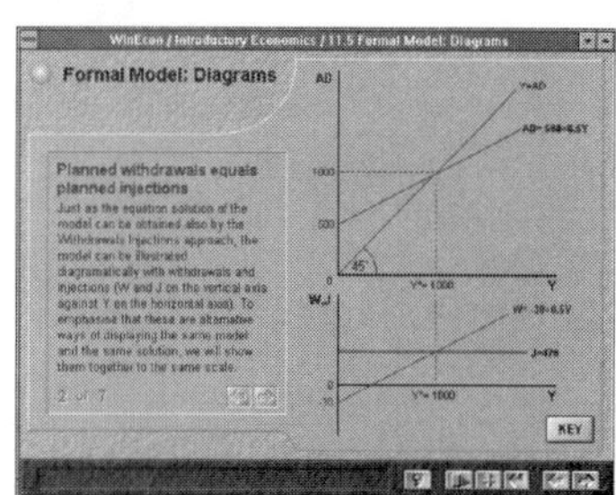

Corresponding to the two equation methods are two diagrams, the Keynesian cross or 45 degree line diagram (showing AD as a function of *Y*, and equilibrium supply *Y* = AD) and the withdrawals–injections diagram (*W* as a function of *Y*, exogenous *J* horizontal). In both diagrams the intersection of the two lines corresponds to the same equilibrium *Y*, which is readily apparent if the two diagrams are placed one above the other.

Diagrammatic representation of equilibrium *Y*

Draw the AD, *Y*, *W* and *J* functions corresponding to the equations in the previous topic to illustrate the equilibrium *Y*. Mark values at all the axis intersections.

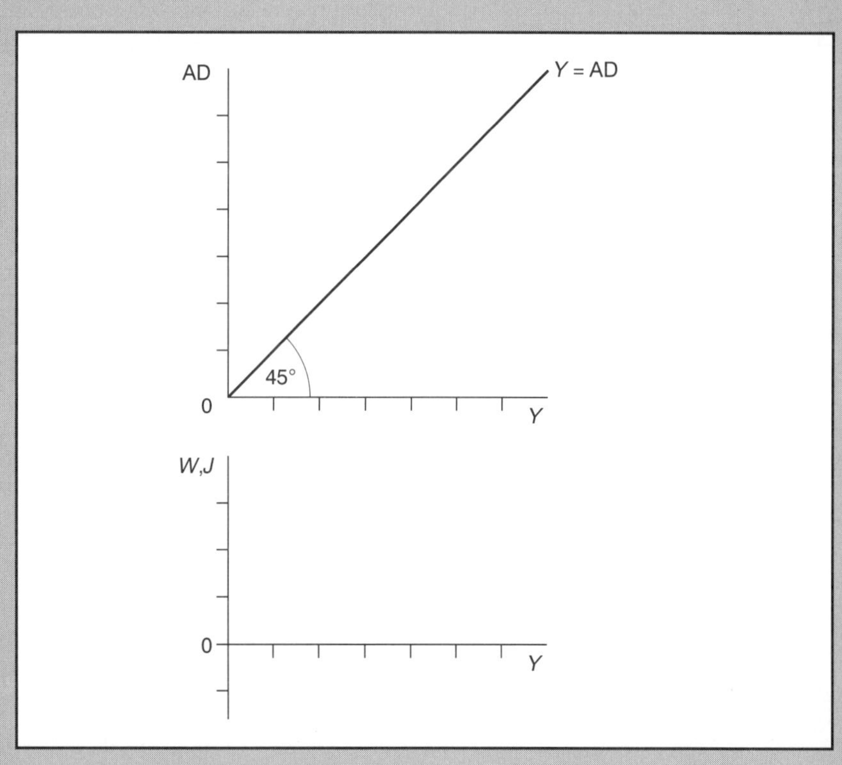

With reference to the diagrams, consider the situation with *Y* below its equilibrium value.

81 AD is **(greater than/less than/equal to)** *Y*.

82 *W* is **(greater than/less than/equal to)** *J*.

83 So *Y* will then **(increase/decrease/stay the same)** .

84 And consequently AD and *W* will **(increase/decrease/stay the same)**.

85 So *Y* will then **(increase/decrease/stay the same)** .

86 And this continues until *Y* = ______.

Section 11.6: Exogenous Changes in Aggregate Demand

One of the more famous and important implications of the income–expenditure model is known as 'the multiplier' process. From the logic of the model we can deduce that any exogenous change in expenditure will cause a larger change in total output and income. As a result any shocks to the economy will have a magnified impact, which is obviously important for understanding boom and recession phenomena, and for designing stabilization policy. In this section we find out why this happens.

A Change in Injections

The explanation of the multiplier effect relates directly to the circular flow structure of the economy. The first of the two screens here demonstrates the multiplier effect to you, while the second screen quantifies the changes taking place at each stage.

Assume an initial equilibrium, and then consider the consequences of an exogenous change in injections. This could be a change in any one or a combination of investment, government expenditure or exports flows. Similar effects would also follow a change in consumption occurring at the initial income level, which could be caused by a change in tax rates or saving preferences. The traditional exposition has tended to use the example of a change in investment expenditure, since in practice this component of aggregate demand does fluctuate considerably.

It can be seen that an increase in demand initially causes producers to raise production by an equivalent amount, assuming spare resources are available. But this yields increased household income, which in turn yields increases in consumer expenditure (and taxation and saving), which leads producers to respond by increasing production of consumer goods and services to meet this extra demand, causing income to increase again, and so on. The cumulative change in income is already at this stage greater than the initial change in injections. But the circularity in the income–expenditure flow structure sustains what in theory is an infinite sequence of adjustments of this kind.

The multiplier process quickly fades, however, because at each 'round' some part of the increase in income leaks out as withdrawals – saving, tax, imports. The size of the fraction which is the marginal propensity to spend on domestic output is critical to the overall quantitative effect on total income. This marginal propensity is the proportion of each increment of income which flows all round the circuit to become the next increment of income. Note that the process also works in the opposite direction following an inital exogenous decrease in injections: firms cut production, household income falls, consumption falls, production and income fall again, etc.

The mathematics of the multiplier process confirms that there is convergence to a new equilibrium. You can see this on the second screen.

Try these questions on the effects of exogenous changes

87 **List three possible exogenous changes which could start a multiplier process of adjustment.**

88 **The initial change in each of the flows is calculated by multiplying the initial change in ______ by the appropriate ______ ______.**

89 **If the consumption function is $C = 50 + 0.63Y$ and income rises by 100, the marginal propensity to consume (MPC) is ______ so, therefore, consumption rises by ______.**

90 **With a marginal propensity to save (MPS) of 0.12 and a marginal propensity for taxation (MPT) of 0.25, an increase in income of 100 will mean saving rises by ______ and taxation rises by ______.**

Now consider an example of a multiplier process. Let the marginal propensity to spend on domestic output be 0.4 and let export orders for UK production fall by 2500.

91 **What is the sequence of income changes (through five rounds) as producers respond to the initial fall?**

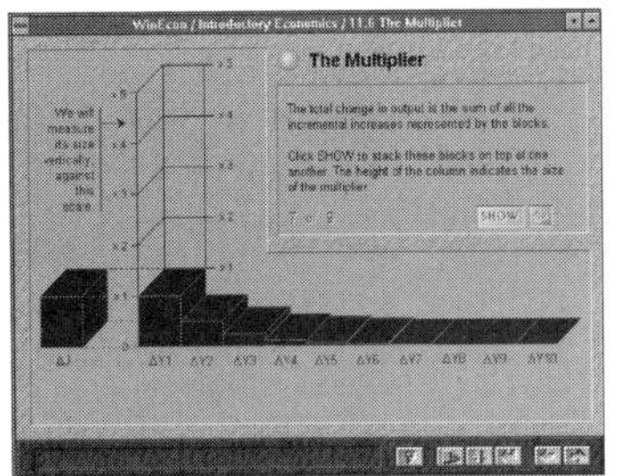

The Multiplier

Here WinEcon provides a different illustration of the multiplier, and shows you that the size of the multiplier effect is related to the marginal propensity to spend on domestic output. On text card 9 of this screen you can experiment to see how changing the marginal propensity to spend on domestic output affects the multiplier process.

The Size of the Multiplier

The multiplier ratio is defined as the total change in equilibrium output/income divided by the initial exogenous change in expenditure which caused it. Here WinEcon shows you how a formula can be derived to give the size of the multiplier. The size of this multiplier ratio – traditionally denoted by k – is given by the formula

$$k = 1/(1-b)$$

where b is the marginal propensity to spend from total income on domestic output. This formula can be derived quickly using calculus or more laboriously without it (see the WinEcon screen). You should memorize the formula. (In the screen example, $b = 0.5$ so we have $k = 1/(1-0.5) = 2$.)

Try these questions on the multiplier

92 **What will be the size of the multiplier ratio if the marginal propensity to spend on domestic output is 0.1, 0.2, 0.6, 0.7?**

93 **In the model used here the marginal propensity to spend on domestic output is given by the marginal propensity to ______ minus the marginal propensity to ______.**

94 **The multiplier ratio becomes larger as the marginal propensity to spend on domestic output ______.**

Equilibrium Values and Exogenous Changes

The overall effect on equilibrium output/income of an exogenous change in injections clearly depends firstly on the scale of the initial change, and secondly on the size of the multiplier ratio. The general calculation required is:

(Change in equilibrium income) = k (initial exogenous change in expenditure)

In these aggregate demand models $k > 1$, which is why it is named the multiplier.

Once a new equilibrium is reached, the change in withdrawals which has taken place always equals the initial change in injections. This must be so because, in equilibrium, $W = J$ and whilst an exogenous change disturbs that balance, the process of adjustment to a new equilibrium restores it. On this screen, WinEcon shows you an example and then on the last text card allows you to experiment with different initial changes. You click the Change Injections button, use the buttons to increase or decrease the changes shown, and then click the Calculate Equilibrium button.

Examine equilibrium values

Use the Change Injections mechanism on the WinEcon screen to set values as follows: $\Delta I = +70$, $\Delta G = -30$, $\Delta X = +100$. Click Calculate Equilibrium and record the new equilibrium values in the table below.

	Before	After	Change
Y^*	1000		
C^*	650		
I^*	120		70
G^*	200		–30
X^*	150		100
S^*	100		
T^*	250		
Z^*	120		

95 **In the above table, what is the net exogenous change in injections? Calculate *k* times this value. Does this equal the change in equilibrium income?**

96 **What is the total change in withdrawals in the table? Does it equal the initial change in injections?**

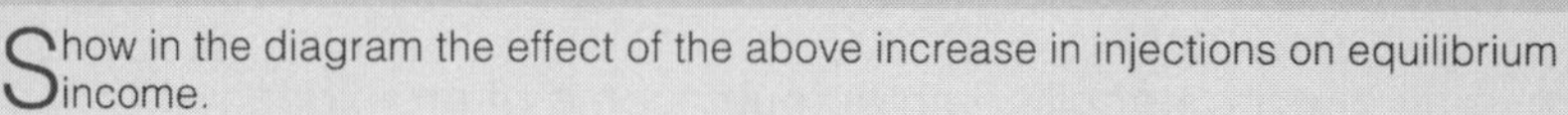

Show in the diagram the effect of the above increase in injections on equilibrium income.

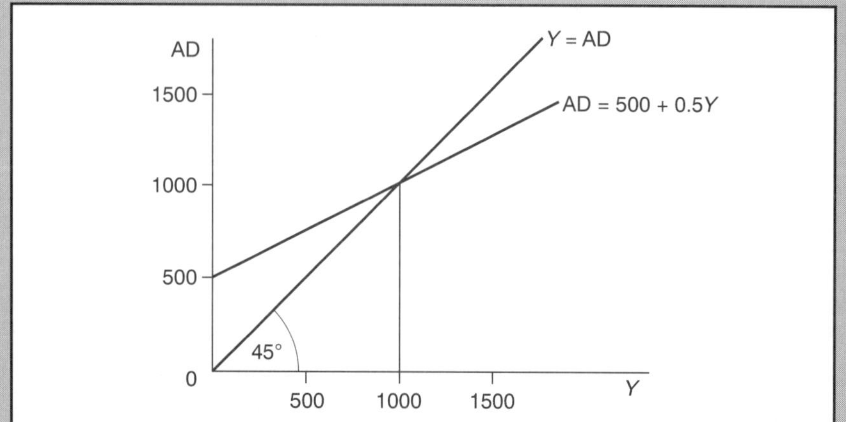

Use the same WinEcon screen to investigate another example:

97 Select changes in injections which give a net overall change of –100, and find the resultant changes in *Y*, *C*, *S*, *T* and *Z*.

The Multiplier: Withdrawals/Injections

The idea of the multiplier effect and the calculation of the size of the multiplier ratio can be approached through a withdrawals–injections perspective just as easily as through the goods market expenditure–production–income perspective. From the initial equilibrium, an exogenous increase in injections will begin to increase the income flow, and as income increases so too will withdrawals since saving, taxation and imports are all functions of income. The process continues until income has increased far enough to bring the total of withdrawals up to the new higher level of injections. This is the new equilibrium.

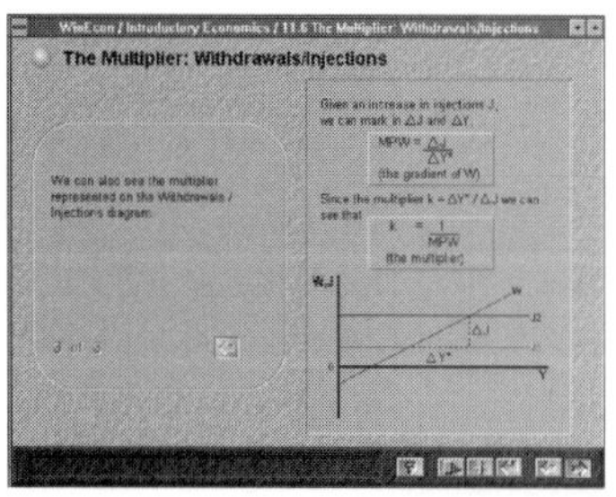

Notice that in the diagram shown on text card 3 the multiplier effect is apparent visually from comparison of the change in equilibrium income (along the horizontal axis) with the change in injections (upward shift of AD and *J* lines, measured against the vertical axis). The income change is clearly larger. A steep AD gradient (high marginal propensity to spend on domestic output) will accentuate the effect, as will a shallow *W* gradient (low marginal propensity to withdraw).

It can be seen that

$$k = 1/w$$

where w is the marginal propensity to withdraw (the sum of the marginal propensities for saving, taxation and imports). This of course is consistent with the earlier formula, so we have $k = 1/(1-b) = 1/w$.

The withdrawals–injections approach

98 As an aid to memory, write down the equation for yourself: k = [ ] = [ ], where b is the marginal propensity to [ ] [ ] [ ] [ ].

Calculate the size of the multiplier ratio in the following cases (where lower case letters represent marginal propensities).

99 When $c = 0.62$, $s = 0.13$, $t = 0.25$ and $z = 0.22$, k = [ ].

100 When $c = 0.9$ and $z = 0.1$, k = [ ].

101 When $s = 0.06$, $t = 0.2$ and $z = 0.14$, k = [ ].

What is the change in equilibrium income when:

102 X increases by 80 and $k = 3.0$? [ ]

103 I falls by 200 and $k = 1.7$? [ ]

104 G increases by 120 and $k = 2.0$? [ ]

Section 11.7: Policy Implications of the Model

Any national government wishing to maintain a general state of economic well-being should be aware that exogenous changes in the components of aggregate demand can produce even larger movements in national income. In this sense, the lessons of the income–expenditure model have general relevance. But it was a more specific concern with unemployment which led to the development of the theory, and the policy implications here are quite striking.

Unemployment and Macroeconomic Policy

Keynes developed his theory to explain the persistence of large-scale unemployment in Britain in the late 1920s and early 1930s. The basic income–expenditure model is at the core of this theory, although there are other (particularly, monetary) aspects of the Keynesian theory we have not incorporated yet. The crucial conclusion is that the economy can settle into an equilibrium at any level of production and income, depending on the level of aggregate demand at the time.

See chapters 12, 13 and 14 for further development of the Keynesian theory.

Keynesian macroeconomic equilibrium and full employment are two quite distinct situations. If aggregate demand for goods and services is low, so too will be the demand for labour and other factors of production, leaving many people unemployed. There is nothing in the situation to create an automatic return to full employment. Firms will not increase production and take on more workers until they can foresee an increase in sales. Households will not increase their purchases until more of their people get jobs and incomes rise. The economy is then stuck in a low-level equilibrium with 'demand deficient unemployment'.

When the problem is insufficient demand, a government can step in to do something about it. For instance, in the model, an increase in G or a decrease in T (which, by giving households more disposable income, induces an increase in C) will have a multiplier effect in increasing Y and, with it, employment. Such changes using the government budget are known as fiscal policy. As a more general political-economic philosophy, 'Keynesianism' advocates that governments should 'manage' aggregate demand using fiscal and monetary policy, to ensure that the economy is stabilized at a level close to full employment. If private spending falls, increased public spending and/or tax cuts can be used to keep aggregate demand and employment high.

Check your understanding of governmental demand management

105 **Demand management by government is advocated by ________ economists as a way of maintaining ______ ________ in the economy.**

106 **The tools of demand management are ________ policies (changing government spending and/or taxation) and ________ policies (changing money supply and interest rate).**

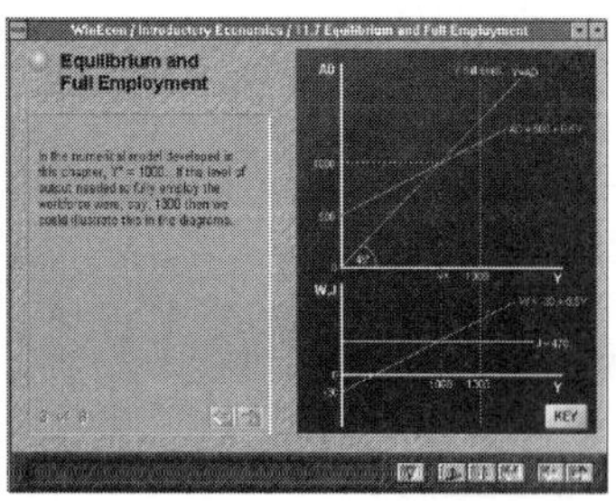

Equilibrium and Full Employment

WinEcon demonstrates, with diagrams, how the income–expenditure model suggests that full employment can be achieved starting from a situation of less than full employment. What is required is an increase in aggregate demand to move the equilibrium of the economy to coincide with full employment.

Policy Implications: A Few Cautions

Things are not always as easy in practice as the income–expenditure model might suggest. (The WinEcon screen mentions some government objectives

Try these questions on equilibrium and full employment

107 Keynesian equilibrium need not be at full employment. True or false? [ ]

108 According to the income–expenditure model, persistent large-scale unemployment is attributable to a [ ] [ ] [ ] [ ].

109 In unemployment equilibrium, firms will not offer more [ ] until they see an increase in [ ], and households will not increase their [ ] for products until they have more [ ] and income.

To revise the use of the income–expenditure model in this context, consider a situation with equilibrium income below full employment. Let full employment output/income be 8000 whilst the current economic situation is given by AD = 2400 + 0.6*Y*, *J* = 2000 and *W* = –400 + 0.4*Y*, such that equilibrium income is 6000. (Check this figure before proceeding.)

Complete the diagrams to show this situation. Mark the 'deflationary gap'. Then show in both diagrams how a sufficient increase of government expenditure would close that gap and move the equilibrium to coincide with full employment.

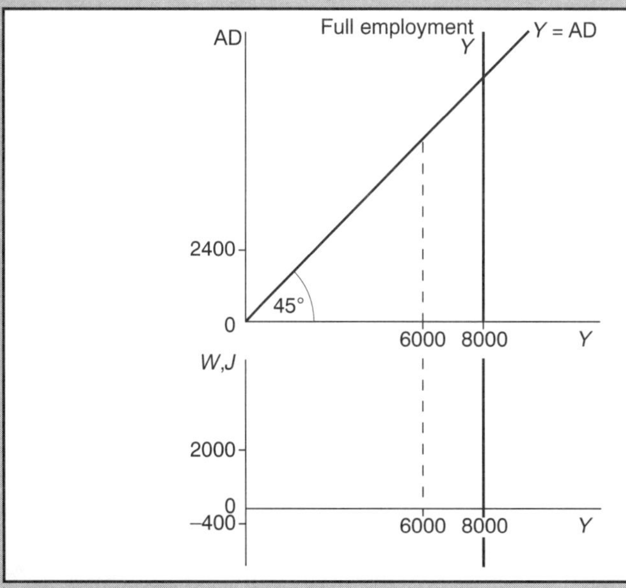

110 How much extra *G* is needed? [ ]

that would preclude the use of the income–expenditure model.) Nevertheless, this relatively simple model provides a sound basis for furthering your understanding of macroeconomics and policy.

See chapter 15 for more on macroeconomic policy.

Section 11.8. Summary

By first identifying the main sectors of activity, firms and households, and the payments flows between them, it is possible to build up a picture of the economic structure. To complete the full circular flow of income and expenditure, the injections and withdrawals flows must be added. We note that for the economy to achieve equilibrium the total of actual injections must equal the total of actual withdrawals.

We have seen how to model the economic behaviour of households and firms using equations and diagrams to represent the main functional relationships. Planned consumer spending is modelled by the consumption function. This has particular importance in the income–expenditure model and depicts the consumer expenditure flow as dependent on the total flow of income. The equilibrium of the system is seen to require a consistency between the plans of different groups of economic agents, with adjustments taking place until this is achieved. The model shows that equilibrium output/income can be at any level up to full employment, depending on the state of aggregate demand at the time.

Exogenous changes in demand initiate a multiplier effect, with continuing repercussions around the circular flow converging to a new equilibrium. This helps to explain fluctuations in economic activity, one of the important requirements for a believable macroeconomic model. The income–expenditure model, originating from the pioneering work of Keynes in the 1930s, provides a very useful basis for further study of macroeconomics.

Self-test revision questions on the income–expenditure model

111 **In the consumption function $C = 350 + 0.55Y$, the MPC is ______.**

112 **In this same function, the APC at $Y = 1000$ is ______.**

113 **MPC + MPS + MPT = ______.**

114 **In terms of the addition and subtraction of components, AD = ______.**

115 **The multiplier is defined as:**

116 **State two formulas for the size of the multiplier ratio.**

Chapter 12:
Money Supply and Demand

The money supply is more than just notes and coins. To understand it we need to look at the principles of banking and learn about some of the institutional features of the financial sector of a modern economy. The demand for money depends on other economic variables. People may want money for buying goods and services, or they may keep it instead of buying other financial assets such as bonds. Different theories are explored in this chapter, and problems in interpreting empirical evidence are noted.

Contents

KEYWORDS

- Assets
- Bank deposit multiplier
- Bills
- Bonds
- Cash
- Deposits
- Liabilities
- LM curve
- Loans
- Quantity theory
- Rate of interest
- Reserve ratio
- Speculative demand
- Transactions demand
- Velocity of circulation

Section 12.1: Introduction

This chapter has two distinct parts, one concerned with money supply and the other with money demand. They are introduced in this section by a screen which gives you an overview of the chapter as a whole. The concept which links both parts is money – the following screen lets you examine some fundamental questions about the functions of money.

Different sections of this chapter present the 'classical', 'Keynesian' and 'monetarist' analyses of the money market. The Keynesian approach leads to the derivation of the 'LM curve', showing where the money market is in equilibrium. This curve is used with the 'IS curve' which we derive in chapter 13. Together the curves let us analyse situations where the economy is in equilibrium using IS–LM analysis.

See the topics The IS Equation and Curve: Graphical Approach and others, especially IS–LM Equilibrium, in section 13.4.

Money Supply and Demand: Introduction

Money supply is in the hands of the banking system, with the central bank endeavouring to exercise some control over the whole process – not always with great success. We investigate how this all works in principle and in the major economies of the late twentieth century.

When we turn to money demand, and ask what determines the extent of money holding by households and firms, we are led to consider different theories. These have importance for the wider question of how monetary variables interact with real activity in the economy.

Functions of Money

What is money? The answer to this may seem obvious; it is something we all take for granted. However, we need to appreciate what it is that is special about the things we use as money. What justifies their being described as 'money'? What else could be 'money'? WinEcon throws more light on these questions, and you find that they are best answered by considering what functions are performed by money. In our society bank accounts rather than notes and coins provide the predominant form of money.

Record what you have learnt about money

01 **Successful barter exchange requires:**

02 **Legal tender is:**

03 **Three major functions of money are:**

04 **Bank deposits are money because:**

Section 12.2: Money Supply

To discover how the money supply is measured and to appreciate its importance we need to understand how the banking system works.

The Money Stock: Aggregate Measures

How much money is being moved around in our economy today? For some economists (e.g. 'monetarists') this is a matter of the greatest importance because they believe the available total stock of money determines the aggregate flow of spending on goods and services and the general rate of increase in prices (i.e. inflation).

WinEcon gives you more information about how the quantity of money in existence at a point in time may be measured. In a modern economy the total stock of money comprises cash (notes and coin) plus bank deposits, and measurement is in currency units. Notice particularly that the total value of bank deposits nowadays is many times greater than the value of the cash issue.

In measuring the money stock (i.e. money supply) it is necessary to ask which bank deposits, or deposits with other financial institutions, qualify for inclusion. There is no single correct answer here; it depends on the context. WinEcon gives you more information about the official 'monetary aggregates' statistics, which include narrow and broad measures of the money stock. 'Narrow money' is more directly available for making payments, so may link more closely to, say, retail spending. 'Broad money' may be a better indicator of total wealth in the community.

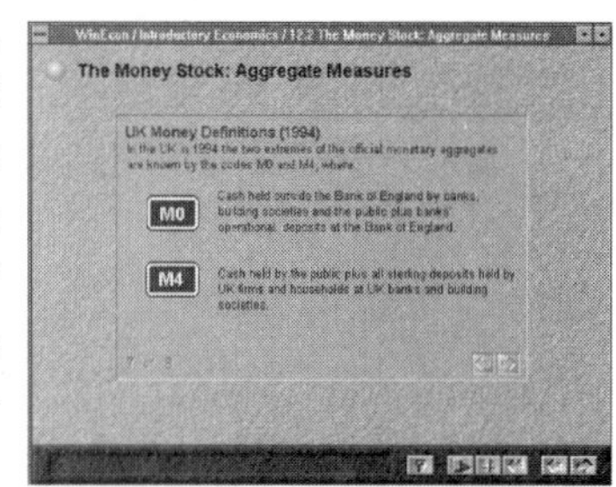

Complete the following statements about the money stock

05 **Time deposits differ from sight deposits (i.e. demand deposits) in requiring:**

06 **In the UK the M0 monetary aggregate is made up of:**

07 **In the UK the M4 monetary aggregate is made up of:**

08 **Money is different from income or spending because:**

Flows of Funds Accounts

As you have seen, money is a stock of 'means of payment'. However, apart from its use in the flows of payments for goods and services, parts of the money stock may be transferred from one holder to another in lending and borrowing transactions. WinEcon shows you how such financial transfers are recorded in 'flows of funds accounts'. These flows of funds can be direct from lender to borrower, or indirect through financial markets and institutions.

Complete the following accounting definitions

09 **Income from current production – current expenditure =** [ ].

10 **Saving –** [ ] [ ] **= financial balance.**

11 **Financial balance = change in** [ ] [ ] **– change in** [ ] [ ].
= [N] [A] **of** [F] [A].

12 **Current income – current expenditure – capital expenditure =** [ ] [ ].

13 **Increase in assets – increase in liabilities =**

Assets and Liabilities

We need to clarify the definition of assets and liabilities. Assets are any items of monetary value which are owned. Apart from money itself, there are other financial assets and there are real assets (e.g. land, buildings, machinery and equipment, stocks of materials or finished goods) which could be sold to obtain money. Liabilities are monetary obligations which are owed to someone else (i.e. debts). Check with the examples in WinEcon that you can correctly identify assets and liabilities.

For every financial asset owned there is a corresponding liability which is owed. Financial assets are created in a lending/borrowing transaction where the lender or depositor has (owns) a claim for repayment, and the borrower has (owes) an obligation to repay. The lender therefore has an asset, the

borrower has a liability of corresponding amount. It follows that for every separate category of financial asset (e.g. loan, certificate of deposit, bond), total assets equal total liabilities in monetary value.

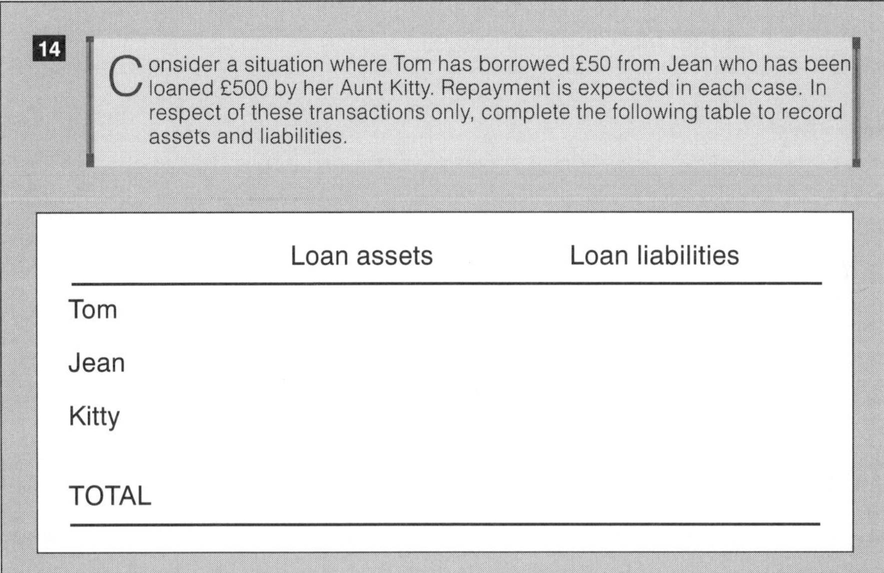

14 Consider a situation where Tom has borrowed £50 from Jean who has been loaned £500 by her Aunt Kitty. Repayment is expected in each case. In respect of these transactions only, complete the following table to record assets and liabilities.

	Loan assets	Loan liabilities
Tom		
Jean		
Kitty		
TOTAL		

Financial Accounts and the Flows of Funds

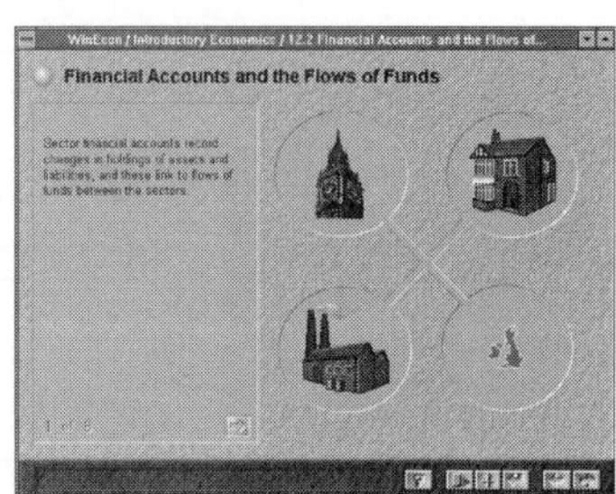

By defining sectors of the economy (such as personal, corporate, government and overseas sectors) and recording the aggregate flows of funds between them, we can gain interesting insights into the overall macroeconomic situation. WinEcon shows you some actual figures for the UK economy to illustrate this.

Test your understanding of flows of funds

15 **Across all sectors, total surpluses + total deficits =** ________.

The Banking System: The Role of the Central Bank

We know what a bank is, but how many other different kinds of 'financial institutions' (whose business is mainly in handling money rather than producing goods) can you identify? WinEcon takes you through three screens to consider the various kinds of institutions which make up the financial sector of a modern economy, beginning with the central bank. We can create a simple picture of the financial system as a triangle with a central bank at the

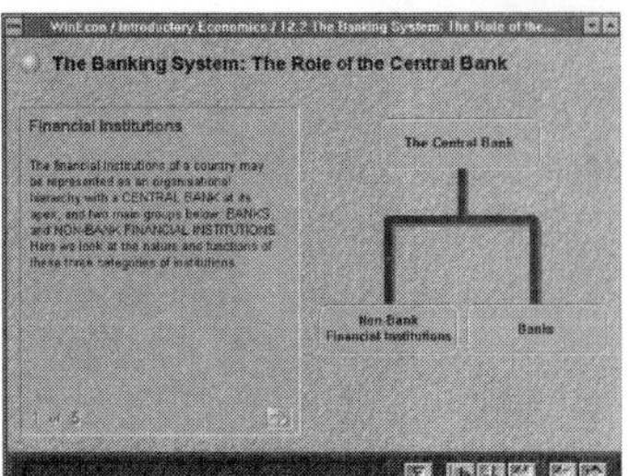

apex and commercial banks and non-bank financial institutions (NBFIs) below. To find out more, work through the WinEcon screens.

From the description of its functions, you now appreciate why a central bank is so called.

About central banks

16 **List six functions of a central bank.**

17 **For three countries, name the central bank.**

The Banking System: The Other Banks

From the information given in WinEcon, you should be able to recognize the various financial institutions, distinguished here by the nature of their business. All financial institutions are financial intermediaries: they take money in and pass it on in different ways. Banks, however, as we see later, do more than this: they create new money as well as circulating existing money.

Try the following question

18 **Name four large clearing banks.**

Non-Bank Financial Institutions (NBFIs)

This WinEcon screen describes briefly the workings of building societies, pension funds, finance companies and unit trusts. These non–bank financial institutions cover a wider range of business than the banks.

The Banking System: Operations

Historically, banks began business by offering safe keeping for people's precious metal money, and the gold and silver deposited in their vaults counted as an asset whilst the claim of customers to withdraw what they had deposited was the corresponding liability. The bank note was originally a receipt for a deposit but once these notes became acceptable for payment in their own right, modern paper money was born. These origins explain the wording on British notes: 'I promise to pay the bearer on demand the sum of XX.'

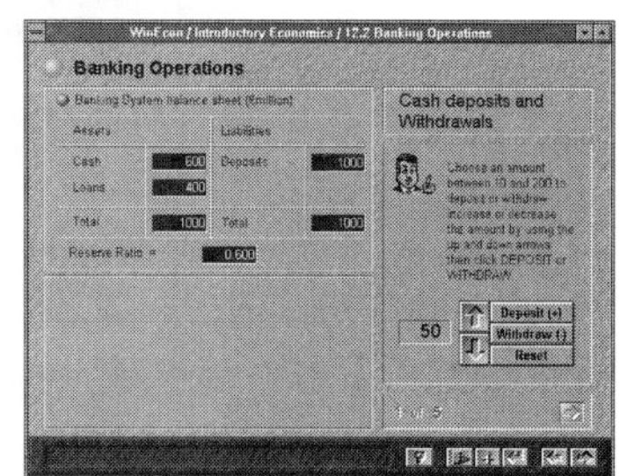

With WinEcon you now begin to consider the basic banking functions in rather more detail, through four screens. This first screen introduces a simplified banking balance sheet with which to record holdings of assets and liabilities in the banking system at one point in time. With the next three screens (Banking Operations (1)–(3)) you then use this balance sheet framework to explore different banking operations.

Modern banks offer more than just safe keeping of deposits; they also make loans. Loans are an asset to the bank (claim for repayment) and an equal liability (obligation to make payments up to this amount on behalf of the borrower). You can draw cash or make payments from your account in the same way, whether your credit balance was created for you by the bank giving you a loan, or by you depositing the money at the bank in the first place. So we normally only show one deposits total in the balance sheet. We will look into bank credit creation more deeply later, because it is a crucially important feature of modern banking, but for the moment we just recognize that loans appear in this way in the balance sheet. New loans will increase the deposits total.

Your attention is drawn to the bank 'reserve ratio'. It is important in controlling bank lending.

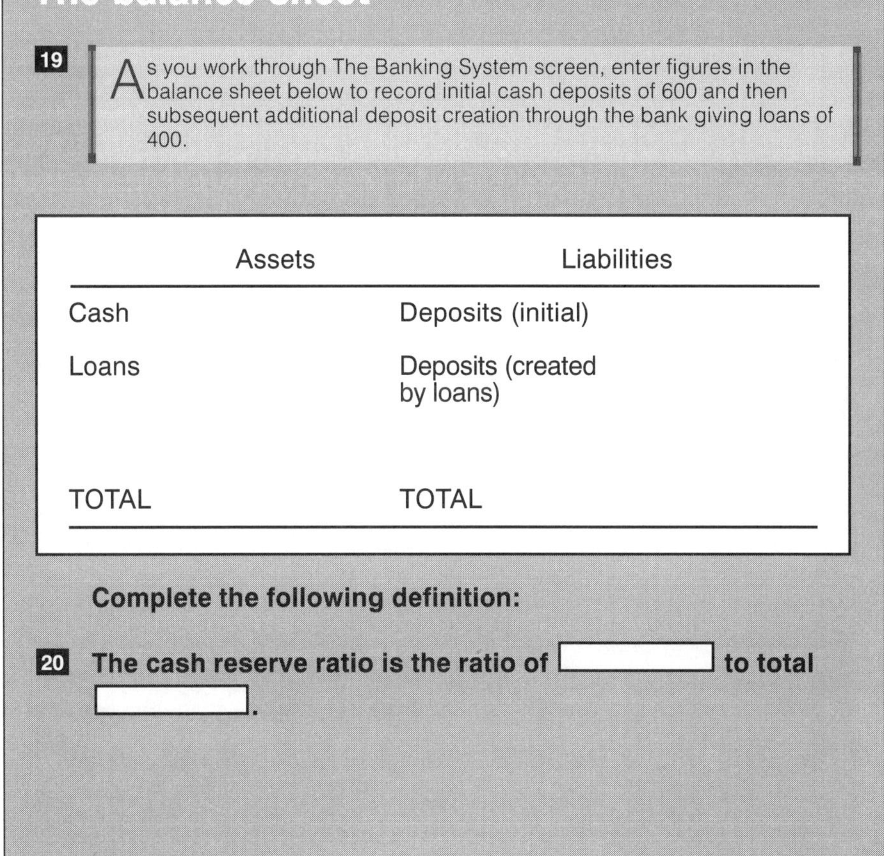

The balance sheet

19 As you work through The Banking System screen, enter figures in the balance sheet below to record initial cash deposits of 600 and then subsequent additional deposit creation through the bank giving loans of 400.

Assets		Liabilities	
Cash		Deposits (initial)	
Loans		Deposits (created by loans)	
TOTAL		TOTAL	

Complete the following definition:

20 **The cash reserve ratio is the ratio of ________ to total ________.**

Banking Operations

Apart from deposits, withdrawals and loans, another fundamental service offered by clearing banks is to make payments for the customer, on instructions provided in the form of a cheque. The WinEcon screen Banking Operations allows you to experiment to see how different deposits, withdrawals and cheque transfers affect the banking system balance sheet and the reserve ratio (with bank loans being held constant for the purposes of this illustration). Banking Operations (2), a supplementary screen accessed with the Next Page button, considers these transactions in a multi–bank system. Banking Operations (3) returns to consideration of how new loans affect the balance sheet. Spend some time with these screens until you are confident about the balance sheet adjustments.

Notice a number of things. Cheque transfers between customers of the same bank involve a bookkeeping transfer between accounts, but no change in the overall totals of assets and liabilities, or in the reserve ratio. Cheque transfers between customers of different banks affect assets, liabilities and the reserve ratio for the individual banks concerned, but not for the banking system as a whole.

Although in a competitive banking system some banks may gain an increased market share at the expense of others, we need not be distracted by such effects here because, as you see, the banking system consolidated balance sheet is not affected. We therefore continue to use a balance sheet for the banking system as a whole because the principles of banking can be most clearly illustrated at this level.

New loans increase assets (loans) and liabilities (deposits) by the same amount, and they cause a decline in the cash reserve ratio. Conversely a reduction of loans outstanding – more loans repaid than new loans issued – will reduce assets and liabilities equally and increase the reserve ratio. The significance of this becomes apparent with the next topic.

The reserve ratio

21 From the balance sheet position shown in card 3 of Banking Operations (3), if new loans increase by 300, the reserve ratio changes from ________ to ________.

The Minimum Reserve Ratio

Banks are in business to make a profit. They charge a higher rate of interest on their loans than they pay on deposits, and the differential is the main source of their profits. Hence, in general, banks will want to extend their loans business (subject to the creditworthiness of applicants). But increasing loans reduces the cash reserve ratio. This means that banks are vulnerable to running out of cash if too many of their customers simultaneously want to make withdrawals. Even a suspicion that a bank is short of cash could precipitate a rush to withdraw, so a bank must acknowledge the imperative need to protect its reputation for soundness, and always maintain sufficient reserves.

This balance between the desire for profits and the need for prudence is at the heart of banking business. To expand business and profits, a bank must promote an image of financial security, which is enhanced by achieving good profits. Yet over-emphasizing security by keeping a high margin of reserves will diminish profitability.

The prudential requirement for adequate reserves to cover foreseeable fluctuations in withdrawals may be imposed by banking law as a statutory minimum reserve ratio. In Britain since 1981 banks have been free to make a commercial decision about the optimal level of reserves, but we can consider this to be equivalent to imposing upon themselves a minimum reserve ratio (mrr).

Why can a relatively low reserve ratio suffice? Consider what happens to cash that is withdrawn. It is used to make payments in shops, cinemas, restaurants, etc. Every day these businesses will 'bank' their takings (i.e. deposit the cash back into the banks). As more is withdrawn, more is spent and, therefore, more is re-deposited. Hence, cash circulates in and out of the banking system, and it is not likely that every customer will want to withdraw at the same time. This is why banks don't need to keep reserves equivalent to 100 per cent of their liabilities.

Loan Expansion and the Bank Deposit Multiplier

A modern banking system is a fractional reserve banking system. It is founded on the assumption that not all customers will wish to withdraw cash at the same time, thereby allowing banks to make loans at levels that cause their reserve ratios to drop to just a fraction of their total liabilities without jeopardizing customer confidence.

This screen shows you that, given a minimum acceptable reserve ratio, there are limits to loan expansion. Loans create additional deposits, and you see that what is known as the bank deposit multiplier gives a mathematical link between a change in reserves and the maximum consequential change in total liabilities (deposits). The actual cash reserve ratio of a bank at any time is given by dividing the cash by the total deposits. This ratio diminishes as total deposits increase when loans are expanded.

Assuming that banks always profit maximize by expanding their loans to the maximum consistent with the minimum reserve ratio, a change in their reserves will lead to a larger change in the same direction in their total deposits. With the mrr a fraction less than one, the bank deposit multiplier is greater than one.

The minimum reserve ratio and deposit multipliers

For the situation where the minimum reserve ratio (mrr) is reached, complete the following:

22 **mrr = cash / [ ].**

23 **Deposits = ([ ]/ [ ]) × cash reserves.**

24 **Change in deposits = ([ ] / [ ]) × change in cash reserves.**

25 **The item in the brackets above is called the [ ] [ ] [ ].**

26 **The bank deposit multiplier is defined here as (the maximum change in bank [ ])/(change in [ ] [ ]) consistent with a given minimum reserve ratio.**

Given mrr = 0.05

27 **If deposits = 24,000, the level of cash reserves needed is [ ].**

28 **The bank deposit multiplier in this case is [ ].**

29 **Given an initial actual reserve ratio at the minimum of 0.05, if there was a cash withdrawal of 100 the decrease in loans outstanding needed to restore the 0.05 ratio is [ ].**

Section 12.3: Monetary Control

This section considers the ways in which the central bank exercises control over the quantity of money in the economy. It may wish to restrict monetary growth to try to restrain inflation, or in the other direction it may wish to stimulate an expansion of real output and employment. Monetary policy is used to support the general economic aims of the government.

Control of the Money Supply

This topic introduces control of the money supply by showing how the total money supply is related to the availability of reserves. If the banks always maintain maximum lending consistent with their minimum reserve ratio, this gives a fixed ratio between reserves and deposits. Given that the central bank controls the 'total cash issue' (which is also known in this context as 'high-powered money', or the 'monetary base', on which banks can build their lending), this gives it leverage also over total deposits. To model this requires making some assumption about the cash in circulation outside the banks. To illustrate, we assume a fixed ratio between the public's desire for cash and their bank deposits.

With WinEcon you discover that in this framework the total money stock is a function of the cash issue. Hence, since the central bank controls the cash issue, this gives it control over the money supply in the country. Specifically, the money supply here is a multiple of the cash issue. Note that if the public's cash holding were fixed, with no change in cash in circulation when the cash issue changed, all of the money supply effect would then be via bank reserves and deposits and the multiplier in the above expression reduces to the simpler bank deposit multiplier used earlier (1/mrr).

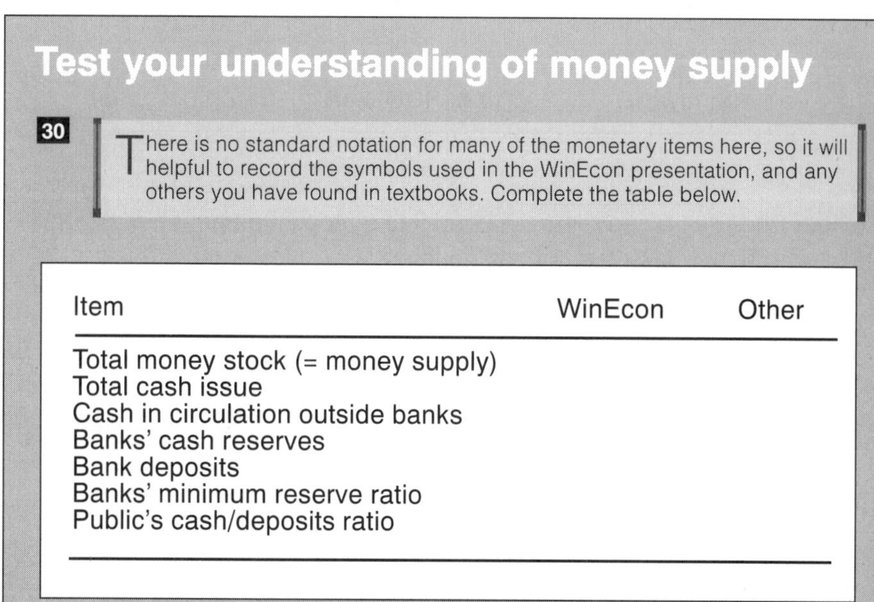

Test your understanding of money supply

30 There is no standard notation for many of the monetary items here, so it will helpful to record the symbols used in the WinEcon presentation, and any others you have found in textbooks. Complete the table below.

Item	WinEcon	Other
Total money stock (= money supply)		
Total cash issue		
Cash in circulation outside banks		
Banks' cash reserves		
Bank deposits		
Banks' minimum reserve ratio		
Public's cash/deposits ratio		

31 **Complete the multiplier formula below:**

MS = [(______ + ______)/(______ + ______)] × HPM

Try the following calculations:

32 **If mrr = 0.04, cdr = 0.08 and HPM is increased by 100, by how much will total money supply (MS) increase?**

33 **If mrr = 0.05, CSH is fixed and HPM is reduced by 60, what is the change in MS?**

Exogenous and Endogenous Money

It can be argued that in a modern liberalized financial system, monetary control does not operate according to the model described above and that money supply is 'endogenous' (banks provide as much money as is demanded) rather than 'exogenous' (fixed in quantity by the central bank). Being aware of this alternative view, we shall need to look more carefully at monetary control processes in theory and practice. Let us first pursue the principles of monetary control a stage further. By what methods does the central bank try to exercise control over reserves in the banking system? The traditional method is known as 'open market operations', where the market referred to is the market for bills and bonds. If the central bank buys or sells bills and bonds this affects the level of reserves in the banking system. Bills and bonds are described in the next topic, followed by an explanation of open market operations.

Bills and Bonds

Do you know what bills and bonds are? With this screen, WinEcon helps you find out more about them. 'Bills' (bills of exchange) are issued by governments, companies, banks etc. to raise funds for a short period of time (months).They are sold at a price below their face value. 'Bonds' are issued to raise funds for a longer period of time (years). A bond has a face value payable at maturity and rewards the purchaser by paying interest.

If you purchase a bond after the issue date, the price may vary in the bond market depending on supply and demand, and your rate of return depends on the price you pay. Financial pages in the newspapers quote yesterday's bond prices (per £100) and 'interest-only (IO) yield' and 'gross redemption yield' (to maturity). Have a look (e.g. at British Funds).

Note that bond prices vary inversely with interest rates. For a perpetual bond (with no maturity date, so the only return is the interest income) prices vary so that the yield equalizes with current interest rates (buyers will not pay a

higher price giving a lower yield, sellers need not accept a lower price). We can summarize this as:

IO yield = fixed coupon payment/bond price = current interest rate

Bond price = fixed coupon payment/current interest rate

As fixed term bonds approach their maturity date this formula does not give the price because the repayment of the face value ('principal') outweighs the interest income in calculating the overall return to the purchaser. It is still true, however, that interest rate changes cause bond prices to change in the other direction.

Test your knowledge of bills and bonds

Complete the following statements:

34 **A bill promises to pay the holder the [ ] [ ] on the [ ] date.**

35 **Bills are sold at a [ ] below the [ ] [ ].**

36 **The interest rate declared at issue, applied to the face value of the bond, gives the '[ ]' interest payment which is then [ ] throughout the life of the bond.**

Try the following calculations:

37 **If a £100 3-month bill yields approximately 4% to the holder over that period, what to the nearest pound was the price paid? [ ]**

38 **For this bill, what is the equivalent annual rate of return, to the nearest integer percentage? [ ]**

39 **If a £100 bond has a coupon interest rate of 12% per annum, what is the annual interest payable? [ ]**

40 **What is the interest-only yield on this bond to a purchaser who pays £120 for it? [ ]**

41 **Imagine you bought a £100 15% perpetual bond at issue (i.e. you paid £100 and receive £15 per annum interest). Since then, interest rates have fallen to 10% per annum. If you now sell your bond, what is your capital gain or loss?**

Open Market Operations: In Theory

The central bank uses open market operations, selling or buying bills and bonds, to influence the money supply. The WinEcon screen shows you the theory of how open market operations work.

Check your understanding of the theory of open market operations

42 **If the central bank sells bills or bonds to non-bank purchasers, the reserves in the banking system are** [increased/reduced] **by a** [larger/equal/smaller] **amount.**

43 **Open market sales lead to a multiple** [expansion/contraction] **in the money supply.**

Open Market Operations: In UK Practice

The effect of open market operations is not so straightforward when banks hold (as they do in practice) a much greater variety of assets and liabilities than we have been showing in our illustrative but over-simplified bank balance sheets.

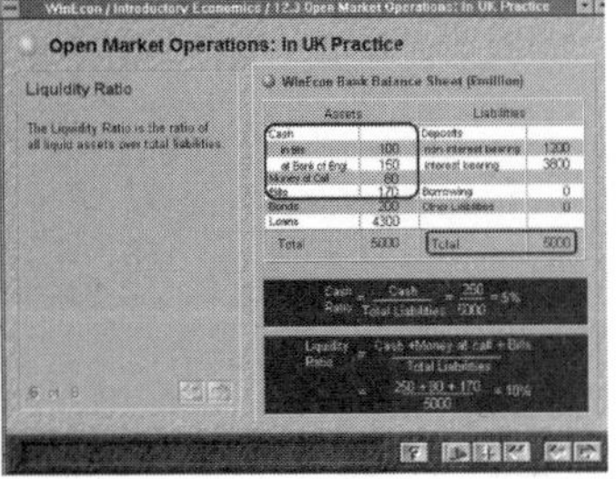

Here we introduce some further items to the balance sheet. In this more realistic context, banks will wish to minimize their cash reserves (which earn them nothing) but supplement these with liquid assets, like money at call and bills, which can be converted to cash quickly and easily if more cash is needed. This translates into maintaining both a minimum cash ratio and a minimum liquidity ratio. In the UK, banks' responses to open market operations will reflect such considerations.

Open Market Sales and Banks' Responses

In practice, in a monetary system like that of the UK in the 1990s, the banks may not react to open market operations by implementing a multiple change in loans. Given open market sales, banks may seek to offset the decline in their reserves by obtaining more reserves in other ways, rather than cut

their loans which are their most profitable asset. In this topic we acknowledge the increased variety of possible responses to open market sales in a liberalized financial system.

Because banks have other assets apart from cash and loans, they may adjust their holdings of these rather than their holdings of loans to restore their cash and liquid asset ratios. Withdrawing/selling liquid assets can replenish cash, and bond holdings might be reduced to replenish liquid assets. Alternatively, banks may adjust their liabilities. More reserves can be obtained by offering higher interest rates to attract new deposits or, more importantly nowadays, by issuing bank bills or borrowing funds in the wholesale inter-bank money market, which is an international market.

In these ways central bank monetary control is made less effective. It is partly in recognition of this that some economists, post-Keynesians in particular, take the position that money supply is endogenous not exogenous. Others hold to the traditional view, but accept that monetary control in practice is imperfect. Some monetarist economists would like to change banking law and regulations to reinstate firmer central bank control over the quantity of money.

Other Monetary Control Measures

Various other methods of control may be available to a central bank, depending on the institutional arrangements in place at the time. Here, WinEcon draws your attention to some other possible means of control.

Interest Rate Control Methods

Interest rate controls are now, in many countries, more important than control of the quantity of money. With this screen you can appreciate some of the ways in which such controls are used.

Control over interest rates is important even when the money supply is endogenous. The central bank provides funds when the other banks are short, to maintain stability and confidence in the system. It may do this through direct lending ('lender of last resort') or through purchasing bills etc. The central bank determines the interest rate (re-discount rate) on such transactions. This rate may be fixed by announcement, or may be engineered through market transactions, and other interest rates in the system adjust accordingly.

Check your understanding of interest rate control methods

44 **List three control measures to reduce the money supply.**

45 **If the central bank indicates a willingness to buy bills at a higher price than previously, which way will interest rates change?**

Section 12.4: Classical Theory of Money Demand

After a general introduction, we look in this section at the classical theory of money demand. Keynesian and monetarist theories are covered later.

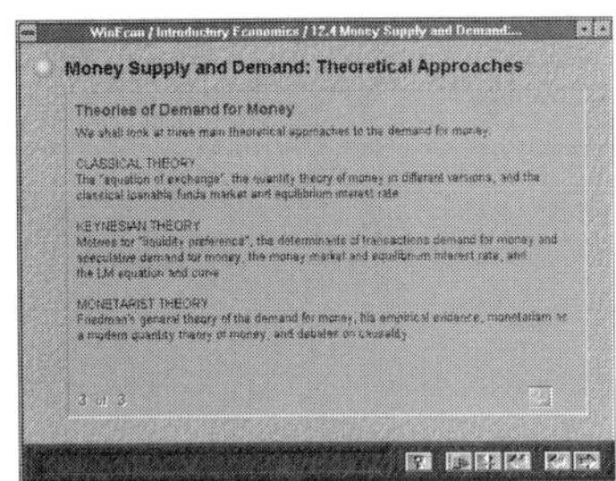

Money Supply and Demand: Theoretical Approaches

The earliest theories of money did not distinguish money demand from money supply. Money flowed in exchange for goods and services and made trade much easier than under barter arrangements. But once the stock of money held between transactions becomes the focus of attention, the total amount of money available (money supply) may not always be the same as the total amount that firms, households and other agents desire to hold (money demand). Money demand should always be understood as a stock demand.

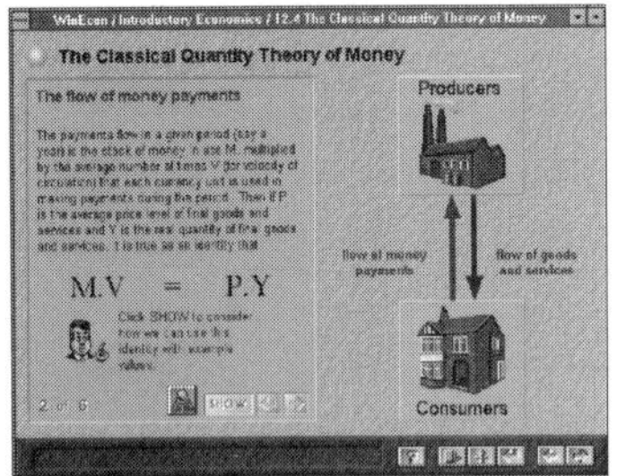

The Classical Quantity Theory of Money

The classical approach revolves around the quantity of money. WinEcon begins here by introducing you to the basic classical theory. The earlier versions of the 'quantity theory of money' are expressed through the 'equation of exchange'. The equation of exchange is in one sense a truism or accounting identity, since the $M.V$ is the flow of money payments in a period, and $P.Y$ is the money value of the goods and services paid for, so $M.V$ and $P.Y$ are necessarily equal. V can be calculated from P, Y and M. To develop this into a theory requires the assumption that V is independently determined and stable, or, at its simplest, a constant. Early thinking justified this in terms of institutional regularities in payments – weekly wages etc. If V is fixed independently of the other three terms, then these must adjust to give the necessary equality $M.V = P.Y$. From here, a more general macroeconomic model can be developed.

The screen The Quantity Theory and Aggregate Demand in section 13.2 gives further details.

If the central bank determines the money quantity M, then $M.V$ is a fixed amount of money expenditure per period. From that, if average price rises, aggregate demand will fall, and vice versa. Or, if Y is given, P must adjust to give equilibrium in the goods market.

About the classical quantity theory of money

46 Fill in what the letters stand for:

M

V

P

Y

Test your understanding:

47 **How is the velocity of circulation of money defined?**

48 **The equation of exchange is** ______

49 **The crucial assumption to develop this from an accounting identity into a theory is** ______

50 **If P = £2, Y = £12 million per annum, M = £6 million, calculate V.**

The Cambridge Version of Quantity Theory of Money

At Cambridge University in the early years of this century, a different version of the quantity theory of money was taught to the young John Maynard Keynes. The emphasis had switched to money balances held rather than money flowing in exchange. This screen examines the question of what determines the aggregate demand to hold money balances.

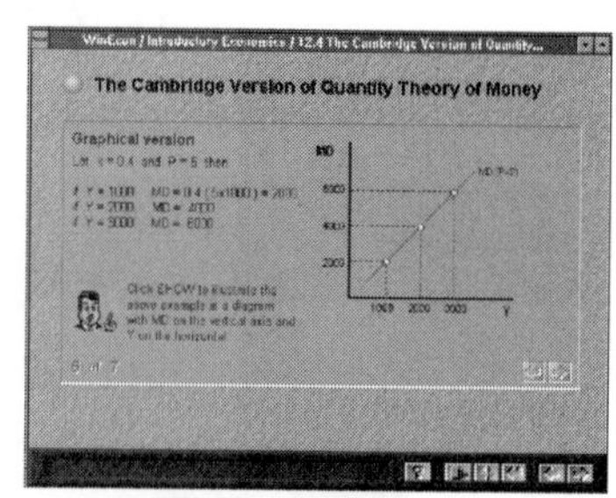

The 'Cambridge k' can be considered to be a constant. If the money market is in equilibrium, MD = MS = M, and then, numerically, k is the reciprocal of velocity (i.e. k = 1/V). But we now have a different emphasis. Economic agents, firms and households, in aggregate, demand money in proportion to the money value of their purchases (quantity × price).

The Cambridge theory

51 **If MD represents money demand (the demand to hold money balances), complete the following expression for the Cambridge version of the quantity theory: MD =** ______.

52 If k = 0.4, P = £2.00 and Y = £120 billion, MD is: ______.

The Classical Loanable Funds Market

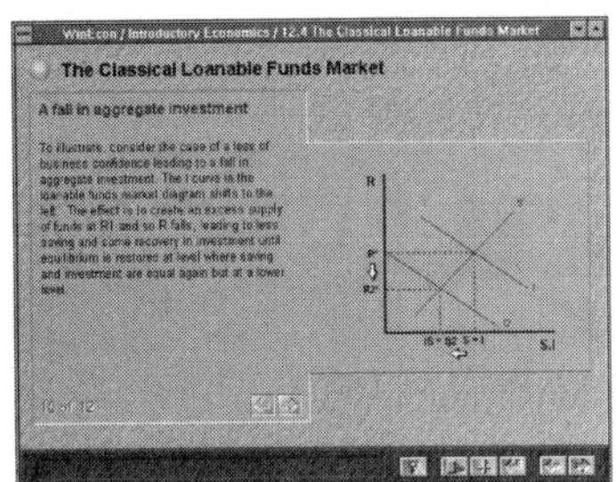

Although a monetary variable, the rate of interest in classical theory is explained not by the quantity theory of money but by reference to a market for loanable funds. WinEcon shows you what this entails. The supply of loanable funds through saving is a positive function of the rate of interest, and the demand for funds to finance investment expenditure is an inverse function of the rate of interest. The rate of interest adjusts in the market until supply and demand for funds are in equilibrium.

Section 12.5: Keynesian Theory of Demand for Money

Keynes identified a number of reasons why people and organizations might want to hold money balances, and we see how his theory is built up from looking at each of these in turn. Keynesian analysis of the money market then explains how the rate of interest is determined. By considering different possible levels of real income, Y, for the economy, we see what interest rate would correspond to each level and so obtain the LM curve, which will be used in chapter 13 for IS–LM analysis.

The Keynesian Theory of Money Demand

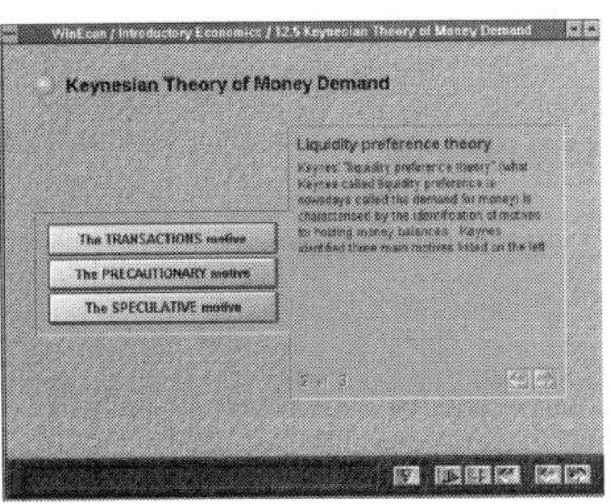

This screen introduces you to the Keynesian theory of money demand. Keynes referred to three main motives for holding money. First, the 'transactions motive', is the need for money to make routine purchases. Second is the 'precautionary motive', which describes the holding of some additional money for unforeseen costs or opportunities – keeping a little extra in reserve over and above normal transactions requirements. The third is quite different: the'speculative motive' refers to the holding of money as an asset or store of value, and is unrelated to current period expenditure on goods and services.

Keynes's 'liquidity preference' is what we now call demand for money. The total demand for money is the sum of the different kinds of demand.

The Transactions Demand for Money

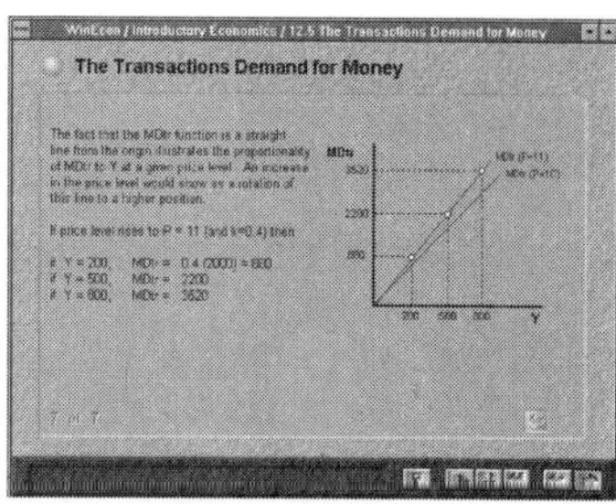

Keynes's theory starts from the transactions demand, MD_{tr}, and we incorporate the precautionary element. This demand is stated to be directly proportional to income, which is of course similar to the Cambridge version of the quantity theory. For transactions purposes, the money needed in aggregate is proportional to average price, *P*, and real aggregate output/income, *Y*. As you use the WinEcon screen you find a graphical approach, and can see how the demand function changes if the price level alters.

Complete the expression for transaction demand

53 MD_{tr} =

The Speculative Demand for Money

The total demand for money is

$$MD = MD_{tr} + MD_{sp}$$

where MD_{sp} is the speculative holding of money, and this additional term makes all the difference in monetary theory. No longer will there be a constant velocity relationship between the money supply and current spending.

Speculative (or asset) demand for money should be understood in the wider context of 'portfolio choice'. For individuals or organizations owning assets (savings, wealth) it is necessary to choose how much of each kind of asset to hold. Keynes posed the question: given a choice between money and bonds, which would be preferred and why? The speculative demand for money derives from the idea that under some circumstances money will be preferred to bonds. Remember that bond prices rise and fall inversely with interest rate movements (see section 12.3). A variable price asset like this carries a risk that the owner might need to sell it to raise money at a time when prices are low, and perhaps receive less than was paid for it (i.e. sustain a capital loss). So, why hold bonds at all? Because, on average, over time they offer a higher return than holding money.

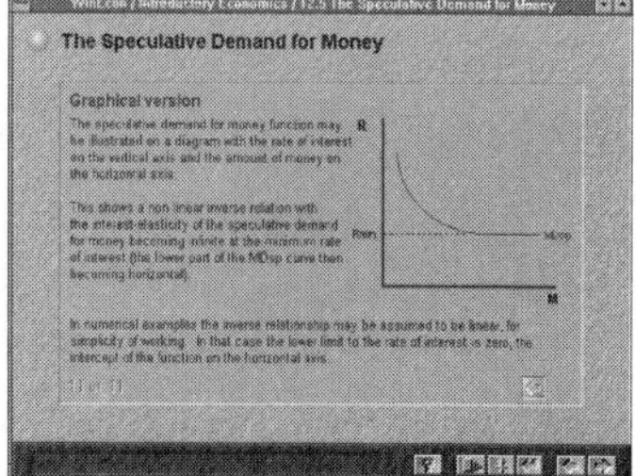

With WinEcon you see that Keynes proposed a particular theory of expectations about the risks and likely returns from bondholding, to explain how people choose between money and bonds. From this he deduced that the aggregate speculative demand for money is an inverse function of the rate of interest, which is a crucial idea in Keynesian monetary theory. If it is assumed that there is a positive minimum rate of interest (R_{min}), below which nobody wants to hold bonds because the return is not enough

to compensate for the risk, then the graph of MD_{sp} against R, the interest rate, shows curvature down to that value as shown by the graph on the screenshot. It is essential to note the inverse relationship between MD_{sp} and R, which for many purposes can be shown equally well by a linear function.

Note that the interest rate, R, is strictly the rate of return on the alternative asset to money (i.e. the interest rate yield on bond purchases).

Check your understanding of bonds and interest rates

54 **The risk of capital loss from bondholding is perceived to be greatest when bond prices are considered to be high/low.**

55 **The risk of capital loss from purchasing a bond is perceived as greater when interest rates are high/low.**

56 **If potential purchasers of bonds prefer to wait, and hold speculative money for the time being, this shows that they expect interest rates to rise/fall.**

57 **As the interest rate rises, progressively more and more people prefer money to bonds/use their speculative money to buy bonds.**

The Total Demand for Money Function

Total demand for money is given by:

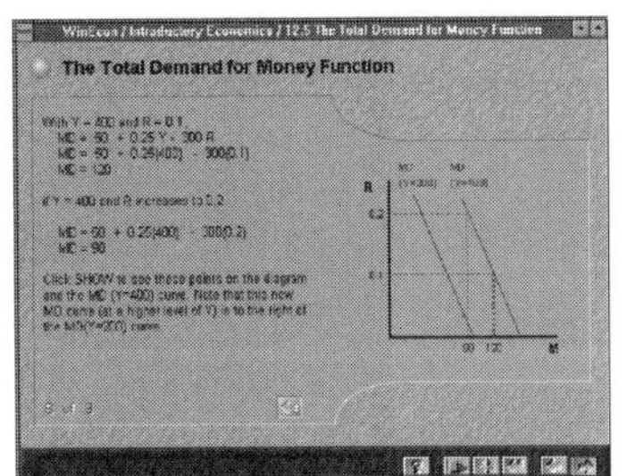

$$MD = MD_{tr} + MD_{sp}$$

It is therefore a function of P, Y (from MD_{tr}) and R (from MD_{sp}). WinEcon here shows you a numerical example and a diagrammatic illustration of the MD function. Notice in the numerical example that the rate of interest, R, is expressed as a fraction. Alternatively, it could be multiplied by 100 and so given as a percentage. If you change the units in which R is measured, you must alter the expressions in which R is used to compensate. In this case the demand for money function would become $MD = 50 + 0.25Y - 3R$, where R is a percentage. Try substituting R = 10 per cent and you should again find that MD = 70.

The diagram is drawn with M, the real quantity of money, on the horizontal axis, and the analysis lets you see how MD is affected by changes in any of the independent variables. In what follows we shall normally assume that P is constant.

Consolidate your learning

58 The three main Keynesian motives for holding money are:

59 Which category of money demand is proportional to *P.Y*?

60 When bond prices fall, interest yields [rise/fall/are unchanged].

61 As a rational person, you would prefer to buy bonds when interest rates are [high/low].

62 The speculative demand for money [rises/falls/ is unchanged] when interest rates fall.

63 If MD = $20 + 0.5Y - 2000R$ and $Y = 1200$ and $R = 0.08$, calculate MD. [ ]

The Money Market and Equilibrium Interest Rate

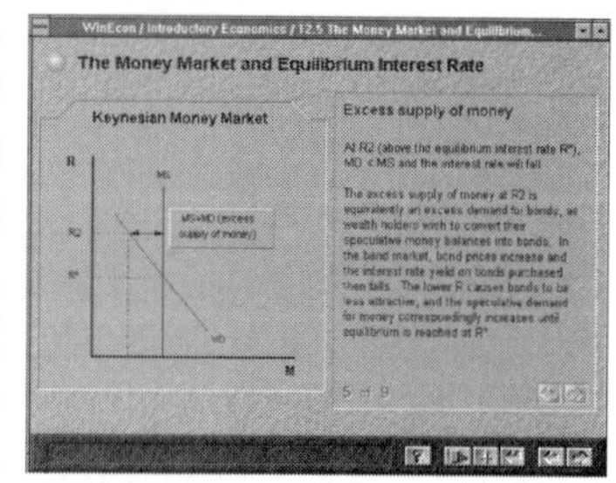

We now have the Keynesian theory of demand for money. Assuming that the money supply is exogenous (i.e. controlled by the central bank), we can proceed to analyse the aggregate money market. This screen helps you build up a picture of the money market and its equilibrium. In the money market diagram, fixed MS is shown as a vertical at the appropriate quantity, and MD is inversely sloped. The intersection gives the equilibrium MD = MS, and the rate of interest on bonds (R) will vary to bring this about. The model therefore explains the determination of the rate of interest.

Exogenous Changes and their Money Market Effects

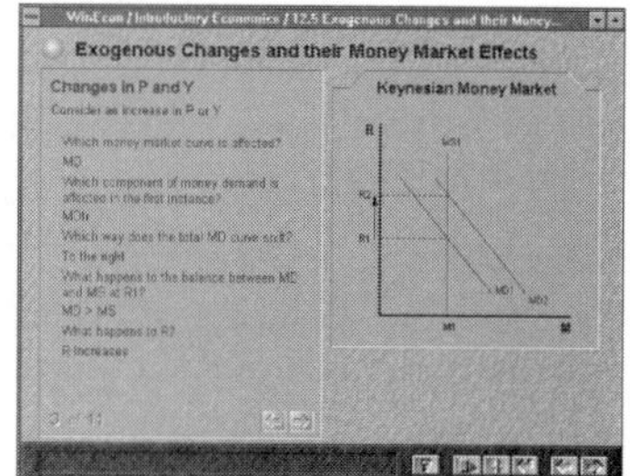

Changes in Y affect MD_{tr} at all interest rates and shift the MD curve horizontally, causing R to adjust to restore equilibrium with the fixed MS. For example, if Y increases so does MD_{tr}, and bond supply increases to obtain more money, so bond prices fall and interest yields rise until MD_{sp} has fallen enough to provide for the rise in MD_{tr}. Some holders of ('idle') speculative balances have been induced to buy bonds with their money, thus transferring the money into ('active') balances for transactions use.

The effect of changes in *Y*

64 Given MD = 20 + 0.5 *Y* – 2000 *R* (where *R* is a fraction and MS = 460), calculate equilibrium *R* for *Y* = 1000 and *Y* = 1400.

Complete this money market diagram to illustrate the numerical example above by showing the two MD = f(*R*) curves corresponding to *Y* = 1000 and *Y* = 1400. Mark in the intercept values on the *M* axis and the equilibrium values on the *R* axis.

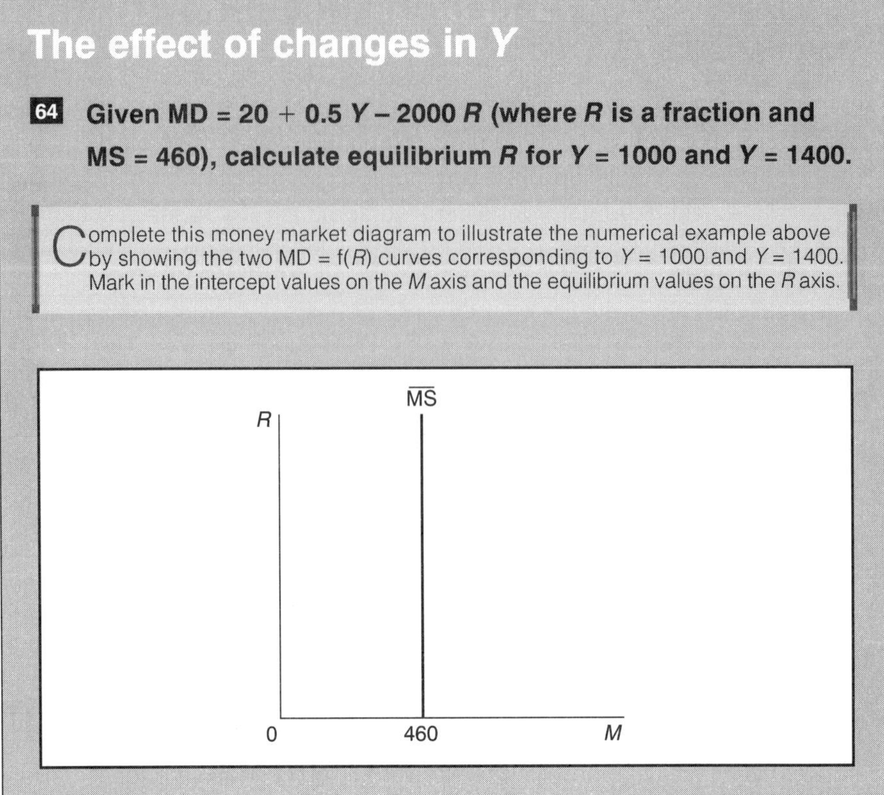

The LM Curve and Equation

Having analysed the money market directly, we now need to consider the LM curve/LM equation, first presented by the Oxford economist John Hicks. This expresses the relationship between *Y* and equilibrium *R*. The L stands for liquidity preference (MD) and the M for money supply (MS), and the relationship corresponds to the money market equilibrium MD = MS. It is important to examine this relationship because one of the major features of Keynesian theory as a whole is its demonstration of how the financial part of the economy interacts with the real economy to determine aggregate levels of demand, production and employment. Here we have one of those links between financial and real variables, namely *R* and *Y*.

See section 13.4 for an explanation of the IS relationship and the combined IS–LM theory.

The LM locus of equilibrium possibilities is another way of representing the same information as already covered, but it has become widely used in a generalized 'IS–LM' version of Keynesian macroeconomic theory. The LM relationship between *R* and *Y* shows that as *Y* increases, MD increases, so money market equilibrium *R* increases. Therefore, we have a forward–sloping curve.

 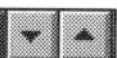

LM Curve: Graphical Derivation

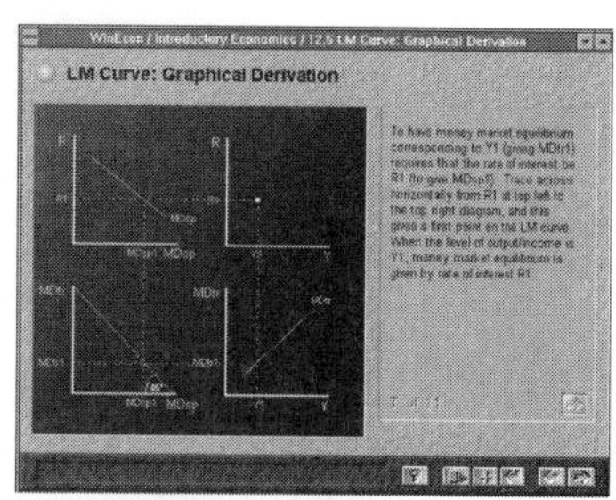

In this screen, WinEcon takes you through the traditional graphical derivation of the LM curve, which rests on the assumption that transactions money balances are held separately from speculative money balances. Notice that real income, *Y*, is plotted on the horizontal axis, and the interest rate, *R*, on the vertical axis.

Plotting the LM curve

Derive the position of the LM curve in the diagram by tracing out equilibrium *R* for the two *Y* values shown.

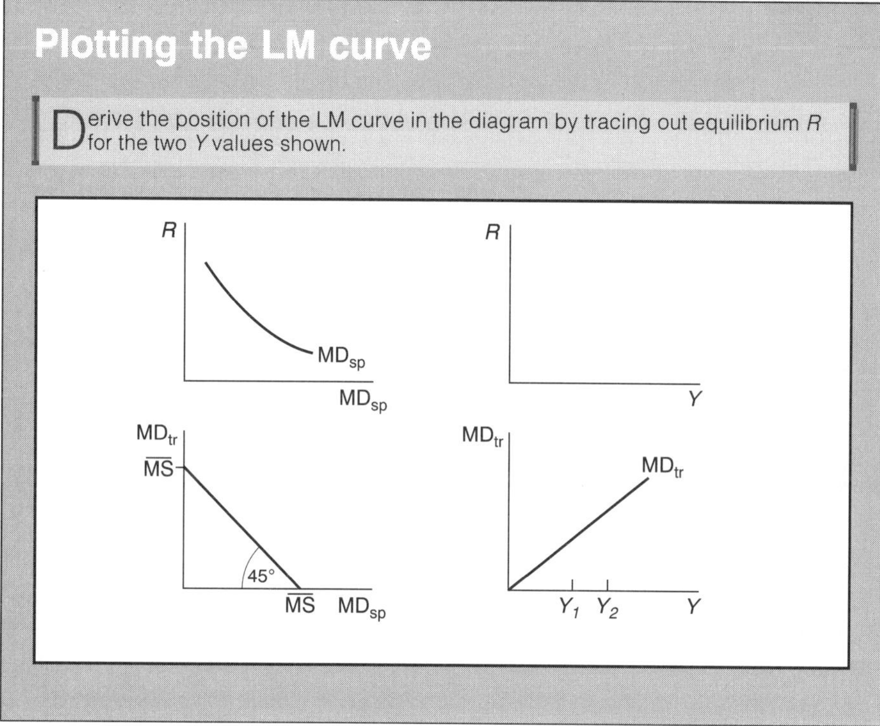

LM Curve and Equation: Exogenous Changes

Here, WinEcon shows you how exogenous changes can be illustrated in the diagram to discover their effects.

The effect of exogenous changes

Exogenous changes in money supply or demand shift the LM curve. State which way it shifts in each of the following cases.

65 **If the preference for holding money increases, LM shifts ________.**

66 **If the money supply increases, LM shifts ________.**

67 **If the price level increases, LM shifts ________.**

LM Curve: Equation Derivation

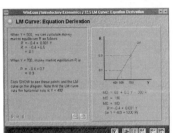

Here you discover how to derive the LM equation from the equations for money demand and money supply. WinEcon uses a numerical example, and the LM equation obtained is then illustrated in a diagram. Notice that in WinEcon the LM curve is derived for values of R which are expressed as fractions of one (e.g. 0.1 and 0.3). These interest rates can alternatively be written as percentages (e.g. 10 per cent and 30 per cent, respectively) and you may find numerous other books use percentage values of R as the convention in their derivations of the LM equation.

With equations it is no longer necessary to assume the separability of transactions and speculative money balances, so this approach is more general.

Deriving the LM curve equation

If MD = 500 + 0.25 Y – 1000R, where R is expressed as a fraction and MS = 1200:

68 **Derive the LM equation.**

69 **What is equilibrium R when Y = 3000 and when Y = 3200 ?**

Section 12.6: Monetarist Theory

We now come to the third approach to money demand to be considered in this chapter. This has been developed by the US economist Milton Friedman and others, and draws from both classical and Keynesian ideas, but develops these in a way which is in keeping with the classical tradition. Friedman's theory relies heavily on empirical evidence to support his particular interpretation, so we look at the issues raised by that. Also, we see that the theory of money demand here is one component in the much broader economic approach known as monetarism.

Friedman's Theory of Money Demand

Friedman treats the demand for money like the demand for anything else – as a function of a scale variable ('permanent income', related to total wealth) and of relative prices (rates of return on this and alternative assets). For Friedman, money is essentially 'a temporary abode of purchasing power' and it is the purchasing power equivalent – real money rather that nominal money – which is the underlying focus in this description of money demand behaviour.

The general formulation of the demand for money function above can be simplified for statistical investigation against long-run data series to:

$$MD = f(P, Y, R)$$

The evidence, too – from a number of national studies – tends to confirm that nominal MD is proportional to *P*, and that MD shows approximately unit elasticity to changes in *Y*, and inelastic inverse response to changes in *R*.

Friedman's general theoretical formulation of the demand for money is, as just that, acceptable to most economists. But Friedman develops a particular interpretation of it which is more open to debate, quoting statistical evidence in support. His statistical methodology has been challenged, and the econometric issues will not be pursued here. Suffice it to say that, in effect, the form of the function in the long run is interpreted by Friedman as:

$$MD = f(R).P.Y$$

in which MD is a stable function of the other variables. This is similar to the Cambridge equation (MD = $k.P.Y$) and justifies Friedman's description of his approach as a 'modern quantity theory of money'.

Friedman's expression

70 **Complete fully Friedman's expression for money demand:**

$$MD/P = f(\quad\quad\quad)$$

where Y_p is permanent income (= expected long-run average income, not current income); the *R* values are rates of return on money itself, on bonds, on equities and on real assets respectively; *w* is the ratio of non-human to total wealth; and *u* represents tastes, etc. Rates of return are understood to include expected capital gain, etc.

In Friedman's theory, which way will real demand for money change in each of the following cases?

71 **When Y_p rises, MD/*P*** ________

72 **When R_m falls, MD/*P*** ________

73 **When R_b rises, MD/*P*** ________

74 **When inflation increases, MD/*P*** ________ **(Hint: inflation is the rate of increase in prices of real commodity assets.)**

Monetarism – The General Approach

Chapters 13 and 14 cover monetarist theory of aggregate demand and aggregate supply respectively.

If the money demand function in the above form is stable, this is equivalent to saying that the velocity of circulation is stable, and this then becomes the basis of a theory of aggregate demand in the goods market. In monetarist macroeconomics this is allied to the 'natural rate hypothesis' for aggregate supply (i.e. in the long run there is one unique equilibrium value for aggregate output).

Monetarism as a political-economic philosophy includes a preference for a private enterprise market economy, with the government pursuing a *'laissez-faire'* approach – leaving economic agents to make their own decisions. However, a major exception is made in respect of monetary control, where strong central bank restraint of money supply growth is advocated to prevent inflation. It is implied that institutional arrangements must be devised to make this possible, perhaps with statutory reserve ratios imposed on banks, and the central bank the only provider of eligible reserves. This is at odds with a liberalized financial system.

Money, Price Level and Output: Debates on Causality

Here, WinEcon gives you a flavour of the (sometimes heated) debates about causality between money supply and other variables.

Empirical Evidence on the Money Demand Function

This WinEcon topic reports briefly on some of the empirical results. Empirical evidence quoted in favour of a monetarist interpretation of events cannot be conclusive because statistical correlation of itself never proves causality. Theoretical debates are therefore likely to continue, as are debates about how to interpret the empirical evidence.

Section 12.7: Summary

This chapter is concerned with money, and with the analysis of how it is supplied, why it is demanded and what implications follow.

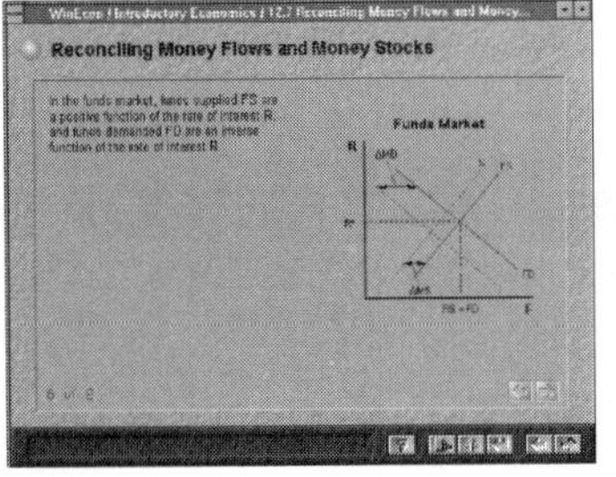

Reconciling Money Flows and Money Stocks

The flows of funds picture of the economy considered earlier can be more formally linked with the analysis of money supply and demand by amending the classical loanable funds market model. The supply of funds in total comes not just from saving existing money but also from bank credit creation of new money. The demand for funds is not just for investment expenditure but also to add to money balances.

Money Supply and Demand: Review

Because it is agreed that the linkages between the financial sector and real activity are important in explaining macroeconomic phenomena, this is an area of continuing theoretical and empirical debates. This chapter has looked mainly at the institutional considerations in explaining money supply, and at three theoretical approaches to modelling the demand for money.

Cash in the form of notes and coins forms just part of the money supply. More important are bank deposits. You should now understand that banks can create money by offering loans. This process of credit creation is limited by the minimum reserve ratio which UK banks now determine for themselves. Given the minimum reserve ratio, the bank deposit multiplier shows the change in total liabilities that results from a particular change in reserves.

Government monetary policy operates through the central bank exercising control over the money supply. It can control the cash issue, but this may merely lead to inconvenience for people wishing to trade. Instead it may engage in open market operations by selling or buying bonds, or it may influence interest rates by the rate at which it lends to the banking system. It can also exert various direct controls.

In studying the demand for money we considered first the classical approach. The quantity theory and the Cambridge equation give slightly different explanations of the demand for money, and the interest rate is determined from the loanable funds market. The Keynesian analysis of money demand separates different motives for holding money. Overall demand for money is therefore a function both of income and of the rate of interest. We use a money market diagram to determine the interest rate, and by considering different levels of income derive the LM curve.

Monetarists treat money as any other commodity. The long-run formulation of the demand for money is similar to the Cambrige equation, and so the approach is sometimes called the modern quantity theory of money.

Money supply and demand: review

75 A nation's money supply has two main components: what are they?

76 Define assets and liabilities.

77 Is a bank deposit an asset or a liability?

78 State the equation of exchange and define all terms.

79 What is the crucial assumption in developing the quantity theory of money?

80 What does the LM curve show?

81 Write out Friedman's general theoretical money demand function and define all terms in the expression.

Chapter 13: Theories of Aggregate Demand

What determines the aggregate quantity of goods and services that customers want to buy from producers in our economy? This is a central concern in macroeconomics. For some economists it is the key to explaining fluctuations in employment and unemployment; for others it is more crucial to explaining inflation. Either way, it is of great practical and policy relevance.

Contents

KEYWORDS

- Aggregate demand
- Aggregate output/income
- BP (balance of payments) curve
- Consumer demand
- Exchange rate
- Exports
- Government expenditure
- Imports
- Interest rate
- Investment demand
- IS curve
- IS–LM analysis
- Real balance effect
- Saving
- Taxation

Section 13.1: Introduction

See particularly the screen Aggregate Demand in the Goods Market in section 11.4.

Aggregate demand, AD, is the quantity of final goods and services produced in the economy that people plan to buy. From chapter 11 we know that aggregate demand is made up of the planned values of a number of components:

$$\text{AD} = C + I + G + X - Z$$

In this chapter we seek to define a relationship between the quantity of real GDP (Y) that is demanded and the price level (P). When we obtain an AD curve it can be used with an AS (aggregate supply) curve, which we derive in chapter 14, for AD–AS analysis.

We consider different approaches to obtaining an AD schedule, and examine aggregate demand in the context of each of the main schools of thought in macroeconomics. Some theories focus in more depth on the real demands represented by each component in the total, whilst other theories emphasize the monetary total of expenditures.

The Keynesian model depicts aggregate demand as depending both on the level of real income and the interest rate. From this we obtain the IS curve showing combinations of real income and the interest rate at which the goods market is in equilibrium. This curve is used with the LM curve in IS–LM analysis. From considering different price levels and the interest rates that are then required to keep the money market in equilibrium, we deduce the AD curve in this model.

Theories of Aggregate Demand

We are going to examine three different theoretical approaches to modelling the aggregate demand for goods and services. These theories have been developed as closed economy models, but we shall see that they can be extended to incorporate the effects of international trade and payments.

Classical and monetarist ideas about aggregate demand are very closely related, and for most purposes we can lump them together as 'classical/monetarist'. The Keynesian approach stands in marked contrast. Neoclassical theory draws from both traditions, although as its name perhaps suggests it carries forward the conventional modelling of individual maximizing behaviour.

Section 13.2: Classical/Monetarist Aggregate Demand

The quantity theory of money developed by the classical/monetarist school leads to the description of aggregate demand as depending (in a fairly simple relationship) on the aggregate money stock and the velocity of its circulation. (Chapter 12 describes these monetary variables, their definition and measurement etc.)

All markets are assumed to be competitive and to exhibit price flexibility, meaning that when demand exceeds supply, prices rise, and when supply exceeds demand, prices fall. Producers and customers react to the price changes by decreasing demand and increasing supply when prices rise, and vice versa when they fall. It follows that temporary disequilibria between demand and supply quantities are cleared via the price mechanism, giving continuous market clearing equilibrium.

The Quantity Theory of Money

At the core of this approach is the quantity theory of money, summarized in the equation of exchange we saw in section 12.4:

$$M.V = P.Y$$

where M is money stock (quantity of money), V is the velocity of circulation of money (assumed constant), P is the average price level and Y is the aggregate quantity of goods and services. We repeat this equation again here because we are about to reinterpret it to give a theory of aggregate demand.

The Quantity Theory and Aggregate Demand

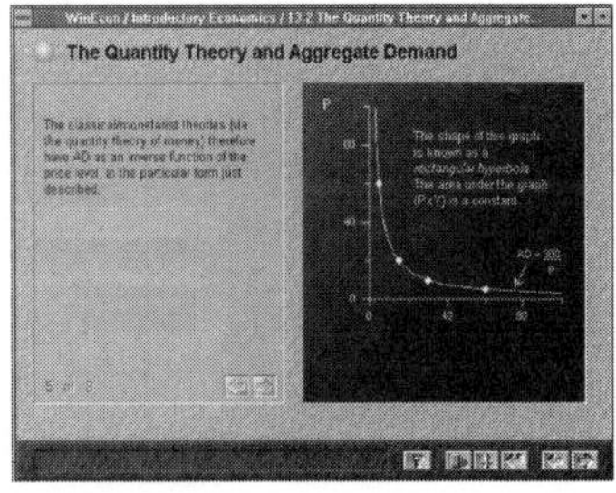

To develop the quantity theory of money as a theory of aggregate demand in the goods market, we need to recognize that the equation of exchange is saying that the flow of money payments (from purchasers on the demand side of the goods market) equates to the total money value of the goods and services they purchase (i.e. have demanded). The Y can therefore be interpreted not just neutrally as aggregate output, but also as aggregate output demanded, AD. Substituting AD for Y in the equation of exchange, and rearranging, gives the aggregate demand function. The function is downward-sloping and its form implies a particular curved shape.

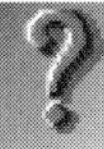

Record the classical/monetarist aggregate demand function

01 AD = [ ]

where *M* is determined by the central bank and *V* is constant, such that *M.V* is the [ ] in the period and within this the demand quantity varies inversely with the [ ] .

Try a numerical example. Let $M = 450$ (£bn) and $V = 2$ (per annum) and explore what is involved in a quantity theory approach.

02 What is total annual expenditure? [ ]

03 For price levels P = £1, £2, £3, £4, £5, £6 calculate AD per year.

04 Plot your results in the diagram below and label the curve.

05 Now repeat the exercise with *M* increased to 600 and plot the values on the diagram.

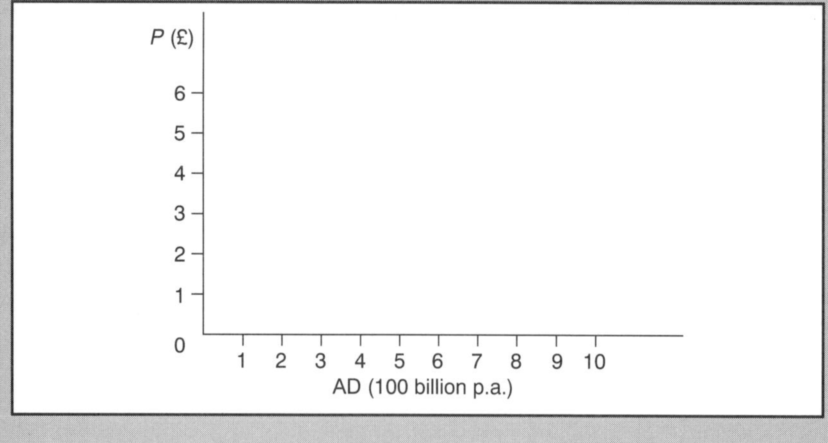

The Monetarist Transmission Mechanism

Assume, as monetarist theory does, that the money supply is controlled by the central bank, which has now decided to increase the quantity of money. Traditionally it would achieve this through open market purchases of bills and bonds. How does that action work through to become an increase in aggregate demand for goods and services? This cause-and-effect chain is known as the 'transmission mechanism'.

The transmission mechanism operates via a process of portfolio adjustment, where the action of the central bank temporarily gives some agents more money than they wish to continue to hold, so they spend some of it. They may spend some on other assets, the prices of which will therefore rise (and interest yield fall). They may spend some on newly produced capital assets (investment expenditure). Or they may increase consumption by spending on durables and non-durables. These adjustments continue until the balance between money holdings, other asset holdings and current consumption meets all preferences again. In the process, more is being spent on goods and services from current production (i.e. AD increases).

This view of the transmission mechanism reflects a monetarist belief that money is widely substitutable with all other assets and current expenditures. In contrast, Keynesian analysis views money mainly as a substitute for bonds.

Check your understanding of substitutability

06 **List six or more possible substitutes for money.**

Policy Implications

In classical/monetarist theory the money stock, given constant velocity of circulation, determines the money flow of aggregate demand. This is the basis of a theory of inflation, which is why monetarists attach such importance to monetary policy.

Monetarist theory

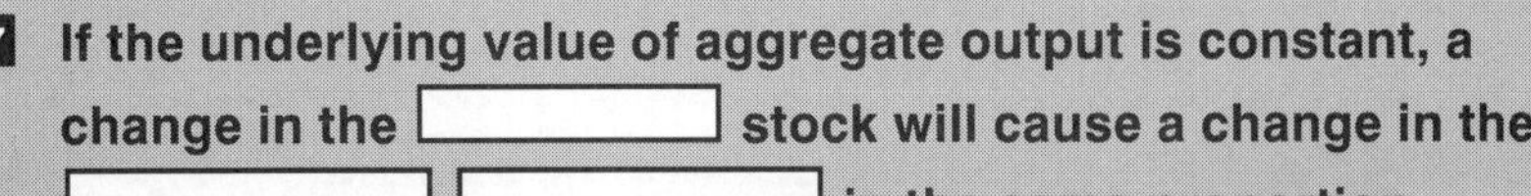

07 **If the underlying value of aggregate output is constant, a change in the ______ stock will cause a change in the ______ ______ in the same proportion.**

08 **In monetarist theory, inflation is caused by**

Section 13.3: Classical/Monetarist Open Economy

Classical/monetarist theory assumes competitive markets within an economy. The model can also be extended to include competitive international markets for goods and services. In principle, exports add to aggregate demand for domestic production, and imports subtract from it. However, as we shall see,

the theory suggests that market forces will bring about a trade equilibrium such that net aggregate demand is not changed.

The opportunities for profitable trade depend on differences in the price of the same good between countries. Traders will then buy in the country where prices are low to sell at a profit in countries where a higher price can be obtained. This is the essence of 'arbitrage' trade. Its effect is to reduce the price differential until the same price holds in both markets.

International Trade: An Example

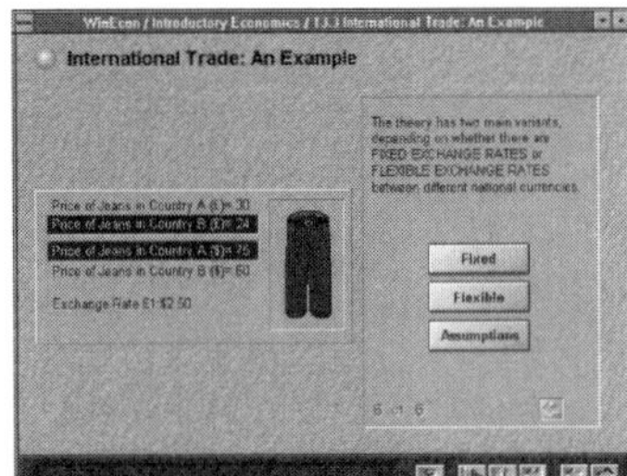

Here, WinEcon illustrates this idea with the example of international trade in jeans, and you see the relevance of currency exchange rates.

It is apparent that the effects of trade will be different under different exchange rate regimes, but with both fixed and flexible exchange rates the 'Law of One Price' will apply. Adjustments take place until, when price equalization is achieved, there is no profit from further trade.

International trade and exchange rates

09 **Price equalization in international trade is achieved as follows. With ________ exchange rates, prices of goods in the domestic currencies will change. With ________ exchange rates, prices in domestic currencies can remain fixed whilst the ________ ________ adjusts.**

Check your understanding. Consider the trade opportunities when an equivalent pack of photocopier paper sells at £10 in country A and $21 in country B, when the exchange rate is £1 = $1.50 and transport costs are negligible.

10 **What is (a) the $ equivalent of the market price in country A, and (b) the £ equivalent of the market price in country B?**

11 **As a profit maximizing trader, (a) in which country would you buy paper to transport to the other market, and (b) at the prices given, how much profit per pack of paper would you make, in £ and in $?**

12 **If the exchange rate remains fixed, what is the effect of the trade on the price of the paper (a) in country A, and (b) in country B? (Hint: consider the supply and demand in each market to explain the direction of price changes.)**

13 **The name given to this process by which prices of the same good in different markets tend to be equalized by trade is ______.**

14 **What exchange rate would make the price of the pack of paper the same in both markets if domestic currency prices remained as quoted?**

Fixed Exchange Rates

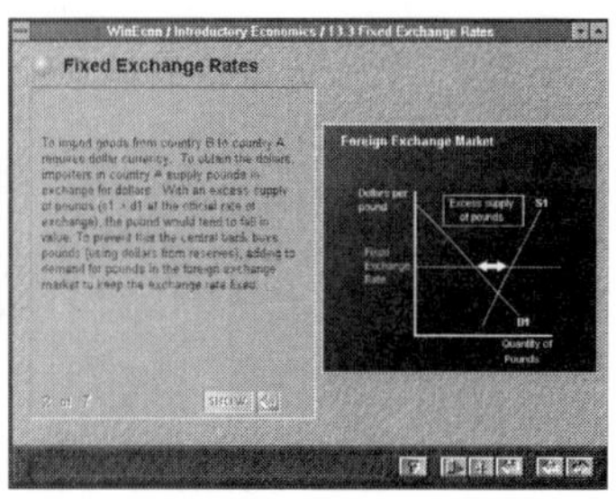

Extrapolating from what would happen to a single traded good to cover all trade between the countries, we make use of a foreign exchange market diagram. To buy goods in country A traders need pounds (supply \$ and demand £); to buy goods in country B traders need dollars (supply £ and demand \$). We construct the market diagram with the amounts of currency offered for exchange represented in pound value on the horizontal axis, and the exchange rate as the price of pounds (\$ per £1) on the vertical axis.

A rise in the value of the pound (£ appreciation) will make country A's goods less competitive and so the demand for £ will have a negative slope in the diagram. But the pound appreciation will increase the demand for country B's goods, so the supply of pounds to obtain dollars will increase (subject to some assumptions about elasticities of demand and supply in the goods markets) and we draw the supply of pounds curve with a positive slope. The equilibrium exchange rate corresponds to the intersection of the curves.

WinEcon shows you how this analysis fits with the quantity theory analysis for the domestic economy. The quantity theory has domestic price levels determined by domestic money supplies. The trade analysis, with fixed exchange rates, shows that domestic price levels are determined by trade flows affecting supply and demand. However, these are compatible because with fixed exchange rates an imbalance in trade requires simultaneous central bank action to hold the exchange rate at its official value, and this action will change the domestic money supply.

Fixed exchange rates

Sketch the supply and demand curves in the foreign exchange market diagram, mark the equilibrium exchange rate, and mark in also a fixed exchange rate above the equilibrium.

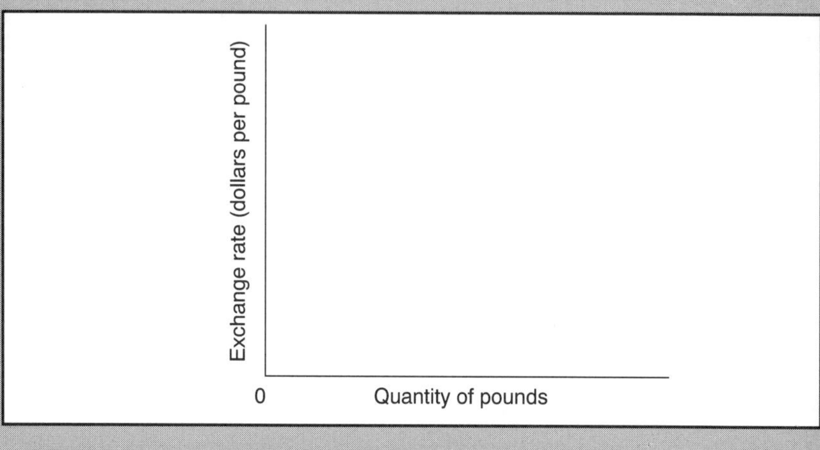

15 **At the fixed exchange rate, is there excess supply or demand (a) for £, and (b) for $?**

16 **What intervention is required from the central bank of country A?**

17 **How would this intervention be shown in the diagram?**

Check your understanding. For the fixed exchange rate case when the exchange rate is below equilibrium:

18 **In this case, net [imports/exports] will cause domestic prices to [rise/fall].**

19 **In this case, the central bank [buys/sells] domestic currency which [increases/decreases] domestic money supply.**

20 **In this case, the changes in money supply cause the domestic price level to [increases/decreases].**

21 **With fixed exchange rates a central bank loses its independent control over its domestic [   ] [   ] because this is subordinated to control of the exchange rate.**

Flexible Exchange Rates

With flexible exchange rates it is the exchange rate which adjusts to give equilibrium in the exchange market and the traded goods markets. Central banks in this case retain their control over domestic money supplies and price levels, and exchange rate changes bring consistency between these separate price levels such that at the equilibrium exchange rate there is 'purchasing power parity' (PPP) between the currencies. In practice PPP is not always apparent, largely because international currency markets nowadays are dominated by huge movements of capital funds and deposit money unrelated to the needs of trade. PPP theory is more relevant in the long run in explaining exchange rate trends.

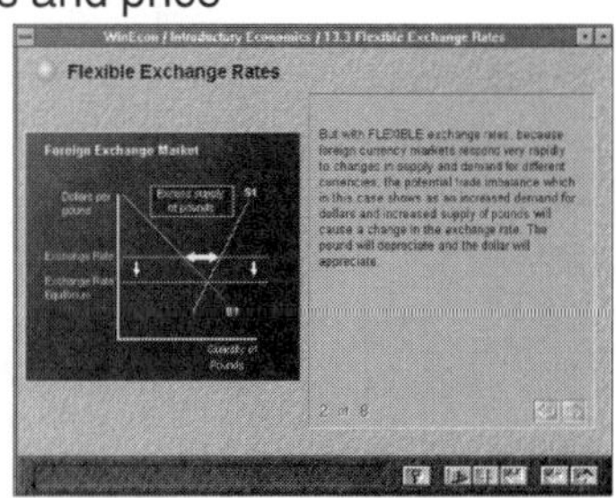

Flexible exchange rates

22 **In the case shown, a depreciation of the pound makes [ ] more competitive and [ ] dearer, and the pound will [ ] until the trade gap is closed.**

23 **In the [ ] theory of exchange rates, given the domestic currency price levels of different nations, exchange rates will adjust until a given sum of money converted at those rates purchases the [ ] quantity of goods in each country.**

Summary: Trade and Exchange Rates

We have found that the classical/monetarist theory, based on markets and money, is applicable to aggregate demand in the open economy, where export flows add to domestic demand and imports reduce it. The adjustment processes differ depending on the exchange rate system, but the outcome is a trade equilibrium with exports equal to imports.

Trade equilibrium

Fill in the country references (A and B) in the diagram.

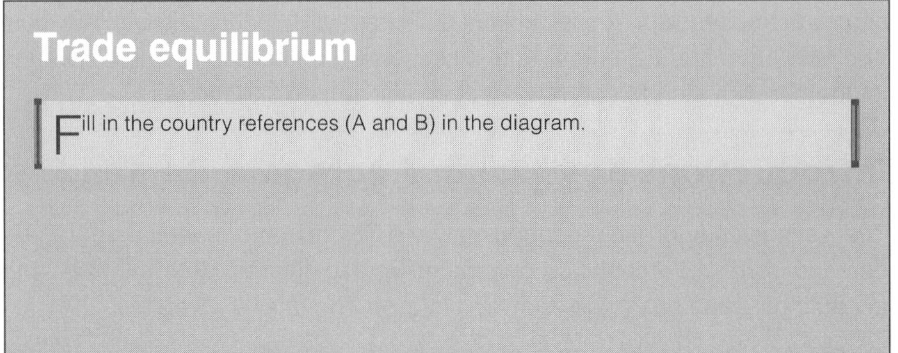

Goods in country B are cheaper than in country A → Consumers in buy goods from firms in which offer lower prices → To buy goods from , needs dollars to pay with → Country buys dollars and sells pounds

Fixed → The Central Bank intervenes to keep exchange rates fixed → Goods flow from country to country . In country , the supply curve shifts out, reducing the equilibrium price. In country , the supply curve shifts back, increasing equilibrium price → Trade continues until the prices equalize

Flexible → So the price of dollars goes up → Exchange rate changes occur faster than changes in supply → The dollar appreciates to a level where goods are the same price in both countries

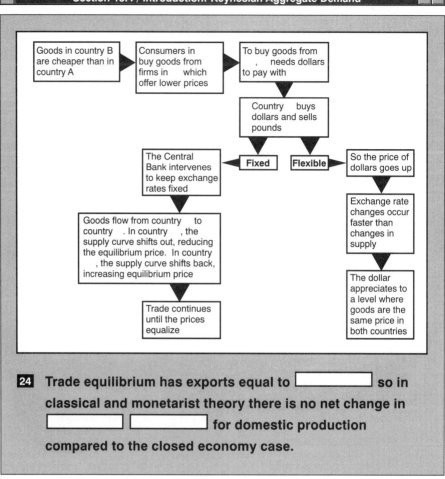

24 Trade equilibrium has exports equal to ______ so in classical and monetarist theory there is no net change in ______ ______ for domestic production compared to the closed economy case.

Section 13.4: Keynesian Aggregate Demand

We now move to consider the Keynesian theory of aggregate demand. This is the most crucial element of the Keynesian model, and we shall see that it involves analysis of the interaction of the real production sector with the financial markets in a way that makes a break with the classical tradition.

The interaction between goods market and money market is usually modelled in terms of what is known as 'IS–LM analysis'. The LM curve, representing money market equilibrium, is explained in chapter 12, beginning with the topic The LM Curve and Equation. In this section we obtain the IS curve and use it together with the LM curve to analyse equilibrium situations.

Introduction: Keynesian Aggregate Demand

The Keynesian approach recognizes that different components of aggregate demand (AD) for domestic production may have different determinants, and accordingly each has to be analysed in turn. The total is given by

$$\text{AD} = C + I + G + X - Z$$

where, on the right-hand side, we have the planned values for consumption, investment, government expenditure, exports and imports respectively.

In this chapter we acknowledge that some components of aggregate demand are influenced by the rate of interest. We develop an analysis of goods market equilibrium which is more sophisticated than that of the introductory income–expenditure model described in chapter 11.

Section 11.5, Equilibrium in the Goods Market.

The IS curve we derive represents possible equilibrium positions for the goods market. Its name comes from the condition:

$$I + G + X = S + T + Z$$

For domestic economy analysis we shall regard G and X as exogenous (i.e. determined outside our model). This assumption is relaxed later in the open economy analysis. Modern treatments recognize that both consumption and investment are functions of income, Y, and interest rate, R, (i.e. $C = f(Y,R)$ and $I = f(Y,R)$), but we will also show a graphical version in which $C = f(Y)$ and $I = f(R)$. Assuming $Z = f(Y)$, both variants give $AD = f(Y,R)$. For simplicity, our illustrations always use linear equations. Imports depend directly on Y, partly because higher domestic output in the firms sector requires more imported supplies of materials, and partly because higher household income means more purchases of imported consumer goods.

Test your understanding of the Keynesian model

25 **In the Keynesian model we are developing here, which of the variables are (a) exogenous (determined outside our model), (b) endogenous (determined within the model)?**

26 **AD = f (______ , ______).**

WinEcon now takes you through three screens leading to a specification of the consumption demand function for our model. This first screen is on consumer demand and disposable income, the second is on consumer demand and the rate of interest, and the third depicts consumer demand as a function of both the variables.

For a basic treatment of consumption as a function of income, see section 11.3.

Consumer Demand and Disposable Income

Planned consumer expenditure depends most directly on the after-tax-and-benefits income of the household sector. This total is known as disposable income. If we measure taxation, T, net of benefits (part of gross taxation is returned to the household sector as benefits payments to those in need, or as state pensions, etc.) disposable income is $Y - T$. We then have:

$$C = a + b\,(Y - T)$$

where $a > 0$ and $0 < b < 1$, with b as the marginal propensity to consume out of disposable income. This has all the usual properties of the consumption function introduced in chapter 11.

Consumer Demand and the Rate of Interest

In a modern economy consumers also save and borrow, and their decisions about their financial arrangements reflect opportunity cost considerations in the usual way. On this screen you explore these considerations.

The rate of interest is a cost of borrowed funds and an opportunity cost of consumption. It follows that a change in the rate of interest will normally have an impact on aggregate consumer expenditure.

Check you understand the effect of interest rates

27 **If the interest rate decreases:**

(a) saving will [**increase/decrease/be unchanged**];

(b) payments on existing variable interest rate debt will [ ];

(c) the cost of borrowing to finance consumption will [ ].

28 **Which of the above will affect consumer demand?**

29 **Which way will aggregate consumer demand change if interest rates fall?**

The Consumption Demand Function

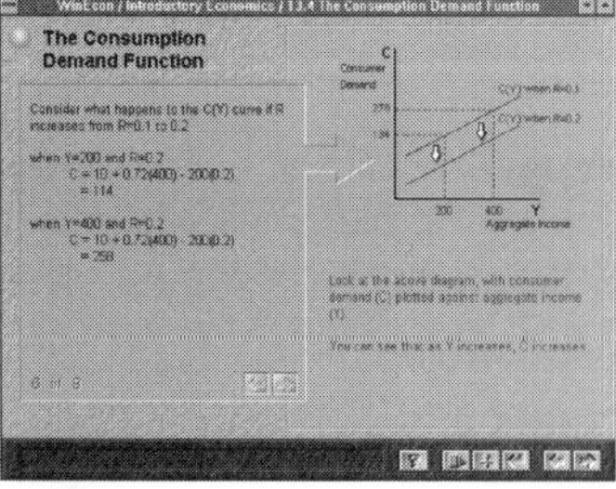

We now re-specify the consumption equation to make it explicitly an inverse function of the rate of interest as well as a positive function of income. The WinEcon screen shows how we can fix either the rate of interest or disposable income and plot consumption against the other variable. Notice how each type of curve can be caused to shift.

Calculating consumption demand

Try this numerical example. Let $C = 400 + 0.8 (Y - T) - 1000 R$ and $T = 0.25 Y$.

30 **Given $R = 0.1$, calculate C at $Y = 1000$, $Y = 2000$ and $Y = 3000$.**

31 **Given $Y = 2000$, calculate C at $R = 0.05$, $R = 0.1$ and $R = 0.15$.**

Show these six points in each of the diagrams and be sure you understand how a change in R affects $C(Y)$ and a change in Y affects $C(R)$.

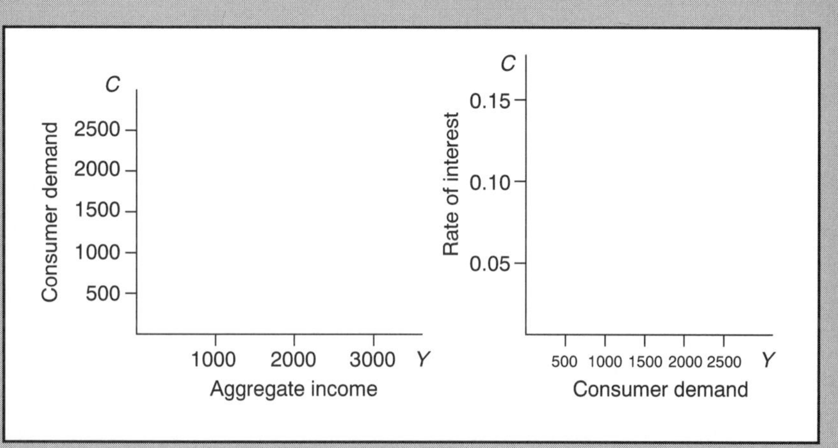

The Investment Decision and the Rate of Interest

WinEcon now takes you through four screens leading to a specification of the investment demand function for our model. With this first screen you consider investment decisions at the level of the firm and the relevance of the rate of interest, R. By generalizing, the second screen builds from this to an aggregate investment demand function. With the third screen you look at investment demand as a function of aggregate output/income, Y, and the fourth consolidates the model of investment demand as a function of both R and Y. Simpler Keynesian models assume aggregate investment expenditure is exogenous.

In section 11.4, the topic Aggregate Demand in the Goods Market makes the assumption that investment is exogenous. From this, section 11.5 develops the 45 degree diagram in the topic Formal Model: Diagrams.

Whilst investment may be affected by changes in factors like business confidence which are hard to model, at the microeconomic level investment decisions reflect rational choices about the use of resources where considerations of costs and returns and opportunity costs are amenable to normal economic analysis.

As an example of an investment project, a profit-maximizing firm may consider the purchase of some new machinery. It would be used in future production where the extra output would add to sales revenues, and after allowing for additional materials and operating costs would yield net receipts to the firm. The amounts of these net receipts in each year can be estimated (perhaps as

a range between a cautious estimate and an optimistic estimate) over the expected life of the machinery. These receipts provide the financial return to be compared to the initial cost in judging whether the investment is worth while. This profitability calculation has to make allowance for the fact that receipts accrue at intervals over future time.

For more details of discounting and the IRR method, see the topic Net Present Value and the following screens in section 8.8.

Investment appraisal calculations require discounting of future money values to (lower) present values to compare costs and returns on a consistent basis. There are different project appraisal methods but we adopt the 'internal rate of return' (IRR) method here.

Check your understanding of discounting and IRR

32 **What is the present value of £144 receivable in two years' time, discounting at 20% per annum?**

33 **Define the internal rate of return on an investment expenditure.**

34 **An investment project costs £100,000 now and has expected net receipts of £60,000 at the end of one year and a final £72,000 at the end of the second year. What is the IRR? (Hint: 72 is half of 144, see earlier question.)**

Investment Demand and the Rate of Interest

In aggregate across the whole economy, how much investment expenditure in total will go ahead? This depends on a comparison between the IRRs in these business investments, and interest rates in the financial system. Projects with an IRR above the current interest rate will be profitable, the others will not, so the total of investment expenditure can be calculated by summing the total costs of the profitable projects.

We find that as the rate of interest rises, less of the business investment projects are profitable, so aggregate investment falls. The rate of interest here is an increasing external cost squeezing net profitability for firms which need borrowed finance, or a higher opportunity cost for those firms which have internal funds available. An investment demand curve, $I = f(R)$, therefore has a negative slope. We have derived this result from IRR calculations, but Keynes's own concept of 'marginal efficiency of capital' and the later adaptation, 'marginal efficiency of investment', are similar in principle. Note that changes in business confidence cause a re-estimation of future sales revenues and IRRs, which will shift the investment demand curve in the diagram shown on the WinEcon screen.

Shifts in the investment demand curve

35 **A fall in business confidence will shift the $I = f(R)$ curve which way?**

Investment Demand and Aggregate Output/Income

In this topic, we see that aggregate investment, I, is likely to be a function of aggregate output/income, Y, as well as a function of the interest rate, R. There are several reasons for this. In a boom situation when Y has increased to a historically high level, business optimism tends to be high (giving higher estimated IRRs), profits are likely to be good (giving more internal finance for investment), existing capital equipment may be fully utilized (indicating a need for expansion), so investment spending is typically high – contributing of course to the boom itself. Conversely, in a recession all of these indicators work the other way, depressing investment and deepening the recession.

The 'accelerator theory' of investment specifically links the level of investment, I, to the change in (rather than level of) aggregate output, Y. The naive version of the accelerator assumes a fixed relationship between the stock of capital equipment and the flow of output from it, so that an increase in output requires net investment (i.e. over and above replacement investment) as a technical imperative. The flexible accelerator, or 'capital stock adjustment' principle, allows the changing of capital stock through net investment (to reach an optimal level in relation to output) to be spread over several periods of time. Often, investment projects have long gestation and construction periods.

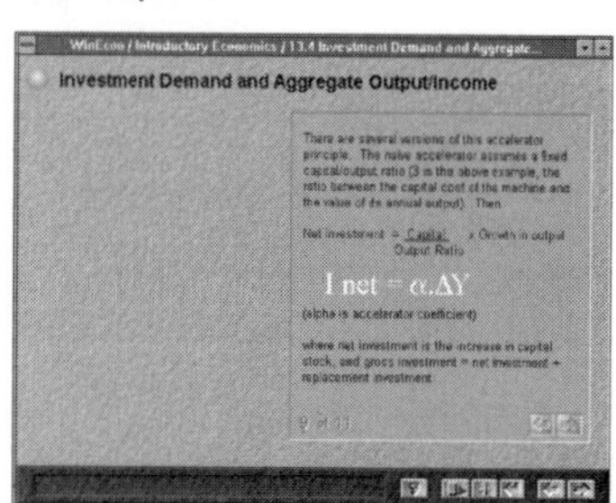

Check your understanding of investment and the accelerator theory

36 **Gross investment = net investment + ______.**

37 **The naive accelerator model can be expressed as Net investment = fixed ______ / ______ ratio × ______.**

38 **If the accelerator coefficient (= capital/output ratio) is four and the desired increase of aggregate output is from £500 billion to £520 billion, what net investment is required?**

The Investment Demand Function

Acknowledging the positive effects of aggregate output on investment, we can include these explicitly in the investment demand function. For simplicity we make I a linear function of the level of Y, so not incorporating an accelerator principle as such.

Calculating investment demand

Try a numerical example. Let $I = 600 + 0.1Y - 4000R$.

39 Given $Y = 5000$, calculate I at $R = 0.05$, $R = 0.1$ and $R = 0.15$.

40 Given $R = 0.1$, calculate I at $Y = 4000$, $Y = 5000$ and $Y = 6000$.

The IS Equation and Curve: Graphical Approach

Section 12.5 explains the derivation of the LM curve.

The next stage of the Keynesian analysis is to derive the IS curve. When this curve is superimposed on the LM curve, which we derived in chapter 12, we have a powerful analytical tool which can be used to analyse policy changes.

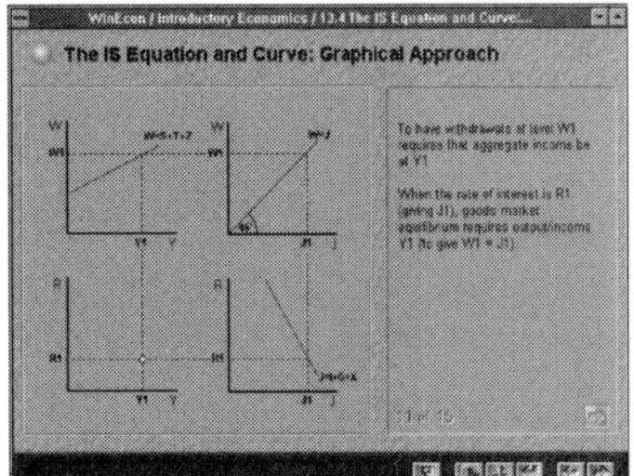

The WinEcon screen shows a traditional derivation of the IS curve using four linked diagrams. These diagrams can only be linked if the same scale is used for each of the axis variables in every diagram in which they appear. This allows us to read values across from one diagram to the next. We now assume that I depends on R but not on Y, and that C (and therefore S) is a function of Y but not R. This simplification lets us plot two of the graphs shown. At the bottom right we see that the total of injections ($J = I + G + X$) is specified just as a function of R, since G and X are both exogenous. At the top left of the screen we have total withdrawals ($W = S + T + Z$) depicted as a function of Y, because all of these components depend on Y. These graphs are linked by the one in the top right corner which imposes the equilibrium condition that $W = J$. Notice that the W and J axes must have the same scales.

Any specified interest rate, R, will induce a particular amount of investment and so will imply the associated value for total injections, J. Marking R on the bottom diagrams, reading J and taking this value upwards to the top right-hand diagram lets us see the value that W must have if equilibrium is to be achieved. We take the value of W across to the top left-hand diagram where we read off the corresponding value of Y. This is the value of Y that will generate the level of withdrawals needed to ensure that $W = J$. We now have a value of R and the Y value which must be associated with it if equilibrium in the goods market is to be achieved. The point corresponding to these values is plotted in the bottom left diagram, and is the first point on our IS curve. By choosing another interest rate we can obtain a second point in the same way, and these can be joined to give the IS curve.

We see that the IS curve is drawn against the *R* (vertical) and *Y* (horizontal) axes. It represents goods market equilibrium and has an inverse slope. At a higher rate of interest, *R*, the level of real income, *Y*, at which equilibrium will be achieved is lower. Notice that, in this model, aggregate demand is a function of both *Y* and *R*, although its separate elements of *C*, *I* and *G* are a function of one or the other, or exogenous.

About the IS curve

41 **The IS curve shows combinations of the _____ _____ and _____ _____ at which the _____ market is in equilibrium.**

Plot the IS curve in the diagram, tracing out the equilibrium *Y* corresponding to each *R* value shown.

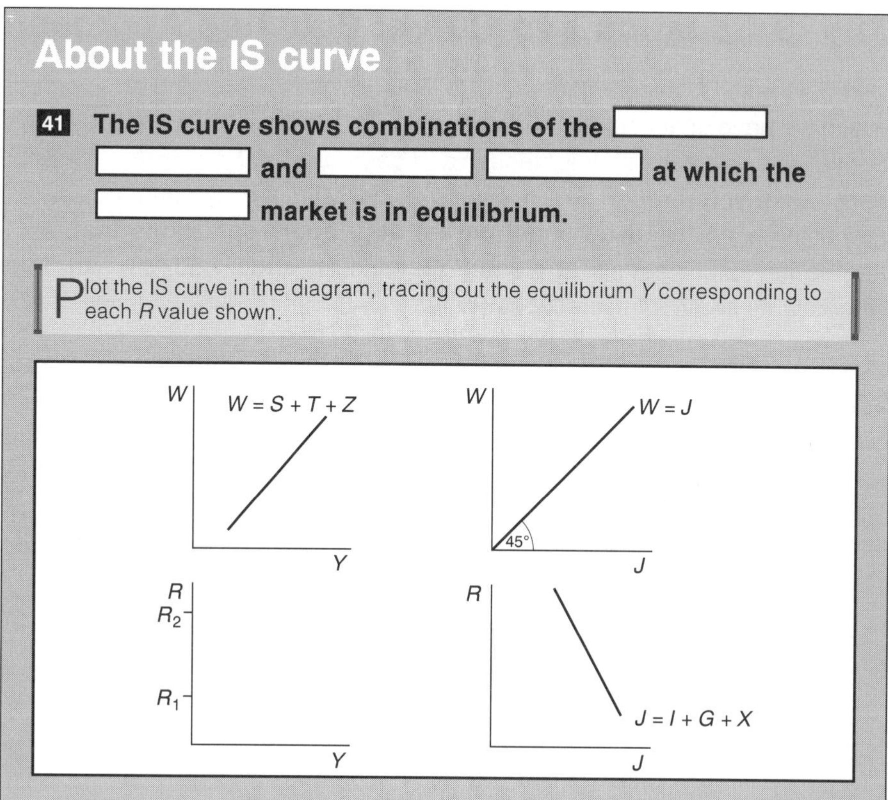

Changes in Injections and Withdrawals

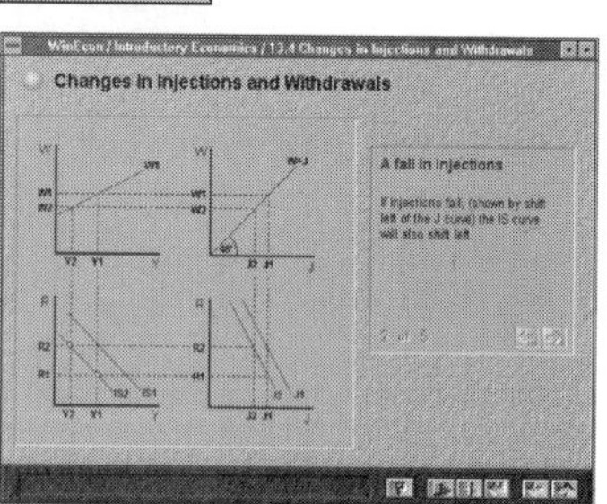

Government policy may affect firms' willingness to invest or alter taxation. With this screen you consider how changes in injections and withdrawals affect the IS curve. Learning about why the IS curve may swivel or shift lets you later analyse the effects of policy changes.

The effect of changes in injections and withdrawals

In this framework, which way does the IS curve shift (left or right) in each of the following cases?

42 **If government expenditure increases, IS shifts _____.**

43 If exports fall, IS shifts ______.

44 If taxation is cut, IS shifts ______.

The IS Equation and Curve: Equation Approach

Using equations we can model $C = f(Y,R)$ and $I = f(Y,R)$, giving an approach which we have suggested is more satisfactory. We have seen previously that both C and I increase as Y increases and decrease as R increases. WinEcon here takes you through two methods of deriving the IS equation, based respectively on the two goods market equilibrium conditions that, first, aggregate output equals aggregate demand (Y = AD) and, second, total withdrawals equal total injections ($W = J$).

Try a complete Keynesian goods market equation system

Let $C = 400 + 0.8\,(Y - T) - 1000\,R$; $S = -400 + 0.15Y + 1000R$; $T = 0.25Y$; $I = 600 + 0.1Y - 4000R$; $G = 2000$; $X = 3000$; and $Z = 700 + 0.2Y$.

45 Derive the AD equation.

46 Derive the equation for total injections, J.

47 Derive the equation for total withdrawals, W.

48 Using the goods market equilibrium condition Y = AD, derive the IS equation.

49 Using the equilibrium condition $W = J$, check your IS equation.

Show this IS curve in the diagram.

R

0 Y

The IS Curve and Aggregate Demand

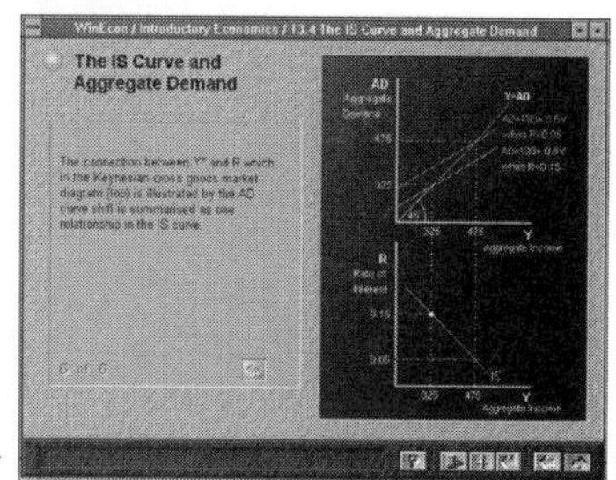

Here, WinEcon shows us how the IS curve links with aggregate demand in the Keynesian cross 45 degree line diagram used earlier. A change in the rate of interest, *R*, shifts the simple aggregate demand function and gives us a new point on the IS curve.

Check your understanding of aggregate demand movement

50 **The IS equation and curve indicate that, as *R* increases, equilibrium *Y* in the goods market ______.**

51 **This is because, as *R* increases, AD ______ and producers respond by ______ output *Y*, which equivalently ______ household sector income *Y*.**

The IS–LM Analysis and Aggregate Demand

The IS relationship between *Y* and *R* corresponds to goods market equilibrium, but does not yet give a single value result for equilibrium *Y*. Still missing is the relevant value of *R*. Real aggregate demand in the goods market is seen to depend on financial conditions. To proceed, we need to integrate the Keynesian money market analysis, using the LM curve and equation, with the goods market analysis summarized in the IS curve.

See Section 12.5 for Keynesian monetary theory and an explanation of the LM relationship.

The LM curve represents money market equilibrium, also against *R* (vertical) and *Y* (horizontal) axes, and it has a positive slope in the diagram. As *Y* increases, so too does the transactions demand for money, and if the total money supply is fixed then *R* must increase until money market equilibrium is restored at a higher *R*. The rise in *R* will cause speculative money holdings to fall to accommodate the increased transactions demand. In this screen, WinEcon reminds you of the LM relationship.

Real–Financial Sector Interactions

Now we combine the IS and LM curves on one diagram to see the result of the real and financial sector interactions. The IS and LM curves at first appear separately on the WinEcon screen, but drawn to the same scale. Each represents possible equilibrium combinations of *Y* and *R*, the former from consideration of the goods market and the latter from the analysis of the money market. Clearly there will be interactions between real and financial sectors, with feedback in both directions. Combining IS and LM curves in the same diagram, we see that there is one intersection position (i.e. one pair of values for *Y* and *R*) at which there is joint equilibrium of goods and money markets.

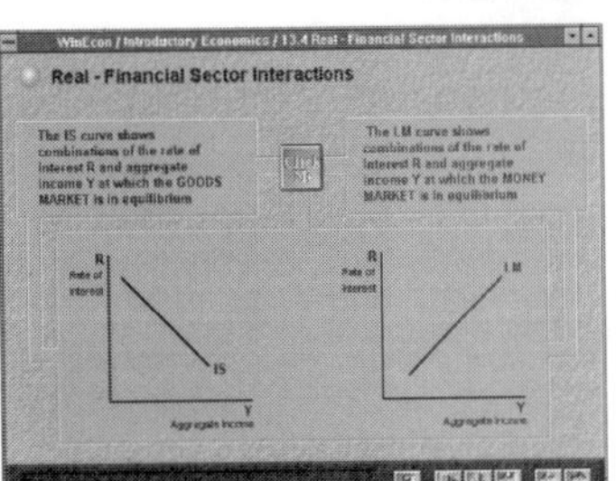

From any initial disequilibrium, the interactions between the goods and money markets logically continue indefinitely, with changes in money market *R* causing changes in goods market AD and hence in *Y*, and changes in goods market *Y* causing changes in money market MD and hence in *R*. However, the adjustments become smaller and smaller and converge on a new equilibrium.

The beauty of IS–LM analysis is that it shows directly where the equilibrium will be, given the economic conditions reflected in a given pair of IS and LM curves or equations.

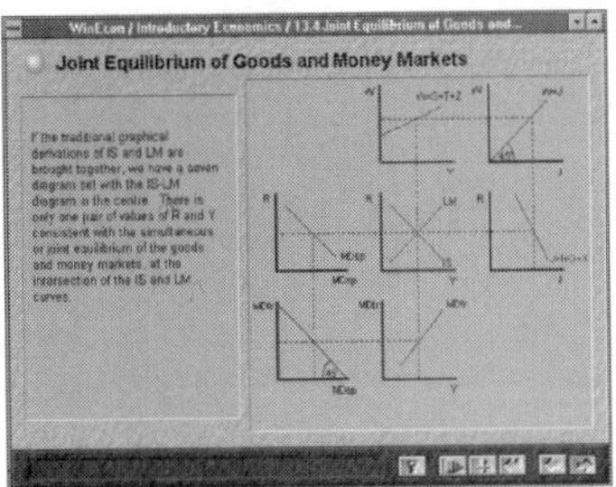

Joint Equilibrium of Goods and Money Markets

WinEcon now develops the full Keynesian IS–LM analysis as you work through the next six screens. This first screen gives you the overall equilibrium in a seven-diagram graphic, which emphasizes the variety of behavioural functions underlying the outcome.

IS–LM Equilibrium

Using a numerical example, we see here how to solve the equations to find the equilibrium values in the model. We also identify the characteristics of different disequilibrium zones in the diagram.

Calculating IS–LM equilibrium

Now add to the equation model used above in the topic The IS Equation and Curve: Equation Approach by including a money market. Let MD = 800 + 0.5*Y* – 6000 *R* and MS = 5000.

52 **Derive the LM curve.**

53 **From the IS and LM equations, solve to find equilibrium *R* and *Y*.**

54 Add this LM curve to the diagram with the Is curve above, and show the equilibrium values.

R

0 *Y*

Exogenous Changes in the IS–LM Model

Here, we examine the effects of exogenous changes in this IS–LM framework. An exogenous change in one of the components of aggregate demand will shift the IS curve. An exogenous change in money demand or supply will shift the LM curve. The final impact on equilibrium *Y* and *R* can then be identified in the IS–LM diagram or from the equations.

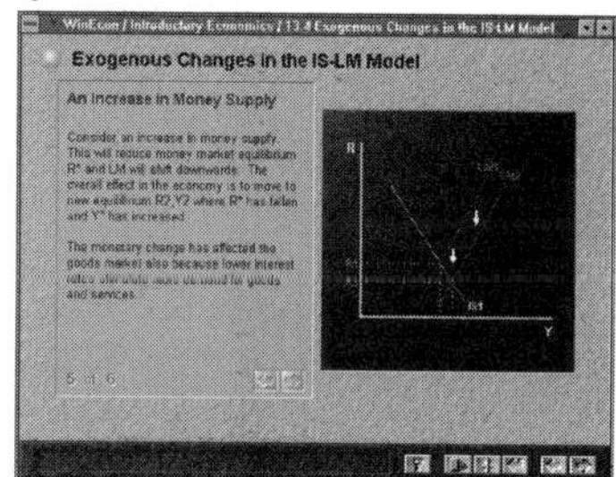

It is this usage of the IS–LM framework to investigate the results of exogenous changes which has made it so valuable as a tool of Keynesian macroeconomic analysis. Notice that when IS shifts, *Y* and *R* change in the same direction, but that when LM shifts *Y* and *R* change in opposite directions.

Check your understanding of exogenous changes

For the following exogenous changes, state which curve (IS or LM) is shifted, the direction of shift, and the direction of change in *Y* and *R*. (It will be helpful if you sketch an IS–LM diagram for each case, starting each with one IS and one LM curve, and showing the initial *R* and *Y* equilibrium values drawn from the intersection. Then introduce the appropriate curve shift to discover the direction of effects on *R* and *Y*.)

55 **An increase in exports.**

56 **An increase in money supply.**

57 **A reduction in public expenditure.**

58 **Tax cuts.**

59 **Increased liquidity preference (i.e. demand to hold money).**

Relative Effects of Exogenous Changes

This WinEcon screen shows that the relative effects on *R* and *Y* of any exogenous changes will depend on the slopes of the curves, and invites you to experiment by changing the slopes in the diagram and considering what economic conditions they represent.

IS–LM Models

With this screen we briefly compare classical/monetarist and Keynesian 'cases' in this framework. It is sometimes suggested that the differences between the two are summed up by different slope combinations, steep IS plus shallow LM being Keynesian while steep LM plus shallow IS is more representative of the classical model

Policy Implications of the IS–LM Theory

This screen, and the one that follows, give you some pointers to the policy implications of this IS–LM theory. Note particularly that the economy can come to equilibrium at any level of *Y*, dependent on the level of AD derived from the real–financial sector interactions. There is absolutely no guarantee that this equilibrium will provide full employment for the workforce. This is the characteristic Keynesian result that leads to consideration of policy interventions by the government to bring about full employment. In the IS–LM context we also see that both fiscal policy (changing *G* and/or *T*) and monetary policy (changing MS and *R*) can change the macroeconomic equilibrium, so that the government has a choice of policy instruments with which to undertake aggregate demand management.

See chapter 15 for further consideration of these policy issues.

Policy implications

60 **Keynesian equilibrium output *Y* is the same as full employment output.** **True/False**

61 **Fiscal policy is shown in the IS–LM framework by shifting the ______ curve, and monetary policy by shifting the ______ curve.**

62 **In Keynesian theory, which fiscal and monetary actions by government could stimulate aggregate demand?**

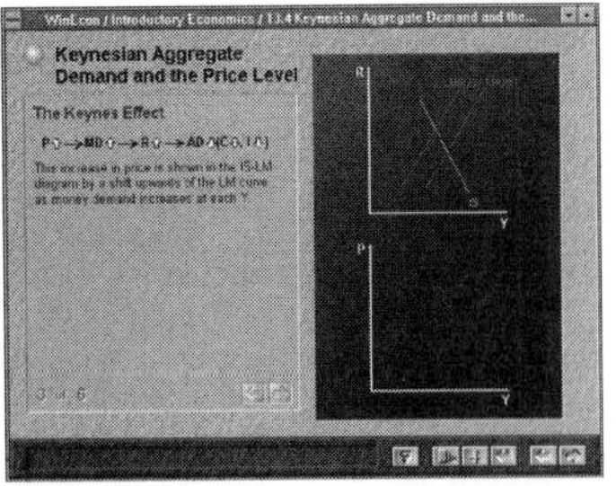

Keynesian Aggregate Demand and the Price Level

Keynesian analysis usually assumes that firms produce the quantity of goods and services demanded at current advertised prices. In other words, the emphasis is on quantity adjustment not price adjustment. However, there is a mechanism through which changes in the general price level can affect aggregate demand. This is known as the 'Keynes effect' of a change in price level, and it operates indirectly via the monetary sector. Through this we obtain the Keynesian aggregate demand schedule.

An increase in the price level P increases the transactions demand for money (remember $MD_{tr} = k.P.Y$) and therefore total MD also increases. This raises equilibrium R in the money market (shifting the LM curve upwards). With increased R, goods market AD falls because C and I both fall in the general case.

In a diagram with P on the vertical axis and Y on the horizontal, the AD curve will therefore have a negative slope because of the Keynes effect. Aggregate demand is an inverse function of the price level, but not for the reasons applicable in a microeconomic context. The outcome due to the Keynes effect of an increase in price level (ceteris paribus) is that equilibrium Y falls, as firms react to the fall in AD by cutting output. This is clearly shown by the IS–LM analysis.

The Keynes effect

Now check your understanding by applying this idea to a fall in the price level.

63 The Keynes effect of a decrease in the price level is that MD increases/decreases, so R increases/decreases and, therefore, AD increases/decreases.

Section 13.5: Keynesian Open Economy

The IS–LM analysis as described so far takes account of exports and imports in the AD function, but does not allow for international capital flows and the balance of payments as a whole. Here we see that this can be rectified by incorporating a further curve or equation in the system. The IS curve represents goods market equilibrium, the LM curve represents money market equilibrium, and the BP curve represents ‘balance of payments’ equilibrium (which is also foreign exchange market equilibrium).

The BP Curve

See the topic Balance of Payments in section 9.3 for more information.

The balance of payments account of a country is made up of two parts, the ‘current account’ and the ‘capital account’.

The current account balance of payments with other countries, CUR, is

$$\text{CUR} = X - Z$$

where X denotes exports, Z represents imports and Z is a function of Y such that Z increases if Y increases. An increase in Y therefore reduces CUR, so

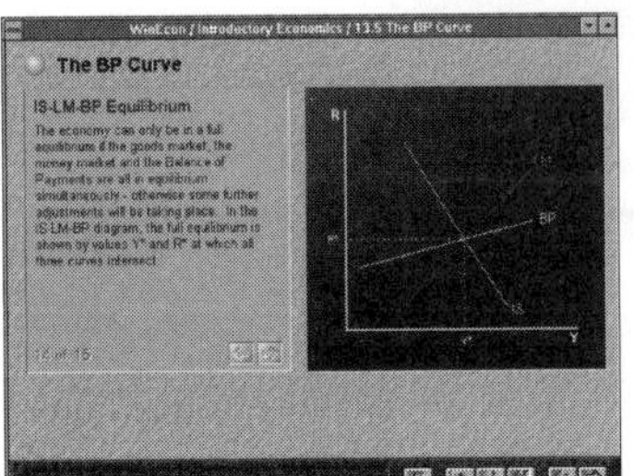

these variables are inversely related. The capital account balance, CAP, increases as *R*, the rate of interest, increases. This is because net inflows of capital and monetary deposits will increase if interest rates here increase (given that foreign interest rates are unchanged).

It follows that if an initial overall balance of payments equilibrium is disturbed by a change in *Y* which affects the current account, equilibrium can be restored by a counterbalancing change in *R*, which affects the capital account. From this analysis, the BP curve is shown to be upward sloping in the IS–LM diagram.

We will assume that international capital flows are very highly interest-elastic such that the slope of BP is less than the slope of LM. In the combined IS–LM–BP diagram, macroeconomic equilibrium for *Y* and *R* now requires an intersection of all three curves at one point.

In using this analysis, the IS–LM intersection is always the reference point. If this is above BP, there is a balance of payments surplus (interest rates are higher than is needed for balance of payments equilibrium), and if it is below BP there is a deficit. What happens in consequence depends on whether there are fixed or flexible exchange rates.

Balance of payments equilibrium

64 **CUR + CAP = ______.**

65 **From initial balance of payments equilibrium, an increase in *Y* which raises ______ and causes a move into ______ could be counterbalanced by ______ *R* which raises net ______ ______, thus providing the foreign currency finance to restore overall equilibrium.**

IS–LM–BP Analysis with Fixed Exchange Rates

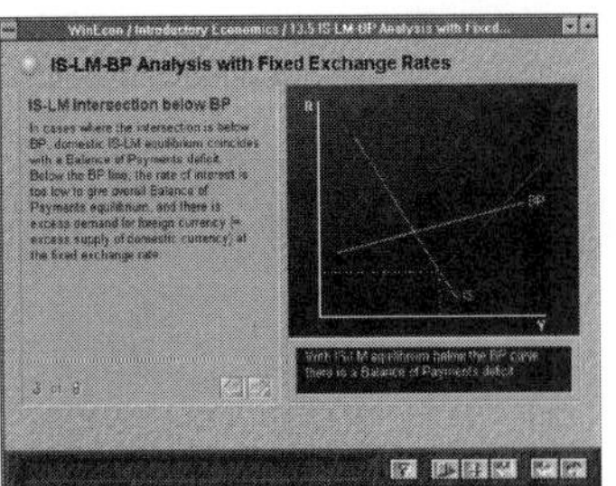

The BP curve remains fixed if exchange rates are fixed, and adjustment to open economy equilibrium rests on monetary changes. These shift the LM curve as the central bank intervenes in the exchange market to maintain the currency value.

Analysis with fixed exchange rates

66 A balance of payments surplus tends to cause currency [ ] such that the central bank has to [ ] its currency to hold the official exchange rate.Conversely, a deficit requires the central bank to [ ] the currency to prevent [ ].

67 Central bank interventions to keep a fixed exchange rate change the [ ] [ ] [ ] and shift the [ ] curve until it reaches the intersection of the [ ] curve and the [ ] curve, giving overall macroeconomic equilibrium at this triple intersection.

In this context:

68 With fixed exchange rates, a balance of payments deficit causes the economy to move towards a [higher/lower] level of output.

IS–LM–BP Analysis: Exchange Rate Changes

This WinEcon screen lets you investigate how currency appreciation or depreciation is illustrated on the IS–LM–BP diagram. With flexible exchange rates a balance of payments surplus causes an appreciation of the currency, and deficit causes depreciation. Taking the surplus case, appreciation makes a country's goods less price-competitive, and exports fall and imports increase, shifting IS left as aggregate demand falls and also shifting BP upwards because a higher interest rate is then required in order for the capital account to improve to offset the worsened current account. Conversely, depreciation shifts IS right and BP downwards. With flexible exchange rates it is the LM curve which remains fixed.

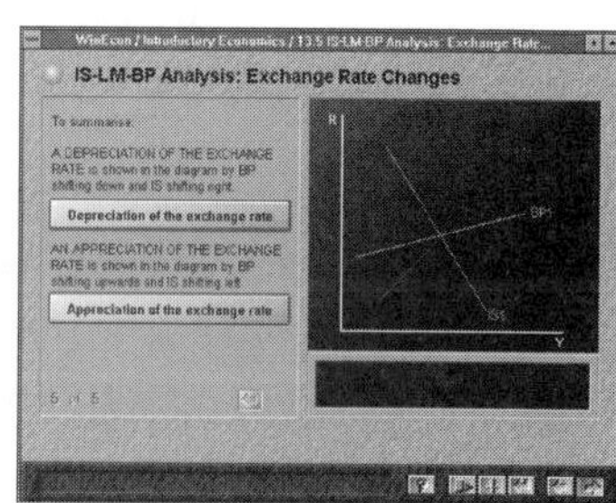

Check you understand the effect of exchange rate changes

69 With fixed exchange rates, a balance of payments deficit requires the central bank to do what?

70 **With flexible exchange rates, a balance of payments deficit causes the currency to** appreciate/depreciate **which in turn causes the balance of trade to** improve/deteriorate **.**

IS–LM–BP Analysis with Flexible Exchange Rates

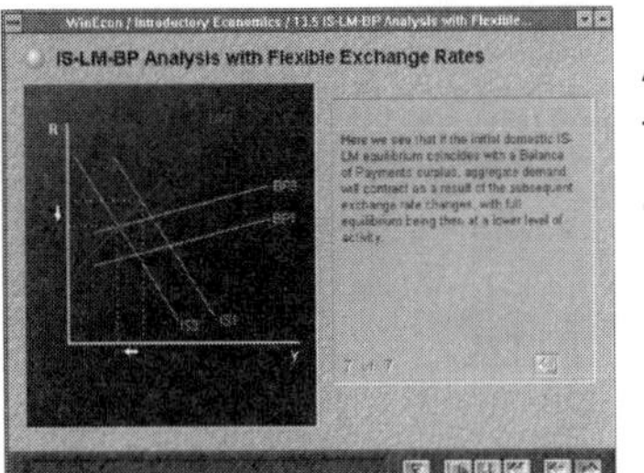

Applying the adjustment process explained in the previous topic, this WinEcon screen lets you follow the IS–LM–BP analysis of adjustments to equilibrium when exchange rates are flexible.

Analysis with flexible exchange rates

Assuming flexible exchange rates, show in the diagram what happens to restore balance of payments equilibrium. Be sure you can explain why.

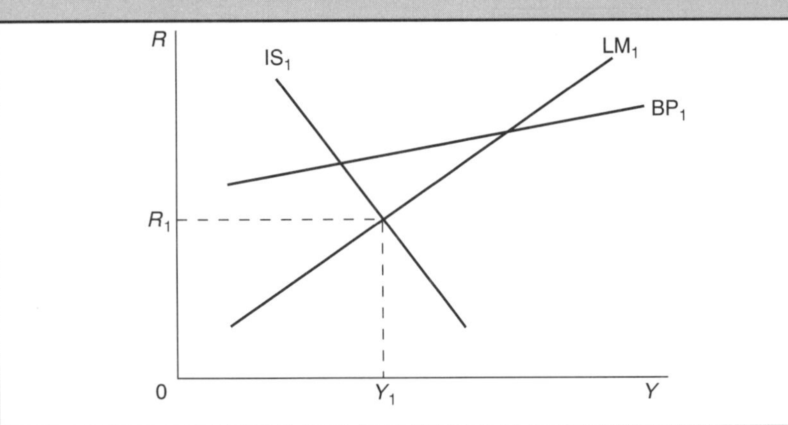

71 **What is the effect of currency depreciation on domestic aggregate demand?**

Exogenous Changes

Starting from full IS–LM–BP equilibrium, the effect of various exogenous changes can be explored in an open economy framework. The main issue here is whether, having allowed for the balance of payments adjustments, the net effect of an exogenous change on Y is greater than or less than in the two-market IS–LM model used previously. To put it another way, are multiplier effects amplified or reduced by recognizing that the economy is open?

Section 13.5 / Exogenous Changes

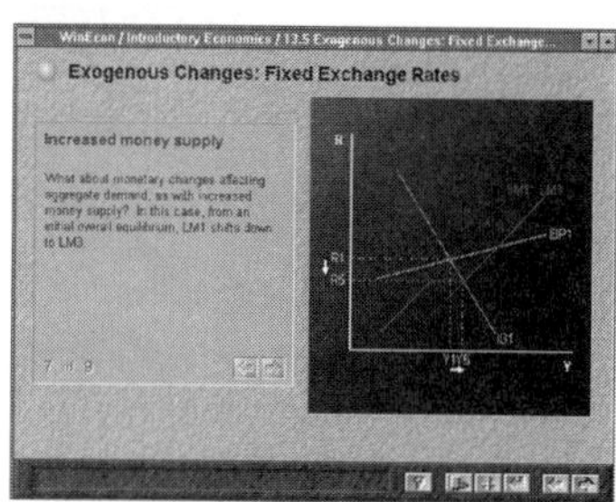

WinEcon takes you through two screens here, dealing with the effects of exogenous changes in fixed and flexible exchange rate systems. One important result is that, with fixed exchange rates, a discretionary change in money supply cannot be sustained. The initial shift of LM is reversed as the central bank has to intervene to hold the exchange rate, so that independent monetary policy is not possible. For a central bank to determine its own national money supply, there must be flexible exchange rates.

The effect of exogenous changes

72 Assuming LM is steeper than BP, an exogenous change in AD causes equilibrium *Y* to change by ________ than in the closed economy case when exchange rates are fixed, and by ________ than in the closed economy case when exchange rates are flexible.

73 With fixed exchange rates, a decrease in money supply is shown by LM shifting ________ which puts the IS–LM intersection ________ BP, corresponding to a balance of payments ________, and to prevent currency ________ the central bank ________ its own currency, thus causing money supply to ________, shown by LM shifting ________, which negates the initial change.

74 Fiscal policy is relatively more powerful than monetary policy when exchange rates are ________ and monetary policy is more powerful than fiscal policy when exchange rates are ________.

Section 13.6: Neoclassical Aggregate Demand

We come finally to a brief review of neoclassical theory in this branch of macroeconomics. There is no entirely distinct model. Instead, there is a series of refinements that bring together elements from classical and Keynesian theory. In particular, there is consideration of the 'microeconomic foundations' of macroeconomics, and increased recognition of the role of assets, or wealth. We shall emphasize considerations of 'inter-temporal choice' and 'real balance effects' in the modelling of consumer demand.

Neoclassical Theory of Consumer Expenditure

This WinEcon screen lets you explore the principles of inter-temporal choice. You apply indifference curve analysis to choosing between consumption in two different time periods. The budget line shows different consumption possibilities, where you can spend more than your income in either one of the time periods by spending less than your income in the other. Spending more than your income in time period 1 implies borrowing and repaying the money with interest in the next time period from the second period's income. Or, if you save some of your income from the first time period, you can spend the saving, together with the interest it has earned, in addition to the second period's income in that time period.

Consumer preferences between consumption in the two time periods are represented by indifference curves. The point of tangency with the budget line represents the chosen consumption combination.

The analysis can be generalized to more than two time periods. It shows that given rational behaviour and the possibility of saving or borrowing, current aggregate consumption does not depend solely on other current period variables (current income and the rate of interest). Also relevant are assets brought forward from the past and expectations of income in the future.

Consumer expenditure

75 **In two-period analysis, a borrower in period 1 will consume above/below income in period 2.**

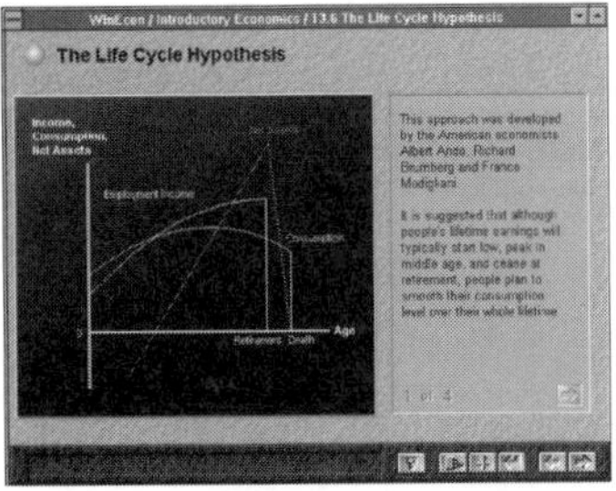

The Permanent Income Hypothesis/Life Cycle Hypothesis

These two screens look at two specific formal models which incorporate in different ways these ideas about longer term influences on consumption. (Note that in this context, Keynes's theory of consumer expenditure is known as the 'absolute income hypothesis'.)

Check your recall

76 **Who proposed the permanent income hypothesis?**

77 **What is permanent income?**

78 **In the life cycle hypothesis, how is consumption financed in retirement?**

79 **With the life cycle hypothesis, what additional variable will affect aggregate consumption?**

Neoclassical Consumption Theories

This screen summarizes the position we have reached. Note that we will now formally include wealth as a third independent variable in the consumption function, together with income, *Y*, and interest rate, *R*.

Real Balance Effects in Aggregate Demand

What are 'real balance effects'? With this screen you consider the idea that changes in the price level will cause changes in the real purchasing power equivalent of some nominal assets, and hence will change real wealth. As the price level increases, the real value of money-denominated assets (money balances, bonds, etc.) is reduced, and with people then less well off this will reduce real consumption and aggregate demand.

When wealth is acknowledged as a further independent variable in the consumption function, we have:

$$C = \text{f}(Y, R, \text{wealth})$$

with higher wealth inducing higher consumption for given values of *Y* and *R*. This means that aggregate demand also becomes a function of wealth:

$$\text{AD} = \text{f}(Y, R, \text{wealth})$$

The appropriate measure of wealth for these purposes is subject to debate, but in principle it is real wealth which matters and so 'real money balances' are certainly relevant. However, the real value or purchasing power of money balances (including savings, deposits, etc.) will depend inversely on the price level of goods and services. Increases in the price level reduce real wealth.

It is real wealth which affects real aggregate demand, and real wealth is equal to nominal wealth divided by price level. Hence, when the overall real balance effect of a change in price level is recognized, real aggregate demand becomes an inverse function of the price level, *P*:

$$\text{AD} = \text{f}(Y, R, \text{nominal wealth}/P)$$

See what you have learnt

80 **If you have savings of £3000, how many units of output would it buy if the average price was £2, £3 and £4?**

81 **The real balance effect of rising prices is that, for given *Y* and *R*, aggregate demand will ________.**

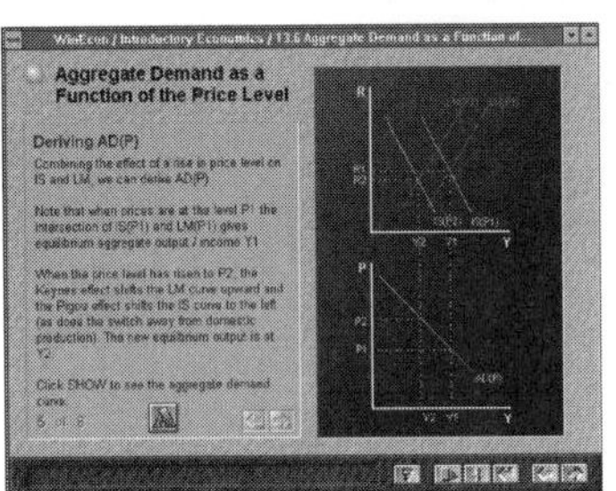

Aggregate Demand as a Function of the Price Level

Here you see how the real balance effect is incorporated into the model alongside other price effects to give a neoclassical analysis of aggregate demand as a function of the price level. The AD = f(*P*) curve (against *P* and *Y* axes) is formally derived from the IS–LM illustration of price effects.

In neoclassical theory, AD = f(*P*) not just because of the Keynes effect considered earlier but also because of the real balance effect or 'Pigou Effect' (Pigou drew attention to it in 1943) and, possibly, open economy effects as well. The neoclassical aggregate demand curve therefore shows a more elastic response to changes in the price level than the Keynesian case considered earlier.

The effect of price level changes

82 **In the IS–LM diagram, the Keynes effect of price changes shifts the ________ curve, but the Pigou effect shifts the ________ curve.**

83 **If the price level ________, aggregate demand will increase.**

The Neoclassical Synthesis

The classical model assumed that market forces would bring about full employment, as unemployment would lead to wage reductions, thereby increasing demand for labour, and price reductions, which would increase demand for goods. Keynes denied this, arguing that this analysis ignored income effects on demand and that even if wage–price reductions could be achieved, increases in real demand might not result, or might not be enough to create full employment.

With the aid of real balance effects, it is possible to show that wage–price deflation in the model will bring full employment equilibrium. Thus the Pigou

effect has a special place in the history of macroeconomics, since it provides the basis of a theoretical refutation of Keynes's argument that market forces would not automatically restore full employment. This type of theory was developed more fully by economists like Don Patinkin in the 1940s and 1950s.

Pigou himself recognized, however, that these theoretical wealth effects might in practice be weak and slow-working, such that Keynesian demand management policy might be helpful in the short run. On that note, a truce was called between classical and Keynesian economists. The classical economists won the theoretical point, but Keynesian ideas were seen to be of practical importance for government policy. This compromise position in the Keynes versus classics debate is known as the 'neoclassical synthesis'.

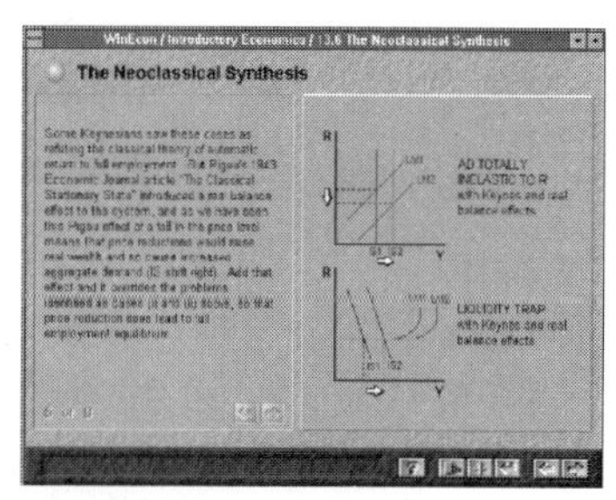

What is the neoclassical synthesis?

84 **The neoclassical synthesis claims to be a general theory in which is incorporated the Keynesian analysis as the special case where there are wage–price ______ and no ______ ______ ______.**

Criticisms of the Neoclassical Synthesis

Not all economists accept this sort of compromise between the two earlier approaches, but it became the conventional mainstream macroeconomics for a quarter of a century from the 1950s onwards. WinEcon here briefly indicates some criticisms of this position.

Section 13.7: Summary

We have looked at three approaches to modelling aggregate demand. All of them agree that the AD schedule is a downward-sloping curve showing the level of real income, Y, that corresponds to different price levels, P. Different theories, however, derive the relationship in different ways. The classical/monetarist theory has AD = f(M, P). Keynesian theory has AD = f(Y, R). Neoclassical theory combines elements of both, and in some versions has AD = f(Y, R, M/P). The AD schedule is needed once the aggregate supply schedule, AS, has been obtained for AD–AS analysis.

The classical or monetarist approach to aggregate demand obtains the relationship by rewriting and interpreting the equation of exchange. Shifts in aggregate demand through a change in the money supply are explained by the transmission mechanism. The theory can be applied to an open economy. If exchange rates are fixed, the need for the central bank to maintain the

exchange rate inhibits its ability to determine the domestic money supply. With flexible exchange rates, aggregate demand in each country is determined as it would be in a closed economy, and the exchange rate adjusts to give international compatibility.

The Keynesian approach models separately the various components of aggregate demand. Since AD is a function of both Y and R, we find combinations of Y and R at which AD = Y, so that the goods market is in equilibrium. Such combinations form the IS curve. This curve is then used with the LM curve from chapter 12 in IS–LM analysis. By looking at the effect of a change in prices on the transactions demand for money, and from this on the rate of interest and then on aggregate demand, a downward-sloping AD curve is deduced.

An open economy is analysed by augmenting IS–LM analysis with the addition of a BP curve. This shows combinations of Y and R at which balance of payments equilibrium is achieved. If this curve does not pass through the intersection of the IS and LM curves, some adjustment is required. If exchange rates are fixed, the BP curve remains static and the LM curve shifts as the central bank intervenes to maintain the exchange rate at its official level. With flexible exchange rates, the value of the currency alters and the BP curve shifts. Macroeconomic equilibrium is achieved in the open economy when the IS, LM and BP curves all cross at the same point.

Neoclassical analysis introduces income in previous and future time periods as relevant to aggregate demand. Another factor is the effect of price changes on the value of real wealth. The model thus derived is capable of refuting Keynes's assertion that market forces do not automatically restore an economy to full employment.

Chapter 14:

Theories of Aggregate Supply

During the 1980s and 1990s there has been a growing interest in 'supply-side' fiscal policies, after the limits of aggregate demand policies became all too obvious. The effects of income tax changes are a good illustration. In the 1960s and 1970s attention was focused almost exclusively on the effects of a change in income tax on aggregate spending, whereas more recently increasing attention has been given to the effects of tax changes on labour supply and work incentives. This chapter lets you discover three quite different approaches to aggregate supply: the 'classical', 'Keynesian' and 'monetarist' models.

Contents

KEYWORDS

- Aggregate production function
- Aggregate supply
- Classical theory
- Keynesian theory
- Labour demand
- Labour supply
- Monetarist theory
- Phillips curve
- Price expectations
- Real consumption wage
- Real product wage

Section 14.1: Introduction

Aggregate supply (AS) is the sum total (in the national economy) of goods and services that firms are able and willing to produce. From chapter 13 we have the aggregate demand (AD) curve showing levels of output and prices for which the level of aggregate demand equals the level of output. Bringing together aggregate supply AS and aggregate demand AD in AS–AD analysis allows us to determine the output level for the economy. It also completes our macroeconomic theory of output and the price level.

Much controversy has surrounded the theory of aggregate supply, and the various schools of thought in macroeconomics take very different theoretical approaches when seeking to explain it. There are, as a result, a large number of theories of aggregate supply, each theory making distinctive assumptions about the objectives and behaviour of firms and workers, and the operations of labour and product markets. In this chapter we consider three broad approaches: classical, Keynesian and monetarist. It may help you if, at the outset, you understand the main differences between these theories, and for this reason the main assumptions made by each are set out below.

	Labour market	*Information*
Classical	Equilibrium	Complete
Keynesian	Disequilibrium	Complete
Monetarist	Equilibrium	Incomplete

In the classical model, the labour market is assumed to clear continuously (i.e. it is assumed to be in equilibrium) and workers are assumed to possess complete information about the prices of the goods they consume. The classical model may be viewed as the 'base case' against which alternative theories depart. The key assumption of the Keynesian theory is that the labour market may not be in equilibrium. In particular, the labour market may be characterized by persistent excess supply (or unemployment). The monetarist approach maintains the classical assumption of market clearing but relaxes the assumption of full information, workers being assumed instead to have imperfect knowledge of the price level. We show in this chapter how these varying assumptions lead to important differences in aggregate supply.

The policy implications of alternative models of aggregate supply are examined in chapter 15 and the models we develop in this chapter are used to analyse macroeconomic fluctuations in chapter 16.

Section 14.2: Basic Tools for Aggregate Supply

Theories of aggregate supply are constructed from four elements: a theory of the aggregate production function, a theory of the demand for labour, a theory of the supply of labour and an assumption about how flexible wage rates are. The first of these shows how much output will be produced by the quantity of labour employed in the economy; the others determine what that quantity of labour will be and what variables will influence it. For the three aggregate supply models covered in this chapter, the theories of the aggregate production function and the demand for labour are the same, so these components are covered first in this section. The relationship between labour supply and unemployment is also common to all theories so again we cover it in this section.

The Aggregate Production Function

The aggregate production function describes the relationship between the input of factor services and the output of goods and services in the macro-economy. It exactly parallels the production function for an individual firm, as described in chapter 4. The function may be formally written as

$$Y = f(K_0, L)$$

where K is the economy-wide capital stock, L is the flow of labour services in the economy (say, the total number of hours worked) and the form of the function reflects the current state of technology. If work effort and hours of work are assumed to be constant, the supply of labour services is determined by the level of employment. For short-run problems, it is convenient to assume that the capital stock is constant (i.e. the effect of current investment expenditure on the stock of capital can be ignored). In the production function above the capital stock is fixed at a particular value (K_0). Therefore, in the short run, over which the state of technology and the stock of capital are fixed, aggregate output can only change by variations in employment.

Using the WinEcon screen, step through to the second text card and note the shape of the production function. The function is upward sloping (aggregate output is assumed to rise as employment rises), but it rises at a diminishing rate. This reflects diminishing returns to additional inputs of labour, as the Show button illustrates. The slope of the function describes the 'marginal product of labour' at a specific level of employment. Work through the quick quiz to make sure you understand the relationship between the slope of the production function and the marginal product of labour.

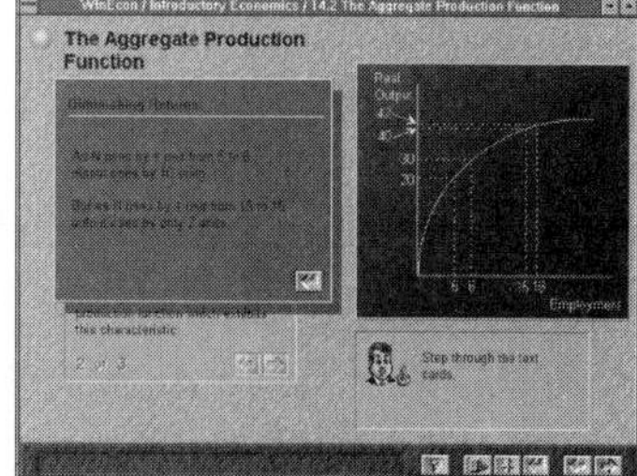

The aggregate production function describes a relationship between the inputs of labour in all firms in an economy and the total output of the economy. The conditions required for the existence of such a function are very demanding, as the following question illustrates.

What the aggregate production function implies

01 The data below are for an imaginary economy consisting of just two firms (A and B). The aggregate level of employment doubles between period one and two. Calculate the aggregate level of real output and comment on the implications of your result for the aggregate production function.

Year 1:

Firm A	Employment: 100,	Real Output: £200
Firm B	Employment: 100,	Real Output: £400

Year 2:

Firm A	Employment: 200,	Real Output: £333
Firm B	Employment: 200,	Real Output: £667

02 This next set of data is for a second imaginary economy, again consisting of just two firms (A and B). The aggregate level of employment remains constant between period 1 and 2. Calculate the aggregate level of real output and comment on the implications of your result for the aggregate production function. Also comment on the nature of each firm's production function.

Year 1:

Firm A	Employment: 100,	Real Output: £200
Firm B	Employment: 100,	Real Output: £400

Year 2:

Firm A	Employment: 50,	Real Output: £120
Firm B	Employment: 150,	Real Output: £500

03 Given the lessons you learnt from the previous two questions, what key assumption is required for the existence of a 'well-behaved' aggregate production function?

04 Assume that the aggregate production function for the UK is upward sloping and subject to decreasing returns to labour. In 1960 the number of labour hours used by firms

(employment) was 56.2 billion and total output (GDP) was £165 billion (in 1985 prices). By 1989 these figures were 52.1 billion labour hours and £355 billion (again in 1985 prices). Explain how these figures can be reconciled with the assumed production function.

The Aggregate Demand for Labour

The demand for labour from individual firms in different market situations is derived in chapter 8. In section 8.4, the topic Short-Run Demand for Labour: competitive input and output markets shows the result used below.

The next building block needed for all our aggregate supply theories is the demand for labour function. Its main implication is that the quantity of labour firms demand will increase as the 'real product wage' (the nominal wage deflated by the price of the firm's product) falls.

With competitive factor and product markets each firm can hire any quantity of labour at the relevant going wage rate (W_i for firm i), and can sell any quantity of its output at the going price (P_i for firm i). A profit maximizing firm will employ labour up to the point where $W_i = \text{MPPL} \times P_i$. Re-arranging this expression gives the result that firms will employ labour up to the point where $W_i/P_i = \text{MPPL}$ (i.e. firms will employ labour up to the point where the real product wage (the nominal wage divided by the price of the product) equals the marginal physical product of labour).

Work through the WinEcon text cards to card six, then click the Show button. You are presented with a range of wage rates, product prices and marginal products of labour and, in each case, you decide whether the firm should expand, contract or maintain constant the level of employment.

If the marginal product of labour falls as output and employment rise (a feature of the production function presented earlier in the topic The Aggregate Production Function), then firms will only raise output if the real product wage falls (as explained by the remaining text cards on this screen).

Test your understanding of the demand for labour

05 **A firm can employ as much labour as it wishes at a money wage rate of £30, and the firm can sell its product for £2. The real product wage is therefore _____. If the firm is maximizing its profit, it will employ workers up to the point where the _____ is equal to the real product wage. If the real product wage is greater than the marginal product, the firm can raise its profits by _____ the level of employment.**

06 **What is the relationship between the aggregate production function and the demand for labour?**

07 **What is the difference between the nominal or money wage and the real product wage?**

08 **Assume that the demand for labour in the UK rises with the real wage. In 1978 the actual real wage rate was £3.58 per hour and employment was 50.7 billion labour hours. In 1988 the respective figures for the real wage and employment were £4.56 and 51.5 billion. Reconcile these facts with the assumed demand for labour function.**

Labour Supply and Unemployment

The final feature that is common to all theories of labour supply is the distinction between the labour force and labour supply. The labour force consists of men and women either in employment or actively seeking work. Labour supply may be defined as the supply of labour actually available to firms at the real wage rates being offered. A worker seeking a job may prefer to remain unemployed for longer, rather than accept the current wage offer. The labour force is thus larger than the supply of labour actually available for employment by the firm. The difference between these is referred to as 'frictional unemployment'. We can also view this unemployment as 'voluntary' because workers remain unemployed by choice.

The individual's decisions firstly about whether to join the labour force and secondly about whether to accept a particular job depend on the real purchasing power of the wage rate being offered – the 'real consumption wage'. This is defined as the money (or nominal) wage rate (*W*) divided by the average price of goods typically purchased by the individual. As the real consumption wage rises, two effects may be noted. First, more individuals may wish to enter the labour force, and, second, more individuals will be keen to accept the wages on offer rather than search for improved offers from other firms.

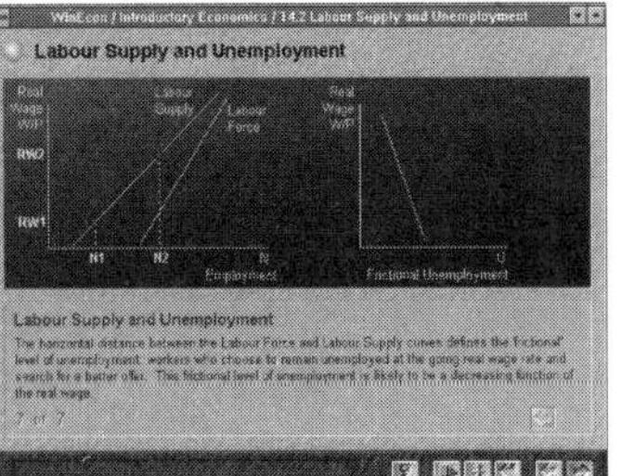

The effective supply of labour will thus rise for two reasons following a real consumption wage increase: the labour force itself may expand, and the frictional level of unemployment will fall, further raising labour supply. To see these effects graphically, work through the text cards on the WinEcon screen. Notice that labour supply is likely to be more responsive than the total labour force to changes in the real consumption wage. Make sure you understand why.

Test your understanding of labour supply and unemployment

09 **What can you say about someone who is part of the labour force but not part of the labour supply?**

10 **If the labour force were independent of the real wage, the labour supply curve would be vertical – true, false or uncertain? Give reasons.**

11 **Labour demand is a function of the real product wage (money wage rate divided by the product price of the firm). Labour supply is a function of the real consumption wage (the money wage rate divided by the price of goods purchased by workers). Given that some goods are not purchased by workers (e.g. investment goods like aircraft), what assumptions are required to ensure that movements in the average real product wage and average real consumption wage are identical?**

Section 14.3: The Classical Theory of Aggregate Supply

In the classical theory of aggregate supply, the labour market is assumed to be continuously in equilibrium (labour demand and supply are always equal so there is no unemployment) and workers are assumed to be fully and correctly informed about the prices of the goods they buy (so that they know with certainty the real consumption wage). Later theories relax one or other of these assumptions, so we view the classical theory as a 'base case' against which others may be compared. The central prediction of the classical model can be stated simply: the level of output supplied is determined by real factors in the economy (e.g. the state of technology, the size of the labour force and the stock of physical capital) and it is independent of the price level.

Classical Aggregate Supply at a Glance

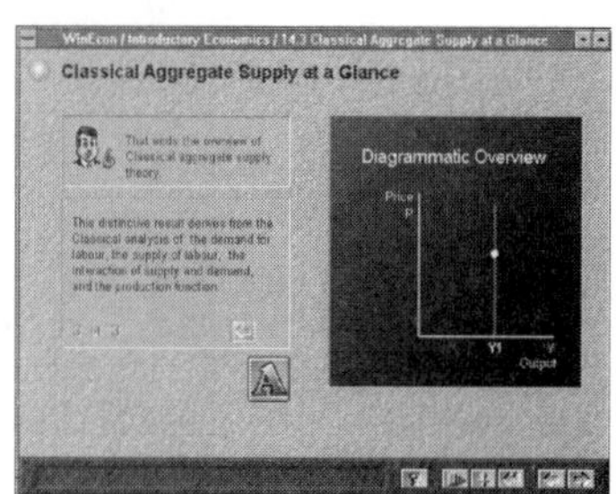

We begin with a simple diagrammatic illustration of the classical model in which you discover at the outset the nature of the aggregate supply curve. You find the shape of the aggregate supply curve assuming the price level has no effect on output. When you reach card three of the screen, you can find out more about individual economists whose work has been generally associated with the classical model by clicking the Advanced Information button.

Classical Labour Supply Theory

The central feature of the classical theory of labour supply is that the quantity of labour supplied is assumed to increase as the real (consumption) wage increases. The important idea here is that it is the real wage, *W/P*, not the nominal wage which affects labour supply. The reason for this is that money wages are only useful for what they will buy: it makes no difference to workers whether the nominal wage is £1 per hour and the typical price of a good is £1, or if the nominal wage is £100 per hour and the typical price of a good is £100. In both cases, an hour's work provides the worker with ability to buy one unit of goods. Hence, in the classical view, in both cases the quantity of labour supplied will be the same. But if the nominal wage is £100 and the price of a typical good is £50 then an hour's work provides the worker with the ability to buy two units of goods and, in the classical view, the quantity of labour will be higher. In general then, the supply of labour rises as the real wage rises.

Of course, other things might affect the aggregate quantity of labour supplied: the size of the population; its age distribution; its geographic mobility and so on. These factors can be seen as determinants of the position of the supply of labour curve and, in the classical view, are relatively slow moving and so can be treated as constant.

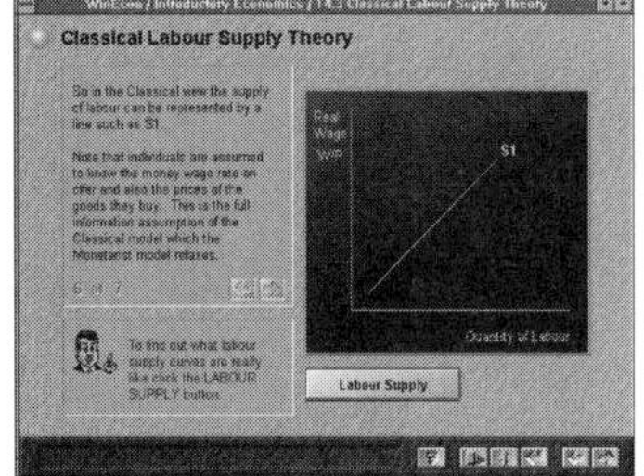

Read the WinEcon text cards and follow their instructions. After you have read card seven, work through the simple exercise. The aim of the exercise is to emphasize the fact that it is real (and not nominal or money) wages that influence labour supply.

Wages and labour supply

12 **What is the relationship between the real wage and the nominal wage rate?**

13 **If the money wage rate doubles and the average price of consumption goods halves, the classical model predicts that labour supply is unchanged – true, false or uncertain? Give your reasons.**

14 **Why might the labour supply curve bend backwards?**

Are You Prone to Money Illusion?

Deciding whether or not the real consumption wage has changed is not as easy a task as it may first appear. Typically, we buy a wide range of goods – from daily newspapers to the occasional mountain bike, and from regular pints of beer to wedding rings. On this WinEcon screen you can tackle an exercise

in which you discover how perceptive you are when deciding in which direction the real consumption wage has changed. The exercise is designed to illustrate the difficulties individuals may face when they purchase four goods and services. These difficulties are compounded with increasing numbers of goods and more varied frequencies of purchase.

Classical Model: Employment Determination

The classical model assumes wage flexibility. This ensures that the labour market is in continuous equilibrium. The level of employment and the real wage rate are determined at the intersection of labour supply and demand curves. The role played by wage flexibility is made clearer when you consider what happens in disequilibrium. You can see this on the Winecon screen by clicking the Show button on cards three and four. The real wage can change either by a change in the money wage rate (the numerator) or by a change in the price level (the denominator). When the labour market is in disequilibrium, we expect the money wage to adjust to ensure labour market equilibrium (with the price level constant).

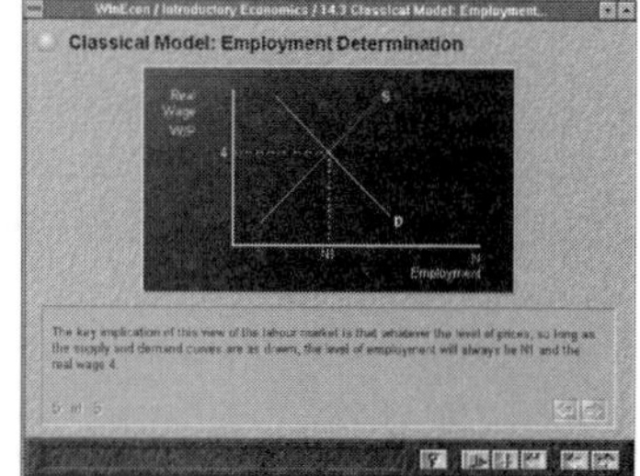

At card six, click the Show button and complete the revision quiz, which checks your understanding of the equilibrium process assumed in the classical model.

The classical view of the labour market

15 **If the labour market has vacancies unfilled (or excess demand), which of the following will reduce the number of unfilled vacancies: (a) a fall in the money wage rate; (b) a rise in the money wage rate; (c) a fall in the real wage rate? Give reasons for your selection.**

16 **A labour market has unemployment: explain why a rise in the general price level will reduce this unemployment. What does the classical model predict when a labour market has unemployment?**

17 **Why, in the classical model, does a rise in the price level lead, ceteris paribus, to a rise in the nominal wage rate?**

18 **The following equations describe the classical labour market: labour supply = 100 + 2(W/P), labour demand = 200 – 8(W/P). Find the levels of the real wage and employment in equilibrium.**

19 **Now assume that demand falls, so that the demand equation is labour demand = 190 – 8(*W*/*P*). Find the new real wage and employment levels in equilibrium and explain why the real wage rate falls by a larger percentage than employment.**

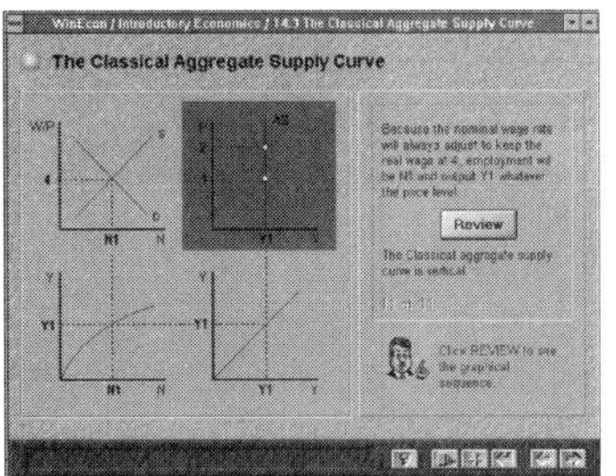

The Classical Aggregate Supply Curve

We now have the building blocks with which we can derive the complete classical aggregate supply model. WinEcon shows you the analysis using four linked diagrams. Work carefully through the text cards, and make sure you understand why the derived aggregate supply (AS) curve is vertical.

See what you have learnt about classical aggregate supply

20 **The WinEcon screen shows an initial price level of 1, a real wage of 4, employment level N_1 and output Y_1. When the price level increases to 2, the classical model shows employment and output remaining at their previous values of N_1 and Y_1 respectively. Why does the employment level remain the same, and what are the new values of the real wage and the nominal wage?**

21 **An economy is initially in full equilibrium and the equilibrium is disturbed by a doubling of the general level of prices. Workers and firms correctly perceive this rise. If the money wage rate remains unchanged, the real wage would [fall/rise], and this would [increase/decrease] labour demand and [increase/decrease] labour supply. Because the labour market has [excess demand/excess supply], the money wage rate will [fall/rise], restoring equilibrium. Following the disturbance, all real variables [double/remain unchanged] and all nominal variables [double/remain unchanged].**

22 **If the price level doubles, what happens to (a) real output and (b) nominal output in the classical model?**

AS Curve Shifts: Technology Shocks

The classical model does not predict that the level of aggregate output is constant – it simply asserts that output will depend only on real variables (like technology) and it will be independent of nominal variables (like the price level). Indeed, in an economy where the labour force is growing (due to population growth) or where there are improvements in technology, the AS curve will shift to the right. On this WinEcon screen, we examine the effects of a favourable change in technology.

Read the first four text cards and follow the animation carefully. Notice that the aggregate production function shifts upwards and this causes a shift in the demand for labour function. On card five the effects of a technology shock are summarized.

The effect of technology shocks on the AS curve

23 **Is it always the case that an upward shift in the production function leads to an upwards shift in the labour demand curve? (Hint: imagine a shift in the production function that preserves its slope at all levels of employment.)**

24 **What determines the increase in output following a technology shock? Obviously the magnitude of the technology improvement is important, but what else matters?**

25 Show the effect of an improvement in technology on the aggregate supply curve when the labour supply curve, *S*, is vertical. How does this compare with the shift shown on the WinEcon screen?

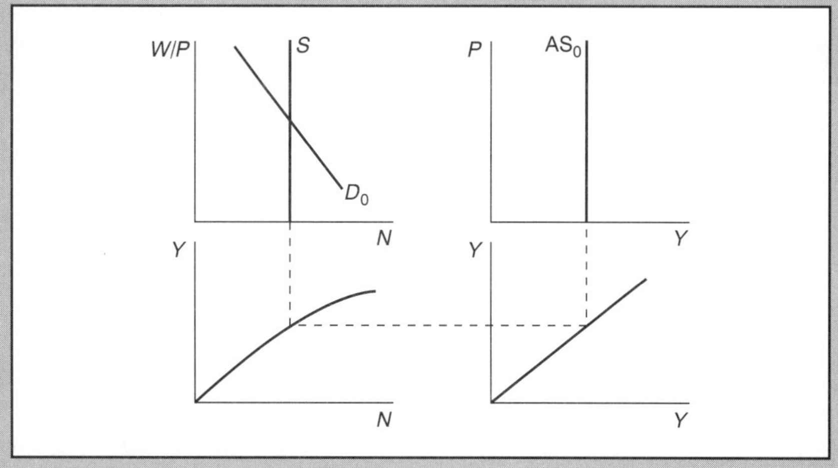

AS Curve Shifts: Income Tax Changes

The aggregate supply curve may be influenced by policies pursued by governments, as this topic illustrates. Indeed, government policies in the 1980s in the UK and elsewhere gave more emphasis to 'supply side' effects than to policies aimed at changing the level of aggregate demand. On this WinEcon screen we consider one such policy instrument: the rate of income tax. You will see how changes in the income tax rate can shift the aggregate supply curve by altering the supply of labour.

Follow the screen to card six, making sure you understand clearly why the introduction of an income tax makes the labour supply curve pivot upwards. Text cards eight and nine show the effect of an income tax when labour supply is unresponsive to the real wage. Intuitively, if labour is supplied at a fixed level independently of the real wage, then tax rate changes will have no effect on the levels of employment and output.

The income tax policies pursued by the British government in the 1980s provide a useful case-study of the effects of tax cuts on labour supply (and output). Professor C. V. Brown ('Will the 1988 Income Tax Cuts Either Increase Work Incentives or Raise More Revenue?', *Fiscal Studies* , Vol 9, No 4, pp 93–107, 1988) found that the increase in allowances had a small favourable effect on work effort (0.5 per cent extra hours), but he found that the cut in the basic tax rate had no detectable effect, except on part-time workers. The cut in higher rates of tax had a small incentive in stimulating work effort amongst the higher-paid workers. On reviewing this evidence, however, the Chancellor of the Exchequer largely identified with the tax reforms, Nigel Lawson, insisted that there should be no more funding for this research project which he describes in his memoirs as being 'particularly unimpressive'. His reasons for this judgement are primarily that most of the field work was done during the recession of 1981 when there was little scope for workers to increase their work effort.

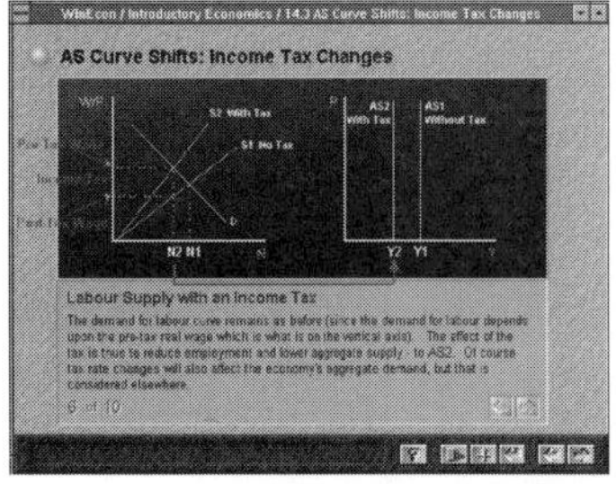

Test your understanding of income tax changes

26 **With a vertical labour demand curve (i.e. labour demand is unresponsive to changes in the real wage rate), a new tax rate would [increase/leave unchanged/reduce] aggregate supply.**

Now illustrate this case by sketching appropriate curves on the following diagram.

W/P

N

27 **The basic rate of income tax was reduced from ________ to ________ over the period 1979 to 1990 in the UK. The change in the higher rate of tax was even more dramatic: from ________ to ________ .**

Unemployment in the Classical Model

This WinEcon screen explains how unemployment can arise in the classical model, even when the labour market is assumed to be in continuous equilibrium. When labour markets are functioning efficiently, there is still a continuous turnover in jobs, many new jobs being created to replace jobs which have been 'destroyed'. It inevitably takes time for workers to move between jobs, and there is a process of job search as workers who are laid off (and workers who quit voluntarily) look for a suitable new job. If workers take a great deal of time searching, the stock of 'frictional' unemployment may be quite large. The quicker workers move between jobs, the smaller will be the number of workers searching at any point in time. As we discussed in section 14.2 in the topic Labour Supply and Unemployment, if the market real wage is high, workers will be inclined to accept jobs offers earlier and their search will be relatively short-lived. It follows that high (low) real wages will be associated with low (high) levels of frictional unemployment.

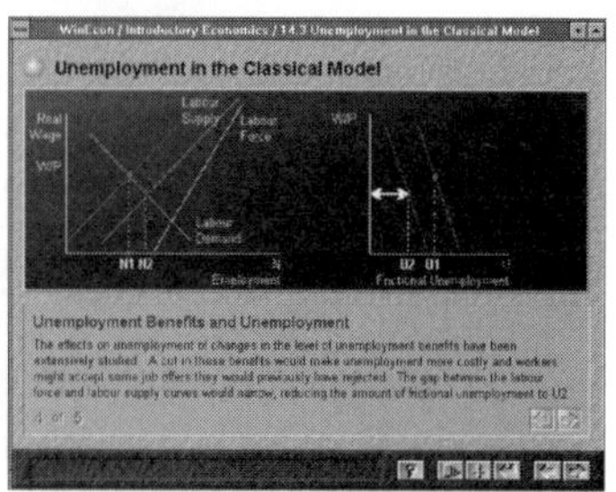

The payment of unemployment benefits to those without work may influence the level of frictional unemployment. Benefits effectively reduce the costs of search and so are likely to prolong the search procedure, raising the numbers of searching workers at each point in time. Step through the WinEcon text cards and click the Advanced button for more information on the impact of unemployment benefits.

About benefits and unemployment

28 **How can unemployment arise in the classical model?**

29 **The ratio of unemployment benefit to average earnings (net of tax) is called the 'replacement ratio'. The replacement ratio in the UK declined during the 1970s and 1980s, as the following figures illustrate.**

Year	Replacement ratio (%)	Unemployment rate (%)
1970	68.7	2.6
1975	65.6	3.1
1980	55.9	5.1
1985	39.0	10.9

On the basis of these figures, which of the following do you believe to be correct?

(a) Unemployment benefits have no effect on unemployment.

(b) Unemployment benefits have a positive effect on unemployment.

(c) Unemployment benefits have a negative effect on unemployment.

(d) It is impossible to determine the effects of benefits from these figures alone.

Classical Aggregate Supply: A Summary

Now check your understanding of the classical model by reading the text cards on the WinEcon summary screen and noting the diagram for the aggregate supply curve.

Section 14.4: Keynesian Theory of Aggregate Supply

The classical model may be viewed as the outcome of a perfectly functioning economy, in which wages and prices are fully flexible and economic agents in labour and product markets are well informed. In our first departure from the classical model, we consider the possibility that the labour market may not function in the fashion assumed by the classical economists. This second model was inspired by the work of John Maynard Keynes. It assumes that the money wage rate may not be sufficiently flexible to ensure equilibrium in the labour market. We therefore relax the classical assumption of labour market equilibrium and, as we shall see, this has important implications for the short-run aggregate supply curve.

The Keynesian theory of aggregate supply is based on *The General Theory of Employment, Interest and Money*, written by Keynes and published in 1936. This book expounds the macroeconomic theory which Keynes developed in the 1930s in an attempt to explain the severe recession that gripped the UK economy in the 1920s and which was exacerbated by the Great Depression in the United States which began towards the end of 1929. Keynes's target was what he called 'classical' theory, which to a certain extent he invented to provide a contrast with his own approach. Classical theory – one ingredient of which is the classical theory of aggregate supply developed above – appeared to suggest that the economy would always be operating at or near full employment. The obvious contrast in the 1920s and 1930s between the facts and this classical theory was what stimulated Keynes to challenge the classical model, and in many respects invent the subject of macroeconomics.

Keynesian Aggregate Supply at a Glance

To appreciate the key features of the Keynesian aggregate supply curve, step through the cards on this introductory WinEcon screen. Clicking the More button will reveal some biographical information on Keynes.

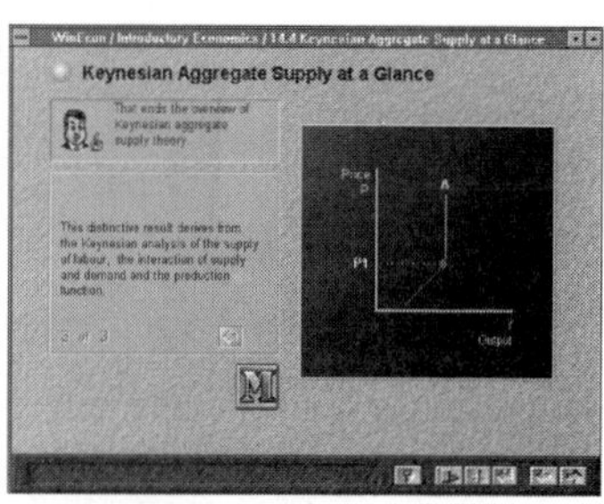

Keynesian Theory of Labour Supply

Keynes assumed that whilst workers are concerned with the real value of their wages they are also concerned about the value of their wages relative to those of other groups of workers. This latter concern induces some downward stickiness in the nominal wage rate because any group of workers will be reluctant to be the first to accept a wage cut that would reduce their wages relative to those of other workers. The average nominal wage will therefore tend not to fall in the way the classical economists assumed when there is excess supply of labour. Of course, the same stickiness will not occur when the nominal wage rate has to rise to equate

supply and demand: all groups will be willing to be the first to accept a nominal wage rise. So when excess demand exists in the labour market it will eliminated by a rise in nominal wages equally quickly in the Keynesian and classical model.

Keynesian Model: Employment Determination

After working through the above topic, Keynesian Theory of Labour Supply, go through this associated WinEcon screen and then tackle the following questions.

Test your understanding of Keynesian employment determination

30 **A company's skilled workers are each paid £500 per week and the average price level is £1. They wish to maintain a real differential of 2:1 over average workers, whose wage rate is £250 (the relative wage ratio is 2:1 at the outset).**

(a) Calculate the real wage of the skilled workers, the average real wage and the real wage differential if all prices doubled but wages were unchanged.

(b) Assuming an average price level of £2, if the money wage rate of the skilled workers were cut by half, calculate the real wage rate of the skilled workers, the average real wage and the real wage differential.

31 **Why are nominal wages sticky downwards but not upwards?**

32 **Why does the real wage sometimes remain the same and sometimes fall in response to a rise in the price level?**

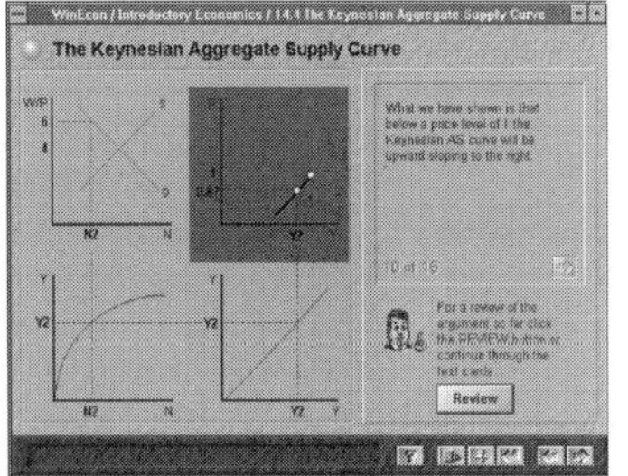

The Keynesian Aggregate Supply Curve

The asymmetric adjustments in the labour market are reflected in a similar asymmetric aggregate supply curve, as this WinEcon screen demonstrates. The Keynesian model has two components: the first segment of the aggregate supply curve is upward sloping and covers a range of prices where the money wage has reached its floor. Step through to text card ten to see the derivation of this segment. The second segment covers a higher range of prices where excess demand for labour is followed by money wage increases and, as in the classical case, the aggregate supply curve is vertical. Text cards eleven to sixteen of the screen show the derivation of this segment.

Develop your understanding of Keynesian aggregate supply

33 Complete the following table using the example on the WinEcon screen. Note whether there is excess supply, excess demand or equilibrium in the labour market. Write whether each value of employment is equal to, greater than or less than N_1, and whether each level of real output is equal to, greater than or less than Y_1. (Notice that some of the information you require is given to you directly on the screen. Work out the rest for yourself.)

Price level	Nominal wage	Real wage	Employment level	Labour market	Real output	Shape of AS curve
0.5						
0.67						
1						
2						
3						

34 **The Keynesian aggregate supply curve is in two segments: the first is [upward/downward] sloping, and in this segment the labour market is in [excess demand/excess supply]. The second segment is vertical, and here the labour market is in [excess demand/excess supply equilibrium]. The vertical segment of the Keynesian model is [identical to/the reverse of] the classical aggregate supply curve.**

35 The following diagram shows two rather different assumptions about labour supply. Labour supply curve A indicates that labour supply is more responsive to changes in the real wage than labour supply curve B. Construct Keynesian aggregate supply curves corresponding to each case.

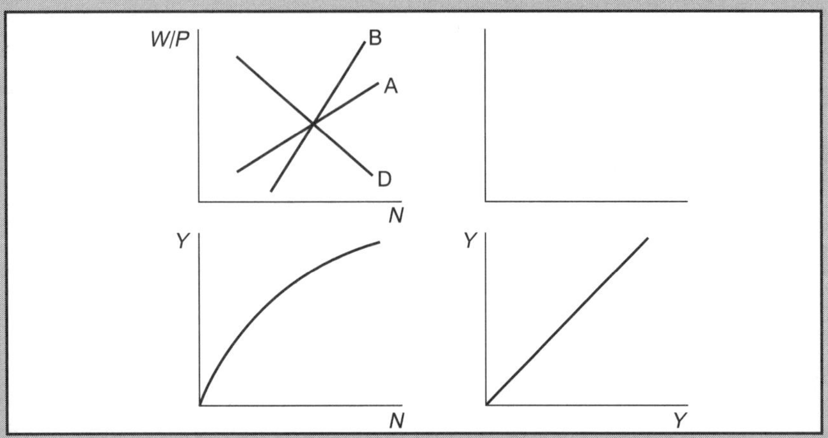

36 In the following diagram we present two labour demand curves – A and B. They make different assumptions about the responsiveness of labour demand to changes in the real wage. In which case is the wage elasticity of labour demand greater? Construct Keynesian aggregate supply curves corresponding to each case.

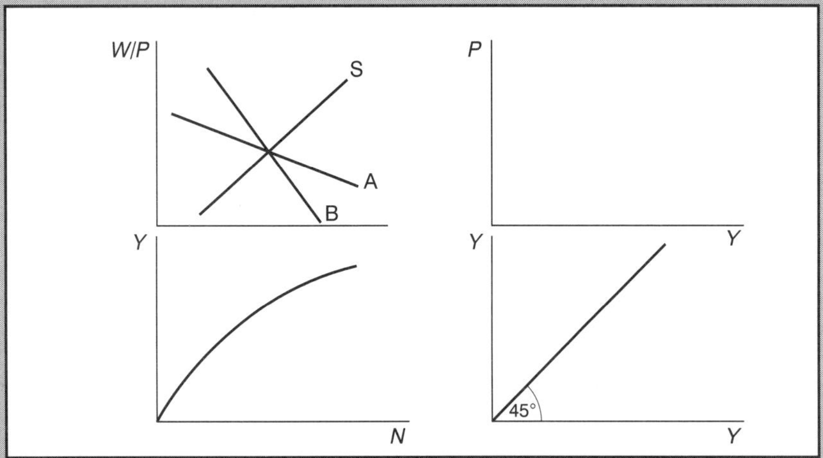

37 Why according to Keynesian aggregate supply theory might you observe different employment levels associated with the same nominal wage?

38 According to Keynesian aggregate supply theory, will the real wage rise or fall as output falls? Justify your answer.

Unemployment in the Keynesian Model

The assumption of a nominal wage floor leads to the possibility of disequilibrium and unemployment in the labour market. Unemployment, however, is now no longer simply caused by job search activities of workers between jobs. As you will see, in the Keynesian model the failure of the wage rate to adjust to its equilibrium level leads to excess supply, which we refer to as 'demand deficient' unemployment. Work through the text cards on the WinEcon screen and note carefully the distinction between frictional unemployment and demand deficient unemployment.

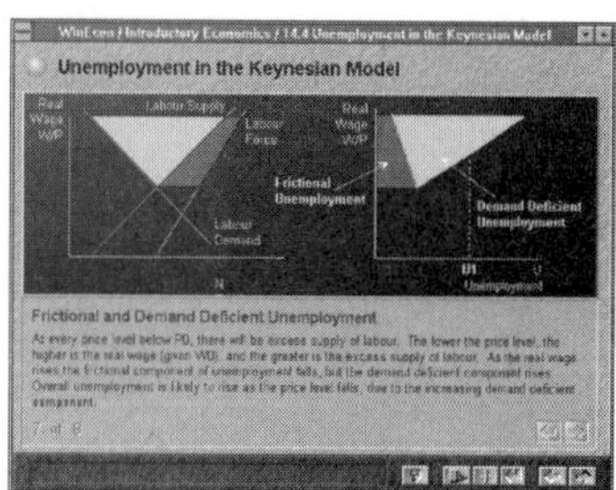

Test your understanding of Keynesian model unemployment

39 **As the real wage rises above its equilibrium level, caused by a __________ in the price level, there is excess __________ labour. The frictional component of unemployment __________ and the demand deficient component __________.**

40 **The labour market is in equilibrium at the current nominal wage rate and price level. If there is an increase in the price level: (a) will the level of frictional unemployment rise, fall or remain unchanged; (b) will the level of demand deficient unemployment rise, fall or remain unchanged? Briefly explain your answer.**

41 **The labour market is in equilibrium at the current nominal wage rate and price level. There is a decrease in the price level and the level of unemployment rises. Which of the following statements correctly describes the effects on the labour market? Give a brief explanation.**

(a) Frictional and demand deficient unemployment rise.

(b) Demand deficient unemployment rises and frictional unemployment falls.

(c) Frictional unemployment rises and demand deficient unemployment falls.

(d) Demand deficient unemployment rises and frictional unemployment remains unchanged.

Keynesian Aggregate Supply: A Summary

Now use this WinEcon screen to check your understanding of the Keynesian model and see under what wage rate conditions the aggregate supply curve will kink at a particular price level.

Section 14.5: The Monetarist Model of Aggregate Supply

The Keynesian theory of aggregate supply departed from the classical model in its assumption about wage flexibility and market clearing. In the monetarist theory of aggregate supply, we restore the classical assumptions concerning the operation of the labour market: the wage rate is assumed to be flexible and labour supply and demand are assumed to be in continuous equilibrium. The monetarist model differs from the classical framework by relaxing the assumption that labour market agents are fully informed.

The main innovative idea in the monetarist model of aggregate supply is that because in any economy information is imperfect, decisions have to be made with reference not to the *actual* value of certain important variables but to their *expected* values. In its most familiar form, the model assumes that the main consequence of imperfect information is that suppliers of labour–workers, when making decisions about how much labour to supply, cannot know the actual real value of the nominal wages they are being offered because they do not know the value of the current price level. They need to form expectations of the price level in order to evaluate their money wage in real terms.

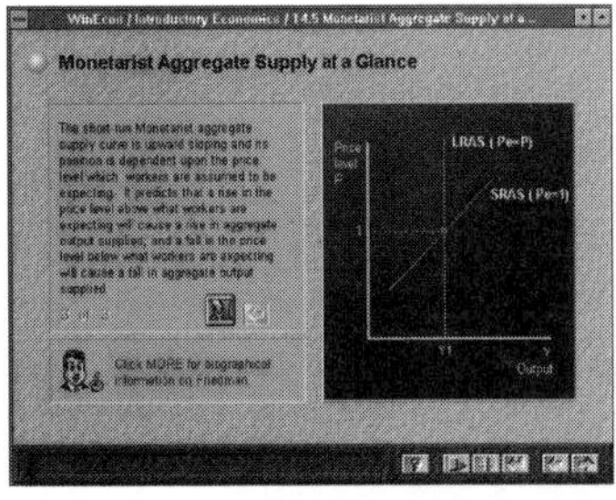

Monetarist Aggregate Supply at a Glance

To appreciate the key features of the monetarist aggregate supply curve, step through the cards on this introductory WinEcon screen. Clicking the More button gives you some biographical information about Milton Friedman, a leading exponent of the monetarist theory.

Time periods in the monetarist model

42 **What is assumed about workers' expectations of the price level in the short run?**

43 **Over what time period is it assumed that any price changes which occur are fully expected?**

Monetarist Theory of Labour Supply

This WinEcon screen lets you discover the role of price expectations in the monetarist theory of labour supply. This is a key concept and you are advised to make sure that you fully understand it before proceeding.

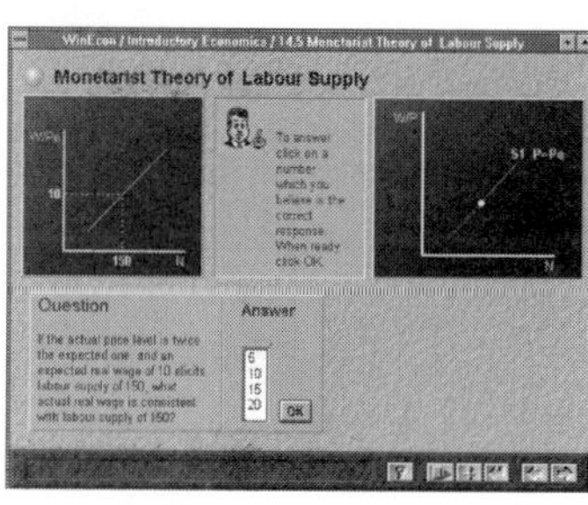

Because the average price level is not known to workers, labour supply decisions are based on the *expected* (and not the actual) real wage. Read the text cards carefully and check your understanding at each stage in the argument by attempting the test questions as they appear. Notice that, because you divide by prices to calculate real wages, if actual prices are double the expected ones, the actual real wage will in fact turn out to be half the expected one.

Check what you have learnt about wages and price expectations

44 **An expected real wage of 20 leads workers to supply 100 hours. We observe 100 hours being supplied when the actual real wage is 40. What does this imply about the level of price expectations?**

45 The diagram shows the labour supply curve for the case where workers' price expectations are one third of the actual price level. Draw the labour supply curve for (a) the case of correct expectations and (b) the case where the expected price level is three times the actual price level.

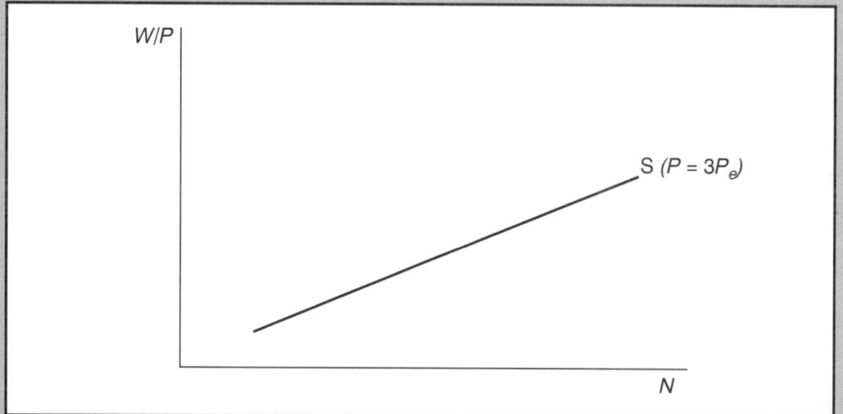

46 **Why might workers supply different quantities of labour at the same real wage rate?**

Monetarist Model: Employment Determination

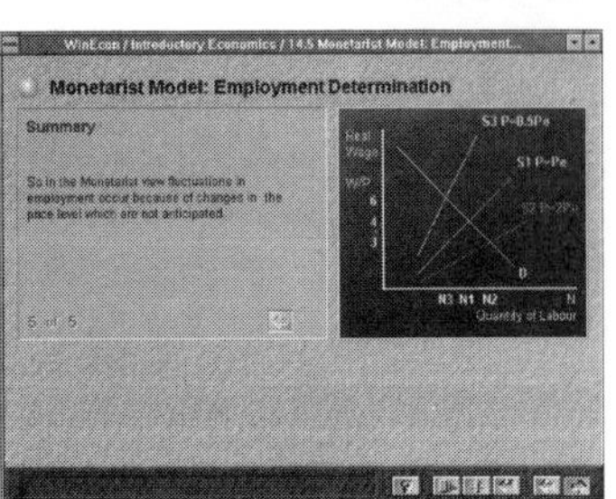

On this WinEcon screen we bring together the theory of labour demand and the monetarist theory of labour supply. As you work through the text cards make sure you appreciate why the demand for labour curve will not shift as expectations of the price level shift. You discover that if a price change occurs that was not anticipated, a different labour supply curve is generated.

Test your understanding of monetarist employment determination

47 Complete the table with data from the screen, then answer the questions which follow.

Actual price level	Expected price level	Nominal wage rate	Expected real wage rate	Actual real wage rate	Employment level	Labour supply
1						
2						
0.5						

48 **When expected prices are the same as before but actual prices rise, what happens to the nominal wage rate, and why?**

49 **What then happens to the level of employment, and why?**

50 **Given constant price expectations, the labour supply is lower when the actual price level is ______, the expected real wage is ______ and the actual real wage is ______.**

51 **Why might workers' decisions about labour supply be affected by misperceptions of the real wage whereas firms' decisions about labour demand would not be?**

52 **A rise in the price level [lowers/raises] the actual real wage, and this encourages firms to [lower/raise] labour. In order to [lower/raise] employment, firms have to offer [lower/higher]**

wage rates. Since price expectations are unchanged, workers interpret the change in the money wage as a [lower/higher] real wage, and they [increase/decrease] their labour supply. The overall effect of a rise in the price level will be to [lower/raise] employment.

The Monetarist Aggregate Supply Curve

We now bring together the components of the monetarist model to derive the aggregate supply curve. The first ten text cards on the WinEcon screen explain the derivation of the aggregate supply curve when workers' expectations are correct. Notice that the same labour supply curve is applicable when a price change occurs because the change is fully anticipated. The nominal wage adjusts so that the real wage remains the same and hence employment is at the same level as before. Not surprisingly, this case corresponds to the classical model, where full information was assumed.

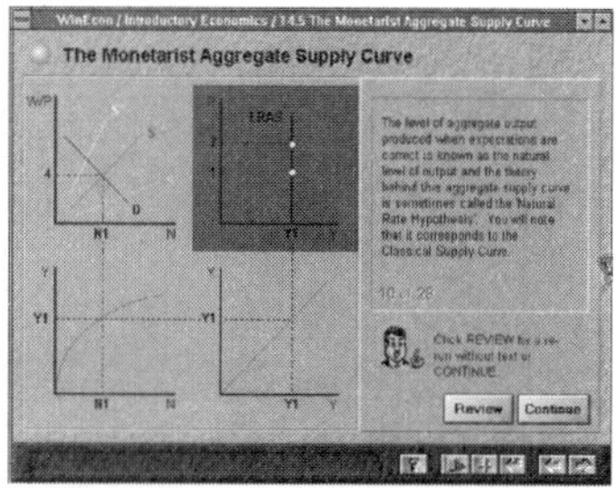

The remaining cards on the screen explain the derivation of the aggregate supply curve when the expected price level departs from the actual price level. Notice how the different labour supply curves are used in this analysis.

In the monetarist model . . .

53 **What is meant by the natural level of output?**

54 **Does the actual real wage rise or fall as output rises? Give a brief explanation.**

55 **Does the expected real wage rise or fall as output rises? Give a brief explanation.**

56 **How can a rise in the price level have different effects on the quantity of aggregate output supplied?**

57 Imagine an initial equilibrium in which the actual price level is 1 and so is the expected price level. Then assume that the actual price level oscillates from 1 to 2 to 1 to 2 and so on. Draw the effects of this behaviour of prices on output, given three different assumptions about the expected price level: (i) it remains constant at 1; (ii) it always equals the actual price level in the previous period; and (iii) it always equals the actual price level.

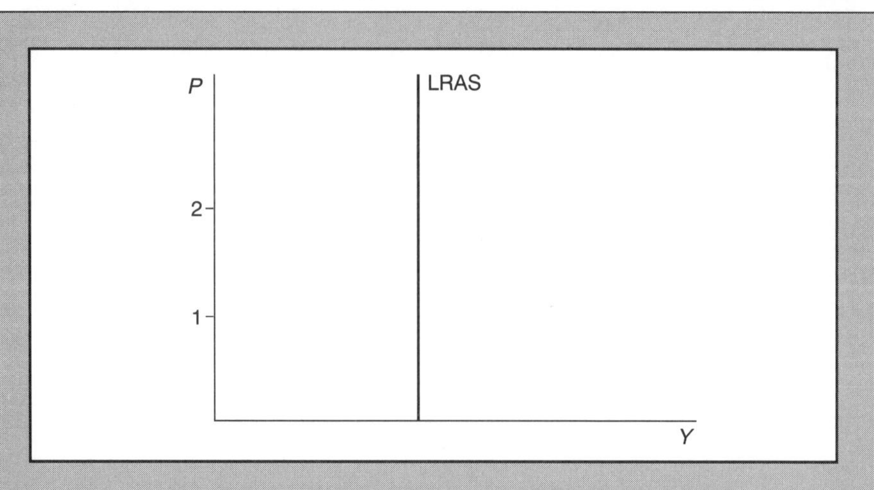

Unemployment in the Monetarist Model

We now turn to the behaviour of unemployment in the monetarist model. As the subject of this topic depends on a clear understanding of the operation of the labour market in the monetarist case, make sure you understand how changes in the actual and the expected price level influence the labour supply curve.

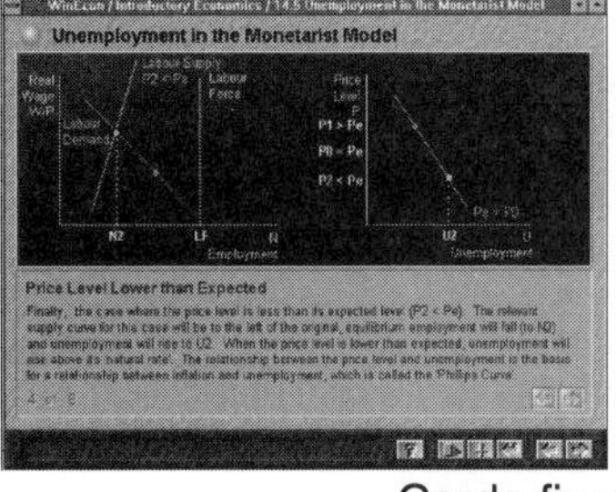

To make the analysis more straightforward, we assume that the overall labour force is independent of the real wage and changes in labour supply arise from differences in the number of workers searching for jobs (frictional unemployment). Work through the first four text cards, where a relationship between the price level and unemployment is derived. Note carefully that this relationship requires an explicit assumption about the level of price expectations. Cards five and six explain what happens when price expectations change. Make sure you understand why an increase in the expected price level leads to an upward shift in the relationship between the price level and unemployment. Cards seven and eight offer a summary of the argument. When you have completed the text cards, answer the questions that follow.

Test your understanding of monetarist unemployment behaviour

58 **What is meant by the natural level of unemployment?**

59 **When the price level is lower than expected, how does unemployment compare with its natural rate?**

60 **When price expectations rise, how does the price level at which the natural rate of unemployment now occurs compare with the previous one?**

61 **Why is there no long run trade-off between the price level and unemployment?**

62 Consider the following imaginary data:

Year	Price level ($)	Expected price level ($)	Unemployment (%)
1980	3	1	2.0
1981	2	1	3.5
1982	2	2	4.0
1983	5	5	4.0
1984	8	9	5.5

(a) Is this data consistent with the monetarist model? Briefly explain why.

(b) What is the natural rate of unemployment?

Logarithms and Growth Rates: A Review

In our analysis so far, we have examined relationships between the levels of unemployment and output and the average price *level*. We now examine the relationship between unemployment and the inflation rate (or the growth rate of the price level). Before we do this it is important to review how growth rates are computed. The reasons for doing this will become clear as you work through the derivation of the Phillips curve. First follow the instructions on this WinEcon screen and when you are sure you understand how a growth rate is computed using logarithms, proceed to the next screen, The Phillips Curve.

Section 22.3 topic Logarithmic Functions (in WinEcon only, not this workbook) explains logarithmic relationships. The topic Trends in Levels and Logarithms in section 9.2 shows how data which plot as a curve may yield a straight line if logarithms are used.

Calculating growth rates

63 **What is the formula for calculating growth rates using logarithms?**

The Phillips Curve

The Phillips curve shows the relationship between inflation and unemployment. The short-run Phillips curve suggests that there is a trade-off between these two variables, with unemployment increasing as inflation falls.

The WinEcon screen begins by explaining that the observed relationship between the price level and unemployment may be log-linear. To build a model of unemployment and inflation, rather than the price level we use an algebraic approach. On the third text card click the Show button to reveal a tableau on which the formal mathematics of the Phillips curve is set out, step by step. The first equation says that unemployment at time t, u_t , is below the natural rate, u_n, if the actual price level, p_t ,is above the expected price level, p_t^e. The third equation uses the logarithmic method in calculating growth rates to define the inflation rate π_t and the expected inflation rate $\pi_t{}^e$. Click the equation check boxes, making sure you understand each step in the logic (read the commentary carefully). The fourth equation shows that unemployment at time t is below the natural rate if the actual rate of inflation is greater than the expected rate of inflation, whilst if inflation is lower than expected, unemployment is above the natural rate. (Card 3 also gives you the opportunity to read a biographical sketch of A. W. Phillips, whose name is associated with the unemployment–inflation trade-off.) If the expected inflation rate and the natural rate of unemployment are fixed, there is then a simple relationship between unemployment and inflation. You can see this shown diagrammatically on card 4. With a different expected inflation rate the curve shifts, as shown on card 5. In the long run, expectations about inflation are fulfilled and therefore unemployment must be at the natural rate, giving a vertical long-run curve.

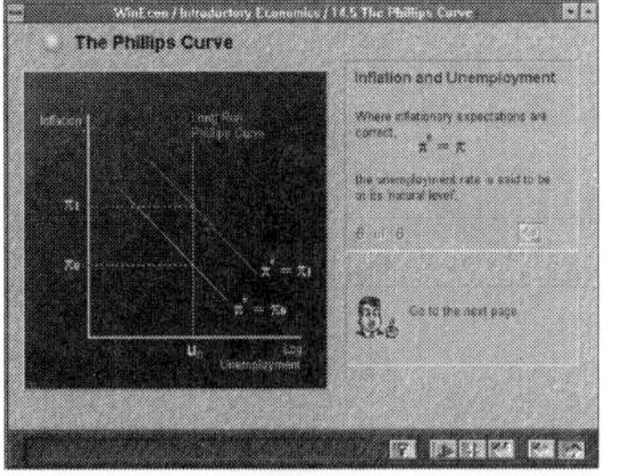

Inflation and unemployment

64 **Which of the following definitions is correct? Provide a short explanation.**

(a) The expected inflation rate is the growth rate of the price level.

(b) The expected inflation rate is the growth rate of the expected price level.

(c) The expected inflation rate is the proportionate difference between the expected current price level and the actual price level the previous period.

65 **What is the unemployment rate called when the expected inflation rate is equal to the actual inflation rate?**

66 **Why can the Phillips curve only be drawn given an explicit assumption about the expected inflation rate?**

67 **Why might an economy experience high levels of both unemployment and inflation?**

68 **If agents in an economy expect zero inflation, what is the actual inflation rate in this economy if unemployment is equal to its natural rate?**

69 **The lagged price level in an economy is £5. If the actual inflation rate in an economy is 10 per cent and if unemployment is less than its natural rate, which of the following is true? Briefly state your reasons.**

(a) The expected price level is £5.5.

(b) The expected price level is £5.2.

(c) The expected price level is £5.7.

Section 14.6: Summary

Contemporary controversies in macroeconomics are perhaps most heated in the area of aggregate supply. To a large extent, economists are in agreement on the determinants of aggregate demand, but they often differ substantially in their approaches to aggregate supply. In this chapter you have examined three key theories of aggregate supply – the classical, Keynesian and monetarist models.

The basic tools used in all three approaches are the aggregate production function, and the aggegate demand for and supply of labour functions. Each of these is similar to its microeconomic counterpart. In addition we distinguish between the labour force and labour supply, with the difference comprising frictional unemployment.

With its assumptions that the labour market always reaches equilibrium and that workers have full information about prices, the classical model depicts aggregate supply as a vertical line at the level of output corresponding to full employment. Flexible nominal wages are the key to this result. In the classical theory, unemployment is explained as frictional.

Section 14.6 / Summary

The Keynesian model assumes that nominal wages are flexible upwards but not downwards, and so derives a kinked aggregate supply curve. If the labour market is initially in equilibrium, a rise in prices will induce a corresponding rise in nominal wages and the aggregate supply curve will be vertical above the initial price level. But if prices fall below the level at which they have become established, there will be resistance to lowering nominal wages, and so excess supply will occur in the labour market. Employment will be lower than before, and so will output. Hence, the Keynesian aggregate supply curve has a forward-sloping section at low price levels. The Keynesian model distinguishes between two different types of unemployment, frictional and demand deficient.

Expectations are the key feature of the monetarist approach. The analysis of labour supply involves the expected real wage. In the short run, expectations about prices may not be correct and an upward-sloping aggregate supply curve results. This curve assumes a particular level of price expectations, and different short-run curves are appropriate if expectations change. In the long run, expectations are fulfilled and the aggregate supply curve is vertical. The level of unemployment that occurs when price expectations are correct is called the natural rate of unemployment. In the short run, unemployment may be either above or below the natural rate, and the Phillips curve analysis suggests a trade-off with inflation. In the long run, unemployment is at the natural rate and the Phillips curve is vertical.

The various theories make quite different assumptions about the operation of the labour market and the information available. These controversies are still largely unresolved. Modern macroeconomic research is still very active in all three schools of thought.

The aggregate supply curves we have derived are used with their corresponding aggregate demand curves in chapter 15, Monetary and Fiscal Policies, and we analyse the impact of policy changes as predicted by each of the approaches.

Chapter 15:

Monetary and Fiscal Policies

An increase in interest rates makes borrowing more expensive and is one measure frequently adopted by governments who wish to reduce inflation and to restrain economic growth. Cutting the rate of income tax on the other hand is likely to lead to higher prices and higher output. These are examples of monetary and fiscal policies and their effects. Governments use such policies to influence key economic variables. This chapter analyses their effects utilizing the IS–LM and AS–AD models.

Contents

KEYWORDS

- BP (balance of payments) locus
- Crowding out
- Endogenous
- Exogenous
- Fiscal policy
- Fixed and flexible exchange rates
- Income elasticity of withdrawals and of the demand for money
- Interest elasticity of investment and of the demand for money
- Keynes and the Classics
- Monetary policy
- Natural rate of unemployment
- Policy effectiveness
- Policy lags

Section 15.1: Introduction

Monetary and fiscal policy are two methods by which the government manages the economy and influences the level and composition of aggregate demand. Monetary policy operates through the central bank and is concerned with controlling the supply of money. It works through interest rates, open market operations and direct controls.

This is described in section 12.3, Monetary Control.

The modelling approach is discussed in the topic Taxation in section 11.3. Recent information about taxes and benefits in the UK is available in the WinEcon topics Types of Tax in the U.K. and Benefit Payments in section 18.7. A recent figure for government final consumption can be found in the WinEcon topic The Expenditure Approach in section 10.4.

Fiscal policy determines taxes, benefit payments and government expenditure on goods and services. In economic modelling we measure the government's tax revenue net of transfer payments such as social security benefits payments to households. This lets us examine the effects of fiscal policy simply by considering changes in taxation, *T*, or government expenditure on goods and services, *G*.

If the government wishes to reduce unemployment and decides to increase aggregate demand it may attempt to bring this about using either monetary or fiscal policy or a combination of the two. Expansionary monetary policy involves increasing the money supply or reducing the interest rate. Expansionary fiscal policy often entails a government budget deficit, with the govenment spending more on goods and services, paying out more in benefits or taking less in taxation.

See also the topics Exogenous Changes in the IS–LM Model and Policy Implications of the IS–LM Theory in section 13.4.

In this chapter we use the theoretical frameworks of IS–LM and AS–AD analyses to explore the operation and effectiveness of monetary and fiscal policy. Both monetary policy (changing MS and *R*) and fiscal policy (changing *G* and/or *T*) can change the macroeconomic equilibrium, giving the government a choice of policy instruments with which to undertake aggregate demand management.

Building on the theories of aggregate demand (AD) and aggregate supply (AS), and the IS–LM and AS–AD models, developed in chapters 13 and 14, we consider the extent to which governments can affect the level of real output in an economy either by manipulating taxation and government expenditure (fiscal policy) or by changing the money supply or the interest rate (monetary policy). Our analysis uses first the IS–LM model, and then the AS–AD model. The second of these superimposes an AS curve on the corresponding AD curve. The intersection of the two curves gives the equilibrium income and price level for the economy. Another section looks at the policy implications of an economy being open to trade. The effectiveness of active stabilization policy is also considered.

Every government has various macroeconomic goals. These may include: steady growth in real GDP, low unemployment, or low inflation and a steady exchange rate. Unfortunately, policies which help to attain some of these targets may act against the achievement of others. There are also practical difficulties in taking the appropriate action at the right time. This chapter focuses on predicting policy effects. In practice other considerations must also be taken into account.

Section 15.2: Macroeconomic Policy and Aggregate Demand

In this section you use the IS–LM model to explore the mechanisms through which fiscal and monetary policy affect the level of aggregate demand. You also examine the factors which determine the effectiveness of fiscal and monetary policy.

A Key Assumption in IS–LM

This section concentrates on the demand side of the economy and assumes that the price level is fixed. This is equivalent to making the assumption that the actual supply of goods and services adjusts to the planned demand for them. Cards 1–3 on the WinEcon screen demonstrate this assumption with an AS–AD diagram. Notice the shape of the AS curve and compare it with those you constructed in chapter 14. Cards 4–8 remind you of how changes in fiscal and monetary policy can be represented graphically on an IS–LM diagram and also link the analysis with the AS–AD diagram. If you want to review the effects of policy changes on the IS and LM curves, return to the topic Exogenous Changes in the IS–LM Model in section 13.4.

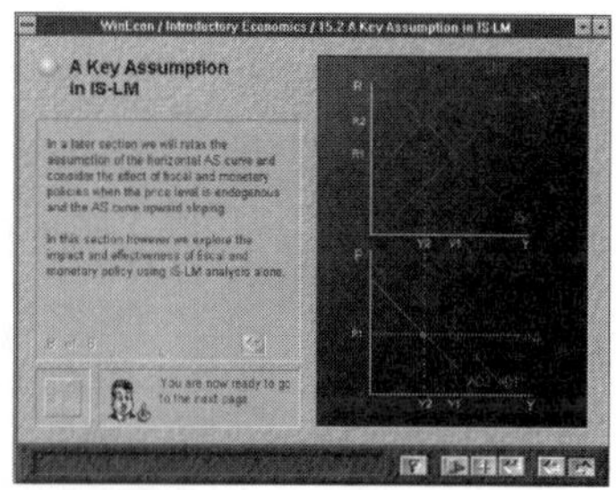

See what you have learnt about this key assumption in IS–LM

01 **What is the 'key assumption', and what does it imply about the slope of the aggregate supply curve?**

02 **What assumption is made about government policy changes and the general price level?**

03 **What shape are the aggregate supply curves derived in chapter 14?**

04 **When a government alters its fiscal policy, which of the IS or LM curves must shift? Explain why. How is the AS–AD diagram affected?**

05 **When a government alters its monetary policy, which of the IS or LM curves must shift? Explain why. How is the AS–AD diagram affected?**

Fiscal Policy and Crowding Out

The multiplier is described in the topics A Change in Injections and Equilibrium Values and Exogenous Changes in section 11.6.

This topic explores the effect of expansionary fiscal policy and introduces the concept of crowding out. Expansionary fiscal policy is planned to increase income, and here we assume that an increase in government expenditure takes place. The multiplier suggests that the resulting increase in income is greater than the amount of the initial change.

The inverse relationship between investment and the interest rate is shown in the topic Investment Demand and the Rate of Interest in section 13.4.

The simple multiplier assumes the interest rate is fixed. With IS–LM analysis, however, we see that this is not so. As a policy change increases income, a further effect comes into play. The rise in income increases the demand for money. Given that the money supply is fixed, this raises the interest rate. At a higher rate of interest less private investment takes place. We say that some investment is crowded out. The new equilibrium level of income is lower than the simple multiplier predicts because of the crowding out that occurs.

Crowding out is important in the context of fiscal policy because it tends to negate a planned expansion. Using the WinEcon screen, make sure that you understand the mechanisms which operate following an increase in government final expenditure.

Develop your understanding of fiscal policy

06 The IS–LM model is a more sophisticated framework than the income–expenditure model. Why is this? Is it (1) because the goods and money markets are treated as interdependent in the IS–LM model whereas the income–expenditure model focuses solely on equilibrium in the goods market or (2) because the price level was assumed to be fixed in the income–expenditure model but is assumed to be variable in IS–LM? Explain your choice.

07 Is fiscal policy apparently more or less powerful according to the IS–LM model than it appeared in the income–expenditure model in chapter 11? Explain.

Draw a diagram to represent the effect of expansionary fiscal policy and mark clearly on the diagram the initial equilibrium point, the final equilibrium point and the output crowded-out by the policy change.

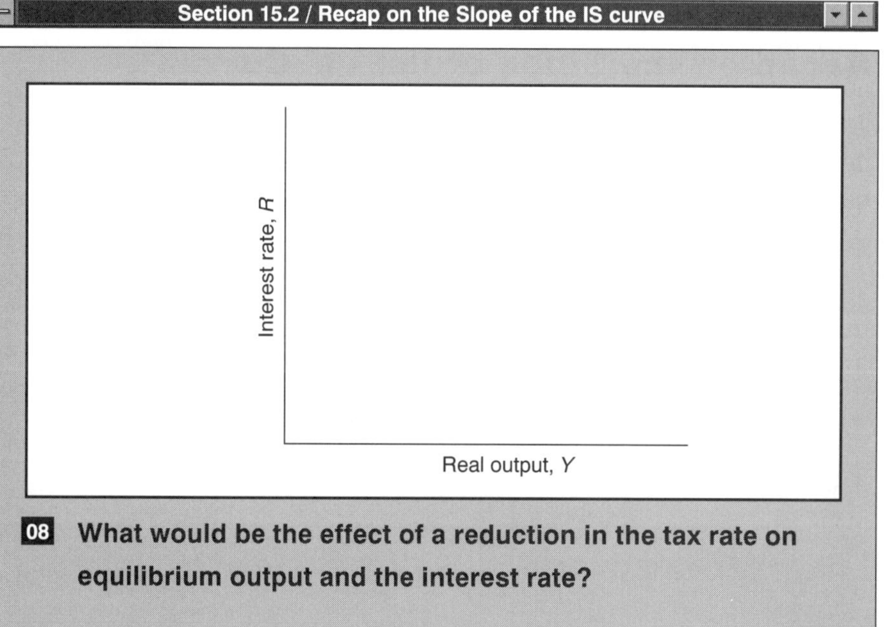

08 **What would be the effect of a reduction in the tax rate on equilibrium output and the interest rate?**

Recap on the Slope of the IS curve

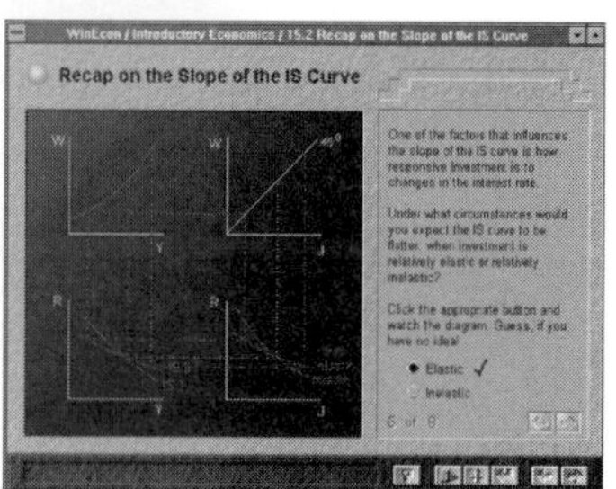

The extent to which fiscal and monetary policy affect aggregate demand depends on the slopes of the IS and LM curves, which in turn depend on certain key elasticities. On this WinEcon screen you can review what the IS curve represents and which factors determine its slope. The questions below can be answered directly by working through the WinEcon cards.

Test what you know about the IS curve

09 **There are two relationships and an equilibrium condition which underpin the IS curve. What are they?**

10 **The IS curve shows combinations of ______ ______ and ______ ______ that give equilibrium in the ______ market.**

11 **The slope of the IS curve depends on the interest elasticity of investment and the income elasticity of withdrawals. It is relatively steep when investment is relatively interest ______ and withdrawals are relatively income ______.**

Recap on the Slope of the LM Curve

With this WinEcon topic you can review the LM curve and the factors which determine its slope. Notice that on this screen LT represents the money demand for transactions purposes and LS the demand for speculative purposes.

Test what you know about the LM curve

12 **There are two relationships and an equilibrium condition which underpin the LM curve. What are they?**

13 **The LM curve shows combinations of ______ ______ and ______ ______ that give equilibrium in the ______ market.**

14 **The slope of the LM curve depends on the interest and income elasticities of the demand for money. It is relatively steep when the demand for money is relatively interest ______ and relatively income ______.**

The Effectiveness of Fiscal Policy

The effect of fiscal policy on the level of real output may be different in different circumstances. The concept of elasticity is useful in describing these differences. The WinEcon screen lets you compare the effectiveness of an expansionary fiscal policy for two different cases. It shows you explanations of the changes seen in the IS–LM diagram in terms of what happens in the goods market or in the money market. The first case shown in WinEcon (on cards 3–7) assumes that investment is relatively interest inelastic and money demand relatively elastic. The second case (on cards 8–12) assumes that investment is relatively interest elastic and money demand relatively inelastic. As you work through the screen complete the diagrams and answer the questions below.

Investment interest inelastic, money demand elastic

Assuming the point (Y_1,R_1) is consistent with equilibrium in both the goods and money markets, draw appropriate IS and LM curves. (Hint: one curve is relatively steep and the other is relatively shallow.)

Now suppose the government engages in expansionary fiscal policy, shifting the IS curve parallel to its original position, so that it now passes through the point (Y_2,R_1). Complete the diagram, marking the new equilibrium position and the amount of crowding out.

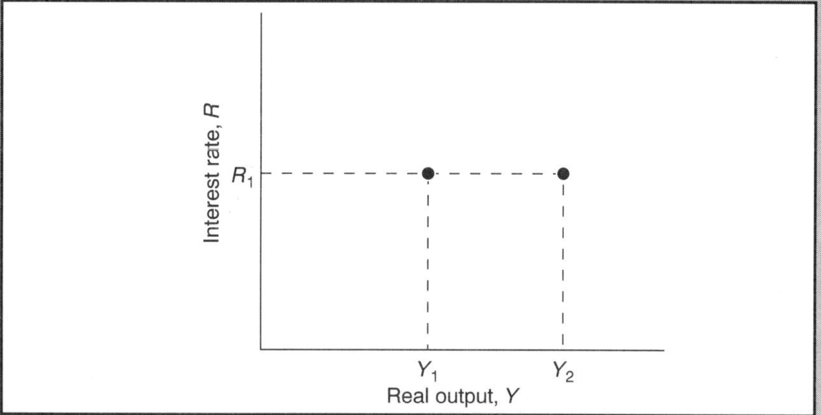

15 **Given the elasticity assumptions above, the change in fiscal policy causes a relatively large/relatively small increase in real output.**

16 **Why is the increase in the interest rate that follows the expansion in fiscal policy relatively small?**

17 **Why is crowding out relatively small?**

Investment interest elastic, money demand inelastic

Assuming the point (Y_1,R_1) is consistent with equilibrium in both the goods and money markets, draw appropriate IS and LM curves.

Now, once more, suppose the government engages in expansionary fiscal policy, shifting the IS curve parallel to its original position, so that it now passes through the point (Y_2,R_1). Complete the diagram, marking the new equilibrium position and the amount of crowding out.

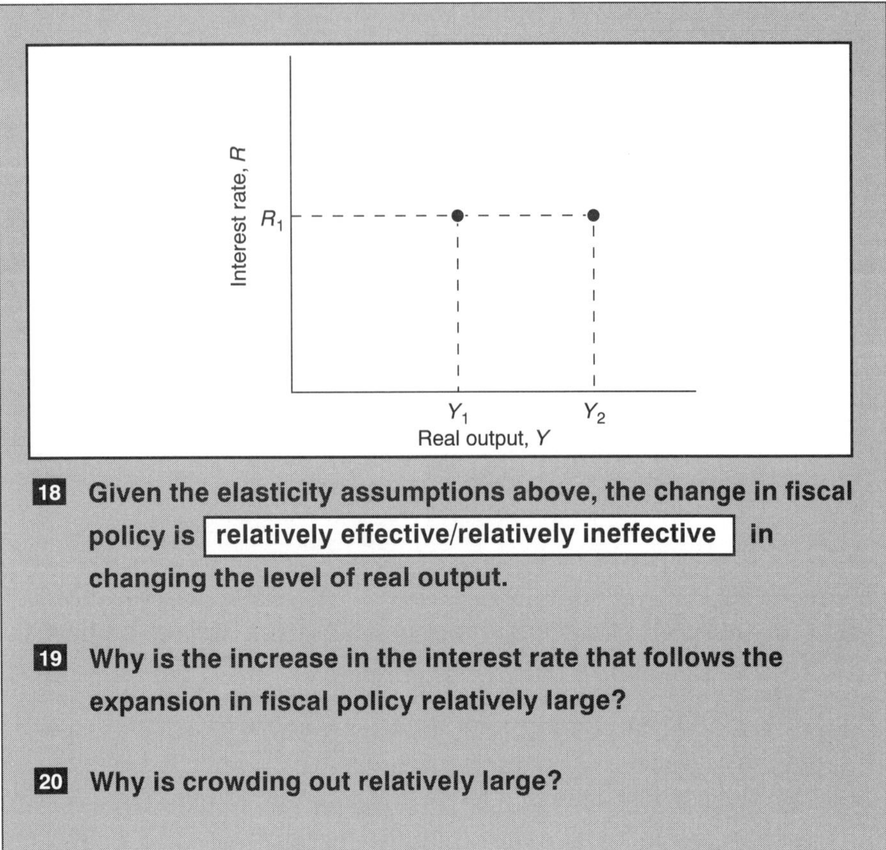

18 **Given the elasticity assumptions above, the change in fiscal policy is [relatively effective/relatively ineffective] in changing the level of real output.**

19 **Why is the increase in the interest rate that follows the expansion in fiscal policy relatively large?**

20 **Why is crowding out relatively large?**

Fiscal Policy Exercise

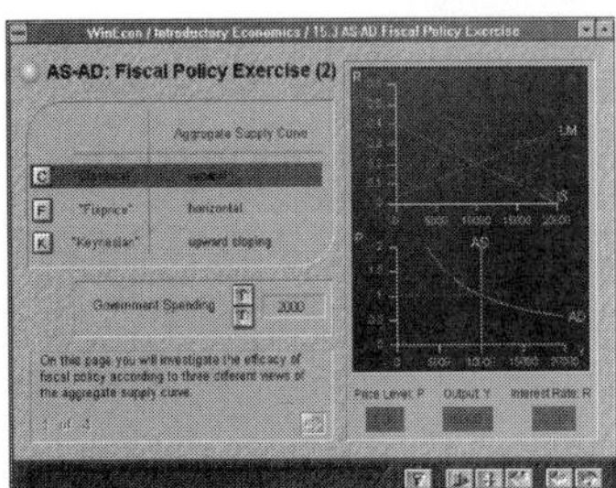

The aim of this exercise is to reinforce the idea that the effect of a change in fiscal policy on aggregate demand depends on the slopes of the IS and LM curves. After reading the introductory screen, use the Next Page button to access a second screen (Fiscal Policy Exercise (2)) which offers you three different scenarios. These correspond to fiscal optimism, fiscal pessimism and a compromise view. You are asked to explore the effect of increasing government expenditure from 2000 to 4000 under each scenario. Use the buttons to enter your answers. Move to card 4 and click Confirm to see whether you are correct. Record your answers and complete the relevant diagrams below.

Fiscal policy exercise

Increasing government expenditure under three analytical frameworks

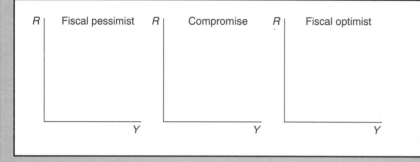

	Final output	Government spending multiplier	Crowding out
Fiscal pessimist			
Compromise			
Fiscal optimist			

R Fiscal pessimist Y

R Compromise Y

R Fiscal optimist Y

Monetary Policy

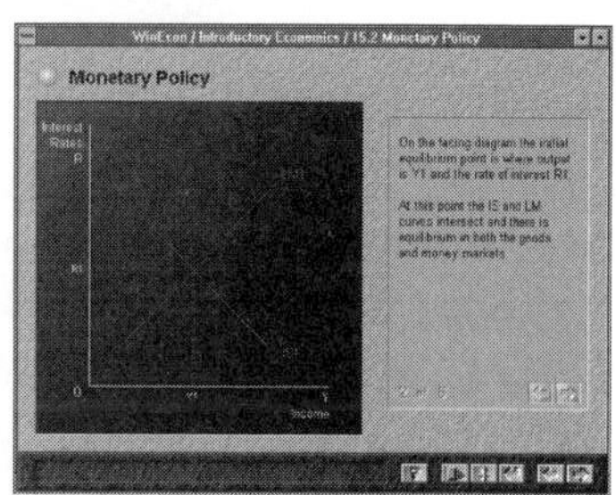

On this WinEcon screen you examine the way that a change in monetary policy can affect real output. WinEcon explores the effect of expansionary monetary policy on real output and the interest rate. As you use this screen, make sure you understand the transmission mechanism through which an increase in the money supply causes an increase in real output.

Develop your understanding of monetary policy

21 **Which of the IS or LM curves is shifted by an increase in the money supply and in which direction?**

22 **What is the effect of an increase in the money supply on the interest rate and real output?**

23 **An expansion of the money supply causes a ______ in the interest rate, which in turn boosts ______ ______. This results in ______ in real output.**

Illustrate your answers above by completing the diagram.

Interest rate, R

Real output, Y

The Effectiveness of Monetary Policy

Monetary policy can be seen to be more or less effective in achieving changes in the level of real output depending on the slopes of the IS and LM curves. The WinEcon screen explores two cases. The first (shown on cards 3–7) assumes that the IS curve is relatively steep and the LM curve is relatively shallow. The second case shown in WinEcon (cards 8–11) assumes that the IS curve is relatively flat and the LM curve is relatively steep.

Steep IS, shallow LM

Draw a steep IS curve and a shallow LM curve, making them intersect at (Y_1, R_1).

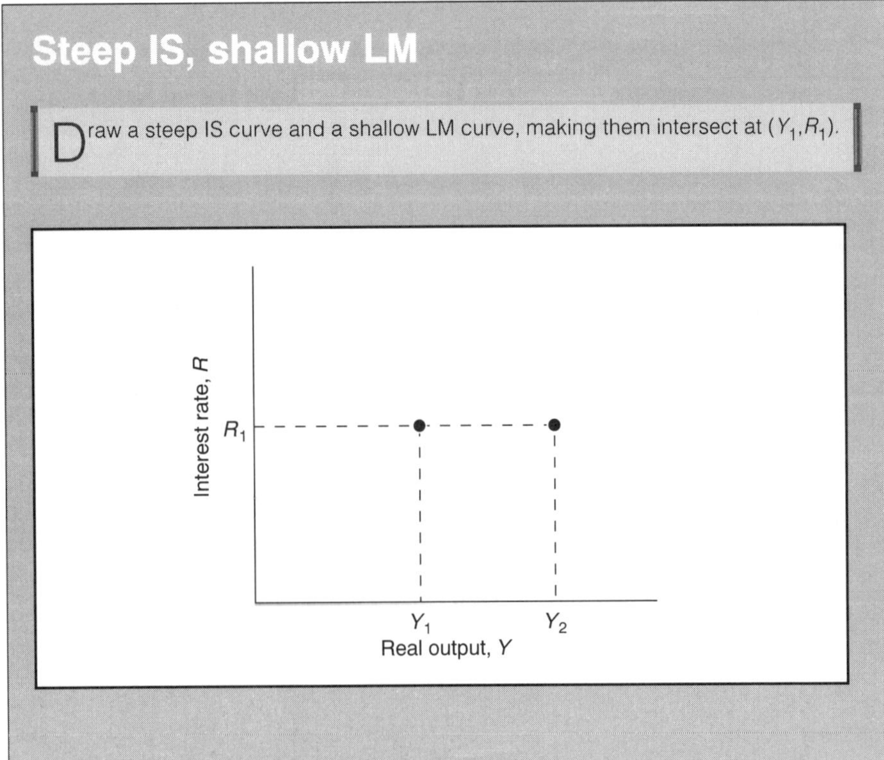

24 **This diagram suggests that the interest elasticity of investment is relatively ______ and the interest elasticity of the demand for money is relatively ______.**

Complete your diagram to show what happens if the government engages in expansionary monetary policy, shifting the LM curve parallel to its original position and to the right, so that it now passes through the point (Y_2,R_1). Mark the new equilibrium position.

25 **Given the assumptions above, the change in monetary policy causes a relatively** large/small **increase in real output.**

26 **Why is the fall in the interest rate that follows the expansion in monetary policy relatively small?**

27 **Why is the increase in private investment relatively small?**

Shallow IS, steep LM

28 **This suggests that the interest elasticity of investment is relatively ______ and the interest elasticity of the demand for money is relatively ______.**

Draw a shallow IS curve and a steep LM curve, making them intersect at (Y_1,R_1). Now, once more, suppose that the government engages in expansionary monetary policy, shifting the LM curve to the right so that it now passes through the point (Y_2,R_1). Complete the diagram, marking the new equilibrium.

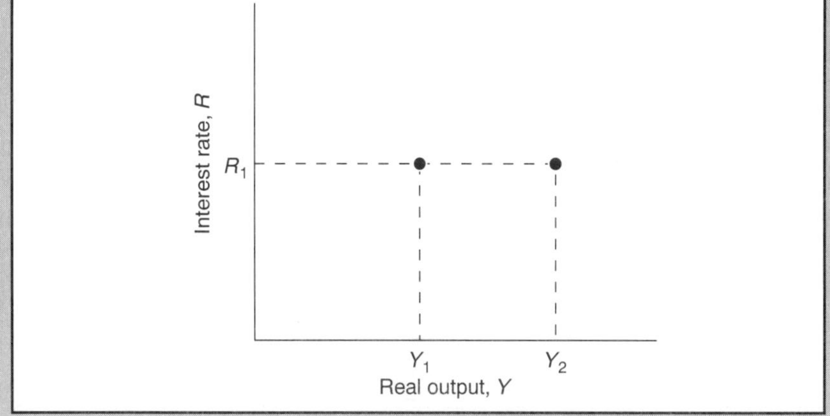

29 **Given the assumptions above, is the change in monetary policy relatively effective or relatively ineffective in changing the level of real output?**

30 **Why is the fall in the interest rate that follows the expansion in monetary policy relatively large?**

31 **Why is the increase in private investment relatively large?**

Monetary Policy Exercise

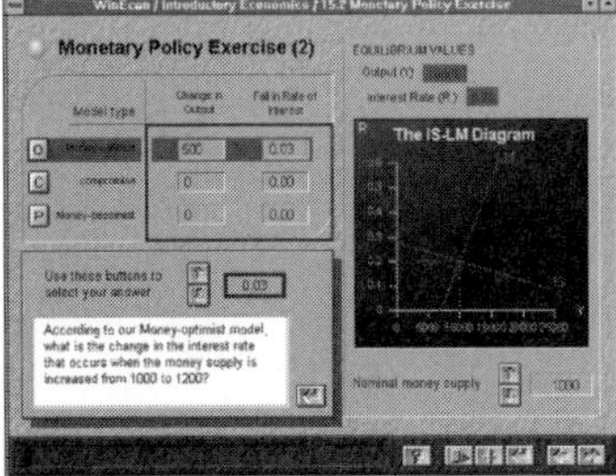

The aim of this WinEcon exercise is to reinforce the idea that the effect of a change in monetary policy on aggregate demand depends on the slopes of the IS and LM curves. Work your way through the WinEcon screens. They are structured in the same way as the fiscal policy exercise (i.e. the Next Page moves you to the second screen, Monetary Policy Exercise (2)). On the second screen you are asked to explore the effect of increasing the money supply from 1000 to 1200 under three different scenarios. Record your answers and complete the relevant diagrams below.

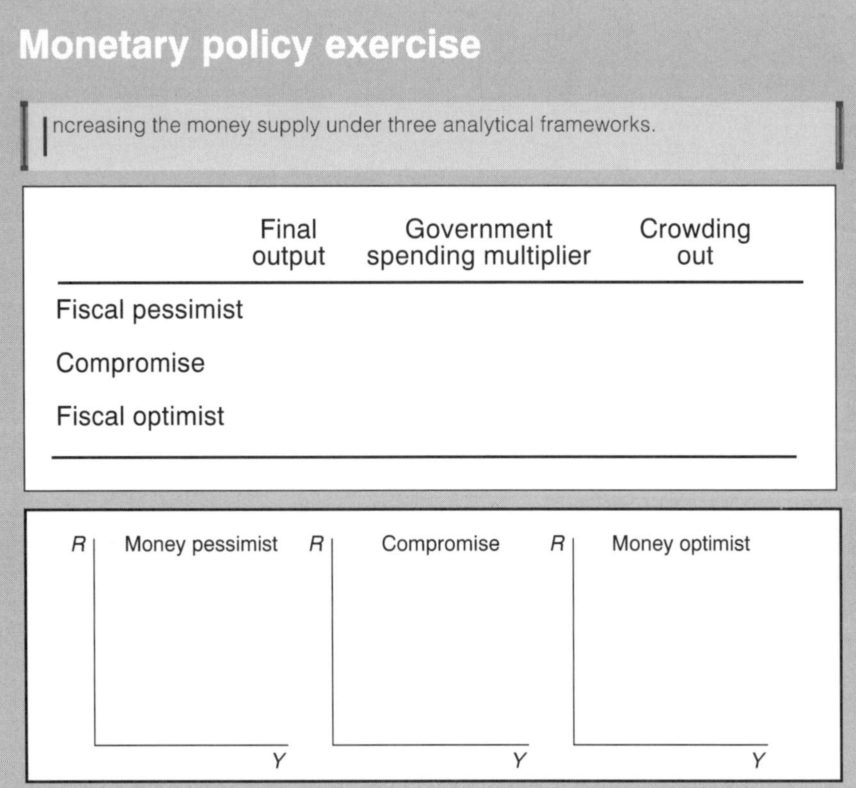

Monetary policy exercise

Increasing the money supply under three analytical frameworks.

	Final output	Government spending multiplier	Crowding out
Fiscal pessimist			
Compromise			
Fiscal optimist			

Section 15.3: Fiscal and Monetary Policy in the AS–AD Framework

This section brings together the aggregate supply, AS, curve and the aggregate demand, AD, curve. You then examine the effects of fiscal and monetary policy using the AS–AD model. An important difference between the model used in this section and the one used in the previous section, is that prices are now assumed to be flexible rather than fixed.

Keynes versus the Classics

In macroeconomics there is an important policy debate between Keynesian and classical economists. Keynesians believe that changes in monetary and fiscal policy can produce lasting changes in real output and employment. Classical economists disagree. These different conclusions stem from the different aggregate supply curves shown in chapter 14 and the premises from which they are derived. The topic Classical Aggregate Supply: A Summary shows a vertical AS curve, while Keynesian Aggregate Supply: A Summary shows an AS curve which is upward sloping at lower price levels and vertical at the full employment level of output.

This topic is covered by three WinEcon screens. The first demonstrates that IS–LM analysis only looks at what happens to aggregate demand when an exogenous change occurs. Now that the price level is assumed to be flexible and endogenous, we must close the model so that all the endogenous variables are determined simultaneously. The way this is done is by specifying the supply side of the economy. This is discussed in chapter 14, but up until this point has been largely ignored in considering policy effectiveness. The interaction of the aggregate supply and demand then determines the equilibrium price level and equilibrium output.

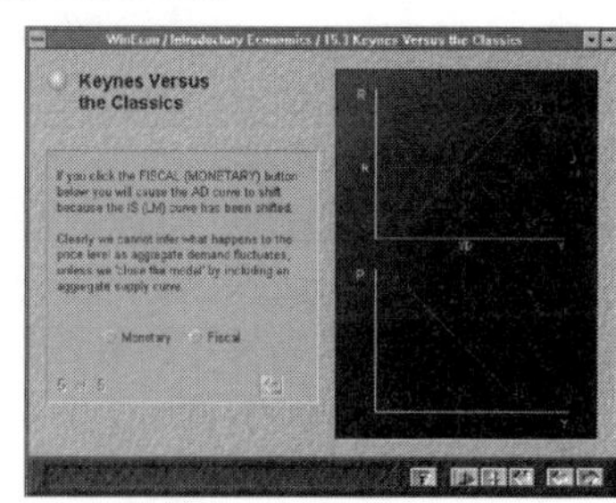

We now address the debate between Keynesian and classical economists on two screens accessed via the Next Page button (Fiscal Policy Under Flexible Prices and Monetary Policy Under Flexible Prices). The first lets you consider the effect of expansionary fiscal policy in Keynesian and classical models. The second is similar but deals with an expansionary monetary policy. On each screen you first review a world of fixed prices, using IS–LM analysis. Then from card 3 you explore the effects in a world where prices are flexible. Up to card 6 you study the Keynesian AS–AD model. From card 7 to 9 you can explore the classical version of events.

Test your understanding of the Keynesian and classical viewpoints

32 What is the classical view of the effectiveness of fiscal and monetary policy?

33 The aggregate supply curve is a way of representing how the supply side of the economy adjusts to changes in aggregate demand. On what does the slope of the aggregate supply curve depend?

34 Why is the effect of fiscal policy on real output not as great according to the Keynesian AS–AD model as it is in the IS–LM model with fixed prices?

35 Why, in the Keynesian model, does the supply of real output increase at all following an expansion of demand?

36 According to the Keynesian model, expansionary fiscal policy causes real output to ________, the price level to ________, the real wage to ________ and employment to ________.

Complete the left-hand panels of the diagram to illustrate the Keynesian case.

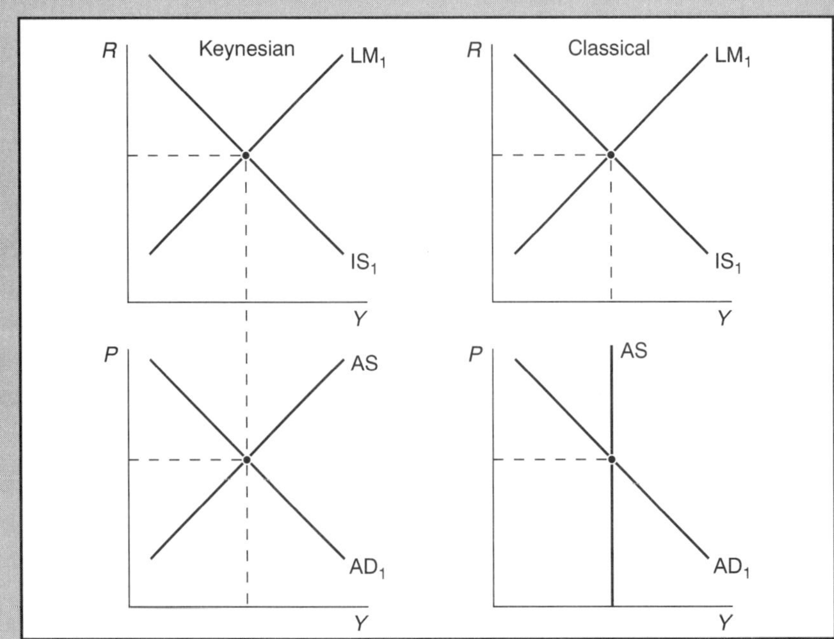

37 **Why, according to the classical model, does the supply of real output not increase following an expansion of demand?**

38 **According to the classical model, expansionary fiscal policy causes real output to ☐, the price level to ☐, the real wage to ☐ and employment to ☐.**

Complete the right-hand panels of the diagram to illustrate the classical case.

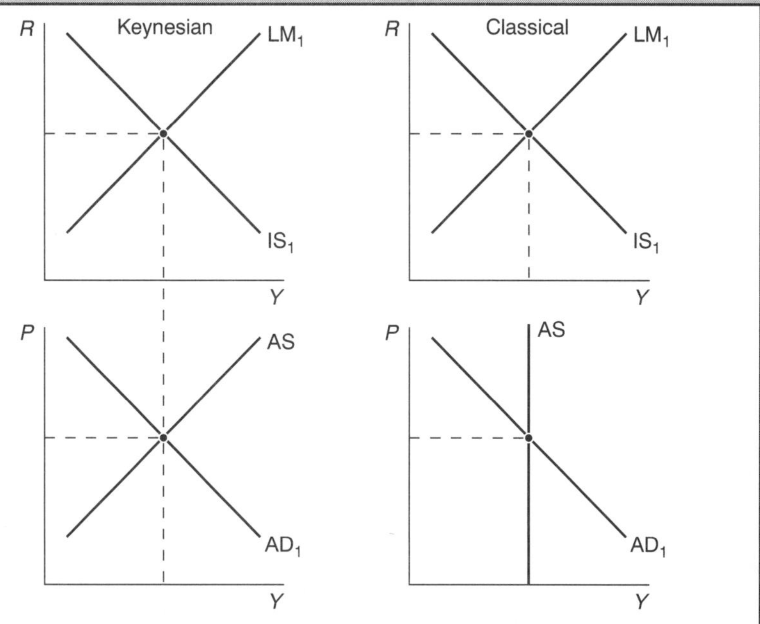

39 **Why is the effect of monetary policy on real output not as great according to the Keynesian AS–AD model as it is in the IS–LM model with fixed prices?**

40 **According to the Keynesian model, expansionary monetary policy causes real output to ☐, the price level to ☐, the real wage to ☐ and employment to ☐.**

41 **According to the classical model, expansionary monetary policy causes real output to ☐, the price level to ☐, the real wage to ☐ and employment to ☐.**

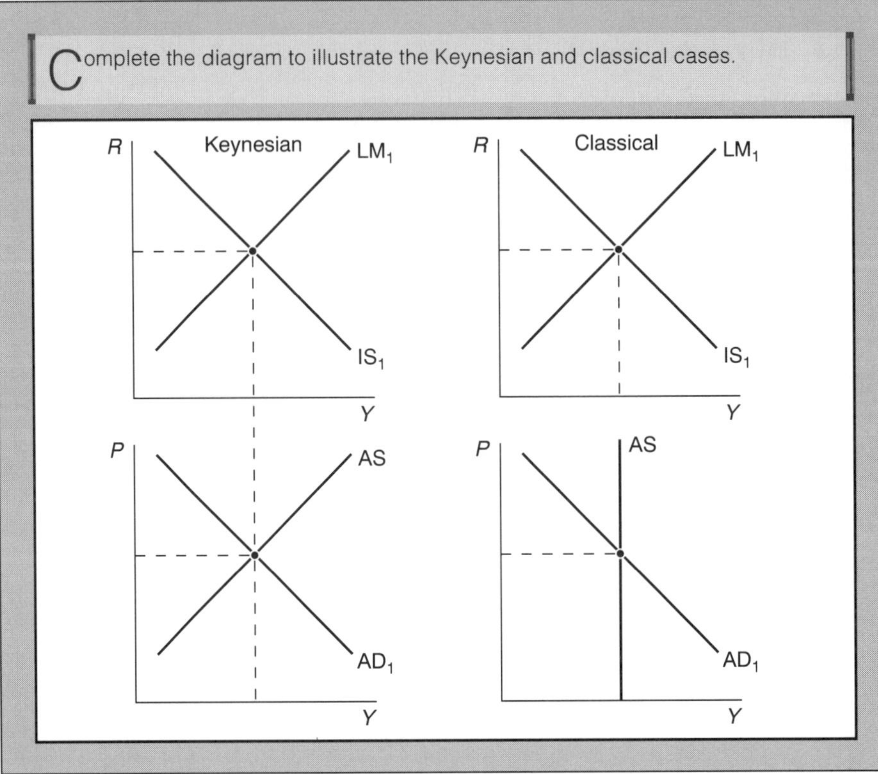

AS–AD Fiscal Policy Exercise

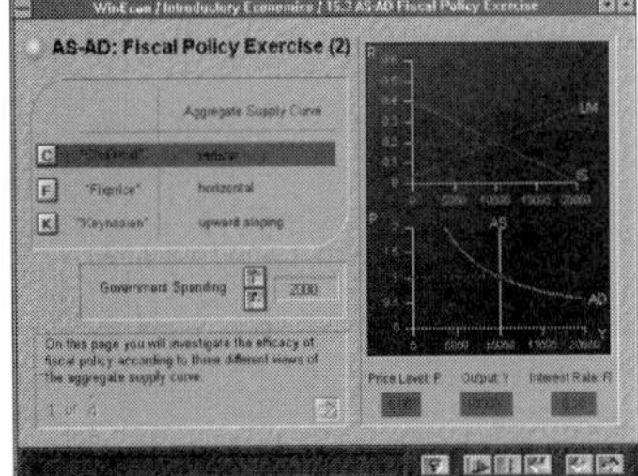

In this two-screen topic you are asked to explore the changes in real output and prices that result from expansionary fiscal policy, according to three different numerical models (classical, fixprice and Keynesian). Work your way carefully through the text cards. Use the buttons to answer the screen questions about the changes in output and the price level that result when government expenditure is increased from 2000 to 4000. The important point to note is what each analytical framework predicts about the effects of a fiscal expansion on both real output and the general price level. Record your answers and complete the relevant diagrams below.

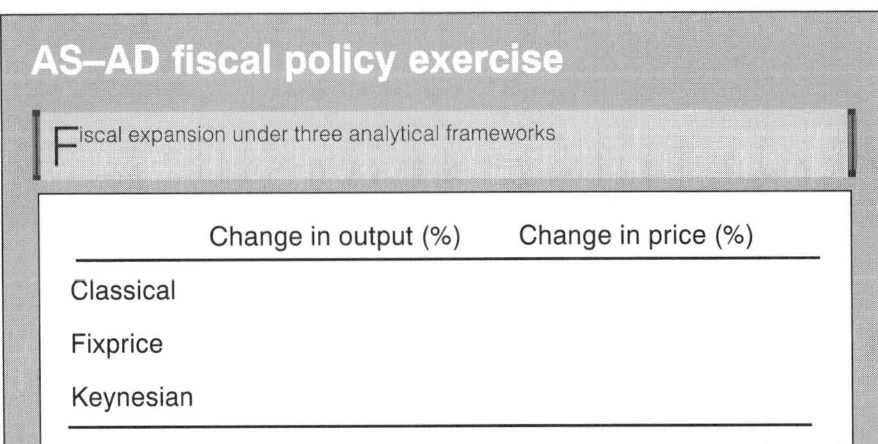

AS–AD fiscal policy exercise

Fiscal expansion under three analytical frameworks

	Change in output (%)	Change in price (%)
Classical		
Fixprice		
Keynesian		

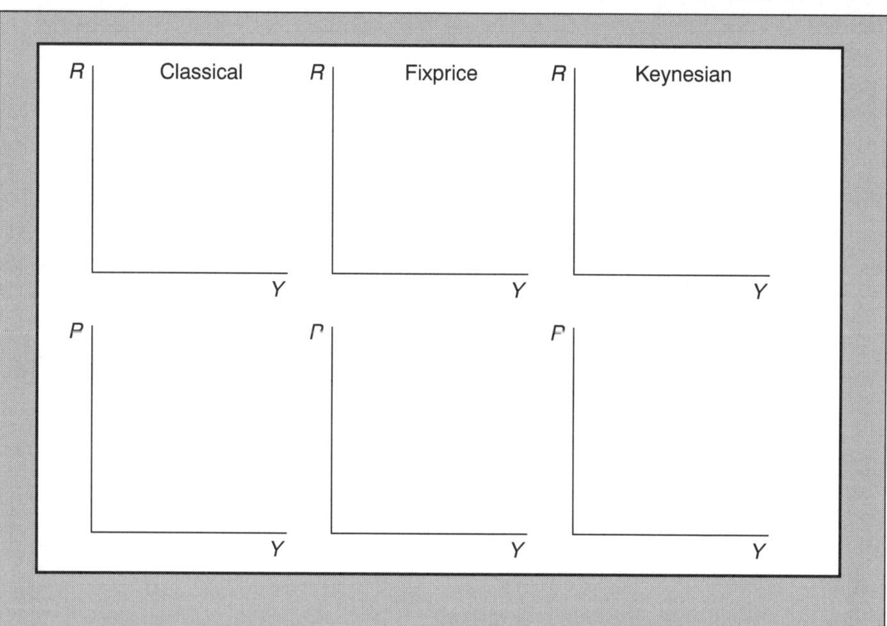

Section 15.4: Policy in the Open Economy

So far our analysis of the effects of monetary and fiscal policy has been carried out in the context of a closed economy. In this section we consider the effect of monetary and fiscal policy in an open economy. Our analysis utilizes IS–LM–BP analysis.

The analysis is introduced in section 13.5 where the topic The BP Curve derives the balance of payments locus. The topic Exogenous Changes provides examples of the effects of policy changes.

We now look further at how the balance of payments (BP) curve is derived, using four linked diagrams to show the underlying balance of payments equilibrium. We then examine the impact of fiscal and monetary policy under different kinds of exchange rate regime.

The IS–LM–BP Framework

The BP curve shows the combinations of the interest rate and real output which are consistent with balance of payments equilibrium. Use WinEcon to see which factor most influences the current account and which the capital account. As the BP curve is derived, answer the questions below.

Understanding the BP curve

42 **What are the two main behavioural relationships which underpin the BP curve? (To answer this question examine the first three cards on the WinEcon screen.)**

43 **What is the condition for equilibrium in the balance of payments and how is it represented?**

44 Consider any point such as B in the diagram below. Mark on the diagram whether this point is one of balance of payments surplus or deficit. Explain why this is so.

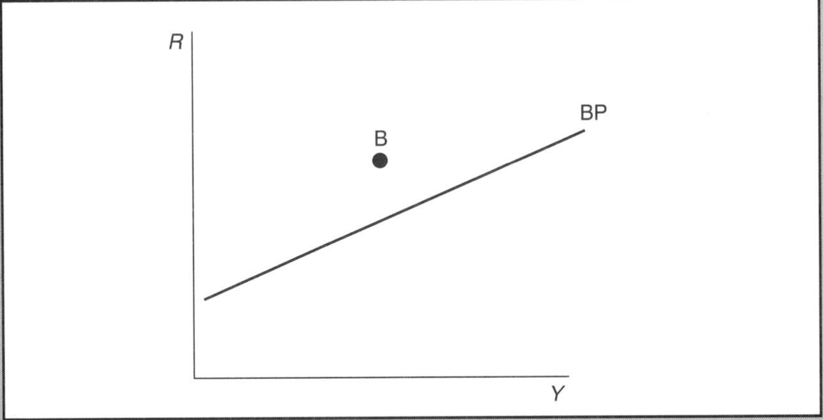

45 **If the effect of an appreciation in the domestic currency is to increase net imports, what would be its effect on the BP curve?**

46 **If the effect of an appreciation in the domestic currency is to increase net imports, what would be its effect on the IS curve?**

47 **If net capital inflows are perfectly interest elastic, what is the slope of the BP curve?**

Policy Effectiveness In The Open Economy

There are two distinct types of exchange rate regime: fixed exchange rates and flexible exchange rates. Under a system of fixed exchange rates, the exchange rate between any two currencies is fixed for an indefinite period and any disequilibrium in the balance of payments must be sustained by the appropriate action of the monetary authorities. Under a (pure) flexible exchange rate regime, the exchange rate adjusts swiftly to eliminate any disequilibrium in the balance of payments. Under such a regime, exchange rates will change continuously.

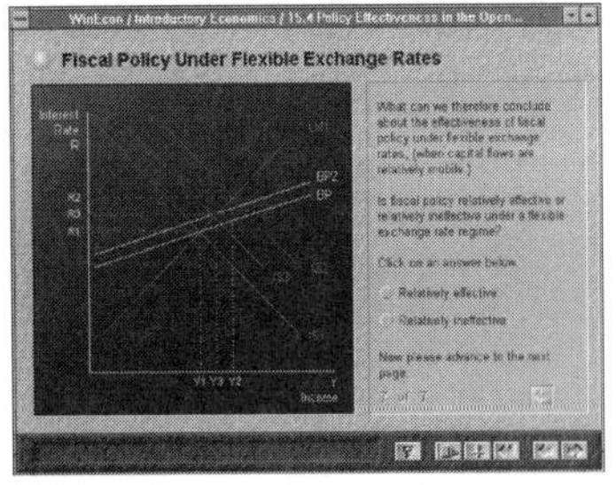

Now we will analyse the effects of expansionary monetary and fiscal policy under fixed and flexible exchange rate regimes. Use the four screens accessed via the Next Page button to explore the effectiveness of fiscal and monetary policy under different exchange rate regimes. These screens are headed Fiscal Policy in a Fixed Exchange Rate

Regime, Monetary Policy in a Fixed Exchange Rate Regime, Fiscal Policy Under Flexible Exchange Rates, and Monetary Policy Under Flexible Exchange Rates.

Fiscal Policy Effectiveness with Fixed Rates

48 **Fiscal policy is likely to be ______ under a regime of fixed exchange rates. Suppose the government increases its final spending from an initial balance of payments equilibrium. The IS curve shifts to the ______, causing real output and interest rates to ______. If capital flows are highly mobile, the balance of payments will move into ______. As a result the money supply will ______ and the LM curve will shift to the ______. Balance of payments equilibrium will be restored at a much ______ level of real output.**

Complete the diagram to illustrate this case.

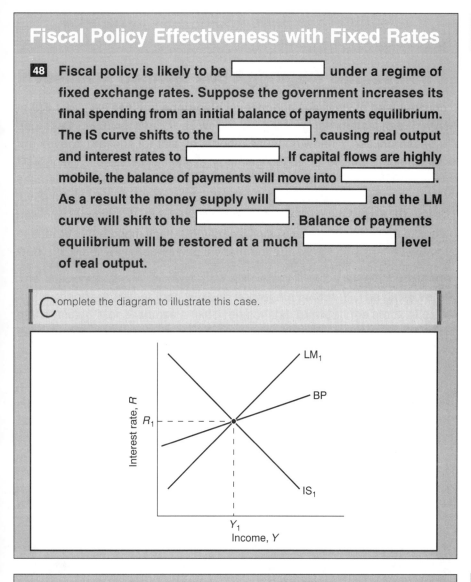

Monetary Policy Effectiveness with Fixed Rates

49 **Monetary policy is likely to be ______ under a regime of fixed exchange rates. Suppose the government expands the money supply from an initial balance of payments equilibrium. The LM curve shifts to the ______, causing real output to ______ and interest rates to ______. The balance of payments will move into ______. As a result the**

money supply will [ ] and the LM curve will shift to the [ ]. Balance of payments equilibrium will be restored at the [ ] level of real output.

Complete the diagram to illustrate this case.

Fiscal Policy Effectiveness with Flexible Rates

50 **Fiscal policy is likely to be [ ] under a regime of flexible exchange rates. Suppose the government increases its final spending from an initial balance of payments equilibrium. The IS curve shifts to the [ ], causing real output and interest rates to [ ]. If capital flows are highly mobile, the balance of payments will show a tendency towards [ ]. As a result the exchange rate will [ ]. This will result in the BP shifting to the [ ] and the IS curve shifting to the [ ]. Balance of payments equilibrium will be restored at a level of real output [ ] than the original level.**

Complete the diagram to illustrate this case.

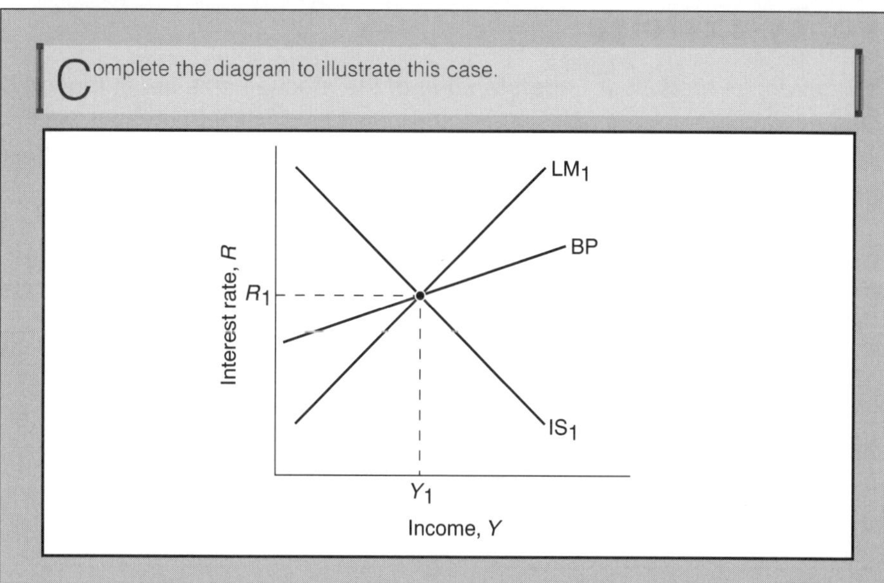

Monetary Policy Effectiveness with Flexible Rates

51 **Monetary policy is likely to be ________ under a regime of flexible exchange rates. Suppose the government increases the money supply. The LM curve shifts to the ________, causing real output to ________ and interest rates to ________. The balance of payments will show a tendency towards ________. As a result the exchange rate will ________. This will result in the BP shifting to the ________ and the IS curve shifting to the ________. Balance of payments equilibrium will be restored at a level of real output considerably ________ than the original level.**

Complete the diagram to illustrate this case.

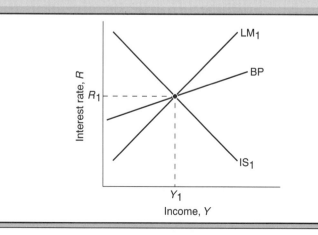

LM1
BP
R1
Interest rate, R
IS1
Y1
Income, Y

Policy Exercise

This exercise tests your understanding of the mechanisms set in motion by changes in government policy. Work through it to check you understand how recognition of the 'openness' of the economy alters the analysis of the effects of policy changes. You can record your answers below.

	New level of output	New interest rate
Fixed exchange rate:		
Fiscal policy		
Monetary policy		
Flexible exchange rate:		
Fiscal policy		
Monetary policy		

Section 15.5: The Monetarist Critique of Active Stabilization Policy

A major aim of government policy is to achieve steady growth in real GDP. The models in this chapter show, apparently, how this can be done, yet practical experience over many years does not bear this out. Difficulties arise in applying the policies we have been studying. Demand management has not proved easy.

This section examines two kinds of criticism of active stabilization policy. First we consider the monetarist contention that governments cannot use macroeconomic policy to boost output and employment in the long run. Second we consider problems relating to the timing of policy and the magnitude of its impact.

The Natural Rate Hypothesis

Here we build on the topics Unemployment in the Monetarist Model and The Phillips Curve which we saw in section 14.5.

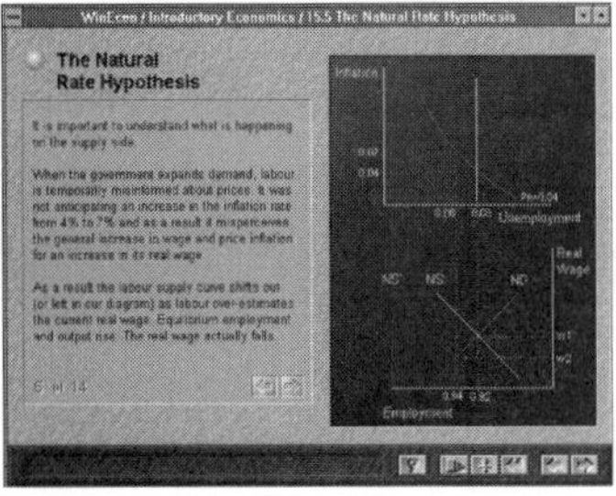

The natural rate hypothesis is the monetarist claim that only one level of unemployment – the natural rate – is consistent with stable inflation. Any attempt to hold unemployment below its natural rate will, according to monetarists, result in ever-increasing rates of inflation. This hypothesis is based on an equilibrium analysis of the labour market, in which short-run changes in employment (and unemployment) are caused by shifts in the labour supply curve.

WinEcon cards 1 to 3 reveal a diagram that represents equilibrium in the labour market. Cards 4 to 6 set out the monetarist analysis of the short-run

effects of attempting to hold unemployment below the natural rate. Later cards explore the long-run effects of such policies.

Test your understanding of the natural rate hypothesis

52 **According to the natural rate hypothesis, why does an expansionary monetary policy cause an increase in output and employment in the short run?**

53 **Why does the short-run increase in output and employment not persist unless monetary policy is expanded still further?**

54 **Why is increased inflation the inevitable consequence of trying to hold unemployment below its natural rate?**

55 **Is the natural rate of unemployment consistent with very high rates of inflation? Explain.**

Policy Timing and Magnitude

In practice it is difficult to ensure that the use of monetary and fiscal policy reduces economic fluctuations. Data are not instantly available, and one month's figures might be considered insufficient evidence for policy intervention. Time is needed for analysis and decision making. Some policy changes, especially fiscal ones, are normally only made at particular times of the year. And, once a policy change *is* announced, it often takes time to come into effect. Since there may be lags in the implementation of a policy, by the time it actually takes effect the situation may have changed and the policy may no longer be appropriate. It is also difficult to assess by how much government expenditure, taxes or the money supply should increase or decrease to have the desired effect.

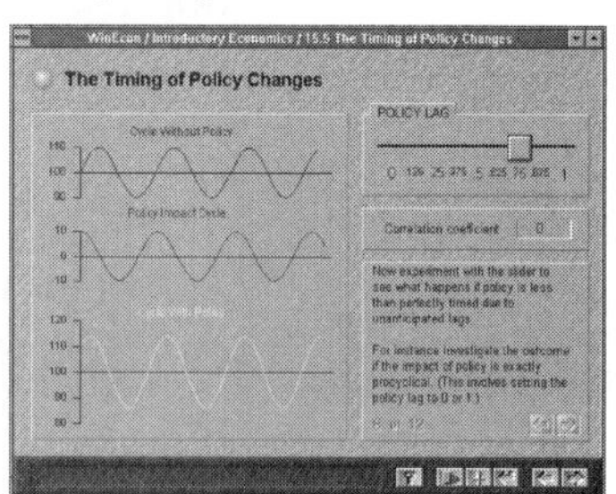

The Timing of Policy Changes and Timing and Magnitude are two associated screens in this topic. Both are accessed by clicking the Next Page button. On these screens you can explore some of the difficulties associated with the timing and magnitude of policy changes.

Test your understanding of policy timing and magnitude

56 **Identify the policy lags which make the timing of macroeconomic policy difficult.**

57 **If policy is applied with the appropriate strength, what kind of correlation should exist between the impact of the policy and the economic cycle (without policy)?**

The Political Angle

This screen very briefly points out the political implications of the different schools of thought.

Section 15.6: Summary

This chapter examines the effectiveness of monetary and fiscal policy in closed and open economies using simple economic models. The IS–LM model assumes the price level is constant. You discover that when fiscal policy is used to expand the economy, crowding out can occur so that the policy has less effect. In a closed economy, the extent to which fiscal and monetary policy affect aggregate demand depends on the slopes of the IS and LM curves. Fiscal policy is most effective when investment is interest inelastic and the demand for money is elastic, while monetary policy can most effectively be used to manipulate aggregate demand when the IS curve has a shallow slope and the LM curve is steep.

The AS–AD framework allows for flexible prices. You have learnt that the response of the supply side is critical to the success or failure of policy changes. According to classical economists, at least in the long run, fiscal and monetary policy do not alter the level of real output. In the Keynesian model, fiscal and monetary policy are less effective with flexible prices because one effect of expansionary policies is to raise prices.

To analyse policy effectiveness in an open economy we add the BP curve to the IS–LM framework. Fiscal policy is likely to be effective with fixed exchange rates, while monetary policy is likely to be ineffective. Under a flexible exchange rate regime, monetary policy is likely to be effective and fiscal policy moderately effective.

Monetarists are critical of discretionary monetary and fiscal policy. They claim that any attempt to hold unemployment below its natural rate will lead to increasing inflation. There are also practical difficulties in estimating the appropriate magnitude for policy changes, and the lags associated with their implementation.

Chapter 16:

Macroeconomic Fluctuations

Boom followed by bust, recession then recovery. This is part of a familiar pattern. Aggregate economic activity and the level of real GDP do not rise along a smooth, linear path, but are subject to periodic upswings and downswings. Such fluctuations receive a lot of media coverage and are a major public concern. Recessions can cause much uncertainty and unhappiness in terms of unemployment and reduced spending power. To avoid political unpopularity, governments often act to promote recovery. With sustained economic growth in the 1950s and early 1960s, it seemed possible that the introduction of Keynesian policies had, 'exorcised the ghost of the nineteenth-century business cycle'. But, if we look at the closing decades of the twentieth century, the business cycle still apparently exists. It is the focus of this chapter.

Contents

KEYWORDS

- Amplitude
- Deviation from trend
- Peak
- Shocks
- Boom
- Frequency
- Persistence
- Trend
- Business cycle
- Growth rates
- Recession
- Trough

Section 16.1: Introduction

The central focus of this chapter is theories of macroeconomic fluctuations (also referred to as 'business cycles'). Before we examine in turn three key theories, we begin with some basic concepts and definitions. We ask: 'what is a recession or a boom?', 'how do we measure the frequency of business cycles?', 'how do we measure the severity of the cycle?' and 'how do macroeconomic shocks to the economy lead to cycles?'. We then consider specific macroeconomic theories of aggregate fluctuations – classical, Keynesian and monetarist. Before proceeding further in this chapter, if you are unsure of the three core theories of aggregate supply, return to sections 14.3, 14.4 and 14.5.

Section 16.2: Concepts and Definitions

We begin by examining some important concepts and definitions used in the analysis of macroeconomic fluctuations. This includes answering the following questions: 'how is the economic cycle measured?', 'what are the key features of a regular cycle?' and 'how can we best characterize "real world" cycles?'

Measuring a Cycle

See the topic Linear Trends with Constant Growth in section 9.2.

On this screen we look at the pattern of changes in real GDP (which is the value of aggregate output measured in base-year prices). A popular approach to analysing GDP over time is to plot logarithmic values over time. You should recall from chapter 9 that taking logarithms has one attractive property: if real GDP has grown at a constant rate, the logarithm of GDP will be a straight line when plotted against time. Uneven growth of GDP will mean that a plot of the log of GDP will oscillate around a linear, upward-sloping trend.

By stepping through the text cards on this screen you will see how real GDP in the UK has been growing over time (at least on average), but its growth is somewhat uneven. Our first task is to separate the tendency for GDP to grow over time from the year-to-year fluctuations (or cycles), and on this screen we present two popular ways of achieving this. When you click the Show button on the third card you will see the first method displayed graphically. The long-run trend in GDP is captured by fitting a linear (straight line) trend to the data, and the cyclical component is determined as the residual of the actual series from this fitted trend. This uses a statistical technique called linear regression to obtain the line which best fits the data. When you click the Show button on card four, the second method is displayed graphically. In this method the growth rate of GDP is calculated in each year. The long-run trend in GDP is captured by the average (or mean) annual growth rate, and the cyclical component is determined by the variation of actual growth around this mean.

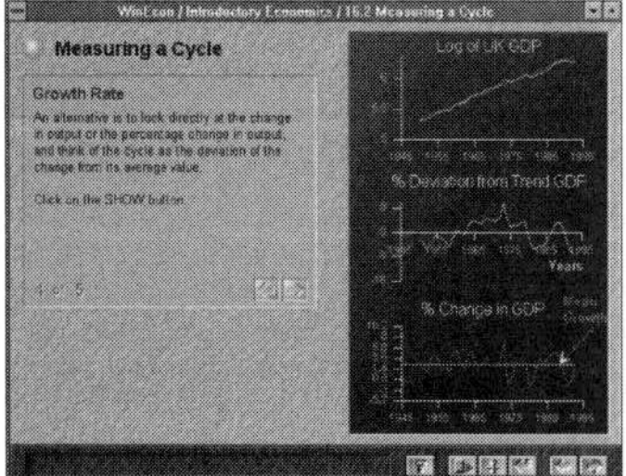

Describing cyclical patterns

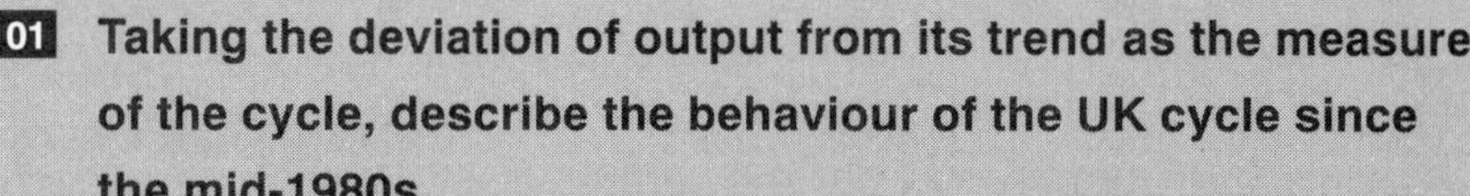

01 **Taking the deviation of output from its trend as the measure of the cycle, describe the behaviour of the UK cycle since the mid-1980s.**

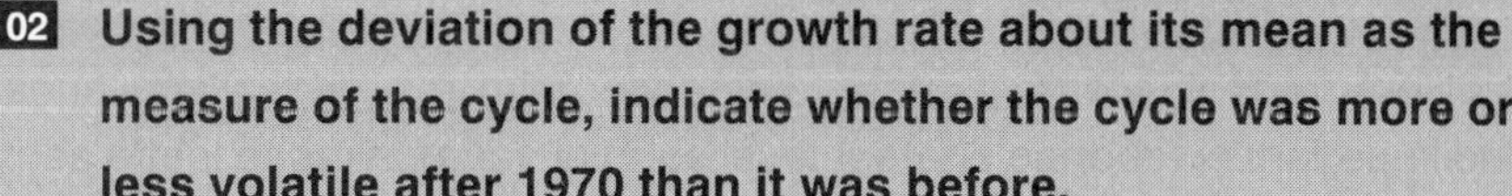

02 **Using the deviation of the growth rate about its mean as the measure of the cycle, indicate whether the cycle was more or less volatile after 1970 than it was before.**

Cycles Terminology

To describe and compare various cycles we need some specific terminology. You can discover the meaning of important terms on this WinEcon screen.

The easiest way to understand the main features of the cycle is to imagine a smooth, regular and symmetric cycle like that shown on the WinEcon screen. As we shall see, real cycles are irregular and asymmetric, but this simplification makes it easier to appreciate the main features of the cycle. As you work through the screen, make sure you understand the differences between the various terms that are used to describe the cycle. You can also discover information on the frequency of the United States business cycle (use the More button which is revealed on card four).

Test your understanding of cycles terminology

Give a brief description of the following key concepts.

03 **Business cycle peak**

04 **Business cycle trough**

05 **Recession**

06 **Boom**

07 **Amplitude**

08 **Frequency (or phase)**

US business cycles

09 **Fill in the following using the information revealed by the More button on card four.**

1945–1982: Number of months from peak to trough: ______

Number of months from trough to peak: ______

On the graph below, draw a simple cycle that corresponds to the data above.

Output, Y

1945 Year 1945

10 **Would you describe this cycle as symmetric? Explain your answer.**

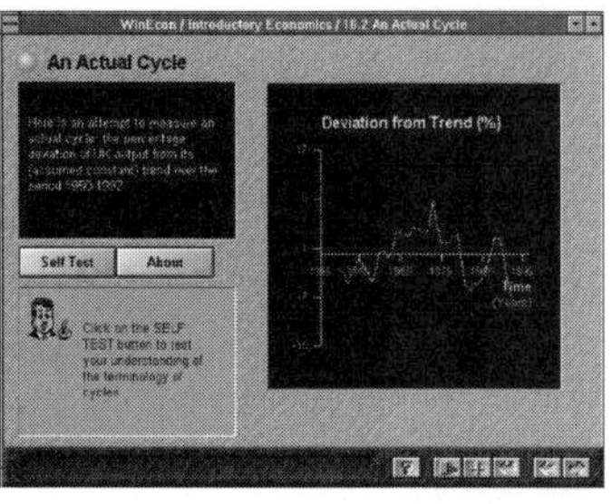

An Actual Cycle

This WinEcon screen examines the percentage deviation of real GDP about its trend in the UK since 1975. Try the self-test exercise to make sure you can correctly identify the peaks and troughs and the periods of boom and recession.

Aggregate Demand and Supply Shocks

Cycles are generated initially by 'shocks', or unexpected events that affect the economy. These are sometimes referred to as 'impulses' that give rise to drawn-out fluctuations. The effects of these shocks may last well beyond the initial impact period, and economists often distinguish between the shocks (or impulses) and the 'propagation mechanism' through which these shocks affect the economy over an extended time.

Precisely how economic cycles are generated by shocks is explained in detail in the next section. On this WinEcon screen you discover that shocks can be classified broadly as aggregate demand shocks or aggregate supply shocks. The former cause the economy's aggregate demand curve to shift and the latter shift its aggregate supply curve. Some shocks may affect both aggregate demand and aggregate supply. Use the buttons on card 3 to discover the appropriate classifications for particular types of shocks and to learn about some actual shocks in the case studies.

Test your understanding of shocks

11 **When you are sure you understand the nature of demand and supply shocks, indicate what kind of shocks the following might be (supply, demand or both).**

(a) An increase in the amount people wish to spend on consumption at any income level. ☐

(b) A rise in the rate of income tax. ☐

(c) A tightening of monetary policy. ☐

(d) An introduction of a minimum national wage. ☐

(e) An increase in benefits paid to the unemployed. ☐

Complete the following statements.

12 **A reduction in the rate of income tax changes aggregate demand because:**

13 **A reduction in the rate of income tax changes aggregate supply because:**

Shocks and Persistence

On this WinEcon screen we explain how shocks or impulses (which may arise randomly in any period) can give rise to persistent deviations in aggregate output. If an economy is in equilibrium, the value of national income is always at its trend value. To study the effects of shocks we consider the values of the deviations of output from its trend values in successive time periods. These values are zero if the economy is in equilibrium. The occurrence of a shock generates a deviation from trend. The 'ripple' effects that we assume ensue

are modelled by explaining each deviation in terms of the previous one. How similar successive deviations are determines how persistent the shock is and therefore how long the ripples take to die away.

The first three WinEcon text cards of this screen explain the terms 'persistence' and 'first-order difference equation'. On cards four and five these terms are illustrated diagrammatically. The key point that we make here is that the value of the deviation of output from trend in any one period may be related to the value of the deviation in the previous period. The reasons for this are potentially numerous. For example, if there is increased demand for goods, output would rise above its trend value. Similarly, if firms partly meet an increase in demand by running down their stocks of finished goods, output may have to be above trend again in the following period in order to replenish these stocks. In this way output would be above trend in the current period because output was above trend (and stocks reduced) in the previous period.

That successive values of a variable are related to previous values does not on its own explain cyclical patterns. We explain on WinEcon cards 6 to 9 what happens when Y is affected both by its lagged value and by periodic shocks (either supply or demand in origin). Complete the spreadsheet exercise on the screen and when you have read the text cards, complete the following questions.

Shocks and Persistence Exercise

Consider the following imaginary economy:

$$Y_t = 100 + b\, Y_{t-1} + e_t$$

where Y is real GDP, e is a 'shock' to GDP and b is a constant parameter which measures 'persistence'. Note that Y now refers to the level of output rather than its deviation from trend.

14 **If equilibrium exists when output is the same in successive time periods and there is no external shock, derive an expression for the equilibrium solution for Y.**

15 **What is the equilibrium solution for Y when (a) b = 0.75, and (b) b = 0.25?**

16 Suppose the data given in the table relates to the economy modelled above and that b = 0.75. Complete the table.

Year	Current GDP (Y_t)	Lagged GDP (Y_{t-1})	Shock (e_t)
1970	600	400	200
1971			0
1972			0
1973			0
1974			0
1975			0
1976			0
1977			0

17 **Notice in the table above that the economy is subject to a single shock. Does it achieve or move towards equilibrium by 1977?**

18 For the same economy, complete the following table when b = 0.75.

Year	Current GDP (Y_t)	Lagged GDP (Y_{t-1})	Shock (e_t)
1970	600	400	200
1971			0
1972			150
1973			–100
1974			100
1975			–50
1976			–100
1977			0

19 **Briefly describe the main differences in *Y* between the two tables.**

Effects of Shocks and Persistence

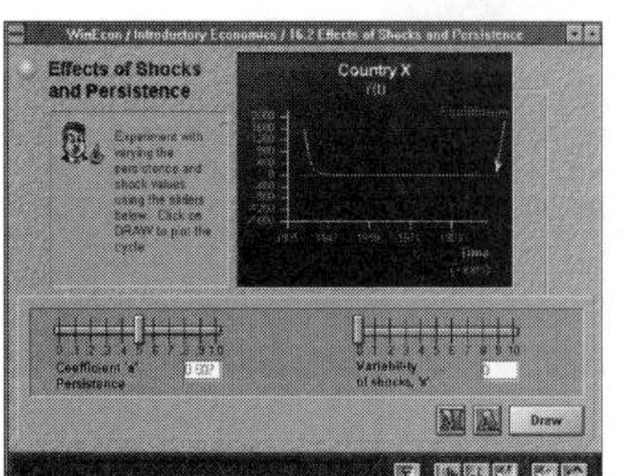

The character of the business cycle (its phase and amplitude, or frequency and severity) will depend on the size of the shocks that affect the economy and also on the degree of persistence. On this WinEcon screen you can see the effects of these on the cycle by using the sliders. Notice that the variable *Y* on the screen denotes deviations around trend output. The More button will give you a hint on how to proceed.

For the technically minded, the size of the shocks is determined by fixing its standard deviation (recall that the mean or average value for the shocks is, by definition, zero). When you adjust the 'Variability' slider the computer adjusts the standard deviation of the stocks. When you have understood how the variability of the shocks and the degree of persistence influence the character of the cycle, proceed to the next topic.

Section 16.3: Macroeconomic Theories of Fluctuations

How do supply and demand shocks affect real output and the price level? This is the central question we answer in this section. The answer to this question depends largely on how the economy is thought to work. For example, a Keynesian economist will give a very different answer to this question from that given by a classical economist (or his contemporary equivalent). The patterns of output and price change following aggregate supply and demand shocks will vary between the three key theories of aggregate supply – classical, monetarist and Keynesian. And the policy implications for avoiding fluctuations will also differ between these theories.

In this section we use aggregate demand and supply diagrams to examine the effects of shocks on output and the price level in each of the three theories.

Theories of Cycles: Overview

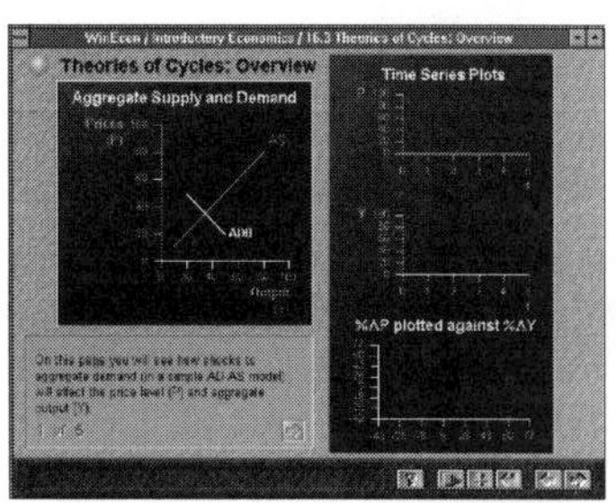

We begin by explaining the diagrammatic framework which we use throughout the rest of this chapter. An aggregate demand and supply diagram is drawn on the left-hand side of the WinEcon screen. The periodic shocks affecting the economy shift the aggregate supply or aggregate demand curves as appropriate. On the right-hand side of the screen we show the effects of these shocks on the behaviour over time of output and the price level, though the time plots do not allow for any persistence in output (i.e. any dependence of output on its lagged value). We also show on the right-hand side of each screen a cross-plot of inflation (the growth rate of the price level) and output growth.

This screen lets you discover the kinds of diagrams generated by the models we shall study. By shifting the aggregate demand curve either up or down (using the mouse), you see the implications this has for the time series behaviour of output and prices. Notice that if you increase aggregate demand, both *P* and *Y* increase. The time series plots start with the initial values of *P* and *Y*, and plot the values corresponding to the positions you choose for the AD curve in periods 1 to 5. The cross-plot is then derived by calculating between each pair of values for *P* and *Y* the change in each of the variables. If AD has increased, both ΔP and ΔY are positive, whilst if AD has decreased ΔP and ΔY are both negative. The cross-plot is upwards sloping and the placing of the points on it no longer necessarily corresponds to the order in time in which the values occur.

The following topics in this section analyse the effects of aggregate supply and demand shocks under the classical, Keynesian and monetarist theories of aggregate supply.

Classical Model: AD Shock, AS Shock

We begin with the classical model of aggregate supply which we introduced in section 14.3. In this model, wages and prices are fully flexible, and the labour and goods markets are always in equilibrium. Moreover, workers and firms are assumed to be correctly informed of the aggregate price level (i.e. we assume full information). Since the Keynesian model relaxes the equilibrium assumption and since the monetarist model relaxes the assumption of full information, we can view the classical model as providing a base case against which the others may be compared.

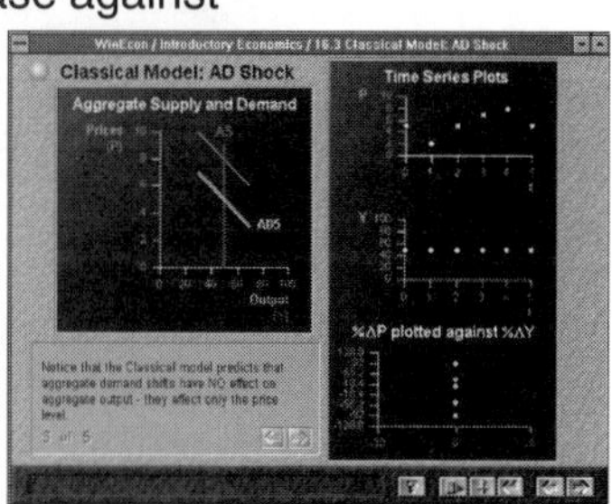

As you work through the two related WinEcon screens, make sure you understand why AD shocks do not generate a business cycle in the classical model. Also check carefully the relationship between inflation and output growth when the classical model is subjected to periodic AS shocks. When you have completed the analysis of AD and AS shocks in the classical model, answer the following questions.

Effects of shocks in the classical model

20 **AD shocks do not generate cycles in the classical model because:**

(a) AS always adjusts to equal AD. ☐

(b) AS never adjusts to equal AD. ☐

(c) AD adjusts through price level changes to equal a fixed AS. ☐

21 **Explain carefully why the following imaginary data could be consistent with a classical economy subjected to periodic AS shocks.**

Year	Output growth (% p.a.)	Inflation (% p.a.)
1950	7.4	3.0
1951	5.2	4.4
1952	–1.0	5.2
1953	4.7	2.9
1954	8.3	–2.3

In the classical model, explain what happens to aggregate output and the price level in the following cases?

22 **Increase in money supply.**

23 **Unexpected depletion of oil reserves.**

24 **Cut in income taxes.**

25 Show on the diagram the effects of an adverse AS shock, and identify its effects on output and the price level.

Price, *P*

Output, *Y*

26 **If the government wished to maintain price stability, what would be the appropriate monetary policy response to the AS shock? Show this on the diagram.**

Stabilizing Prices in the Classical Model

Our aim on this WinEcon screen is to explain how stabilization policy can have a role even in the classical model. You are asked to control the level of aggregate demand in a 'classical economy' which is subject to aggregate supply and demand shocks. Your aim is to stabilize prices by keeping the price level as close as you can to P_0.

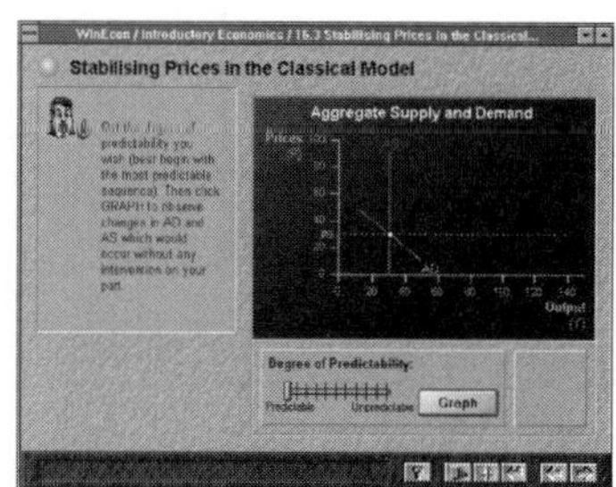

To begin the exercise, select the degree of predictability (it is best to start with the most predictable shocks) and view the sequence of shocks by clicking the Graph button. When you have clicked the Reset and Start buttons, the graph will be refreshed and the sequence will recommence. But this time you are able to affect the movement in AD by adjusting the slide bar. A negative value on the slide bar will shift the new AD curve to the left; a positive value shifts it to the right. Your aim is to keep the price level as close to P_0 as possible. Check your score against the maximum attainable. To repeat the exercise, click the Reset button and start again.

The lesson you should learn from this exercise is the need to control aggregate demand to stabilize prices when the economy is subject to repeated aggregate supply shocks, even in the classical model.

Keynesian Model: AD Shock, AS Shock

In the classical model, labour and product markets are assumed to be in continuous equilibrium and workers and employers are assumed to have correct expectations of the aggregate price level. In the Keynesian model, we relax the assumption of continuous equilibrium (or market clearing), at least in the labour market. The aggregate supply curve is constructed on the assumption that the labour market may not be in equilibrium and that labour supply may, at times, exceed labour demand.

Keynes suggested that fluctuations in aggregate real ouptut are caused principally by changes in aggregate demand (or aggregate spending). When we introduce aggregate demand shocks to the Keynesian model, we only consider movements in AD along the upward-sloping section of the supply curve. Of course, if the shock to AD were to lead to an intersection on the vertical section, the aggregate supply curve would shift upwards (since the price level and the money wage would both have risen). If you are unsure of this, return to section 14.4 which explains the Keynesian theory of aggregate supply.

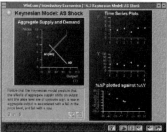

Note the difference in the relationship between inflation and output growth on these two WinEcon Screens. Check you understand why aggregate demand shocks imply a positive relationship between inflation and output growth whereas aggregate supply shocks imply the reverse. When you have completed the animation sequences on these screens, answer the questions that follow.

Test your understanding of shocks in the Keynesian model

27 If the economy has unemployed resources, an increase in aggregate spending will raise the prices of goods and services. This raises the value of the [marginal/average] product of labour. Because the [real/money] wage is fixed, profit maximizing firms will raise the level of employment (or the [supply/demand] for labour). The increase in employment will [raise/lower] the level of output. As long as output is less than demand, prices will continue to [fall/rise] until the excess demand is removed. The key assumption we have used is that the money wage rate is [flexible/fixed].

Locate the shocks Examine the following imaginary data for a country with a Keynesian AS curve and answer the question that follows.

Year	Output growth (% p.a.)	Inflation (% p.a.)
1980	–5.0	3.0
1981	7.4	4.4
1982	0.0	5.0
1983	–4.7	0.0

28 When did the following shocks take place?

(a) An increase in imported oil prices. [ ]

(b) An increase in imported oil prices accompanied by a rise in the money supply. [ ]

(c) An increase in government spending. [ ]

(d) An increase in imported oil prices accompanied by a fall in the money supply. [ ]

Monetarist Model: AD Shock

In the monetarist model, wages and prices are assumed to adjust to ensure the equality of supply and demand in both the labour market and goods market. The monetarist model differs from the classical model by assuming that workers may be incorrectly informed about the aggregate price level. The aggregate supply curve in this model is drawn on the assumption of a given expectation of the price level, and there will be a 'family' of short-run aggregate supply curves, each one based on a specific value for price level expectations.

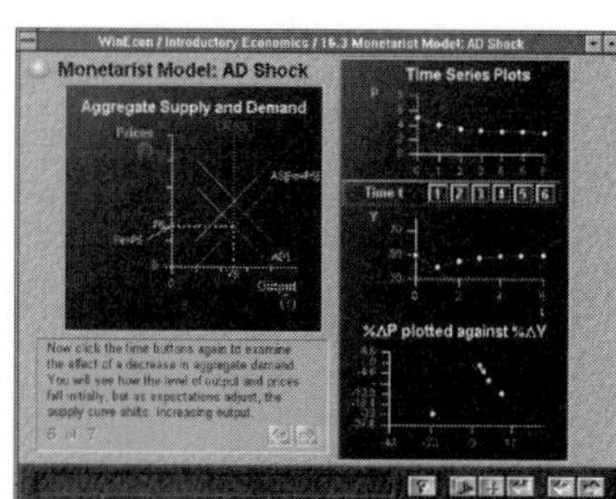

We consider the effects of aggregate demand shocks in two stages and on two WinEcon screens. In the first we examine the effects (on output and prices) of a *single* shock to aggregate demand and, in the following screen, we consider the effect of a *sequence* of aggregate demand shocks. Before we turn to the case of multiple shocks, work through the first screen and then answer the questions that follow. As you follow the animation, note the importance of the assumption we make about price expectations.

Test your understanding of an AD shock in the monetarist model

29 **An economy is initially in equilibrium and workers and employers have correct price expectations. The economy is subject to an unexpected positive AD shock. The shock shifts the aggregate [demand/supply] curve to the right and, since it is unexpected, the AS curve [remains unchanged/ shifts to the right] This is because, initially, price expectations [adjust/remain unchanged] . Output and prices [fall/rise]. If workers expect the price level to equal its value in the previous period, in the second period their price level expectations will be revised [upwards/downwards] and this shifts the aggregate [supply/demand] curve to the left. In subsequent periods, the AS curve continues to shift to the [right/left] , so that output will [fall/rise] and the aggregate price level will [fall/rise] .**

Examine the following data for an imaginary economy and answer the questions below.

Year	Output growth (% p.a.)	Inflation (% p.a.)
1980	1.0	0.0
1981	3.4	3.6
1982	–2.5	2.0
1983	–1.0	1.5
1984	–0.5	0.9

30 **Explain whether the data could describe an economy with a monetarist AS curve and subjected to a single AD shock.**

31 **At what date did the shock to AD occur?** ☐

32 **If price expectations are naive, what is the expected inflation rate in 1983 and 1984?** ☐ ☐

33 **Is the supply curve for 1984 above or below the supply curve for 1983? Give reasons for your answer.**

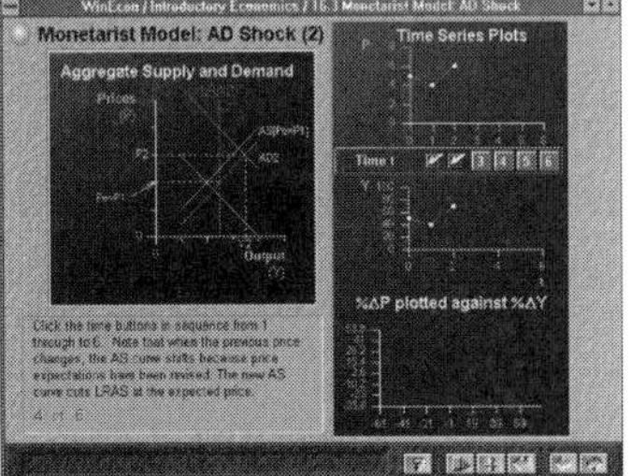

Monetarist Model: AD Shock (2)

Moving forward to this WinEcon screen with the Next Page button, you examine the effects on output and the price level of a *sequence* of aggregate demand shocks (rather than the effects of a single shock). Make sure you fully understand why the short-run aggregate supply curve shifts in the way it does.

Monetarist Model: AS Shock

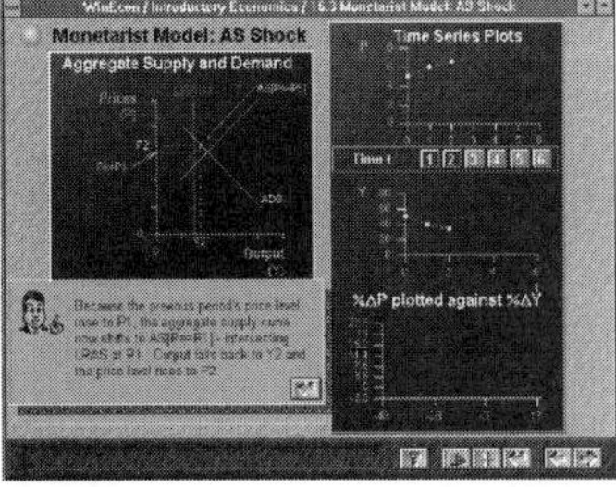

In general, aggregate demand shocks lead to a business cycle in which the inflation rate is pro-cyclical. We now examine the effects of aggregate supply shocks in the monetarist model. Once again we begin by examining the effects of a single shock, and then on the second WinEcon screen study a sequence of shocks. Begin studying the topic with Winecon, and work through the first four text cards. Examine the effects of a single adverse aggregate supply shock and make sure you understand why the aggregate supply curves move as they do.

Test your understanding of an adverse AS shock in the monetarist model

34 **Why does the short-run AS curve shift when there is a shift in the long-run AS curve?**

35 **Why does output continue to fall after the initial shock to AS?**

36 **Explain intuitively why output growth and inflation are negatively correlated.**

Now proceed to card six and examine the effects of a favourable aggregate supply shock.

Test your understanding of a favourable AS shock in the monetarist model

37 **'The short-run AS curve (labelled 'AS') cuts the long-run AS curve (labelled 'LRAS') at a price level below the expected price level.' Give your reasons for believing this statement to be true, false or uncertain.**

38 **An economy is initially in equilibrium and workers and employers have correct price expectations. The economy is subject to a favourable AS shock. The shock shifts the aggregate [demand/supply] curve to the right. Aggregate output [falls/rises] and the price level [falls/rises] . If workers expect the price level to equal its value in the previous period, in the second period their price level expectations will be revised [upwards/downwards] and this shifts the aggregate [supply/demand] curve to the [right/left]. In subsequent periods, the AS curve continues to shift to the [right/left] , so that output will [fall/rise] and the aggregate price level will [fall/rise] .**

Monetarist Model: AS Shock (2)

On this WinEcon screen you will see what happens to output, the price level and the cross-plot of output growth and inflation when an economy with a monetarist aggregate supply curve is subjected to *repeated* aggregate supply shocks. Once again be sure you follow why the short-run aggregate supply curve moves in response to shocks to the long-run aggregate supply curve.

Section 16.4: Summary

Macroeconomic fluctuations remain an important feature of the modern economy. We have discovered that they arise through a combination of shocks to the economy and a tendency of the economy's output to depend on its immediate past.

The nature of the cycle depends on whether the shocks are predominantly demand or supply in origin and on whether the economy is classical, Keynesian or monetarist in character. In general, if demand shocks predominate we expect output growth and inflation to be positively associated, whereas the reverse is true if supply shocks are dominant. In the classical model, aggregate demand shocks do not generate a business cycle.

If governments can influence the effects of demand shocks – for example, by adjusting their own monetary and fiscal policies to counteract a private sector demand shock – they may reduce macroeconomic fluctuations when they arise from aggregate demand. Government aggregate demand policies (monetary or fiscal) should generally aim at accommodating aggregate supply shocks to avoid excessive price fluctuations.

Chapter 17:

Development Economics

What is economic development and how is it measured? Why is economic development not synonymous with economic growth? How do you explain the rapid development of countries like South Korea, Taiwan, Hong Kong and Singapore? In what respect does the government play an important role in the development process? In this chapter, we attempt to answer these questions.

Contents

KEYWORDS

- Deprivation index
- Development
- Export-oriented industrialization
- Human development index
- Import substitution industrialization
- Income elasticity of demand
- Least developed countries
- Newly industrialized countries
- Terms of trade
- Third World

Section 17.1: Introduction

This chapter focuses on some of the major issues which are central to understanding the economies of developing countries. A large number of developing countries are low income countries, in which the level of income per head is very low. The rest are middle income countries, in contrast to developed countries with high incomes. As a starting point this chapter introduces you to the unequal distribution of world income as well as its measurement.

In the next section, discussion focuses on the concept of development and its measurement. You learn that development is a normative concept and hence there is no single definition of what development is. However, for practical purposes certain criteria are used to define and measure development.

You are then introduced to the major policy issues that dominated the development debates in the last three decades. The early emphasis on 'import substitution industrialization', which governed development thinking in the 1960s, was replaced by 'export-oriented industrialization' strategy in the 1970s. However, these issues were overshadowed by debt crisis in the 1980s.

The last section of this chapter provides a brief discussion of the direction and the structure of international trade. Developing countries are very dependent on trade with developed countries. You also learn that the export composition of most developing countries is dominated by agricultural and primary products. However, a few developing countries are exporters of manufactured goods and the compositions of their exports resemble those of developed countries.

Section 17.2: The Distribution of Income

In this section you are introduced to the classification of countries on the basis of their income and type of economy, as well as classification on a regional basis. These classifications enable you to distinguish developing countries from developed industrialized countries and the former socialist countries of eastern Europe and the former USSR. You also learn how to use Lorenz curves to measure income inequality. Lorenz curves are useful for comparing income inequalities among countries, as well as in one particular country over time.

The Distribution of Income

The World Bank classifies countries into three broad income groups – low income, middle income and high income countries. Developing countries by and large fall into the first and second groupings while developed countries belong to the third group. The majority of the world's population lives in developing countries.

Until recently a widely used and popular classification grouped countries into First, Second and Third World. Developing countries used to be labelled as Third World. Developed industrialized countries were considered as the First World and the former USSR and the socialist countries of Eastern and Central Europe were grouped into the Second World.

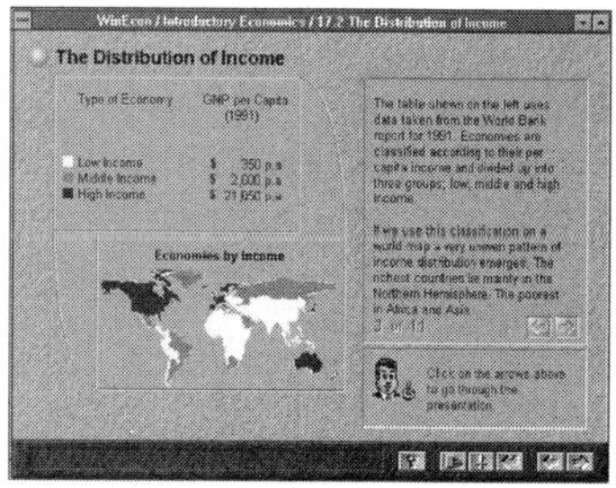

Developing countries are not a homogeneous group of countries but can be classified into different sub-groupings, such as 'newly industrialized countries' (NICs), OPEC (oil exporting) countries, and 'least developed countries' (LDCs). Most of the least developed countries are located in Africa.

Use the WinEcon screen to find out more about the classification of countries and the different sub-groupings of developing countries. Move to the supplementary screen (The Distribution of Income (2)) by clicking the Next Page button. You can then explore the different classifications of countries and see where each is located.

Test what you have learnt about income distribution and classifications

01 **Developing countries used to be classified as (a) Second World, (b) middle income countries, (c) least developed countries, or (d) none of the above.** ☐

02 **Why has the classification of countries into three worlds become obsolete?**

03 **In which continent are most of the least developed countries located?** ☐

04 **Name some countries which are classified as NICs.**

Distribution of Income – The Lorenz Curve

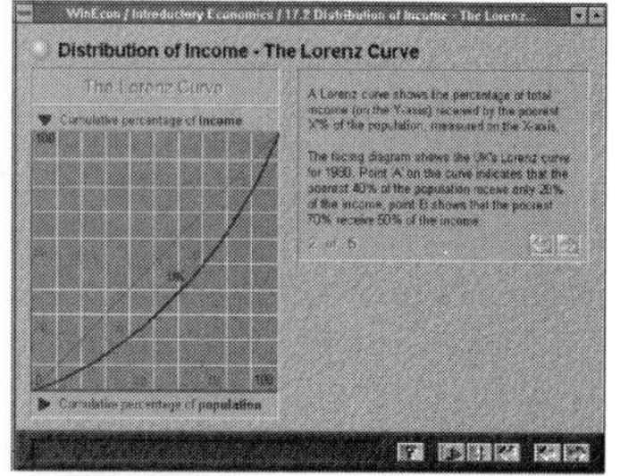

In 1905 the American statistician M. O. Lorenz devised a diagram which is still the one most used to depict income inequality. The Lorenz curve represents the degree of inequality in the distribution of income. It shows the relation between the cumulative percentage of income and the cumulative percentage of population. Click on the screen buttons from card 1 to 6 to see why a Lorenz curve is bowed out. Also use the arrow buttons below card 3 to change the percentage of income belonging to 50 per cent of the population and see the effect on the Lorenz curve.

There are two supplementary screens in this topic. They are both reached with the Next Page button. The first asks you about the poorest countries in the world, those that share the lowest third of the world's income. You can discover where these countries are on a map. Clicking the Next Page button again takes you to the Distribution of Income (3) screen. Here you are shown the Lorenz curves for five different countries.

What Lorenz curves show

On the basis of data in the table on WinEcon screen (3), you are asked to click and drag the countries to the colour coded boxes on the screen graph. Note your answers here.

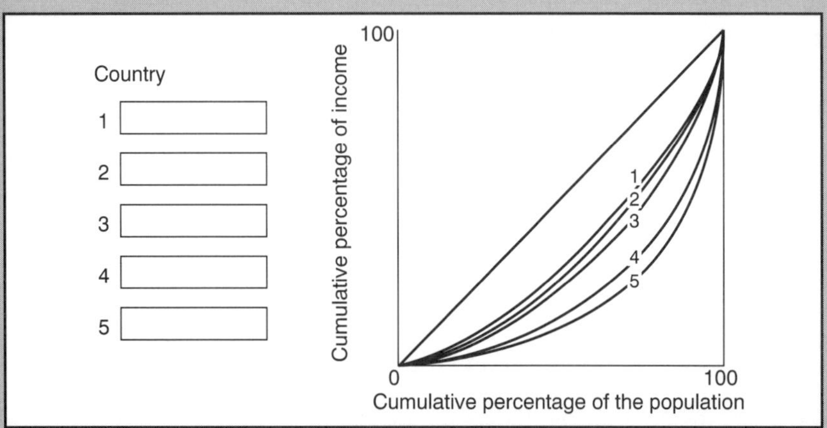

05 **Which two countries have the most unequal distribution of income?**

06 **Define the Lorenz curve.**

07 **What pattern of income distribution would allow a 45 degree line Lorenz curve?**

08 **Why is a Lorenz curve bowed out?**

09 **On the screen diagram showing the UK Lorenz curve for 1980, what percentage of the income is received by the poorest 50 per cent of the population?**

10 **On the basis of the data in the screen table, what percentage of the income is received by the poorest 20 per cent of the population in Brazil and Kenya?**

11 **On the basis of the same data find out what is the income share of the richest 20 per cent of the population in Kenya and Sweden.**

Section 17.3: Measuring Development

In this section you will become familiar with the normative concept of development, which is concerned with the enhancement and improvement of human welfare. You will also learn why growth is not synonymous with development.

Later on you will be introduced to a composite index of development, known as the 'human development index' (HDI). The HDI is a broad measure of development, which is useful for comparing development amongst countries. To construct the HDI, however, you need to know how to measure the 'deprivation index' for different countries. Data in this section will enable you to measure the deprivation index and, later, to construct the HDI for different countries.

Development – Concepts and Measurements

Development is a process of improvement and enhancement of 'human welfare'. Yet there is no unique definition as to what human welfare entails. Human welfare is defined differently by different people. For some, for example, it entails material improvement for life sustenance in terms of food, clothing, housing, minimal education and health, which are considered as basic human needs. For others the definition is broader. It also includes political and social objectives such as democratic freedom and self-esteem arising from feelings of fulfilment and independence.

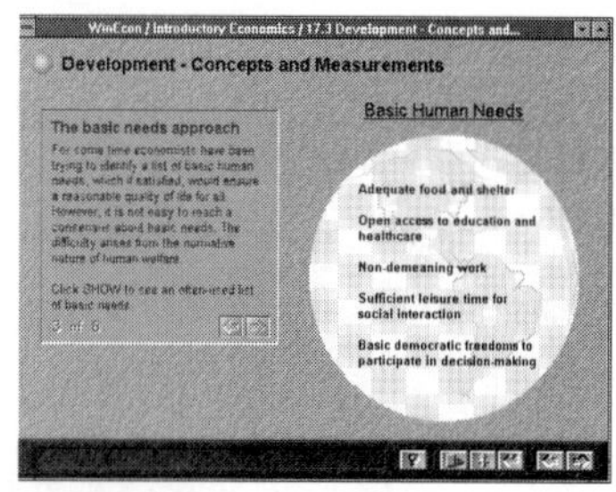

Another source of confusion is the distinction between economic growth and development. There is general agreement that steady growth of GNP per capita is a necessary, but not a sufficient, condition for economic development. GNP per capita is not entirely an appropriate indicator of human welfare. For one thing, it does not reflect the distributional effects of economic growth. It is possible for an increase in GNP per capita to arise from the increased incomes and consumption of a relatively small number of elite individuals, leading to a more uneven income distribution.

Another shortcoming of GNP per capita as an indicator of human welfare relates to non-marketed items and externalities. The value of GNP captures only those economic activities that are transacted in the market. This leaves out non-marketable activities, such as externalities, that affect human welfare.

More details about externalities can be found in the topics Production Externalities and Consumption Externalities in section 7.5.

It also omits goods and services produced and consumed without any market transactions. These include food crops grown and eaten by those who produced them, DIY activities, and the services of housewives. Non-marketed goods may form a higher proportion of the total output of the economy for developing countries.

See what you have learnt about development

12 **Why is development not a value free concept?**

13 **Describe two of the shortcomings of GNP per capita as an indicator of development.**

14 **Name three externalities that reduce human welfare.**

The Basic Development Indicators (1)

You can discover more about the shortcomings of GNP per capita as an indicator of development from the supplementary WinEcon screens in this topic (The Basic Development Indicators (1) and (2)). These screens let you compare how various countries can be ranked by using different criteria of human welfare.

The table on screen (1) initially ranks eight developing countries on the basis of their GNP per capita. In the next stage, 'life expectancy at birth' (LEB) as a social indicator of development is introduced in another column and countries are ranked according to this indicator. You can see that the introduction of this social indicator changes the initial impression about ranking based on GNP per head.

Basic development indicators

On the basis of data in the table on supplementary screen (1), fill in the answers to the following questions.

15 **Which country is seventh in terms of income per head but second in terms of LEB?** ______

16 **Which country is the first in terms of income and fourth in terms of LEB?** ______

The Basic Development Indicators (2)

This screen allows you to explore the world's countries and discover how they are rated, based on a variety of indicators.

The Human Development Index

In this topic you learn how to construct a composite index of development that incorporates income, health and education. This broad indicator of development is called the 'human development index' (HDI). Construction of the HDI is based on deprivation ratios for the three variables involved, namely GDP per capita, life expectancy at birth and the literacy rate.

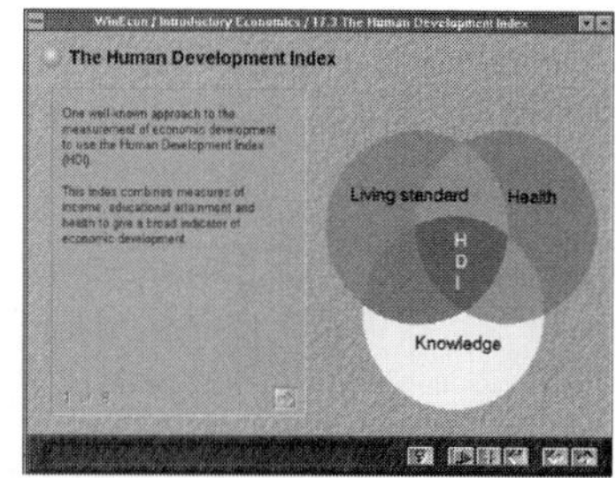

Deprivation is treated as a relative concept and is measured against a desired target. Deprivation ratios are in the range of zero to one. A deprivation ratio of one implies maximum deprivation while a zero ratio suggests no deprivation.

As you work through the screen you should make sure you know how to measure deprivation ratios for health, education and income appropriate to different countries. You see that deprivation ratios for health and education are measured against the best possible target. The deprivation ratio for income, however, is not measured against the world's highest GDP per capita. Instead the level of 'adequate income' is taken as a target.

There are four further screens within this topic. They can be accessed in turn by clicking the Next Page button. Of these, Human Development Index (2) and (3) present data for selected countries as examples. Screen (2) shows how the HDI is calculated, and screen (3) lets you investigate how it can be increased. Moving to the next WinEcon screen (The Human Development Indicator) lets you explore how values of the HDI are made up for many countries in the world.

The final screen (Basic Development Indicators) gives you an opportunity to look in more detail again at some of the countries highlighted in this section.

Comparisons of indicators and the human development index

On the basis of data in the table on screen (2), record the following details.

17 **Deprivation ratio for LEB for Iran and China.** ☐ ☐

18 **HDI for Congo and Sri Lanka.** ☐ ☐

19 **Which country has the lowest HDI?** ____

20 **Which country has the highest HDI?** ____

Section 17.4: The Last Three Development Decades

In this section you learn about some of the main issues which dominated development thinking and development policies in 1960s, 1970s and 1980s.

In the 1960s the main emphasis in development literature was on the acceleration of economic growth through large-scale investment in manufacturing industries. This emphasis on investment in the industrial sector was born out of considerable disenchantment with specialization in the production of primary products in developing countries. A policy of 'import substitution industrialization' was pursued in many developing countries in the 1960s, and even earlier in some others. However, import substitution did not prove to be a successful industrial policy. Instead, 'export-led growth' has acquired great importance as a development strategy since the 1970s.

From WinEcon you learn that developing countries borrowed heavily in the 1970s, during the time of credit abundance and low interest rates. In consequence they faced severe debt crises in the 1980s following the rise in interest rates, which adversely affected their ability to service debt payments.

The Last Three Development Decades

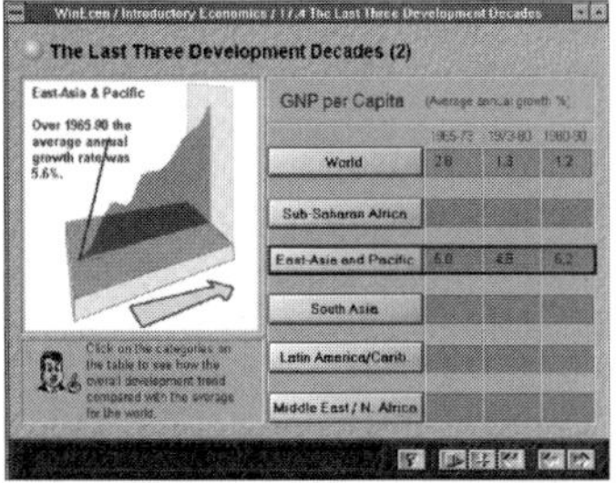

As you work through the text cards on the opening screen you learn that in the 1960s there was great optimism about the future growth prospects of developing countries. Clicking the Next Page button takes you to a supplementary screen, The Last Three Development Decades (2). Here you are asked to state how key groups of developing countries actually fared in comparison with average world growth rates. The screen then gives you the actual figures and shows how the expected growth did not always materialize.

Actual growth 1965–90

On the basis of data in the table on the screen, record answers to the following questions.

21 **Which region of the developing world had the lowest growth rate over the period 1965–90?**

22 **Which region of the developing world had the highest growth rate over the period 1965–90?**

The 1960s

There are four WinEcon screens in this topic. After this introductory screen the Next Page button takes you first to The Problems of Primary Producers, then to Import Substitution Industrialization, and finally to Import Substitution Industrialization – An Example.

The Problems of Primary Producers

Developing countries, historically, were exporting primary products to developed countries and importing manufactured goods from them. This reliance on the production and export of primary products, however, was not conducive to the rapid development and transformation of these economies. One of the characteristics of primary products, which include agricultural as well as mineral products, is their low income elasticity of demand. In this respect primary products contrast with manufactured goods, which have a high income elasticity of demand.

To refresh your memory, see Income Elasticity of Demand in section 2.5.

The different income elasticities imply that as incomes rise the terms of trade turn against exporters of primary products and in favour of exporters of manufactured goods. The terms of trade express the relative price at which a country trades, measured as the price of exports divided by the price of imports.

As you move from card 1 to card 6 on this screen, use the questions and comments on the answers to make sure that you know about the demand fluctuations facing minerals products and the supply uncertainties affecting agricultural goods.

Review what you have learnt about primary production

23 **Define income elasticity of demand.**

24 **Over time, why do the terms of trade tend to turn against exporters of primary products?**

25 **What uncertainties affect the price of minerals and the income of agricultural producers?**

Import Substitution Industrialization

During the 1960s developing countries embarked on a policy of import substitution industrialization (ISI) to alter their production and export structure. There were great expectations that ISI would boost the growth and development prospects of developing countries, eliminating poverty and underdevelopment. You will learn later that this policy was not a successful development strategy.

Import substitution industrialization, it was hoped, would reduce the dependence of developing countries on imported manufactured goods. The strategy was implemented through active state intervention in the economy. Domestic industries were set up and were protected and promoted through tariffs, quotas and a host of fiscal and monetary measures. Import substitution started with the last stage of production (i.e. the assembly of the final products) and was then supposed to advance into the production of intermediate inputs and machinery.

Import Substitution Industrialization – An Example

As buttons are clicked on this WinEcon screen you are provided, in cards 1 to 5, with an example of a step-by-step process of ISI based on the production of cars. You see that in the first stage of the ISI strategy the extent of domestic production is very limited. It is at the second and third stage of ISI that domestic production of parts and components reduces the import dependency of the economy.

Test your understanding of ISI

26 **What were the main objectives of ISI strategy?**

27 **What was the role of the state in the industrialization of developing countries during the 1960s?**

28 **At what stage/stages of the ISI strategy is the import dependence of the import substituting industry reduced?**

The 1970s

After this introduction there are two supplementary WinEcon screens in this topic – The Four Tigers of Asia, and The 1970s: The First Oil-shock, Borrowing and Debt.

Since the 1970s there has been growing disenchantment with import substitution policy. The high level of protection granted to domestic industries in the 1960s gave rise to the establishment of high-cost industries that were not capable of competing in the world market. Furthermore, progress into the production of parts, components and machinery that constituted the second

and third stage of ISI strategy, proved to be far more difficult than was originally assumed. Many parts and components, such as car engines, need to be produced on a large scale to be economic. Most developing countries have relatively small markets because of their limited purchasing power. Thus production of parts and components was not a feasible strategy for the majority of developing countries. This meant that import substituting industries remained highly dependent on imported parts and components.

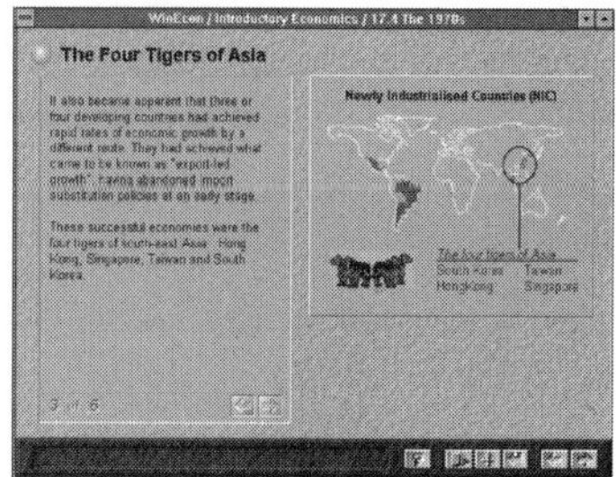

Simultaneously, the 1970s witnessed the success story of 'export-oriented industrialization', based on the performance of the 'four tigers of Asia'. The Four Tigers of Asia screen illustrates some of the salient features of export-led industrialization.

Another major feature of the 1970s was heavy borrowing by developing countries from commercial banks. Move to the next page (The 1970s: The First Oil-shock, Borrowing and Debt) to find out more about borrowing conditions in the 1970s. You will see that the availability of petrodollars, following the first oil-price shock, provided ample scope for borrowing.

Strategy changes in the 1970s

29 **Why did the policy of import substitution, in many instances, get stuck in the first stage?**

30 **In what respects did the ISI strategy differ from that of export-led growth followed by the four tigers?**

31 **What were the two factors that led to heavy borrowing by developing countries during the 1970s?**

The 1980s

In this three-screen WinEcon topic, we discover that the developing countries faced a serious financial crisis during the 1980s. This was, primarily, caused by their inability to pay their debt service payments. From the initial screen, click the Next Page button to learn first about The Debt Crisis, and then Borrowing and Indebtedness.

Test your understanding of the debt crisis

32 **State one of the main causes of the debt crisis in the 1980s.**

Section 17.5: The Direction and Composition of International Trade

This section introduces you to the structure of international trade in goods, with emphasis on the magnitude, composition and direction of trade flows between developed and developing countries.

The first question to address concerns the significance of international trade and trade patterns. To begin with, a country's export composition reflects the country's pattern of specialization in the international market. This stems from countries being endowed with different types of resources and factors of production. OPEC countries, which are mainly located in west Asia, for instance, are endowed with petroleum, which they export to the rest of the world. Developed countries, on the other hand, usually have highly developed and efficient manufacturing industries, which enable them to export industrial goods. Thus a country exports those goods which it can produce efficiently and at a competitive price. Furthermore, international trade allows consumers in different countries to diversify their choice by consuming different types of the same products.

The Direction of International Trade

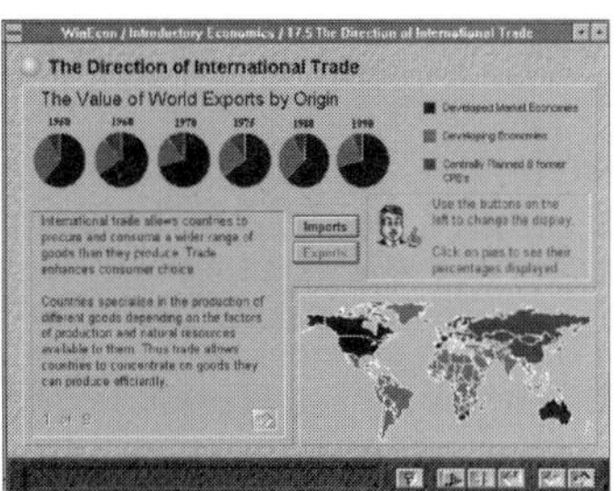

This WinEcon topic provides you with pie diagrams showing the shares of exports and imports by three broad categories of countries: developed, developing and the former socialist countries. You should be familiar with these country groupings, which are described in section 17.2. The pie diagrams cover data for 40 years. By clicking the Exports or Imports button you see that most world trade takes place between developed countries. On screen (2) you also see that most of the developing countries' imports and exports go to or come from developed countries.

Review the direction of international trade

33 Which group of countries accounts for the major share of world export? [ ]

34 Define and provide an example of intra-industry trade.

Click on the pie diagrams showing the value of world imports/exports to answer the following questions.

35 The developed countries [increased/decreased] their share of world exports between 1960 and 1990.

36 **What were the respective shares in world exports of the developed and developing countries in 1990?** ☐ ☐

37 **What has been the lowest percentage of world imports purchased by the developing countries since 1950?** ☐

38 **What were the shares of developing countries in world exports in 1960, 1970 and 1980?** ☐ ☐ ☐

Recap: The Direction of International Trade

This supplementary screen, accessed by clicking the Next Page button, provides a summary of the direction and structure of international trade.

The Composition of International Trade

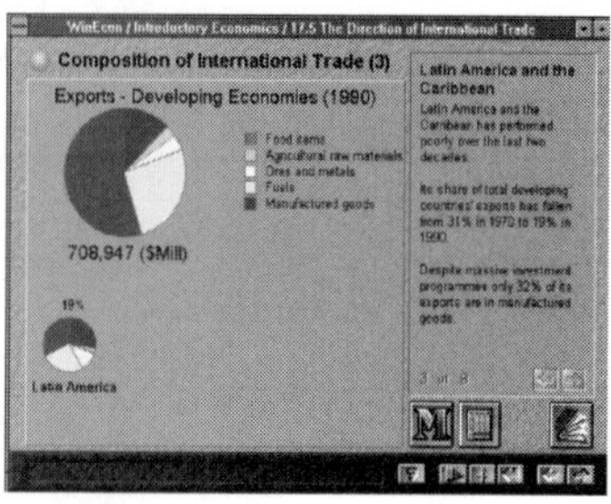

There are five WinEcon screens in this sub-topic. The pie diagrams displayed on screens (1) and (2) show the composition of world exports in 1970, 1980 and 1990. By clicking the pies you see that most world trade is in manufactured goods. Trade in manufactured goods, over time, has also grown faster than that in primary products. You also learn that it is predominantly developed countries that are exporters of manufactured goods.

The Composition of International Trade (3)

As buttons are clicked on this screen you see that food, raw materials and fuel still account for a substantial share of exports by developing countries. However, you will also see that there is substantial variation in the export composition of different groupings of developing countries. It is worth learning about the differences in export composition of various groupings of developing countries because you should be able to compare, for example, the export composition of Latin America and the Caribbean with that of Africa, or West Asia, or any other region. You can find out about these by clicking the pies showing export composition of these regional groupings of developing countries. Screens (4) and (5) let you explore further the variation in trade composition among different countries.

About trade shares

39 **What is inter-industry trade?**

40 **What products constitute the major share of developed countries' exports to developing countries?**

41 What were the respective shares of West Asia, Africa and South and SE Asia in the total exports of developing countries in 1990? [ ] [ ] [ ]

Click on pie diagrams in screen (3) showing the export composition of different groupings of developing countries to answer the following questions.

42 What was the share of food items in total exports of Latin America in 1990? [ ]

43 What were the shares of manufactured goods in total exports from Latin America, Africa and West Asia in 1990?
[ ] [ ] [ ]

44 What were the respective shares of manufactured goods and food items in the total exports of South and SE Asia in 1990? [ ] [ ]

Section 17.6: Summary

In this chapter you have learned that developing countries are, by and large, low income and middle income countries. In contrast, developed countries have high incomes. Lorenz curves are used to compare how equally incomes are distributed in different countries or at different times.

Although it is a convenient measure, GNP per capita has various shortcomings for comparisons of economic development. The Human Development Index is a broad measure of development, encompassing deprivation ratios for GDP per capita, life expectancy at birth and the literacy rate.

The dominant industrialization strategy in most developing countries was based on Import Substitution, which failed to promote competition and efficiency. Hence, the export composition of most developing countries is still mainly comprised of agricultural, food and fuel products. However, a few countries in South-East Asia pursued an export-oriented industrial strategy and are exporters of manufactured goods. Most world trade takes place between developed countries and is in manufactured goods. There are variations in trade composition amongst different groups of developing countries.

Chapter 18:

Welfare Economics

Which output and allocation decisions are best for society as a whole? The analysis of this question forms the subject matter of this chapter. It involves subjective choice, and is said to be normative. By comparison, the rest of economic theory is called positive economics. While disputes about positive statements can, in principle, be resolved by appealing to the evidence, arguments about normative statements usually end in an agreement to differ. The special nature of the subject matter of welfare economics is perhaps the reason why it continues to fascinate many economists.

Contents

KEYWORDS

- Allocative efficiency
- Consumer surplus
- Deadweight loss
- Direct taxation
- Horizontal equity
- Indirect taxation
- Pareto optimum
- Producer surplus
- Social efficiency
- Social surplus
- Social welfare
- Vertical equity

Section 18.1: Introduction

Welfare economics is concerned with comparing different economic situations open to society and saying which is preferable, given specified assumptions. To make some headway in this matter, welfare economists have tried to create generally acceptable criteria by which statements concerning 'best' or 'better than' can be judged. In this way, comparisons become, if not objective, at least generally agreed. You can discover the Pareto criterion for a socially efficient allocation in this chapter, and see examples of its application.

The efficiency criterion forms the basis of much of the analysis in this chapter. Equity criteria are also defined and demonstrated. There are examples of what happens when we try to use them to say which of alternative situations is best. A contrast is shown between efficiency and equity judgements.

We consider what allocation and production decisions should be arrived at by a market economy. Sometimes the decision arrived at depends on choices made by different people in the economy, and their choices are partly dependent on their incomes. The existing distribution of income therefore influences what society considers the optimal allocation of goods.

Market failure, when the economy fails to reach an optimal position, is covered in chapter 7. The present chapter extends that analysis to include public and merit goods. In addition, the concepts of consumer, producer and social surplus are explained and used to compare alternative market positions. Government actions that might bring about an efficiency improvement include making changes to the tax and benefits system of the country. Such changes may also alter the distribution of income, and so may have equity implications. The section which analyses this provides details of the current taxes and benefits in the UK, and also lets you explore the concept of tax incidence.

The analysis of welfare economics builds on many of the concepts that are developed in earlier chapters. Before starting this chapter you should be familiar with demand curves, indifference curves, cost functions, market failure, and the determination of equilibrium in perfect competition and in monopoly.

Section 18.2: Efficiency and Equity Criteria

This section is concerned with efficiency and equity as two approaches to assessing what is best for society as a whole. You find an efficient choice requires that net social benefit is maximized, or that a Pareto optimum is achieved. On the grounds of horizontal or vertical equity, however, different situations may be preferred.

Given the possible conflict between criteria, economic analysis has generally concentrated on assessing whether allocative efficiency, sometimes called social efficiency, is achieved in a particular situation. This is the approach that WinEcon takes. It is convenient to assume that equity considerations are taken care of by the tax/benefit system.

Judgements made by economists about allocative efficiency depend on certain assumptions. The comparisons made in WinEcon are based on being able to value changes in money terms. We abstract from the difficulty of making interpersonal comparisons, and assume the distribution of income remains unaltered.

Allocative Efficiency for Society

When a market is in equilibrium, both buyers and sellers are satisfied with the quantity they are trading at the market price. The market price/output combination, however, may not be the one that society as a whole would choose. This WinEcon topic introduces the idea that to find the best allocation of resources from society's point of view we should distinguish between private and social costs and benefits, and select the output which maximizes 'net social benefit'. When this is achieved, 'allocative efficiency' occurs. WinEcon asks you to complete a statement defining the optimal output for society.

You should remember this statement from section 7.2, topics Allocative Efficiency, and Perfect Competition and Allocative Efficiency.

About society's choice

01 Why might society as a whole not agree with the quantity of good X, Q_x, traded by producers and consumers in equilibrium?

Net Social Benefit

Net social benefit is found as the difference between total social benefit (TSB) and total social cost (TSC). It is, therefore, the vertical distance between the curves in the top diagram on this WinEcon screen. The lower diagram shows the corresponding marginal social benefit (MSB) and marginal social cost (MSC) curves. On card 3, use the buttons to change the amount of good X produced and observe what happens to net social benefit. Note the important result shown by the lower diagram.

There is more information on external production costs and benefits in section 7.5 in the topic What are Social Costs and Externalities?

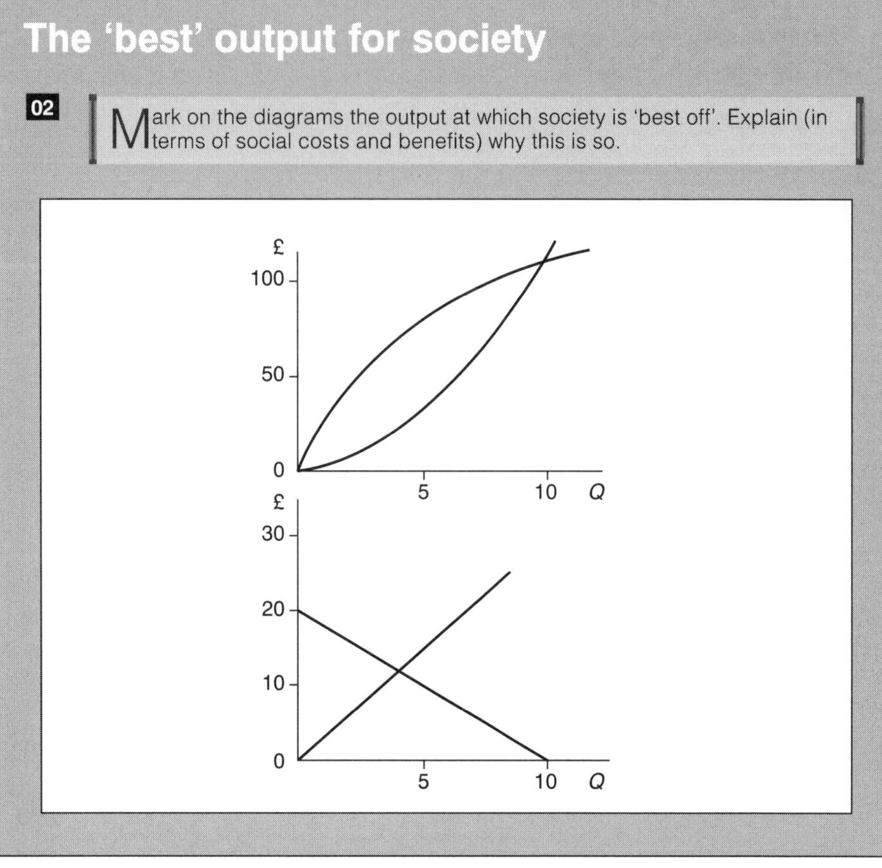

Section 18.2 / Types of Effiency – Quiz
The 'best' output for society
02
Mark on the diagrams the output at which society is 'best off'. Explain (in terms of social costs and benefits) why this is so.
£
100
50
0
5
10
Q
£
30
20
10
0
5
10
Q

Types of Efficiency – Quiz

This screen lets you test your understanding of efficiency concepts. To revise for this quiz you can use the WinEcon topics Allocative Efficiency, and Reasons for Market Failure in chapter 7.

Record what you know about efficiency

03 Once you have completed the screen correctly, record the information in the table below.

Type of efficiency	Involves	Achieved when
	no resources being wasted	
	maximum output from given inputs	
	chosen input mix minimizes costs	
	goods purchased give maximum satisfaction for given income	

The Pareto Principle

The Pareto principle gives us a criterion for judging whether a change is beneficial from the viewpoint of society as a whole. It was first put forward by Vilfredo Pareto, who is sometimes regarded as the founder of modern welfare economics. A Pareto optimum is said to occur if it is not possible to make anyone better off without simultaneously making someone else worse off. The generality of this criterion makes it acceptable to many people but also limits its usefulness because it is powerless to distinguish between many situations.

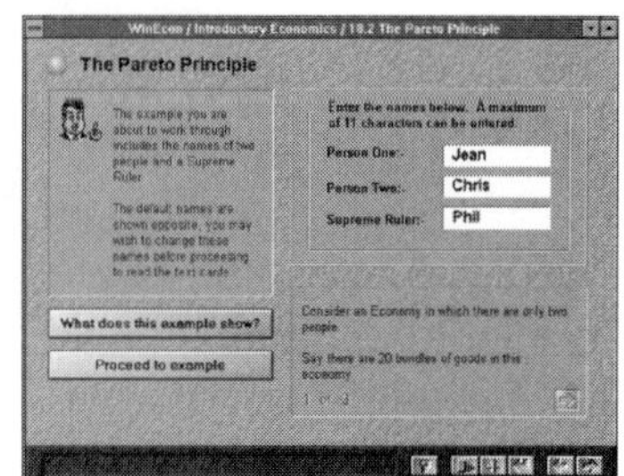

Many interesting questions involve gainers and losers, and when confronted with that kind of choice the Pareto criterion falls silent. We say such alternatives are Pareto non-comparable. The reason is that the Pareto criterion is really only concerned with the efficient use of resources and not at all with the distribution of those resources.

Here WinEcon gives you the opportunity to customize the example you are going to study. You can type names of your choice and delete those given by default. When you proceed through the example you discover how the Pareto criterion operates. It is applied to provide descriptions of the welfare impact of various changes. The situations considered are possible allocations of 20 bundles of goods between two people. As the various points marked on the graph are compared, we judge that a Pareto improvement occurs if one person is made better off without the other being made worse off. Work through the screen cards, clicking the buttons when asked, to discover what comparisons can be made between the various points on the diagram.

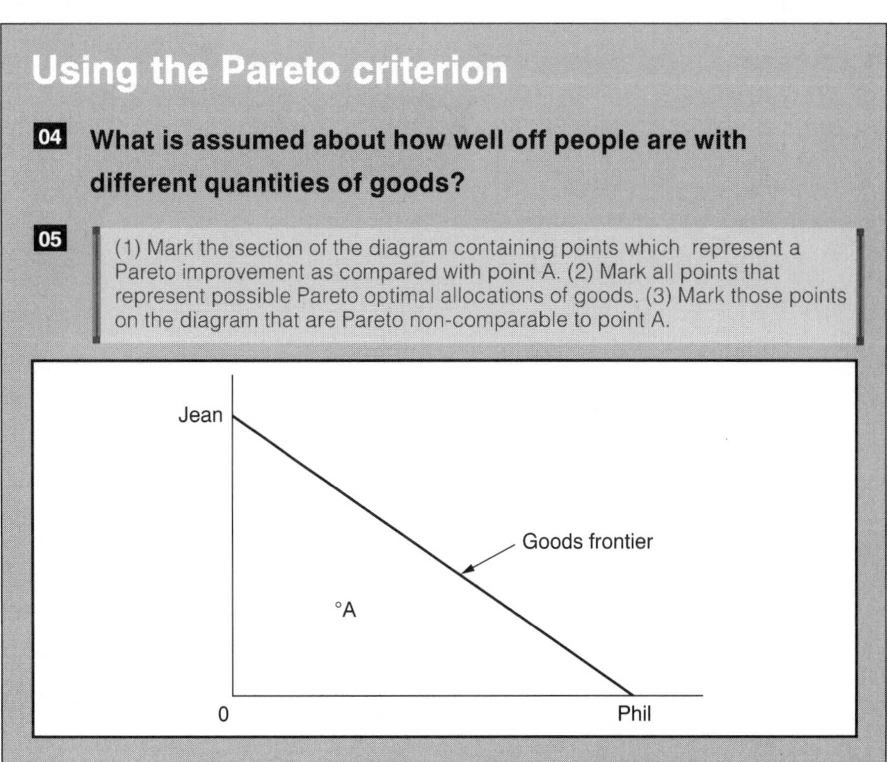

Using the Pareto criterion
04 What is assumed about how well off people are with different quantities of goods?
05 (1) Mark the section of the diagram containing points which represent a Pareto improvement as compared with point A. (2) Mark all points that represent possible Pareto optimal allocations of goods. (3) Mark those points on the diagram that are Pareto non-comparable to point A.
Jean
Goods frontier
°A
0
Phil
What does this example show?

06 What is optimal at a Pareto optimum?

07 At a Pareto optimum it is impossible to reallocate goods so as to

08 Why can't the Pareto criterion be used to compare all changes in society's allocation of goods?

09 Why is more than one Pareto optimum possible?

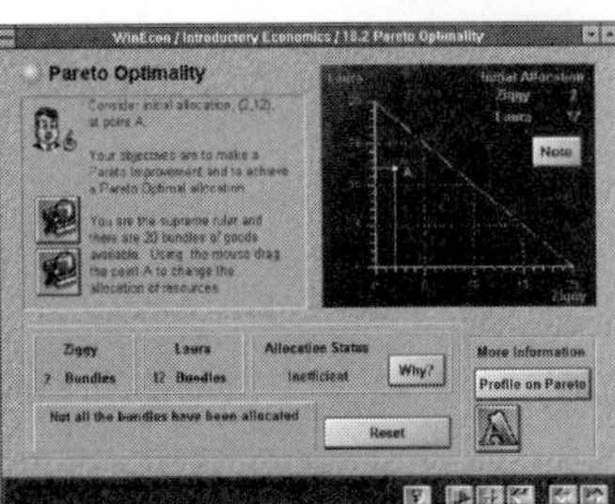

Pareto Optimality

By dragging the point marked A on the WinEcon screen to different positions, you can investigate how various allocations of goods compare with the initial one. Make sure you understand the distinction between a Pareto improvement and a Pareto optimal allocation. Notice there are several buttons available that offer additional information.

Investigate Pareto optimality

Ignore the stated objectives on the screen, and investigate what happens if you drag point A to a place on the frontier where Laura has less goods than in the initial allocation.

10 What are the initial and final allocations?

11 Why is the initial allocation inefficient?

12 Why does the new allocation represent a Pareto efficient allocation, but not a Pareto improvement?

Equity and Efficiency

Considerations of efficiency alone cannot determine the best situation for society. Another criterion used is equity, which is concerned with fairness. We distinguish between horizontal equity, which is the equal treatment of equal people, and vertical equity, which is the appropriately different treatment of different people. Examples follow the definitions on card 1 of this WinEcon topic. They will test your understanding of various of the concepts encountered so far in this topic.

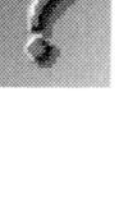

Using equity and efficiency criteria

Work through the examples in WinEcon, answering the questions on the screen and then those below.

13 **Why is there a Pareto improvement in moving from Allocation One to Allocation Two?**

14 **Why is Allocation Three more efficient than Allocation Two?**

15 **Why is the movement from Allocation Three to Allocation Four *not* a Pareto improvement?**

Section 18.3: Production Possibility Frontier

The 'production possibility frontier' (referred to as the PPF) is a graph showing what alternative sets of goods can be produced by an economy having, like any real economy, only limited resources. Simple cases typically involve only two goods – in WinEcon they are beer and pizza – so that the frontier attainable by using all the available resources to produce different mixes of the two goods can be drawn in two dimensions: more pizza implies less beer and vice versa. Points outside (to the north east of) the PPF are unattainable with the present level of resources. Points within it are inefficient, or wasteful, because not all factors of production are being used and more beer and pizza could be enjoyed if they were. Use WinEcon to investigate possible production combinations, and discover reasons for the shape and position of the PPF.

The Five Assumptions for the PPF

In the simple example given in WinEcon, the only variable is labour – capital and resources are both fixed. Relaxing this assumption would complicate matters but would not fundamentally change the analysis. Other assumptions are also used. You can investigate what they are and why they are required by clicking the appropriate buttons.

About the model assumptions

16 **How much of the economy's output is consumed?**

17 **What implication does this have for investment?**

18 **What important simplification arises from the assumption that there is only one person in the economy?**

Production Possibilities

see chapter 4 for more information.

The production possibilities in a particular period of time are limited by the available inputs of labour and capital and the production function. The simple model set out in WinEcon assumes the capital used in producing beer and pizza is fixed, as is the total labour supply in the economy. What can be chosen is the amount of each working day that is spent making each item. The quantities made can then be read from the table at the left of this screen.

Click the Show button on card 2 for an explanation of the information given. Card 3 determines the length of the working day. The only way the output of one of the goods can be increased is by reducing the output of the other. Labour must be transferred between the two industries. Several of the possible combinations for beer and pizza are tabulated as you work through text cards 3 and 4. Notice that the pairs of output possibilities are obtained by deciding how much of one good to produce, seeing how long this takes and hence finding how much time can be devoted to making the other item. The production function then determines how much can be produced in the time available. You are asked to input some of the values for yourself on card 5.

Find the production possibilities

19 You plan to work for 8 hours per day, spending L_c hours baking cakes and L_s hours drawing sketches. Your production function for cakes is:

$$Q_c = 5L_c^{1.2} + L_c.L_s$$

That for sketches is:

$$Q_s = 2L_s^{1.5} + L_c.L_s$$

Complete the table below, rounding values to 1 decimal place.

Hours baking cakes	Hours drawing sketches	No. of cakes	No. of sketches
0			
1			
2			
3			
4			
5			
6			
7			
8			

The Production Possibility Frontier

Once the production possibilities have been calculated, the production possibility frontier can be drawn. The first point is located by assuming that all resources are to be used in beer production. This will result in the production of some beer but, of course, no pizza, which means the first point on the PPF is actually on the beer axis. For the next point some labour is going to be used in pizza production, so beer output will be less than before but pizza output will be greater. This will produce a point on the PPF which is below and to the right (south east) of the first. It can be seen that, by starting with all labour allocated to one of these goods and steadily reallocating labour, the PPF can be drawn up. Use WinEcon to see how this is done. (The values plotted are those from the previous topic.)

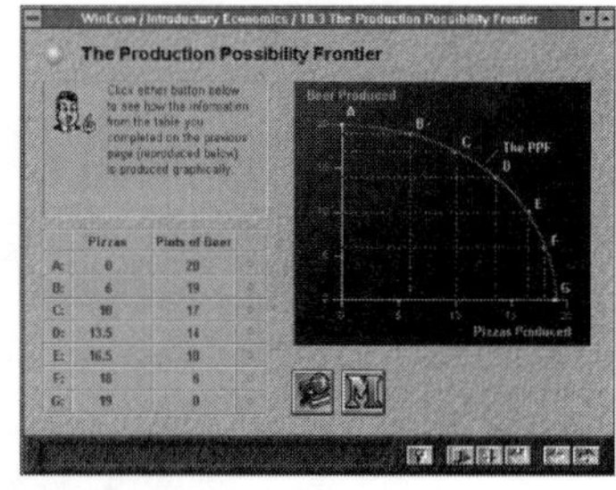

You should notice from the shape of the graph that the trade-off between the two goods that can be produced is not constant. The PPF is curved (bowed away from the origin of the axes of the diagram). This reflects the usual assumption that some of the productive resources are more suited to one industry than the other. If both products are made, the more suitable resources can be employed in their respective industries where they will be more productive than when all resources are used in one or other of the industries only.

Develop your understanding of the PPF

20 **In the beer and pizza example given, how can the curved shape of the PPF be justified?**

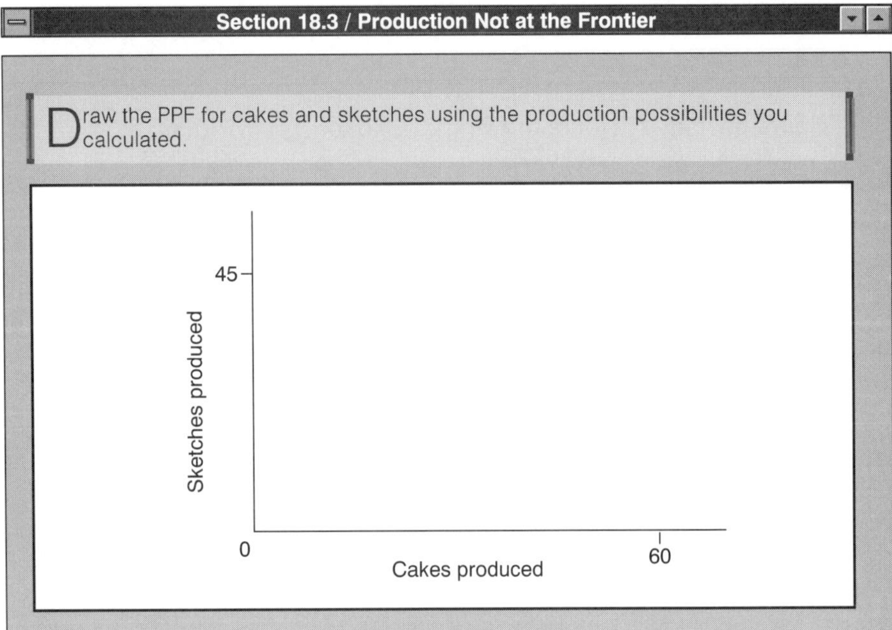
Draw the PPF for cakes and sketches using the production possibilities you calculated.
45
Sketches produced
0
Cakes produced
60

Production Not at the Frontier

Production points within the PPF are not desirable because not all resources are fully and efficiently used.

Comparing the PPF with alternative production combinations

21 **Points on the PPF show combinations that can be produced when all resources are __________. Points on the frontier are __________.**

22 **What are the assumptions about economic behaviour which make us conclude that points within the PPF are not desirable?**

23 Move to card 2 on this screen and drag the point T so you can record the appropriate information in the table below.

Point	Beer produced	Pizzas produced	Use of resources
Initial			
On PPF		8	
On PPF		0	
On PPF	0		
On PPF	Equal to no. of pizzas	Equal to no. of beers	

24 What can you say about the number of items produced if the economy is operating efficiently and producing approximately equal amounts of beer and pizza, by comparison with if it were to use all its resources to produce just one of the items?

25 Drag the point T outside the PPF. What do you discover about the quantity of resources used?

Changing the PPF

Here you can use WinEcon to investigate two ways in which the PPF may move outwards.

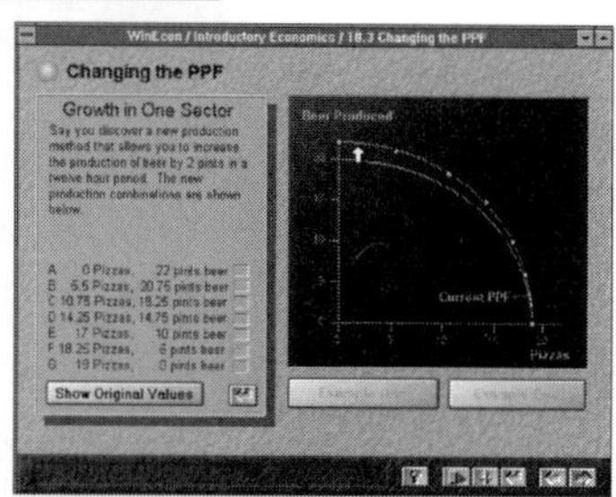

Why the PPF changes

26 What is needed for the PPF to shift outwards?

27 What may bring this about?

28 What may cause the PPF to pivot outwards?

Section 18.4: Public and Merit Goods

If a good posesses certain key characteristics, it is said to be a public good, while different features identify other commodities as merit goods. Both public and merit goods cause market failure.

For more details see the topic Reasons for Market Failure in section 7.3.

You can discover the key characteristics of each of these special types of goods in this section, and analyse how much of such goods should be produced. You investigate the problem of free riders, and can test your understanding of the appropriate classification of goods with quick quizzes.

Public versus Private Goods

The basic distinction between public and private goods lies in how many people can enjoy the consumption benefits of just a single item. This is explained, with examples, in WinEcon.

Consumption of public and private goods

29 Fill in the grid.

	Each unit of a good which is	
	public	private
is consumed by		

Key Characteristics of a Public Good

The key characteristics of a public good are succinctly described by the terms on this WinEcon screen. Click the buttons to discover their meaning, then use the quiz to test your understanding.

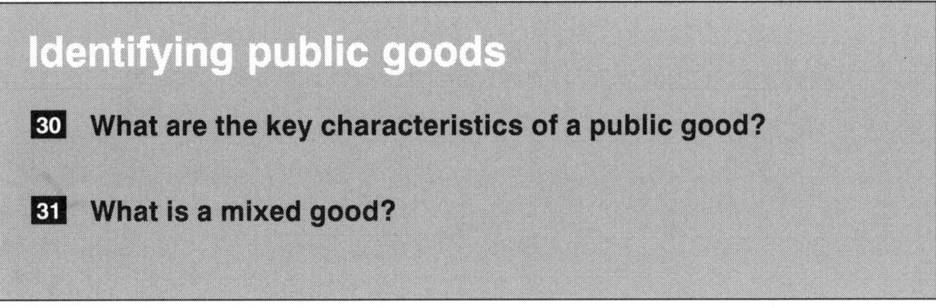

Identifying public goods

30 What are the key characteristics of a public good?

31 What is a mixed good?

Public Goods and Free Riders

You can use WinEcon to discover how the free rider problem arises. You find that if public goods are provided by a private market it is rational for some consumers not to buy any of the goods, but to use what is bought by other people.

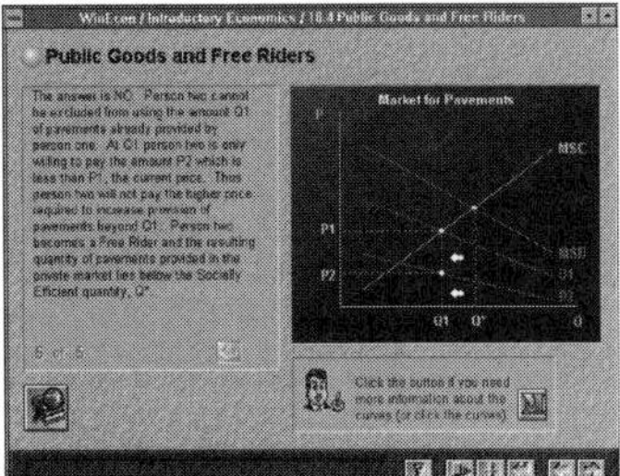

The analysis used to determine the socially efficient level of output and that which would be provided in a free market adds the individual demand curves vertically. This is because at any level of output everyone in society benefits from it. The method contrasts with the usual horizontal summation of demand curves. Notice the conclusion that the socially efficient output of a public good is larger than the output that the free market will provide.

Understanding the analysis

32 **Look at the diagram on card 3 concerning the public good, pavements. Consider the point where marginal social cost (MSC) and marginal social benefit (MSB) intersect. How is that value on the MSB function obtained? (Hint: you can get help by clicking on the curves of the diagram.)**

33 **How is MSC determined?**

34 **How would the output of pavements be determined if the market were a private one? (Hint: you can see how demand in a private market would be aggregated in The Product Demand Curve topic in section 2.2.)**

How Much of a Public Good to Produce

This WinEcon topic lets you discover possible problems that may arise in estimating the appropriate amount of a public good to be produced. Information on the current solution is also available.

How output is chosen

35 **What determines how much of a public good is produced?**

Key Characteristics of a Merit Good

Merit goods (and bads) are shown to arise because individuals are not the best judges of their own welfare, or because they do not account for externalities in deciding how much of a good to consume. Use the WinEcon quick quiz to check that you can recognize merit goods and bads when they occur.

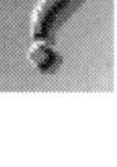

About merit goods

36 **If it were left to private provision, on average, people would spend too ________ on education. When there is state provision of education, children educated in private schools have (on average) too ________ spent on their education. Complete and explain these statements.**

Section 18.5: Consumer and Producer Surplus

The concepts of consumer and producer surplus allow economists to make welfare comparisons between alternative situations. By considering the changes in these surpluses we can say whether consumers or producers or both are better off.

WinEcon's animated examples show how consumer surplus arises and how it changes for different demand curves. The concept is explained and measured both for an individual and for the market. Producer surplus is also defined, and the two are added to obtain social surplus.

Understanding Consumer Surplus

When consumers buy several units of a good, the total price they pay may underestimate what the goods are worth to them. To find their full value we must add the consumer surplus generated by the purchase to the total price paid. Consumer surplus is the extra benefit which someone feels they have gained from a purchase. The example on the WinEcon screen shows how consumer surplus arises.

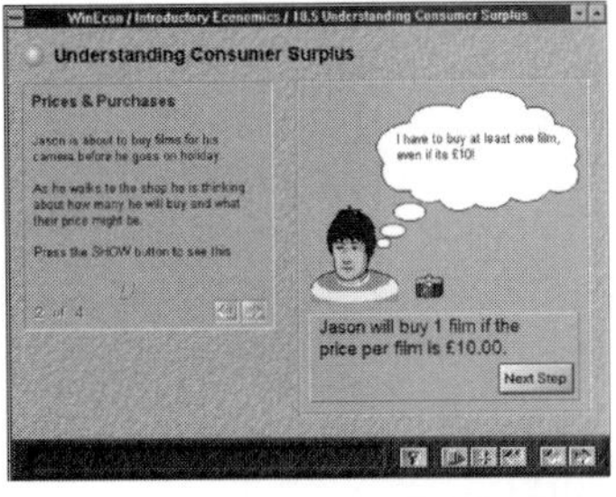

On card 2 of this screen you can see what Jason is thinking by clicking the Next Step button. A summary of what he would buy is available in spreadsheet form on card 3. After you have clicked to display a chart of Jason's consumer surplus on card 4, try the short quiz to check you understand the concept.

Consumer surplus calculations

37 **How many films should Jason purchase to maximize his consumer surplus? Can you draw any general conclusion from this answer?**

38 **If I refuse to pay more than £1.70 for a pint of beer, but I will buy three pints at the current price of £1.20 each, how much consumer surplus will I enjoy with my three pints? What might cause your estimate to be slightly wrong?**

39 Draw Jason's demand curve for films and mark on it his consumer surplus. What would happen to his surplus if the sale price of films were reduced to £1.50 per film?

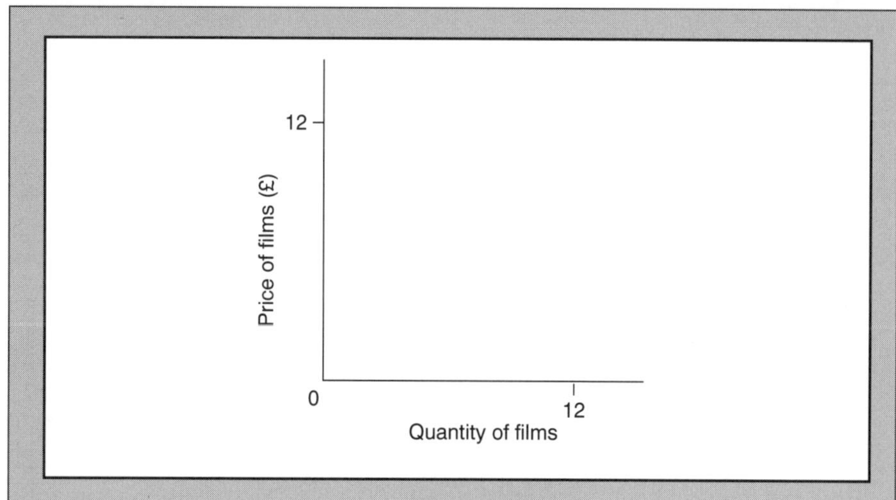

Individual Consumer Surplus

The relationship between marginal utility and demand (explained in the topic Utility and Demand in section 3.3) implies that consumer surplus can also be defined in terms of utility. The Change button at the bottom right of this screen lets you switch the labelling on the diagram to obtain alternative descriptions of areas marked on the graph shown. Another button gives access to Alfred Marshall's original definition of the term 'consumer surplus'.

Consumer surplus in terms of utility

40 **Define individual consumer surplus in terms of that person's utility.**

41 **What was the original definition of consumer surplus?**

Market Consumer Surplus

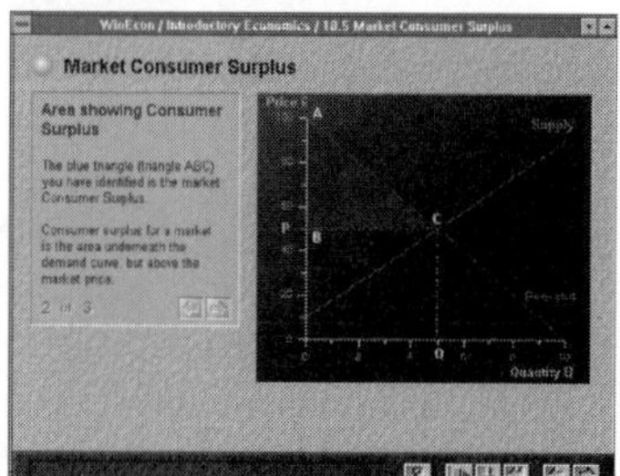

Since individual's demand curves can be summed to obtain the market demand curve, as shown in The Product Demand Curve topic in section 2.2, this allows us to define consumer surplus for the market. Notice that while the graph explaining individual consumer surplus showed blocks for separate units of the good, the total quantities purchased in the market as a whole are so much greater that the aggregated diagram appears smooth.

Consumer surplus when demand is linear

42 **Explain why the area under the demand curve, but above the market price, represents consumer surplus.**

43 **For a straight line demand curve, if the market price is £5.50 and the quantity sold is 8.5 units, what is the consumer surplus if the demand curve intersects the vertical axis at *P* = £7.50?**

44

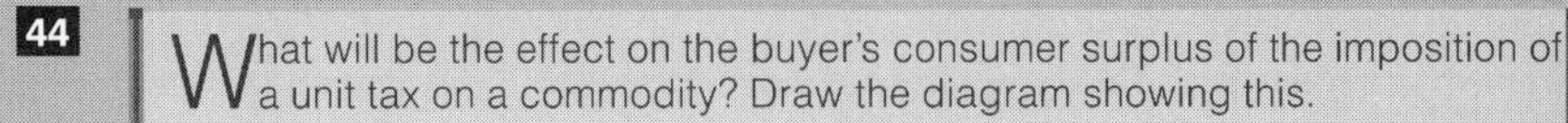

What will be the effect on the buyer's consumer surplus of the imposition of a unit tax on a commodity? Draw the diagram showing this.

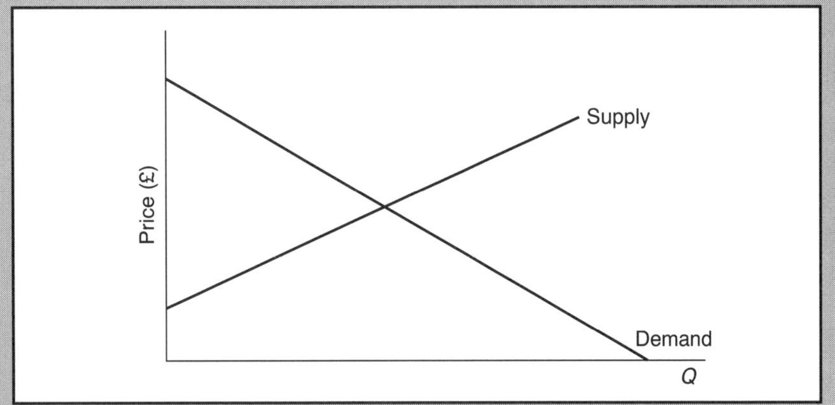

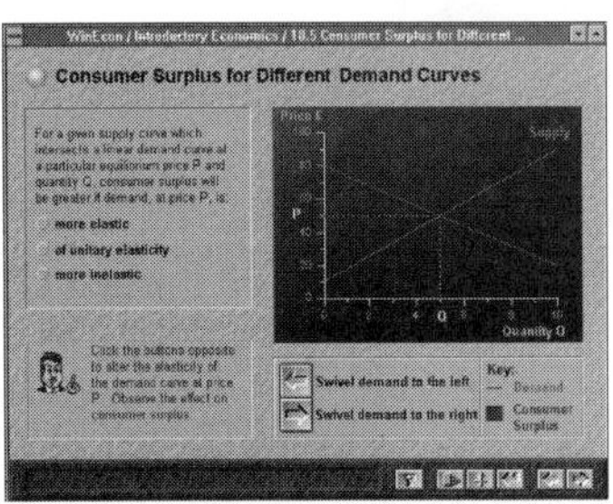

Consumer Surplus for Different Demand Curves

Since consumer surplus is found from the demand curve, altering the shape of the demand curve, and hence its elasticity at the current market price, will change consumer surplus. This screen lets you investigate the effects of different kinds of changes.

Some special demand curves

45 **If the demand curve is vertical, what can you say about consumer surplus?**

46 **If the demand curve is horizontal, what can you say about consumer surplus?**

Defining Producer Surplus

Producer surplus is defined in an analogous way to consumer surplus. It is the amount by which the revenue received exceeds production costs for each of the units of output produced. Any fixed costs in the short run are incurred as the first unit is produced, while the production costs for successive units of output are represented by the MC curve. Notice we identify as producer surplus something that is already familiar to us under a different name.

Measuring producer surplus

47 **What is the other name for producer surplus?**

48 Mark producer surplus on this diagram, as shown on card 4 of the screen. How else might it be measured?

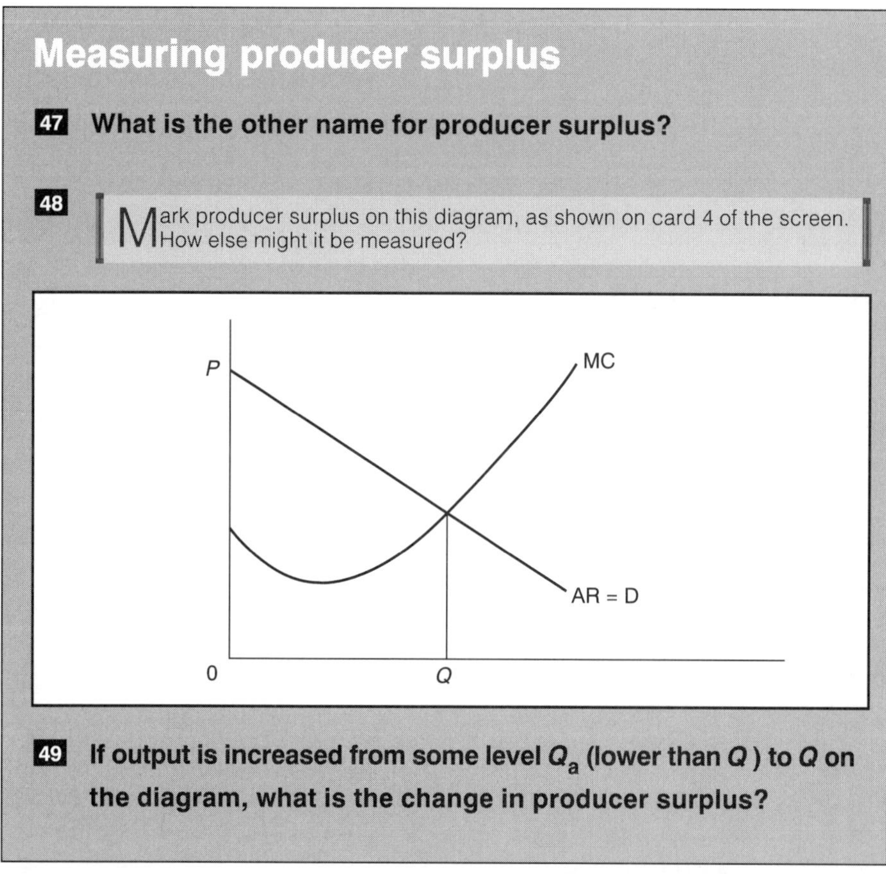

49 **If output is increased from some level Q_a (lower than Q) to Q on the diagram, what is the change in producer surplus?**

Producer Surplus in Different Markets

We know that the extent to which producers can make long-run profits is different under alternative market conditions. It follows that the amount of producer surplus in the long run is different under competition than in monopoly.

About producer surplus

50 **In equilibrium, a monopolist will** not/still **have some producer surplus. In equilibrium, a perfectly competitive firm will** not/still **have some producer surplus.**

51 Mark producer surplus on this diagram for a profit maximizing monopolist. Is this equal to profit?

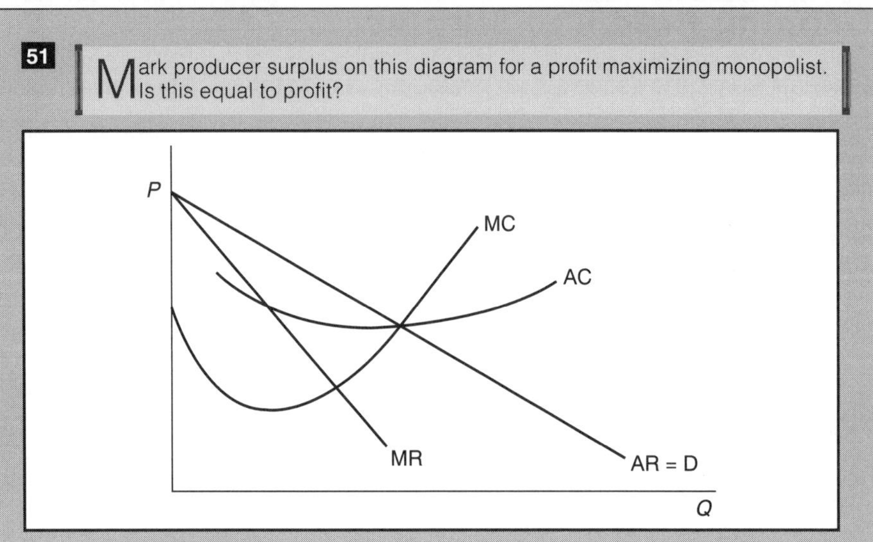

Social Surplus

Economists wish to assess the welfare effects of changes on society as a whole. Since society is comprised of both consumers and producers, the overall effect can be gauged by taking together the consumer surplus and the producer surplus. This gives us social surplus.

About social surplus

52 Social surplus is the sum of

Label the diagram to show consumer surplus, producer surplus, and social surplus at the level of output *Q*.

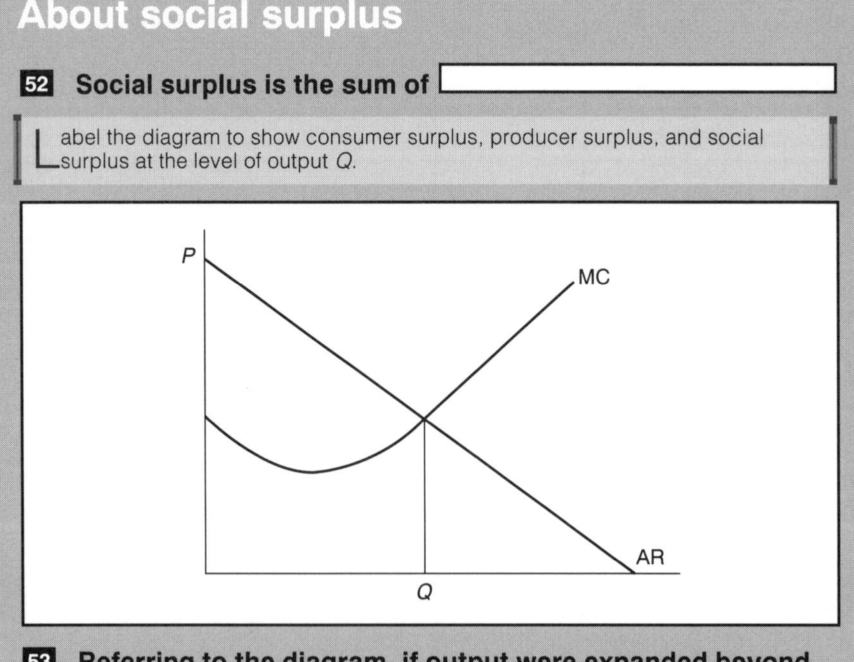

53 Referring to the diagram, if output were expanded beyond *Q*, what would happen to consumer surplus? What would happen to producer surplus? And what would happen to social surplus?

Section 18.6: Welfare Effects of Monopoly

The Competitive Industry

This screen is a reminder of how equilibrium price and output are determined in a perfectly competitive industry.

Social Surplus in Competition

By considering each of the surpluses separately, we find how to measure social surplus in a perfectly competitive market.

Note your result

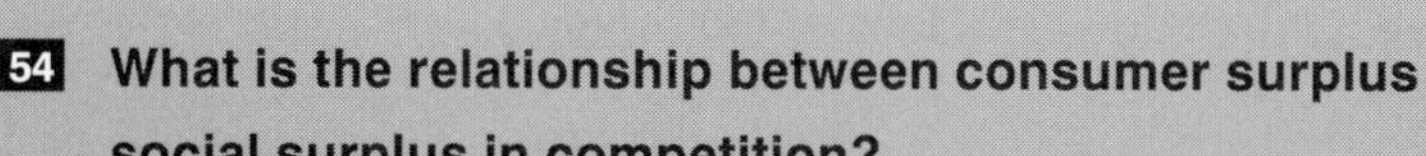

54 What is the relationship between consumer surplus and social surplus in competition?

Social Surplus in Monopoly

The analysis of how equilibrium output is determined under monopoly should already be familiar to you. This WinEcon screen steps you through the various curves that are required. Once you have found the equilibrium output you can reveal areas that represent consumer and producer surplus.

Surplus in Monopoly

Mark consumer surplus, producer surplus, and social surplus on the diagram.

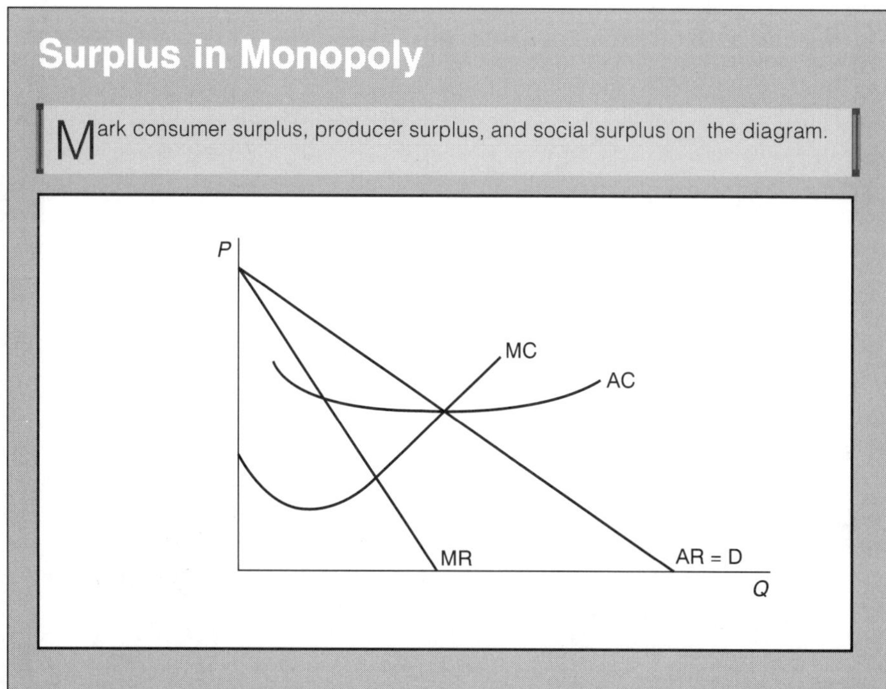

Changes Resulting from Monopolization

Because of the horizontal demand curve each faces, when perfectly competitive firms choose their outputs to maximize profits and produce where MC = MR, they set price equal to marginal cost since MR = AR. Providing there are no externalities, firms in perfect competition produce at a socially efficient level of output. In this situation MSC = MC and is also equal to price which equals MSB, as price measures what people are willing to pay to have the last unit of the good produced.

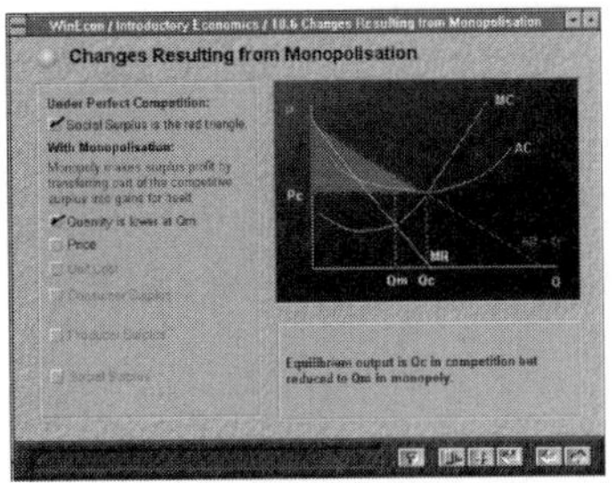

This WinEcon screen summarizes the changes that result from monopolization of an industry. The model assumes that costs remain the same, and we see that the monopolist chooses to produce a lower output than the perfectly competitive industry. This is accompanied by a price which is above marginal cost, a signal of monopoly power. The reduction in social surplus is identified with the deadweight loss of monopoly.

Test your understanding of monopoly

55 **What effect does monopolization of a competitive industry have on (a) market price, (b) market quantity, (c) consumer surplus, (d) producer surplus and (e)social surplus?**

Draw a diagram showing a competitive industry, then add the MR curve which arises if the industry is monopolized as it stands. Indicate the competitive and monopolistic equilibria.

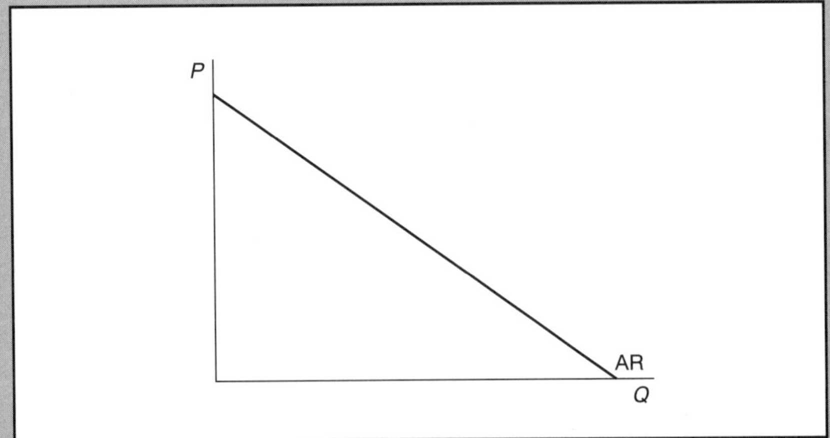

56 **On your diagram, what are the features which show (a) a reduction of allocative efficiency, and (b) a redistribution of income?**

Deadweight Loss of Monopoly – An Alternative Measure

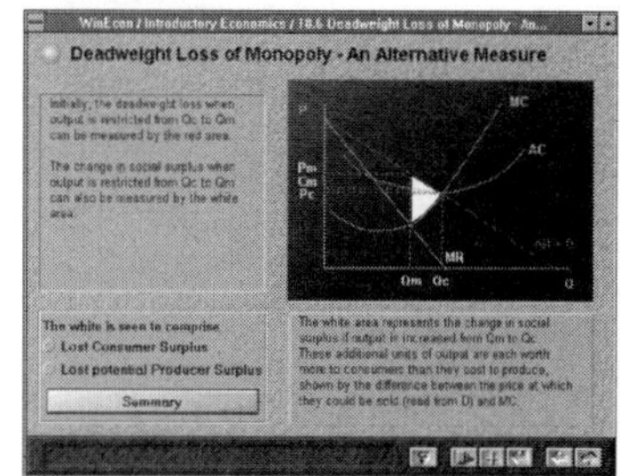
Deadweight Loss of Monopoly - An Alternative Measure
Summary

The deadweight loss of monopoly arises because the market demand curve is downward sloping and, assuming the industry costs are the same as under perfect competition, a monopolist restricts output. As output is reduced from Q_c to Q_m (see the screen diagram), there is a loss of social surplus as indicated by the white area. The deadweight loss represents the social cost of monopoly power.

Monopolization of a Constant Cost Industry

When an industry has constant returns to scale the diagram simplifies somewhat, with long-run average and marginal costs both being represented by the same horizontal line. Use the WinEcon screen to check you understand, and can apply, the concepts of the various surpluses and the deadweight loss of monopoly.

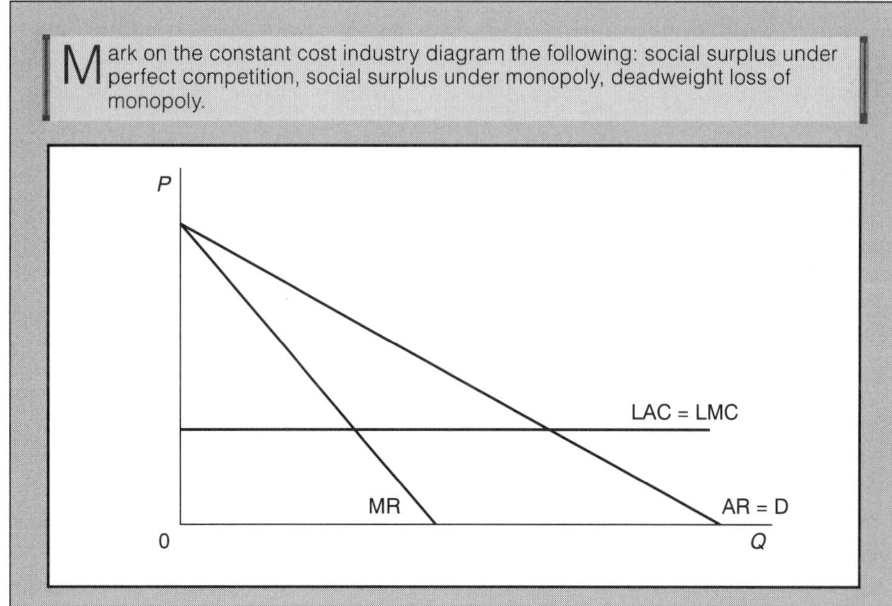
Mark on the constant cost industry diagram the following: social surplus under perfect competition, social surplus under monopoly, deadweight loss of monopoly.
P
LAC = LMC
MR
AR = D
0
Q

Section 18.7: Taxation, Benefits and Tax Incidence

This section of WinEcon provides information about all the main kinds of taxes and transfer payments in operation in the UK. You learn about the way different taxes operate, and discover the principles of a good taxation system. Although a particular person is liable to pay a tax, he or she may be able to pass on at least part of it to someone else, perhaps by charging them a higher price. We analyse the extent to which this happens by looking at tax incidence.

Information about how income is distributed in different countries is available in the topic Distribution of Income – The Lorenz Curve in Chapter 17.

The tax benefit system is often presumed to be the appropriate medium for dealing with equity considerations. Income can be redistributed by taxing some members of society more than others, and also by making benefit payments to people who fulfil certain criteria, either of need or of family circumstances.

Types of Tax in the UK

A tax is a compulsory levy payable to central or local government. Criteria for liability to the tax must be laid down. They are different for different kinds of taxes. This WinEcon screen lets you discover information about the various types of taxes: (direct, indirect and wealth taxes) that exist in the UK.

Direct taxes such as income tax and national insurance are often only charged on incomes above a certain level. Fiscal drag is said to exist when a tax allowance or threshold is fixed in nominal (money) terms and is not automatically adjusted for inflation. In this way, as time goes on, the real value of the allowance falls and the effective starting point at which the tax is levied falls with it. This was a regular feature of the UK income tax system until tax allowances became index-linked to retail prices. Even then the government was able explicitly to override the index-linking provisions, which they have sometimes done as a way of increasing direct taxation without risking the political opposition which would follow an increase in the rate of income tax.

Sources of Tax Revenue

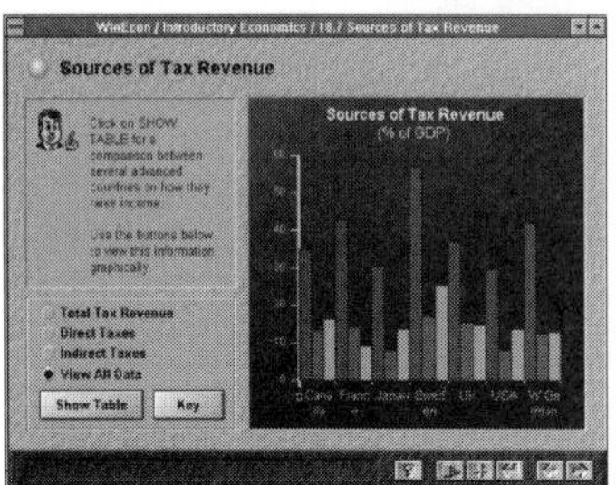

Governments in different countries raise their tax income in different ways. This WinEcon screen gives information for several advanced economies on the proportions of their tax revenue raised by direct and by indirect taxation.

Progressive, Regressive and Proportional Taxes

Progressive taxation reduces post-tax differences in income by comparison with pre-tax differentials, so there is greater equality in the distribution of incomes after tax. An example of this is an income tax system that charges a higher rate of tax on higher incomes.

Regressive taxation does the opposite: it increases post-tax differences. Indirect taxation may be regressive if it is levied on basic commodities such as food, fuel and housing. People with lower incomes spend a higher proportion of their income on such items than richer persons, and so may pay a higher proportion of their income in tax if, say, an *ad valorem* tax is charged on these goods.

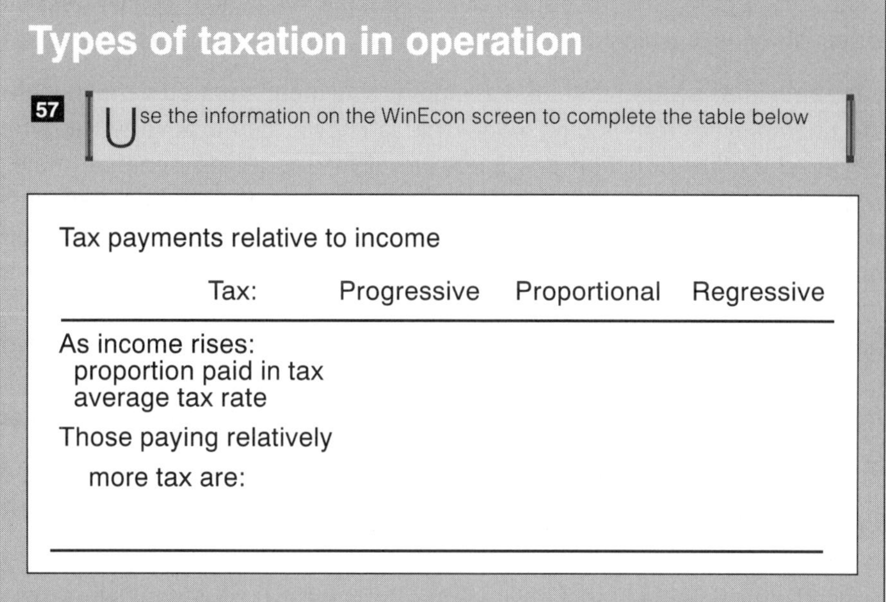

Types of taxation in operation

57 Use the information on the WinEcon screen to complete the table below

Tax payments relative to income

Tax:	Progressive	Proportional	Regressive
As income rises: proportion paid in tax average tax rate			
Those paying relatively more tax are:			

Requirements of a Good Tax System

This WinEcon screen sets out the principles of taxation against which each tax can be judged. There is often some trade-off between the various principles. For example, the benefit principle may conflict with the aims of horizontal and vertical equity, which was a reason for the unpopularity of the Community Charge or Poll Tax. It is very difficult in a civilised society to insist that the poor should pay for the benefits they receive. A tax (VAT) on fuel is convenient to the government and difficult to evade, but it is argued that it is inequitable since the poor spend a much higher proportion of their incomes on fuel than do the rich. Efficiency of taxation is that the tax should achieve its intended aim without side effects, while equity in taxation means that a tax is based on the taxpayer's ability to pay. An income tax is usually based on ability to pay, and so is equitable, but if it has serious disincentive effects on working it may not be efficient.

Tax avoidance and evasion are different reasons for not paying taxes. The first is legal, but the second is not. Tax avoidance involves looking for ways of reducing or not having to pay tax, such as avoiding inheritance tax by giving away property during one's lifetime. Obviously the higher the rate of tax the more time and energy is devoted to avoiding it. Tax evasion involves concealing assets or incomes which are taxable, which is criminal since there is a legal duty to report such taxable items to the taxation authorities.

Benefit Payments

Benefit payments, also called transfer payments, are made by the government to eligible claimants. They provide a means of redistributing income to members of society who are deemed appropriate recipients because of their age, ill health, family circumstances or other reason. This

WinEcon screen provides details of the benefits available in the UK and the circumstances in which they are paid.

It is sometimes argued that the rules governing means-tested benefits deter the unemployed from finding work. This is known as the poverty trap. It is triggered by the reduction or withdrawal of means-tested benefits (mainly social security transfer payments) in response to increases in a claimant's income, perhaps from finding some work. Obviously any reduction in benefit means that, in total, the claimant receives less than the full increase in income, but in many cases the benefit cut is so great that the claimant is actually worse off as a result of the notional increase in his/her income. Not only unemployment benefit but also free NHS prescriptions, infant milk and free school meals may be lost. As a result, those in receipt of means-tested benefits have no incentive to take employment.

What is Tax Incidence?

A distinction is made in this topic between the person who nominally pays a tax, its formal incidence, and the person who finally pays it after it has possibly been passed on, its effective incidence. An illustrative example of a value added tax is given.

As you work through the WinEcon cards you discover how VAT is added to the price of both intermediate goods and final goods. Although the formal incidence of VAT is on producers, the effective incidence of the tax is on the purchasers of the final goods, since they pay a price which includes VAT.

VAT example

58 **A truck load of wood is sold for £1,000 (excluding VAT). A furniture producer adds value worth £2,500 (including profit) as the wood is manufactured into tables. If VAT at 17.5% is chargeable at each stage, what will be the total amount paid by the purchasers of the tables?**

Unit Tax – An Example of Tax Incidence

Work through the screen cards and tackle the questions below.

Tax incidence

59 **Why can we analyse the effect of a unit tax by shifting the supply curve on a diagram?**

The diagram shows a market initially in equilibrium at e_1, and in equilibrium at e_2 after the imposition of a unit tax. Mark on the diagram the size of the unit tax, the amount of the tax revenue, and the deadweight loss to society of the tax.

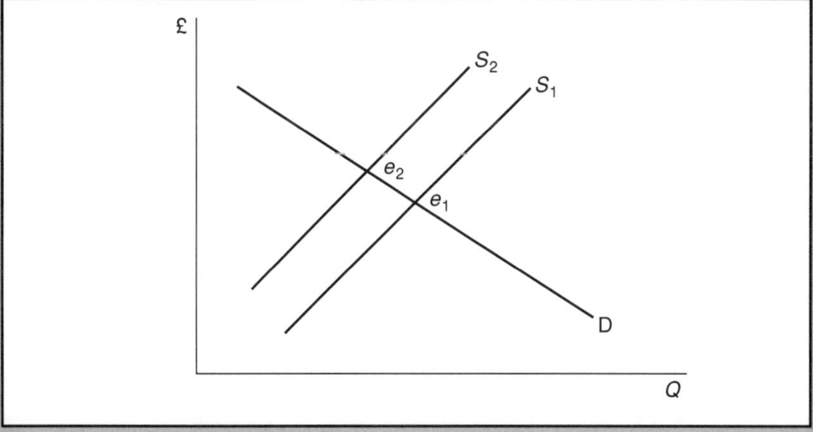

60 **In the above diagram, what can you say about the quantity purchased and the price in the pre- and post-tax situations?**

61 **What can you say about the incidence of the tax in the diagram above?**

62 **What is the incidence of a unit tax if demand is perfectly elastic, and if it is perfectly inelastic?**

Section 18.8: Summary

Welfare economics is often appropriate for analysing questions containing the word 'should', which asks for a value judgement, or for comparing situations and saying which is best. For example, if you are given the title "Should monopolies be regulated?", as well as explaining the term regulated and analysing how monopolies operate you are required to make a judgement. To do this you should use the efficiency criteria of welfare economics, comparing the change in social welfare between two different situations, describing the change in social surplus, and explaining the term deadweight loss. You have learnt the basic analysis required in this chapter.

Welfare economics can be applied to a wide variety of issues, and there will usually be other WinEcon topics that you need to study also in conjunction with the basic analysis. For example, in your analysis of "Should monopolies be regulated?" you will also find the following topics helpful: UK regulation of Private Monopolies & Oligopolies, Regulation of Privatized Utilities, Perfect Competition and Monopoly Compared.

Welfare economics provides you with efficiency and equity criteria which can be applied to judge which situation is preferable from the viewpoint of society as a whole. As in chapter 7 Regulation of Markets and Market Failure we recognize that the output where MSC = MSB is optimal from society's point of view and we see this as equivalent to requiring net social benefit to be maximized.

According to the Pareto principle an improvement in allocative efficiency occurs if someone is make better off without anyone else being made worse off. We see that situations involving gainers and losers are Pareto non-comparable.

Much of our welfare economic analysis is concerned with choosing positions which are optimal from an efficiency point of view. Equity is usually assumed to be taken care of through the taxation and benefit payments system.

The principle of horizontal equity is concerned with ensuring equal people receive equal treatment, while vertical equity deals with providing appropriately different treatments to different people.

The production possibility frontier represents the maximum possible combinations of goods that can be produced with the resources available to the economy. Efficient production positions occur on the frontier. Technological change or economic growth may cause the production possibility frontier to shift.

Public goods are items whose consumption benefits can be enjoyed simultaneously by many people. The analysis of how much should be produced involves the vertical summation of demand curves. If such goods are provided by the market system, less than the optimal quantity is chosen. The problem of free riders also occurs. Merit goods arise when people are not the best judges of their own welfare and choose to consume either more or less of a good than society deems beneficial for them.

Consumer surplus is an extra benefit which consumers feel they have gained if they pay less than the maximum amount they were prepared to pay for items they buy. It is measured by the area between the demand curve and the price line. Producer surplus is measured by the area between the price line and marginal cost. As we consider the effects of changes in output, changes in producer surplus are identical with profit changes. The sum of consumer and producer surplus gives us social surplus. This provides a useful indicator of whether a proposed change is worthwhile. In the context of monopoly, the deadweight loss can be interpreted as the loss of social surplus.

The main types of taxes are direct, indirect and wealth taxes. A proportional tax is shown to absorb a constant proportion of income, while a progressive tax takes a higher proportion of income as income rises and a regressive tax takes relatively more from those on lower incomes. A good tax system has requirements such as horizontal and vertical equity, convenience and efficiency. The various objectives are unlikely to be all mutually consistent. The concept of tax incidence distinguishes between the person who formally pays a tax and the one on whom it eventually falls if it is passed on, for example as a higher price. Benefit payments are made to persons who qualify for them, for example the retired, the unemployed and those with children. The payments may or may not be means tested.

Chapter 19:

Insurance and Risk

Our knowledge of economic matters is rather like our knowledge of the weather – highly specific and uncertain. We may know whether we are employed or unemployed today, but we have no certainty about our employment prospects for the future. Yet decisions we make today, such as the purchase of an item on credit require us to make some sort of judgement about our future earning powers. This demonstrates that we do make decisions in the face of uncertainty, although we may not fully understand what we are doing. This chapter helps to unravel the issues involved in evaluating risk and provides a framework to assist decision making.

Contents

KEYWORDS

- Diversifiable risk
- Diversification
- Forward markets
- Futures markets
- Portfolio
- Probability
- Risk
- Risk aversion
- Uncertainty

Section 19.1: Introduction

The main theme of this chapter is the handling of risk. We look at how risk affects the kind of decisions people make and we consider the main ways in which the costs of bad outcomes can be reduced. The issue is complicated by the fact that people are willing to take a risk and, at the same time, wish to avoid it. This is shown on the one hand by the popularity of lotteries and other forms of gambling, where the odds are clearly stacked against participants, and on the other hand by the thriving market in all forms of insurance against accidents, theft and loss of life.

There is clearly a spectrum of attitudes to risks and this helps to explain the existence of institutions which allow individuals who wish to avoid risks to pass on these risks to those who are more willing to accept them. As in all economic transactions there is a mutual benefit to those involved and the purpose of this chapter is to explore how such benefits are translated into market behaviour.

We explore different situations in economics where risks are relevant to the decisions that are made. We analyse markets in insurance and in spot and futures trading. Reasons for holding a portfolio of assets are also examined.

Section 19.2: Risk in Economics

This section sets out different aspects of risk that apply to economic issues. We distinguish between different types of risk and see examples of their occurrence. You learn what is meant by a fair risk, and find that people can be classified in particular situations as risk averse, risk loving or risk neutral.

Examples of Certainty and Risk

The existence of risk has a number of different impacts on decision making. Often we know that particular events can or will occur but we cannot foresee when they might happen. For example, we may know that certain favourable weather conditions go hand in hand with a good holiday. However, we do not know whether the weather will be anything like we had hoped on the day we arrive at our holiday destination. Thus we can predict the consequences of an occurrence but not its specific timing.

At other times we are sure that something must occur, but the incidence is uncertain. Hence, we must, if we buy a fridge, pay value added tax on our purchase. However, the exact amount and timing is within our control to some extent. There are also other events which are beyond our control, as you will be reminded when you work through the list of situations where the outcome is certain but at least one aspect of the event is uncertain.

Now work through the list on the WinEcon screen. How would you classify the events you see? Some are unavoidable, like death, taxes and course fees. Some are partly optional and partly mandatory, like insurance. Lotteries and investments may appear to have much in common. What similarities and differences do you see in betting on the national lottery and buying shares in a well-run company?

Risk in Economics

Apart from the somewhat dramatic examples in the previous topic, all economic decisions involve some element of risk. This is because the consequences of any decision can never be fully known at the time the decision is made. For example, in purchasing this book you have decided that the (uncertain) future gains in terms of increased understanding of economics exceed the value of the next best item you could buy today.

Purchasing major durable goods involves a judgement about their future running costs as well as about performance reliability. Taking out a loan to finance any major expenditure – like an educational programme or an extension to a company's premises – requires us to evaluate an uncertain future. Owners of firms may decide to borrow for the purchase of plant or equipment because they believe it will generate revenue over a fixed period of time. Risk attaches to lenders' decisions also. Bank managers have to be persuaded that borrowers will be able to repay loans. Given this uncertainty it is surprising that any such decisions are made at all, and yet in fact they are made all the time.

Types of Risk

Economists distinguish between various kinds of risk. Some events are known to occur with a fixed probability. Thus it is known that ordinary domestic electric light bulbs will fail after a certain amount of use and that their failure pattern will follow a clearly defined probability distribution. This means that we can predict failure rates with some accuracy and make sensible predictions of the demand for replacement bulbs. Such events are described as risky.

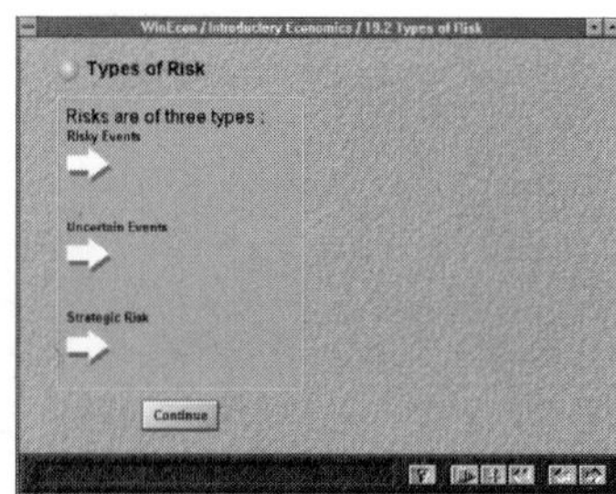

Quite different is the case of events like earthquakes or tidal waves. Little is known about the complex set of factors which determine the occurrences of such events. But even if it were possible to predict accurately the timing of the event, the severity of impact would depend on its location and its magnitude. The extra dimensionality of the event makes even a rough estimate that much more difficult and these events have been called uncertain events.

Many events in economics occur as a result of strategic considerations. We cannot predict with certainty events like a labour strike, a major investment decision designed to pre-empt a market, or a newspaper price war. They can, however, be explained as the result of logical economic reasoning designed to achieve particular advantages for the decision-makers involved in the events. The proprietors of the Times newspaper group in 1994 calculated that undercutting the market would increase market share and ultimately profits, and made a decision to lower the price of *The Times*, *The Sun* and other papers in the group.

The strange aspect of risk from an economic viewpoint is that people do not behave entirely consistently in their response to risk. They may take steps to reduce their exposure by taking care, improving security for their property and by buying insurance, whilst in other situations they may heighten their exposure to risk by gambling.

Your attitude to risk

If you had £100 to spend dealing with risk, what proportion would you spend on (a) insurance ________ and (b) gambling (including National Lottery) ________.

Now compare yourself with the national averages. Note from the WinEcon screen that in the UK in 1993, out of the total of £82 billion spent on insurance and gambling combined, 84 per cent went on insurance and the remaining 16 per cent on gambling. Are you more attracted or repelled by risk than the average?

One problem of interpreting the data is that corporate spending is included and so individual attitudes to risk may not be accurately represented. However, it is clear that more economic activity is directed towards reducing risk than heightening it, although there are some well-known states in the USA where a much greater proportion of economic activity is given over to gambling. Can you think of any examples?

Risks – Fair or Not?

In this topic you use the concept of 'expected value' to analyse situations involving uncertainty. The expected value of a set of outcomes is the value of each outcome multiplied by the probability of its occurrence. It represents the average value that would be obtained in the long run from many such investments, each with the same particular set of outcomes.

Work through the WinEcon text cards to discover the concept of a fair gamble in a simple example with just two possible outcomes. Notice that an investment with favourable odds produces a positive expected value (return), so that if such an investment is repeated you can expect to win in the long run.

See if you have understood if a risk is fair or not

01 **The expected value of a fair gamble is ________. If an investment has an expected value of £10, the odds are said to be ________.**

02 **What kind of odds produce a loss in the long run? ________.**

03 **Suppose an investment returns profits which depend on the state of the economy. The economy can be either in recession (State 1), no growth (State 2), or booming (State 3). In these cases profits are –£100, +£4, and +£100 respectively. If the probability of recession is known to be 0.3, that of 'no growth' to be 0.3 and that of boom to be 0.4, is investment in this project a 'fair gamble' or not?**

04 **In the question above, what would be the impact of reducing the probability of boom to 0.25 and increasing that of the recession to 0.45? Is the investment a better or worse gamble than before?**

Risk Aversion

The concept of 'odds' is of course linked with that of probability. If the odds are 10:1 (10 to 1) against a particular horse winning a race, this means that should I bet £1 that the horse will win, and it does win, I will receive not only my original stake (£1) back but an extra £10. Translated into probability terms this means that the probability that the horse wins is 1/(10 + 1) = 1/11. The probability that it does not win is therefore 10/11, or 1 minus the probability of the opposite outcome. There is in fact a formula linking the ideas of odds and probability: *If the odds are* a:b *against an event occurring, the probability of the event is* b/(a + b).

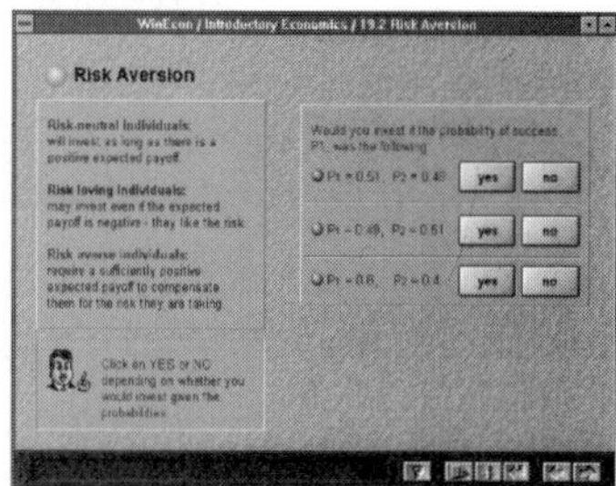

We can see that the phrase 'the odds are just favourable' means that the probability of occurrence is just greater than 0.5. Risk aversion is where people only invest if the odds are more than favourable (i.e. if the probability of success is well over 0.5).

Identifying risk aversion

05 Study the WinEcon screen, then identify the circumstances in which, if a person chooses not to invest, he or she may be described as risk averse: probabilities of failure of [0.2, 0.3–0.49, 0.49–0.51, 0.51, 0.55–0.66]; odds of success of [1:1 against, 2:1 in favour].

Test Your Understanding of Risk

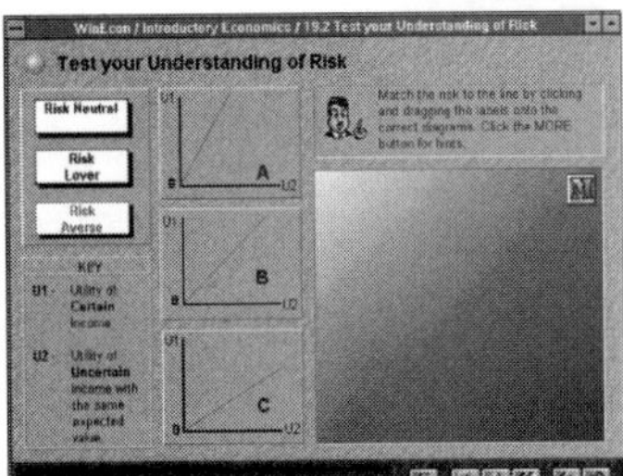

Work through the tasks on this WinEcon screen. Each of the graphs has the same scale on both axes, and each line plots a relationship between U_1, the utility of a certain or non-risky income, and U_2, the utility of the same expected value of income from an uncertain investment.

It is probably easiest to start with risk neutrality. Why is the relationship a 45 degree line? Risk neutrals make no distinction between certain income and expected values. They do not pay any attention to the possibility that the uncertain income may be totally different from its expected value on any specific occasion. They ignore risk. They therefore get the same amount of utility from a certain income of a particular amount and from an uncertain income of the same expected value. U_1 and U_2 are the same for all points on the line.

Risk preference, by contrast, is the enjoyment of taking risks. This is shown by the line representing the relationship between certain and expected incomes of the same amount being closer to the U_2 axis. Points on this line have greater utility from a risky income of a particular expected amount than from that value of fixed income. Preference is shown for the risky outcome as opposed to the safe certain value. This diagram would apply to the compulsive gambler, or the highly optimistic speculator.

Risk aversion is the more important of the conditions. The line pulled towards the U_1 axis shows that the individual needs to be compensated by higher expected value in order to cope with any given amount of risk. At any point on the line, the individual gets less utility from a risky outcome with expected income the same as the certain amount. For example, the amount of income that yields a utility of 10 on the U_1 axis when the income is certain gives a utility (on the U_2 axis) of only 5.6 if the amount is an expected value. A risk averse individual will only take the risky alternative to a safe income by being offered a higher expected value. Mostly in economics, we assume people are risk averse. This at least ensures that our economic predictions turn out to favour those aspects of economic life which promote security rather than those which increase risk.

Section 19.3: Insurance

Insurance is one of the main ways in which people attempt to reduce their exposure to risk. This section explains in more depth how the demand for insurance arises. It focuses on the ways in which relative risk aversion shapes the demand curve for insurance. Then it shows why the supply of insurance is never quite as great as consumers would wish. This leads to a frequently encountered problem that insurance markets do not work perfectly.

Insurance and Risk

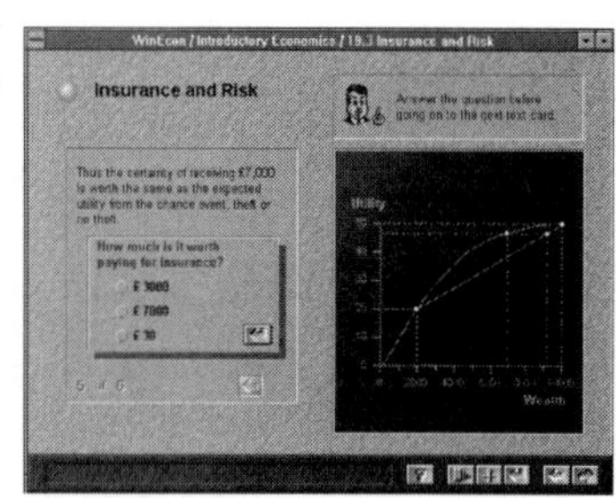

This section shows clearly how both the demand for and supply of insurance can arise for a risk with fixed probability of occurrence. You should follow the example carefully to make sure that you understand why (a) a risk averse individual facing particular risks would wish to have insurance, and why (b) an insurer would find it worth while to supply insurance at premiums which the insurance seeker would be likely to find attractive. Work through the WinEcon text cards and then answer the following questions.

Is insurance worth while?

Suppose that your sole wealth consists of a guitar worth £1000 and you are worried about accidental damage to it which could reduce its value to £100. You have been told by a friend who works in insurance that the risk of accidental damage is 0.1. Your utility at various levels of wealth is as follows.

Wealth	Utility
100	10
700	26.5
800	28.3
867	29.4
900	30
910	30.2
1000	31.6

06 **What is your utility when there is no damage to the guitar?**

07 **What is your utility if the guitar is damaged?**

08 What is your expected utility? (Hint: the probability of damage is 0.1.)

09 What certain income corresponds to this level of expected utility? (Hint: read table.)

10 What premium would you pay to have this certain income? (Hint: subtract this value from what the insurance company's payout would bring your wealth back to.)

11 What profit does this premium provide the insurer? (Hint: multiply the payout by the probability of damage to find the expected cost to the insurer.)

12 Will the insurer be willing to supply £900 worth of insurance at the premium you are just willing to pay? **Yes/No**

13 If your answer to the previous question was 'Yes', you will see that a market can indeed exist for insurance services. You would wish to reduce the premium to as low as possible. If you *were* able to do so, what would be the premium paid?

The Supply of Insurance

This section shows that insurance is possible because of the ability of the insurer to spread risks. Losses made on one client can be offset by gains made on other clients. On balance, the insurer faces no more than the statistical risk from the group of individuals who are insured.

Why do we assume that, unlike those seeking insurance, the insurer is not risk averse? There are two reasons: firstly, the insurer has spread the risks over a large number of individuals so the unique risk facing any one individual is not so important to the insurer; and, secondly, the insurer may be a company owned by shareholders who themselves have spread their risks over a number of companies. In the latter case, the managers of the insurance company can ignore the risk aversion of its shareholders.

Problems with Insurance

Although you have seen that insurance markets can satisfy both clients and insurers at a mutually agreed premium, in many cases insurance is either inadequate or not supplied. The text card illustrates circumstances in which the provision of insurance cover is unsatisfactory. Some of these relate to major disasters which have the potential for bankrupting insurance providers because risks cannot be pooled and neither are they independent. If a major disaster could hit many insured parties at the same time, and if the liability is unlimited or very high, insurers will be reluctant to supply insurance.

In less extreme cases, the market fails because the act of insurance increases the chance of the payout occurring. 'Moral hazard' describes the extra risk born by the insurer when the client takes less care after becoming insured than before. Insurers deal with this problem by offering less than full insurance. An excess clause in the policy means that the insured must share in the risk of loss, and provides an incentive not to change the risks faced by the insurer. The market only supplies part of the insurance required.

When the insured possesses better information than the insurer, costs to the insurer can be raised above expected levels. If premiums are based on average risks, a person who knows that their own individual risk is higher than average will find it worth while to become insured, whilst those with below average risk will not want to be fully insured. The insurer will end up facing higher than expected risks with only limited pooling capability. Anticipating this, insurers will either raise premiums to cope with the highest risk individuals, in which case low-risk individuals will not be insured, or exit from the market altogether, leaving no one insured. In either case, overall welfare is reduced.

Section 19.4: Forward and Futures Markets

One risk facing producers is that of price changes between purchase of inputs and sale of output. Farmers, for example, who must wait between sowing and harvest for receipt of income, are often acutely sensitive to downward price movements, as are firms with large investment programmes where capital needs to be raised at the beginning of the program but revenue comes in slowly over a long period of time. One method of overcoming risk is to tie up purchasers in long-term contracts. Examples of these are the long-term contracts signed between coal producers and the main electricity generators in England and Wales following privatization of the UK coal industry.

A more sophisticated remedy is for firms to engage in forward or futures markets transactions. For such transactions to work it is necessary that there should be both a seller seeking to avoid low prices in the future and also a buyer seeking to remove the opposite risk of high prices. A wheat producer wants to prevent prices falling before harvest: a miller wants to prevent prices rising before harvest. Bringing both together in a futures market can lead to an agreed futures price which removes risk from both parties.

Spot and Forward Markets

Commodity or oil markets often quote prices as either spot or forward. Spot means 'for on the spot or immediate delivery' whereas forward refers to price on delivery at a specific date in the future. Work your way through the oil market example to discover the incentives that are created for sellers and buyers to make forward market transactions.

Futures Markets

As an industry develops, forward markets are often replaced or supplemented by futures markets. The difference relates to the specificity of the forward market which is designed solely for the operators in that business. Forwards markets work smoothly when the purchaser is committed to taking delivery of goods on exactly the day specified in the contract. However, if the purchaser does not want the commodity at that time then delivery could be costly. Imagine what you would do with a ton of unwanted crude oil!

Futures contracts are more flexible and allow others to take the risks created by such specific provisions. Futures markets are larger and have better access to financial sources. This helps to minimize the credit risk, which can have serious consequences for a relatively specialized forward market facing adverse price movements.

How Does a Futures Market Work?

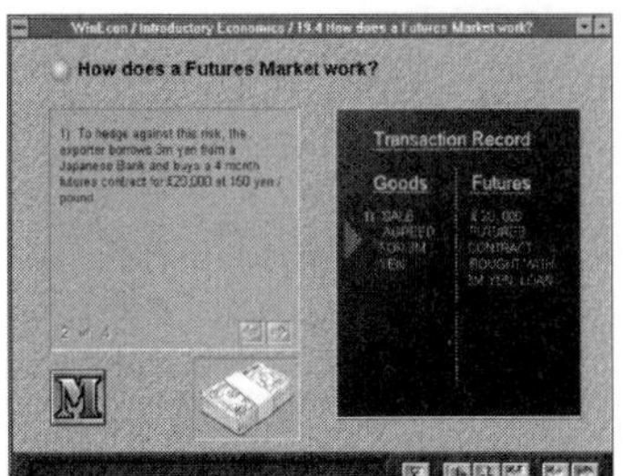

One important use of a futures market is to hedge risk in a 'real' market by buying offsetting contracts in a financial market. International trading transactions involving foreign currencies are particularly vulnerable to exchange rate risk. To avoid risk, a matching futures contract in the relevant currency can be taken out at the time of the trade contract.

Work through the WinEcon text cards to see how a futures contract in Yen is used to balance exactly the risk in the export transaction. Note that the UK exporter wishes solely to avoid one type of risk – that sterling might appreciate against the Yen and thereby yield a lower sterling return from exports. This possibility is reflected in the futures price of the Japanese currency. Using sterling to buy future Yen means that when the transaction is completed any loss made as a result of adverse currency movements is counterbalanced by gains in the futures contract.

Of course, the exporter is only insured against loss. Futures markets do not ensure that maximum profits are made, only that certain types of risks can be accommodated.

Section 19.5: Investment and Uncertainty

This section considers the impact of uncertainty on investment decisions. It is widely known that increased uncertainty has adverse effects on aggregate investment. Two ways of handling investment risk are investigated – 'portfolio management' and 'diversification'.

Holding a Portfolio

Just as an insurer can offer advantageous insurance contracts to individual owners seeking to reduce risks of asset loss by pooling independent risks, so an investor can reduce risk by holding a portfolio of assets. The crucial point has to do with combined probabilities of loss. If asset returns are independent, the likelihood of identical losses on two or more assets will be less than the individual likelihoods. If the probability of shares in company 1 falling in value has been assessed at 10 per cent and the same probability is attached to shares of company 2, it is less likely that they will fall together or at the same time. Thus the combined likelihood of loss will be less than 10 per cent.

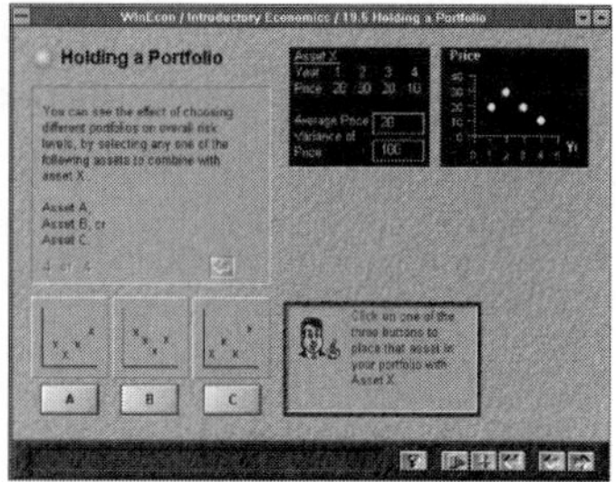

The WinEcon text cards illustrate the portfolio effect rather dramatically. Working through option A you will see that two assets with the same average price but different variances, when added together over time, produce a portfolio with no variation in price whatever. Movements in one market exactly counterbalance movements in the other. In fact, in all the cases (A, B and C), combining the assets results in lower variance of returns, and therefore lowers risk on the investment.

Diversification

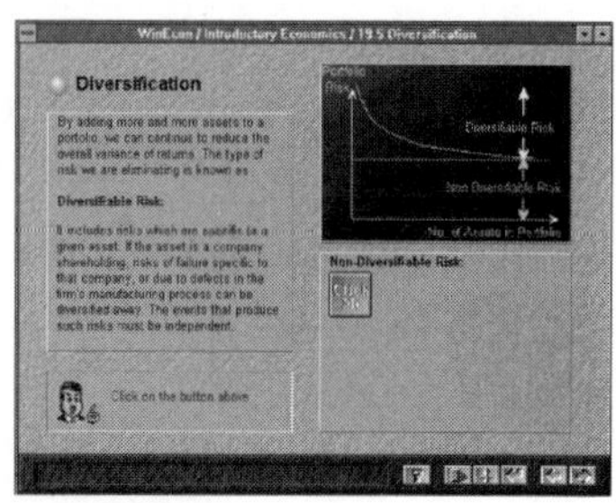

The process of adding more and more assets to a portfolio of assets is called 'diversification'. Economists like to consider the effect of taking a desirable policy to its limits, and diversification provides a good example of this tendency. As more and more assets are added, eventually there will be no further reduction of risk.

At this point all the risk specific to that asset will have been diversified away and we are left with an amount of risk which is called 'non-diversifiable risk'. These includes risks to which all companies are exposed through being involved in the same economy – risks created by unanticipated government policy actions and risks created by general trends in society (e.g. the rise in crime levels, increasing the risk of theft).

The economic analysis of portfolios is carried much further in texts on financial economics where methods of measuring risk characteristics are developed. These methods are used widely in modern financial management, and have considerable influence on the observed behaviour of firms.

Section 19.6: Summary

This chapter explains how risk and uncertainty affect economic behaviour. Various types of risk are distinguished, including uncertainty about both the occurrence and consequences of events. A fair risk is found to have an expected value of zero. Someone who is risk averse gets more utility from a certain income of a particular amount than from a risky outcome with the same expected income.

Risk of loss of assets provides the motivation for insurance provision. Where individuals are risk averse and insurers are risk neutral, profitable opportunities exist for the supply of insurance. The existence of moral hazard and adverse selection, however, increase the costs of insurance and may lead to market failure.

Other ways of coping with risk are to use forward and futures markets. These provide contracts which remove some of the uncertainty about price movements. For the individual firm, risk exposure can be reduced even further by choosing an appropriate portfolio of investments. Diversification of asset holdings can lead to removal of all risks except those created by influences from outside an economy, including unanticipated government intervention.

Chapter 20:

Nationalization and Privatization

Privatization has become fashionable in recent years. Firms nationalized several decades ago when state ownership was in vogue have been returned to private hands. The process has gone a long way in many countries, as in the UK, and whole areas of state activity which have never been in private ownership, such as local authority housing, water, telephones, gas and electricity generation, have been sold to the private sector.

Profitability, levels of employment and regulation are all important issues in this controversial area. We now try to inject into it some 'positive' economics.

Contents

KEYWORDS

- Adverse selection
- Agency
- Allocative efficiency
- Average cost pricing
- Countervailing (monopoly) power
- Externalities
- Internal market
- Marginal cost pricing
- Merit goods
- Moral hazard
- Nationalization
- Natural monopoly
- Privatization
- Productive efficiency
- Public goods
- Regulation
- Skimming

Section 20.1: Introduction to Nationalization and Privatization

With privatization, millions of individuals around the globe have bought shares in companies such as British Gas and British Telecom which were once publicly owned utilities. Thousands of jobs have been lost as the newly privatized firms have sought to become more profitable by cutting costs and becoming more efficient.

Whether in the public or private sectors, the monopolistic public utilities have been distrusted by their customers, and governments have decided to subject them to various forms of regulation. This highly controversial topic of public or private ownership is one where the positive and normative aspects of economics are difficult to disentangle.

WinEcon tries to take a 'positive economics' approach in two ways. The first is to provide relevant facts. WinEcon offers you historical information about the changes which have taken place in public sector/state ownership in the UK, and data on the performance of nationalized and privatized businesses, concentrating on their productive and allocative efficiency. The second approach is to identify economic analysis developed elsewhere in WinEcon which can be used to examine the motives for, and the results of, privatization or nationalization in any country. However, you will see in WinEcon some areas of the controversy where the positive and normative economics are hopelessly entangled, and you may sometimes disagree with the 'facts' that we have chosen to present as evidence of the relative merits of nationalized and privatized organizations.

The content is split into three main sections. One deals with the nationalizations that took place in the UK between 1945 and 1985 and the reasons adduced for them. The second looks at recent UK privatizations and their effects. The third main section is a detailed case-study of healthcare, mainly in the UK, showing how economic analysis can illuminate the political choices that have to be made when deciding on the boundaries of the public and private sectors in any 'industry'.

Section 20.2: Nationalization

This section combines a factual account of nationalization in the UK with some of the economic concepts which were used to both justify and analyse it. You can find out when industries were nationalized, and the way in which successive UK governments sought to regulate their activities 'in the public interest'.

Reference is made to the economic case that was put forward to justify nationalization, and you can consult material on 'natural monopoly', 'externalities', 'public goods', 'market failure' and 'productive and allocative efficiency' both here and elsewhere in WinEcon.

Reasons for Market Failure and the topics which follow in chapter 7 present the relevant theory. Public and Merit Goods are described in chapter 18.

The Major UK Nationalizations

Use the table below to record information about when the different nationalizations took place. Details are given on the WinEcon screen after you click the decade buttons.

Decade	*Nationalizations that took place*
1920s	
1940s	
1950s	
1960s	
1970s	

You may like to verify this information. Use an economics textbook or any other source that seems appropriate to check the validity of these details. Record any discrepancies or further details, and the source you have used.

The Case for Nationalization

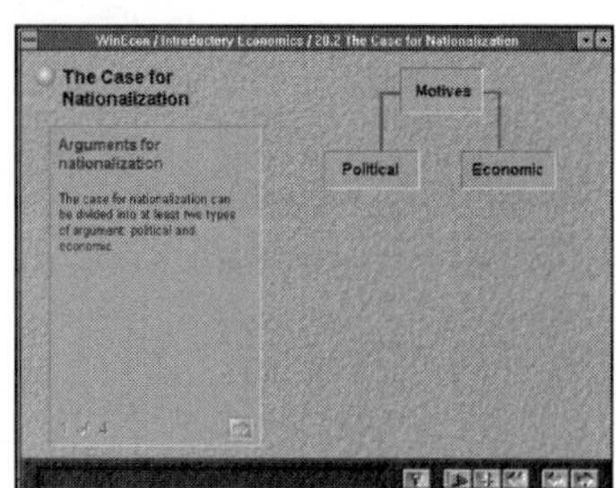

Nationalization provides a possible solution to problems of market failure. If the market system left to itself does not achieve allocative efficiency, government intervention may improve the allocation of resources from society's point of view. There may also be equity concerns which can be addressed by nationalization. It is generally agreed that nationalization has also taken place for ideological reasons. The WinEcon screen sets out various reasons for nationalization, classifying them as either political or economic.

The Economic Case for Nationalization

This supplementary screen allows you to investigate the main arguments for nationalization by using sliders to change the nature of the imaginary industry you are considering. Record any terms and concepts that are new to you for future reference.

The Emergence of a Natural Monopoly

Economies of scale are an inducement to firms to expand and merge to create larger sized units. Given the total market demand, this may imply that only a small number of firms can exist in the industry in the long run. If the minimum efficient scale of an industry is so large that it is not reached

This is shown in the topic The Case for Imperfect Competition in section 6.4.

even if a single producer supplies the whole market, the industry constitutes a natural monopoly.

This WinEcon screen uses an animated model to show you how a natural monopoly can arise. The third cue card suggests that the firms depicted can be thought of as competing in different regions of a national economy.

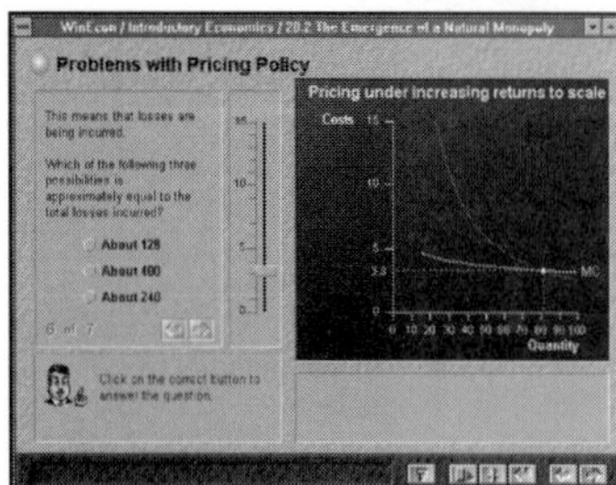

The topic Monopoly Power and Allocative Inefficiency in section 7.3 shows the analysis for a monopoly with U-shaped cost curves.

Problems with Pricing Policy

This supplementary WinEcon screen is accessed via the Next Page button. It deals with the conflict in running a natural monopoly between charging a price that is profitable (which a private sector firm would have to do) and a price that satisfies economists' criteria for efficient resource allocation (which would make a loss for the firm). A monopolist usually charges a higher price than the one at which allocative efficiency is achieved. But in the case of a natural monopoly the problem is accentuated because of the downward-sloping average cost curve faced by the firm. If a natural monopolist were to set price equal to marginal cost, losses would be incurred.

Price under a natural monopoly

01 What pricing rule generates allocative efficiency, assuming there are no externalities?

02 What makes a monopoly 'natural'?

If the market has a demand curve as shown and is supplied by a natural monopoly, sketch appropriately shaped average and marginal cost curves in the diagram. Deduce and sketch the marginal revenue curve. Mark the monopolist's chosen output and price. Indicate the socially efficient output and show the loss the monopolist would make.

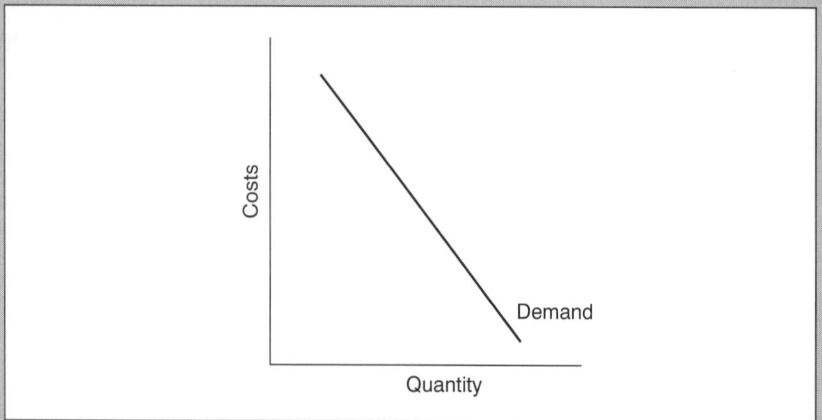

03 Give three ways of dealing with the 'natural monopoly' problem other than nationalization.

Externalities and Public Goods

Externalities and public goods are possible causes of market failure, so nationalization might be thought appropriate in markets in which they occur. This WinEcon screen outlines their characteristics. After working through the WinEcon cards you can test your understanding of the concepts by dragging items into their appropriate category.

For more details see the Externalities and Social Costs section of chapter 7, and the Public and Merit Goods section of chapter 18.

The Nationalized Industries in the UK – A Potted History

This WinEcon topic shows how government control of the nationalized industries in the UK sought to achieve economic objectives in the period 1945 to 1980. It is an excellent case study of the interaction between economics and politics – economists showing what was happening or likely to happen, and governments deciding what they wanted to happen. Above all it shows how regulation of public utilities has evolved over the years, responding to problems as they have occurred.

History of nationalization

The early years of UK nationalized industries – 1945 to 1960

04 Nationalized industries were to maximize welfare. What was the financial constraint?

05 What were the nationalized industries not allowed to do?

06 What pricing policy was usually adopted?

07 What did this policy lead to?

Economic objectives 1960–1977

08 What was the main control imposed by the 1961 White Paper on nationalized industries?

09 What were the policies for pricing and investment in the 1967 White Paper?

10 With what were these two policies consistent?

11 How were non-commercial activities to be treated?

The new emphasis in the 1978 White Paper

12 **What was the stated reason for setting financial rather than economic targets?**

13 **What was the other new emphasis in this White Paper?**

Productive Efficiency

The underlying analysis is covered in chapter 7 and chapter 18.

The next two WinEcon sub-topics look at the UK nationalized industries over the last four decades, asking whether they achieved the objectives of productive and allocative efficiency.

About productive efficiency

14 **Give the two main aspects of productive efficiency.**

As regards labour productivity

15 **Which nationalized industries performed better than the private sector (manufacturing) in all three time periods?**

16 **Which were worse in all three periods?**

17 **Which were better in 1978–85?**

18 **Which were worse in 1978–85?**

As regards total factor productivity

19 **How was the productivity of UK nationalized industries restricted between 1973 and 1978?**

20 **What happened between 1978 and 1985?**

UK Allocative efficiency

Economic analysis shows us that an unregulated monopoly is unlikely to achieve allocative efficiency. A major aim of nationalization was to maximize welfare. This WinEcon screen allows you to explore the extent to which allocative efficiency was achieved by UK nationalized industries between 1945 and 1985.

Was allocative efficiency achieved?

21 What is a necessary condition for allocative efficiency?

22 If NIs are monopolistic what should they do to achieve allocative efficiency?

23 If NIs are in a competitive industry, what is the test of whether allocative efficiency has been achieved?

24 Which NIs are said to have been allocatively efficient?

25 Which NIs are said to have not been allocatively efficient?

26 Which are said to have been partially efficient?

Section 20.3: Privatization

This section tries to help you make sense of the recent, and controversial, UK privatization programme by discovering information about it in WinEcon and recording the details by answering the questions below.

We first look at differing definitions of privatization, and you discover the one we are using. Then we structure the UK privatizations into two main groups, and suggest a strong connection between competition and efficiency. You investigate the possible economic arguments for privatization, and see how they relate to the history of privatization in the UK. The final topic gives an overview of the 'RPI-X' approach to regulating public utilities in relation to other types of regulatory policies in use. Some of the screens invite you to test your knowledge and understanding.

Definitions of Privatization

Four uses of the term privatization

27 List the four usages

28 This section of WinEcon concentrates on

UK Privatizations

There are two screens in this WinEcon topic. The first lets you discover when various enterprises were privatized. The Next Page button takes you to screen (2).

Privatization peaks

29 **Which five years (of those shown on the screen) had the highest privatization proceeds? List the years and the firms or industries privatized in each.**

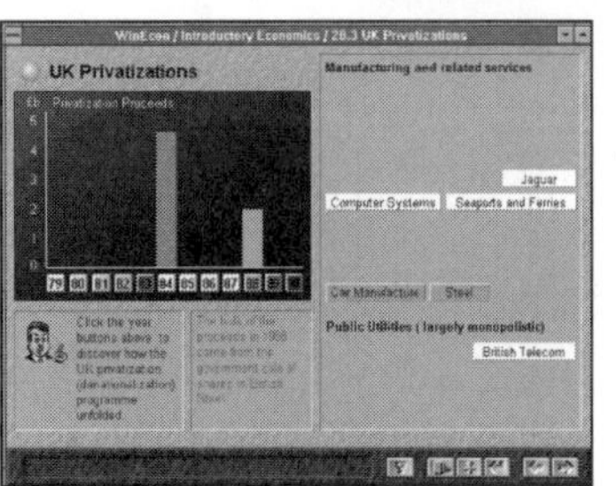

UK Privatizations (2)

As privatization gathered pace, larger public corporations were sold to private shareholders. This WinEcon screen asks you to identify when a change occurred so that from then on the process of privatization became a much larger project.

The two phases of UK privatization

30 **When was the first phase?**

31 **Which kind of industries were privatized?**

32 **When was the second phase?**

33 **Which kind of industries were privatized?**

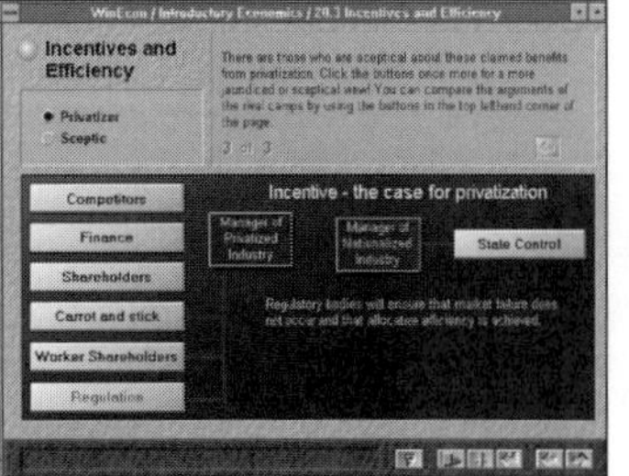

Incentives and Efficiency

Privatized firms are subject to market pressures. Shareholders and banks have to be satisfied with a company's performance for it to be able to raise capital. Firms facing competition have to be efficient if they are to survive. The case for privatization is largely based on the premise that market forces promote efficiency. But the public utilities which have been privatized could have monopoly power – public transport and the supply of electricity may generate externalities, and the provision of a pure water supply has elements of a public good. These are the kinds of circumstances in which market failure,

with its attendant loss of social efficiency, occurs. As such industries have been privatized, regulatory bodies have been set up to ensure the industries act in the public interest.

See the topic Examples of Regulation in section 7.6.

You can discover more about why firms may be more efficient under private ownership than when nationalized on this WinEcon screen. Notice that you can also view some contrary arguments. Card 3 lets you view the pros and cons alternately so that you can compare them.

About incentives

What are the incentives to efficiency that management has? Discover from the WinEcon screen one for nationalized industries and six for privatized industries and summarize them below. Note also the possible counter arguments to each.

34 Nationalized industry

35 Privatized industry

Seven Reasons to Privatize

Various motivations lay behind the privatization programme that took place in the UK during the 1980s. Use this WinEcon screen to find out about them and discover how their relative importance changed as the programme proceeded.

What motivations were most important:

36 **In the early 1980s?**

37 **In the mid-1980s?**

38 **From 1986?**

39 **What were the other subsidiary policy aims? Explain what each entailed.**

Ownership and Efficiency

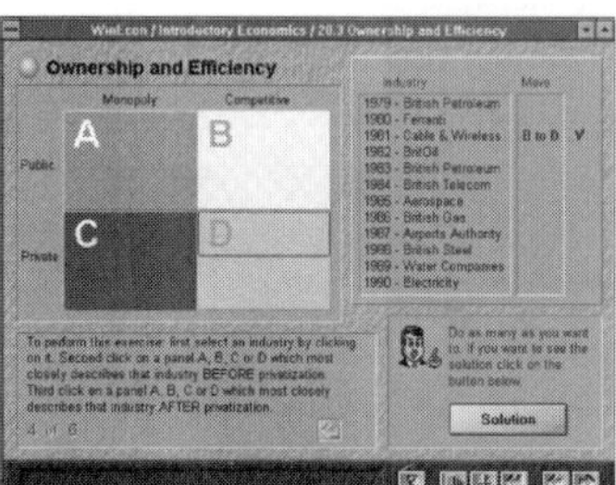

While some of the nationalized industries were natural monopolies and have remained the sole suppliers of particular areas after privatization, there were also individual firms within the public sector which formed part of a competitive industry.

This WinEcon screen asks you to decide how the market structure of various firms changed at the specified dates. You will be told immediately whether each individual response is right. If you need them, the correct answers are also offered.

Private vs public

40 **Which of the businesses listed on the WinEcon screen became more competitive when privatized?**

Ownership and Efficiency (2)

The second screen in this topic discusses the conflict the government faced as it decided how privatization of a particular industry should take place. Use the WinEcon screen to discover the problems encountered in dividing a publicly owned monopoly into private competitive firms.

Efficiency vs profitability

41 **Give two reasons why Conservative governments in the UK in the 1980s chose *not* to make public monopolies competitive when they privatized them.**

Regulation of Privatized Utilities

For an industry which in some respects forms a natural monopoly, there may still be some aspects of its business in which competition is feasible. It would be wasteful to have a multiplicity of pipes or cables laid down the same street to provide the same service to different households, but it may be possible for different companies to supply their products down the same pipes or cables.

If competition does not exist, regulation offers a way of protecting the public interest. This WinEcon screen explains possible methods of regulating privatized utilities and some of the economic issues raised. British Telecom, British Gas, water supply and electricity are used as sources for examples.

The regulatory framework for the four large utilities

Use the information in WinEcon to complete the table below.

Company	Method of regulation	Formula used	Comments
BT			
British Gas			
Water			
Electricity			

42 **What sanction is available to the regulator of a utility if the company does not comply with the terms of its licence?**

Do different methods cause different problems?

43 **Which of the three problems (lower quality/over-investment/higher prices) does rate of return regulation cause?**

44 **Which of the three problems (lower quality/over-investment/higher prices) does RPI-X regulation cause?**

45 **What is the Averch-Johnson effect?**

46 **Does price-cap regulation prevent it?**

The Privatization of Electricity

This screen looks at some of the issues involved in the privatization of the electricity generation industry.

Privatization principles

Summarize each of the six stated objectives for the privatization of electricity, and say if you think that the Secretary of State seriously expected them to be achieved, or if they were included mainly for cosmetic purposes.

(1)

(2)

(3)

(4)

(5)

(6)

Section 20.4: A Case Study on the Provision of Healthcare

The UK NHS (National Health Service) was set up by the 1945–50 Labour government in the face of almost total hostility from the Conservative opposition. The health professions themselves were divided, the main opposition coming from the doctors' professional body. President Clinton faced similar opposition recently in attempting to make the market-driven US system a little more 'socialistic'.

Why was there this opposition to a healthcare 'industry' financed mostly by taxation, and why is the UK Conservative government carrying out market-oriented 'reforms' in the 1990s? The answer is that we are all acutely aware of our own mortality, and afraid that when we are ill or old we might not be cared for, but also that there are very different reactions to this problem, as varied as our other attitudes to life.

For some people the solution lies in insuring against illness, just as we insure against any other mishap, and then choosing how to spend our insurance money on treatment. For these people financing healthcare by taxation takes away the incentive for individuals to care for themselves, and removes competition between healthcare providers. For other people, the community (state) is the only body capable of guaranteeing that however expensive our medical bills are, they will be paid. They also point out that the US market-driven insurance system is much more expensive than the UK NHS, and Americans are no more healthy. Obviously the UK NHS is not completely taxation-funded, and the US system is partly paid for by taxation, but they do provide interesting contrasts which we can use to illuminate the issues.

When resources are limited, how can we ensure that everyone gets the best possible health care? In this topic we try to introduce some light into what is usually a heated ideological and emotional debate. Is there a 'positive economics' contribution to the debate over how market-oriented the UK health service should become?

WinEcon addresses these issues in two main ways. One is to discover some facts about the 'product' itself, and what makes it unique. The second is to see if the concepts and analysis developed elsewhere in WinEcon can be used to inform the choices being made by governments, health professionals, managers and voters.

We start the topic by looking at the main issues at stake, and the key characteristics of healthcare which place it on the boundary between public and private sectors. We then collect 'expert' testimony on the two main options (i.e. the UK and US systems). We finish by looking at the current 'reforms' of the UK NHS, linking them to what we know of the operation of markets.

Case Study: The UK's National Health Service (NHS)

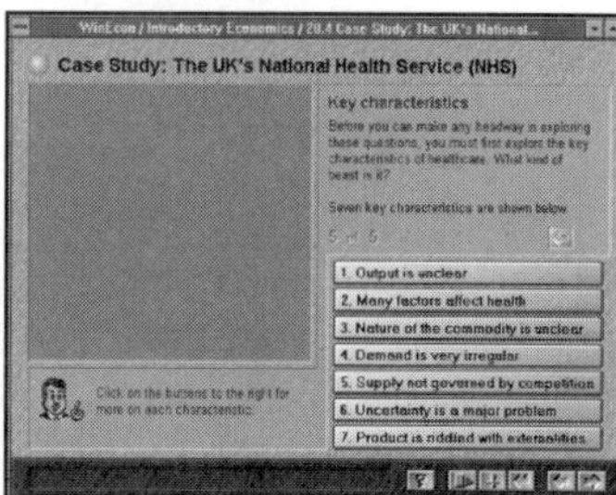

This WinEcon screen lets you discover the basic issues involved in making decisions about the provision of healthcare. Once you have learnt what are the three key questions, you study some important aspects of healthcare as a product. There are seven special characteristics which distinguish healthcare from most other products and services.

The issues

47 **What are the three main questions about the provision of healthcare?**

48 **List the seven key characteristics, with a brief explanation of each.**

Private vs Public Control of Health Care Resources

This WinEcon screen sets out various reasons that lend support to one or other of the views about how healthcare should be provided, either privately or by the state. Use the screen to discover which arguments are appropriate to each case, and note them below.

The arguments

49 Fill in the table using the screen data

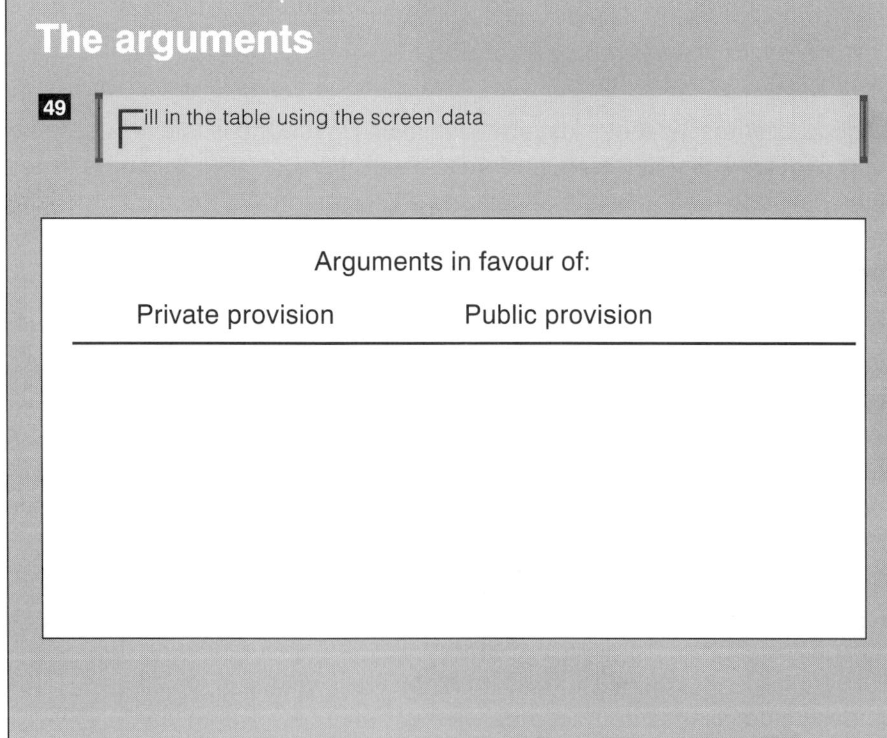

Arguments in favour of:

Private provision	Public provision

Private vs Public Control – Ask the Experts

Healthcare is provided by two different systems in the UK and in the USA. Explore the differences between the systems and the case for each of them with this WinEcon screen.

Key differences between the UK and US systems

50 Is there competition in the provision of healthcare services (a) in the UK and (b) in the USA?

51 How are healthcare services allocated (a) in the UK and (b) in the USA?

Arguments for state and private provision

52 What case can be made on the basis that healthcare is a merit good?

53 What case can be made on the basis of consumers making rational choices?

54 What case can be made on the grounds of equity?

Case Study NHS: What are the Benefits of a Mixed System?

Given that there are arguments in favour both of public and of private provision for healthcare services, a mixed system may be appropriate, combining the best elements of each. You consider this possibility here.

On adverse selection and moral hazard see the topic Problems with Insurance in section 19.3.

The weaknesses of a market system

55 What is meant by the doctor acting as 'agent'?

56 Why does this agency raise problems if the doctor is trying to make profits?

57 What is 'skimming', and who suffers?

58 What is 'adverse selection', and who suffers?

59 What is 'moral hazard', and who is subject to it?

60 **What is the main result of moral hazard in this case?**

61 **What is 'countervailing monopoly power', and how does this operate in the UK?**

Lessons to be learnt from the free market in the USA

62 **List three practices that can be copied from private systems.**

63 **Give two reasons why the cost implications of decisions are not always considered in the NHS.**

64 **What was a result of basing one year's spending on the previous year's spending?**

65 **Give three criticisms of NHS spending on GP (family doctor) services.**

Complete the table to compare data from the UK and USA.

	UK	USA
Expenditure on healthcare as a percentage of GDP		
Infant mortality rate per 1000 live births		
Life expectancy for men in years		

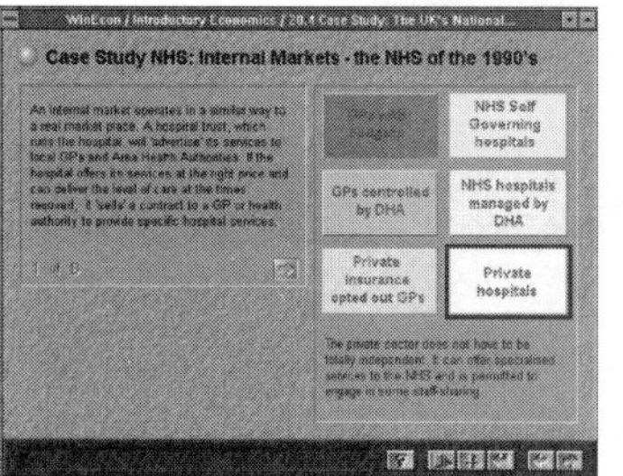

Case Study NHS: Internal Markets – The NHS of the 1990s

The management structure under which the NHS is run in the 1990s is designed to provide a framework for decision making which imitates a market system. In the NHS internal market there are people who demand healthcare services, and those who supply them. They are represented by boxes at the right of this WinEcon screen. The three boxes in the left-hand column indicate the people in the system who demand the services. Notice that patients are not included in this list. They obtain their healthcare through their GP. The three boxes in the right-hand column show the main suppliers of healthcare services in the UK.

Demand and supply in the internal market

66 **Who are the main demanders (customers)?**

67 **Who are the main suppliers?**

68 **What is said to be the key to making the healthcare internal market work?**

69 **What else is needed to ensure choice of supplier?**

70 **Does this exist?**

Section 20.5: Summary

This chapter provides history and analysis of nationalization and privatisation in the UK. A nationalization programme began after World War II and continued through to the 1970s, sometimes in response to a particular crisis in an industry. Privatization, or denationalization, began at the end of the 1970s and gathered pace from 1984.

The nature of a public utility makes it likely that it constitutes a natural monopoly. Nationalization is one possible solution to the problem of monopoly power that may then arise. Other sources of market failure, such as externalities, public goods and merit goods, may also be cited as reasons for nationalization. Marginal cost pricing is desirable to achieve allocative efficiency, but if used by a natural monopoly it would lead to a loss.

Since nationalized industries were at first required to break even, average cost pricing was usually used. From the 1960s they were required to achieve a set rate of return on assets. Marginal cost pricing was advocated in the 1967 White Paper. From then on separate accounts were to be kept of non-commercial activities instead of them being cross-subsidized by profitable activities. Financial targets, including covering the opportunity cost of capital, were set in 1978. Despite these guidelines, productivity and efficiency in the nationalized industries were somewhat disappointing.

The case for privatization rests to a considerable extent on the view that market forces promote efficiency, and arguments are presented as to why

management should be more efficient under private ownership. Given the nature of utilities which are amongst the industries that have been privatized, it was perhaps inevitable that some monopolistic elements should remain. The desire to split up monopolies to promote competition may also have been countered by the requirement that the newly privatized industries should earn profits for their shareholders. Regulatory frameworks have been established to protect the public interest. Price-cap regulation is used, with formulae of the type RPI-X for industries where technological advances are expected to reduce costs.

The case study on the provision of healthcare compares arguments for public and for private provision. Healthcare may be viewed as a merit good, and equity arguments also support public provision. Doctors act as agents for their patients in demanding healthcare. If healthcare is paid for through insurance schemes, skimming, adverse selection and moral hazard may arise. As the single purchaser of doctors' services, the NHS may have countervailing monopoly power, which may keep down the cost of doctors' salaries. To obtain the benefits which are gained with a market system, the NHS is now run with an internal market which imitates a market system.

Chapter 21:

Financing Business

In 1937 Ronald Coase posed the question: 'why do firms exist?' Before his time, economists had taken their existence for granted. Coase, however, showed that the entrepreneur could use either the market mechanism or the firm to organize economic activities. He concluded that firms are used where the costs involved in running the firm are less than the transaction costs associated with using the market. Later economists have shown that the firm has other advantages as well, such as being a relatively efficient way to raise finance.

Contents

KEYWORDS

- Capital gearing
- Rights issues
- Stock market
- Entrepreneur
- Share capital
- Transactions costs
- Long-term finance
- Short-term finance
- Value chain

Section 21.1: Introduction

This chapter of WinEcon consists partly of economics related subjects and partly of accounting related materials. We concentrate on the economics areas in this text: this means investigating the nature of the firm and looking at the associated topic of examining the various sources of finance available to it. The term 'firm' is used in this chapter as a general term to describe all of the different legal forms; from sole traders to public limited companies.

The topics in WinEcon which cover accounting issues are not discussed here. For further information on sections 21.4 and 21.5, you should consult the textbook references given in WinEcon.

Section 21.2: What is a Firm?

This section begins by examining the wide diversity that exists in the sizes of firms and also the diversity found in the different legal forms they can adopt. It continues by introducing the concept of the 'value chain' ; no matter how large or how small the firm is, it can be viewed as a mechanism which can be used to link various elements of this chain. The chain contains all the linkages from the owners of the raw materials used in the production process to the final consumer. Some large firms operate at each link in the chain whilst some small firms only operate at a single link. This leads to another issue raised in this chapter; the question of when should co-ordination between the links in the value chain be undertaken by the market and when should it be undertaken by the firm. This is the question asked by Ronald Coase.

Types of Firms

WinEcon gives you examples of the wide variety of size and legal forms firms can take in the UK and overseas. In the UK there are approximately 2.5 million firms of all different sizes. At one extreme the UK's largest firm is Royal Dutch/Shell which in 1993 had sales approaching $100 billion and profits close to $10 billion. At the other extreme there are many thousands of sole traders who have low turnovers and small profits.

WinEcon shows you that firms of different sizes take different legal forms or status. These include public limited companies, private limited companies, private unlimited companies, partnerships, sole traders and non-profit makers. Usually large firms become public limited companies whilst the smaller ones tend to become partnerships and sole traders.

By requesting details of size on this WinEcon screen and working through the text cards you gain access to company information, which is also available directly from the menu in the topic called Company Information. The screen offers you information about the largest firms in selected countries.

The size and legal form of the firm

01 Use the WinEcon database to find out the turnover and profits of the largest companies in the UK, USA, Germany, France and Japan. Choose whichever size criterion you wish and record the values in the table provided.

Size criterion:

Country	Largest company	Turnover	Profits
UK			
USA			
Germany			
France			
Japan			

02 **Use WinEcon to find out the number of UK firms in each of the various categories of legal forms and record this in the table.**

Legal Form	Numbers of UK firms
Public companies	
Private companies with limited liability	
Private companies with unlimited liability	
Partnerships, sole traders and non-profit makers	
Total	

The Value Chain

The 'value chain' comprises all the linkages from the owners of the raw materials used in the production process to the final consumer. It includes production, distribution and marketing elements. At each link in the chain, the economic agent adds value, and firms take part of the value added as their profits.

The chain has firms operating at each and every link, which raises the question of what determines the size of the firm. Some large firms operate at each link in the chain whilst other small firms are only found at a single link. The various links can be categorized into three distinct stages which correspond to different types of economic activities. These are: the purchase

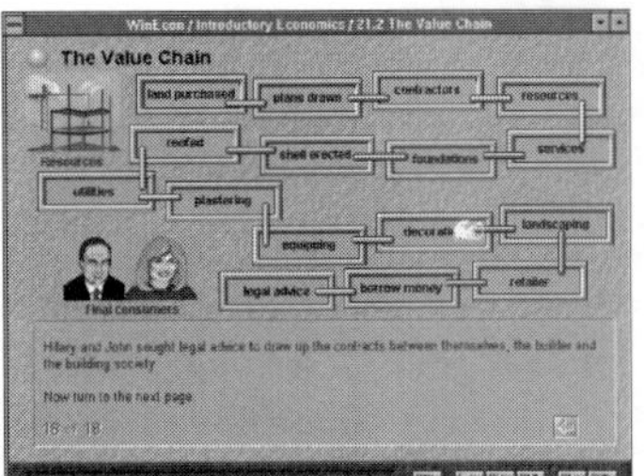

or manufacturing of components; final product manufacturing or assembly; and marketing of the final product.

As you work through the three WinEcon screens in this topic, you see the value chain involved in building a house. Firms may be involved in one or more of the links in the chain. Some large housebuilding firms (e.g. Wimpey) may be involved in several links in the chain. They employ workers such as architects, bricklayers, electricians, plumbers and salesmen. Other smaller firms are involved in, perhaps, just one or two links in the chain. If a firm is involved in more than one link then an element of 'vertical integration' can be seen to have occurred. This integration can be either backwards or forwards. For example, if a housebuilding firm buys a firm of architects then 'backward integration' has occurred. If the building firm then buys an estate agent to sell the houses produced, this is an example of 'forward integration'. We can use vertical integration to help explain why some firms are large and why some are small. Large firms tend to be vertically integrated organizations whilst small firms specialize on a limited number of specific links in the value chain.

Value Chain Exercise

On this screen you find an exercise that tests your understanding of the stages of production in the brewing industry and car manufacture.

Now use the value chain concept

03 Which of the three main elements of the personal computer value chain are the following companies involved in?

	Components	Manufacture	Marketing
IBM			
Dixons			
Currys			
Amstrad			
Sega			
Nintendo			

04 In the following diagram, draw the value chain associated with the manufacture and selling of personal computers. Remember that there are three main elements of the chain: purchase or manufacture of components; final product manufacture or assembly; and marketing.

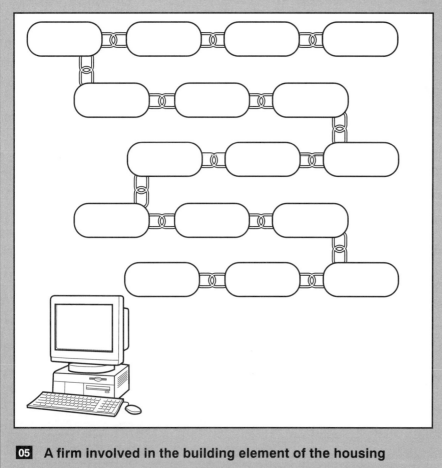

05 **A firm involved in the building element of the housing industry is involved in which part of the value chain?**

Market or Firm Co-ordination?

Ronald Coase saw the choice between using the firm or the market to co-ordinate the different links of the value chain as a question of cost. There are costs associated with using both approaches. Consequently, profit maximizing entrepreneurs will want to use the cheapest in order to maximize their profits. If the market is used, transactions costs are incurred. If the firm is used, costs associated with running the firm are incurred.

Turning to the four WinEcon screens we can see that our entrepreneurs, Hilary and John, are faced with the question of whether they should use the market, a firm, or a combination of the two, to co-ordinate each activity in the building of their house. If they use the market at each link in the value chain they will incur the costs of identifying suppliers, obtaining quotations, negotiating prices and drawing up contracts, making sure the terms of the contract are fulfilled and arranging payments to their contractors. If they use a firm to build the house, however, all the costs of organization are incurred by the firm. The method Hilary and John use will depend on which approach

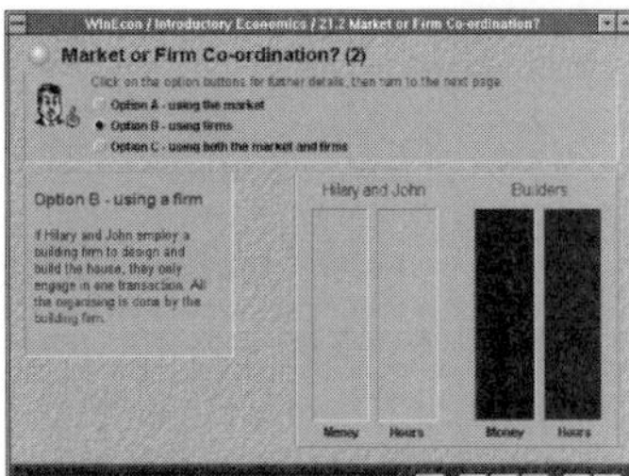

is the cheaper. The second WinEcon screen in this topic depicts these alternatives.

The firm may prove to be a cheaper option than the market because the various transactions costs at each link in the chain are eliminated. The firm employs workers which means that the costs of searching, negotiating and monitoring compliance to contracts at each link are absent. The firm does, however, incur management and organization costs but these are likely to be lower than the transactions costs associated with using the market. Look at the second screen of this WinEcon topic to see if this is the case with Hilary and John's house.

We should be aware that there are additional cost advantages which the firm may also enjoy. The firm is likely to enjoy economies of scale and economies of team production. These will give further unit production costs advantages to the firm in addition to the advantage gained from the absence of transaction costs. You can discover more information about this in the screen (3) of this WinEcon topic.

Develop your understanding of co-ordinating the value chain

06 **The firm will normally represent the cheapest way of organizing the value chain because it does not incur ______________. It will also have additional cost advantages derived from ______________ ______________.**

07 **Use WinEcon to find the major cost advantages associated with using the firm rather than the market to co-ordinate the value chain. Use your own words to record what these advantages are.**

08 **Refering to the WinEcon screen for The Value Chain topic, assess what transactions costs would be involved if Hilary and John decided to use the market to organize the marketing component of the value chain.**

09 **The firm does not incur transactions costs but will incur other costs instead. Produce a list of the types of management and organization costs which a firm building Hilary and John's house will incur.**

Forms of Business Organization

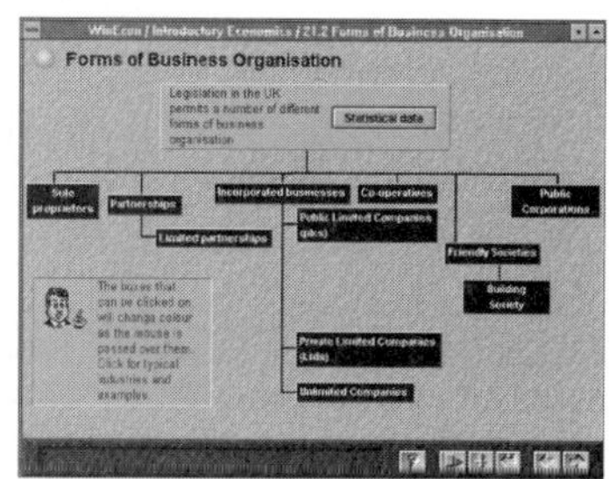

We said in the introduction that firms can take a variety of legal forms. These differences relate to aspects such as whether the organization is public or private, and whether it is a profit or non-profit making organization. We concentrate here on private sector profit making firms. Their different legal forms relate mainly to the amount of legal liability which their owners face.

Smaller legal forms of private business organization tend to be sole traders and partnerships. The liabilities of the sole trader and at least one of the partners in a partnership are unlimited. This means that if the business runs up large debts the owner(s) will be personally liable to repay the money owed. The result could be that they could lose their personal assets, most often their houses, which makes this type of legal form unpalatable to many entrepreneurs.

Larger profit making business organizations tend to be formed either as public or private limited companies. In these cases the liability of the shareholder (i.e. the owner) is limited to that of the value of their share capital. This means that if the firm runs up large debts or losses, the owners may lose all of their share capital but creditors cannot make claims against the shareholders' personal assets.

Another interesting form of the firm is the co-operative. This is owned and run by the people working in it. Each member has one vote in making company decisions, regardless of the capital they have invested. The liability of the owners is also limited in this case to the value of their share holding. This means that, as in the case of the public limited company, creditors cannot make claims against private assets.

Work through the three WinEcon screens in this topic (Forms of Business Organization, Forms of Business Organization: Liability, and Legal Forms of Business Organization) and then tackle the questions below.

About the legal forms of business organization

10 **Refering to the WinEcon sub-topic Legal Forms of Business Organization, find which legal forms of the firm have unlimited liability and which have limited liability.**

11 **Explain why many entrepreneurs are unwilling to operate as sole traders or in partnerships.**

12 **Refering to WinEcon sub-topic Legal Forms of Business Organization, what form of business organization is appropriate for a non-profit making firm? Identify a legal difference between that firm and profit making firms.**

13 **In the same WinEcon sub-topic, find out the legal difference between a private limited company and a public limited company in terms of what the latter must have open to public inspection.**

14 **What types of legal forms are found most often in the following industries: accountancy, oil companies, pharmaceutical firms, solicitors, market stall holders, football pools companies, and computer games writers.**

There are two further screens in this topic section. The first (Business Organization: Matching Game) is a quiz based on the card game, pairs. You have to match legal forms of firms to the obligations associated with those forms. The second (Company Information) gives direct access to the database you saw earlier in the topic Types of Firm.

Section 21.3: Financing Firms

Business organizations (firms) need capital to operate. If the firm is a large production and manufacturing company, like Royal Dutch/Shell or Unilever, it needs capital to purchase plant and machinery to produce its products. Even a firm at the other end of the size spectrum, such as a sole trader, will need capital (e.g. a flower and plant wholesaler needs to be able to buy a delivery lorry). The capital which a firm needs is not just that required to buy plant and equipment. All organizations also need working capital to finance the items used in the day-to-day running of the firm, such as the holding of stocks.

A wide variety of different forms of finance is available, ranging from bank loans to debt and equity. These are normally split into short-term and long-term categories; as a rough rule of thumb the type used should correspond to the length of the life of the asset being financed.

Why Do Firms Need Finance?

A firm's need for finance can be illustrated by looking at what a building firm requires to finance its operations. On this WinEcon screen we see that the firm needs to finance the purchase of necessary plant and equipment. These

assets are what we call 'fixed assets'. Such assets have a long life and remain in the business without being sold. For the builder, they include a lorry to transport equipment, a cement mixer, a Kango hammer, ladders, spades and tools, scaffolding, a pneumatic drill and miscellaneous other equipment. Finance is needed also for holding current assets, which are mainly the stock materials used. For the building firm, these will include items like tiles, wood, cement, bricks and nails.

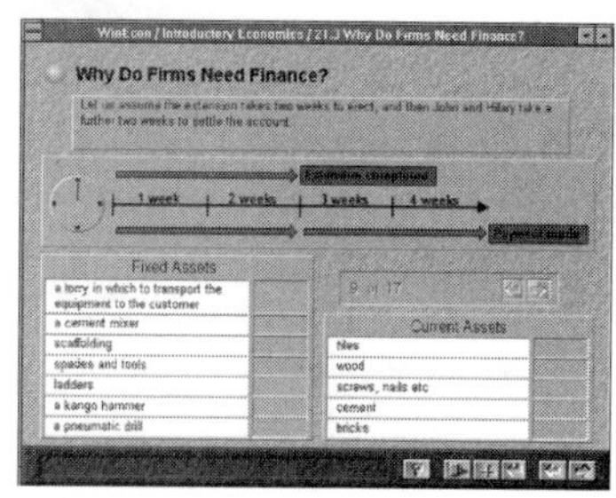

The types of finance which the builder uses should depend on the types of assets being bought. Short-term finance is appropriate for current assets, whilst long-term finance is needed for the fixed assets. Generally the type of finance used should reflect the life of the asset.

How firms finance assets

15 **Explain what types of assets the firm will finance with, firstly, long-term finance and, secondly, short-term finance.**

16 **Produce examples of the types of assets for which a computer manufacturer will require (a) long-term finance and (b) short-term finance.**

Finance For Industry

There are numerous potential sources of finance for firms. For a small firm, such as a sole trader, the sources are likely to be fairly limited. The firm will have to obtain any finance needed partly from its own profits and partly through bank loans. However, in general, the larger the firm, the wider the range of sources of finance available. Limited companies can raise money from the owners of the business and/or borrow money. Finance from owners is called 'share capital' whilst finance from borrowing is called 'loan capital'. Share capital is long term whilst loan capital can take many different forms and can be for differing periods. This supplementary screen describes these two methods of raising finance.

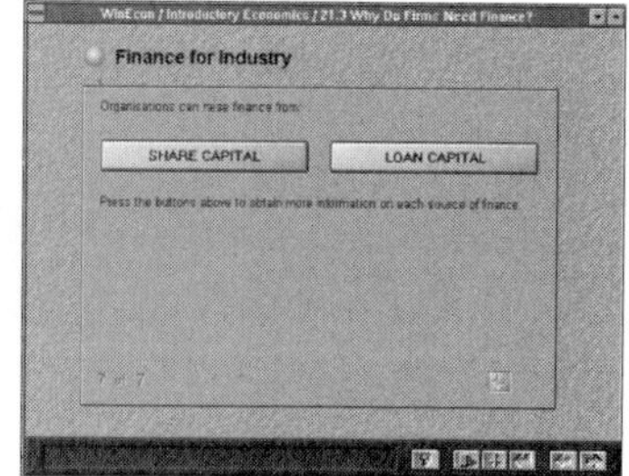

Types of Security

Collectively, share and loan capital are known as securities. These take forms such as 'preference shares', 'ordinary shares', 'debentures' and 'convertibles'. For more details on these various forms you can consult WinEcon.

Forms of securities

17 Use WinEcon to find what the following forms of finance are: preference shares, ordinary shares, and debentures. Record the definitions using your own words.

Sources of Short-Term Finance

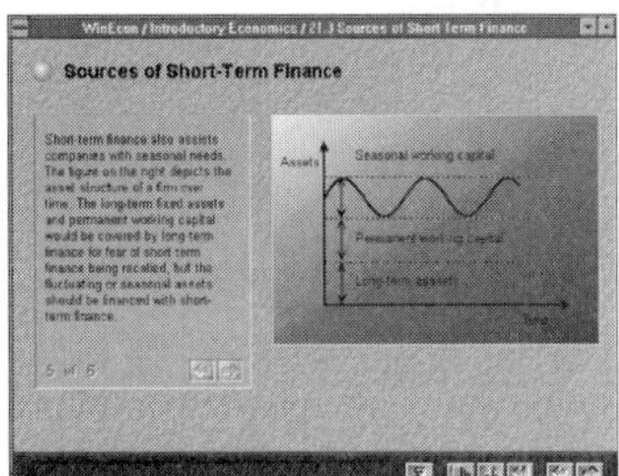

There are a number of reasons why firms use short-term finance. The most important is that their requirements for finance may fluctuate over the short term. Firms will want flexibility to take account of this; they will not want to be left holding large amounts of money for which they have no use, given that interest charges will be being incurred. Similarly, they will not want to be left short of money if there is a short-term increase in their needs.

There are several reasons why the short-term demand for finance can fluctuate. One of the most common reasons is that many firms face seasonal fluctuations in their demand during the year. This will result in them requiring different levels of working capital during the year to finance stock holdings. A manufacturer of Christmas crackers, for example, will be faced by such a problem.

Card 6 of this WinEcon screen offers you the opportunity to explore sources of short-term credit. You find that a wide range of short-term finance is available, including 'trade credit', 'accrued expenses', 'bank loans', 'overdraft' (or 'line of credit'), 'commercial bills of exchange', 'factoring/invoice discounting'. For details on these you should refer to WinEcon.

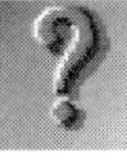

Discovering sources of short-term finance

Use WinEcon to find seven forms of short-run finance and, in your own words, record the nature of these forms below.

18 **Explain the main reasons why firms need short-term finance. Why will each of the following firms need it: UK car manufactures, fireworks manufacturers, Easter egg producers and Christmas card producers?**

Capital Gearing

The firm's long-term finance can take the form of equity, or a combination of equity and debt. The relationship between the relative proportions of debt and equity capital used by the firm can be analysed using the concept of capital gearing. As the name suggests, gearing looks at the ratio of the two forms of finance.

If there is a high proportion of fixed-cost finance (preference shares and debt) in relation to ordinary shares then the firm is said to be highly geared. In practice, some companies can have gearing of well over 100 per cent. Recently there have been numerous so-called management buyouts where most of the finance has come in the form of loan capital and where the gearing is very high. If gearing is high, the financial markets perceive the company to be a risky investment, as large amounts of the profit are paid out in fixed interest payments. In such circumstances, when the economy goes into recession and profits fall the survival of these types of firms can be at risk; they will find it hard to make enough profit to cover the fixed interest payments on the debt finance, and they can go bankrupt. This has happened to several famous name companies in the past few years (e.g. Brent-Walker and the Maxwell Communications empire).

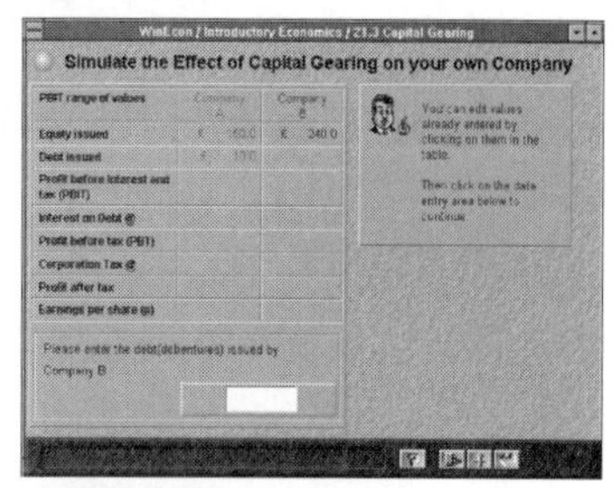

Discover more about capital gearing with this WinEcon screen. Card 6 gives access to a simulation to help you investigate the effects of capital gearing.

See what you have learnt about capital gearing

19 **Use WinEcon to find out how we normally calculate the capital gearing of a firm. Record the formula below.**

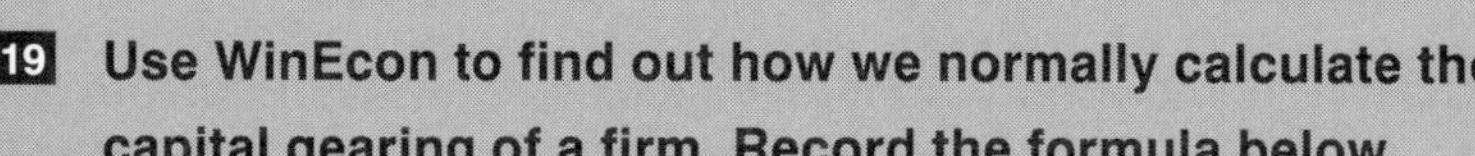

20 **Use WinEcon to find out some of the advantages and disadvantages to a firm of having high gearing ratio and make a record of them.**

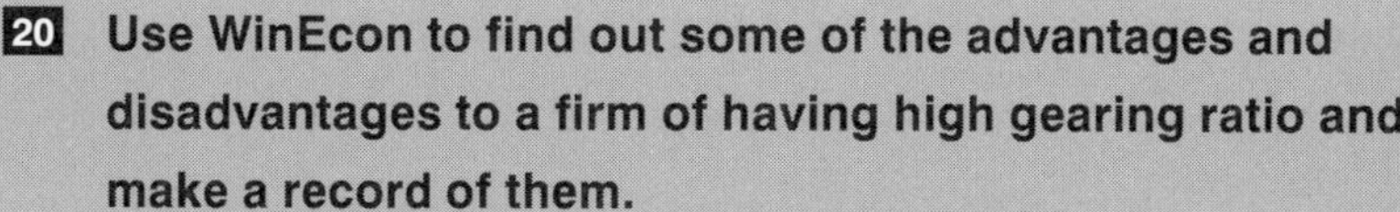

21 Using the definition of capital gearing you have recorded above, work out the capital gearing of the following firms and complete the table.

	Firm 1	Firm 2	Firm 3	Firm 4
£1 preference shares	100,000	50,000	20,000	0
Debt (in £1)	500,000	100,000	50,000	100,000
£1 ordinary shares	1,000,000	2,000,000	50,000	10,000
Gearing ratio (%)				

22 **For each of the firms above assess whether you think it is risky to invest in their ordinary shares given their gearing**

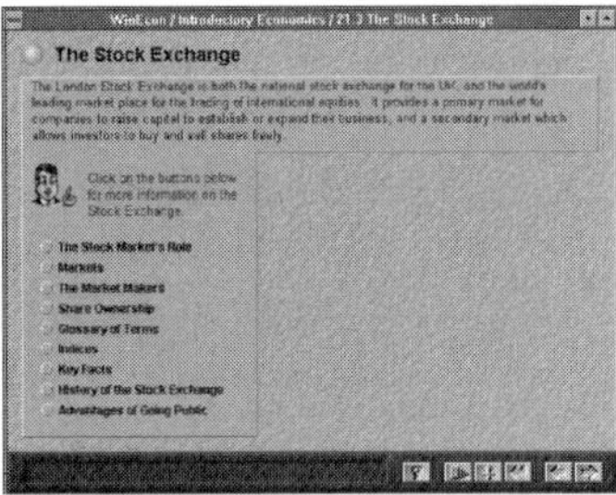

The Stock Exchange

The stock exchange is a very important source of long-term finance for firms. Existing firms can issue new ordinary shares through what are called 'rights issues'. In 1993, firms raised £18.6 billion through such issues on the UK market. Some firms use this form of finance to reduce levels of gearing which are thought to be too high. In other cases, an expanding company may use rights issues to raise more money, as this will often represent the cheapest source of new funds.

As well as providing finance for established firms, newly listed firms can raise capital on the market for the first time. In 1993, £6.1 billion was raised through this channel. An example of this is the satellite television company BSkyB which is a recent debutante in the stock market.

In addition to providing finance, the stock market has the equally important role of ensuring liquidity in the market by making it easy for existing shareholders to sell their shares. This is important as people will be more willing to buy shares if they know that these can be sold if the money is needed.

If you would like to know more about the stock market, WinEcon provides a survey of it. You can see how the market operates; learn its terminology; discover key facts; and explore the history of the market.

There are two further screens in this section (Ways of Issuing Securities and The Stock Exchange – Conditions for Listing). Use these to find out how a company goes about getting a listing on the market.

Develop your understanding of the role of the stock market

23 **Existing companies can raise additional finance from the stock market using a ________ ______. The names of three UK companies which have raised money this way in the UK in the last few years are:**

24 **In your own words explain why the liquidity provided by the stock market is so important.**

25 **Use WinEcon to examine how the stock market has developed from its foundation until today. Explain what has happened in your own words.**

Section 21.4/.5:

As explained in the introduction, these two sections relate to accounting issues and are therefore not covered in this workbook. There are screens in WinEcon that cover these areas (Company Accounts, and Measuring Profits and Costs: Differing Perspectives) but you should refer to references given in the WinEcon Glossary for further information.

Section 21.6: Summary

This chapter looks at firms, and addresses the question of why they exist. The different forms a firm can take are described. We see that the different economic activities in each value chain can be co-ordinated by using either the market mechanism or the firm. A profit seeking entrepreneur uses a firm if this represents the cheapest way of organizing the economic activities. Reasons why a firm may be cheaper include lower transactions costs, economies of scale and team production.

A second advantage of the firm is that it represents an efficient vehicle for the entrepreneur to use to raise finance. The forms of finance which can be raised may be split into two main categories, short-term finance and long-term finance. We have also seen in this chapter that the size of a firm and its legal form influence the sources of finance available to it. These sources range from bank loans for the small sole trader to share and debt capital for public limited companies.

The WinEcon screen Company Information at the end of section 21.2 provides data on large companies in several countries according to various size criteria.

Answers to Questions

Chapter 1

1.1 Introduction

Economics

01 (1) Individuals have objectives (what they wish to achieve/produce/consume etc.) and (2) they are constrained by their limited resources.

Micro/macroeconomics

02 Studies the decisions of relatively small economic units such as individuals or firms.

03 Studies economic aggregates or average variables such as output or unemployment.

Positive/normative economics

04 Attempts to find out what is, and predict what will happen if certain circumstances occur.

05 Asks questions about what should be, and deals with value judgements.

Mixed economy

06 The government decides what will be produced, how it will be produced and who will receive it.

07 Decisions by consumers and producers interact via the market to decide what will be produced, how it will be produced and who will receive it.

08 (a) Who produced the item (but see the question on defence equipment)

Open/closed economy

09 One which can be analysed as if the economy in question were cut off from world trade.

10 One which must be analysed in a way that takes account of influences from other countries.

11 If the result of the analysis will be changed a great deal by this assumption.

The Economic Approach – Rationality

12 That people (consumers or producers) have the intelligence to adopt courses of action which will get them as close as to their objectives as the constraints will allow.

13 The assumption is needed because (a) irrational behaviour is more difficult to predict and (b) the assumption helps to explain many economic phenomena.

Students and debt

14 Rational.

15 Higher rates make debt less attractive.

16 People who value the present more highly than the future.

17 In itself, the above phenomenon (called positive time-preference, or in some books myopia (short-sightedness)) has no necessary connection with rationality as defined in this chapter.

Advertising

18 Rational.

19 Advertisers.

20 Yes, if they judge it to be in their interests.

21 What is rational for one person is not necessarily rational for the community/family/clan/tribe/country/world etc.

Water shortages

22 Rational for water companies interested in profits.

23 Rational (as defined in this simple case study).

24 A water consumer who values present consumption highly (consumption now probably reduces consumption in the future).

25 (As defined here) someone who conserves water!

Objectives and Actions: The Squash Club

26 (1) There will be less members if the membership fee is higher
(2) Less people will use the courts if the court fees are higher.

27 (1) Took into account the constraints on your decisions (your resources and the members

probable reactions to your pricing decisions)
(2) Changed your decisions/strategy when your objectives changed.

28 Lower Lower
Lower Higher
Higher Higher

Objectives and Actions: Allocating a Health Budget

29 Disease A

30 20%, 80%, 0%

31 Disease A is much cheaper to treat, so the cheapest way of saving patients' lives is to first treat everyone with disease A. After that we treat as many as possible with disease B, since this is the more cost effective than treating those with disease C

32 £5,400,000.

33 20%, 64%, 16%.

Objectives and Actions: Looking Ahead

34 The formula can be accessed from card 4 of this screen by using the [A] button.

35 104 (100 + 120+ 150 + 150 + 0 = 520 (the income in the five time periods) divided by five time periods gives 104 per year).

Economic Modelling

36 The WinEcon screen gives answers to this exercise.

Chapter 2

2.2 Factors Affecting Demand

01 The quantity of a good that prospective purchasers wish to buy at all conceivable prices.

02 Price, income, price of related commodities, tastes and other factors.

03 Price.

04 Price.

The Demand Curve of an Individual

05 Lower; down.

06 Other factors affecting demand do not change; the three points in a straight line are assumed to imply a straight line relationship that holds beyond the points. (Mathematically, simple linear extrapolation is assumed.)

Shifts in an Individual's Demand Curve

07 Price.

08 Income, prices of complements, prices of substitutes, changes in tastes.

09 A reduction in demand.

The Product Demand Curve

10 It is the sum of the amounts demanded by all individuals in the market.

11 They are the horizontal sum of the individual demand curves.

Shifts in the Product Demand Curve

12 Goods whose demand increases when income increases.

13 Goods whose demand decreases when income increases.

2.3 Factors Affecting Supply

14 Quantities of a good that prospective producers wish to produce and sell at each conceivable price.

15 Price, costs of inputs, taxes and subsidies, the state of technology.

16 Price, causing a movement along the supply curve

17 Price

The Supply Curve of a Firm

18 All factors other than the one we are considering are held constant.

19 So that we can isolate the effect of price on the firm's willingness to supply.

20 That costs per unit rise as output rises.

21 That three points in a straight line imply a straight line relationship that holds between the points and beyond them. (Mathematically, linear interpolation and extrapolation are assumed.)

Shifts in the Supply Curve of a Firm

22 Price.

23 Costs of production, taxation, subsidies, weather.

24 An increase in supply.

The Product Supply Curve

25 The sum of a number of individual firms' supply curves.

26 That three points in a straight line imply a straight line relationship that holds between the points. (Mathematically, simple linear interpolation is assumed.)

2.4 Market Equilibrium

27 Any arrangement which facilitates the trading of goods or services.

28 When the quantity demanded does not equal the quantity supplied.

29 Excess demand, excess supply.

30 Because the quantity demanded and the quantity supplied are equal at that price.

31 That when there is a disequilibrium the customers and suppliers will quickly move along their curves to the new equilibrium.

Comparative Statics

32 The demand curve shifts to the right, price rises, quantity supplied increases.

33 The supply curve shifts to the left, price rises, quantity demanded falls.

34 That any change that we wish to analyse will affect *either* the demand curve *or* the supply curve but not both – this is the assumption which makes supply and demand analysis 'elegant' (simple and powerful).

Agricultural Support

35 Fluctuating agricultural incomes; agricultural incomes growing more slowly due to low income elasticity of demand for agricultural products.

36 Producers, because their incomes are raised and more stable; consumers, because they continue to pay world (by implication, low) prices.

37 Producers and merchants who store 'mountains' and sell them off to poorer countries.

38 By reducing the prices producers receive, or controlling production.

Government Intervention

Rent controls

39 Setting the controlled rent above the market (equilibrium) rent.

40 There are many possible reasons, for instance: they regard housing as a public or merit good; they gain; they gain in the short term; the supply and demand analysis shown here is too simple.

Subsidies

41 The size of the subsidy and the slopes of the curves.

42 Yes, if it were of an 'equivalent' amount, and if suppliers reacted in the simple way suggested by static demand and supply analysis.

Taxes

43 Consumers; the extent of their suffering depends on their price elasticity of demand which is discussed in the next section of this chapter. In this (simple) analysis producers are assumed to be able to cease production if their profits are affected and move to another product – for an extensive discussion of the 'burden of taxation', see chapter 18.

The Cobweb Model

44 They base their decision about what to supply in the next time period on the current price.

45 None; the crop takes time to grow, and when it is harvested it is all supplied to the market.

46 Once price is dislodged from equilibrium it is alternately above and below the equilibrium price, with the quantity alternately below and above the equilibrium amount.

47 Price adjusts so that the quantity demanded will match the quantity that is actually being supplied.

48 Agricultural products.

The Cobweb Model (2)

49 When the slope of the supply curve is greater than the slope of the demand curve (in terms of absolute slope values – i.e. not taking the sign into account).

50 When the slope of the demand curve is greater than the slope of the supply curve (using absolute slope values).

51 When the slopes are equal (again, absolute values).

2.5 Elasticity and Smoking

52 If price elasticity of demand (in this case for tobacco) is low.

53 It increases – this explains why governments try to put larger taxes on goods and services which have price inelastic demand such as alcohol, tobacco and petrol (gasoline).

54 Yes, because (a) it could use the revenue to pay for other ways of reducing consumption such as advertising, education and the extra expenses involved in providing segregated facilities, and (b) a sudden increase in price could have a shock effect and thus cause people to give up smoking – simple economic models tend to assume that consumers always react smoothly to any change, but in reality there may be 'thresholds' (sudden changes in slope) in their response to price changes.

Price Elasticity of Demand

55 Proportionate change in quantity demanded divided by the proportionate change in price, or, more generally, proportionate change in the dependent variable divided by the proportionate change in the independent variable.

56 Arc elasticity is calculated over a range of prices, point elasticity is measured at a particular price.

57 Proportionate change in demand/proportionate change in price, using the averages of the new and old quantities and of the new and old prices in the calculation.

58 209.6 litres (PED = (% change in D)/(% change in P) = ?/–4 = –1.2, so the % change in D is 4.8, and therefore the new demand is 200 + 4.8% of 200 = 209.6 litres).

59 450 tonnes (same method as above).

Price Elasticity and Total Revenue

Maximizing Total Revenue

60 At the price where price elasticity is –1.

61 Because at prices below this, demand is price inelastic and a reduction in price reduces revenue; at prices above this an increase in price reduces revenue as demand is price elastic.

62 At a price of £5 per visitor there would be 250 visitors bringing in the maximum total revenue, which is £1250. You could have used several different methods such as: (1) find (by trial and error) where total revenue is maximized; (2) find (by trial and error) where arc elasticity is roughly –1; (3) find (by trial and error) where point elasticity is –1; (4) read/recall that price elasticity is –1 at the centre of a straight line demand curve which cuts both axes.

Point Elasticity – Demand

63 $(\Delta Q/\Delta P) \times (P/Q)$.

64 Point price elasticity of demand = (P/Q)/(slope of demand curve).

Demand Curves with Constant Elasticity

65 Total revenue is the same at all these points.

Factors Affecting PED

66 Number and closeness of substitutes; proportion of income spent on the commodity; absence of advertising; time period.

Income Elasticity of Demand

67 An Engel curve plots quantity demanded of a product against income.

68 A line with a slope of 45 degrees.

69 The Engel curve for a superior good starts at the origin and curves. (If the product axis is vertical, the Engel curve becomes steeper.) Its IED is greater than 1.

70 Over the range of income where it is inferior, the quantity bought of the product declines as incomes rises. (As card 4 shows the good may be superior over other ranges of income.) Its IED is less than 0 (i.e. negative).

71 Normal goods are usually income inelastic. (On average they must be because we observe that saving (i.e. not spending) increases as a proportion of income as incomes increase – saving is 'superior'.)

Cross Elasticity of Demand

72 (Proportional change in quantity demanded of good X)/(proportional change in price of good Y).

73 Negative.

74 Positive.

Ruby Earrings and the Price Elasticity of Supply

75 Inelastic.

76 Not in this case – given the initial values of *P* and *Q*, the slope is enough (but, of course, this is only a simple straight line case).

Price Elasticity of Supply

77 (Proportionate change in quantity supplied)/(proportionate change in price).

78 When the supply curve is a straight line through the origin (0,0).

Price Elasticity and the Slope of the Supply Curve

79 No (see the next two questions).

80 Those which cut the price axis.

81 Those which cut the quantity axis.

Point Elasticity – Supply

82 Use the formula on the card 2 pop up.

83 Where PES > 1.

84 Where PES < 1.

85 Those which do not go through the origin (0,0).

Factors Affecting the Price Elasticity of Supply

86 (1) The price elasticities of the inputs used in production of the good in question; (2) time.

87 Positively (elasticity increases with time).

Chapter 3

3.2 Consumption Decisions

01 Utils.

02 They spend limited income so as to maximize satisfaction.

03 Yes, but buying one good usually affects buying other goods.

04 All consumers seem to plan at least some of their spending, which suggests they are rational.

05 We may find out some previously unknown information.

06 We each have different definitions of what is good – what we 'ought' to buy is a 'normative' economic decision, as discussed in chapter 18.

3.3 Total and Marginal Utility

07 The missing column is 10, 5, 2, 0, –1.

08 Zero.

09 Negative.

10 Extra units add successively smaller amounts to a person's total utility. Marginal utility decreases as that person has more of the good.

Utility and Demand

11 A demand curve is a marginal utility curve expressed in money terms, for instance by valuing each (marginal) util at £2.

12 The marginal utility of money is constant.

Choice of Goods

13 Equi-marginal utility (EMU).

14 Consumers change their purchases until the ratio MU/*P* is the same for all of their purchases.

3.4 Elements of the Consumer Choice Model

15 No: one of the axes can be for good X and the other axis can be for 'all other goods'.

16 –(price of X)/(price of Y).

17 No: prices are assumed to affect only the budget line while tastes and preferences are assumed to be incorporated into the IC curve map.

(Obviously there are commodities for which a change in price will affect the image of a good, and thus our feelings about it, but, as usual in economics, we have simplified our model so that any change affects only one of the two curves – *either* the budget line *or* the ICs.

18 Because there is diminishing MRS for both goods (see the diagram on the screen).

19 Optimization *or* constrained maximization.

Discovering Indifference Curves

20 The consumer likes equally all combinations of goods represented by points on the same indifference curve. He or she is indifferent between all points on the same curve.

21 The assumption that the ICs shown are only a few of those that could be drawn.

22 Higher indifference curves are further out from the origin.

23 The shape is standard (convex to the origin of the diagram).

24 Utility is not measurable (but can be compared).

Assumptions of Indifference Curves

25 Both goods give satisfaction.

26 C.

27 D.

28 The marginal rate of substitution is the amount of Y a consumer is willing to give up to gain an extra unit of X.

29 MRS = (marginal utility of X)/(marginal utility of Y) *or* MRS = (fall in Y)/(increase in X).

30 Refer to the screen explanation under Rational and draw the diagram.

Non-Standard Indifference Curves

31 Good X has negative utility (the consumer requires more Y to compensate him/her for taking more X).

Perfect substitutes (either good can replace the other, so the consumer will swap them at a constant rate).

Perfect complements (the consumer gets no extra satisfaction from more of one good unless he/she also has more of the other).

Increasing MRS (the consumer prefers to have all of one good or all of the other).

3.5 The Budget Line

32 (1) price of good X; (2) price of good Y; and (3) income (or budget for the period).

33 Affordable combinations lie on or below the budget line.

34 All points on the budget line exactly match the consumer's income.

3.6 Optimal Consumption Choice

35 (1) not affordable; (2) not on a higher indifference curve.

36 A point on an indifference curve just allowed by the budget line.

37 A point at which the slope of the IC equals the slope of the budget line.

38 MRS = $P_x/P_y = MU_x/MU_y$.

Income–Consumption Curve

39 Indifference curves have the standard shape; budget lines are parallel.

40 Use the glossary definition.

41 Yes, but only if both prices change by the same amount. (This is known as a real income change – a 10% fall/rise in both prices would have the same effect as a rise/fall in income if these were the only two goods bought and all income was spent on them.)

42 The position of indifference curves in relation to each other – try drawing some indifference curves which produce a straight ICC.

The Engel Curve

43 Use the glossary definition.

44 Yes, but not a simple one. The slope of the Engel curve is also decided by the scale on the income axis – try changing the scale.

Price–Consumption Curve

45 As the price of X falls, the budget line pivots at its intersection with the Y axis so it just touches higher and higher indifference curves.

46 Use the glossary definition.

47 It pivots around the point on the axis of the good whose price has not changed.

3.7 The Substitution Effect

48 The change in demand due solely to the change in relative prices.

49 The consumer is assumed to remain on the same indifference curve.

50 A 'hypothetical' budget line parallel to the new one is drawn which just touches the old indifference curve.

The Income Effect

51 The change in demand due to the real income effect of a price change.

52 Use the definition in the pop-up box.

Inferior Goods

53 Use the definition in the pop-up box.

54 Only the income effect is unusual.

55 Use the definition in the pop-up box.

Chapter 4

4.2 Production and Factor Inputs

01 Land; labour; capital. Production = f(land, labour, capital). This shows how output changes as inputs are changed.

The Short-Run Production Function

02 Land; capital; labour.

03 When the first unit of labour is added, one sack of corn is produced, but one unit of capital on its own produces nothing. Adding one unit of capital to one unit of labour increases output to four units. As factor inputs are increased more output is produced, and more is produced when inputs are used jointly rather than using each separately.

Diminishing Returns in Production

04 Factors; fixed; diminishing marginal returns.

05 At least one factor of production.

06 As the stock of agricultural land was fixed, Malthus said that food production would exhibit diminishing returns.

The Law of Variable Proportions

07 The extra (physical) output produced by employing one additional unit of labour.

08 Increasing; decreasing.

09 Increasing returns occur when the output produced by an additional labourer is more than

the last additional labourer produced. Constant returns occurs when they produce the same, and decreasing returns when the additional person produces less.

Short-Run Production Functions: A Numerical Example

Marginal and Average Product of Labour: A Numerical Example

10

Lab	TP	AP	MP
1	278	278	
2	608	304	330
3	978	326	370
4	1381	345	403
5	1806	361	425
6	2245	374	439
7	2688	384	443
8	3126	391	438
9	3550	394	424
10	3950	395	400
11	4317	392	367
12	4642	387	325
13	4915	378	273
14	5127	366	212
15	5269	351	142
16	5331	333	62

11 APPL is the average output produced by all labourers combined.

12 The APP at first rises and then falls. The MPP rises then falls but at a different rate.

13 Total physical product; labour; capital; increasing returns; constant returns; decreasing returns.

14 Diminishing returns set in because the amount of land used is fixed and as more and more labour is added the MPP starts to fall.

4.3 The Isocost Line

15 Labour; capital; budget; capital; labour.

Isoquants and Production Rays

16 Output.

17 Labour and capital combinations.

18 It has increased.

19 For point X: labour units = 3, capital units = 4, so capital cost = 2000, labour cost = 1500 and total cost = 3500.

20 This assumes imperfect substitutability between labour and capital.

21 No they do not, especially when we take account of scale factors in the production process.

Producing at Minimum Cost

22 Slope; labour; capital.

23 Isoquant; isocost.

24 MPP/P is the same for all factors.

25 If the isocost cuts the isoquant this shows that a different factor combination can be found which produces the same output level but at a cheaper total cost.

Changes in Factor Prices

26

Price of labour	Price of capital	Isocost slope	Capital used	Labour used
200	1000	–0.20	98	285
300	900	–0.33	117	220
800	200	–4.00	220	116

27 The firm chooses a combination which minimizes costs. It will substitute between the two up to the point where the MRS = slope of the isocost. If the slope of the isocost changes the new point of tangency is where relatively less is used of the factor that has risen in price.

4.4 Short-Run Cost Definition

28 Use the opening screen of this WinEcon topic.

The Shape of the Marginal Cost Curve

29 At low output levels, AFC will be high and will dominate ATC. AVC may also be relatively high.

30 The marginal cost is the additional cost of producing an extra unit. It will depend on what each labourer can produce. If the MPP is high the extra cost of producing each unit will be low and vice versa.

31 AFC; AVC or MC; fall; below; rise.

32 This is because as long as MC is below AC each additional unit of output will be produced at a lower cost than AC, and AC will therefore fall.

33

Lab	TP	AP	MP	FC	TVC	TC	AFC	AVC	AC	MC
1	278	278		55,000	25,000	80,000	198	90	288	
2	608	304	329	55,000	50,000	105,000	90	82	173	76
3	978	326	371	55,000	75,000	130,000	56	77	133	68
4	1381	345	403	55,000	100,000	155,000	40	72	112	62
5	1806	361	425	55,000	125,000	180,000	30	69	100	59
6	2245	374	439	55,000	150,000	205,000	24	67	91	57
7	2688	384	443	55,000	175,000	230,000	20	65	86	56
8	3126	391	438	55,000	200,000	255,000	18	64	82	57
9	3550	394	424	55,000	225,000	280,000	15	63	79	59
10	3950	395	400	55,000	250,000	305,000	14	63	77	63
11	4317	392	367	55,000	275,000	330,000	13	64	76	68
12	4642	387	325	55,000	300,000	355,000	12	65	76	77
13	4915	378	273	55,000	325,000	380,000	11	66	77	92
14	5127	366	212	55,000	350,000	405,000	11	68	79	118
15	5269	351	142	55,000	375,000	430,000	10	71	82	176
16	5331	333	62	55,000	400,000	455,000	10	75	85	403

34 (1) TFC, AFC, TC and AC shift upwards. (2) TVC, TC, AVC, AC and MC shift upwards. (3) If the cost of capital and its amount is the same, greater output will be produced. Or to produce a given output, less variable factors are needed. Hence, TVC, TC, AVC, AC and MC fall.

4.5 CVP: Graphical Analysis

35 Value added.

36 Because at low levels the fixed costs are not covered, but they are at high levels.

CVP: Algebraic Analysis

37 1667 and 2667.

38 28,571 and 30,000.

39 100 and 5100.

4.6 Expansion Paths

40 Short run; straight line.

41 The points of tangency between isocost and isoquant will change. The new points will be where relatively more labour is used, and the cost of producing particular levels of output will fall.

42 Because of the shape of the curves and the isocost being a straight line.

43 It is a straight line because the level of capital used is fixed.

44 One; tangential; isocost.

45 This can be explained by looking at the isocost–isoquant diagram. Note that on each short-run expansion path there is only one point of tangency; at all other output levels the curves cut. This shows therefore that at these other output levels the goods could be produced more cheaply in the long run by moving to another level of capital.

46 Because this output level can be produced more cheaply in the long run by altering the amount of capital used.

4.7 The Three Scale Effects

47 U; fall; economies; constant returns; diseconomies of scale; rise.

48 Economies: production , marketing. Diseconomies: managerial.

49 Because the firm reaps the economies of scale but avoids diseconomies.

Long-Run Average Costs in Practice

50 Downwards.

51 Survive in the long run.

Economies of Scale and Market Structure

52 Because each firm needs a 50 per cent market share to reach the point of MES.

53 1 , 20, 8, 3, 10.

Chapter 5

5.2 Characteristics of Market Structure

01 Monopolistic competition.

02 Oligopoly or monopoly.

03 Perfect competition or oligopoly.

04 Product differentiation.

Profit Maximization

05 AR = (TR)/Q.

MR = $(P_1 \times Q_1 - P_2 \times Q_2)/(Q_1 - Q_2)$.

06

Rides	Total revenues	Total costs	Profit	Marginal revenue	Marginal cost
10	100	114	–14		
				10	1
11	110	115	–5		
				10	1
12	120	116	4		
				10	10
13	130	126	4		
				10	14
14	140	140	0		
				10	15
15	150	155	–5		

07 13.

08 MC < MR; MC = MR; MC > MR

09 MR = AR = 10. Marginal and average revenue are the same horizontal line.

Normal and Supernormal Profit

10 Supernormal profits; 2 per cent.

11 Normal profits are included in production costs.

12 Supernormal profits equal total revenue minus total cost.

13 Normal profit.

14 Both are alternatives for profit or supernormal profit.

5.3 Four Key Assumptions in Perfect Competition

15 In the long run, firms are free to enter or leave the industry. Long-run equilibrium exists in the industry when firms do not wish to do so.

16 Factor mobility is the ability of factors such as labour and capital to move if they wish. In perfect competition this exists and so factors move to the occupation where they are best paid.

17 Goods are not branded. There is no product differentiation.

Firm and Industry Demand in Perfect Competition

18 Price falls by 0.0002 per cent.

19 Downward sloping.

20 Horizontal.

21 Infinite.

Profit Maximization in Perfect Competition

22 20 and 43.

23 Lower at 20; higher at 43.

24 Supernormal profits, in the short run.

25 No, because MC cuts MR from above.

Fixed and Variable Costs

26 In the short run it stays in business if average variable costs are covered.

27 Yes, in the short run, because some contribution to fixed costs is being made.

28 The smallest.

29 Yes. Note that we are ignoring firm's expectations about the future in the static analysis.

30 MC; the intersection with AVC.

5.4 Profits and Losses in the Short Run

31 F is the lowest output that sells for as much revenue as it cost to produce (losses are at a local maximum at this output); G is a break-even point; at H, the firm operates at the minimum point on its short-run average cost curve (profits are made in the short run – this is the minimum efficient scale); J is the profit maximizing output (this is the output the firm should choose to produce) K is another break-even point.

32 G, H, J, K.

Comparative Static Effects of Demand Changes

33 Price rises so they supply more. The profits they make attract entrants to the industry, so supply increases and price falls back to its original level.

34 Not exactly. Higher prices certainly stimulated a leftward shift in demand as industrial energy consumers disinvested. It also produced a rightward shift in supply, however, as other producers expanded output. The combined effects can be seen in the low oil prices in the late 1980s.

Comparative Static Effects of Changing Costs

35 (a) All firms are earning normal profits; (b) each firm produces at the minimum point on its LAC curve; (c) no firms wish to enter or leave the industry.

The Effect of a Tariff on Imports

36 $P_d = 10$ and $P_w = 6$ so the tariff is $P_d - P_w = 4$.

5.5 Two Key Assumptions in Monopoly

37 Downward sloping.

38 They prevent new firms entering to compete away the monopolist's profits, so supernormal profits can be earned in the long run.

Barriers to Entry

39 Gas, electricity and architecture.

A Monopolist's Revenue

Price	Quantity	Total revenue	Change in TR	MR
160	0	0		
			1400	140
140	10	1400		
			1000	100
120	20	2400		
			600	60
100	30	3000		
			200	20
80	40	3200		
			–200	–20
60	50	3000		
40	60	2400	–600	–60
20	70	1400	–1000	–100

40 Q = 40; TR = 3200 is at its maximum value.

41 MR falls twice as steeply as AR. When Q increases by 10, MR falls 40 whereas AR, or price, falls 20.

42 MR is below AR and pulls down successive values of AR as Q increases.

43 TR is falling when MR is negative.

Profit Maximization by a Monopolist

44 50 (from intersection of MC and MR).

45 45 (moving vertically up to AR line).

46 1000 [(AR − AC) × 50].

Monopoly and Supply

47 The monopolist has no supply curve. The amounts supplied are determined by both demand and cost conditions.

48 Less.

49 Fall; rise.

50 More.

Demand, Elasticity and Monopoly

Point	Price	Quantity	Revenue	Elasticity
A	80	20	1600	elastic
B	50	50	2500	unitary elasticity
C	20	80	1600	inelastic
D	63	36	2268	elastic

51 a) Of unitary elasticity; (b) elastic.

Price Discrimination Under Monopoly

52 (a) Yes; (b) Yes.

53 Worse

Main Differences between Perfect Competition and Monopoly

The supplementary WinEcon screen shows how to fill in the table.

54 Price control.

Chapter 6

6.2 Key Assumptions in Monopolistic Competition

01 An insignificantly small portion; set its own.

02 Some; product differentiation.

03 Characteristics recognized by consumers.

04 Set their own prices.

05 Brewing involves only a small number of large firms. Each firm produces a variety of often rivalrous brands. Thus the individual firm has a complex problem in deciding prices and quantities. Building is more dispersed amongst smaller firms. There is little within-firm competition. Building is more like the textbook view of monopolistic competition than brewing.

06 Hairdressing services and jewellery.

07 Different.

Short-Run Equilibrium of a Monopolistic Firm

08 Output is chosen where MC = MR to maximize profits.

09 In the short run it may happen to produce at the point where AC is a minimum if MR happens to pass through that point.

10 Price > MC

Adjustment to Long-Run Equilibrium

11 (a) With constant average costs, minimum average cost is achieved at all levels of output. (b) Where the cost curve is declining, minimum average cost is achieved at the point where AC = AR (market demand). One such firm in monopolistic competition cannot produce at this level of output.

12 60; 420; supernormal; 8400; enter; left; diminishes; AC; no; less; minimum.

6.3 The Key Assumptions of Oligopoly

13 The small number of firms in oligopoly.

14 Monopolist.

Interdependence in Oligopoly

15 Less; cannot.

16 Less; less.

17 Less; difficult.

Cartels

18 Where the sum of the MCs equals MR for the market.

19 Where each firm's MC equals the value of the market MR at the output that has been chosen.

20 An individual firm could raise its profits by increasing its output.

21 To increase its individual profits.

Cartel Disintegration

22 Firms which cheat increase their output and, if other members adhere to agreed limits, industry output increases, price falls and profits fall. The cheats increase their market share. The cartel may break down, leading to a price war.

23 Increased competition.

24 Oil; other goods; recession.

25 Political tensions.

26 It must be registered and then justified by showing that it passes one of seven tests, called 'gateways'. It must not be judged by the Restrictive Practices Court to be contrary to the public interest.

27 Combined supply.

28 Residual.

29 Zero.

Non-Collusive Oligopoly

30 Mutual interdependence between firms.

31 Firms have to guess how their rivals will act or react.

32 All firms are happy with their present strategies, given the strategies their rivals have adopted.

33 No firm wishes to change its strategy; each has correctly guessed its rivals' strategies and chosen its own best strategy in the circumstances.

34 If it has guessed wrongly its rivals' moves (or, of course, if its own calculations are wrong).

Assumptions of Cournot's Oligopoly Model

35 Each firm assumes the other will not react in any way but will continue producing as at present.

36 Each firm assumes the other will continue to supply the quantity of goods it is supplying at present, so it views its own demand curve as the market demand curve minus that quantity.

37 Costs are zero, so marginal costs are zero at all output levels.

38 It chooses the output where MC = 0 = MR.

39 0.5.

40 It constructs its demand curve (as described above), it finds the corresponding MR curve and sets MR = MC = 0.

41 0.75.

42 The first firm's price is double that of the second firm.

43 The first firm now assumes the second firm will continue to produce 0.25 of the maximum total output, so the maximum available to it is 0.75 of that total. Its demand curve is therefore reduced, and it reduces its output and price.

44 The second firm now sees a greater market share available, and it increases its output and price.

45 ⅔, of which each firm supplies half. The firms sell at the same price, which is ⅓ of the value at which the market demand curve intersects the price axis.

Successive Cournot Price/Quantity combinations

		Position				
		1	2	3	4	Equilibrium
Helen:	Price	50	37.5	34.375	33.594	33.333
	Quantity	50	37.5	34.375	33.594	33.333
Jim:	Price	25	31.25	32.813	33.203	33.333
	Quantity	25	31.25	32.813	33.203	33.333

Kinked Demand Theory

46 Elastic.

47 Inelastic.

48 Greater.

49 P_1; P_1; P_1.

Other Explanations for Stable Prices

50 Petrol; high costs of adjusting filling station equipment.

51 Personal computers; prices are used to indicate large differences in quality.

52 Clothing; optimal production is at a smaller scale than glass.

Non-Price Competition

53 Informative; persuasive

54 Advertise if the MR from advertising is greater than the MC of advertising.

55 Advertising is not worth while; profits fall from 3.5 to –1 after advertising.

56 If the product is newer, or less well known, or more of a luxury; if the economy is booming, and there is low unemployment, and there is high overall demand; if there is little competitive advertising, and the product has a small share of the market; if there has already been some expenditure on sales promotion, but not a very large amount.

Game Theory

57 A strategy which yields a better pay-off than any other, whichever strategy the opposing player may choose.

Here each firm wishes to gain the largest pay-offs possible.

		Firm B		
		Low price	High price	
Firm A	Low price	8, 8	200, 1	Dominant strategy for A
	High price	1, 200	150, 150	
		Dominant strategy for B		

The rational outcome is that each firm charges a low price.

58 Firm B will feel that firm A will face an irresistible temptation to break its promise. This would leave firm B with a pay-off of only 1 if it chose the high price strategy, so it is unlikely to do so.

6.4 The Case for Imperfect Competition

59 Lack of competition reduces the incentive to discover lower cost methods.

60 The firms that earn them may have economies of scale.

61 Savings due to economies of scale.

62 The benefits are higher. Investment generates economies of scale, R&D generates new products; both give the firm that undertakes them strategic advantages.

63 They are differentiated, so consumers have a choice.

Differences Within Imperfect Competition

Use the WinEcon screen to complete the table.

Chapter 7

7.2 Allocative Efficiency

01 Resources: land, labour, capital.

02 When a person says he or she is better off we assume he/she is actually better off.

03 Technological efficiency is getting the maximum possible output from given inputs.

04 Technical efficiency is achieved when an input mix is chosen which minimizes costs.

05 Ask individuals how they feel about a possible alternatives. If you cannot make anyone better off without making someone worse off, the existing situation is Pareto optimal.

06 Marginal social cost equals marginal social benefit.

07 Yes. We are comparing how individuals regard different combinations of goods. We consider whether they could be made better off without giving them more income.

08 Economic efficiency; consumer efficiency; MSC = MSB.

Marginal Private Cost and Benefit

9 It takes into account only the private viewpoints of buyers and sellers of the good.

10 MC = *P* = AR.

11 It is the value the purchaser puts on the last unit of output, so it is what he or she feels that output is worth.

12 *P* = MC.

Perfect Competition and Allocative Efficiency

13 Efficiency; MC; price; AR. Perfect competition. Social; private. Externalities; social; private. MSC; MSB.

On the diagram, MSC coincides with MC, and MSB with demand.

14 This happens if there are no externalities. It is important because private and social efficiency then occur together.

15 The individual firms in the competitive industry.

16 It is the allocatively efficient output.

17 When there are no external costs or benefits.

18 No externalities.

The Six Competitive Market Assumptions

19 A large number of consumers. A large number of suppliers. No barriers to entry. Homogeneous product from the firms. All resources are owned. Perfect information to consumers and producers.

20 Constant and complete preferences: no. Assumptions 2–6: yes.

7.3 Reasons for Market Failure

21 If firms maximize profits this will generally ensure market failure through economic inefficiency does not occur.

22 Consumers are assumed to maximize utility and this prevents consumer inefficiency leading to market failure.

23 When more than one cause of allocative efficiency is present. The problem is particularly difficult to solve.

24 Externalities, public goods and monopoly power.

Monopoly Power and Allocative Inefficiency

25 Less.

26 Equal to the social optimum.

27 The optimum is where MC and D cross. At lower quantities, such as the monopolist's output, D > MC and there is under-production; at higher quantities D < MC and there is over-production.

Externalities and Allocative Efficiency

28 The presence of social costs reduces the socially optimal output, so it may become closer to that chosen by the monopoly.

7.4 Price, Output and Profit in Competition and Monopoly

29 Demand or AR; supply or MC.

30 Price; equal to AVC (in the short run).

31 MC, MR.

32 Output is lower and price is higher in monopoly.

33 Costs are the same under monopoly as with perfect competition.

34 $(P - \text{AC}) \times Q$.

Efficiency in Competition and Monopoly

35 MSC = MSB.

36 No externalities, no monopoly

37 Technological and technical inefficiency are ruled out by profit maximization. Consumer inefficiency is ruled out because consumers buy on the demand curve.

38 Policies to prevent monopolies forming (e.g. the role of the Monopolies and Mergers Commission) and the regulation of firms with monopoly power.

7.5 Production externalities

39 With external production costs present, over-production occurs.

40 No, resources would not be better allocated without the training, so the training does not cause misallocation of resources.

Consumption externalities

41 Yes.

Finding Marginal Social Cost and Benefit

42 External production costs increase MC to give MSC. External production benefits decrease MC to give MSC. External consumption costs decrease demand to give MSB. External consumption benefits increase demand to give MSB.

7.6 Demand for Regulation

43 Pressure groups lobby politicians.

Supply of Regulation

44 Governments prefer to implement policies that have clear benefits, as this helps their chances of re-election.

Equilibrium Amount of Regulation

45 No, because people have different views. But nobody thinks it is worth trying to alter it.

46 The regulatory body is captured by the producers in the industry.

47 Under the public interest theory, yes, but not under the capture theory.

48 It remains at its existing level.

7.7 Monopoly Policy in a First-Best World

49 Monopolists may restrict output to raise prices. Subsidies would encourage the firm to expand output.

50 A lump sum tax is a possible way of removing the supernormal profits of a monopolist without altering the amount of output produced by the firm.

Externality Policy in a First-Best World

51 If production of a good causes pollution, a tax could lead to less of the good being produced, thereby reducing pollution.

52 A subsidy will encourage output. Works of art may be subsidized.

7.8 UK Regulation of Private Monopolies and Oligopolies

53 The Director General of Fair Trading refers the firm. A special investigation is conducted to see whether the firm is acting against the public interest.

54 If the firm supplies more than 25 per cent of output of the good, or if there is an explicit agreement between two firms which restricts competition.

UK Merger Policy

55 If the merger will create a new monopoly with a share of over 25 per cent of the market, or if at least £30 million of assets will be transferred by the merger.

56 The company may abandon its proposal because the MMC investigation would take too long; the merger may be in the public interest; the merged size of the firm may be small relative to its market.

Regulation due to Membership of the European Union

57 If combined world-wide turnover exceeds £3.7 bn, and if EU-wide turnover of at least two of the firms involved exceeds ECU 250 million.

Chapter 8

8.3 Supply of Labour: Derivation of the Budget Constraint

01 (a) £0, 10 hours; (b) £16, 8 hours; (c) £64, 2 hours; (d) £80, 0 hours.

The Labour Supply Decision

02

Hours	Income Wage rate £6.25)	Income (Wage rate £10)	Income (Wage rate £12.50)
1	6.25	10	12.5
2	12.5	20	25
3	18.75	30	37.5
4	25	40	50
5	31.25	50	62.5
6	37.5	60	75
7	43.75	70	87.5
8	50	80	100
9	56.25	90	112.5
10	62.5	100	125
11	68.75	110	137.5
12	75	120	150

03

	Wage rate £6.25	Wage rate £10	Wage rate £12.50
Hours worked	8.5	9	8
Income	53.125	90	100

04 This occurs because the individual is on the backward-bending part of the labour supply curve.

05 Increase; fall.

06 More leisure is taken as an hour of leisure is relatively cheaper.

07 Less leisure is taken, assuming leisure is a normal good.

08 Real income is defined as being a constant level of utility.

09 More leisure is taken. There is a fall in hours worked; the labour supply curve bends backwards.

10 Substitution effect dominates.

11 Most of an increase in wages will be used to buy more leisure time.

8.4 Short-Run Demand for Labour

12 MPP; MR.

13 MPP; price.

14 Wage rate = MRP.

15 In competition, price equals MR as the demand curve is perfectly elastic.

16 (and 18)

Wage rate	C-C Workers employed	C-I Workers employed
70	4	3
40	5	4
10	6	5

Competitive Input Market and Imperfect Output Market

17 The price charged falls as output increases so MR is below price.

18 See table above.

Imperfect Input and Output Markets

19 Even if price is a constant the MPP of labour falls as output rises, hence the downward slope.

20 This is because the MRP differs. The price of the good falls in the imperfect goods market as output rises but not in the competitive goods market.

21 VMP = MPP × P, MRP = MPP × MR and P = MR in the perfectly competitive goods market but not in the imperfect one.

22 Since MRP = MPP × MR, a technological advance will increase the MPP and will therefore increase MRP.

23 The ACF is the wage rate. If the labour market is competitive it is horizontal. If the market is imperfect, to attract more workers it has to rise, hence the upward slope.

Aggregate Demand for Labour

24 This is because a fall in wages will shift the MC curve in the goods market, which in turn shifts supply, thus reducing the price of the good, MR and MRP.

25 An increase in the wage rate will shift the MC and therefore reduce supply. This will increase the goods price and therefore also MR. This in turn will increase the MRP since MRP = MPP × MR.

26 This will reduce MC and therefore increase the supply in the goods market. This will reduce the price of the goods and therefore MR. This in turn will reduce the MRP since MRP = MPP × MR.

27 Left; increase; reduce; up; MPP × MR.

28 Right; increase; fall; downwards.

8.5 The Market for Skilled Labour: TV Weather Presenters

29 Opportunity cost is the next best use of the factor (e.g. the next best job available); transfer earnings are the minimum payment required to keep someone in their present job (i.e. their opportunity cost); economic rent is the payment made over and above transfer earnings (i.e. payments not necessary to keep people in their present job).

30 High rent: pop stars, top actors; low rent: cleaners, bar staff. The difference is explained by supply and demand: if demand is high relative to supply, rent will be high, and vice versa

31 The area under the supply curve is the minimum amount presenters would be willing to work for in this job, as another could be obtained at the same pay rate. The upper area is the amount they are paid over and above the rate required to keep them in the job.

32 £1 million; £1 million.

33

Presenter	Transfer earnings	Economic rent
1	10,000	40,000
2	20,000	30,000
3	30,000	20,000
4	40,000	10,000
5	50,000	0

34 Transfer earnings = £5000; economic rent = £10,000.

The Market for Unskilled Labour: Bar staff

35 Zero; transfer earnings.

The Market for City Centre Office Space

36 Zero; economic rent; inelastic.

37 Examples include agricultural products (e.g. rubber), newly developed components, highly trained personnel.

8.6 Discrimination in the Labour Market

38 Arbitrage.

39 Between young and adult workers; wage rates that vary from region to region.

The Aggregate Supply Curve faced by a Monopsonist

40 60; 30; 90.

41 This occurs because the labour supply markets are not perfectly competitive. To increase employment, the wage rate paid to all rises. Therefore, the MCF is not just the wages of the new workers but also the increase paid to the existing workers. This would not be the case if the labour supply was perfectly elastic.

Discriminating and Non-Discriminating Monopsony Compared

42 £1555; £1600; £45.

43 They will employ workers up to the point where MRP = MCF. Because the two groups have a different MCF, this will result in different levels being employed at a given MRP.

8.7 Minimum Wage

44 10; 40.

On the graph the combinations are, respectively: youth £3, adult £7; youth £5, adult £8; youth £7, adult £9.

8.8 Net Present Value

45 Because of its opportunity cost. It could receive interest if put in a bank which will mean £100 now is worth more than the future £100 that does not accrue interest

46 1/[(1 + cost of capital)^{year}].

47 If they do, not the value of future profits are over estimated and the wrong decision is made.

48

		10%	12.5%	15%
Year	Investment/earnings	Present value	Present value	Present value
0	(70,000)	(70,000)	(70,000)	(70,000)
1	20,000	18,182	17,778	17,391
2	40,000	33,058	31,605	30,246
3	30,000	22,539	21,070	19,725
4	20,000	13,660	12,486	11,435
5	10,000	6209	5549	4972
		------	------	------
NPV		23,649	18,488	13,769
Decision		Go ahead	Go ahead	Go ahead

The Cost of Capital

49 The IRR is the discount rate producing a NPV of zero.

50 No, it depends of the opportunity cost of using this capital. It should look at the next best use and, if it offers a greater return, use it in that way.

51 The IRRs are (1) 4%; (2) 6.5%; (3) 9.5%; (4) 6.5%; (5) 6.5%. The project with the highest IRR would be preferable, providing it exceeds the cost of capital.

52 23.8%.

Chapter 9

9.2 Trended and Non-Trended Variables

01 Investment.

02 The nominal £/$ exchange rate was fixed until 1972 and subsequently has been allowed to float. Since 1972 the £/$ exchange rate has fallen on average, though the graph shows how volatile floating exchange rates can be. The £ was devalued by the Wilson government in 1967, and this is clearly seen in the graph.

The Behaviour of Real and Nominal Variables.

03 Nominal variables have shown particularly pronounced upward trends since the early 1970s whereas the trends in real variables and ratios are less pronounced and they do not show any acceleration over time.

04 The statement is true. If both prices and quantities are rising, nominal spending must rise at a faster rate than real spending on its own.

Nominal and Real Interest Rates

05 (a) $[(1 + R)/(1 + p)] - 1$; (b) $R - p$.

06 False. Falling prices means negative inflation, so the real interest rate is greater than the nominal interest rate.

07

Interest rate (%)	Inflation rate (%)	Correct real rate (%)	Short-cut method (%)
5	2	2.9	3
20	18	1.7	2
10	15	–4.3	–5
5	–1	6.1	6

08

Interest-bearing rate (%)	Inflation rate (%)	Difference (%)
10	4	9.615
20	14	17.544
5	8	4.630
10	–4	10.417

09

Inflation rate (%)	Price in year 2 (£)
50	1.5
100	2
200	3
10,000	101

10

Year	Variable	Deviation from Trend
1980	100	0
1981	105	0
1982	110	0
1982	115	0
1983	120	0

Trends in Levels and Logarithms

11 Your trend should look like this.

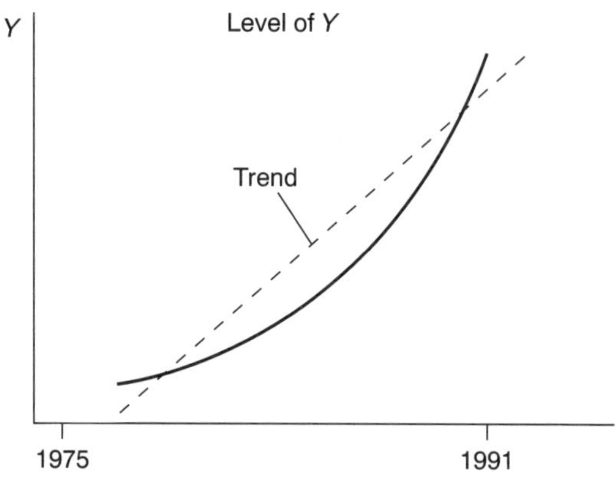

12 No. As time goes by the linear trend will increasingly under-predict the future value of *Y*.

13 (c)

14 110 and 10; 550 and 50. A constant growth rate means the absolute increase in the variable is greater the higher its initial value.

15 4.60517, 4.70048, 0.09531; 6.21461, 6.30992, 0.09531. The difference in the logarithms of the variable does not vary with the initial value.

Deviations from Linear and Log-Linear Trends

16 (c)

Annual Real GDP growth Rates

17

Year	Real GDP ($m)	Growth Rate (%)
1980	1500	–
1981	1800	20.0
1982	1600	–11.1
1983	2500	56.25
1984	3125	25.0

Quarterly GDP Growth Rates

18 Early 1980s and early 1990s.

9.3 Measuring the Price Level and Inflation

19 Refer to the Advanced popup on this screen.

20

Year	A Price (£)	A Quantity (kg)	B Price (£)	B Quantity (pints)	Base-weighted index	Current-weighted index
1980	0.50	1	5.0	30	100.00	100.00
1981	0.60	4	5.0	25	100.07	100.32
1982	0.75	5	6.2	30	124.09	124.43
1983	0.60	10	6.0	25	120.00	120.00
1984	0.80	26	7.0	30	140.07	141.60
1985	1.50	40	6.0	25	120.60	144.83

21 Base-weighted: –13.90%, current-weighted, 2.28%.

22 The base-weighted index falls because the price of B falls and the base weight (quantity consumed in 1980) is relatively high. The current-weighted index rises because the 1985 quantity of A is more important than in the base year, and the price of A rises.

Calculating the GDP Deflator

23 100.

24 £300 million.

The Balance of Payments

25 £600 million deficit.

26 (a) Invisible debit item; (b) visible export item ;(c) does not appear; (d) invisible credit item; (e) capital credit item.

9.4 Comovements with GDP Growth

27 No. It represents a strong negative correlation, indicating a counter-cyclical association.

28 No. Association between two variables does not necessarily imply causation. To determine causation we require a theory – in this case it is more likely that it is the rise in GDP that stimulates imports.

Lead and Lag Comovements

29 Interest Rates, Both; Money supply, Neither; Unemployment, Lag

30 Not necessarily. The fact that a change in one variables (like GDP growth) is followed by a change in another (unemployment) may suggest causation, but this may be misleading at times. For example households' money balances often increase just before Christmas, when expenditures typically rise. But it is not correct to infer the money supply causes expenditure to rise at Christmas. The money supply increase just before Christmas may be caused by the anticipated increase in spending over the festive season.

31 Yes, as the example of interest rates makes clear.

Money Supply and Inflation

32 Not necessarily. Once again correlation does not imply causation. If individuals wish to hold increased money balances in anticipation of future inflation, this correlation would be observed. Although this would seem to be an unlikely explanation in this case, you should never interpret correlation in terms of causation without reference to an explicit economic theory.

Chapter 10

10.2 Defining Output

01 Money.

02 It would involve double counting and would include transfer payments.

Transfer Payments

03 Double counting does not reflect unproductive activity. It is simply when certain outputs are counted more than once.

04 When a new car is purchased, money is exchanged in return for a newly produced good – the car. The payment of a pension is not made in return for any newly produced good or service.

05 Money flows one way, a newly produced good or service flows the other.

06 This is generally true, though not without exception.

07 This is because it is a 'domestic' activity (i.e. within the home).

08 Besides housework, the sale of an undetected (newly produced!) forgery of a Van Gogh painting would be such an example.

09 The profit made on the sale of a second-hand car.

Double Counting

10 Coal and iron ore are raw materials; steel is the intermediate good; cutlery is the final product.

11 Three times: once as the coal and iron ore itself, once as part of the value of the steel and once as part of the value of the cutlery.

12 Either count only final goods produced or sum the values added at each stage of production.

13

Firm/product	Value-added	Final sales
Earth		
Corn	8100	5400
Grapes	3600	2400
Milk	4200	2800
Wind		
Bread	7300	10,000
Wine	3800	5000
Cheese	6600	8000
Total	33,600	33,600

14 The income generated by each sector are the same as the values-added.

10.3 The Circular Flow of Income

15 Factor services; factor payments (income); wages, rent, profits. Final goods, services; revenue. Factor, factor services.

16 The net output of (value added by) a firm creates an equivalent amount of factor payments or income. Therefore, total output (the sum of values added) equals total income (the sum of all factor payments).

17 Expenditure is defined as the money flow necessary to purchase current output.

Investment and Saving

18 An addition to the income of firms (households) that does not come from the spending of households (firms).

19 Income received by households that is not spent on current consumption.

20 The amount households spend on consumer goods and services over a period.

21 Any revenue received by firms (net of tax) not distributed as factor payments.

22 Investment is defined as fixed investment plus inventory investment.

23 Fixed investment is expenditure on new capital goods, such as plant and machinery, land and buildings. Inventory investment is the net increase in the stocks of finished goods, work-in-progress and raw materials over a period. (It can be positive or negative.)

24 Any output produced but not sold is reflected in the expenditure total as inventory investment.

The Inclusion of Government

25 Governments levy indirect taxes such as VAT. Total expenditure incurred by purchasers is equal to GDP at market prices. Firms receive an amount equal to GDP at factor cost.

26 Governments levy direct taxes on household income and provide transfer benefits such as unemployment benefit and income support.

27 It is spending on goods and services that does not arise from the spending of households.

28 The existence of taxation means that some of the payments made by households (firms) are not received by firms (households); they leak into the government sector.

29 Gross domestic product at factor cost.

30 Yes. Just as before, net output generates an equivalent amount of factor income. Expenditure is defined as the expenditure necessary to purchase current output.

31 Use the supplementary WinEcon screen Injections Equal Withdrawals.

The Foreign sector

32 It is the money flow arising from exports that is relevant to the circular flow of income. This represents an injection into the circular flow.

33 A leakage. They are the payments for imports.

34 Three: investment, government consumption and exports.

35 Three: saving, taxation and imports.

36 GDP at market prices = C + I + G + (X − Z). Part of C, I and G represent spending on goods imported from overseas and such expenditure does not imply domestic production. Therefore, imports are netted out, giving a negative term.

37 Use the supplementary WinEcon screen Injections Equal Withdrawals (Again).

10.4 The Output Approach

38 No, these numbers are not comparable. The index numbers in any one sector can only be compared with other index numbers for the same sector from different periods (calculated using the same base year), not with those of other sectors.

39 Yes, for the above reason

40 To estimate the value added, we need data both on gross output and input. It is rare that both are available.

41 Passenger transport, for example, can be measured in passenger miles.

42 They are combined as a weighted sum, where the weights are determined by the values of sector outputs in the base period.

43 Yes, because nominal outputs are measured in terms of a common unit, money.

44 It has fallen steadily while the other services trend has risen.

45 It peaked in the 1980s due to high production of North Sea oil and gas at that time.

46 Services accounted for 63% of GDP in 1990, goods 37%.

The Expenditure Approach

47 Consumers' expenditure, investment, government consumption and exports.

48 Consumers' expenditure includes all spending on consumer durables in a period. Consumption includes the value of consumer durables (old and new) used up in a period.

49 No. It is included under investment.

50 Market prices.

51 Consumers' expenditure made up about 50% of TFE in 1990.

52 Investment.

53 Exports.

The Income Approach

54 Wages, profit, rent.

55 Factor cost. GDP at factor cost is what firms actually receive and, after depreciation and taxation, is what is available for distribution to factors of production.

56 Wages and salaries.

57 The Inland Revenue.

58 The mid-1970s, which was a highly inflationary period.

10.5 GNP and NNP

59 GDP is output produced within the borders of the domestic economy, whereas GNP also includes factor income generated by domestically owned assets located abroad but excludes factor incomes generated by foreign-owned assets located domestically. Hence GNP = GDP + net property income.

60 NNP = GNP – depreciation. NNP is national income because it equals total factor payments.

61 Because depreciation is notoriously difficult to measure.

GNP and Economic Welfare

62 It includes the production of bads, it ignores externalities, it ignores distributional questions, it measures production not consumption.

63 A regrettable necessity is output which does not add to economic welfare (e.g. defence expenditure and commuting). Not included in MEW.

64 Certain items are counted as final output in the national accounts, although it can be argued that they are in fact intermediate goods. Government spending on sanitation and civilian safety, for example, does not confer final benefit. Not included in MEW.

65 Certain non-market activities are productive, but are not included in the national accounts because they are difficult to measure (e.g. cooking, cleaning, washing etc.). These are included in MEW.

Chapter 11

11.2 Basic Concepts

Firms and households

01 Produce; consume.

02 Household.

03 Firm.

04 Household (the activity is performed by someone in his or her role as a member of a household).

05 Firm.

06 Household.

07 Firm.

Aggregate Markets

08 (a).

09 Sales revenue.

10 Money; real.

11 (a) Wages and salaries; (b) rent; (c) profits, interest and dividends.

12 Factor income.

The Circular Flow of Income and Expenditure

13 Such expenditures are called injections.

14 Such money flows are called withdrawals or leakages.

15 Investment expenditure, government expenditure, exports.

16 Saving, taxation, imports.

17 Withdrawal (taxation).

18 Withdrawal (import).

19 Injection (export).

20 Injection (investment).

21 Injection (government expenditure).

22 Withdrawal (saving).

23 Factor income and consumer expenditure.

Accounting Identities in the Circular Flow

24 Check you have recorded the notation correctly by referring to text card 2 of this screen.

25 Revenues are received from consumer expenditure, investment expenditure, government expenditure, and exports.

26 Income is used for consumer expenditure, or saved, or it goes as taxation.

27 $Y + Z$ (or E + Z, where E is aggregate real expenditure on domestic output, which equates to the quantity of domestic output (Y) supplied and purchased).

28 Y (or E).

29 Y.

Planned Versus Actual Flows

30 Alternative terms include *ex ante*, desired, and intended.

31 Alternative terms include *ex post*, and measured.

32 C, S, T, I, G, X, Z, aggregate output Y.

11.3 The Consumption Function

33 As income increases, consumer expenditure increases.

34 As income increases, not all of the increase will be consumed.

35 As income increases, a decreasing proportion will be consumed.

36 The proportion of an increase in income which is consumed ($\Delta C/\Delta Y$).

37 The proportion of total income which is consumed (C/Y).

38 130, 22, 48.

The Consumption Function Diagram

39 50; 0.6.

40 6400; 9200.

41 0.8; 0.766 recurring.

42 0.7.

Taxation

43 Examples include unemployment benefits, state pensions, subsidies to firms, student grants, etc.

Saving

44 Total income minus total taxation. (Taxation is direct taxation net of transfer payments.)

45 True.

46 0; 400.

47 $S = -800 + 0.1Y$.

48 0.1.

49 $Y - T = Y - 0.2Y = 0.8Y$

50 $0.9(0.8) = 0.72$.

51 $0.1(0.8) = 0.08$.

11.4 Constructing the Aggregate Demand Function

52 Because, as domestic output increases, the country's firms will need more imported materials and component parts, and, as income increases, domestic households will purchase more imported goods and services.

53 Planned expenditures.

54 In terms of its components, $AD = C + I + G + X - Z$.

55 $AD = 4700 + 0.6Y$.

56 1200; 1400; 1600.

57 0.1.

58 0.6.

Aggregate Supply: Equation and Diagram

59 Stocks of finished goods will decrease.

60 Respectively, decrease or increase the quantity of output.

61 Price lists; quantity adjustment rather than price adjustment.

62 8000.

63 $Y = AD$.

11.5 Goods Market Equilibrium

64

Aggregate output/income (Y)	$AD = 1000 + 0.6Y$	Firms' response
1500	1900	increase Y
2000	2200	increase Y
2500	2500	no change
3000	2800	decrease Y
3500	3100	decrease Y

65 Decrease.

66 Decrease.

67 Decreases.

68 Decreases.

69 Decrease.

70 Equilibrium.

71 Demand (supply); supply (demand).

The Formal Model: Equations and Solutions

72 Aggregate demand; withdrawals; injections.

73 AD = 3600 + 0.6Y.

74 Y = 3600 + 0.6Y which gives 0.4Y = 3600, so Y = 9000.

75 W = –100 + 0.4Y.

76 –100 + 0.4Y = 3500 which gives 0.4Y = 3600, so Y = 9000.

77 7080, 120, 1800, 1580.

78 Taxation minus government expenditure.

79 Exports minus imports.

80 (a) 300; (b) –280.

The Formal Model: Diagrams

81 Greater than.

82 Less than.

83 Increase.

84 Increase.

85 Increase.

86 9000.

11.6 A Change in Injections

87 Changes in investment, government spending or exports.

88 Income; marginal propensity.

89 0.63; 63.

90 12; 25.

91 –2500, –1000, –400, –160, –64.

The Size of the Multiplier

92 1.11; 1.25; 2.5; 3.33 recurring.

93 Consume; import.

94 Increases.

Equilibrium Values and Exogenous Changes

95 140; 280; yes.

96 42 + 70 + 28 = 140; yes.

97 –200; –120; –30; –50; –20.

The Multiplier: Withdrawals – Injections

98 $k = 1/(1 - b) = 1/w$; spend on domestic output.

99 1.66 recurring.

100 5.

101 2.5.

102 240.

103 –340.

104 240.

11.7 Unemployment and Macroeconomic Policy

105 Keynesian; full (or high) employment.

106 Fiscal; monetary.

Equilibrium and Full Employment

107 True.

108 Deficiency in aggregate demand.

109 Employment; demand; demand; employment.

110 800.

11.8 Self-test Revision Questions

111 0.55.

112 0.9.

113 1 (by definition).

114 $C + I + G + X - Z$.

115 The total change in equilibrium output/income divided by the exogenous change in expenditure which caused it

116 $1/(1 - b)$, $1/w$, $1/(1 - c + z)$ and $1/(s + t + z)$ are all correct.

Chapter 12

12.1 Functions of Money

01 A double coincidence of wants.

02 The official currency issue of notes and coin.

03 Means of payment; unit of account; store of value.

04 They are generally transferable as means of payment.

12.2 The Money Stock: Aggregate Measures

05 Notice of withdrawal.

06 Notes and coin held outside the Bank of England plus banks' operational balances at the Bank of England.

07 Cash held by the public plus all sterling deposits held by UK firms and households at UK banks and building societies.

08 Money is a stock of 'means of payment'; income and spending are flows of payments.

Flows of Funds Accounts

09 Income from current production – current expenditure = saving.

10 Saving – capital expenditure = financial balance.

11 Change in financial assets – change in financial liabilities; or net acquisition of financial assets.

12 Financial balance.

13 Net acquisition of financial assets (financial balance).

Assets and Liabilities

14

	Loan assets	Loan liabilities
Tom	0	50
Jean	50	500
Kitty	500	0
TOTAL	550	550

Financial Accounts and the Flows of Funds

15 Zero.

The Banking System: The Role of the Central Bank

16 (1) Banker to the other banks; (2) banker to the government; (3) issuer of domestic currency notes; (4) holder of national reserves of foreign currencies; (5) supervision of the financial sector; (6) operation of monetary policy.

17 For example: Germany, Deutsche Bundesbank; UK, Bank of England; USA, Federal Reserve Board.

The Banking System: The Other Banks

18 In the UK, Barclays, Lloyds, Midland, National Westminster.

The Banking System

19

Assets		Liabilities	
Cash	600	Deposits (initial)	600
Loans	400	Deposits (created by loans)	400
TOTAL	1000	TOTAL	1000

20 The ratio of cash to total liabilities.

Banking Operations (1)–(3)

21 From 0.6 to 0.462.

Loan Expansion and the Bank Deposit Multiplier

22 mrr = cash/deposits.

23 Deposits = (1/mrr) × cash reserves.

24 Change in deposits = (1/mrr) × change in cash reserves.

25 The bank deposit multiplier.

26 Maximum change in bank deposits/change in cash reserves.

27 1200.

28 20.

29 1900 (given a bank deposit multiplier of 20, total deposits must fall by 2000, but a 100 fall occurred with the cash withdrawal itself so it is the remaining 1900 which must come through a decrease in loans).

12.3 Control of the Money Supply

30 Check your table against the WinEcon screen.

31 MS = [(1 + cdr)/(mrr + cdr)] HPM.

32 900.

33 –1200.

Bills and Bonds

34 It pays the holder the face value on the maturity date.

35 Bills are sold at a discount below the face value.

36 It gives the 'coupon' interest payment which is then fixed.

37 £96.

38 16% per annum.

39 £12.

40 10% per annum.

41 £50 gain.

Open Market Operations: In Theory

42 Reduced by equal amount.

43 Contraction.

Interest Rate Control Methods

44 Impose an increased minimum reserve ratio; direct banks to reduce their lending; raise interest rates.

45 Interest rates fall.

12.4 The Classical Quantity Theory of Money

46 M = money stock; V = velocity of circulation of money; P = average price of goods and services; Y = aggregate output of goods and services.

47 The average number of times that each unit of the currency is used in making payments during the period.

48 $M.V = P.Y$.

49 That velocity, V, is constant.

50 4 per annum.

The Cambridge Version of Quantity Theory of Money

51 MD = k.P.Y.

52 £96 billion.

12.5 The Transactions Demand for Money

53 MD_{tr} = k.P.Y.

The Speculative Demand for Money

54 High.

55 Low.

56 Rise.

57 Use their speculative money to buy bonds.

The Total Demand for Money Function

58 Transactions; precautionary; speculative.

59 Transactions.

60 Rise.

61 High.

62 Rises.

63 460.

Exogenous Changes and their Money Market Effects

64 (Y = 1000) MD = 520 – 2000R = MS = 460, so 2000R = 60, making R = 0.03; (Y = 1400) MD = 720 – 2000R = MS = 460, so 2000R = 260, making R = 0.13.

LM Curve and Equation: Exogenous Changes

65 Left (because R increases).

66 Right (R falls).

67 Left (R increases).

LM Curve: Equation Derivation

68 MD = MS gives 500 + 0.25Y – 1000R = 1200, so 0.25Y = 700 + 1000R. Therefore, Y = 2800 + 4000R, or R = –0.7 + 0.00025Y.

69 (Y = 3000) R = 0.05; (Y = 3200) R = 0.1.

12.6 Friedman's Theory of Money Demand

70 MD/P = f(Y_p ; R_m, R_b, R_e, R_c ; w ; u).

71 MD/P increases.

72 MD/P falls.

73 MD/P falls.

74 MD/P falls.

12.7 Money Supply and Demand: Review

75 Cash and deposits.

76 Assets are items of monetary value which are owned; liabilities are monetary obligations which are owed.

77 A bank deposit is an asset for the bank customer, but a liability for the bank itself.

78 $M.V = P.Y$ where M = money stock quantity, V = velocity of circulation of money, P = average price of goods and services, Y = aggregate quantity of goods and services.

79 V is constant (or at least, independently determined and stable).

80 Values of R and Y at which the money market is in equilibrium.

81 MD/P = f(Y_p ; R_m, R_b, R_e, R_c ; w ; u) (see section 12.6).

Chapter 13

13.2 The Quantity Theory and Aggregate Demand

01 AD = M.V/P.
M.V is the total money expenditure in the period and within this the demand quantity varies inversely with the price.

02 £900 billion.

03 900, 450, 300, 225, 180, 150 (billions).

04 Plot curve; label AD = M.V/P = 900/P.

05 1200, 600, 400, 300, 240, 200 (billions), labelled AD = 1200/P.

The Monetarist Transmission Mechanism

06 Examples include bonds, equities, property, investment expenditure on capital goods for production, consumer durables, non-durables consumption, human capital.

Policy Implications

07 Money; price level.

08 Excessive increases in money supply.

13.3 International Trade: An Example

09 Fixed; flexible; exchange rate.

10 (a) \$15; (b) £14.

11 (a) A; (b) £4, \$6.

12 (a) Price increases; (b) price decreases.

13 Arbitrage.

14 £10 = \$21 (i.e. £1 = \$2.10).

Fixed Exchange Rates

15 (a) Excess supply of £; (b) Excess demand for \$.

16 Buy pounds.

17 The demand for pounds curve would be shifted to the right.

18 Exports; rise.

19 Sells; increases.

20 Increase.

21 Money supply.

Flexible Exchange Rates

22 Exports; imports; fall.

23 Purchasing power parity; same.

Summary: Trade and Exchange Rates

24 Imports; aggregate demand.

13.4 Introduction: Keynesian Aggregate Demand

25 (a) G, X; (b) C, I, S, T, Z, W, J, Y, R and AD.

26 AD = f(Y, R).

Consumer Demand and the Rate of Interest

27 (a) Decrease; (b) decrease; (c) decrease.

28 All.

29 C increases.

The Consumption Demand Function

30 900; 1500; 2100.

31 1550; 1500; 1450.

The Investment Decision and the Rate of Interest

32 £100.

33 The rate of discount which makes the present value of expected net receipts over the life of the project equal to the present cost.

34 0.2 (£60,000/1.2 = £50,000 and £72,000/1.44 = £50,000).

Investment Demand and the Rate of Interest

35 Downwards (estimated IRRs will be lower).

Investment Demand and Aggregate Output/Income

36 Gross investment = net investment + replacement investment

37 Net investment = (fixed capital/output ratio) × change in output.

38 £80 billion (4 × £20 billion output increase).

The Investment Demand Function

39 900; 700; 500.

40 600; 700; 800.

The IS Equation and Curve: Graphical Approach

41 Interest rate; real income; goods.

Changes in Injections and Withdrawals

42 Right.

43 Left.

44 Right.

The IS Equation and Curve: Equation Approach

45 $AD = C + I + G + X - Z = 5300 + 0.5Y - 5000R$.

46 $J = I + G + X = 5600 + 0.1Y - 4000R$.

47 $W = S + T + Z = 300 + 0.6Y + 1000R$.

48 $Y = 5300 + 0.5Y - 5000R$ so $0.5Y = 5300 - 5000R$, giving $Y = 10{,}600 - 10{,}000R$.

49 $300 + 0.6Y + 1000R = 5600 + 0.1Y - 4000R$ so $0.5Y = 5300 - 5000R$, giving $Y = 10{,}600 - 10{,}000R$.

The IS Curve and Aggregate Demand

50 Decreases.

51 Decreases; reducing; cuts.

IS–LM Equilibrium

52 MD = MS gives $800 + 0.5Y - 6000R = 5000$ so $0.5Y = 4200 + 6000R$. Therefore, $Y = 8400 + 12{,}000R$, or $R = -0.7 + 0.00008333Y$.

53 From the IS equation, $Y = 10{,}600 - 10{,}000R$, subtract the LM equation, $Y = 8400 + 12{,}000R$ to give $0 = 2200 - 22{,}000R$. Hence, equilibrium is at $R = 0.1$, $Y = 9600$.

54 Mark these IS–LM intersection values in diagram.

Exogenous Changes in the IS–LM Model

55 IS shifts right, Y increases and R increases.

56 LM shifts right, R decreases and Y increases.

57 IS shifts left, Y decreases and R decreases.

58 IS shifts right, Y increases and R increases.

59 LM shifts left, R increases and Y decreases.

Policy Implications of the IS–LM Theory

60 False.

61 IS curve; LM curve.

62 Fiscal: increasing government expenditure, G, decreasing taxation, T. Monetary: increasing money supply, MS, decreasing rate of interest, R.

Keynesian Aggregate Demand and the Price Level

63 MD decreases; R decreases; AD increases.

13.5 The BP Curve

64 CUR + CAP = 0.

65 Imports; deficit; increasing; capital inflow.

IS–LM–BP Analysis with Fixed Exchange Rates

66 Appreciation; sell; buy; depreciation.

67 Domestic money supply; LM curve; IS curve; BP curve.

68 Lower *Y*.

IS–LM–BP Analysis: Exchange Rate Changes

69 Purchase its own currency with foreign currency from reserves.

70 Currency depreciates, trade balance improves.

IS–LM–BP Analysis with Flexible Exchange Rates

71 AD increases (because exports are more competitive, imports less).

Exogenous Changes

72 More; less.

73 Left; above; surplus; appreciation; sells; increase; downwards.

74 Fixed; flexible.

13.6 Neoclassical Theory of Consumer Expenditure

75 Below.

The Permanent Income/Life Cycle Hypotheses

76 Milton Friedman.

77 Expected long-run average income, consistent with maintaining wealth intact.

78 By running down assets.

79 The age structure of the population.

Real Balance Effects in Aggregate Demand

80 £1500; £1000; £750.

81 Decrease.

Aggregate Demand as a Function of the Price Level

82 LM curve; IS curve.

83 Decreases.

The Neoclassical Synthesis

84 Wage–price rigidities; real balance effects.

Chapter 14

14.2 The Aggregate Production Function

01 Aggregate output rises from £600 to £1,000. That is output less than doubles following a doubling of labour input. This is consistent with diminishing marginal productivity. Note that the shares in employment and output are the same for each firm in both years (firm A has a half and one third respectively).

02 Aggregate output rises from £600 in year 1 to £620 in year 2. The aggregate production function would appear to have shifted. In fact there has been a distribution shift towards firm B, where productivity was higher (output per worker in B in year 1 was £4, cf £2 in A). The average product in both firms falls as employment rises, which is consistent with diminishing productivity.

03 The aggregate production function requires there to be no change in the distribution of employment from high to low productivity firms.

04 Between 1960 and 1989 the other determinants of aggregate output – the capital stock and technology – have not remained constant. And the quality of the labour input may also have improved. So the production function will have shifted upwards.

The Aggregate Demand for Labour

05 £15; MPPL; lowering.

06 The demand for labour is given by the marginal product of labour, which is the slope of the aggregate production function.

07 The real product wage is the nominal wage divided by the price of the firm's output.

08 Changes in technology and the capital stock have caused the demand for labour to have increased at every real wage – the labour demand curve has shifted outwards.

Labour Supply and Unemployment

09 That person is unemployed and looking for work but not willing to accept a job at the wage currently on offer. This kind of unemployment is described as frictional.

10 False. As the real wage falls, the number of job searchers will increase (frictional unemployment), so the labour supply curve will be upward sloping even when the labour force is constant.

11 We require that the relative price of wage goods and non-wage goods remains constant over time, so that movements in consumer prices and the real consumption wage are identical to movements in all prices and the real product wage.

14.3 Classical Labour Supply Theory

12 The real wage equals the nominal wage rate divided by the price level = W/P, where P is the price of consumption goods.

13 False. The real consumption wage will have increased four-fold. Labour supply would only be unchanged if the real wage were unchanged.

14 As the real wage rises, workers might decide to work fewer hours, taking more leisure as their income rises.

15 (b). The other two will increase demand and lower supply, increasing the amount of excess demand in the labour market.

16 A rise in the price level will lower the real wage and this will raise the quantity of labour demanded and lower that supplied. The classical model predicts that the nominal wage rate will fall, removing the excess supply.

17 Assume initial labour market equilibrium. A rise in the price level will lower the real wage, raising the amount of labour demanded and lowering its supply. The excess demand for labour will raise the nominal wage to its equilibrium level.

18 Real wage = 10; employment = 120.

19 Real wage = 9; employment = 118. The labour demand curve shifts to the left, so the amount by which the real wage falls depends on the slope of the labour supply curve.

The Classical Aggregate Supply Curve

20 The nominal wage rate adjusts to allow the real wage to remain the same, keeping labour supply = labour demand. New values are 4 and 8 respectively.

21 Fall; increase; decrease; excess demand; rise; remain unchanged; double.

22 (a) Real output remains unchanged; (b) nominal output (real output × price level) doubles.

AS Curve Shifts: Technology Shocks

23 No. If the slope of the production function remained the same at each level of employment, the demand for labour function would not be affected.

24 Output rises because of the upward shift in the production function at each level of employment and because the level of employment changes in the labour market. The slope of the labour supply curve will determine the change in employment.

25 Compare your AS_1 curve with text card 5, Show clicked, of the WinEcon screen. You should see that the AS curve shifts less when the labour supply curve is vertical since there is no change in the quantity of labour employed.

AS Curve Shifts: Income Tax Changes

26 Leave unchanged. Your illustration should look like this.

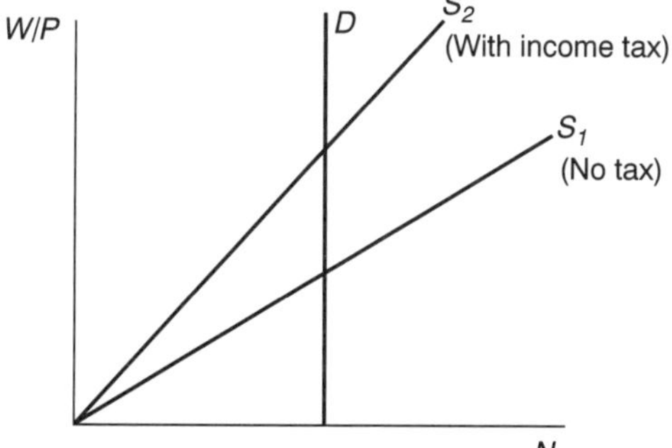

27 33%; 25%; 83%; 40%.

Unemployment in the Classical Model

28 Frictional unemployment arises in the classical model as workers search for better jobs. It is represented as the amount by which the labour force exceeds the labour supply at the equilibrium real wage.

29 (d). It is not possible to be sure of the effects of falls in the replacement ratio. Although unemployment has risen, it is possible that unemployment may have risen even more if the replacement ratio was unchanged.

14.4 Keynesian Model: Employment Determination

30 (a) 250, 125 and 2:1; (b) 125, 125 and 1:1.

31 Workers wish to maintain or improve their wage differentials with other workers, so they will resist a cut in their money wage (which lowers these differentials) even when they would be prepared for a real wage cut through a price increase. A rise in the money wage of one group of workers only will not worsen the wage differentials with others.

32 If the labour market were in equilibrium, a rise in the price level creates excess demand for labour and the money wage will rise, restoring equilibrium at the same real wage. If the money wage were at its floor, and there is unemployment in the labour market, a rise in the price level will increase the demand for labour without creating excess supply. Employment will rise but the money wage will be unchanged. The real wage falls.

Keynesian Aggregate Supply Curve

33

Price level	Nominal wage	Real wage	Employment level	Labour market	Real output	Shape of AS curve
0.5	4	8	$N_4 < N_2$	excess supply	$Y_4 < Y_2$	upward slope
0.67	4	6	$N_2 < N_1$	excess supply	$Y_2 < Y_1$	upward slope
1	4	4	N_1	equilibrium	Y_1	kinks here
2	8	4	N_1	equilibrium	Y_1	vertical
3	12	4	N_1	equilibrium	Y1	vertical

34 Upward; excess supply; equilibrium; identical.

35 Your AS curves should look like this.

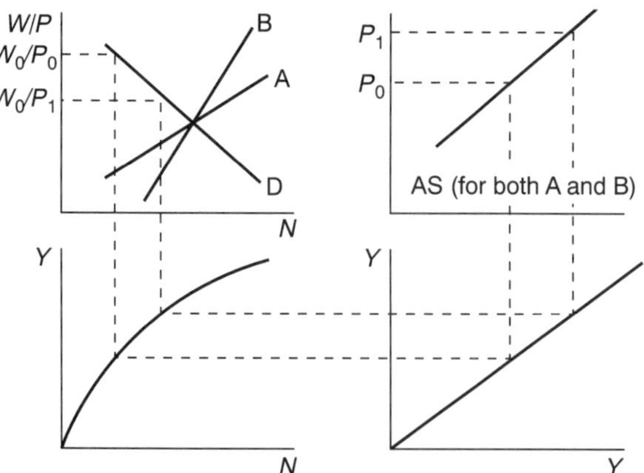

36 Your AS curves should look like this. The wage elasticity is greatest for A.

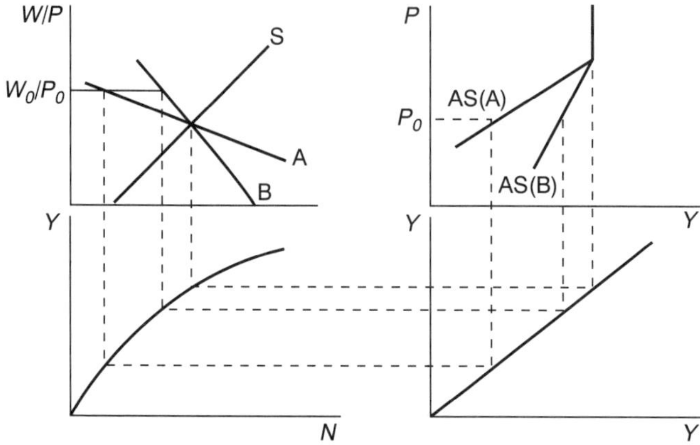

37 Assume initial equilibrium in the labour market. The price level and the wage both increase, and the level of employment remains unchanged. Now assume the price level falls back to its original level. The wage rate will not fall (as it is now the new wage floor), so the quantity of labour demanded and the level of employment will fall.

38 The real wage will rise as output (and therefore employment) falls because the level of employment is determined in the Keynesian model by the demand for labour, which is downward sloping.

Unemployment in the Keynesian Model

39 Fall; supply of; falls; rises.

40 (a) Remain unchanged; (b) remain unchanged. Because the labour market is initially in equilibrium, any rise in the price level will be followed by an equi-proportionate rise in the money wage, leaving the real wage unchanged. Frictional unemployment will equal its 'equilibrium' level and there will be no change in the level of demand deficient unemployment (it remains at zero).

41 (b). The fall in price raises the real wage, and this will persuade unemployed workers to spend less time searching, lowering frictional unemployment. The increase in the real wage reduces labour demanded and raises the quantity of labour supplied. This increases demand deficient unemployment.

14.5 Monetarist Aggregate Supply at a Glance

42 Expectations are fixed in the short run and may be wrong.

43 The long run.

Monetarist Theory of Labour Supply

44 Price expectations are double actual prices.

45 Your labour supply curves should look like this.

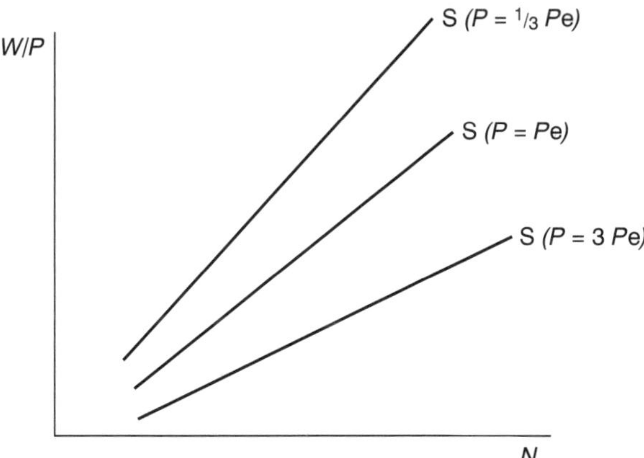

46 They supply different quantities of labour if their price expectations change.

Monetarist Model: Employment Determination

47

Actual price level	Expected price level	Nominal wage rate	Expected real wage rate	Actual real wage rate	Employment level curve	Labour supply
1	1	4	4	4	N1	S1
2	1	6	6	3	N2 > N1	S2 > S1
0.5	1	3	3	6	N3 < N1	S3 < S1

48 It rises, because employers see the real wage is falling and want to employ more workers. They raise the nominal wage to attract them.

49 It rises, because employees (wrongly) think the real wage has risen.

50 Lower; lower; higher.

51 Workers need to have information on a range of consumer goods when calculating their real wage, and mistakes are likely. Firms need only know the price of their output and they can safely be assumed to have full knowledge of this.

52 Lowers; raise; raise; higher; higher; increase; raise.

The Monetarist Aggregate Supply Curve

53 The level of output produced when workers have correct price expectations.

54 The actual real wage falls as output rises. This is because the economy is always on the labour demand curve, and since firms are correctly informed about the real wage, employment and output will only rise when the real wage falls.

55 The expected real wage must rise as employment and output rise. Otherwise workers would not be willing to supply the extra effort required to raise output.

56 If the rise in the price level were anticipated, employment and output would be unchanged. If the rise in the price level were unanticipated, then output and employment would rise. In this case workers interpret the rise in the money wage as a rise in the real wage.

57 Your graph should look like this.

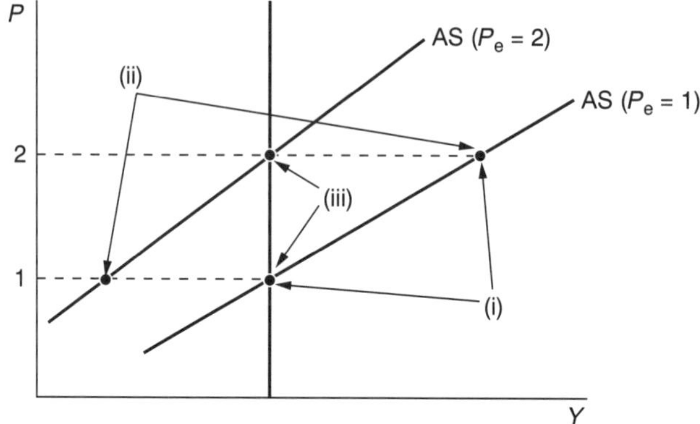

Unemployment in the Monetarist Model

58 The level of unemployment that is consistent with correct price expectations.

59 Unemployment is above the natural rate.

60 It is higher.

61 In the long run, expectations are correct, so unemployment is at the natural rate.

62 (a) Yes. If actual prices are higher than expected, unemployment is below its natural level. (b) 4%.

Logarithms and Growth Rates: A Review

63 $[\ln(x_t) - \ln(x_{t-1})] \times 100$.

The Phillips Curve

64 (c). It is found by comparing the expected price level with the known previous price level.

65 The natural rate of unemployment.

66 The short-run Phillips curve shifts as the expected inflation rate changes.

67 If the expected inflation rate is high.

68 Zero.

69 (b). Since unemployment is less than its natural rate the actual price level is greater than the expected price level. The actual price level is £5.5, so the expected price level can only be £5.2.

Chapter 15

15.2 A Key Assumption

01 It implies that the aggregate supply curve is horizontal.

02 The general price level is assumed to be exogenous. It is taken as a given and is independent of any policy changes the government might make.

03 Vertical or upward sloping.

04 A change in fiscal policy will cause the IS curve to shift. The change in fiscal policy means that, at a given rate of interest, goods market equilibrium will now occur at a different level of real output. For instance, if the government increases its final expenditure the IS curve will shift to the right. The aggregate demand curve will shift in the same direction as the IS curve as a result of any change in fiscal policy.

05 A change in monetary policy will cause the LM curve to shift. The change means that, at a given rate of interest, money market equilibrium will now occur at a different level of real output. For instance, if the government increases the money supply, the LM curve will shift to the right. The aggregate demand curve will shift in the same direction as the LM curve as a result of any change in monetary policy.

Fiscal Policy and Crowding Out

06 Answer 1 is correct. It is because the goods and money markets are treated as being interdependent. For instance, in the IS–LM model expansionary fiscal policy not only increases real output, but because increasing output causes the transactions demand for money to increase, it also causes the interest rate to rise. This in turn results in the crowding out of some private investment. Answer 2 is not correct because in the IS–LM model, as it is used here, the price level is also assumed fixed. (The model can be extended to include flexible prices, but it then becomes what is later termed the AS–AD model.)

07 Fiscal policy is apparently less powerful according to the IS–LM model because it takes account of crowding out. The simple income–expenditure model does not.

08 According to the IS–LM model a reduction in the tax rate would cause the interest rate and real output to rise. The tax cut will cause the IS curve to shift to the right (and to become steeper). Real output will rise (as consumption demand rises). Simultaneously the increased demand for transactions balances will cause the interest rate to rise.

Recap on the Slope of the IS curve

09 Withdrawals are a function of Y, injections are a function of R, $W = J$.

10 Interest rate; real output; goods.

11 Inelastic; elastic.

Recap on the Slope of the LM curve

12 Transactions demand for money, a function of Y; speculative demand for money; a function of R; money supply = money demand.

13 Interest rate; real output; money.

14 Inelastic; elastic.

The Effectiveness of Fiscal Policy

15 Relatively large. (In your diagram the IS curves should be relatively steep and the LM curve relatively flat.)

16 This is because the demand for money is relatively elastic. Only a small increase in the rate of interest is necessary to restore equilibrium in the money market.

17 Partly because the interest rate has not risen by much and partly because investment is relatively interest inelastic.

18 Relatively ineffective. (In your diagram the IS curves should be relatively flat and the LM curve relatively steep.)

19 This is because the demand for money is relatively inelastic. A large increase in the rate of interest is necessary to restore equilibrium in the money market.

20 Partly because the interest rate has risen significantly and partly because investment is relatively interest elastic.

Monetary Policy

21 The LM curve is shifted to the right. Whatever the rate of interest, the money market is now in equilbrium at a higher level of real output.

22 The effect is to lower the interest rate and to increase real output.

23 Reduction; private investment; an increase.

The Effectiveness of Monetary Policy

24 Low; high.

25 Relatively small. (In your diagram the IS curves should be relatively steep and the LM curve relatively flat.)

26 This is because the demand for money is relatively elastic. Only a small fall in the rate of interest is necessary to restore equilibrium in the money market.

27 Partly because the interest rate has not fallen by much and partly because investment is relatively interest inelastic.

28 High; low.

29 Relatively effective. (In your diagram the IS curves should be relatively flat and the LM curve relatively steep.)

30 This is because the demand for money is relatively inelastic. A large fall in the rate of interest is necessary to restore equilibrium in the money market.

31 Partly because the interest rate has fallen significantly and partly because investment is relatively interest elastic.

15.3 Keynes versus the Classics

32 At least in the long run, fiscal and monetary policy do not affect the level of real output.

33 It depends on the way in which the labour market behaves and whether or not wages are flexible downwards. Or, in the monetarists' view, it depends on whether workers' expectations of the price level are correct.

34 This is because one effect of expansionary fiscal policy is to push the prices of goods and services up. If the nominal money supply is fixed, then the result is that the real money supply falls. This reduces the overall expansionary effect of the policy change.

35 The money wage is taken as given (exogenous). Therefore, when the price level rises, the real wage falls, thereby increasing the demand for labour and the supply of output.

36 Rise, rise, fall, rise.

37 This is because wages are assumed to be perfectly flexible in the classical model. As prices rise, so money wages rise in the same proportion. The real wage is unchanged. Therefore, the demand for labour and the supply of output are unchanged.

38 Remain unchanged; rise; remain unchanged; remain unchanged.

39 This is because in the AS–AD model prices will rise as a result of the expansionary monetary policy, limiting the size of the increase in the *real* money supply.

40 Rise; rise; fall; rise.

41 Remain unchanged; rise; remain unchanged; remain unchanged.

15.4 The IS–LM–BP Framework

42 They are that net imports are a positive function of real income and that net capital inflows depend positively on the interest rate.

43 It is that net imports must equal (autonomous) net capital inflows. It is represented by a 45 degree line on a graph where net imports are measured on the vertical axis and net capital inflows are measured on the horizontal axis.

44 B is a point of surplus, because it lies above the BP curve. To see why, mark on the diagram a point, 'A', that lies on the BP curve vertically below B. 'A' is a point of balance of payments equilibrium. Point B represents the same level of output as A, but with a higher interest rate. Therefore, at B, net imports are the same as at A, but net capital inflows are greater. Since A is a point of equilibrium, B must be a point of surplus.

45 If an appreciation causes net imports to rise (or net exports to fall), then this means that, at every interest rate, the balance of payments is now in equilibrium at a lower level of output than previously. This amounts to a leftward shift in the BP curve.

46 If an appreciation in the exchange rate causes net exports to fall (or net imports to rise), it must also cause the IS curve to shift to the left. Net exports are a component of aggregate expenditure.

47 The BP is horizontal if net capital inflows are perfectly interest elastic.

Policy Effectiveness in the Open Economy

48 Effective; right; rise; surplus; increase; right; higher.

49 Ineffective; right; rise; fall; deficit; fall back; left; original.

50 Moderately effective; right; rise; surplus; appreciate; left; left; higher.

51 Effective; right; rise; fall; deficit; depreciate; right; right; higher.

15.5 The Natural Rate Hypothesis

52 In the short-run, the labour force mistakes the increase in nominal money wages for a real increase. They therefore increase their supply of labour causing the equilibrium real wage to fall and employment and output to rise.

53 After a while the labour force realizes that prices have risen faster than they had anticipated and that, therefore, their real wages are not higher. Consequently, they reduce their supply of labour back to its original level. Output and employment are then restored to their original levels.

54 The only circumstance under which the level of unemployment is below its natural level is when labour underestimates the general price level and hence overestimates its real wage. Since labour eventually adapts to any new (in this case higher) level of prices engineered by government, the only way in which labour can be continuously fooled into increasing its supply is if the price level is continuously being increased at a faster and faster rate. Therefore, the inevitable consequence of holding unemployment below its natural rate must be increasing inflation.

55 Yes. The natural rate of unemployment is consistent with any rate of inflation. The key point about the natural rate of unemployment is that inflation will be constant. This constant rate can be very high or very low. If it is high this may be because a previous government attempted to hold unemployment below its natural rate for several periods, causing inflation to rise. When it eventually gave up, unemployment returned to its natural rate, but inflation was then at a high level.

Policy Timing and Magnitude

56 There is an inside lag, consisting of a recognition, decision and implementation lag and an outside lag.

57 Ideally there should exist a correlation coefficient of –1. In other words, the policy impact should exactly counterbalance the economic cycle, which may seem rather unlikely. The correlation coefficient needs to be less than zero, at any rate. The nearer it is to –1, the better.

Chapter 16

16.2 Measuring a Cycle

01 In the late 1980s GDP increased well above its trend, but it fell significantly below trend in the early 1990s.

02 Growth rates were more volatile after 1970 than they were before.

Cycles Terminology

03 The maximum value of real GDP in the boom.

04 The minimum value of real GDP in the recession.

05 A period of real GDP decline (comprising at least two consecutive quarters).

06 A period of real GDP growth (comprising at least two consecutive quarters).

07 The difference in GDP between peak and trough.

08 The time between two peaks (or two troughs).

09 Peak to trough = 11 months; Trough to peak = 34 months. Your graph should have a saw-tooth appearance. The curve should rise for 34 months and then fall for 11 months, and so on throughout the period covered.

10 No. The period of recession is shorter than the period of boom.

Aggregate Demand and Supply Shocks

11 (a) Demand shock; (b) both demand and supply shocks; (c) demand shock; (d) supply shock; (e) supply shock, and also demand shock.

12 It changes disposable income, and this can be expected to have an effect on the level of consumer spending.

13 It increases net real wages, and this may have an effect on labour supply and work incentives.

Shocks and Persistence

14 Y = 100/(1 – b).

15 (a) 400; (b) 133.33.

16

Year	Current GDP (Y_t)	Lagged GDP (Y_{-1})	Shock (e_t)
1970	600	400	200
1971	550	600	0
1972	512.5	550	0
1973	484.375	512.5	0
1974	463.281	484.375	0
1975	447.461	463.281	0
1976	435.596	447.461	0
1977	426.697	435.596	0

17 The economy is moving towards the equilibrium value of 400.

18

Year	Current GDP (Y_t)	Lagged GDP (Y_{t-1})	Shock (e_t)
1970	600	400	200
1971	550	600	0
1972	662.5	550	150
1973	496.875	662.5	–100
1974	572.656	496.875	100
1975	479.492	572.656	–50
1976	359.619	479.492	–100
1977	369.714	359.619	0

19 In the first case there is a single shock. The economy is disturbed from its equilibrium (400) and over time it slowly returns to it. In the second case repeated random shocks cause output to fluctuate around 400.

16.3 Classical Model: AD Shock, AS Shock

20 (c).

21 If price and output movements were generated by supply shocks, you would expect output growth and inflation to be negatively correlated. This is true of the data – a rise in output growth is associated with lower inflation rates.

22 Output unchanged; rise in the price level.

23 Output falls; price level rises.

24 Uncertain. The tax change shifts both AD and AS.

25 AS moves left, output falls and the price level rises.

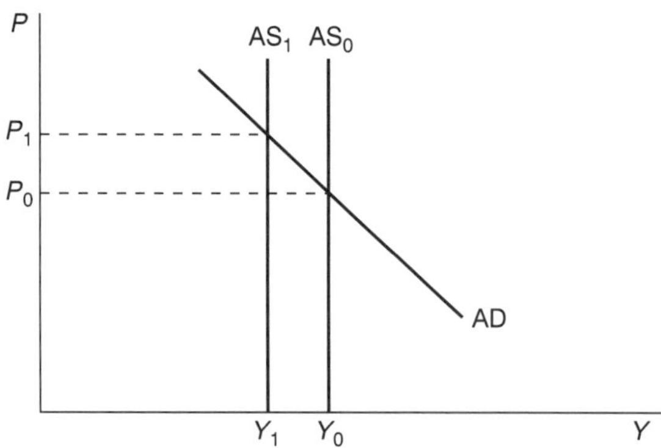

26 The government should reduce the money supply so that the AD curve moves with the AS curve. This is sometimes referred to as an 'accommodating' policy response.

Keynesian Model: AD Shock, AS Shock

27 Marginal; money; demand; raise; rise; fixed.

28 (a) 1980; (b) 1982; (c) 1981; (d) 1983.

Monetarist Model: AD Shock

29 Demand; remains unchanged; remains unchanged; rise; upwards; supply; left; fall; rise.

30 Yes. A positive AD shock leads to an increase in the price level and output. Subsequent movements in the AS curve cause output to fall and prices continue to rise, but at a slower rate.

31 1981

32 1983: 2.0%; 1984: 1.5%.

33 Above. This is because price expectations have been revised upwards.

Monetarist Model: AS Shock

34 The intersection of the short-run AS curve with the long-run curve occurs where price expectations are correct. If the level of price expectations is unchanged, the short-run curve must intersect the long-run curve at the same price level as before.

35 Because price expectations are revised upwards, causing a shift in the short-run aggregate supply curve.

36 Shifts in the AS curve mean that price and output are determined by the AD curve, which is downward sloping.

37 False. The AS curve cuts the LRAS curve at a price level equal to the expected price level.

38 Supply; rises; falls; downwards; supply; right; rise; fall.

Chapter 17

17.2 The Distribution of Income

01 (d).

02 Because developing countries are becoming more and more differentiated and also the Second World is no longer the 'socialist camp' it used to be.

03 Africa.

04 South Korea, Taiwan, Singapore, Hong Kong, Brazil, Thailand and Malaysia are classified as NICs.

The Lorenz Curve

05 Kenya and Brasil.

06 It represents the degree of inequality in the distribution of income. It shows the relation between the cumulative percentage of income and the cumulative percentage of population.

07 If income is exactly equally distributed.

08 Because income is not equally distributed.

09 24%.

10 2.1% and 2.7% respectively.

11 60.9% and 36.9% respectively.

17.3 Development – Concepts and Measurements

12 Development is a process of improvement and enhancement of human welfare. However, human welfare is defined differently by different people depending on their value judgements.

13 (1) It does not take into account the distributional effects of economic growth. (2) It does incorporate non-market transactions such as externalities.

14 Pollution, congestion and the depletion of natural resources.

15 China.

16 Iran.

The Human Development Index

17 0.3 and 0.2 respectively.

18 0.34 and 0.57 respectively.

19 Senegal.

20 Sri Lanka.

17.4 The Last Three Development Decades

21 Sub-Saharan Africa.

22 East Asia and Pacific.

The 1960s

The Problems of Primary Producers

23 Percentage change in quantity demanded divided by the corresponding percentage change in income.

24 Because most primary products have a low income elasticity of demand. In contrast manufactured goods have a high income elasticity of demand.

25 Demand factors, which depend on the overall economic condition, affect mineral prices. Climatic conditions, which are beyond the control of farmers, affect the income of agricultural producers.

Import Substitution Industrialization – An Example

26 Diversification of production and export structure of developing countries.

27 An active role.

28 Second and third.

The 1970s

29 Domestic production of parts and components, in many instances, was not economically feasible.

30 ISI is primarily oriented towards the domestic market and domestic industries are sheltered from foreign competition. Export-led growth is, however, oriented towards the international market.

31 (1) The oil-price rise increased the import bill of non-oil exporting developing countries; (2) the availability of petro-dollars.

The 1980s

32 The rise in international interest rates.

17.5 The Direction of International Trade

33 Developed.

34 Trade within the same industry or in the same products, such as trade in car components.

35 Increased.

36 71% and 22% respectively.

37 18%.

38 22%, 18% and 29% respectively.

The Composition of International Trade

39 Trade in different industries and products.

40 Manufactured goods.

41 15%, 9% and 54% respectively.

42 28%.

43 32%, 15% and 19% respectively.

44 79% and 8% respectively.

Chapter 18

18.2 Allocative Efficiency for Society

01 Externalities may exist.

Net Social Benefit

02 The amount by which social benefits exceed social costs is greatest at this output.

Types of Efficiency – Quiz

03 Allocative; there's perfect competition and no externalities. Technological; firms maximize profits. Technical; firms maximize profits. Consumer; purchasing decisions accord with demand curves.

The Pareto Principle

04 People are better off with more goods, and they are able to judge for themselves how well off they are.

05 (1) Points within and on the frontier that are above and/or to the right of A. (2) All points on the frontier. (3) Points above but to the left of A, or below but to the right of A.

06 Allocative efficiency.

07 Make someone better off without making at least one other person worse off.

08 It cannot be used when someone's gain is at the expense of a loss to someone else.

09 Different optima imply different distributions of income.

Pareto Optimality

10 The screen will show you your allocations.

11 Not all the goods are allocated.

12 All the goods are allocated but Laura is worse off.

Equity and Efficiency

13 There is an increase in efficiency as less pizzas are left unallocated.

14 All pizzas are allocated in Allocation Three, while one was left unallocated in Allocation Two.

15 Allocation Three is Pareto optimal, so no further Pareto improvements are possible. In moving to Allocation Four, person one is made worse off.

18.3 The Five Assumptions for the PPF

16 Everything produced is consumed.

17 There is no build up of stocks.

18 There is no need to answer questions about how or by whom the output will be produced.

Production Possibilities

19

Hours (cakes)	Hours (sketches)	No. (cakes)	No. (sketches)
0	8	0.0	45.3
1	7	12.0	44.0
2	6	23.5	41.4
3	5	33.7	37.4
4	4	2.4	32.0
5	3	49.5	25.4
6	2	54.9	17.7
7	1	58.7	9.0
8	0	60.6	0.0

The Production Possibility Frontier

20 Spending all day producing either beer or pizza may be monotonous Productivity is greater when some of each is made.

Production Not at the Frontier

21 Fully employed; technologically efficient.

22 It is assumed more would be preferred, yet when some resources are unemployed more goods could be made.

23

Point	Beer produced	Pizzas produced	Use of resources
Initial	10	8	15 available
On PPF	17.6	8	0 available
On PPF	19.8	0	0 available
On PPF	0	18.9	0 available
On PPF	13.6	13.7	0 available

24 The economy produces about 27 items when it makes approximately equal quantities of each. The total is substantially more than when a single product is produced.

25 There are not enough resources available to produce at that point.

Changing the PPF

26 Economic growth.

27 Improved technology.

28 Technological improvements in one sector but not in another.

18.4 Public versus Private Goods

29 Many people; one person.

Key Characteristics of a Public Good

30 Non-excludability, non-rivalry.

31 A mixed good has characteristics of a public good up to a certain level of consumption.

Public Goods and Free Riders

32 MSB is the vertical summation of all individual demand curves.

33 With no production externalities, MSC equals MPC, marginal private cost.

34 To analyse a private market, add the demand curves horizontally and find the intersection with MPC.

How much of a public good to produce?

35 Voters elect a government which has stated in its election manifesto how much of various public goods it will supply and how it will finance their provision.

Key Characteristics of a Merit Good

36 Little; much. Individuals would often choose to consume less education than it would be beneficial for them to have. When children are privately educated their parents pay the full cost of this. They also contribute through the tax system to making public education available to their children.

18.5 Understanding Consumer Surplus

37 Seven films. Continue purchasing until consumer surplus from the last unit purchased is zero.

38 75p. This is on the assumption that the second pint gives a consumer surplus of 25p.

39 Consumer surplus would increase by £3.50.

Individual Consumer Surplus

40 Consumer surplus is the additional utility over and above what has been paid for.

41 The excess of what the consumer would be willing to pay over that which he actually does pay.

Market Consumer Surplus

42 For quantities below the equilibrium market quantity, consumers would be willing to pay prices indicated by the demand curve that are above the market price that they actually pay.

43 £8.50.

44 It will be reduced as the price of the commodity rises.

Consumer Surplus for Different Demand Curves

45 It is infinite.

46 There is none.

Defining Producer Surplus

47 Profit.

48 As TR – TC.

49 It is the area between the price line and the MC curve between Qa and Q.

Producer Surplus in Different Markets

50 Still; not.

51 The area between AR, MC and the price axis. This takes no account of fixed cost, but in the long run all costs are variable, so producer surplus equals profit.

Social Surplus

52 Consumer surplus and producer surplus.

53 Increase; decrease; decrease.

18.6 Social Surplus in Competition

54 They are equal.

Changes Resulting from Monopolization

55 (a) Raises it; (b) reduces it; (c) reduces it; (d) increases it; (e) reduces it. (Assuming there are not large economies of scale.)

56 (a) Output is below the allocatively efficient level and a deadweight loss exists; (b) the producer is better off while consumers are worse off.

Progressive, Regressive and Proportional Taxes

57 Tax payments relative to income

Tax:	Progressive	Proportional	Regressive
As income rises: proportion paid in tax average tax rate	 increases rises	 is constant stays same	 decreases falls
People who pay relatively more tax are:	 richer	 all pay the same proportion	 poorer

What is Tax Incidence?

58 (£1000 + £2500) × 1.1175 = £4112.50.

Unit tax – An Example of Tax Incidence

59 For any quantity, the suppliers now need to be paid the previous price at which they were willing to supply it, plus the amount of the unit tax which they now have to remit to the government.

60 In the post-tax situation, the price is increased, although not by the amount of the tax, and the quantity purchased is reduced.

61 The tax incidence has been shared between consumers and suppliers.

62 All on the suppliers; all on the consumers.

Chapter 19

19.2 Risks – Fair or Not?

01 Zero; favourable.

02 Unfavourable.

03 The investment is not just a fair gamble. Its expected value is –£100 × 0.3 + £4 x 0.3 + £100 × 0.4 = + £11.2. It is better than a fair gamble.

04 Expected value reduces to –£18.8. The investment is a worse gamble than before.

Risk Aversion

05 P1 = 0.2 and 0.3–0.49; odds of 2:1 in favour.

19.3 Insurance and Risk

06 Utility of £1000 = 31.6.

07 Utility of £100 = 10.

08 Expected utility = 0.9 × (utility of £1000) + 0.1 × (utility of £100) = 0.9 × 31.6 + 0.1 × 10 = 29.4.

09 £867.

10 £1000 – £867 = £133.

11 £133 – 0.1 × 900 = £43.

12 Yes.

13 £133 – £43 = £90 (the expected value of the payout). Of course the insurer would never offer this premium. Can you think why not?

Chapter 20

20.2 The Major UK Nationalizations

The table should look like this.

Decade	Nationalizations that took place
1920s	Electricity
1940s	Gas, coal, railways, airways, road haulage
1950s	Steel
1960s	Airports, buses, post and telecommunications
1970s	Oil (part), water, shipbuilding, aerospace, aeroengines, car manufacturing

Natural Monopolies

01 Price should be set equal to marginal cost.

02 High set-up costs *and* increasing returns to scale.

03 (1) Reduce set-up costs (costs of entry into the industry); (2) remove any legal barriers to competition; (3) encourage competitive imports.

The Nationalized Industries in the UK – A Potted History

04 To break even.

05 Discriminate between customers.

06 Average cost pricing

07 Cross-subsidization.

08 Each industry to achieve a set rate of return on its assets.

09 (1) Marginal cost pricing; (2) investment to be on the basis of economic costs and benefits.

10 Pareto optimality.

11 (1) Kept separate from commercial activities; (2) subject to social cost–benefit analysis.

12 To ensure they covered their costs including the cost of capital.

13 Control and reduction of costs of production.

Productive efficiency

14 (1) Labour productivity; (2) total factor productivity.

15 Airways, gas, electricity (better in all).

16 Post Office, BT, buses (worse in all).

17 BR, steel, coal, airways, gas, electricity (better in 78–85).

18 Post Office, BT, buses (worse in 78–85).

19 By following policies of price, wage and investment restraint aimed at reducing inflation.

20 Large rises in productivity.

UK Allocative Efficiency

21 Prices should reflect the marginal social costs of production.

22 Use marginal cost pricing.

23 Forced to supply its output at market prices (unprotected and unsubsidized).

24 Rail, steel (efficient).

25 Post Office, Coal, Gas, Buses (not efficient).

26 BT, airways, electricity (partially efficient).

20.3 Definitions of Privatization

27 (1) De-nationalization; (2) de-regulation; (3) competitive tendering; (4) transformation of former centrally planned economies (CPEs).

28 De-nationalization.

UK Privatizations

29 84: British Telecom, Jaguar, computer systems, seaports and ferries; 86: gas, weapons manufacture, helicopter carriers, bus and coach carriers; 87: British Petroleum, British Airways, car parts, rolling stock manufacture, bus manufacture; 89: water supply and sewage; 90: regional electricity companies.

30 1979–83.

31 Firms in competitive industries.

32 1984–90 (and continuing in the 1990s).

33 Monopolistic public utilities.

Incentives and Efficiency

34 State control gives the government the opportunity to ensure efficient management. But the state has shifting priorities (e.g. employment may be more important than efficiency).

35 (1) Competition fosters efficiency and responsiveness to consumer wishes. But privatized

industries may be, or attempt to become, monopolies. (2) Privatized firms must demonstrate to financial institutions that they are financially sound to obtain investment funds. But the UK banks lending policy is based on a narrow view which does not necessarily take into account what is best for the country as a whole. (3) Shareholders monitor managers performance. They can sack managers, or they can sell their shares, reducing the share price and leaving the company vulnerable to a takeover. But it is difficult for shareholders to act together to achieve this, and a takeover bid may increase the share price. (4) Performance bonuses and threat of the sack act as carrot and stick. In practice bonuses are very common but sackings are very rare. (5) Workers who hold shares in the company will press for good management. This will only occur if the workers feel they actually have an influence. (6) The regulatory bodies that have been set up will ensure the social interest is given high priority. But regulatory capture may occur, so that management interests are given priority.

Seven Reasons to Privatize

36 Economic efficiency, remove government from business.

37 Reduce PSBR.

38 Popular capitalism; political advantage.

39 Worker share ownership; ease public pay. Worker share ownership gives workers a personal stake in the fortunes of the business, so improving their motivation, perhaps reducing absenteeism, etc. The easing of public pay was important because in the old nationalized industries labour relationships had been unsatisfactory, and unions had seen them as a bottomless purse.

Ownership and Efficiency (2)

40 None.

41 (1) More profitable to sell them off as monopolies; (2) needed the co-operation of existing top management.

Regulation of Privatized Utilities

Your table should look like this.

Company	Method of regulation	Formula used	Comments
BT	price-cap	RPI – 3	technological advances are reducing costs
British Gas	price-cap	RPI – 2	improvements in efficiency are expected to lower costs
Water	price-cap	RPI + K	above the rate of inflation to pay for quality improvements
Electricity	price-cap	RPI to RPI–2.5	under review

42 The regulator can refer it to the Monopolies and Mergers Commission.

43 Over-investment. Firms invest too much in order to lower their rate of return.

44 Lower quality.

45 Over-investment. If profit as a proportion of capital employed is limited, firms may invest more to be able to be able to make larger profits.

46 Not if firms believe that the regulator will set a less restrictive price cap if their rates of return are lower.

20.4 Case Study: The UK's National Health Service (NHS)

47 (1) The general approach: should the main emphasis be on preventive care or on primary care ? (2) How should healthcare be allocated – by need or ability to pay? (3) Should it be provided mainly by public or private sectors?

48 Follow the WinEcon screen.

49 Use the WinEcon screen.

Private vs. Public Control of Healthcare Resources

50 (a) The NHS has a monopoly in healthcare provision, but there are some elements of competition in the internal market. (b) Yes, doctors compete for patients.

51 (a) They are allocated equitably according to need, but rationed by waiting lists. (b) Through markets, with the poor and chronic sick being covered by government schemes.

52 Individuals may not be the best judges of how much healthcare they need. It should be available to all regardless of ability to pay.

53 Private provision allows consumer choice on how much healthcare to purchase, and when.

54 Poorer people may have worse health, and therefore greater need for healthcare. State provision leads to a more equitable distribution of healthcare.

Case Study NHS: What are the Benefits of a Mixed System?

The weaknesses of a market system

55 The doctor decides what care the patient will 'demand'.

56 The doctor has an incentive to recommend expensive care.

57 Health insurers trying to only insure the healthy – the sufferers are the unhealthy.

58 Unhealthy people are more likely to insure than those who think they are healthy – the number of claims is relatively high and the healthy suffer higher premiums.

59 Those insured have little incentive not to claim – doctors and patients make more claims.

60 Drives up the cost of health insurance.

61 The NHS, as almost the only employer, can keep down doctors' incomes

Lessons to be learnt from the free market in the USA

62 (1) Some services can be contracted out; (2) private sector cost-control methods can be used; (3) standardization of treatments and drugs can keep costs down.

63 (1) Poor financial information; (2) doctors have 'clinical freedom'.

64 Areas tend to keep spending at the same level as in the past. High spenders continue high, low spenders continue low.

65 (1) It is difficult to allocate costs between the GP and hospital sectors; (2) doctors were not trained how to manage what was really a small business; (3) doctors were not encouraged to do much preventive medicine.

Your table should look like this.

	UK	USA
Expenditure on healthcare as a percentage of GDP	6	11
Infant mortality rate per 1000 live births	9.5	10.4
Life expectancy for men in years	71.5	71.3

Internal Markets – the NHS of the 1990s

66 GPs (family doctors), DHAs (District Health Authorities) and private insurance companies.

67 NHS Trusts (self-governing hospitals etc.), NHS hospitals managed by DHAs and private hospitals.

68 Good information flows.

69 Spare capacity (you cannot buy from someone else if they have no spare capacity).

70 Not yet (spare capacity may be one of the results of the internal market).

Chapter 21

21.2 Types of Firms

01 The companies depend on the size criterion you choose. Using 'turnover' at the criterion, for example, gives:

Country	Largest company	Turnover ($m)	Profits ($m)
UK	Shell Transport	99,170	9,059.2
USA	General Motors Corp	135,696	2,465.8
Germany	Daimler-Benz	63,100.9	729.6
France	Elf Aquitaine	39,578.5	603.5
Japan	Sumitomo Corporation	172,154.8	255.6

02

Legal Form	Numbers of UK firms
Public companies	11,700
Private companies with limited liability	945,100
Private companies with unlimited liability	38,00
Partnerships, sole traders and non profit makers	590,500
Total	2,500,000

The Value Chain

03

	Components	Manufacture	Marketing
IBM	y	y	y
Dixons	n	n	y
Currys	n	n	y
Amstrad	n	y	y
Sega	n	y	y
Nintendo	n	y	y

04 Purchase or manufacture of components: design computer, obtain casing, motherboard, video card, sound card, monitor, keyboard, mouse, MS-DOS, Windows packages. Final product manufacture or assembly: build computer, test it, load software. Marketing: advertise, sales reps, retailers.

05 Final product manufacture or assembly.

Market or Firm Co-ordination?

06 Transactions costs; economies of scale and economies of team production.

07 Using the firm will not incur transactions costs of using the market such as finding out prices and drawing up contracts and monitoring contracts. The firm will only have single contracts with their employees and suppliers.

08 Costs incurred will be those associated with using the estate agent, solicitors and building society

09 Contracts with employees and suppliers; monitoring of employment contracts (i.e. employing foremen etc.); offices.

Forms of Business Organization

10 Plc – limited; private companies – both; co-ops – limited; partnerships – unlimited; sole trader – unlimited; public corporations – limited; friendly societies – limited (normally).

11 Liability is unlimited and they put at risk houses, cars, and other personal assets.

12 Friendly society; does not have to pay corporation tax.

13 The private company does not need to disclose the same amount of financial information. Accounts of public companies are open to public inspection.

14 Accountancy – partnerships; oil companies – plc; pharmaceutical firms – plc; solicitors – partnerships; market stall holders – sole traders; football pools companies – private company; computer games writers – sole traders.

21.3 Why Do Firms Need Finance?

15 Short-term finance for short-term assets (e.g. stock and debtors); long-term finance for fixed assets (e.g. plant and equipment, and buildings).

16 Long term: buildings, assembly lines, chip producing machines. Short term: stock holding, debtors.

Types of Security

17 Preference shares are fixed interest shares but do not pay if the firm makes no profits. Ordinary shares are the last equity to be paid. They are paid dividends from residual profits. Debentures constitute debt capital and are paid fixed interest before the other two. This security must be paid.

Sources of Short-Term Finance

Your table should contain the following categories.

Trade credit

Accrued expenses

Bank loans

Overdraft

Factoring

Commercial bills of exchange

Invoice discounting

18 They need to finance stock holding because of fluctuations in demand. Each of the firms has a different peak time in demand: August, November, Easter, and Christmas.

Capital Gearing

19 Gearing ratio = $\frac{\text{long-term loans} + \text{preference shares}}{\text{ordinary and preference capital} + \text{long-term loans}}$

20 Debt is cheaper than equity, and is tax deductible. But, the company may be forced into liquidation.

21

	Firm 1	Firm 2	Firm 3	Firm 4
Gearing ratio (%)	37.5	6.98	58.3	90.9

22 The higher the gearing, the higher the risk from fixed interest payments.

The Stock Exchange

23 Rights issue; Burton Group; Scottish Power; Barclays; Medeva; Eurotunnel.

24 Liquidity is the fact that shares can be bought and sold. If they could not be sold they would not be bought.

25 Use WinEcon to check your answer.

Index